⑤ REASONS
to buy your textbooks and course materials at

CENGAGE**brain**.com

 SAVINGS:
Prices up to 75% off, daily coupons, and free shipping on orders over $25

 CHOICE:
Multiple format options including textbook, eBook and eChapter rentals

 CONVENIENCE:
Anytime, anywhere access of eBooks or eChapters via mobile devices

 SERVICE:
Free eBook access while your text ships, and instant access to online homework products

 STUDY TOOLS:
Study tools* for your text, plus writing, research, career and job search resources
*availability varies

 Find your course materials and start saving at:
www.cengagebrain.com

MindTap

1. To get started, navigate to www.cengagebrain.com and select "Register a Product."

A new screen will appear prompting you to add a Course Key. A Course Key is a code given to you by your instructor — this is the first of two codes you will need to access MindTap. Every student in your course section should have the same Course Key.

2. Enter the Course Key and click "Register."

If you are accessing MindTap through your school's Learning Management System, such as BlackBoard or Desire2Learn, you may be redirected to use your Course Key/Access Code there. Follow the prompts you are given and feel free to contact support if you need assistance.

3. Confirm your course information above and proceed to the log in portion below.

If you have a CengageBrain username and password, enter it under "Returning Students" and click "Login." If this is your first time, register under "New Students" and click "Create a New Account."

4. Now that you are logged in, you can access the course for free by selecting "Start Free Trial" for 20 days or enter in your Access Code.

Your Access Code is unique to you and acts as payment for MindTap. You may have received it with your book or purchased separately in the bookstore or at www.cengagebrain.com. Enter it and click "Register."

NEED HELP?

Western Civilization

A BRIEF HISTORY

Western Civilization

A BRIEF HISTORY
Volume II: Since 1500

NINTH EDITION

JACKSON J. SPIELVOGEL

The Pennsylvania State University

CENGAGE
Learning·

Australia • Brazil • Mexico • Singapore • United Kingdom • United States

CENGAGE
Learning·

Western Civilization: A Brief History,
Volume II: Since 1500, Ninth Edition
Jackson J. Spielvogel

Product Director: Paul R. Banks

Product Manager: Scott Greenan

Senior Development Editor: Margaret
McAndrew Beasley

Product Assistant: Andrew Newton

Marketing Development Manager: Kyle
Zimmerman

Senior Content Project Manager: Carol
Newman

Senior Art Director: Cate Rickard Barr

Manufacturing Planner: Fola Orekoya

IP Analyst: Alexandra Ricciardi

IP Project Manager: Nick Barrows

Production Service and Compositor:
Cenveo Publisher Services

Text and Cover Designer: Dale Porter, Real
Time Design

Cover Image: "Village Fete," 1927 (oil on
canvas), Hegedusic, Krsto (1901-1971)/
Moderna Galerija, Zagreb, Croatia/
Alinari/The Bridgeman Art Library.

For product information and technology assistance, contact us at
Cengage Learning Customer & Sales Support, 1-800-354-9706
For permission to use material from this text or product,
submit all requests online at **www.cengage.com/permissions.**
Further permissions questions can be emailed to
permissionrequest@cengage.com.

Library of Congress Control Number: 2015942011

Student Edition:
ISBN: 978-1-305-63348-3

Loose leaf Edition:
ISBN: 978-1-305-86532-7

Cengage Learning
20 Channel Center Street
Boston, MA 02210
USA

Cengage Learning is a leading provider of customized learning solutions with
employees residing in nearly 40 different countries and sales in more than 125
countries around the world. Find your local representative at
www.cengage.com.

Cengage Learning products are represented in Canada by Nelson
Education, Ltd.

To learn more about Cengage Learning Solutions, visit **www.cengage.com.**
Purchase any of our products at your local college store or at our preferred
online store **www.cengagebrain.com.**

Printed in Canada
Print Number: 01   Print Year: 2015

ABOUT THE AUTHOR

JACKSON J. SPIELVOGEL is associate professor emeritus of history at The Pennsylvania State University. He received his Ph.D. from The Ohio State University, where he specialized in Reformation history under Harold J. Grimm. His articles and reviews have appeared in such journals as *Moreana, Journal of General Education, Catholic Historical Review, Archiv für Reformationsgeschichte, and American Historical Review*. He has also contributed chapters or articles to *The Social History of the Reformation, The Holy Roman Empire: A Dictionary Handbook,* the *Simon Wiesenthal Center Annual of Holocaust Studies,* and *Utopian Studies*. His work has been supported by fellowships from the Fulbright Foundation and the Foundation for Reformation Research. At Penn State, he helped inaugurate the Western civilization courses as well as a popular course on Nazi Germany. His book *Hitler and Nazi Germany* was published in 1987 (seventh edition, 2014). He is the author of *Western Civilization*, first published in 1991 (ninth edition, 2015), and the coauthor (with William Duiker) of *World History*, first published in 1994 (eighth edition, 2016). Professor Spielvogel has won five major university-wide teaching awards. During the year 1988–1989, he held the Penn State Teaching Fellowship, the university's most prestigious teaching award. In 1996, he won the Dean Arthur Ray Warnock Award for Outstanding Faculty Member, and in 2000, he received the Schreyer Honors College Excellence in Teaching Award.

TO DIANE,
WHOSE LOVE AND SUPPORT MADE IT ALL POSSIBLE
J.J.S.

Brief Contents

Detailed Contents

30 After the Fall: The Western World in a Global Age (Since 1985)   739

Documents

Maps

Features

FILM & HISTORY

OPPOSING VIEWPOINTS

IMAGES OF EVERYDAY LIFE

Preface

DURING A VISIT to Great Britain, where he studied as a young man, Mohandas Gandhi, the leader of the effort to liberate India from British colonial rule, was asked what he thought of Western civilization. "I think it would be a good idea," he replied. Gandhi's response was as correct as it was clever. Western civilization has led to great problems as well as great accomplishments, but it remains a good idea. And any complete understanding of today's world must take into account the meaning of Western civilization and the role Western civilization has played in history. Despite modern progress, we still greatly reflect our religious traditions, our political systems and theories, our economic and social structures, and our cultural heritage. I have written this brief history of Western civilization to assist a new generation of students in learning more about the past that has shaped them and the world in which they live.

At the same time, for the ninth edition, as in the eighth, I have added considerable new material on world history to show the impact that other parts of the world have had on the West. Certainly, the ongoing struggle with terrorists since 2001 has dramatized the intricate relationship between the West and the rest of the world. It is important then to show not only how Western civilization has affected the rest of the world but also how it has been influenced and even defined since its beginnings by contacts with other peoples around the world.

Another of my goals was to write a well-balanced work in which the political, economic, social, religious, intellectual, cultural, and military aspects of Western civilization would be integrated into a chronologically ordered synthesis. Moreover, I wanted to avoid the approach that is quite common in other brief histories of Western civilization—an approach that makes them collections of facts with little continuity from section to section. Instead, I sought to keep the story in history. Narrative history effectively transmits the knowledge of the past and is the form that best enables students to remember and understand the past. At the same time, I have not overlooked the need for the kind of historical analysis that makes students aware that historians often disagree in their interpretations of the past.

Features of the Text

To enliven the past and let readers see for themselves the materials that historians use to create their pictures of the past, I have included in each chapter **primary sources** (boxed documents) that are keyed to the discussion in the text. The documents include examples of the religious, artistic, intellectual, social, economic, and political aspects of Western life. Such varied sources as a description of the life of an upper-class Roman, marriage negotiations in Renaissance Italy, a debate in the Reformation era, and the diary of a German soldier at Stalingrad all reveal in vivid fashion what Western civilization meant to the individual men and women who shaped it by their activities. Questions at the end of each source aid students in analyzing the documents.

A second primary source feature, **Opposing Viewpoints**, introduced in the seventh edition, presents comparisons of two or three primary sources along with focus questions to facilitate student analysis of historical documents. A visual feature, **Images of Everyday Life**, combines two or more illustrations with a lengthy caption to provide insight into various aspects of social life. Another boxed feature, **Film & History**, presents a brief analysis of a film's plot as well as its historical significance, value, and accuracy. (For more specifics about all of these features, see "New to This Edition.")

A section entitled "Studying from Primary Source Materials" appears in the front of the book to introduce students to the language and tools of analyzing historical evidence—documents, photos, artwork, and maps.

Each chapter has an **introduction and an illustrated chapter summary** to help maintain the continuity of the narrative and to provide a synthesis of important themes. Anecdotes in the chapter introductions dramatically convey the major theme or themes of each chapter. **Detailed chronologies** reinforce the events discussed in the text, and a **timeline** at the end of each chapter enables students to review at a glance the chief developments of an era. Many of the timelines also show parallel developments in different cultures or nations. **Suggestions for Further Reading** at the end of each chapter reviews the most recent literature on each period and also points readers to some of the older "classic" works in each field. Also at the end of each chapter, a chapter review that includes **Upon Reflection essay questions and a list of Key Terms** provides valuable study aids.

Updated maps and extensive illustrations serve to deepen readers' understanding of the text. **Detailed map captions** are designed to enrich students' awareness of the importance of geography to history, and numerous spot maps enable students to see at a glance the region or subject being discussed in the text. Map captions also include a map question to guide students' reading of the map. To facilitate understanding of cultural movements, illustrations of artistic works discussed in the text are placed near the discussions. Throughout the text, illustration captions have been revised and expanded to further students' understanding of the past. **Chapter outlines and focus questions, including critical thinking questions**, at the beginning of each chapter give students a useful overview and guide them to the main subjects of each chapter. The focus questions are then repeated at the beginning of each major section in the chapter. A **glossary of important terms** (boldfaced in the text when they are introduced and defined) is provided at the back of the book to maximize reader comprehension. A **guide to pronunciation** is now provided in the text in parentheses following the first mention of a complex name or term. **Chapter Notes** are now at the end of each chapter rather than at the end of the book.

New to This Edition

As preparation for the revision of *Western Civilization: A Brief History*, I re-examined the entire book and analyzed the comments and reviews of colleagues who have found the book to be a useful instrument for introducing their students to the history of Western civilization. In making revisions for the ninth edition, I sought to build on the strengths of the previous editions and above all to maintain the balance, synthesis, and narrative qualities that characterized those editions. To keep up with the ever-growing body of historical scholarship, new or revised material has been added throughout the book on all of the following topics:

Chapter 1 religion and society in the Neolithic Age; new Opposing Viewpoints feature on "The Great Flood"; Akhenaten of Egypt; new historiographical

subsection, "The Spread of Humans: Out of Africa or Multiregional?"

Chapter 2 the Persians; new document on "Customs of the Persians"

Chapter 3 Minoan Crete; the role of the phalanx and colonies in the rise of democracy; sports and violence in ancient Greece

Chapter 4 new historiographical subsection, "The Legacy: Was Alexander Great?"; Demosthenes and Isocrates; Alexander; military institutions; new document on "Relations Between Greeks and Non-Greeks"

Chapter 5 the origins of the Etruscans; early Rome, especially the influence of the Etruscans

Chapter 6 new critical thinking question on the Roman military; client kingdoms; the *pax Romana*; new Images of Everyday Life feature on "Children in the Roman World"

Chapter 7 the labor of women in Frankish society; Pope Gregory the Great; the Byzantine military; new document on "A Byzantine Emperor Gives Military Advice"

Chapter 8 the *missi dominici*; new historiographical subsection, "What Was the Significance of Charlemagne?"; new Opposing Viewpoints feature on "Lords, Vassals, and Samurai in Europe and Japan"; new section on "Women in Byzantium"; new section on "Women in the Slavic World"; women in the world of Islam

Chapter 9 roles of peasant women; commercial capitalism; women in medieval cities; new document on "Goliardic Poetry: The Archpoet"

Chapter 10 the Crusades; new historiographical section, "What Were the Effects of the Crusades?"

Chapter 11 reorganized material on art and the Black Death: new subsection on "Art and the Black Death" located in section on "The Black Death in Europe" and another new subsection on "A New Art: Giotto" located in section on "Culture and Society in an Age of Adversity"; *condottieri* in Italy; new document on "A Liberated Woman in the Fourteenth Century"

Chapter 12 new section on "The Birth of Modern Diplomacy"; shortened section on Machiavelli; the impact of printing; new historiographical subsection, "Was There a Renaissance for Women?"; new subsection on "The Artist and Social Status"; new document on "The Genius of Leonardo da Vinci"; the English civil wars in the fifteenth century

Chapter 13 Luther's conservatism; new historiographical subsection, "Catholic Reformation or Counter-Reformation?"; new document on "Queen Elizabeth I: 'I Have the Heart of a King'"

Chapter 14   the West Indies; new section on "Disease in the New World"

Chapter 15   Bernini; new document on "The King's Day Begins"

Chapter 16   Galileo's telescope; new document on "Margaret Cavendish: The Education of Women"

Chapter 17   women and salons; new document on "The Punishment of Crime"

Chapter 18   agricultural practices and taxation

Chapter 19   de-Christianization and the new calendar; Treaties of Tilsit

Chapter 20   the cotton industry; new document on "The Great Irish Potato Famine"; new historiographical subsection, "Did Industrialization Bring an Improved Standard of Living?"

Chapter 21   the revolution of 1848 in Austria; Romanticism

Chapter 22   the Crimean War; Robert Koch and health care; new document on "Flaubert and an Image of Bourgeois Marriage"

Chapter 23   the Latin American economy; food and population growth; mass consumption; new document on "Bismarck and the Welfare of the Workers"

Chapter 24   Impressionism; imperialism; new document on "Does Germany Need Colonies?"

Chapter 25   new historiographical subsection, "The Assassination of Franz Ferdinand: A Blank Check?"; trench warfare; women and work

Chapter 26   the democratic states; new historiographical subsection, "The Retreat from Democracy: Did Europe Have Totalitarian States?"; Nazi culture

Chapter 27   new focus questions; invasion of Poland; the *Einsatzgruppen* in the Holocaust; new document on "Heinrich Himmler: 'We Had the Moral Right'"

Chapter 28   new historiographical subsection, "Confrontation of the Superpowers: Who Started the Cold War?"; the Algerian revolution; the denazification of postwar Germany; the European Common Market; new document on "The Burden of Guilt"

Chapter 29   new document on "Betty Friedan: The Problem That Has No Name"; new Film & History feature on "*The Iron Lady* (2011)"; land art

Chapter 30   the global economy; Great Britain, Germany, France, the United States, and Canada; Russia and Ukraine; new historiographical section, "Why Did the Soviet Union Collapse?"; new section on "The West and Islam"; the war in Afghanistan; the Catholic Church; technology; new Images of Everyday Life feature on "The New Global Economy: Fast Fashion"

The enthusiastic response to the primary sources (boxed documents) led me to evaluate the content of each document carefully and add new documents throughout the text, including new comparative documents in the feature called **Opposing Viewpoints**. This feature has been expanded and now appears in most chapters, including such new topics as "Lords, Vassals, and Samurai in Europe and Japan," "Causes of the Black Death: Contemporary Views," "Attitudes of the Industrial Middle Class in Britain and Japan," and "Czechoslovakia, 1968: Two Faces of Communism." Two additional features have also been revised. **Images of Everyday Life** can now be found in twelve chapters, including such new topics as "Children in the Roman World" and "The New Global Economy: Fast Fashion." **Film & History features** now appear in twelve chapters, including the addition of *The Iron Lady*.

A new focus question has also been added at the beginning of each chapter. Entitled **Connections to Today**, this question is intended to help students appreciate the relevance of history by asking them to draw connections between the past and present.

Also new to the ninth edition are **historiographical sections**, which examine how and why historians differ in their interpretation of specific topics. Examples include "Was There a United Kingdom of Israel?"; "Was There a Renaissance for Women?"; "The Retreat from Democracy: Did Europe Have Totalitarian States?"; and "Why Did the Soviet Union Collapse?"

Because courses in Western civilization at American and Canadian colleges and universities follow different chronological divisions, the text is available in both one-volume and two-volume versions to fit the needs of instructors. Teaching and learning ancillaries include the following.

Instructor Resources

MindTap[TM]   MindTap for *Western Civilization: A Brief History* 9e is a personalized, online digital learning platform providing students with an immersive learning experience that builds critical thinking skills. Through a carefully designed chapter-based learning path, MindTap allows students to easily identify the chapter's learning objectives, improve their writing skills by completing unit-level essay assessments, read short, manageable sections from the e-book, and test their content knowledge with a Chapter Test that employs Aplia[TM] (see Chapter Test description on next page).

- **Setting the Scene:** Each chapter of the MindTap begins with a brief video that introduces the chapter's major themes in a compelling, visual way that encourages students to think critically about the subject matter.
- **Review Activities:** Each chapter includes reading comprehension assignments designed to cover the content of each major heading within the chapter.
- **Chapter Test:** Each chapter within MindTap ends with a summative Chapter Test. It covers each chapter's learning objectives and is built using Aplia critical thinking questions. Aplia provides automatically graded critical thinking assignments with detailed, immediate explanations on every question. Students can also choose to see another set of related questions if they did not earn all available points in their first attempt and want more practice.
- **Reflection Activity:** Every chapter ends with an assignable, gradable reflection activity, intended as a brief writing assignment through which students can apply a theme or idea they've just studied.
- **Unit Activities:** Chapters in MindTap are organized into multi-chapter units. Each unit includes a brief set of higher-stakes activities for instructors to assign, designed to assess students on their writing and critical thinking skills, and their ability to engage larger themes, concepts, and material across multiple chapters.
- **Classroom Activities:** MindTap includes a brief list of in-class activity ideas for instructors. These are designed to increase student collaboration, engagement, and understanding of selected topics or themes. These activities, including class debate scenarios and primary source discussion guides, can enrich the classroom experience for both instructors and students.

MindTap also includes a variety of other tools that will make history more engaging for students:

- ReadSpeaker reads the text out-loud to students in a voice they can customize.
- Note-taking and highlighting are organized in a central location that can be synced with Ever Note on any mobile device a student may have access to.
- Questia allows professors to search a database of thousands of peer reviewed journals, newspapers, magazines, and full-length books – all assets can be added to any relevant chapter in MindTap.
- Kaltura allows instructors to insert inline video and audio into the MindTap platform.

- ConnectYard allows instructors to create digital "yards" through social media–all without "friending" students

MindTap for *Western Civilization: A Brief History* 9e goes well beyond an eBook and a homework solutions. It is truly a Personal Learning Experience that allows you to synchronize the reading with engaging assignments. To learn more, ask your Cengage Learning sales representative to demo it for you—or go to www.cengage.com/MindTap.

Instructor Companion Website This website is an all-in-one resource for class preparation, presentation, and testing for instructors. Accessible through Cengage.com/login with your faculty account, you will find an Instructor's Manual, Powerpoint presentations (descriptions below), and testbank files (please see Cognero description).

- **Instructor's Manual:** This manual contains for each chapter: chapter outlines and summaries, lecture suggestions, suggested research topics, map exercises, discussion questions for primary source documents, and suggested readings and resources.
- **PowerPoint® Lecture Tools:** These presentations are ready-to-use, visual outlines of each chapter. They are easily customized for your lectures. There are presentations of only lecture or only images, as well as combined lecture and image presentations. Also available is a per chapter JPEG library of images and maps.

Cengage Learning Testing, powered by Cognero® for *Western Civilization: A Brief History* 9e is accessible through Cengage.com/login with your faculty account. This test bank contains multiple-choice and essay questions for each chapter. Cognero® is a flexible, online system that allows you to author, edit, and manage test bank content for *Western Civilization: A Brief History* 9e. Create multiple test versions instantly and deliver through your LMS from your classroom, or wherever you may be, with no special installs or downloads required.

The following format types are available for download from Instructor Companion Site: Blackboard, Angel, Moodle, Canvas, Desire2Learn. You can import these files directly into your LMS to edit, manage questions, and create tests. The test bank is also available in Word and PDF format from the Instructor Companion Website.

MindTap Reader for Western Civilization: A Brief History 9e MindTap Reader is an eBook specifically designed to address the ways students assimilate content and media assets. MindTap Reader combines thoughtful navigation ergonomics, advanced student annotation, note-taking, and search tools, and embedded media assets such as video and interactive (zoomable) maps. Students can use the eBook as their primary text or as a multimedia companion to their printed book. The MindTap Reader eBook is available within the MindTap found at www.cengagebrain.com.

Cengagebrain.com Save your students time and money. Direct them to www.cengagebrain.com for choice in formats and savings and a better chance to succeed in your class. Cengagebrain.com, Cengage Learning's online store, is a single destination for more than 10,000 new textbooks, eTextbooks, eChapters, study tools, and audio supplements. Students have the freedom to purchase a-la-carte exactly what they need when they need it. Students can save 50% on the electronic textbook, and can pay as little as $1.99 for an individual eChapter.

Custom Options Nobody knows your students like you, so why not give them a text that is tailor-fit to their needs? Cengage Learning offers custom solutions for your course—whether it's making a small modification to *Western Civilization: A Brief History* 9e to match your syllabus or combining multiple sources to create something truly unique. You can pick and choose chapters, include your own material, and add additional map exercises along with the Rand McNally Atlas to create a text that fits the way you teach. Ensure that your students get the most out of their textbook dollar by giving them exactly what they need. Contact your Cengage Learning representative to explore custom solutions for your course.

Student Resources

MindTap^TM The learning path for *Western Civilization: A Brief History* 9e MindTap incorporates a set of resources designed to help students develop their own historical skills. These include interactive, autogradable tutorials for map skills, essay writing, and critical thinking. They also include a set of resources developed to aid students with their research skills, primary and secondary source analysis, and knowledge and confidence around proper citations.

MindTap Reader MindTap Reader is an eBook specifically designed to address the ways students assimilate content and media assets. MindTap Reader combines thoughtful navigation ergonomics, advanced student annotation, note-taking, and search tools, and embedded media assets such as video and interactive (zoomable) maps. Students can use the eBook as their primary text or as a multimedia companion to their printed book. The MindTap Reader eBook is available within the MindTap found at www.cengagebrain.com.

Cengagebrain.com Save time and money! Go to www.cengagebrain.com for choice in formats and savings and a better chance to succeed in your class. Cengagebrain.com, Cengage Learning's online store, is a single destination for more than 10,000 new textbooks, eTextbooks, eChapters, study tools, and audio supplements. Students have the freedom to purchase a-la-carte exactly what they need when they need it. Students can save 50% on the electronic textbook, and can pay as little as $1.99 for an individual eChapter.

Writing for College History, 1e [ISBN: 9780618306039] Prepared by Robert M. Frakes, Clarion University. This brief handbook for survey courses in American history, Western Civilization/European history, and world civilization guides students through the various types of writing assignments they encounter in a history class. Providing examples of student writing and candid assessments of student work, this text focuses on the rules and conventions of writing for the college history course.

The History Handbook, 2e [ISBN: 9780495906766] Prepared by Carol Berkin of Baruch College, City University of New York and Betty Anderson of Boston University. This book teaches students both basic and history-specific study skills such as how to read primary sources, research historical topics, and correctly cite sources. Substantially less expensive than comparable skill-building texts, The History Handbook also offers tips for Internet research and evaluating online sources.

Doing History: Research and Writing in the Digital Age, 2e [ISBN: 9781133587880] Prepared by Michael J. Galgano, J. Chris Arndt, and Raymond M. Hyser of James Madison University. Whether you're starting down the path as a history major, or simply looking for a straightforward and systematic guide to writing a successful paper, you'll find this text to be an indispensible handbook to historical research. This text's "soup to nuts" approach to researching and writing about history addresses every step of the process, from locating your sources and gathering information, to writing clearly and making proper use of various citation styles to avoid plagiarism. You'll also learn how to make the most of every tool available to you—especially the technology that helps you conduct the process efficiently and effectively.

The Modern Researcher, *6e [ISBN: 9780495318705]*
Prepared by Jacques Barzun and Henry F. Graff of Columbia University. This classic introduction to the techniques of research and the art of expression is used widely in history courses, but is also appropriate for writing and research methods courses in other departments. Barzun and Graff thoroughly cover every aspect of research, from the selection of a topic through the gathering, analysis, writing, revision, and publication of findings, presenting the process not as a set of rules but through actual cases that put the subtleties of research in a useful context. Part One covers the principles and methods of research; Part Two covers writing, speaking, and getting one's work published.

Acknowledgments

I would like to thank the many teachers and students who have used previous editions of *Western Civilization: A Brief History*. I am gratified by their enthusiastic response to a textbook that was intended to put the *story* back in *history* and capture the imagination of the reader. I especially thank the many teachers and students who made the effort to contact me personally to share their enthusiasm. I am deeply grateful to John Soares for his assistance in preparing the map captions and to Charmarie Blaisdell of Northeastern University for her detailed suggestions on women's history. Daniel Haxall of Kutztown University provided valuable assistance with materials on postwar art, popular culture, postmodern art and thought, and the digital age. I am especially grateful to Kathryn Spielvogel for her work as a research associate. Thanks to Cengage's comprehensive review process, many historians were asked to evaluate my manuscript and review each edition. I am grateful to the following for the innumerable suggestions that have greatly improved my work:

Patricia Adelle
William Paterson University

Paul Allen
University of Utah

Gerald Anderson
North Dakota State University

Susan L. H. Anderson
Campbell University

Letizia Argenteri
University of San Diego

Roy A. Austensen
Illinois State University

James A. Baer
Northern Virginia Community College—Alexandria

James T. Baker
Western Kentucky University

Patrick Bass
Morningside College

John F. Battick
University of Maine

Frederic J. Baumgartner
Virginia Polytechnic Institute

Phillip N. Bebb
Ohio University

Anthony Bedford
Modesto Junior College

F. E. Beemon
Middle Tennessee State University

Joel Benson
Northwest Missouri State University

Robert L. Bergman
Glendale Community College

Leonard R. Berlanstein
University of Virginia

Douglas T. Bisson
Belmont University

Charmarie Blaisdell
Northeastern University

Stephen H. Blumm
Montgomery County Community College

Hugh S. Bonar
California State University

Werner Braatz
University of Wisconsin—Oshkosh

Alfred S. Bradford
University of Missouri

Maryann E. Brink
College of William & Mary

Blaine T. Browne
Broward Community College

J. Holden Camp, Jr.
Hillyer College, University of Hartford

Jack Cargill
Rutgers University

Martha Carlin
University of Wisconsin—Milwaukee

Elizabeth Carney
Clemson University

Kevin K. Carroll
Arizona State University

Yuan-Ling Chao
Middle Tennessee State University

Eric H. Cline
Xavier University

Michael Clinton
Gwynedd Mercy College

Robert Cole
Utah State University

William J. Connell
Rutgers University

Nancy Conradt
College of DuPage

Marc Cooper
Southwest Missouri State

Caitlin Corning
George Fox University

Richard A. Cosgrove
University of Arizona

David A. Crain
South Dakota State University

Michael A. Crane, Jr. (student)
Everett Community College

Steve Culbertson
Owens Community College

Luanne Dagley
Pellissippi State Technical Community College

Marion F. Deshmukh
George Mason University

Michael F. Doyle
Ocean County College

Michael Duckett
Dawson College

Laura Dull
Delta College

Roxanne Easley
Central Washington University

James W. Ermatinger
University of Nebraska—Kearney

Charles T. Evans
Northern Virginia Community College

Porter Ewing
Los Angeles City College

Carla Falkner
Northeast Mississippi Community College

Steven Fanning
University of Illinois—Chicago

Ellsworth Faris
California State University—Chico

Gary B. Ferngren
Oregon State University

Mary Helen Finnerty
Westchester Community College

Eve Fisher
South Dakota State University

Lucien Frary
Rider University

Erik Freas
Borough of Manhattan Community College—CUNY

A. Z. Freeman
Robinson College

Marsha Frey
Kansas State University

Frank J. Frost
University of California—Santa Barbara

Frank Garosi
California State University—Sacramento

Lorettann Gascard
Franklin Pierce College

Richard M. Golden
University of North Texas

Manuel G. Gonzales
Diablo Valley College

Amy G. Gordon
Denison University

Richard J. Grace
Providence College

Hanns Gross
Loyola University

John F. Guilmartin
Ohio State University

Jeffrey S. Hamilton
Gustavus Adolphus College

J. Drew Harrington
Western Kentucky University

James Harrison
Siena College

Derek Hastings
Oakland University

A. J. Heisserer
University of Oklahoma

Fred Heppding
Maranatha Baptist University

Rowena Hernández-Múzquiz
Old Dominion University

Betsey Hertzler
Mesa Community College

Robert Herzstein
University of South Carolina

Shirley Hickson
North Greenville College

Martha L. Hildreth
University of Nevada

Boyd H. Hill, Jr.
University of Colorado—Boulder

Sean Hill
Irvine Valley College

Michael Hofstetter
Bethany College

Donald C. Holsinger
Seattle Pacific University

Frank L. Holt
University of Houston

W. Robert Houston
University of South Alabama

David R. C. Hudson
Texas A&M University

Paul Hughes
Sussex County Community College

Richard A. Jackson
University of Houston

Fred Jewell
Harding University

Jenny M. Jochens
Towson State University

Carolyn Johnston
Marian College

William M. Johnston
University of Massachusetts

Allen E. Jones
Troy State University

George Kaloudis
Rivier College

Jeffrey A. Kaufmann
Muscatine Community College

David O. Kieft
University of Minnesota

Patricia Killen
Pacific Lutheran University

William E. Kinsella, Jr.
Northern Virginia Community College—Annandale

James M. Kittelson
Ohio State University

Doug Klepper
Santa Fe Community College

Mark Klobas
Scottsdale Community College

Cynthia Kosso
Northern Arizona University

Clayton Miles Lehmann
University of South Dakota

Diana Chen Lin
Indiana University, Northwest

Ursula W. MacAffer
Hudson Valley Community College

Andrea Maestrejuan
Metropolitan State University—Denver

Anthony Makowski
Delaware County Community College

Harold Marcuse
University of California—Santa Barbara

Mavis Mate
University of Oregon

Tom Maulucci
State University of New York—Fredonia

Meghean Mayeur
Southeastern Louisiana University

T. Ronald Melton
Brewton Parker College

Jack Allen Meyer
University of South Carolina

Eugene W. Miller, Jr.
The Pennsylvania State University—Hazleton

David Mock
Tallahassee Community College

John Patrick Montano
University of Delaware

Rex Morrow
Trident Technical College

Thomas M. Mulhern
University of North Dakota

Pierce Mullen
Montana State University

Frederick I. Murphy
Western Kentucky University

William M. Murray
University of South Florida

Otto M. Nelson
Texas Tech University

Sam Nelson
Willmar Community College

John A. Nichols
Slippery Rock University

Lisa Nofzinger
Albuquerque Technical Vocational Institute

Heather O'Grady-Evans
Elmira College

Chris Oldstone-Moore
Augustana College

Donald Ostrowski
Harvard University

James O. Overfield
University of Vermont

Matthew L. Panczyk
Bergen Community College

Kathleen Parrow
Black Hills State University

Michael Pascale
SUNY, Suffolk County Community College

Jonathan Perry
University of Central Florida

Carla Rahn Phillips
University of Minnesota

Keith Pickus
Wichita State University

Linda J. Piper
University of Georgia

Janet Polasky
University of New Hampshire

Thomas W. Porter
Randolph-Macon College

Charles A. Povlovich
California State University—Fullerton

Nancy Rachels
Hillsborough Community College

Charles Rearick
University of Massachusetts—Amherst

Jerome V. Reel, Jr.
Clemson University

Paul Reuter
Jefferson State Community College

Joseph Robertson
Gadsden State Community College

Jonathan Roth
San Jose State University

Constance M. Rousseau
Providence College

Julius R. Ruff
Marquette University

John Saddler
George Mason University

Richard Saller
University of Chicago

Magdalena Sanchez
Texas Christian University

Bonnie F. Saunders
Glendale Community College

Jack Schanfield
Suffolk County Community College

Richard Schellhammer
University of West Alabama

Linda Scherr
Mercer County Community College

Roger Schlesinger
Washington State University

Joanne Schneider
Rhode Island College

Alexandra Tolin Schultz
SUNY—Oneonta

Thomas C. Schunk
University of Wisconsin—Oshkosh

Denise Scifres
Hinds Community College

Kyle C. Sessions
Illinois State University

Colleen M. Shaughnessy
Zeena Endicott College

Linda Simmons
Northern Virginia Community College—Manassas

Donald V. Sippel
Rhode Island College

Douglas R. Skopp
State University of New York—Plattsburgh

Glen Spann
Asbury College

John W. Steinberg
Georgia Southern University

Paul W. Strait
Florida State University

James E. Straukamp
California State University—Sacramento

Brian E. Strayer
Andrews University

Fred Suppe
Ball State University

Ruth Suyama
Los Angeles Mission College

Roger Tate
Somerset Community College

Tom Taylor
Seattle University

Jack W. Thacker
Western Kentucky University

Janet A. Thompson
Tallahassee Community College

David S. Trask
Guilford Technical Community College

Thomas Turley
Santa Clara University

John G. Tuthill
University of Guam

Maarten Ultee
University of Alabama

Donna L. Van Raaphorst
Cuyahoga Community College

Nancy G. Vavra
University of Colorado—Boulder

Janet Walmsley
George Mason University

Allen M. Ward
University of Connecticut

Richard D. Weigel
Western Kentucky University

Michael Weiss
Linn-Benton Community College

Richard S. Williams
Washington State University

Arthur H. Williamson
California State University—Sacramento

Julianna Wilson
Pima Community College

Katherine Workman
Wright State University

Judith T. Wozniak
Cleveland State University

Walter J. Wussow
University of Wisconsin—Eau Claire

Edwin M. Yamauchi
Miami University

The editors at Cengage Learning have been both helpful and congenial at all times. I especially wish to thank Margaret McAndrew Beasley, who thoughtfully, wisely, efficiently, and pleasantly guided the overall development of the ninth edition. I also thank Cara St. Hilaire for her valuable managerial skills. Holly Collins of Cenveo was as cooperative and cheerful as she was competent in matters of production management. And finally, I wish to thank Clark Baxter, whose faith in my ability to be a single author of a Western civilization textbook made it all possible.

Above all, I thank my family for their support. The gifts of love, laughter, and patience from my daughters, Jennifer and Kathryn; my sons, Eric and Christian; my daughters-in-law, Liz and Laurie; and my sons-in-law, Daniel and Eddie, were enormously appreciated. I also wish to acknowledge my grandchildren, Devyn, Bryn, Drew, Elena, Sean, Emma, and Jackson, who bring great joy to my life. My wife and best friend, Diane, contributed editorial assistance, wise counsel, good humor, and the loving support that made it possible for me to accomplish a project of this magnitude. I could not have written the book without her.

Introduction to Students of Western Civilization

CIVILIZATION, AS HISTORIANS define it, first emerged between five and six thousand years ago when people in different parts of the world began to live in organized communities with distinct political, military, economic, and social structures. Religious, intellectual, and artistic activities assumed important roles in these early societies. The focus of this book is on Western civilization, a civilization that many people identify with the continent of Europe.

Defining Western Civilization

Western civilization itself has evolved considerably over the centuries. Although the concept of the West did not yet exist at the time of the Mesopotamians and Egyptians, their development of writing, their drafting of law codes, and their practice of different roles based on gender all eventually influenced what became Western civilization. Although the Greeks did not conceive of Western civilization as a cultural entity, their artistic, intellectual, and political contributions were crucial to the foundations of Western civilization. The Romans produced a remarkable series of accomplishments that were fundamental to the development of Western civilization, which came to consist largely of lands in Europe conquered by the Romans, in which Roman cultural and political ideals were gradually spread. Nevertheless, people in these early civilizations viewed themselves as subjects of states or empires, not as members of Western civilization.

With the rise of Christianity during the late Roman Empire, however, peoples in Europe began to identify themselves as part of a civilization different from other civilizations, such as that of Islam, leading to a concept of a Western civilization different from other civilizations. In the fifteenth century, Renaissance intellectuals began to identify this civilization not only with Christianity but also with the intellectual and political achievements of the ancient Greeks and Romans.

Important to the development of the idea of a distinct Western civilization were encounters with other peoples. Between 700 and 1500, encounters with the world of Islam helped define the West. But after 1500, as European ships began to move into other parts of the world, encounters with peoples in Asia, Africa, and the Americas not only had an impact on the civilizations found there but also affected how people in the West defined themselves. At the same time, as they set up colonies, Europeans began to transplant a sense of Western identity to other areas of the world, especially North America and parts of Latin America, that have come to be considered part of Western civilization.

As the concept of Western civilization has evolved over the centuries, so have the values and unique features associated with that civilization. Science played a crucial role in the development of modern Western civilization. The societies of the Greeks, the Romans, and the medieval Europeans were based largely on a belief in the existence of a spiritual order; a dramatic departure to a natural or material view of the universe occurred in the seventeenth-century Scientific Revolution. Science and technology have been important in the growth of today's modern and largely secular Western civilization, although antecedents to scientific development also existed in Greek and medieval thought and practice, and religion remains a component of the Western world today.

Many historians have viewed the concept of political liberty, belief in the fundamental value of every individual, and a rational outlook based on a system of logical, analytical thought as unique aspects of Western civilization. Of course, the West has also witnessed horrendous negations of liberty, individualism, and reason. Racism, slavery, violence, world wars, totalitarian regimes—these, too, form part of the complex story of what constitutes Western civilization.

The Dating of Time

In our examination of Western civilization, we also need to be aware of the dating of time. In recording the past, historians try to determine the exact time when events occurred. World War II in Europe, for example, began on September 1, 1939, when Hitler sent German troops into Poland, and ended on May 7, 1945, when Germany surrendered. By using dates, historians can place events in order and try to determine the development of patterns over periods of time.

If someone asked you when you were born, you would reply with a number, such as 1997. In the United States, we would all accept that number without question because it is part of the dating system followed in the Western world (Europe and the Western Hemisphere). In this system, events are dated by counting backward or forward from the year 1. When the system was first devised, the year 1 was assumed to be the year of the birth of Jesus, and the abbreviations B.C. (before Christ) and A.D. (for the Latin words *anno Domini*, meaning "in the year of the Lord") were used to refer to the periods before and after the birth of Jesus, respectively. Historians now generally refer to the year 1 in nonreligious terms as the beginning of the "common era." The abbreviations B.C.E. (before the common era) and C.E. (common era) are used instead of B.C. and A.D., although the years are the same. Thus, an event that took place four hundred years before the year 1 would be dated 400 B.C.E. (before the common era)—or the date could be expressed as 400 B.C. Dates after the year 1 are labeled C.E. Thus, an event that took place two hundred years after the year 1 would be dated 200 C.E. (common era), or the date could be written as A.D. 200. It could also be written simply as 200, just as you would not give your birth year as 1997 C.E. but simply as 1997. In keeping with the current usage by most historians, this book will use the abbreviations B.C.E. and C.E.

Historians also make use of other terms to refer to time. A decade is ten years, a century is one hundred years, and a millennium is one thousand years. Thus "the fourth century B.C.E." refers to the fourth period of one hundred years counting backward from the year 1, the beginning of the common era. Since the first century B.C.E. would be the years 100 B.C.E. to 1 B.C.E., the fourth century B.C.E. would be the years 400 B.C.E. to 301 B.C.E. We could say, then, that an event in 350 B.C.E. took place in the fourth century B.C.E.

Similarly, the "fourth century C.E." refers to the fourth period of one hundred years after the beginning of the common era. Since the first period of one hundred years would be the years 1 to 100, the fourth period or fourth century would be the years 301 to 400. We could say, then, that an event in 350 took place in the fourth century. Likewise, the first millennium B.C.E. refers to the years 1000 B.C.E. to 1 B.C.E.; the second millennium C.E. refers to the years 1001 to 2000.

The dating of events can also vary from people to people. Most people in the Western world use the Western calendar, also known as the Gregorian calendar after Pope Gregory XIII, who refined it in 1582. The Hebrew calendar uses a different system in which the year 1 is the equivalent of the Western year 3760 B.C.E., considered to be the date of the creation of the world according to the Bible. Thus, the Western year 2015 is the year 5775 on the Hebrew calendar. The Islamic calendar begins year 1 on the day Muhammad fled Mecca, which is the year 622 on the Western calendar.

Studying from Primary Source Materials

ASTRONOMERS INVESTIGATE THE universe through telescopes. Biologists study the natural world by collecting plants and animals in the field and then examining them with microscopes. Sociologists and psychologists study human behavior through observation and controlled laboratory experiments.

Historians study the past by examining historical "evidence" or "source" materials—church or town records, letters, treaties, advertisements, paintings, menus, literature, buildings, clothing—anything and everything written or created by our ancestors that give clues about their lives and the times in which they lived.

Historians refer to written material as "documents." Excerpts of more than 150 documents—some in shaded boxes and others in the text narrative itself—appear in every chapter of this textbook. Each chapter also includes several photographs of buildings, paintings, and other kinds of historical evidence.

As you read each chapter, the more you examine all this "evidence," the more you will understand the main ideas of the course. This introduction to studying historical evidence, along with the visual summaries at the end of each chapter, will help you learn how to look at evidence the way historians do. The better you become at reading evidence, the better the grade you will earn in your course.

Source Material Comes in Two Main Types: Primary and Secondary

Primary evidence is material that comes to us exactly as it left the pen of the person who wrote it. Letters between King Louis XIV of France and the king of Tonkin (now Vietnam) are primary evidence (p. 343). So is the court transcript of a witchcraft trial in France (p. 360), or a diagram of the solar system drawn by Copernicus (p. 389).

Secondary evidence is an account by someone about the life or activity of someone else. A story about Abraham Lincoln written by his secretary of war would give us primary source information about Lincoln by someone who knew him. Reflections about Lincoln's presidency written by a historian might give us insights into how, for example, Lincoln governed during wartime. But because the historian did not know Lincoln in person, we would consider this a secondary source of information about Lincoln. Secondary sources such as historical essays (and textbooks such as this one) can therefore by very helpful in understanding the past. But it is important to remember that a secondary source can reveal as much about its author as it does about its subject.

Reading Documents

We will turn to a specific document in a moment and analyze it in some detail. For now, however, the following are a few basic things to be aware of—and to ask yourself— as you read any written document.

1. Who wrote it? The author of the textbook answers this question for you at the beginning of each document in the book. But your instructors may give you other documents to read, and the authorship of each document is the first question you need to answer.
2. What do we know about the author of the document? The more you know about the author, the more meaningful and reliable the information you can extract from the document.
3. Is it a primary or secondary document?
4. When was the document written?
5. What is the purpose of the document? Closely tied to the question of document type is the document's purpose. A work of fiction might have been written to entertain, whereas an official document was written to convey a particular law or decree to subjects, citizens, or believers.
6. Who was the intended audience? A play is meant to be performed by actors on a stage before a group of onlookers, whereas Martin Luther's Ninety-Five Theses were posted publicly and intended to be seen by ordinary citizens.
7. Can you detect a bias in this document? As the two documents on the siege of Jerusalem (p. 244) suggest, firsthand accounts of the Crusades written by Christians and Muslims tend to differ. Each may be "accurate" as far as the writer is concerned,

but your job as a historian is to decide whether this written evidence gives a reliable account of what happened. You cannot always believe everything you read, but the more you read, the more you can decide what is, in fact, accurate.

"Reading" and Studying Photographs and Artwork

This book pays close attention to primary source and written documents, but contemporary illustrations can also be analyzed to provide an understanding of a historical period.

A historian might ask questions about a painting like the one at the right to learn more about life in a medieval town. The more you study and learn about medieval social history, the more information this painting will reveal. To help you look at and interpret art like a historian, ask yourself the following questions:

1. By looking closely at just the buildings, what do you learn about the nature of the medieval town dwellings and the allotment of space within the town? Why were medieval towns arranged in this fashion? Why would this differ from modern urban planning?
2. Based on the various activities shown, what kinds of groups would you expect to find in a medieval town? What do you learn about medieval methods of production? How do they differ from modern methods of production? What difference would this make in the nature of community organization and life?
3. Based on what the people in the street are wearing, what do you think their economic status was? Would that be typical of a medieval town? Why or why not?
4. What do you think the artist who created this piece was trying to communicate about life in a medieval town? Based on your knowledge of medieval towns, would you agree with the artist's assessment? Why or why not?
5. What do you think was the social class of the artist? Why?

Reading and Studying Maps

Historical events do not just "happen"; they happen in a specific place. It is important to learn all you can about that place, and a good map can help you do this.

Your textbook includes several kinds of maps. The map of Europe printed on the inside front cover of the textbook is a good place to start. Map basics include taking care to read and understand every label on whatever

Medieval Town

map you study. The map of Europe has labels for six kinds of information. Each of the following is important:

1. Names of countries.
2. Names of major cities.
3. Names of oceans and large bodies of water.
4. Names of rivers.
5. Longitude and latitude. Lines of longitude extend from the North Pole to the South Pole; one such line intersects Iceland in the top left (or northwest) corner of the map. Lines of latitude circle the globe east to west and intersect lines of longitude. These imaginary lines place countries and oceans in their approximate setting on the face of the earth. Not every map includes latitude and longitude.
6. Mileage scale. A mileage scale shows how far apart, in miles and kilometers, each location is from other locations.

Most Maps Include Three Basic Types of Information

1. The boundaries of countries, cities, empires, and other kinds of "political" information. A good map shows each political division in a different color to make them all easy to find. The color of each region or country is the decision of the mapmaker (also known as a cartographer).
2. Mountains, oceans, rivers, and other "physical" or "topographic" information. The mountains on this kind of map have been rendered by the cartographer: Switzerland and Norway are mountainous; Germany and Belarus are relatively flat.

3. Latitude, longitude, a mileage scale, and other information. These elements help the reader place the information in some kind of context. Some maps include an "N" with an arrow that points north. Most maps show northern areas (Alaska, Norway, etc.) at the top. A map that does not do this is not misleading or wrong. But if an "N" arrow does not appear on the map, be sure you know where north is.

"Political" information tends to change a great deal: maps may change after a major war if the winners take more territory, for example. "Physical" information changes slowly: latitude, rivers, distances, and the like do not change or generally change very slowly.

In addition, many maps include information about the spread of disease, the location of cathedrals and universities, trade routes, and any number of other things. There is no real limit to the kinds of information a map can show, and the more information a map can display clearly, the more useful it is. Any good map will include a "legend" stating the information that makes the map useful. The more detailed the map, the more information the mapmaker should provide in the legend.

Again, note that only the oceans, large bodies of water, and rivers—the "physical" features in a map—really exist in nature. They are relatively changeless. All other features on a map are made up and change fairly often. The maps you see here and on the next page all show the same familiar "boot" we call Italy. But all or part of this landmass has also been called Latium, Campania, the duchy of Benevento, the Papal States, the kingdom of the Two Sicilies, Tuscany, Lombardy, Piedmont, and Savoy. Populations and place names change; mountains and oceans do not, at least not much. Whenever you have trouble finding a region or a place on a map, look for a permanent feature to get your bearings.

In addition to kingdoms, cities, and mountains, maps can show the physical proximity of any two or more ideas, movements, or developments. Map 10.5 (p. 243) shows the routes of several crusades of the eleventh and twelfth centuries. Note that the legend associates the color of a crusade's route (shown as a line) with its duration in years. This map makes it possible to see a number of useful things at a glance that could take several maps to describe, including the following:

1. Where each crusade began. (Note the places that send the most crusades and those that send none.)
2. How far each crusade traveled. (Note the mileage key.)

3. Which route each crusade took. (Why did no Crusaders make the trip only on land?)
4. How much time passed between the end of one crusade and the beginning of another. (Did the rate of Crusades accelerate or slow down over time? What does this suggest?)

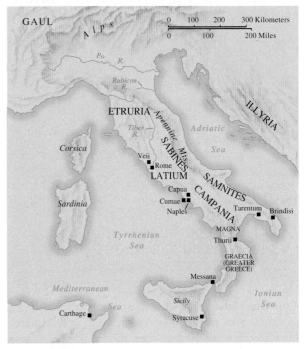

Ancient Italy

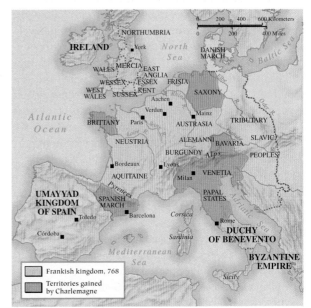

The Carolingian Empire

The Unification of Italy

5. Which Crusaders actually made it to the eastern Mediterranean and which did not. (Consider any correlation between route and timing.)
6. The names of the crusader states themselves.

Another kind of invasion appears in Map 11.1 (p. 253). This map shows the steady progress of the Black Death from the Black Sea and the Mediterranean north and west through Europe. Using the legend, find the shade of color that corresponds to the first outbreak of plague, in December 1347, and follow the spread of disease, shown here in six-month intervals, as you follow the colors northward.

The documents on p. 252 give a sense of how contemporaries tried to explain the plague, and the image on p. 254 vividly illustrates how some people responded to the horrors of the plague. Map 11.1 brings to mind another aspect of this horror by tracking the plague's ruthless and irresistible advance, month by month, year by year. The more information you can gather from the map, the more the document and illustrations can tell you about the horrors of the plague.

A happier kind of movement, the advance of learning, appears in Map 9.2 (p. 212). For this map, it is important to identify the symbols for universities and schools and to see where they appear on the map. Because education does not tend to move as a wave, as the plague did, each symbol represents a place where learning flourished more than it did in places without a symbol of some kind.

Map 11.1 makes it clear that the plague began in one part of Europe and touched nearly every region as it passed through it. Map 9.2 shows that education works differently; some people have better access to it than others. Your job as a historian is to recognize this and then to figure out why.

Putting It Together: Reading and Studying Documents, Supported by Images

Learning to read a document is no different from learning to read a restaurant menu. The more you practice, the quicker your eyes will find the lobster and pastries.

Let Us Explore a Pair of Primary Sources

As the introduction to the reading on the next page makes clear, King Louis XIV of France is writing the king of Tonkin to ask permission to send Christian missionaries to Southeast Asia. But this exchange of letters tells a great deal more than that.

Before you read this document, take a careful look at this portrait of Louis XIV. As this image makes clear, Louis lived during an age of flourishes and excess. Among many other questions, including some that appear later, you may ask yourself how Louis's manner of speaking reflects the public presentation you see in his portrait.

King Louis XIV

A Letter to the King of Tonkin from Louis XIV

1 Most high, most excellent, most mighty and most magnanimous
2 Prince, our very dear and good friend, may it please God to increase
3 your greatness with a happy end!

4   We hear from our subjects who were in your Realm what pro-
5 tection you accorded them. We appreciate this all the more since we
6 have for you all the esteem that one can have for a prince as illustri-
7 ous through his military valor as he is commendable for the justice
8 which he exercises in his Realm. We have even been informed that
9 you have not been satisfied to extend this general protection to our
10 subjects but, in particular, that you gave effective proofs of it to
11 Messrs. Deydier and de Bourges. We would have wished that they
12 might have been able to recognize all the favors they received from
13 you by having presents worthy of you offered you; but since the war
14 which we have had for several years, in which all of Europe had
15 banded together against us, prevented our vessels from going to the
16 Indies, at the present time, when we are at peace after having gained
17 many victories and expanded our Realm through the conquest of
18 several important places, we have immediately given orders to the
19 Royal Company to establish itself in your kingdom as soon as possi-
20 ble, and have commanded Messrs. Deydier and de Bourges to re-
21 main with you in order to maintain a good relationship between
22 our subjects and yours, also to warn us on occasions that might
23 present themselves when we might be able to give you proofs of our
24 esteem and of our wish to concur with your satisfaction as well as
25 with your best interests.

26   By way of initial proof, we have given orders to have brought
27 to you some presents which we believe might be agreeable to you.
28 But the one thing in the world which we desire most, both for you
29 and for your Realm, would be to obtain for your subjects who have
30 already embraced the law of the only true God of heaven and earth,
31 the freedom to profess it, since this law is the highest, the noblest,
32 the most sacred and especially the most suitable to have kings reign
33 absolutely over the people.

34   We are even quite convinced that, if you knew the truths and
35 the maxims which it teaches, you would give first of all to your
36 subjects the glorious example of embracing it. We wish you this in-
37 comparable blessing together with a long and happy reign, and we
38 pray God that it may please Him to augment your greatness with
39 the happiest of endings.

40   Written at Saint-Germain-en-Laye, the 10th day of January, 1681,
41   Your very dear and good friend,
42   Louis

Answer from the King of Tonkin to Louis XIV

43 The King of Tonkin sends to the King of France a letter to express
44 to him his best sentiments, saying that he was happy to learn that
45 fidelity is a durable good of man and that justice is the most impor-
46 tant of things. Consequently practicing of fidelity and justice cannot
47 but yield good results. Indeed, though France and our Kingdom dif-
48 fer as to mountains, rivers, and boundaries, if fidelity and justice
49 reign among our villages, our conduct will express all of our good
50 feelings and contain precious gifts. Your communication, which
51 comes from a country which is a thousand leagues away, and which
52 proceeds from the heart as a testimony of your sincerity, merits re-
53 peated consideration and infinite praise. Politeness toward strangers
54 is nothing unusual in our country. There is not a stranger who is
55 not well received by us. How then could we refuse a man from
56 France, which is the most celebrated among the kingdoms of the
57 world and which for love of us wishes to frequent us and bring us
58 merchandise? These feelings of fidelity and justice are truly worthy
59 to be applauded. As regards your wish that we should cooperate in
60 propagating your religion, we do not dare to permit it, for there is
61 an ancient custom, introduced by edicts, which formally forbids it.
62 Now, edicts are promulgated only to be carried out faithfully;
63 without fidelity nothing is stable. How could we disdain a well-
64 established custom to satisfy a private friendship? . . .

65   We beg you to understand well that this is our communication
66 concerning our mutual acquaintance. This then is my letter. We send
67 you herewith a modest gift, which we offer you with a glad heart.

68   This letter was written at the beginning of winter and on a
69 beautiful day.

Your textbook does not show a corresponding portrait of the king of Tonkin, but you might try to create a picture of him in your mind as you read this response to the letter he receives from his fellow ruler.

The following questions about this document are the kinds of questions your instructor would ask about the document.

1. Why does Louis refer to the king of Tonkin, whom he never met, as his "very dear and good friend" (line 2)? Do you think that this French king would begin a conversation with, say, a French shopkeeper in quite the same way? If not, why does he identify more with a fellow king than with a fellow Frenchman?

2. How often do you imagine that the king of France had to persuade people to do what he wanted rather than order them to do so? Who might the people that he had to persuade have been?

3. Note that Louis uses what is referred to as the "royal we," referring to himself in the plural. When does the king of Tonkin refer to himself in the singular ("he," "my"), and when does he refer to himself in the plural ("we")?

4. Why does Louis say that he is writing at that particular time rather than earlier (lines 13–18)?

5. Why does Louis say that Christian missionaries will be good for Tonkin and its people (lines 28–33)? What reason in Louis's own letter makes you wonder if converting the people of Tonkin to Christianity is "the one thing in the world which we desire most"?

6. Does the king of Tonkin seem pleased to hear from Louis and to receive his request (lines 43–53)? How does he refer to the gift Louis offers him?

7. Louis mentions his gratitude for the good treatment of some French subjects when they were "in

your realm." What do you think these Frenchmen were doing there? Do you think they were invited, or did they arrive on their own? How does the king of Tonkin respond when Louis mentions his appreciation for the "protection" they were accorded (lines 53–58)? Protection from what, do you suppose?

8. What reason does the king of Tonkin give for refusing Louis's offer of Christian missionaries (lines 59–64)? He takes care to explain to Louis that "without fidelity [to edicts] nothing is stable." What does this suggest about the king of Tonkin's attitude toward Louis and the "incomparable blessing" of faith in the Christian god? How many French people (or Europeans, for that matter) is the king of Tonkin likely to have met? What French person or persons might have already expressed to the king the ideas that Louis offers?

9. Compare the final lines of each letter. What significance do you draw from the fact that Louis names the day, month, year, and location in which he writes? Apart from later historians, to whom in particular would this information be of greatest interest? What is the significance of the king of Tonkin's closing line?

If you can propose thoughtful answers to these questions, you will have come to know the material very well and should be ready for whatever examinations and papers await you in your course.

Western Civilization to 1500

ALTHOUGH EARLY CIVILIZATIONS emerged in different parts of the world, the foundations of Western civilization were laid by the Mesopotamians and the Egyptians. They developed cities and struggled with the  problems of organized states. They developed writing to keep records and created literature. They constructed monumental architecture to please their gods, symbolize their power, and preserve their culture. They developed political, military, social, and religious structures to deal with the basic problems of human existence and organization. These first literate civilizations left detailed records that allow us to view how they grappled with three of the fundamental problems that humans have pondered: the nature of human relationships, the nature of the universe, and the role of divine forces in that cosmos. Although later peoples in Western civilization would provide different answers from those of the Mesopotamians and Egyptians, it was they who first posed the questions, gave answers, and wrote them down. Human memory begins with these two civilizations.

By 1500 B.C.E., much of the creative impulse of the Mesopotamian and Egyptian civilizations was beginning to wane. The entry of new peoples known as Indo-Europeans who moved into Asia Minor and Anatolia (modern Turkey) led to the creation of a Hittite kingdom that entered into conflict with the Egyptians. The invasion of the Sea Peoples around 1200 B.C.E., however, destroyed the Hittites, severely weakened the Egyptians, and created a power vacuum that allowed a patchwork of petty kingdoms and city-states to emerge, especially in the area of Syria and Palestine. All of them were eventually overshadowed by the rise of the great empires of the Assyrians, Chaldeans, and Persians. The Assyrian Empire was the first to unite almost all of the ancient Near East. Far larger was the empire of the Great Kings of Persia. Although it owed much to the administrative organization developed by the Assyrians, the Persian Empire had its own peculiar

strengths. Persian rule was tolerant as well as efficient. Conquered peoples were allowed to keep their own religions, customs, and methods of doing business. The many years of peace that the Persian Empire brought to the Near East facilitated trade and the general well-being of its peoples. Many Near Eastern peoples expressed gratitude for being subjects of the Great Kings of Persia.

The Israelites were one of these peoples. Never numerous, they created no empire and were dominated by the Assyrians, Chaldeans, and Persians. Nevertheless, they left a spiritual legacy that influenced much of the later development of Western civilization. The evolution of Hebrew monotheism (belief in a single god) created in Judaism one of the world's great religions  and influenced the development of both Christianity and Islam. When we speak of the Judeo-Christian heritage of Western civilization, we refer not only to the concept of monotheism but also to ideas of law, morality, and social justice that have become important parts of Western culture.

On the western fringes of the Persian Empire, another relatively small group of people, the Greeks, were creating cultural and political ideals that would also have an important impact on Western civilization. The first Greek civilization, known as the Mycenaean, took shape around 1600 B.C.E. and fell to new Greek-speaking invaders five hundred years later. By the eighth century B.C.E., the polis or city-state had become the chief focus of Greek life. Loyalty to the polis created a close-knit community but also divided Greece into a host of independent states. Two of them, Sparta and Athens, became the most important. They were very different, however. Sparta created a closed, highly disciplined society, while Athens moved toward an open, democratic civilization.

The Classical Age in Greece (ca. 500–338 B.C.E.) began with a mighty confrontation between the Greeks and the Persian Empire. After their victory over the Persians, the Greeks began to divide into two large alliances, one headed by Sparta and the other by Athens. Athens created a naval empire and flourished during the age of Pericles, but fear of Athens led to the Great Peloponnesian War between Sparta and Athens and their allies. For all of their brilliant accomplishments, the Greeks were unable to rise above the divisions and rivalries that caused them to fight each other and undermine their own civilization.

The accomplishments of the Greeks formed the fountainhead of Western culture. Socrates, Plato, and Aristotle established the foundations of Western phi-

losophy. Our literary forms are largely derived from Greek poetry and drama. Greek notions of harmony, proportion, and beauty have remained the touchstones for all subsequent Western art. A rational method of inquiry, so important to modern science, was conceived in ancient Greece. Many of our political terms are Greek in origin, and so are our concepts of the rights and duties of citizenship, especially as they were conceived in Athens, the first great democracy. Especially during their classical period, the Greeks raised and debated fundamental questions about the purpose of human existence, the structure of human society, and the nature of the universe that have concerned Western thinkers ever since.

While the Greek city-states were pursuing their squabbles, to their north a new and powerful kingdom—Macedonia—emerged. Under King Philip II, the Macedonians defeated a Greek allied army in 338 B.C.E. and then consolidated their control over the Greek peninsula. Although the independent Greek city-states lost their freedom when they were conquered by the Macedonians, Greek culture did not die. Under the leadership of Alexander the Great, son of Philip II, both Macedonians and Greeks invaded and conquered the Persian Empire. In the conquered lands, Greeks and non-Greeks established a series of kingdoms (known as the Hellenistic kingdoms) and inaugurated the Hellenistic era.

The Hellenistic period was, in its own way, a vibrant one. New cities arose and flourished. New philosophical ideas captured the minds of many. Significant achievements occurred in art, literature, and science. Greek culture spread throughout the Near East and made an impact wherever it was carried. In some areas of the Hellenistic world, queens played an active role in political life, and many upper-class women found new avenues for expressing themselves. Although the Hellenistic era achieved a degree of political stability, by the late third century B.C.E., signs of decline were beginning to multiply, and the growing power of Rome would eventually endanger the Hellenistic world.

Sometime in the eighth century B.C.E., a group of Latin-speaking people built a small community called Rome on the Tiber River in Italy. Between 509 and 264 B.C.E., this city expanded and united almost all of Italy under its control. Even more dramatically, between 264 and 133 B.C.E., Rome expanded to the west and east and became master of the Mediterranean Sea.

After 133 B.C.E., however, Rome's republican institutions proved inadequate for the task of ruling an empire. In the breakdown that ensued, ambitious individuals saw opportunities for power unparalleled in Roman history and succumbed to the temptations. After a series of bloody civil wars, peace was finally achieved when Octavian defeated Antony and Cleopatra. Octavian, who came to be known by the title of *Augustus*, created a

new system of government that seemed to preserve the republic while establishing the basis for a new system that would rule the empire in an orderly fashion.

After a century of internal upheaval, Augustus established a new order that began the Roman Empire, which experienced peace and prosperity between 14 and 180. During this era, trade flourished and the provinces were governed efficiently. In the course of the third century, however, the Roman Empire came near to collapse due to invasions, civil wars, and economic decline. Although the emperors Diocletian and Constantine brought new life to the so-called Late Empire at the beginning of the fourth century, their efforts shored up the empire only temporarily. In the course of the fifth century, the empire divided into western and eastern parts.

The Roman Empire was the largest empire in antiquity. Using their practical skills, the Romans produced achievements in language, law, engineering, and government that were bequeathed to the future. The Romance languages of today (French, Italian, Spanish, Portuguese, and Romanian) are based on Latin. Western practices of impartial justice and trial by jury owe much to Roman law. As great builders, the Romans left monuments to their skills throughout Europe, some of which, such as aqueducts and roads, are still in use today. Aspects of Roman administrative practices survived in the Western world for centuries. The Romans also preserved the intellectual heritage of the ancient world.

During its last two hundred years, the Roman world underwent a slow transformation with the spread of Christianity. The rise of Christianity marked an important break with the dominant values of the Roman world. Christianity began as a small Jewish sect, but under the guidance of Paul of Tarsus it became a world religion that appealed to both Jews and non-Jews. Despite persecution by Roman authorities, Christianity grew and became widely accepted by the fourth century. At the end of that century, it was made the official state religion of the Roman Empire.

The period of late antiquity that saw the disintegration of the western part of the Roman Empire also witnessed the emergence of a new European civilization in the early Middle Ages. This early medieval civilization was formed by the coalescence of three major elements: the Germanic peoples who moved into the western part  of the empire and established new kingdoms, the continuing attraction of the Greco-Roman cultural legacy, and the Christian church. Politically, a new series of Germanic kingdoms emerged in western Europe. Each fused Roman and Germanic elements to create a new society. The Christian church (or Roman Catholic Church, as it came to be called in the west) played a crucial role in the growth of the new European civilization. The church developed an organized government under the leadership of the pope. It also assimilated the classical tradition and through its clergy brought Christianized civilization to the Germanic tribes. Especially important were the monks and nuns who led the way in converting the Germanic peoples in Europe to Christianity.

At the end of the eighth century, a new kingdom—the Carolingian Empire—came to control much of western and central Europe, especially during the reign of Charlemagne. In the long run, the creation of a western empire fostered the idea of a distinct European identity and marked a shift of power from the south to the north. Italy and the Mediterranean had been the center of the Roman Empire. The lands north of the Alps now became the political center of Europe, and increasingly, Europe emerged as the focus and center of Western civilization.

Building on a fusion of Germanic, classical, and Christian elements, the Carolingian Empire was well governed but was held together primarily by personal loyalty to the strong king. The economy of the eighth and ninth centuries was based almost entirely on farming, which proved inadequate to maintain a large monarchical system. As a result, a new political and military order—known as fief-holding—subsequently evolved to become an integral part of the political world of the Middle Ages. Fief-holding was characterized by a decentralization of political power, in which lords exercised legal, administrative, and military power. This transfer of public power into many private hands seemed to provide the security that the weak central government could not provide.

The new European civilization that had emerged in the ninth and tenth centuries began to come into its own in the eleventh and twelfth centuries, and Europeans established new patterns that reached their high point in the thirteenth century. The High Middle Ages (1000–1300) was a period of recovery and growth for Western civilization, characterized by a greater sense of security and a burst of energy and enthusiasm. Climatic improvements that produced better growing conditions, an expansion of cultivated land, and technological changes combined to enable Europe's food supply to increase significantly after 1000. This increase in agricultural production helped sustain a dramatic rise in population that was physically apparent in the expansion of towns and cities.

The development of trade and the rise of cities added a dynamic new element to the civilization of the High Middle Ages. Trading activities flourished first in northern Italy and Flanders and then spread outward from these centers. In the late tenth and eleventh centuries, this renewal of commercial life led to a revival of cities. Old Roman sites came back to life, and new towns  arose at major crossroads or natural harbors favorable to trading activities. By the twelfth and thirteenth centuries, both the urban centers and the urban population of Europe were experiencing a dramatic expansion. The revival of trade, the expansion of towns and cities, and the development of a money economy did not mean the end of a predominantly rural European society, but they did open the door to new ways to make a living and new opportunities for people to expand and enrich their lives. Eventually, they created the foundations for the development of a predominantly urban industrial society.

During the High Middle Ages, European society was dominated by a landed aristocracy whose primary function was to fight. These nobles built innumerable castles that gave a distinctive look to the countryside.  Although lords and vassals seemed forever mired in endless petty conflicts, over time medieval kings began to exert a centralizing authority and inaugurated the process of developing new kinds of monarchical states. By the thirteenth century, European monarchs were solidifying their governmental institutions in pursuit of greater power. The nobles, who rationalized their warlike attitudes by calling themselves the defenders of Christian society, continued to dominate the medieval world politically, economically, and socially. But quietly and surely, within this world of castles and private power, kings gradually began to extend their public powers and developed the machinery of government that would enable them to become the centers of political authority in Europe. The actions of these medieval monarchs laid the foundation for the European kingdoms that in one form or another have dominated the European political scene ever since.

During the High Middle Ages, the power of both nobles and kings was often overshadowed by the authority of the Catholic Church, perhaps the dominant institution of the High Middle Ages. In the early Middle Ages, the Catholic Church had shared in the challenge of new growth by reforming itself and striking out on a path toward greater papal power, both within the church and over European society. The High Middle Ages witnessed a spiritual renewal that led to numerous and even divergent paths: revived papal leadership, the development of centralized administrative machinery that buttressed papal authority, and new dimensions to the religious life of the clergy and laity. A wave of religious enthusiasm in the twelfth and thirteenth centuries led to the formation of new religious orders that worked to provide for the needs of the people, especially their concern for achieving salvation.

The economic, political, and religious growth of the High Middle Ages also gave European society a new confidence that enabled it to look beyond its borders to the lands and empires of the east. Only a confident Europe could have undertaken the Crusades, a concerted military effort to recover the Holy Land of the Near East from the Muslims.

Western assurance and energy, so crucial to the Crusades, were also evident in a burst of intellectual and artistic activity. New educational institutions known as universities came into being in the twelfth century. New literature, written in the vernacular language, appealed to the growing number of people in cities or at courts who could read. The study of theology, "queen of the sciences,"  reached a high point in the work of Thomas Aquinas. At the same time, a religious building spree—especially evident in the great Romanesque and Gothic cathedrals of the age—left the landscape bedecked with churches that were the visible symbols of Christian Europe's vitality.

Growth and optimism seemed to characterize the High Middle Ages, but underneath the calm exterior lay seeds of discontent and change. Dissent from church teaching and practices grew in the thirteenth century, leading to a climate of fear and intolerance as the church responded with inquisitorial instruments to enforce conformity to its teachings. The breakdown of the old agricultural system and the creation of new relationships between lords and peasants led to local peasant uprisings in the late thirteenth century. The Crusades ended ignominiously with the fall of the last crusading foothold in the east in 1291. By that time, more and more signs of ominous troubles were appearing. The fourteenth century would prove to be a time of crisis for European civilization.

In the High Middle Ages, European civilization had developed many of its fundamental features. Monarchical states, capitalist trade and industry, banks, cities, and vernacular literature were all products of that fertile period. During the same time, the Catholic Church, under the direction of the papacy, reached its apogee. Fourteenth-century European society, however, was challenged by an overwhelming number of crises that led to the disintegration of medieval civilization. At midcentury, one of the most destructive natural disasters in history erupted—the Black Death, a devastating plague that wiped out at least one-third of the European population. Economic crises and social upheavals, including a decline in trade and industry, bank failures, and peasant revolts pitting lower classes against the upper classes, followed in the wake of the Black Death. The Hundred Years' War, a long, drawn-out conflict between the English and French, undermined political stability. The Catholic Church, too, experienced a crisis with the absence of the popes from Rome and even the spectacle of two popes condemning each other as the anti-Christ.

The new European society proved remarkably resilient, however. Periods of disintegration are often fertile grounds for change and new developments. Out of  the dissolution of medieval civilization came a rebirth of culture that historians have labeled the Renaissance. It was a period of transition that witnessed a continuation of the economic, political, and social trends that had begun in the High Middle Ages. It was also a movement in which artists and intellectuals proclaimed a new vision of humankind and raised fundamental questions about the value and importance of the individual. The humanists or intellectuals of the age called their period (from the mid-fourteenth to the mid-sixteenth century) an age of rebirth, believing that they had restored arts and letters to new glory after they had been "neglected" or "dead" for centuries. Of course, intellectuals and artists existed only among the upper classes, and the brilliant intellectual, cultural, and artistic accomplishments of the Renaissance were therefore products of and for the elite. The ideas of the Renaissance did not have a broad base among the masses.

The Renaissance did, however, raise new questions about medieval traditions. In advocating a return to the early sources of Christianity and criticizing current religious practices, the humanists raised fundamental issues about the Catholic Church, which was still an important institution. In the sixteenth century, the intellectual revolution of the fifteenth century gave way to a religious renaissance that touched the lives of people, including the masses, in new and profound ways.

When the monk Martin Luther entered the public scene with an attack on the sale of indulgences, few people suspected that he would eventually produce a division of Europe along religious lines. But the yearning for reform of the church and meaningful religious experience caused a seemingly simple dispute to escalate into a powerful movement.

CHAPTER

13

Reformation and Religious Warfare in the Sixteenth Century

A nineteenth-century engraving showing Luther before the Diet of Worms

bpk, Berlin/Art Resource, NY

CHAPTER OUTLINE AND FOCUS QUESTIONS

Prelude to Reformation

Q What were the chief ideas of the Christian humanists, and how did they differ from the ideas of the Protestant reformers?

Martin Luther and the Reformation in Germany

Q What were Martin Luther's main disagreements with the Roman Catholic Church, and what political, economic, and social conditions help explain why the movement he began spread so quickly across Europe?

The Spread of the Protestant Reformation

Q What were the main tenets of Lutheranism, Zwinglianism, Anabaptism, and Calvinism, and how did they differ from each other and from Catholicism? What impact did political, economic, and social conditions have on the development of these four reform movements?

The Social Impact of the Protestant Reformation

Q What impact did the Protestant Reformation have on society in the sixteenth century?

The Catholic Reformation

Q What measures did the Roman Catholic Church take to reform itself and to combat Protestantism in the sixteenth century?

Politics and the Wars of Religion in the Sixteenth Century

Q What role did politics, economic and social conditions, and religion play in the European wars of the sixteenth century?

CRITICAL THINKING

Q Where and how did the reform movements take hold, and how did the emergence of these reform movements affect the political and social realms where they were adopted?

CONNECTIONS TO TODAY

Q How are the religious controversies of the sixteenth century related to religious and social conditions in the Western world today?

ON APRIL 18, 1521, a lowly monk stood before the emperor and princes of the Holy Roman Empire in the city of Worms. He had been called before this august gathering to answer charges of heresy, charges that could threaten his very life. The monk was confronted with a pile of his books and asked if he wished to defend them all or reject a part. Courageously, Martin Luther defended them all and asked to be shown where any part was in error on the basis of "Scripture and plain reason." The emperor was outraged by Luther's response and made his own position clear the next day: "Not only I, but you of this noble German nation, would be forever disgraced if by our negligence not only heresy but the very suspicion of heresy were to survive. After having heard yesterday the obstinate defense of Luther, I regret that I have so long delayed in proceeding against him and his false teaching. I will have no more to do with him." Luther's appearance at Worms set the stage for a serious challenge to the authority of the Catholic Church. This was by no means the first crisis in the church's fifteen-hundred-year history, but its consequences were more far-reaching than anyone at Worms in 1521 could have imagined.

Throughout the Middle Ages, the Christian church continued to assert its primacy of position. It had overcome defiance of its temporal authority by emperors and kings while challenges to its doctrines had been crushed by the Inquisition and combated by new religious orders that carried its message of salvation to all the towns and villages of medieval Europe. The growth of the papacy had paralleled the growth of the church, but by the end of the Middle Ages, challenges to papal authority from the rising power of monarchical states had resulted in a loss of papal temporal authority. An even greater threat to papal authority and church unity arose in the sixteenth century when the unity of Christendom was shattered by the Reformation.

The movement begun by Martin Luther when he made his dramatic stand quickly spread across Europe, a clear indication of dissatisfaction with Catholic practices. Within a short time, new religious practices, doctrines, and organizations, including Zwinglianism, Calvinism, Anabaptism, and Anglicanism, were attracting adherents all over Europe. Although seemingly helpless to stop the new Protestant churches, the Catholic Church also underwent a reformation and managed to revive its fortunes by the mid-sixteenth century. All too soon, the doctrinal divisions between Protestants and Catholics led to a series of religious wars that dominated the history of western Europe in the second half of the sixteenth century.

Prelude to Reformation

Q FOCUS QUESTION: What were the chief ideas of the Christian humanists, and how did they differ from the ideas of the Protestant reformers?

Martin Luther's reform movement was by no means the first in sixteenth-century Europe. During the second half of the fifteenth century, the new classical learning that was part of Italian Renaissance humanism spread to northern Europe and spawned a movement called **Christian** or **northern Renaissance humanism**, whose major goal was the reform of Christendom.

Christian or Northern Renaissance Humanism

The most important characteristic of northern Renaissance humanism was its reform program. Convinced of the ability of human beings to reason and improve themselves, the northern humanists thought that through education in the sources of classical, and especially Christian, antiquity, they could instill a true inner piety or an inward religious feeling that would bring about a reform of the church and society. For this reason, Christian humanists supported schools, brought out new editions of the classics, and prepared new editions of the Bible and writings of the church fathers. In the preface to his edition of the Greek New Testament, the famous humanist Erasmus wrote:

> Indeed, I disagree very much with those who are unwilling that Holy Scripture, translated into the vulgar tongue, be read by the uneducated, as if Christ taught such intricate doctrines that they could scarcely be understood by very few theologians, or as if the strength of the Christian religion consisted in men's ignorance of it.... I would that even the lowliest women read the Gospels and the Pauline Epistles. And I would that they were translated into all languages so that they could be read and understood not only by Scots and Irish but also by Turks and Saracens [Arabs].[1]

Like later intellectuals, Christian humanists believed that to change society, they must first change the human beings who compose it.

ERASMUS The most influential of all the Christian humanists was the Dutch-born scholar Desiderius Erasmus (dez-i-DEER-ee-uss i-RAZZ-mus) (1466–1536). After withdrawing from a monastery, he wandered to France, England, Italy, Germany, and Switzerland, conversing everywhere in the classical Latin that might be called his mother tongue. The *Handbook of the Christian Knight*, published in 1503, reflected his preoccupation with religion. He called his conception of religion "the philosophy of Christ," by which he meant that Christianity should be a guiding philosophy for the direction of daily life rather than the system of dogmatic beliefs and practices that the medieval church seemed to stress. In other words, he emphasized inner piety and de-emphasized the external forms of religion (such as the sacraments, pilgrimages, fasts, veneration of saints, and relics). To return to the simplicity of the early church, people needed to understand the original meaning of the Scriptures and early church fathers.

To Erasmus, the reform of the church meant spreading an understanding of the philosophy of Jesus, providing enlightened education in the sources of early Christianity, and making commonsense criticism of the abuses in the church. This last is especially evident in

Louvre, Paris/Scala/Art Resource, NY

Erasmus. Desiderius Erasmus, the most influential of the northern Renaissance humanists, sought to restore Christianity to the early simplicity found in the teachings of Jesus. This portrait of Erasmus was painted in 1523 by Hans Holbein the Younger, who had formed a friendship with the great humanist while they were both in Basel.

The Praise of Folly, written in 1509, in which Erasmus engaged in humorous yet effective criticism of the most corrupt practices of his own society. He was especially harsh on the abuses within the ranks of the clergy:

> Many of [the monks] work so hard at protocol and at traditional fastidiousness that they think one heaven hardly a suitable reward for their labors; never recalling, however, that the time will come when Christ will demand a reckoning of that which he had prescribed, namely charity, and that he will hold their deeds of little account. One monk will then exhibit his belly filled with every kind of fish; another will profess a knowledge of over a hundred hymns. Still another will reveal a countless number of fasts that he has made, and will account for his large belly by explaining that his fasts have always been broken by a single large meal.[2]

Erasmus's program did not achieve the reform of the church that he so desired. His moderation and his emphasis on education were quickly overwhelmed by the passions of the Reformation. Undoubtedly, though, his work helped prepare the way for the Reformation; as contemporaries proclaimed, "Erasmus laid the egg that Luther hatched." Yet Erasmus eventually disapproved of Luther and the Protestant reformers. He had no intention of destroying the unity of the medieval Christian church; instead, his whole program was based on reform within the church.

Church and Religion on the Eve of the Reformation

Corruption in the Catholic Church was another factor that spurred people to want reform. No doubt the failure of the Renaissance popes to provide spiritual leadership had affected the spiritual life of all Christendom. The papal court's preoccupation with finances had an especially strong impact on the clergy. So did the economic changes of the fourteenth and fifteenth centuries. The highest positions among the clergy were increasingly held by nobles or wealthy members of the bourgeoisie. Moreover, to increase their revenues, high church officials (such as bishops, archbishops, and cardinals) took over more than one church office. This so-called **pluralism** led in turn to absenteeism: church officeholders ignored their duties and hired underlings who sometimes lacked the proper qualifications. There were widespread complaints about the ignorance and ineptness of parish priests.

While many of the leaders of the church were failing to meet their responsibilities, ordinary people were clamoring for meaningful religious expression and certainty of salvation. As a result, for some the salvation process became almost mechanical. As more and more people sought salvation through the veneration of relics, collections of such objects grew. Frederick the Wise, elector of Saxony and Martin Luther's prince, had amassed more than 19,000 relics to which were attached **indulgences** that could reduce one's time in purgatory by nearly 2 million years. (An indulgence is a remission, after death, of all or part of the punishment for sin.) Other people sought certainty of salvation in the popular mystical movement known as the Modern Devotion, which downplayed religious dogma and stressed the need to follow the teachings of Jesus. Thomas à Kempis, author of *The Imitation of Christ*, wrote that "truly, at the day of judgment we shall not be examined by what we have read, but what we have done; not how well we have spoken, but how religiously we have lived."

What is striking about the revival of religious piety in the fifteenth century—whether expressed through external forces such as the veneration of relics and the buying of indulgences or through the mystical path—was its adherence to the orthodox beliefs and practices of the Catholic Church. The agitation for certainty of salvation and spiritual peace was done within the framework of the "holy mother Church." But disillusionment grew as the devout experienced the clergy's inability to live up to their expectations. The deepening of religious life, especially in the second half of the fifteenth century, found little echo among the worldly-wise clergy, and this environment helps explain the tremendous and immediate impact of Luther's ideas.

Martin Luther and the Reformation in Germany

Q **Focus Question:** What were Martin Luther's main disagreements with the Roman Catholic Church, and what political, economic, and social conditions help explain why the movement he began spread so quickly across Europe?

The Protestant Reformation began with a typical medieval question: What must I do to be saved? Martin Luther, a deeply religious man, found an answer that did not fit within the traditional teachings of the late medieval church. Ultimately, he split with that church, destroying the religious unity of western Christendom.

The Early Luther

Martin Luther was born in Germany on November 10, 1483. His father wanted him to become a lawyer, so Luther enrolled at the University of Erfurt. In 1505, after becoming a master in the liberal arts, the young man began to study law. But Luther was not content, due in large part to his long-standing religious inclinations. That summer, while returning to Erfurt after a brief visit home, he was caught in a ferocious thunderstorm and vowed that if he survived unscathed, he would become a monk. He then entered the monastic order of the Augustinian Hermits in Erfurt, much to his father's disgust. In the monastery, Luther focused on his major concern, the assurance of salvation. The traditional beliefs and practices of the church seemed unable to relieve his obsession with this question. Luther threw himself into his monastic routine with a vengeance:

> I was indeed a good monk and kept my order so strictly that I could say that if ever a monk could get to heaven through monastic discipline, I was that monk.... And yet my conscience would not give me certainty, but I always doubted and said, "You didn't do that right. You weren't contrite enough. You left that out of your confession." The more I tried to remedy an uncertain, weak and troubled conscience with human traditions, the more I daily found it more uncertain, weaker and more troubled.[3]

Despite his herculean efforts, Luther achieved no certainty of salvation.

To help overcome his difficulties, his superiors recommended that he study theology. Luther received his doctorate in 1512 and then became a professor in the theological faculty at the University of Wittenberg, lecturing on the Bible. Sometime between 1513 and 1516, through his study of the Bible, he arrived at an answer to his problem.

Catholic doctrine emphasized that both faith and good works were required for a Christian to achieve personal salvation. In Luther's eyes, human beings, weak and powerless in the sight of an almighty God, could never do enough good works to merit salvation. Through his study of the Bible, especially his work on Paul's Epistle to the Romans, Luther discovered another way of viewing this problem. To Luther, humans are saved not through their good works but through faith in the promises of God, made possible by the sacrifice of Jesus on the cross. The doctrine of salvation or justification by grace through faith alone became the primary doctrine of the Protestant Reformation (**justification** is the act by which a person is made deserving of salvation). Because Luther had arrived at this doctrine from his study of the Bible, the Bible became for Luther, as for all other Protestants, the chief guide to religious truth. Justification by faith and the Bible as the sole authority in religious affairs were the twin pillars of the Protestant Reformation.

THE INDULGENCE CONTROVERSY Luther did not regard himself as either an innovator or a heretic, but his involvement in the indulgence controversy propelled him into an open confrontation with church officials and forced him to see the theological implications of justification by faith alone. In 1517, Pope Leo X had issued a special jubilee indulgence to finance the ongoing construction of Saint Peter's Basilica in Rome. Johann Tetzel, a rambunctious Dominican, hawked the indulgences with the slogan "As soon as the coin in the coffer [money box] rings, the soul from purgatory springs."

Luther was greatly distressed by the widespread selling of indulgences, certain that people who relied on these pieces of paper to assure themselves of salvation were guaranteeing their eternal damnation instead. Greatly angered, Luther issued a stunning indictment of the abuses in the sale of indulgences, known as the Ninety-Five Theses (see the box on p. 306). It is doubtful that Luther intended to break with the church over the issue of indulgences. If the pope had clarified the use of indulgences, as Luther wished, Luther would probably have been satisfied. But Pope Leo X did not take the issue seriously and is even reported to have said that Luther was simply "some drunken German who will amend his ways when he sobers up." Meanwhile, thousands of copies of a German translation of the Ninety-Five Theses were quickly printed and were received sympathetically in a Germany that had a long tradition of dissatisfaction with papal policies and power.

THE QUICKENING REBELLION In three pamphlets published in 1520, Luther moved toward a more definite break with the Catholic Church. In *Address to the Nobility of the German Nation*, a political tract written in German, Luther called on the German princes to overthrow the papacy in Germany and establish a reformed German church. *The Babylonian Captivity of the Church* attacked the sacramental system as the means by which the pope and church had held the real meaning of the Gospel captive for a thousand years. Luther called for the reform of monasticism and for the clergy to marry. While virginity is good, he argued, marriage

is better, and freedom of choice is best. *On the Freedom of a Christian Man* was a short treatise on the doctrine of salvation. It is faith alone, not good works, that justifies, frees, and brings salvation through Jesus. Being saved and freed by his faith in Jesus, however, does not free the Christian from doing good works. Rather, he performs good works out of gratitude to God: "Good works do not make a good man, but a good man does good works."[4]

Unable to accept Luther's forcefully worded dissent from traditional Catholic teachings, the church excommunicated him in January 1521. He was also summoned to appear before the Reichstag (RYKHSS-tahk), the imperial diet of the Holy Roman Empire, in Worms (WURMZ or VORMPS), convened by the recently elected Emperor Charles V (1519–1556). Expected to recant the heretical doctrines he had espoused, Luther refused and made the famous reply that became the battle cry of the Reformation:

> Since then Your Majesty and your lordships desire a simple reply, I will answer without horns and without teeth. Unless I am convicted by Scripture and plain reason—I do not accept the authority of popes and councils, for they have contradicted each other—my conscience is captive to the Word of God. I cannot and I will not recant anything, for to go against conscience is neither right nor safe. Here I stand, I cannot do otherwise. God help me. Amen.[5]

The young Emperor Charles was outraged at Luther's audacity and gave his opinion that "a single friar who goes counter to all Christianity for a thousand years must be wrong." By the Edict of Worms, Martin Luther was made an outlaw within the empire. His works were to be burned and Luther himself captured and delivered to the emperor. Instead, Luther's prince, the elector of Saxony, sent him into hiding at the Wartburg (VART-bayrk) Castle, where he remained for nearly a year.

The Rise of Lutheranism

At the beginning of 1522, Luther returned to Wittenberg in Saxony and began to organize a reformed church. While at the Wartburg Castle, Luther's foremost achievement was his translation of the New Testament into German. Within twelve years, his German New Testament sold almost 200,000 copies. Lutheranism had wide appeal and spread rapidly, but not primarily through the written word, as only 4 to 5 percent of the people in Germany were literate at the time.

Luther and the Ninety-Five Theses

To most historians, the publication of Luther's Ninety-Five Theses marks the beginning of the Reformation. To Luther, they were simply a response to what he considered Johann Tetzel's blatant abuses in selling indulgences. Although written in Latin, Luther's statements were soon translated into German and disseminated widely across Germany. They made an immense impression on Germans already dissatisfied with the ecclesiastical and financial policies of the papacy.

Martin Luther, *Selections from the Ninety-Five Theses*

5. The Pope has neither the will nor the power to remit any penalties beyond those he has imposed either at his own discretion or by canon law.

20. Therefore the Pope, by his plenary remission of all penalties, does not mean "all" in the absolute sense, but only those imposed by himself.

21. Hence those preachers of Indulgences are wrong when they say that a man is absolved and saved from every penalty by the Pope's indulgences.

27. It is mere human talk to preach that the soul flies out [of purgatory] immediately the money clinks in the collection box.

28. It is certainly possible that when the money clinks in the collection box greed and avarice can increase; but the intercession of the Church depends on the will of God alone.

50. Christians should be taught that, if the Pope knew the exactions of the preachers of Indulgences, he would rather have the basilica of St. Peter reduced to ashes than built with the skin, flesh and bones of his sheep.

81. This wanton preaching of pardons makes it difficult even for learned men to redeem respect due to the Pope from the slanders or at least the shrewd questionings of the laity.

82. For example: "Why does not the Pope empty purgatory for the sake of most holy love and the supreme need of souls? This would be the most righteous of the reasons, if he can redeem innumerable souls for sordid money with which to build a basilica, the most trivial of reasons."

86. Again: "Since the Pope's wealth is larger than that of the crassest Crassi of our time, why does he not build this one basilica of St. Peter with his own money, rather than with that of the faithful poor?"

90. To suppress these most conscientious questionings of the laity by authority only, instead of refuting them by reason, is to expose the Church and the Pope to the ridicule of their enemies, and to make Christian people unhappy.

94. Christians should be exhorted to seek earnestly to follow Christ, their Head, through penalties, deaths, and hells.

95. And let them thus be more confident of entering heaven through many tribulations rather than through a false assurance of peace.

Q What were the major ideas of Luther's Ninety-Five Theses? Why did they have such a strong appeal in Germany?

Source: From *Martin Luther: Documents of Modern History* by E. G. Rupp and Benjamin Drewery. Palgrave Macmillan, 1970. Reproduced with permission of Palgrave Macmillan.

Instead, the primary means of disseminating Luther's ideas was the sermon. The preaching of evangelical sermons, based on a return to the original message of the Bible, found favor throughout Germany. Also useful to the spread of the Reformation were pamphlets illustrated with vivid woodcuts portraying the pope as a hideous Antichrist and titled with catchy phrases such as "I Wonder Why There Is No Money in the Land" (obviously an attack on papal greed).

Luther was able to gain the support of his prince, the elector of Saxony, as well as other German rulers among the more than three hundred states that made up the Holy Roman Empire. Lutheranism spread to both princely and ecclesiastical states in northern and central Germany as well as to two-thirds of the free imperial cities, especially those of southern Germany, where prosperous burghers, for both religious and secular reasons, became committed to Luther's cause. At its outset, the Reformation in Germany was largely an urban phenomenon. Three-fourths of the early converts to the reform movement were from the clergy, many of them from the better-educated upper classes,

Woodcut: Luther Versus the Pope. In the 1520s, after Luther's return to Wittenberg, his teachings began to spread rapidly, ending ultimately in a reform movement supported by state authorities. Pamphlets containing picturesque woodcuts were important in the spread of Luther's ideas. In the woodcut shown here, the crucified Jesus attends Luther's service on the left, while on the right the pope is at a table selling indulgences.

which made it easier for them to work with the ruling elites in the cities.

A series of crises in the mid-1520s, however, made it apparent that spreading the word of God was not as easy as Luther had originally envisioned—the usual plight of most reformers. Luther experienced dissent within his own ranks in Wittenberg as well as defection from many Christian humanists who feared that Luther's movement threatened the unity of Christendom. The Peasants' War constituted Luther's greatest challenge, however. In June 1524, peasants in Germany rose in revolt against their lords and looked to Luther for support. But Luther, who knew how much his reformation of the church depended on the full support of the German princes and magistrates, supported the rulers, although he also blamed them for helping to cause the rebellion by their earlier harsh treatment of the peasants. To Luther, who proved to be a conservative on economic and social issues, the state and its rulers were ordained by God and given the authority to maintain the peace and put down all revolts. By May 1525, the German princes had ruthlessly suppressed the peasant hordes. By this time,

Luther found himself ever more dependent on state authorities for the growth and maintenance of his reformed church.

Organizing the Church

Justification by faith was the starting point for most of Protestantism's major doctrines. Since Luther downplayed the role of good works in salvation, the sacraments also had to be redefined. No longer regarded as merit-earning works, they were now viewed as divinely established signs signifying the promise of salvation. Luther kept only two of the Catholic Church's seven sacraments: baptism and the Lord's Supper (the Eucharist). Baptism signified rebirth through grace. Regarding the Lord's Supper, Luther denied the Catholic doctrine of **transubstantiation**, which taught that the substance of the bread and wine consumed in the rite is miraculously transformed into the body and blood of Jesus. Yet he continued to insist on the real presence of Jesus's body and blood in the bread and wine given as a testament to God's forgiveness of sin.

Martin Luther and the Reformation in Germany **307**

Ninety-Five Theses	1517
Diet and Edict of Worms	1521
Peasants' War	1524–1525
Peace of Augsburg	1555

Luther took an active role in establishing a reformed church. Since the Catholic ecclesiastical hierarchy had been scrapped, Luther came to rely increasingly on the princes or state authorities to organize and guide the new Lutheran reformed churches. The Lutheran churches in Germany (and later in Scandinavia) quickly became territorial or state churches in which the state supervised and disciplined church members. As part of the development of these state-dominated churches, Luther also instituted new religious services to replace the Mass. These featured a worship service consisting of a German liturgy that focused on Bible reading, preaching the word of God, and song. Following his own denunciation of clerical celibacy, Luther married a former nun, Katherina von Bora (kat-uh-REE-nuh fun BOH-rah), in 1525. His union provided a model of married and family life for the new Protestant minister.

Germany and the Reformation: Religion and Politics

From its very beginning, the fate of Luther's movement was closely tied to political affairs. In 1519, Charles I, king of Spain and the grandson of the Emperor Maximilian, was elected Holy Roman emperor as Charles V (1519–1556). Charles V ruled over an immense empire, consisting of Spain and its overseas possessions, the traditional Austrian Habsburg lands, Bohemia, Hungary, the Low Countries, and the kingdom of Naples in southern Italy (see Map 13.1). The extent of his possessions was reflected in the languages he used: "I speak Spanish to God, Italian to women, French to men, and German to my horse." Politically, Charles wanted to maintain his dynasty's control over his enormous empire; religiously, he hoped to preserve the unity of the Catholic faith throughout his empire. But despite Charles's strengths, his empire was overextended, and he spent a lifetime in futile pursuit of his goals. Four major problems—the French, the papacy, the Turks, and Germany's internal situation—cost him both his dream and his health. At the same time, the emperor's problems gave Luther's movement time to grow and organize before facing the concerted onslaught of the Catholic forces.

Charles V's chief political concern was his rivalry with the Valois king of France, Francis I (1515–1547). Encircled by the possessions of the Habsburg empire, Francis became embroiled in conflict with Charles over disputed territories in southern France, the Netherlands, the Rhineland, northern Spain, and Italy. These conflicts, known as the Habsburg-Valois Wars, were fought intermittently for more than two decades (1521–1544), preventing Charles from concentrating on the Lutheran problem in Germany.

At the same time, Charles faced opposition from Pope Clement VII (1523–1534), who, guided by political considerations, joined the side of Francis I. The advance of the Ottoman Turks into the eastern part of Charles's empire forced the emperor to divert forces there as well. Under Suleiman (soo-lay-MAHN) the

Museo del Prado, Madrid//Erich Lessing/Art Resource, NY

Charles V. Charles V sought to maintain religious unity throughout his vast empire by keeping all his subjects within the bounds of the Catholic Church. Due to his conflict with Francis I of France and his difficulties with the Turks, the papacy, and the German princes, Charles was never able to check the spread of Lutheranism. This portrait by the Venetian painter Titian shows Charles at the height of his power in 1547 after the defeat of the Lutherans at the Battle of Mühlberg.

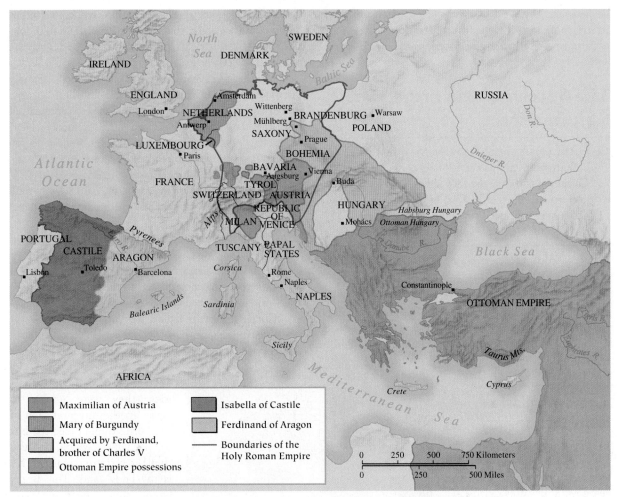

MAP 13.1 The Empire of Charles V. Charles V spent much of his reign fighting wars in Italy, against France and the Ottoman Empire, and within the borders of the Holy Roman Empire. He failed in his main goal to secure Europe for Catholicism: the Peace of Augsburg in 1555 recognized the equality of Catholicism and Lutheranism and let each German prince choose his realm's religion.

Q Why would France feel threatened by the empire of Charles V?

Magnificent (1520–1566), the Ottoman Turks overran most of Hungary, moved into Austria, and advanced as far as Vienna, where they were finally repulsed in 1529.

Finally, the internal political situation in the Holy Roman Empire was not in Charles's favor. Germany was a land of several hundred territorial states—princely states, ecclesiastical principalities, and free imperial cities. Although all owed loyalty to the emperor, Germany's medieval development had enabled these states to become quite independent of imperial authority. They had no desire to have a strong emperor. By the time Charles V was able to bring military forces to

Germany in 1546, Lutheranism had become well established and the Lutheran princes were well organized. Unable to impose his will on Germany, Charles was forced to negotiate a truce. An end to religious warfare in Germany came in 1555 with the Peace of Augsburg, which marked an important turning point in the history of the Reformation. The division of Christianity was formally acknowledged, with Lutheranism granted equal legal standing with Catholicism. Moreover, the peace settlement accepted the right of each German ruler to determine the religion of his subjects (but not the right of the subjects to choose their religion). Charles's hope for a united empire had been completely dashed, and the ideal of medieval Christian unity was irretrievably lost. The rapid proliferation of new Protestant groups served to underscore that new reality.

The Spread of the Protestant Reformation

Q FOCUS QUESTIONS: What were the main tenets of Lutheranism, Zwinglianism, Anabaptism, and Calvinism, and how did they differ from each other and from Catholicism? What impact did political, economic, and social conditions have on the development of these four reform movements?

For both Catholics and Protestant reformers, Luther's heresy raised the question of how to determine what constituted the correct interpretation of the Bible. The inability to agree on this issue led not only to theological confrontations but also to bloody warfare as each Christian group was unwilling to admit that it could be wrong.

The Zwinglian Reformation

In the sixteenth century, the Swiss Confederation was a loose association of thirteen self-governing states called cantons. Theoretically part of the Holy Roman Empire, they had become virtually independent in 1499. The six forest cantons were democratic republics, while the seven urban cantons, which included Zürich, Bern, and Basel, were governed primarily by city councils controlled by narrow oligarchies of wealthy citizens.

The Swiss Cantons

Ulrich Zwingli (OOL-rikh TSFING-lee) (1484–1531) was ordained a priest in 1506 and accepted an appointment as a cathedral priest in the Great Minster of Zürich in 1518. Zwingli's preaching of the Gospel caused such unrest that the city council in 1523 held a public disputation or debate in the town hall. Zwingli's party was accorded the victory, and the council declared that "Mayor, Council and Great Council of Zürich, in order to do away with disturbance and

discord, have upon due deliberation and consultation decided and resolved that Master Zwingli should continue as heretofore to proclaim the Gospel and the pure sacred Scriptures."[6]

Over the next two years, a city council strongly influenced by Zwingli promulgated evangelical reforms in Zürich. It abolished relics and images, removed all paintings and decorations from the churches, and replaced them with whitewashed walls. A new liturgy consisting of Scripture reading, prayer, and sermons replaced the Mass. Monasticism, pilgrimages, the veneration of saints, clerical celibacy, and the pope's authority were all abolished as remnants of papal Christianity.

As his movement began to spread to other cities in Switzerland, Zwingli sought an alliance with Martin Luther and the German reformers. Protestant political leaders attempted to promote an alliance of the Swiss and German reformed churches by persuading the leaders of both groups to attend a colloquy (conference) at Marburg to resolve their differences. Although both the German and Swiss reformers realized the need for unity to defend against the opposition of Catholic authorities, they were unable to agree on the interpretation of the Lord's Supper (see the box on p. 311). Zwingli believed that the scriptural words "This is my body" and "This is my blood" should be taken symbolically, not literally. To Zwingli, the Lord's Supper was only a meal of remembrance, and he refused to accept Luther's insistence on the real presence of the body and blood of Jesus "in, with, and under the bread and wine." The Marburg Colloquy of 1529 produced no agreement and no evangelical alliance. It was a foretaste of the issues that would divide one reform group from another and eventually lead to the creation of different Protestant groups.

In October 1531, war erupted between the Swiss Protestant and Catholic cantons. Zürich's army was routed, and Zwingli was found wounded on the battlefield. His enemies killed him, cut up his body, burned it, and scattered the ashes. This Swiss civil war of 1531 provided an early indication of what religious passions

OPPOSING VIEWPOINTS

A Reformation Debate: Conflict at Marburg

Debates played a crucial role in the Reformation period. They were a primary instrument in introducing the Reformation into innumerable cities as well as a means of resolving differences among like-minded Protestant groups. This selection contains an excerpt from the vivacious and often brutal debate between Luther and Zwingli over the sacrament of the Lord's Supper at Marburg in 1529. The two protagonists failed to reach agreement.

_____

The Marburg Colloquy, 1529

THE HESSIAN CHANCELLOR FEIGE: My gracious prince and lord [Landgrave Philip of Hesse] has summoned you for the express and urgent purpose of settling the dispute over the sacrament of the Lord's Supper.... Let everyone on both sides present his arguments in a spirit of moderation.... Now then, Doctor Luther, you may proceed.

LUTHER: Noble prince, gracious lord! Undoubtedly the colloquy is well intentioned.... Although I have no intention of changing my mind, which is firmly made up, I will nevertheless present the grounds of my belief and show where the others are in error.... Your basic contentions are these: In the last analysis you wish to prove that a body cannot be in two places at once, and you produce arguments about the unlimited body which are based on natural reason. I do not question how Christ can be God and man and how the two natures can be joined. For God is more powerful than all our ideas, and we must submit to his word.

Prove that Christ's body is not there where the Scripture says, "This is my body!" Rational proofs I will not listen to.... It is God who commands, "Take, eat, this is my body." I request, therefore, valid scriptural proof to the contrary.

ZWINGLI: I insist that the words of the Lord's Supper must be figurative. This is ever apparent, and even required by the article of faith: "taken up into heaven, seated at the right hand of the Father." Otherwise, it would be absurd to look for him in the Lord's Supper at the same time that Christ is telling us that he is in heaven. One and the same body cannot possibly be in different places....

LUTHER: I call upon you as before: your basic contentions are shaky. Give way, and give glory to God!

ZWINGLI: And we call upon you to give glory to God and to quit begging the question! The issue at stake is this: Where is the proof of your position? ... You're trying to outwit me.... You'll have to sing another tune.

LUTHER: You're being obnoxious.

ZWINGLI: (*excitedly*) Don't you believe that Christ was attempting in John 6 to help those who did not understand?

LUTHER: You're trying to dominate things! You insist on passing judgment! Leave that to someone else! ... It is your point that must be proved, not mine. But let us stop this sort of thing. It serves no purpose.

ZWINGLI: It certainly does! It is for you to prove that the passage in John 6 speaks of a physical repast.

LUTHER: You express yourself poorly and make about as much progress as a cane standing in a corner. You're going nowhere.

ZWINGLI: No, no, no! This is the passage that will break your neck!

LUTHER: Don't be so sure of yourself. Necks don't break this way. You're in Hesse, not Switzerland.

_____

Q How did the positions of Zwingli and Luther on the sacrament of the Lord's Supper differ? What was the purpose of this debate? Based on this example, why do you think Reformation debates led to further hostility rather than compromise and unity between religious and sectarian opponents? What implication did this have for the future of the Protestant Reformation?

Source: "The Marburg Colloquy," from *Great Debates of the Reformation*, edited by Donald Ziegler, copyright © 1969 by Donald Ziegler.

would lead to in the sixteenth century. Unable to find peaceful ways to agree on the meaning of the Gospel, the disciples of Christianity resorted to violence and decision by force. When he heard of Zwingli's death, Martin Luther, who had not forgotten the confrontation at Marburg, is supposed to have remarked that Zwingli "got what he deserved."

The Radical Reformation: The Anabaptists

Although many reformers were ready to allow the state to play an important, if not dominant, role in church affairs, some people rejected this kind of magisterial reformation and favored a far more radical reform movement. Collectively called the Anabaptists, these radicals were actually members of a large variety of groups who had certain characteristics in common.

To the Anabaptists, the true Christian church was a voluntary association of believers who had undergone spiritual rebirth and had then been baptized into the church. Anabaptists advocated adult rather than infant baptism. No one, they believed, should be forced to accept the Bible as truth. They also tried to return literally to the practices and spirit of early Christianity. Adhering to the accounts of early Christian communities in the New Testament, they followed a strict sort of democracy in which all believers were considered equal. Each church chose its own minister, who might be any member of the community because all Christians were considered priests (though women were often excluded). Those chosen as ministers had the duty to lead services, which were very simple and contained nothing not found in the early church. Calling themselves "Christians" or "Saints," Anabaptists, like the early Christians, accepted that they would have to suffer for their faith. They rejected theological speculation in favor of simple Christian living according to what they believed was the pure word of God. The Lord's Supper was interpreted as a remembrance, a meal of fellowship celebrated in the evening in private houses according to Jesus's example.

Unlike the Catholics and other Protestants, most Anabaptists believed in the complete separation of church and state. Not only was government to be excluded from the realm of religion, but it was not even supposed to exercise political jurisdiction over true Christians. Human law had no power over those whom God had saved. Anabaptists refused to hold political office or bear arms because many took the commandment "Thou shall not kill" literally, although some Anabaptist groups did become quite violent. Their political beliefs as much as their religious beliefs caused the Anabaptists to be regarded as dangerous radicals who threatened the fabric of sixteenth-century society. Indeed, the chief thing Protestants and Catholics could agree on was the need to stamp out the Anabaptists.

One early group of Anabaptists known as the Swiss Brethren arose in Zürich. Their ideas frightened Zwingli, and they were expelled from the city in 1523. As their teachings spread through southern Germany, the Austrian Habsburg lands, and Switzerland, Anabaptists suffered ruthless persecution, especially after the Peasants' War of 1524–1525, when the upper classes resorted to repression. Virtually eliminated in Germany, Anabaptist survivors emerged in Moravia, Poland, and the Netherlands.

Menno Simons (1496–1561) was the man most responsible for rejuvenating Dutch Anabaptism. A popular leader, Menno dedicated his life to the spread of a peaceful, evangelical Anabaptism that stressed separation from the world in order to truly emulate the life of Jesus. The Mennonites, as his followers were called, spread from the Netherlands into northwestern Germany and eventually into Poland and Lithuania as well as the New World. Both the Mennonites and Amish, who are also descended from the Anabaptists, maintain communities in the United States and Canada today.

The Reformation in England

The English Reformation was initiated by King Henry VIII (1509–1547), who wanted to divorce his first wife, Catherine of Aragon, because she had failed to produce a male heir. Furthermore, Henry had fallen in love with Anne Boleyn (BUH-lin or buh-LIN), a lady-in-waiting to Queen Catherine. Anne's unwillingness to be only the king's mistress and the king's desire to have a legitimate male heir made their marriage imperative, but the king's first marriage stood in the way.

Normally, church authorities might have been willing to grant the king an annulment of his marriage, but Pope Clement VII was dependent on the Holy Roman emperor, Charles V, who happened to be Catherine's nephew. Impatient with the pope's inaction, Henry sought to obtain an annulment of his marriage in England's own ecclesiastical courts. As archbishop of Canterbury and head of the highest ecclesiastical court in England, Thomas Cranmer held official hearings on the king's case and ruled in May 1533 that the king's marriage to Catherine was "null and absolutely void." He then validated Henry's secret marriage to Anne, who had become pregnant. At the beginning of June, Anne was crowned queen. Three months later, a child was born. Much to the king's disappointment, the baby was a girl, who was named Elizabeth.

In 1534, at Henry's request, Parliament moved to finalize the Church of England's break with Rome. The Act of Supremacy of 1534 declared that the king was "taken, accepted, and reputed the only supreme head on earth of the Church of England," a position that gave him control of doctrine, clerical appointments, and discipline.

Although Henry VIII had broken with the papacy, little changed in matters of doctrine, theology, and ceremony. Some of his supporters, such as Archbishop Cranmer, sought a religious reformation as well as an administrative one, but Henry was unyielding. When Henry died in 1547, he was succeeded by his son, the underage and sickly Edward VI (1547–1553), the son of Henry's third wife, Jane Seymour. During Edward's reign, Cranmer and others inclined toward Protestant doctrines were able to move the Church of England (also known as the Anglican Church) in a more Protestant direction. New acts of Parliament instituted the right of the clergy to marry, the elimination of religious images, and the creation of a revised Protestant liturgy that was elaborated in a new prayer book known as the Book of Common Prayer. These rapid changes in doctrine and liturgy aroused much opposition and prepared the way for the reaction that occurred when Mary, Henry's daughter by Catherine of Aragon, came to the throne.

Mary (1553–1558) was a Catholic who fully intended to restore England to Roman Catholicism. But her restoration of Catholicism aroused much opposition. First, there was widespread antipathy to Mary's unfortunate marriage to Philip II, the son of Charles V and future king of Spain. Philip was strongly disliked in England, and Mary's foreign policy of alliance with Spain aroused further hostility. The burning of more than three hundred Protestant heretics aroused further ire against "bloody Mary." As a result of her policies, Mary managed to achieve the opposite of what she had intended: England was more Protestant by the end of her reign than it had been at the beginning. When she came to power, Protestantism had become identified with church destruction and religious anarchy. Now people identified it with English resistance to Spanish interference. Mary's death in 1558 ended the restoration of Catholicism in England.

John Calvin and the Development of Calvinism

Of the second generation of Protestant reformers, one stands out as the premier systematic theologian and organizer of the Protestant movement—John Calvin (1509–1564). Calvin was educated in his native France, but after his conversion to Protestantism, he was forced to flee to the safety of Switzerland. In 1536, he published the first edition of the *Institutes of the Christian Religion*, a masterful synthesis of Protestant thought that immediately secured Calvin's reputation as one of the new leaders of Protestantism.

CALVIN'S IDEAS On most important doctrines, Calvin stood very close to Luther. He adhered to the doctrine of justification by faith alone to explain how humans achieved salvation. Calvin also placed much emphasis on the absolute sovereignty of God or the "power, grace and glory of God." One of the ideas derived from his emphasis on the absolute sovereignty of God— **predestination**—gave a unique cast to Calvin's teachings. This "eternal decree," as Calvin called it, meant that God had predestined some people to be saved (the elect) and others to be damned (the reprobate). According to Calvin, "He has once for all determined, both whom he would admit to salvation, and whom he would condemn to destruction."[7] Although Calvin stressed that there could be no absolute certainty of salvation, some of his followers did not always make this distinction. The practical psychological effect of predestination was to give some later Calvinists an unshakable conviction that they were doing God's work on earth. It is no accident that Calvinism became the activist international form of Protestantism.

To Calvin, the church was a divine institution responsible for preaching the word of God and administering the sacraments. Calvin kept the same two sacraments as other Protestant reformers, baptism and the Lord's Supper. Baptism was a sign of the remission of sins. Calvin believed in the real presence of Jesus in the sacrament of the Lord's Supper, but only in a spiritual sense. Jesus's body is at the right hand of God and thus cannot be in the sacrament, but to the believer, Jesus is spiritually present in the Lord's Supper.

CALVIN'S GENEVA In 1536, Calvin began working to reform the city of Geneva, where he established a church government that used both clergy and laymen in the service of the church. The Consistory, a special body for enforcing moral discipline, was set up as a

John Calvin. After a conversion experience, John Calvin abandoned his life as a humanist and became a reformer. In 1536, Calvin began working to reform the city of Geneva, where he remained until his death in 1564. This sixteenth-century portrait of Calvin pictures him in his study in Geneva.

The Social Impact of the Protestant Reformation

Q FOCUS QUESTION: What impact did the Protestant Reformation have on society in the sixteenth century?

Because Christianity was such an integral part of European life, it was inevitable that the Reformation would have an impact on the family and popular religious practices.

The Family

For centuries, Catholicism had praised the family and sanctified its existence by making marriage a sacrament. But the Catholic Church's high regard for abstinence from sex as the surest way to holiness made the celibate state of the clergy preferable to marriage. Nevertheless, because not all men could remain chaste, marriage offered the best means to control sexual intercourse and give it a purpose, the procreation of children. To some extent, this attitude persisted among the Protestant reformers; Luther, for example, argued that sex in marriage allowed one to "make use of this sex in order to avoid sin," and Calvin advised that every man should "abstain from marriage only so long as he is fit to observe celibacy." If "his power to tame lust fails him," then he must marry.

But the Reformation did bring some change to the conception of the family. Both Catholic and Protestant

court to oversee the moral life and doctrinal purity of Genevans. The Consistory had the right to punish people who deviated from the church's teachings and moral principles.

Calvin's success in Geneva enabled the city to become a vibrant center of Protestantism. John Knox, the Calvinist reformer of Scotland, called Geneva "the most perfect school of Christ on earth." Following Calvin's lead, missionaries trained in Geneva were sent to all parts of Europe. Calvinism became established in France, the Netherlands, Scotland, and central and eastern Europe. By the mid-sixteenth century, Calvinism had replaced Lutheranism as the militant international form of Protestantism, and Calvin's Geneva stood as the fortress of the Reformation.

clergy preached sermons advocating a more positive side to family relationships. The Protestants were especially important in developing this new view of the family. Because Protestantism had eliminated any idea of special holiness for celibacy, abolishing both monasticism and a celibate clergy, the family could be placed at the center of human life, and a new stress on "mutual love between man and wife" could be extolled. But were doctrine and reality the same? For more radical religious groups, at times they were. One Anabaptist wrote to his wife before his execution: "My faithful helper, my loyal friend. I praise God that he gave you to me, you who have sustained me in all my trial."[8] But more often reality reflected the traditional roles of husband as the ruler and wife as the obedient servant whose chief duty was to please her husband. Luther stated it clearly:

> The rule remains with the husband, and the wife is compelled to obey him by God's command. He rules the home and the state, wages war, defends his possessions, tills the soil, builds, plants, etc. The woman on the other hand is like a nail driven into the wall ... so the wife should stay at home and look after the affairs of the household, as one who has been deprived of the ability of administering those affairs that are outside and that concern the state. She does not go beyond her most personal duties.[9]

Obedience to her husband was not a wife's only role; her other important duty was to bear children. To Calvin and Luther, this function of women was part of the divine plan. God punishes women for the sins of Eve by the burdens of procreation and feeding and nurturing their children, but, said Luther, "it is a gladsome punishment if you consider the hope of eternal life and the honor of motherhood which had been left to her."[10] Although the Protestant reformers sanctified this role of woman as mother and wife, viewing it as a holy vocation, Protestantism also left few alternatives for women. Because monasticism had been destroyed, that career avenue was no longer available; for most Protestant women, family life was their only destiny. At the same time, by emphasizing the father as "ruler" and hence the center of household religion, Protestantism even removed the woman from her traditional role as controller of religion in the home. Overall, the Protestant Reformation did not noticeably transform women's subordinate place in society.

Religious Practices and Popular Culture

The attacks of Protestant reformers on the Catholic Church led to radical changes in religious practices. The Protestant Reformation abolished or severely curtailed such customary practices as indulgences, the veneration of relics and saints, pilgrimages, monasticism, and clerical celibacy. The elimination of saints put an end to the numerous celebrations of religious holy days and changed a community's sense of time. Thus, in Protestant communities, religious ceremonies and imagery, such as processions and statues, tended to be replaced with individual private prayer, family worship, and collective prayer and worship at the same time each week on Sunday.

In addition to abolishing saints' days and religious carnivals, some Protestant reformers even tried to eliminate customary forms of entertainment. Puritans (as English Calvinists were called), for example, attempted to ban drinking in taverns, dramatic performances, and dancing. Dutch Calvinists denounced the tradition of giving small presents to children on the feast of Saint Nicholas in December. Many of these Protestant attacks on popular culture were unsuccessful, however. The importance of taverns in English social life made it impossible to eradicate them, and celebrating at Christmastime persisted in the Dutch Netherlands.

The Catholic Reformation

Q **FOCUS QUESTION:** What measures did the Roman Catholic Church take to reform itself and to combat Protestantism in the sixteenth century?

By the mid-sixteenth century, Lutheranism had become established in Germany and Scandinavia and Calvinism in parts of Switzerland, France, the Netherlands, and eastern Europe (see Map 13.2). In England, the split from Rome had resulted in the creation of a national church. The situation in Europe did not look favorable for Roman Catholicism. Yet constructive, positive forces for reform were already at work within the Catholic Church.

Catholic Reformation or Counter-Reformation?

There is no doubt that the Catholic Church underwent a revitalization in the sixteenth century. But was this reformation a **Catholic Reformation** or a Counter-Reformation? Some historians prefer to call it a "Counter-Reformation" to focus on the aspects that

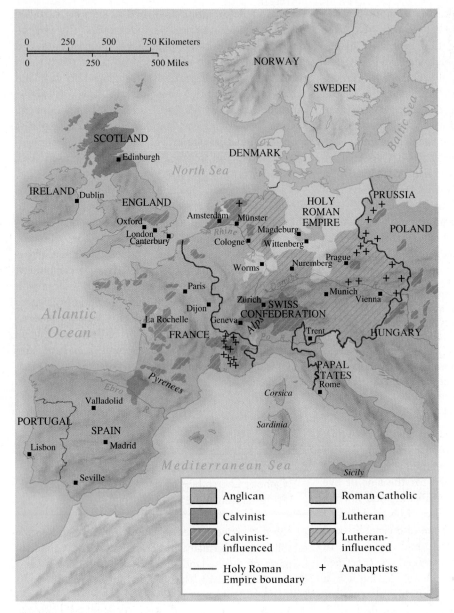

MAP 13.2 Catholics and Protestants in Europe by 1560. The Reformation continued to evolve beyond the basic split of the Lutherans from the Catholics. Several Protestant sects broke away from the teachings of Martin Luther, each with a separate creed and different ways of worship. In England, Henry VIII broke with the Catholic Church for political and dynastic reasons.

Q Which areas of Europe were solidly Catholic, which were solidly Lutheran, and which were neither?

were a direct reaction against the Protestant movement. Historians who prefer to use "Catholic Reformation" point out that elements of reform were already present in the Catholic Church at the end of the fifteenth century and the beginning of the sixteenth, and that by the mid-sixteenth century, they came to be directed by a revived and reformed papacy, giving the church new strength.

No doubt, both positions on the nature of the reformation of the Catholic Church contain elements of truth. The Catholic Reformation revived the best features of medieval Catholicism and then adjusted them to meet new conditions, as is most apparent in the revival of mysticism and monasticism. The emergence of a new mysticism, closely tied to the traditions of Catholic piety, was especially evident in the life of the Spanish mystic Saint Teresa of Avila (1515–1582). While the regeneration of religious orders also proved valuable to the reform of Catholicism, new religious orders and brotherhoods were also created.

The Society of Jesus

Of all the new religious orders, the most important was the Society of Jesus, known as the Jesuits, who became the chief instrument of the Catholic Reformation. The Society of Jesus was founded by a Spanish nobleman, Ignatius of Loyola (ig-NAY-shuss of loi-OH-luh) (1491–1556), whose injuries in battle cut short his military career. Loyola experienced a spiritual torment similar to Luther's but, unlike Luther, resolved his problems not by a new doctrine but by a decision to submit his will to the will of the church. Unable to be a real soldier, he vowed to be a soldier of God. Over a period of twelve years, Loyola prepared for his life work by praying, going on pilgrimages, going to school, and working out a spiritual program in his brief but powerful book, *The Spiritual Exercises*. This was a training manual for spiritual development emphasizing exercises by which the human will could be strengthened and made to follow the will of God as manifested through his instrument, the Catholic Church (see the box on p. 318).

Loyola gathered together a small group of individuals who were eventually recognized as a religious order, the Society of Jesus, by a papal bull in 1540. The new order was grounded on the principles of absolute obedience to the papacy, a strict hierarchical order for the society, the use of education to achieve its goals, and a dedication to engage in "conflict for God." Executive leadership was put in the hands of a general, who nominated all important positions in the order and was to be revered as the absolute head of the order. Loyola served as the first general of the order until his death in 1556. A special vow of absolute obedience to the pope made the Jesuits an important instrument for papal policy.

The Jesuits were active on behalf of the Catholic faith. They established well-disciplined schools, believing that thorough education of young people was crucial to combat the advance of Protestantism. Another prominent Jesuit activity was the propagation of the Catholic faith among non-Christians. Francis Xavier (ZAY-vee-ur) (1506–1552), one of the original members of the Society of Jesus, carried the message of Catholic Christianity to the East. After converting tens of thousands in India, he traveled to Malacca and the Moluccas before reaching Japan in 1549. Thousands of Japanese, especially in the southernmost islands, became Christians. In 1552, Xavier set out for China but died of a fever before he reached the mainland.

Although conversion efforts in Japan proved short-lived, Jesuit activity in China, especially that

Ignatius of Loyola. The Jesuits became the most important new religious order of the Catholic Reformation. Shown here in a sixteenth-century painting by an unknown artist is Ignatius of Loyola, founder of the Society of Jesus. Loyola is seen kneeling before Pope Paul III, who officially recognized the Jesuits in 1540.

Il Gesu, Rome/Scala/Art Resource, NY

of the Italian Matteo Ricci (ma-TAY-oh REE-chee) (1552–1610), was more long-lasting. Recognizing the Chinese pride in their own culture, the Jesuits attempted to draw parallels between Christian and Confucian concepts and to show the similarities between Christian morality and Confucian ethics. For their part, the missionaries were impressed with many aspects of Chinese civilization, and reports of their experiences heightened European curiosity about this great society on the other side of the world.

The Jesuits were also determined to carry the Catholic banner and fight Protestantism. Jesuit missionaries succeeded in restoring Catholicism to parts of Germany and eastern Europe. Poland was largely won back for the Catholic Church through Jesuit efforts.

A Revived Papacy

A reformed papacy was another important factor in the development of the Catholic Reformation. The

Loyola and Obedience to "Our Holy Mother, the Hierarchical Church"

In his *Spiritual Exercises*, Ignatius of Loyola developed a systematic program for "the conquest of self and the regulation of one's life" for service to the hierarchical Catholic Church. Ignatius's supreme goal was the commitment of the Christian to active service in the Church of Christ (the Roman Catholic Church). In the final section of *The Spiritual Exercises*, Loyola explained the nature of that commitment in a series of "rules for thinking with the church."

Ignatius of Loyola, "Rules for Thinking with the Church"

The following rules should be observed to foster the true attitude of mind we ought to have in the Church militant.

1. We must put aside all judgment of our own, and keep the mind ever ready and prompt to obey in all things the true Spouse of Jesus Christ, our holy Mother, the hierarchical Church.
2. We should praise sacramental confession, the yearly reception of the Most Blessed Sacrament [the Lord's Supper], and praise more highly monthly reception, and still more weekly Communion. . . .
3. We ought to praise the frequent hearing of Mass, the singing of hymns, psalmody, and long prayers whether in the church or outside. . . .
4. We must praise highly religious life, virginity, and continency; and matrimony ought not be praised as much as any of these. . . .
6. We should show our esteem for the relics of the saints by venerating them and praying to the saints. We should praise visits to the Station Churches, pilgrimages, indulgences, jubilees, the lighting of candles in churches. . . .
8. We ought to praise not only the building and adornment of churches, but also images and veneration of them according to the subject they represent.
9. Finally, we must praise all the commandments of the Church, and be on the alert to find reasons to defend them, and by no means in order to criticize them.
10. We should be more ready to approve and praise the orders, recommendations, and way of acting of our superiors than to find fault with them. Though some of the orders, etc., may not have been praiseworthy, yet to speak against them, either when preaching in public or in speaking before the people, would rather be the cause of murmuring and scandal than of profit. As a consequence, the people would become angry with their superiors, whether secular or spiritual. But while it does harm in the absence of our superiors to speak evil of them before the people, it may be profitable to discuss their bad conduct with those who can apply a remedy.
13. If we wish to proceed securely in all things, we must hold fast to the following principle: What seems to me white, I will believe black if the hierarchical Church so defines. For I must be convinced that in Christ our Lord, the bridegroom, and in His spouse the Church, only one Spirit holds sway, which governs and rules for the salvation of souls.

Q What are the fundamental assumptions that inform Loyola's rules for "thinking with the church"? What do these assumptions tell you about the nature of the Catholic reform movement?

Source: Excerpt from *The Spiritual Exercises of St. Ignatius of Loyola*, translated by Louis J. Puhl, S.J. (Newman Press 1951). Reprinted with permission of Loyola Press. To order copies of this book, call 1-800-621-1008 or visit www.loyolabooks.org.

pontificate of Pope Paul III (1534–1549) proved to be a turning point in the reform of the papacy. Raised in the lap of luxury, Paul III continued Renaissance papal practices by appointing his nephews as cardinals, involving himself in politics, and patronizing arts and letters on a lavish scale. Nevertheless, he perceived the need for change and expressed it decisively. Advocates of reform, such as Gasparo Contarini (GAHS-puh-roh kahn-tuh-REE-nee) and Gian Pietro Caraffa (JAHN PYAY-troh kuh-RAH-fuh), were made cardinals. In

CHRONOLOGY The Catholic Reformation	
Pope Paul III	1534–1549
Papal recognition of the Society of Jesus (Jesuits)	1540
Establishment of the Roman Inquisition (Holy Office)	1542
Council of Trent	1545–1563
Pope Paul IV	1555–1559

1535, Paul took the audacious step of appointing a commission to study the church's condition. The Reform Commission's report in 1537 blamed the church's problems on the corrupt policies of popes and cardinals. It was also Paul III who formally recognized the Jesuits and summoned the Council of Trent (see the next section).

A decisive turning point in the direction of the Catholic Reformation and the nature of papal reform came in the 1540s. In 1541, a colloquy had been held at Regensburg in a final attempt to settle the religious division peacefully. Here Catholic moderates, such as Cardinal Contarini, who favored concessions to Protestants in the hope of restoring Christian unity, reached a compromise with Protestant moderates on a number of doctrinal issues. When Contarini returned to Rome with these proposals, Cardinal Caraffa and other hardliners, who regarded all compromise with Protestant innovations as heresy, accused him of selling out to the heretics. It soon became apparent that the conservative reformers were in the ascendancy when Caraffa was able to persuade Paul III to establish the Roman Inquisition or Holy Office in 1542 to ferret out doctrinal errors. There was to be no compromise with Protestantism.

When Cardinal Caraffa was chosen pope as Paul IV (1555–1559), he so increased the power of the Inquisition that even liberal cardinals were silenced. This "first true pope of the Catholic Counter-Reformation," as he has been called, also created the Index of Forbidden Books, a list of books that Catholics were not allowed to read. It included all the works of Protestant theologians. Any hope of restoring Christian unity by compromise was fading. The activities of the Council of Trent, the third major pillar of the Catholic Reformation, made compromise virtually impossible.

The Council of Trent

In March 1545, a group of cardinals, archbishops, bishops, abbots, and theologians met in the city of Trent on the border between Germany and Italy and initiated the Council of Trent, which met in three major sessions between 1545 and 1563. Moderate Catholic reformers hoped that compromises would be made in formulating doctrinal definitions that would encourage Protestants to return to the church. Conservatives, however, favored an uncompromising restatement of Catholic doctrines in strict opposition to Protestant positions. The latter group won, although not without a struggle.

The final doctrinal decrees of the Council of Trent reaffirmed traditional Catholic teachings. Scripture and tradition were affirmed as equal authorities in religious matters; only the church could interpret Scripture. Both faith and good works were declared necessary for salvation. The seven sacraments, the Catholic doctrine of transubstantiation (rejected by the Protestant reformers), and clerical celibacy were all upheld. Belief in purgatory and in the efficacy of indulgences was strengthened, although the hawking of indulgences was prohibited.

After the Council of Trent, the Roman Catholic Church possessed a clear body of doctrine and a unified church under the acknowledged supremacy of the popes, who had triumphed over bishops and councils. The Roman Catholic Church had become one Christian denomination among many with an organizational framework and doctrinal pattern that would not be significantly altered for four hundred years. With renewed confidence, the Catholic Church entered a new phase of its history.

Politics and the Wars of Religion in the Sixteenth Century

Q FOCUS QUESTION: What role did politics, economic and social conditions, and religion play in the European wars of the sixteenth century?

By the middle of the sixteenth century, Calvinism and Catholicism had become activist religions dedicated to spreading the word of God as they interpreted it. Although this struggle for the minds and hearts of Europeans is at the core of the religious wars of the sixteenth century, economic, social, and political forces also played important roles in these conflicts. Of the sixteenth-century religious wars, none were more momentous or more shattering than the French civil wars known as the French Wars of Religion.

The French Wars of Religion (1562–1598)

Religion was the engine that drove the French civil wars of the sixteenth century. Concerned by the growth of Calvinism, the French kings tried to stop its spread by persecuting Calvinists but had little success. **Huguenots** (HYOO-guh-nots), as the French Calvinists were called, came from all layers of society: artisans and shopkeepers hurt by rising prices and a rigid guild system, merchants and lawyers in provincial towns whose local privileges were tenuous, and members of the nobility. Possibly 40 to 50 percent of the French nobility became Huguenots, including the house of Bourbon, which stood next to the Valois dynasty in the royal line of succession and ruled the southern French kingdom of Navarre (nuh-VAHR). The conversion of so many nobles made the Huguenots a potentially dangerous political threat to monarchical power. Though the Calvinists constituted only about 10 percent of the population, they were a strong-willed and well-organized minority.

The Catholic majority greatly outnumbered the Calvinist minority. The Valois monarchy was staunchly Catholic, and its control of the Catholic Church gave it little incentive to look favorably on Protestantism. At the same time, an extreme Catholic party—known as the Ultra-Catholics and led by the Guise (GEEZ) family—favored strict opposition to the Huguenots. They received support abroad from the papacy and the Jesuits, who favored their uncompromising Catholic position.

But religion was not the only factor contributing to the French civil wars. Resentful of the growing power of monarchical centralization, towns and provinces were only too willing to join a revolt against the monarchy. This was also true of the nobility, and because so many of them were Calvinists, they formed an important base of opposition to the Crown. The French Wars of Religion, then, presented a major constitutional crisis for France and temporarily halted the development of the French centralized state. The claim of the state's ruling dynasty to a person's loyalties was temporarily superseded by loyalty to one's religious beliefs. For thirty years, battles raged in France between Catholic and Calvinist parties, who obviously considered the unity of France less important than religious truth. But there also emerged in France a group of public figures who placed politics before religion and believed that no religious truth was worth the ravages of civil war. These *politiques* (pul-lee-TEEKS) ultimately prevailed, but not until both sides had become exhausted by bloodshed.

Finally, in 1589, Henry of Navarre, the political leader of the Huguenots and a member of the Bourbon dynasty, succeeded to the throne as Henry IV (1589–1610). Realizing, however, that he would never be accepted by Catholic France, Henry took the logical way out and converted to Catholicism. With his coronation in 1594, the French Wars of Religion finally came to an end. The Edict of Nantes (NAHNT) in 1598 solved the religious problem by acknowledging Catholicism as the official religion of France while guaranteeing the Huguenots the right to worship and to enjoy all political privileges, including the holding of public offices.

Philip II and Militant Catholicism

The greatest advocate of militant Catholicism in the second half of the sixteenth century was King Philip II of Spain (1556–1598), the son and heir of Charles V. Philip's reign ushered in an age of Spanish greatness, both politically and culturally. Philip's first major goal was to consolidate and secure the lands he had inherited from his father. These included Spain, the Netherlands, and possessions in Italy and the New World. For Philip, this meant strict conformity to Catholicism and the establishment of strong monarchical authority. Establishing this authority was not an easy task because Philip had inherited a governmental structure in which each of the various states and territories of his empire stood in an individual relationship to the king.

Crucial to an understanding of Philip II is the importance of Catholicism to the Spanish people and their ruler. Driven by a heritage of crusading fervor, the Spanish had little difficulty seeing themselves as a nation divinely chosen to save Catholic Christianity from the Protestant heretics. Philip II, the "Most Catholic King," became the champion of Catholicism throughout Europe, a role that led him to spectacular victories and equally spectacular defeats. Spain's leadership of a "holy league" against Turkish encroachments in the Mediterranean resulted in a stunning victory over the Turkish fleet in the Battle of Lepanto in 1571. Philip's greatest misfortunes came from his attempts to crush the revolt in the Netherlands and his tortured relations with Queen Elizabeth of England.

Revolt of the Netherlands

As one of the richest parts of Philip's empire, the Spanish Netherlands was of great importance to the

Philip of Spain. This portrait by Titian depicts Philip II of Spain. The king's attempts to make Spain a great power led to large debts and crushing taxes, and his military actions in defense of Catholicism ended in failure and misfortune in both France and the Netherlands.

Most Catholic King. Philip's attempt to strengthen his control in the Netherlands, which consisted of seventeen provinces (modern Netherlands, Belgium, and Luxembourg), soon led to a revolt. The nobles, who stood to lose the most politically if their jealously guarded privileges and freedoms were weakened, strongly opposed Philip's efforts. Resentment against Philip was also aroused by his use of taxes collected in

the Netherlands to further Spanish interests. Finally, religion became a major catalyst for rebellion when Philip attempted to crush Calvinism.

The Netherlands

Violence erupted in 1566 when Calvinists—many of them nobles—began to smash statues and stained-glass windows in Catholic churches. Philip responded by sending the duke of Alva with 10,000 veteran Spanish and Italian troops to crush the rebellion. But the revolt became organized, especially in the seven northern provinces, where the Dutch, under the leadership of William of Nassau, the prince of Orange, offered growing resistance. The struggle dragged on until 1609, when a twelve-year truce ended the war, virtually recognizing the independence of the northern provinces. These seven northern provinces, which began to call themselves the United Provinces of the Netherlands in 1581, soon emerged as the Dutch Republic, although the Spanish did not formally recognize them as independent until 1648. The ten southern provinces remained a Spanish possession.

The England of Elizabeth

After the death of Queen Mary in 1558, her half-sister Elizabeth, the daughter of Henry VIII and Anne Boleyn, ascended the throne of England. During Elizabeth's reign, England rose to prominence as the relatively small island kingdom became the leader of the Protestant nations of Europe and laid the foundations for a world empire (see the Film & History feature on p. 323).

CHRONOLOGY	Wars of Religion in the Sixteenth Century
The French Wars of Religion	1562–1598
Outbreak of revolt in the Netherlands	1566
Battle of Lepanto	1571
Spanish armada	1588
Twelve-year truce (Spain and Netherlands)	1609
Independence of the United Provinces	1648

Queen Elizabeth I: "I Have the Heart of a King"

Queen Elizabeth I ruled England from 1558 to 1603 with a consummate skill that contemporaries considered unusual in a woman. Though shrewd and paternalistic, Elizabeth, like other sixteenth-century monarchs, depended for her power on the favor of her people. When England faced the threat of an invasion by the Spanish armada of Philip II in 1588, Elizabeth sought to rally her troops with a speech at Tilbury, a town on the Thames River. This selection is taken from her speech.

Queen Elizabeth I, Speech at Tilbury

My loving people, we have been persuaded by some, that are careful of our safety, to take heed how we commit ourselves to armed multitudes, for fear of treachery; but I assure you, I do not desire to live to distrust my faithful and loving people. Let tyrants fear; I have always so behaved myself that, under God, I have placed my chiefest strength and safeguard in the loyal hearts and good will of my subjects. And therefore I am come amongst you at this time, not as for my recreation or sport, but being resolved, in the midst and heat of the battle, to live or die amongst you all; to lay down, for my God, and for my kingdom, and

for my people, my honor and my blood, even in the dust. I know I have but the body of a weak and feeble woman; but I have the heart of a king, and of a king of England, too; and think foul scorn that Parma or Spain, or any prince of Europe, should dare to invade the borders of my realm: to which, rather than any dishonor should grow by me, I myself will take up arms; I myself will be your general, judge, and rewarder of every one of your virtues in the field. I know already, by your forwardness, that you have deserved rewards and crowns; and we do assure you, on the word of a prince, they shall be duly paid you. In the mean my lieutenant general shall be in my stead, than whom never prince commanded a more noble and worthy subject; not doubting by your obedience to my general, by your concord in the camp and by your valor in the field, we shall shortly have a famous victory over the enemies of my God, of my kingdom, and of my people.

Q What qualities evident in Elizabeth's speech would have endeared her to her listeners? How was her popularity connected to the events of the late sixteenth century?

Source: From Elizabeth I's Speech at Tilbury in 1588 to the troops.

Intelligent, cautious, and self-confident, Elizabeth moved quickly to solve the difficult religious problem she inherited from her half-sister. Elizabeth's religious policy was based on moderation and compromise. The Catholic laws of Mary's reign were repealed, and the new Act of Supremacy designated Elizabeth as "the only supreme governor" of both church and state. She used this title rather than "supreme head of the church," which had been used by both Henry VIII and Edward VI, because she did not want to upset Catholics, who considered the pope the supreme head, or radical Protestants, who thought that Christ alone was head of the church. The church service used during the reign of Edward VI was revised to make it more acceptable to Catholics. The Church of England under Elizabeth was basically Protestant, but of a moderate sort that kept most of the queen's subjects satisfied.

Elizabeth proved as adept in foreign policy as in religious affairs (see the box above). Fearful of other countries' motives, Elizabeth realized that war could be disastrous for her island kingdom and her own rule. While encouraging English piracy and providing clandestine aid to French Huguenots and Dutch Calvinists to weaken France and Spain, Elizabeth pretended complete aloofness and avoided alliances that would force her into war with any major power. Gradually, however, Elizabeth was drawn into conflict with Spain. After years of resisting the idea of invading England as too impractical, Spain's Philip II was finally persuaded to do so by advisers who assured him that the people of England would rise against their queen when the Spaniards arrived. A successful invasion of England would mean the overthrow of heresy and the return of England to Catholicism, surely an act in accordance with the will of God.

FILM & HISTORY

Elizabeth (1998)

DIRECTED BY SHEKHAR KAPUR, *Elizabeth* opens in 1554 with a scene of three Protestant heretics being burned alive as Queen Mary (Kathy Burke) pursues her dream of restoring Catholicism to England. Mary also contemplates signing a death warrant for her Protestant half-sister Elizabeth (Cate Blanchett) but refuses to do so before dying in 1558. Elizabeth becomes queen and is portrayed in her early years of rule as an uncertain monarch who "rules from the heart instead of the mind," as one adviser tells her. Elizabeth is also threatened by foreign rulers, the duke of Norfolk (Christopher Eccleston), and others who want a Catholic on the throne of England. A plot, which supposedly includes Robert Dudley (Joseph Fiennes), reputedly her former lover, is unraveled with the help of Francis Walsingham (Geoffrey Rush), a ruthless Machiavellian adviser whose primary goal is protecting Elizabeth. The queen avoids assassination, but the attempt nevertheless convinces Elizabeth that she must be a Virgin Queen who dedicates her life to England. As she tells Lord Burghley (Richard Attenborough), her closest adviser, during the procession that ends the film, "I am now married to England."

The strength of the movie, which contains numerous historical inaccuracies, is in the performance of Cate Blanchett, who captures some of the characteristics of Queen Elizabeth I. At one point, Elizabeth explains her reluctance to go to war: "I do not like wars. They have uncertain outcomes." After she rebuffs the efforts of her advisers to persuade her to marry a foreign prince for the sake of maintaining the throne, Elizabeth declares, "I will have one mistress here, and no master." Although the movie correctly emphasizes her intelligence and her clever handling of advisers and church officials, Elizabeth is shown inaccurately as weak and vacillating when she first comes to the throne. In fact, Elizabeth was already a practiced politician who knew how to use power. She was, as she reminds her advisers, her father's (Henry VIII) daughter.

In many other ways, the movie is not faithful to the historical record. It telescopes events that occurred over thirty years of Elizabeth's lengthy reign into the first five years of her reign and makes up other events altogether. Mary of Guise (Fanny Ardant) was not assassinated by

Queen Elizabeth I (Cate Blanchett) and the duke of Norfolk (Christopher Eccleston).

Francis Walsingham, as the movie implies. Nor was Walsingham an important figure in the early years of Elizabeth's reign. Robert Dudley's marriage was well known in Elizabethan England, and there is no firm evidence that Elizabeth had a sexual relationship with him. The duke of Norfolk was not arrested until 1571, much later than in the film. The duc d'Anjou (Vincent Cassel) never came to England, and even if he had come, he would not have addressed Elizabeth with the candid sexual words used in the film. It was the duc's younger brother, the duc d'Alençon, who was put forth as a possible husband for Elizabeth, although not until she was in her forties. And finally, Elizabeth's choice of career over family and personal happiness seems to reflect a feminist theme of our own times; it was not common in the sixteenth century, when women were considered unfit to rule.

Philip therefore ordered preparations for an armada (fleet of warships) to spearhead the invasion of England in 1588.

The armada proved to be a disaster. The Spanish fleet that finally set sail had neither the ships nor the troops that Philip had planned to send. A conversation between a papal emissary and an officer of the Spanish fleet before the armada departed reveals the fundamental flaw:

> "And if you meet the English armada in the Channel, do you expect to win the battle?"
>
> "Of course," replied the Spaniard.
>
> "How can you be so sure?" [asked the emissary]
>
> "It's very simple. It is well known that we fight in God's cause. So, when we meet the English, God will surely arrange matters so that we can grapple and board them, either by sending some strange streak of weather, or, more likely, just by depriving the English of their wits. If we can come to close quarters, Spanish valor and Spanish steel (and the great masses of soldiers we shall have on board) will make our victory certain. But unless God helps us by a miracle the English, who have faster and handier ships than ours, and many more long-range guns, and who know their advantage just as well as we do, will never close with us at all, but stand aloof and knock us to pieces with their culverins [cannons], without our being able to do them any serious hurt. So," concluded the captain, and one fancies a grim smile, "we are sailing against England in the confident hope of a miracle."[11]

The hoped-for miracle never materialized. The Spanish fleet, battered by a number of encounters with the English, sailed back to Spain by a northward route around Scotland and Ireland, where it was further ravaged by storms. Although the English and Spanish would continue their war for another sixteen years, the defeat of the Spanish armada guaranteed for the time being that England would remain a Protestant country. Although Spain made up for its losses within a year and a half, the defeat was a psychological blow to the Spaniards.

Chapter Summary

When the Augustinian monk Martin Luther burst onto the scene with a series of theses on indulgences, few people suspected that his observations would eventually split all of Europe along religious lines. But the yearning for reform of the church and meaningful religious experiences caused a seemingly simple dispute to escalate into a powerful movement.

Martin Luther established the twin pillars of the Protestant Reformation: the doctrine of justification by faith alone and the Bible as the sole authority in religious affairs. Although Luther felt that his revival of Christianity based on his interpretation of the Bible should be acceptable to all, others soon appeared who also read the Bible but interpreted it in different ways. Protestantism fragmented into different sects—Zwinglianism, Calvinism, Anglicanism, Anabaptism—which, though united in their dislike of Catholicism, were themselves divided over the interpretation of the sacraments and religious practices. As reform ideas spread, religion and politics became ever more intertwined.

Although Lutheranism was legally acknowledged in the Holy Roman Empire by the Peace of Augsburg in 1555, it had lost much of its momentum and outside of Scandinavia had scant ability to attract new supporters. Its energy was largely replaced by the new Protestant form of Calvinism, which had a clarity of doctrine and a fervor that made it attractive to a whole new generation of Europeans. But while Calvinism's activism enabled it to spread across Europe, Catholicism was also experiencing its own revival. New religious orders based on reform, a revived and reformed papacy, and the Council of Trent, which reaffirmed traditional Catholic doctrine, gave the Catholic Church a renewed vitality.

By the middle of the sixteenth century, it was apparent that the religious passions of the Reformation era had brought an end to the religious unity of medieval Europe. The religious division (Catholic versus Protestant) was instrumental in beginning a series of religious wars that were also complicated by economic, social, and political forces. The French Wars of Religion,  the revolt of the Netherlands against Philip II, and the conflict between Philip II of Spain and Elizabeth of England, which led to the failed attempt of the Spanish armada to invade England, were the major struggles in the sixteenth-century religious wars.

That people who were disciples of the Apostle of Peace would kill each other over their beliefs aroused skepticism about Christianity itself. As one German writer put it, "Lutheran, popish, and Calvinistic, we've got all these beliefs here, but there is some doubt about where Christianity has got."[12] It is surely no acci-dent that the search for a stable, secular order of politics and for order in the universe through natural laws soon came to play important roles. Before we look at this search for order in the seventeenth century, however, we need first to look at the adventures that plunged Europe into its new role in the world.

CHAPTER TIMELINE

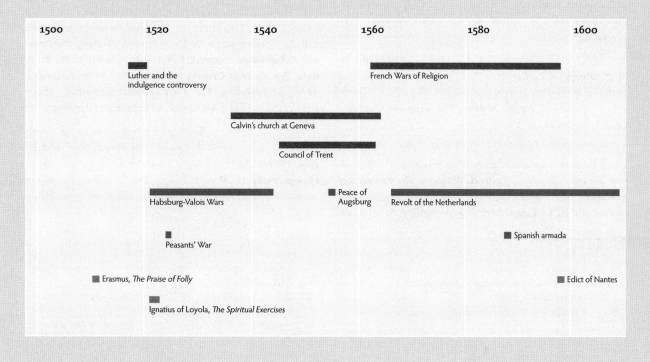

CHAPTER REVIEW

Upon Reflection

Q If attempts at reform of the Catholic Church were unsuccessful in the fifteenth century, why did they succeed in the sixteenth-century Reformation?

Q What role did politics play in the establishment of Lutheranism and Anglicanism?

Q Elizabeth of England and Philip II of Spain were two of Europe's most famous monarchs in the second half of the sixteenth century. Compare and contrast their methods of ruling and their foreign policy. Which was a more successful ruler? Why?

Key Terms

Christian (northern Renaissance) humanism (p. 302)
pluralism (p. 303)
indulgences (p. 304)
justification (p. 304)

transubstantiation (p. 307)
predestination (p. 313)
Catholic Reformation (p. 315)
Huguenots (p. 320)
politiques (p. 320)

Suggestions for Further Reading

THE REFORMATION Basic surveys of the Reformation period include **J. D. Tracy, *Europe's Reformations, 1450–1650*** (Oxford, 1999), and **D. MacCulloch, *The Reformation*** (New York, 2003). See also the brief work by **P. Collinson, *The Reformation: A History*** (New York, 2006).

NORTHERN RENAISSANCE HUMANISM The development of humanism outside Italy is examined in **C. G. Nauert, Jr., *Humanism and the Culture of Renaissance Europe,*** 2d ed. (Cambridge, 2006).

LUTHER AND LUTHERANISM On Martin Luther's life, see **H. A. Oberman, *Luther*** (New York, 1992), and the brief biography by **M. Marty, *Martin Luther*** (New York, 2004). On the role of Charles V, see **W. Maltby, *The Reign of Charles V*** (New York, 2002).

SPREAD OF THE PROTESTANT REFORMATION The most comprehensive account of the various groups and individuals who are called Anabaptists is **G. H. Williams, *The Radical Reformation,*** 2d ed. (Kirksville, Mo., 1992). On the English Reformation, see **N. L. Jones, *English Reformation: Religion and Cultural Adaptation*** (London, 2002). On Calvinism, see **W. G. Naphy, *Calvin and the Consolidation of the Genevan Reformation*** (Philadelphia, 2003).

SOCIAL IMPACT OF THE REFORMATION On the impact of the Reformation on the family, see **J. F. Harrington, *Reordering Marriage and Society in Reformation Germany*** (New York, 1995).

CATHOLIC REFORMATION A good introduction to the Catholic Reformation can be found in **M. A. Mullett, *The Catholic Reformation*** (London, 1999). Also valuable is **M. R. P. Hsia, *The World of Catholic Renewal, 1540–1770*** (Cambridge, 1998). **J. O'Malley, *The First Jesuits*** (Cambridge, Mass., 1995), offers a clear discussion of the founding of the Jesuits.

WARS OF RELIGION For a good introduction to the French Wars of Religion, see **R. J. Knecht, *The French Wars of Religion, 1559–1598,*** 2d ed. (New York, 1996). On Philip II, see **G. Parker, *Philip II,*** 3d ed. (Chicago, 1995). Elizabeth's reign can be examined in **C. Haigh, *Elizabeth I,*** 2d ed. (New York, 1998).

Notes

1. D. Erasmus, *The Paraclesis,* in *Christian Humanism and the Reformation: Selected Writings of Erasmus,* ed. J. Olin, 3d ed. (New York, 1987), p. 101.
2. J. P. Dolan, ed., *The Essential Erasmus* (New York, 1964), p. 149.
3. Quoted in A. E. McGrath, *Reformation Thought: An Introduction* (Oxford, 1988), p. 72.
4. Quoted in E. G. Rupp and B. Drewery, eds., *Martin Luther* (New York, 1970), p. 50.
5. Quoted in R. Bainton, *Here I Stand: A Life of Martin Luther* (New York, 1950), p. 144.
6. Quoted in D. L. Jensen, *Reformation Europe* (Lexington, Mass., 1981), p. 83.
7. J. Calvin, *Institutes of the Christian Religion,* trans. J. Allen (Philadelphia, 1936), vol. 1, p. 228; vol. 2, p. 181.
8. Quoted in R. Bainton, *Women of the Reformation in Germany and Italy* (Boston, 1971), p. 154.
9. Quoted in B. S. Anderson and J. P. Zinsser, *A History of Their Own: Women in Europe from Prehistory to the Present* (New York, 1988), vol. 1, p. 259.
10. Quoted in J. A. Phillips, *Eve: The History of an Idea* (New York, 1984), p. 105.
11. Quoted in G. Mattingly, *The Armada* (Boston, 1959), pp. 216–217.
12. Quoted in T. Schieder, *Handbuch der Europäischen Geschichte* (Stuttgart, 1979), vol. 3, p. 579.

MindTap **MindTap** is a fully online, highly personalized learning experience built upon Cengage Learning content. MindTap combines student learning tools—readings, multimedia, activities, and assessments—into a singular Learning Path that guides students through the course.

C H A P T E R

14

Europe and the World: New Encounters, 1500–1800

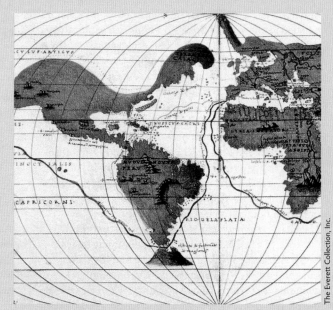

A 1536 Mercator projection map showing the route of Ferdinand Magellan's first circumnavigation of the world

The Everett Collection, Inc.

CHAPTER OUTLINE AND FOCUS QUESTIONS

On the Brink of a New World

Q Why did Europeans begin to embark on voyages of discovery and expansion at the end of the fifteenth century?

New Horizons: The Portuguese and Spanish Empires

Q How did Portugal and Spain acquire their overseas empires, and how did their empires differ?

New Rivals on the World Stage

Q How did the arrival of the Dutch, British, and French on the world scene in the seventeenth and eighteenth centuries affect Africa, India, Southeast Asia, China, and Japan? What were the main features of the African slave trade, and what effects did it have on Africa?

The Impact of European Expansion

Q How did European expansion affect both the conquered and the conquerors?

Toward a World Economy

Q What was mercantilism, and what was its relationship to colonial empires?

CRITICAL THINKING

Q What was the relationship between European overseas expansion and political, economic, and social developments in Europe?

CONNECTIONS TO TODAY

Q Considering both the benefits and the consequences, what are the similarities and differences between the overseas trade that developed in the seventeenth and eighteenth centuries and the global trade of the twenty-first century?

WHILE MANY EUROPEANS were occupied with the problems of dynastic expansion and religious reform, others were taking voyages that propelled Europeans far beyond the medieval walls in which they had been enclosed for almost a thousand years. One of these adventurers was the Portuguese explorer Ferdinand Magellan. Convinced that he could find a sea passage to Asia through America, Magellan persuaded the king of Spain to finance an exploratory voyage. On August 10, 1519, Magellan set sail on the Atlantic with five ships and a Spanish crew of 277 men. After a stormy and difficult crossing of the ocean, Magellan's fleet sailed down along the coast of South America, searching for the strait that would take him through. His Spanish ship captains thought he was crazy: "The fool is obsessed with his search for a strait," one remarked. "On the flame of his ambition he will crucify us all." At last, in October 1520, he found it, passing through a narrow waterway (later named the Strait of Magellan) and emerging into an unknown ocean that he called the Pacific Sea. Magellan reckoned that it would then be a short distance to the Spice Islands of the East, but he was badly mistaken. Week after week, he and his crew sailed on across the Pacific as their food supplies dwindled. According to one account, "When their last biscuit had gone, they scraped the maggots out of the casks, mashed them and served them as gruel. They made cakes out of sawdust soaked with the urine of rats—the rats themselves, as delicacies, had long since been hunted to extinction." At last they reached the islands that would later be called the Philippines (after King Philip II of Spain), where Magellan met his death at the hands of the local inhabitants. Although only one of his original fleet of five ships survived and returned to Spain, Magellan is still remembered as the first person to circumnavigate the world.

At the beginning of the sixteenth century, European adventurers like Magellan had begun launching small fleets into the vast reaches of the Atlantic Ocean. They were hardly aware that they were beginning a new era, not only for Europe, but for the peoples of Asia, Africa, and the Americas as well. Nevertheless, the voyages of these Europeans marked the beginning of a process that led to radical changes in the political, economic, and cultural life of the entire world.

Between 1500 and 1800, European power engulfed the globe. In the Americas, Europeans established colonies that spread their laws, religions, and cultures. In the island regions of Southeast Asia, Europeans firmly implanted their rule. In other parts of Asia and in Africa, their activities ranged from trading goods to trafficking in humans, permanently altering the lives of the local peoples. In all regions touched by European expansion, the indigenous peoples faced exposure to new diseases, alteration of their religions and customs, and the imposition of new laws.

On the Brink of a New World

Q FOCUS QUESTION: Why did Europeans begin to embark on voyages of discovery and expansion at the end of the fifteenth century?

Nowhere has the dynamic and even ruthless energy of Western civilization been more apparent than in its expansion into the rest of the world. By the late sixteenth century, the Atlantic seaboard had become the center of a commercial activity that raised Portugal and Spain and later the Dutch Republic, England, and France to prominence. The age of expansion was a crucial factor in the European transition from the agrarian economy of the Middle Ages to a commercial and industrial capitalistic system. Expansion also brought Europeans into new and lasting contacts with non-European peoples that inaugurated a new age of world history in the sixteenth century.

The Motives for Expansion

Lands outside Europe had long intrigued Europeans as a result of a large body of fantasy literature about "other worlds" that had blossomed in the Middle Ages. In the fourteenth century, the author of *The Travels of John Mandeville* spoke of realms (which he had never seen) filled with precious stones and gold. Other lands were more frightening and considerably less appealing. In one country, "the folk be great giants of twenty-eight foot long, or thirty foot long.... And they eat more gladly man's flesh than any other flesh." Farther north was a land inhabited by "cruel and evil women. And they have precious stones in their eyes. And they be of that kind that if they behold any man with wrath they slay him at once with the beholding."[1] Other writers enticed Europeans with descriptions of mysterious Christian kingdoms: the magical kingdom of Prester John in Africa and a Christian community in southern India that was supposedly founded by Thomas, an apostle of Jesus.

Although Muslim control of Central Asia cut Europe off from the countries farther east, the Mongol conquests in the thirteenth century had reopened the doors. The most famous medieval travelers to the East were the Polos of Venice. Niccolò and Maffeo, merchants from Venice, accompanied by Niccolò's son Marco, undertook the lengthy journey to the court of the great Mongol ruler Khubilai Khan (1259–1294) in 1271. Marco's account of his experiences, the *Travels*, was the most informative of all the descriptions of Asia by medieval European travelers. Others followed the Polos, but in the fourteenth century, the conquests of the Ottoman Turks and then the breakup of the Mongol Empire reduced Western traffic to the East. With the closing of the overland routes, a number of people in Europe became interested in the possibility of reaching Asia by sea to gain access to the spices and other precious resources of the region. Christopher Columbus had a copy of Marco Polo's *Travels* in his possession when he began to envision his epoch-making voyage across the Atlantic Ocean.

An economic motive thus looms large in European expansion in the Renaissance. Merchants, adventurers, and government officials had high hopes of finding new areas of trade, especially more direct access to the spices of the East. In addition to the potential profits to be made from the spice trade, many European explorers and conquerors did not hesitate to express their desire for material gain in the form of gold and other precious metals. One Spanish conquistador said that he went to the New World to "serve God and His Majesty, to give light to those who were in darkness, and to grow rich, as all men desire to do."[2]

The conquistador's statement also expressed another major reason for the overseas voyages—religious zeal. Hernán Cortés (hayr-NAHN kor-TAYSS *or* kor-TEZ), the conqueror of Mexico, asked his Spanish rulers if it was not their duty to ensure that the native Mexicans "are introduced into and instructed in their holy Catholic faith."[3] Spiritual and secular affairs were closely intertwined in the sixteenth century. No doubt, the desire for grandeur and glory, as well as plain intellectual curiosity and a spirit of adventure, also played some role in the European expansion.

The Means for Expansion

If "God, glory, and gold" were the primary motives, what made the voyages possible? First of all, the expansion of Europe was connected to the growth of centralized monarchies during the Renaissance. By the second half of the fifteenth century, European monarchies had increased both their authority and their resources and were in a position to turn their energies beyond their borders. At the same time, by the end of the fifteenth century, European states had achieved a level of wealth and technology that enabled them to make a regular series of voyages beyond Europe. They now had remarkably seaworthy ships and reliable navigational aids, such as the compass and astrolabe (an instrument used to determine the position of heavenly bodies).

One of the most important world maps available to Europeans at the end of the fifteenth century was that of Ptolemy, an astronomer of the second century C.E. Ptolemy's work, the *Geography*, had been known to Arab geographers as early as the eighth century, but it was not until the fifteenth century that a Latin translation was made of the work. Printed editions, which contained his world map, first became available in 1477. Ptolemy's map showed the world as spherical with three major landmasses—Europe, Asia, and Africa—and only two oceans. In addition to showing the oceans as considerably smaller than the landmasses, Ptolemy had also dramatically underestimated the circumference of the earth, which led Columbus and other adventurers to believe that it would be feasible to sail west from Europe to Asia.

New Horizons: The Portuguese and Spanish Empires

Q FOCUS QUESTION: How did Portugal and Spain acquire their overseas empires, and how did their empires differ?

Portugal took the lead in the European age of expansion when it began to explore the coast of Africa under the sponsorship of Prince Henry the Navigator (1394–1460). His motives were a blend of seeking a Christian kingdom as an ally against the Muslims, acquiring trade opportunities for Portugal, and spreading Christianity.

The Development of a Portuguese Maritime Empire

In 1419, Portuguese fleets began probing southward along the western coast of Africa in search of gold. Exploration slowed after Prince Henry's death in 1460, but Portuguese ships gradually crept down the African coast until Bartholomeu Dias (bar-toh-loh-MAY-oo DEE-ush) (ca. 1450–1500) finally rounded the Cape of Good Hope at the southern tip of Africa in 1488 (see Map 14.1). Ten years later, a fleet under the command of Vasco da Gama (VAHSH-koh dah GAHM-uh) rounded the cape and stopped at several ports controlled by Muslim merchants along the coast of East Africa. Da Gama's fleet then crossed the Arabian Sea and reached the port of Calicut, on the southwestern coast of India, on May 18, 1498. On arriving in Calicut, da Gama announced to his surprised hosts that he had come in search of

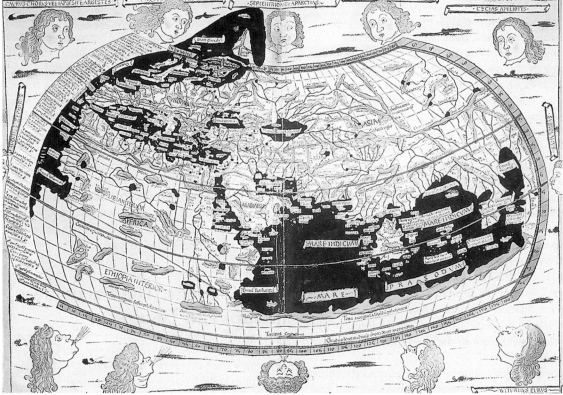

Ptolemy's World Map. Contained in the Latin translation of Ptolemy's *Geography* was this world map, which did not become available to Europeans until the late fifteenth century. Scholars quickly accepted it as the most accurate map of its time. The twelve "wind faces," meant to show wind currents around the earth, were a fifteenth-century addition to the ancient map.

"Christians and spices." He found no Christians, but he did find the spices he sought. Although he lost two ships en route, da Gama's remaining vessels returned to Europe with their holds filled with ginger and cinnamon, a cargo that earned the investors a profit of several thousand percent.

Portuguese fleets returned annually to the area, seeking to destroy Arab shipping and establish a monopoly in the spice trade. In 1510, seeing the need for a land base in the area, Admiral Afonso d'Albuquerque (ah-FAHN-soh day AL-buh-kur-kee) (ca. 1462–1515), took the lead in establishing a ring of commercial-military bases on the western coast of India south of present-day Mumbai (Bombay). The port at Goa became the headquarters for operations throughout the entire region.

The Portuguese now began to range more widely in search of the source of the spice trade (see Images of Everyday Life on p. 332). Albuquerque sailed into the harbor of Malacca (muh-LAK-uh) on the Malay Peninsula, one of the main harbors in the spice trade, and

after a short but bloody battle, the Portuguese seized the city and massacred the local Arab population. From Malacca, the Portuguese launched expeditions farther east, to China and the Spice Islands. There they signed a treaty with a local ruler for the purchase and export of cloves to the European market. The new trading empire was now complete. Within a few years, the Portuguese had managed to seize control of the spice trade from Muslim traders and had garnered substantial profits for the Portuguese monarchy. Nevertheless, the Portuguese Empire remained limited, consisting only of trading posts on the coasts of India and China. The Portuguese lacked the power, the population, and the desire to colonize the Asian regions.

Why were the Portuguese so successful? Basically, their success was a matter of guns and seamanship. By the sixteenth century, Portuguese fleets were heavily armed and were able not only to intimidate but also to inflict severe defeats if necessary on local naval and land forces. The Portuguese by no means possessed a

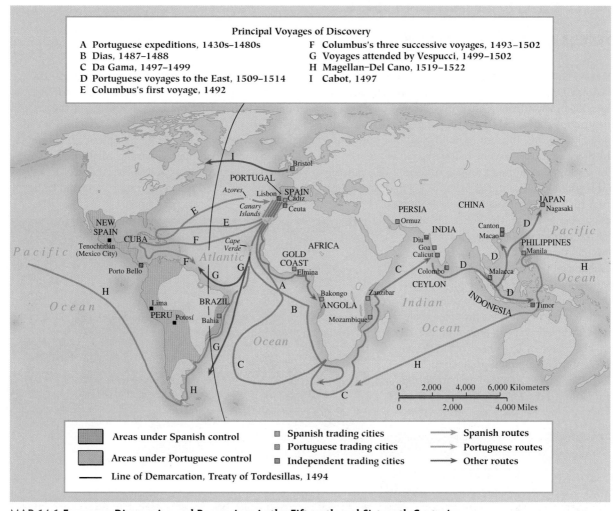

Principal Voyages of Discovery

A Portuguese expeditions, 1430s–1480s
B Dias, 1487–1488
C Da Gama, 1497–1499
D Portuguese voyages to the East, 1509–1514
E Columbus's first voyage, 1492
F Columbus's three successive voyages, 1493–1502
G Voyages attended by Vespucci, 1499–1502
H Magellan–Del Cano, 1519–1522
I Cabot, 1497

Areas under Spanish control
Areas under Portuguese control
Line of Demarcation, Treaty of Tordesillas, 1494

Spanish trading cities
Portuguese trading cities
Independent trading cities

Spanish routes
Portuguese routes
Other routes

MAP 14.1 European Discoveries and Possessions in the Fifteenth and Sixteenth Centuries.
Desire for wealth was the main motivation of the early explorers, although spreading Christianity was also an important factor. Portugal under Prince Henry the Navigator initiated the first voyages in the early fifteenth century; Spain's explorations began at the century's end.

Q Which regions of the globe were primarily explored by Portugal, and which were the main focus of Spain's voyages?

monopoly on the use of firearms and explosives, but their effective use of naval technology, their heavy guns that could be mounted in the hulls of their sturdy vessels, and their tactics gave them military superiority over lightly armed rivals that they were able to exploit until the arrival of other European forces several decades later.

Voyages to the New World

While the Portuguese were seeking access to the spice trade of the Indies by sailing eastward through the Indian Ocean, the Spanish were attempting to reach the same destination by sailing westward across the Atlantic. Although the Spanish came to overseas discovery and exploration after the initial efforts of the Portuguese, their greater resources enabled them to establish a far grander and quite different overseas empire.

An important figure in the history of Spanish exploration was an Italian known as Christopher Columbus (1451-1506). Knowledgeable Europeans were aware that the world was round but had little understanding

IMAGES OF EVERYDAY LIFE
Spices and World Trade

PEPPER, CINNAMON, NUTMEG, and other spices from the East had long been a part of European life. The top right illustration from a fifteenth-century French manuscript shows the harvesting of pepper in Malabar, India. Europeans' interest in finding a direct route to the Spice Islands intensified after the fall of Constantinople to the Ottoman Turks in 1453, causing a thirtyfold increase in the price for pepper. As evident from the number of available spices in the spice seller's shop in the Venetian fresco on the bottom right, Venetians played a dominant role in the spice trade via Constantinople. However, it was Vasco da Gama's success in locating a route to the East by sailing around Africa that shifted much of the control over the spice trade into Portuguese hands. Following the establishment in 1518 of a fort in Ceylon, the center of cinnamon production, the Portuguese were able to dominate Europe's cinnamon trade. The illustration to the left shows a portrait of da Gama from around 1600. The artist depicted the explorer holding a large stick of cinnamon in his right hand, an indication of the significance of the spice to his legacy and its role in his expeditions. Without the desire for spices, men such as da Gama and Christopher Columbus might not have ventured around Africa or across the Atlantic Ocean, thereby opening and forever altering European trade.

Bibliothèque Nationale, Paris/Archives Charmet/The Bridgeman Art Library

Marine Museum, Lisbon//Gianni Dagli Orti/The Art Archive at Art Resource, NY

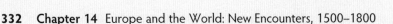

Castello d'Issogne, Val d'Aosta, Italy//Scala/Art Resource, NY

Christopher Columbus. Columbus was an Italian explorer who worked for the queen of Spain. He has become a symbol for two entirely different perspectives. To some, he was a great and heroic explorer who discovered the New World; to others, especially in Latin America, he was responsible for beginning a process of invasion that led to the destruction of an entire way of life. Because Columbus was never painted during his lifetime, the numerous portraits of him are more fanciful than accurate. The portrait shown here is attributed to the Italian painter Ridolfo Ghirlandaio.

of its circumference or the extent of the continent of Asia. Convinced that the circumference of the earth was less than contemporaries believed and that Asia was larger than people thought, Columbus believed that Asia could be reached by sailing directly west instead of around Africa. After being rejected by the Portuguese, he persuaded Queen Isabella of Spain to finance his exploratory expedition.

With three ships, the *Santa María*, the *Niña*, and the *Pinta*, and a crew of ninety men, Columbus set sail on August 3, 1492. On October 12, he reached the Bahamas and then went on to explore the coastline of Cuba and the northern shores of Hispaniola (present-day Haiti and the Dominican Republic). Columbus believed that he had reached Asia, and in his reports to Queen Isabella and King Ferdinand upon his return to Spain, he assured them not only that he would eventually find gold but also that they had a golden opportunity to convert the indigenous peoples—whom Columbus persisted in calling "Indians"—to Christianity. In three subsequent voyages (1493, 1498, and 1502), Columbus sought in vain to find a route to the Asian mainland. In his four voyages, Columbus landed on all the major islands of the Caribbean and the mainland of Central America, still convinced that he had reached the Indies in Asia.

Although Columbus clung to his belief until his death, other explorers soon realized that he had discovered a new frontier altogether. State-sponsored explorers joined the race to the New World. A Venetian seaman, John Cabot, explored the New England coastline of the Americas under a license from King Henry VII of England. The continent of South America was discovered accidentally by the Portuguese sea captain Pedro Cabral (kuh-BRAL) in 1500. Amerigo Vespucci (ahm-ay-REE-goh vess-POO-chee), a Florentine, accompanied several voyages and wrote a series of letters describing the geography of the New World. The publication of these letters led to the use of the name *America* (after *Amerigo*) for the new lands.

The first two decades of the sixteenth century witnessed numerous overseas voyages that explored the eastern coasts of both North and South America. Perhaps the most dramatic of all these expeditions was the journey of Ferdinand Magellan (1480–1521) in 1519. After passing through the strait named after him at the southern tip of South America, he sailed across the Pacific Ocean. Although Magellan himself was killed in the Philippines and only one of his fleet of five ships completed the return voyage to Spain, his name is still associated with the first known circumnavigation of the earth.

The Europeans referred to the newly discovered territories as the New World, even though they held flourishing civilizations populated by millions of people. But the Americas were indeed new to the Europeans, who quickly saw opportunities for conquest and exploitation. The Spanish, in particular, were interested because in 1494 the Treaty of Tordesillas (tor-day-SEE-yass) had divided up the newly discovered world into separate Portuguese and Spanish spheres of influence, and it turned out that most of South America (except for the eastern hump) fell within the Spanish sphere. Hereafter the route east around the Cape of Good Hope was to be reserved for the Portuguese, while the route across the Atlantic was assigned to Spain.

The Spanish Empire in the New World

The Spanish conquerors known as **conquistadors** were hardy individuals motivated by a typical sixteenth-century blend of glory, greed, and religious zeal. Although authorized by the Castilian crown, these groups were financed and outfitted privately, not by the government. Their superior weapons, organizational skills, and determination brought the conquistadors incredible success. They also benefited from rivalries among the native peoples and the decimation of the native populations by European diseases.

EARLY CIVILIZATIONS IN MESOAMERICA
Before the Spaniards arrived in the New World, Mesoamerica (modern Mexico and Central America) had already hosted a number of flourishing civilizations. Beginning around 300 C.E. on the Yucatán peninsula, a people known as the Maya (MY-uh) had developed one of the most sophisticated civilizations in the Americas. The Maya built splendid temples and pyramids, were accomplished artists, and developed a sophisticated calendar, as accurate as any in existence in the world at that time. The Maya were an agrarian people who cleared the dense rain forests, developed farming, and built a patchwork of city-states. Mayan civilization came to include much of Central America and southern Mexico. For unknown reasons, Maya civilization began to decline around 800 and collapsed less than a hundred years later.

Sometime during the early twelfth century C.E., a people known as the Aztecs began a long migration that brought them to the Valley of Mexico. They established their capital at Tenochtitlán (tay-nawch-teet-LAHN), on an island in the middle of Lake Texcoco (now the location of Mexico City). For the next hundred years, the Aztecs built their city, constructing temples, other public buildings, houses, and causeways of stone across Lake Texcoco to the north,

Lands of the Maya

The Aztec Empire

south, and west, linking the many islands to the mainland.

The Aztecs were outstanding warriors, and while they were building their capital city, they also set out to bring the entire area around the city under their control. By the early fifteenth century, they had become the leading city-state in the lake region. For the remainder of the fifteenth century, the Aztecs consolidated their rule over much of what is modern Mexico, from the Atlantic to the Pacific Ocean and as far south as the Guatemalan border. The new kingdom was not a centralized state but a collection of semi-independent territories governed by local lords.

SPANISH CONQUEST OF THE AZTEC EMPIRE In 1519, a Spanish expedition under the command of Hernán Cortés (1485–1547) landed at Veracruz, on the Gulf of Mexico. He marched to the city of Tenochtitlán (see the box on p. 335) at the head of a small contingent of troops (550 soldiers and 16 horses), on the way making alliances with city-states that had tired of the oppressive rule of the Aztecs. Especially important was Tlaxcala (tuh-lah-SKAH-lah), a state that the Aztecs had not been able to conquer. In November, Cortés arrived at Tenochtitlán, where he received a friendly welcome from the Aztec monarch Moctezuma (mahk-tuh-ZOO-muh) (often called Montezuma). At first, Moctezuma believed that his visitor was a representative of Quetzalcoatl (KWET-sul-koh-AHT-ul), the god who had departed from his homeland centuries before and had promised someday to return.

But the Spaniards quickly wore out their welcome. They took Moctezuma hostage and proceeded to pillage the city. In the fall of 1520, one year after Cortés had arrived, the local population revolted and drove the invaders from the city. Many of the Spaniards were killed, but the Aztecs soon experienced new disasters. As one Aztec related, "At about the time that the Spaniards

The Spanish Conquistador: Cortés and the Conquest of Mexico

Hernán Cortés was a minor Spanish nobleman who came to the New World in 1504 to seek his fortune. Contrary to his superior's orders, Cortés waged an independent campaign of conquest and overthrew the Aztec Empire in Mexico (1519–1521). He then wrote a series of five reports to Emperor Charles V to justify his action. The second report includes a description of Tenochtitlán, the capital of the Aztec Empire. The Spanish conquistador and his men were obviously impressed by this city, which was awesome in its architecture yet built by people who lacked European technology, such as wheeled vehicles and tools of hard metal.

Cortés's Description of Tenochtitlán

The great city Tenochtitlán is built in the midst of this salt lake, and it is two leagues [about 6 miles] from the heart of the city to any point on the mainland. Four causeways lead to it, all made by hand and some twelve feet wide. The city itself is as large as Seville or Córdoba. The principal streets are very broad and straight, the majority of them being of beaten earth, but a few and at least half the smaller thoroughfares are waterways along which they pass in their canoes. Moreover, even the principal streets have openings at regular distances so that the water can freely pass from one to another, and these openings which are very broad are spanned by great bridges of huge beams, very stoutly put together, so firm indeed that over many of them ten horsemen can ride at once. . . .

The city has many open squares in which markets are continuously held and the general business of buying and selling proceeds. One square in particular is twice as big as that of Salamanca and completely surrounded by arcades where there are daily more than sixty thousand folk buying and selling. Every kind of merchandise such as may be met with in every land is for sale there, whether of food and victuals, or ornaments of gold and silver, or lead, brass, copper, tin, precious stones, bones, shells, snails and feathers; limestone for building is likewise sold there, stone both rough and polished, bricks burnt and unburnt, wood of all kinds and in all stages of preparation. . . . There is a street of herb-sellers where there are all manner of roots and medicinal plants that are found in the land. There are houses as it were of apothecaries where they sell medicines made from these herbs, both for drinking and for use as ointments and salves. . . .

Finally, to avoid [excess] in telling all the wonders of this city, I will simply say that the manner of living among the people is very similar to that in Spain, and considering that this is a barbarous nation shut off from a knowledge of the true God or communication with enlightened nations, one may well marvel at the orderliness and good government which is everywhere maintained.

The actual service of Moctezuma and those things which call for admiration by the greatness and state would take so long to describe that I assure your Majesty I do not know where to begin with any hope of ending. For as I have already said, what could there be more astonishing than that a barbarous monarch such as he should have reproductions made in gold, silver, precious stones, and feathers of all things to be found in his land, and so perfectly reproduced that there is no goldsmith or silversmith in the world who could better them.

Q What did Cortés focus on in his description of this Aztec city? Why do you think he felt justified in overthrowing the Aztec Empire?

Source: From *The European Reconnaissance: Selected Documents* by John H. Parry. Copyright © 1968 by John H. Parry. Reprinted by permission Walker & Co.

had fled from Mexico, there came a great sickness, a pestilence, the smallpox." With no natural immunity to the diseases of Europe, many Aztecs fell sick and died (see "Disease in the New World" later in this chapter). Meanwhile, Cortés received fresh soldiers from his new allies; the state of Tlaxcala alone provided fifty thousand warriors. After four months, the city capitulated. And then the destruction began. The pyramids, temples, and palaces were leveled, and the stones were used to build Spanish government buildings and churches. The rivers and canals were filled in. The mighty Aztec Empire on mainland Mexico was no more. Between 1531 and 1550, the Spanish gained control of northern Mexico.

THE INCA AND THE SPANISH In the late fourteenth century, the Inca were a small community in the area of Cuzco, a city located at an altitude of ten thousand feet in the mountains of southern Peru. In the 1440s, however, under the leadership of their powerful ruler Pachakuti (pah-chah-KOO-tee), the Inca launched a campaign of conquest that eventually brought the entire region under their control.

Pachakuti created a highly centralized state. Cuzco, the capital, was transformed from a city of mud and thatch into an imposing city of stone. The Inca were great builders. Their roadways extended through the Andes Mountains, in a north-south direction, with connecting routes to another roadway along the coast. Another system of roads covered 24,800 miles from modern-day Colombia to a point south of modern-day Santiago, Chile. Along the roadways, the Inca constructed some of the finest examples of suspension bridges in premodern times. Under Pachakuti and his immediate successors, Topa Inca and Huayna Inca (the word *inca* means "ruler"), the boundaries of the Inca Empire were extended as far as Ecuador, central Chile, and the edge of the Amazon basin. The empire included perhaps 12 million people.

The Inca Empire was still flourishing when the first Spanish expeditions arrived in the area. In December 1530, Francisco Pizarro (frahn-CHESS-koh puh-ZAHR-oh) (ca. 1475–1541) landed on the Pacific coast of South America with a band of about 180 men, but like Cortés, he had steel weapons, gunpowder, and horses, none of which were familiar to his hosts. Pizarro was also lucky because the Inca Empire had already succumbed to an epidemic of smallpox. Like the Aztecs, the Inca had no immunities to European diseases, and all too soon, smallpox was devastating entire villages. In another stroke of good fortune for Pizarro, even the Inca emperor was a victim. Upon the emperor's death, two sons claimed the throne, setting off a civil war. Pizarro took advantage of the situation by seizing Atahualpa (ah-tuh-WAHL-puh), whose forces had just defeated his brother's. Armed only with stones, arrows, and light spears, Inca soldiers were no match for the charging horses of

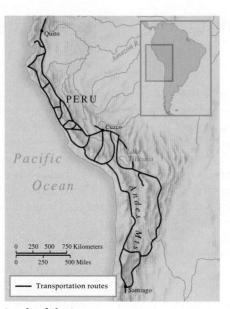

Lands of the Inca

the Spanish, let alone their guns and cannons. After executing Atahualpa, Pizarro and his soldiers, aided by their Inca allies, marched on Cuzco and captured the Inca capital. By 1535, Pizarro had established a capital at Lima for a new colony of the Spanish Empire.

DISEASE IN THE NEW WORLD When Columbus reached the Caribbean island of Hispaniola in 1492, he brought more than gunpowder, horses, and soldiers to the shores of the New World. With no immunity to European diseases, the Indians of America were ravaged by smallpox, influenza, measles, and pneumonic plague, and later by typhus, yellow fever, and cholera.

In 1518, smallpox, a highly contagious disease, spread rapidly along trade routes from the Caribbean to Mesoamerica, killing a third of the Indian population. Its ravages of the Aztecs helped make possible their conquest by Hernán Cortés. The Inca suffered a similar fate from smallpox and measles. By 1630, smallpox had reached New England. The ferocity of the epidemics left few survivors to tend the crops, leading to widespread starvation and higher mortality rates. Although scholarly estimates vary, a reasonable guess is that 30 to 40 percent of the local populations died. The population of central Mexico, estimated at roughly 11 million in 1519, had declined to 6.5 million by 1540 and 2.5 million by the end of the sixteenth century.

The high mortality rates among the native populations resulted in a shortage of workers for the Europeans, which led them to turn to Africa for the labor needed for the silver mines and sugar plantations (see "Africa: The Slave Trade" later in this chapter). Despite the Europeans' technological advantages, the biological weapons that they brought with them from the Old World proved to have an even greater impact on the Americas.

ADMINISTRATION OF THE SPANISH EMPIRE Spanish policy toward the Indians of the New World was a combination of confusion, misguided paternalism, and cruel exploitation. Whereas the conquistadors made decisions based on expediency and their own interests, Queen Isabella declared the indigenous peoples to be subjects of Castile and instituted the Spanish **encomienda** (en-koh-MYEN-dah),

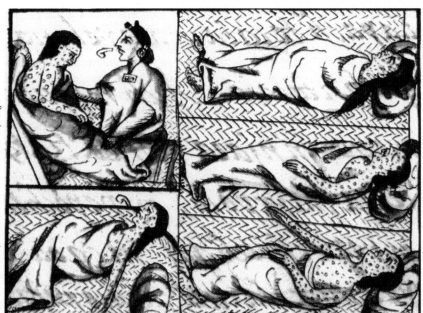

Aztec Victims of Smallpox. The indigenous populations of the New World had no immunities to the diseases of the Old World, such as smallpox. By 1520, smallpox had spread throughout the Caribbean and Mesoamerica. This sixteenth-century drawing by a Franciscan friar portrays Native Americans afflicted with smallpox. The pustules that often covered the body are clearly depicted. The figure at the lower right twists in agony—representing the immense pain experienced by those who contracted the disease.

an economic and social system that permitted the conquering Spaniards to collect tribute from the Indians and use them as laborers. In return, the holders of an encomienda were supposed to protect the Indians, pay them wages, and supervise their spiritual needs. In practice, this meant that the settlers were free to implement the paternalistic system of the government as they pleased. Three thousand miles from Spain, Spanish settlers largely ignored their government and brutally used the Indians to pursue their own economic interests. Indians were put to work on plantations and in the lucrative gold and silver mines. In Peru, the Spanish made use of the *mita*, a system that allowed authorities to draft native labor to work in the silver mines.

In the New World, the Spanish developed an administrative system based on viceroys. Spanish possessions were initially divided into two major administrative units: New Spain (Mexico, Central America, and the Caribbean islands), with its center in Mexico City, and Peru (western South America), governed by a **viceroy** in Lima. Each viceroy served as the king's chief civil and military officer.

By papal agreement, the Catholic monarchs of Spain were given extensive rights over ecclesiastical affairs in the New World. They could appoint all bishops and clergy, build churches, collect fees, and supervise the affairs of the various religious orders that sought to convert the heathen. In the early years of the conquest, Catholic missionaries converted and baptized hundreds of thousands of Indians. Soon after the missionaries came the establishment of dioceses, parishes, cathedrals, schools, and hospitals—all the trappings of civilized European society.

New Rivals on the World Stage

Q **FOCUS QUESTIONS:** How did the arrival of the Dutch, British, and French on the world scene in the seventeenth and eighteenth centuries affect Africa, India, Southeast Asia, China, and Japan? What were the main features of the African slave trade, and what effects did it have on Africa?

Portugal and Spain had been the first Atlantic nations to take advantage of the age of exploration, starting in the late fifteenth century, and both had become great

CHRONOLOGY The Portuguese and Spanish Empires in the Sixteenth Century	
Bartholomeu Dias sails around the tip of Africa	1488
Voyages of Columbus	1492–1502
Treaty of Tordesillas	1494
Vasco da Gama lands at Calicut in India	1498
Portuguese ships land in southern China	1514
Magellan's voyage around the world	1519–1522
Spanish conquest of Mexico	1519–1522
Pizarro's conquest of the Inca	1530–1535

colonial powers. In the seventeenth century, however, their European neighbors to the north—first the Dutch and then the French and English—moved to replace the Portuguese and Spanish and create their own colonial empires. The new rivals and their rivalry soon had an impact on much of the rest of the world—in Africa, Asia, and the Americas.

Africa: The Slave Trade

Although the primary objective of the Portuguese in sailing around Africa was to find a sea route to the Spice Islands, they soon discovered that profits could be made in Africa itself. So did other Europeans.

Traffic in slaves was not new, and at first, the Portuguese simply replaced European slaves with African ones. During the second half of the fifteenth century, about a thousand slaves were taken to Portugal each year. Most wound up serving as domestic servants for affluent families in Europe. But the discovery of the Americas in the 1490s and the planting of sugarcane in South America and on the islands of the Caribbean changed the situation drastically.

Cane sugar had first been introduced to Europeans from the Middle East during the Crusades. During the sixteenth century, sugarcane plantations were set up along the eastern coast of Brazil and on several islands in the Caribbean. Because the growing of cane sugar demands both skill and large quantities of labor, the new plantations required more workers than could be provided by the small American Indian population in the New World, which had been decimated by diseases imported from the Old World. Since the climate and soil of much of West Africa were not conducive to the cultivation of sugar, African slaves began to be shipped to Brazil and the Caribbean to work on the plantations. The first were sent from Portugal, but in 1518, a Spanish ship carried the first boatload of African slaves directly from Africa to the New World.

GROWTH IN THE SLAVE TRADE During the next two centuries, the trade in slaves grew dramatically and became part of the **triangular trade** connecting Europe, Africa, and the American continents that characterized the new Atlantic economy (see Map 14.2).

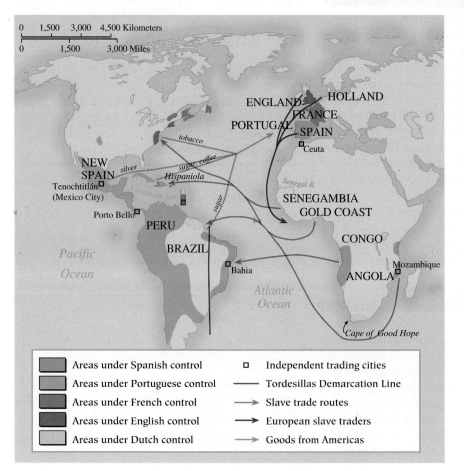

MAP 14.2 Triangular Trade in the Atlantic Economy. As the trade in slaves grew, it became a part of the triangular trade route that characterized the Atlantic economy, involving the exchange of goods and slaves between the western coast of Europe, the slave depots on the African coast, and the ports of North and South America.

Q What were the important source regions for slaves, and where were most of the slaves taken?

European merchant ships (primarily those of England, France, Spain, Portugal, and the Dutch Republic) carried European manufactured goods, such as guns, gin, and cloth, to Africa, where they were traded for a cargo of slaves. The slaves were then shipped to the Americas and sold. European merchants then bought tobacco, molasses, sugar, rum, coffee, and raw cotton and shipped them back to Europe to be sold in European markets.

An estimated 275,000 enslaved Africans were exported to other countries during the sixteenth century, with 2,000 going annually to the Americas alone. The total climbed to over a million in the seventeenth century and jumped to 6 million in the eighteenth century, when the trade spread from West and Central Africa to East Africa. Altogether, as many as 10 million African slaves were transported to the Americas between the early sixteenth and nineteenth centuries.

One reason for the astonishing numbers of slaves, of course, was the high death rate. The journey of slaves from Africa to the Americas became known as the **Middle Passage**, the middle leg of the triangular trade route. African slaves were closely packed into cargo ships, 300 to 450 per ship, and chained in holds without sanitary facilities or room to stand up; there they remained during the voyage to America, which took at least one hundred days (see the box on p. 340). Mortality rates averaged 10 percent; longer journeys due to storms or adverse winds resulted in even higher death rates. The Africans who survived the journey were subject to high death rates from diseases to which they had little or no immunity.

Before the coming of Europeans in the fifteenth century, most slaves in Africa were prisoners of war. When Europeans first began to take part in the slave trade, they bought slaves from local African merchants at slave markets in return for gold, guns, or other European goods such as textiles or copper or iron utensils.

At first, local slave traders obtained their supply from regions nearby, but as demand increased, they had to move farther inland to find their victims. In a few cases, local rulers became concerned about the impact of the slave trade on the well-being of their societies. In a letter to the king of Portugal in 1526, King Affonso of Congo (Bakongo) complained, "So great, Sire, is the corruption and licentiousness that our country is being completely depopulated."[4] But

Europeans as well as other Africans generally ignored protests from Africans.

EFFECTS OF THE SLAVE TRADE The effects of the slave trade varied from area to area. Of course, it had tragic effects on the lives of the slaves and their families. There was also an economic price as the importation of cheap manufactured goods from Europe undermined local cottage industries and forced countless families into poverty. The slave trade also led to the depopulation of some areas and deprived many African communities of their youngest and strongest men and women.

The political effects of the slave trade were also devastating. The need to maintain a constant supply of slaves led to increased warfare and violence as African chiefs and their followers, armed with guns acquired from the trade in slaves, stepped up their raids and wars on neighboring peoples. A few Europeans lamented what they were doing to traditional African societies. One Dutch slave trader remarked, "From us they have learned strife, quarrelling, drunkenness, trickery, theft, unbridled desire for what is not one's own, misdeeds unknown to them before, and the accursed lust for gold."[5] Nevertheless, the slave trade continued unabated.

Despite a rising chorus of humanitarian sentiments from European intellectuals, the use of black slaves remained largely acceptable to Western society. Europeans continued to view blacks as inferior beings fit primarily for indentured labor. Not until the Society of Friends, known as the Quakers, began to criticize slavery in the 1770s and exclude from their church any member adhering to slave trafficking did European sentiment for the abolition of slavery begin to build. Even then, it was not until the radical stage of the French Revolution in the 1790s that the French abolished slavery (see Chapter 19). The British followed suit in 1807. Despite the elimination of the African source, slavery continued in the newly formed United States until the 1860s.

The West in Southeast Asia

Portugal's efforts to dominate the trade of Southeast Asia were never totally successful. The Portuguese lacked both the numbers and the wealth to overcome local resistance and colonize the Asian regions. Portugal's empire was simply too large and

The Atlantic Slave Trade

One of the most odious practices of early modern Western society was the Atlantic slave trade, which reached its height in the eighteenth century. Blacks were transported in densely packed cargo ships from the western coast of Africa to the Americas to work as slaves in the plantation economy. This excerpt presents a criticism of the slave trade from an anonymous French writer.

Diary of a Citizen

As soon as the ships have lowered their anchors off the coast of Guinea, the price at which the captains have decided to buy the captives is announced to the Negroes who buy prisoners from various princes and sell them to Europeans. Presents are sent to the sovereign who rules over that particular part of the coast, and permission to trade is given. Immediately the slaves are brought by inhuman brokers like so many victims dragged to a sacrifice. White men who covet that portion of the human race receive them in a little house they have erected on the shore, where they have entrenched themselves with two pieces of cannon and twenty guards. As soon as the bargain is concluded, the Negro is put in chains and led aboard the vessel, where he meets his fellow sufferers. . . .

The vessel sets sail for the Antilles, and the Negroes are chained in a hold of the ship, a kind of lugubrious prison where the light of day does not penetrate, but into which the air is introduced by means of a pump. Twice a day some disgusting food is distributed to them. Their consuming sorrow and the sad state to which they are reduced would make them commit suicide if they were not deprived of all the means for an attempt upon their lives. Without any kind of clothing it would be difficult to conceal from the watchful eyes of the sailors in charge any instrument apt to alleviate their despair. The fear of a revolt, such as sometimes happens on the voyage from Guinea, is the basis of a common concern and produces as many guards as there are men in the crew. The slightest noise or a secret conversation among two Negroes is punished with utmost severity. All in all, the voyage is made in a continuous state of alarm on the part of the white men, who fear a revolt, and in a cruel state of uncertainty on the part of the Negroes, who do not know the fate awaiting them.

When the vessel arrives at a port in the Antilles, they are taken to a warehouse where they are displayed, like any merchandise, to the eyes of buyers. The plantation owner pays according to the age, strength, and health of the Negro he is buying. He has him taken to his plantation, and there he is delivered to an overseer who then and there becomes his tormentor. In order to domesticate him, the Negro is granted a few days of rest in his new place, but soon he is given a hoe and a sickle and made to join a work gang. Then he ceases to wonder about his fate; he understands that only labor is demanded of him. But he does not know yet how excessive this labor will be. As a matter of fact, his work begins at dawn and does not end before nightfall; it is interrupted for only two hours at dinnertime. The food a full-grown Negro is given each week consists of two pounds of salt beef or cod and two pots of tapioca meal.

Q What does this account reveal about the nature of the slave trade and white attitudes toward blacks in the eighteenth century?

Source: From *European Society in the Eighteenth Century*, ed. Robert and Elborg Forster. New York: Walker & Co., 1969. Reprinted by permission of Walker & Co.

Portugal too small to maintain it. By the end of the sixteenth century, new European rivals had entered the fray.

One of them was Spain. The Spanish had established themselves in the region when Magellan had landed in the Philippines. Although he was killed there, the Spanish were able to gain control over the Philippines, which eventually became a major Spanish base in the trade across the Pacific. Spanish ships carried silk and other luxury goods to Mexico in return for silver from the mines of Mexico.

The primary threat to the Portuguese Empire in Southeast Asia, however, came with the arrival of the Dutch and the English, who were better financed than the Portuguese. The shift in power began in the early seventeenth century when the Dutch seized a Portuguese fort in the Moluccas (muh-LUHK-uhz) and then gradually pushed the Portuguese out of the spice trade.

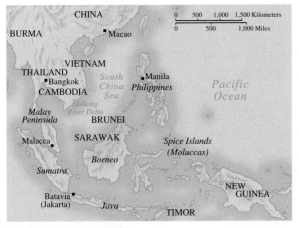

Southeast Asia, ca. 1700

During the next fifty years, the Dutch occupied most of the Portuguese coastal forts along the trade routes throughout the Indian Ocean, including the island of Ceylon (today's Sri Lanka), and seized Malacca in 1641. The aggressive Dutch drove the English traders out of the spice market as well.

The Dutch also began to consolidate their political and military control over the entire area. On the island of Java, where they had established a fort at Batavia (buh-TAY-vee-uh) (modern Jakarta) in 1619, the Dutch found that it was necessary to bring the inland regions under their control to protect their position. On Java and the neighboring island of Sumatra, the Dutch East India Company, which had been founded in 1602, established pepper plantations, which soon became the source of massive profits for Dutch merchants in Amsterdam. By the end of the eighteenth century, the Dutch had succeeded in bringing almost the entire Indonesian archipelago under their control.

Europe in Asia. As Europeans began to move into parts of Asia, they reproduced many of the physical surroundings of their homeland in the port cities they built there. This is evident in comparing these two scenes. Below is a seventeenth-century view of Batavia, which the Dutch built as their headquarters on the northern coast of Java in 1619. The scene at the left is from a sixteenth-century engraving of Amsterdam. This Dutch city had become the financial and commercial capital of Europe and was also the chief port for the ships of the Dutch East India Company, which carried the spices of the East to Europe.

The arrival of the Europeans had less impact on mainland Southeast Asia, where strong monarchies in Burma (modern Myanmar), Siam (modern Thailand), and Vietnam resisted foreign encroachment. In the sixteenth century, the Portuguese established limited trade relations with several mainland states, including Siam, Burma, Vietnam, and the remnants of the old Angkor kingdom in Cambodia. By the early seventeenth century, other nations had followed and had begun to compete actively for trade and missionary privileges. In general, however, these states were able to unite and drive the Europeans out.

In Vietnam, the arrival of Western merchants and missionaries in the mid-seventeenth century coincided with a period of internal conflict among ruling groups in the country. The European powers began to take sides in local politics, with the Portuguese and the Dutch supporting rival factions. The Europeans also set up trading posts for their merchants, but by the end of the seventeenth century, when it became clear that economic opportunities were limited, most of them were abandoned. French missionaries attempted to remain, but their efforts were blocked by the authorities, who viewed converts to Catholicism as a threat to the prestige of the Vietnamese emperor (see the box on p. 343).

The French and British in India

When a Portuguese fleet arrived at the port of Calicut in the spring of 1498, the Indian subcontinent was divided into a number of Hindu and Muslim kingdoms. But it was on the verge of a new era of unity that would be brought about by a foreign dynasty called the Mughals (MOO-guls).

THE MUGHAL EMPIRE The founders of the Mughal Empire were not natives of India but came from the mountainous region north of the Ganges River Valley. The founder of the dynasty, Babur (BAH-ber), had an illustrious background. His father was descended from the great Asian conqueror Tamerlane; his mother, from the Mongol conqueror Genghis Khan. It was Akbar (AK-bahr) (1556–1605), Babur's grandson, however, who brought Mughal rule to most of India, creating the greatest Indian empire since the Mauryan dynasty nearly two thousand years earlier.

THE IMPACT OF THE WESTERN POWERS As we have seen, the first Europeans to arrive in India were the

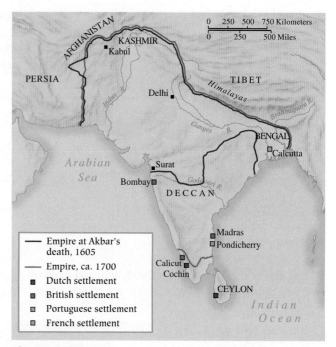

The Mughal Empire

Portuguese. At first, Portugal dominated regional trade in the Indian Ocean, but at the end of the sixteenth century, the English and the Dutch arrived on the scene. Soon both powers were competing with Portugal, and with each other, for trading privileges in the region.

During the first half of the seventeenth century, the English presence in India steadily increased. By 1650, English trading posts had been established at Surat (a thriving port along the northwestern coast of India), Fort William (now the great city of Calcutta) near the Bay of Bengal, and Madras (now Chennai) on the southeastern coast. From Madras, English ships carried Indian-made cotton goods to the East Indies, where they were bartered for spices, which were shipped back to England.

English success in India attracted rivals, including the Dutch and the French. The Dutch abandoned their interests to concentrate on the spice trade in the middle of the seventeenth century, but the French were more persistent and established their own forts on the east coast. For a brief period, the French competed successfully with the British, even capturing the British fort at Madras.

But the British were saved by the military genius of Sir Robert Clive (1725–1774), an aggressive British empire builder who eventually became the chief

OPPOSING VIEWPOINTS

West Meets East: An Exchange of Royal Letters

Economic gain was not the only motivation of Western rulers who wished to establish a European presence in the East. In 1681, King Louis XIV of France wrote a letter to the king of Tonkin (the Trinh family head, then acting as viceroy to the Vietnamese emperor) asking permission for Christian missionaries to proselytize in Vietnam. The king of Tonkin politely declined the request.

A Letter to the King of Tonkin from Louis XIV

Most high, most excellent, most mighty and most magnanimous Prince, our very dear and good friend, may it please God to increase your greatness with a happy end!

We hear from our subjects who were in your Realm what protection you accorded them. We appreciate this all the more since we have for you all the esteem that one can have for a prince as illustrious through his military valor as he is commendable for the justice which he exercises in his Realm. We have even been informed that you have not been satisfied to extend this general protection to our subjects but, in particular, that you gave effective proofs of it to Messrs. Deydier and de Bourges. We would have wished that they might have been able to recognize all the favors they received from you by having presents worthy of you offered you; but since the war which we have had for several years, in which all of Europe had banded together against us, prevented our vessels from going to the Indies, at the present time, when we are at peace after having gained many victories and expanded our Realm through the conquest of several important places, we have immediately given orders to the Royal Company to establish itself in your kingdom as soon as possible, and have commanded Messrs. Deydier and de Bourges to remain with you in order to maintain a good relationship between our subjects and yours, also to warn us on occasions that might present themselves when we might be able to give you proofs of our esteem and of our wish to concur with your satisfaction as well as with your best interests.

By way of initial proof, we have given orders to have brought to you some presents which we believe might be agreeable to you. But the one thing in the world which we desire most, both for you and for your Realm, would be to obtain for your subjects who have already embraced the law of the only true God of heaven and earth, the freedom to profess it, since this law is the highest, the noblest, the most sacred and especially the most suitable to have kings reign absolutely over the people.

We are even quite convinced that, if you knew the truths and the maxims which it teaches, you would give first of all to your subjects the glorious example of embracing it. We wish you this incomparable blessing together with a long and happy reign, and we pray God that it may please Him to augment your greatness with the happiest of endings.

Written at Saint-Germain-en-Laye, the 10th day of January, 1681,

Your very dear and good friend,
Louis

Answer from the King of Tonkin to Louis XIV

The King of Tonkin sends to the King of France a letter to express to him his best sentiments, saying that he was happy to learn that fidelity is a durable good of man and that justice is the most important of things. Consequently practicing of fidelity and justice cannot but yield good results. Indeed, though France and our Kingdom differ as to mountains, rivers, and boundaries, if fidelity and justice reign among our villages, our conduct will express all of our good feelings and contain precious gifts. Your communication, which comes from a country which is a thousand leagues away, and which proceeds from the heart as a testimony of your sincerity, merits repeated consideration and infinite praise. Politeness toward strangers is nothing unusual in our country. There is not a stranger who is not well received by us. How then could we refuse a man from France, which is the most celebrated among the kingdoms of the world and which for love of us wishes to frequent us and bring us merchandise? These feelings

(continued)

of fidelity and justice are truly worthy to be applauded. As regards your wish that we should cooperate in propagating your religion, we do not dare to permit it, for there is an ancient custom, introduced by edicts, which formally forbids it. Now, edicts are promulgated only to be carried out faithfully; without fidelity nothing is stable. How could we disdain a well-established custom to satisfy a private friendship? . . .

We beg you to understand well that this is our communication concerning our mutual acquaintance. This then is my letter. We send you herewith a modest gift, which we offer you with a glad heart.

This letter was written at the beginning of winter and on a beautiful day.

Q What are the underlying beliefs and approaches of these two rulers? How are they alike? How are they different? What is the significance of the way the two rulers date their letters?

Source: From *The World of Southeast Asia: Selected Historical Readings*, Harry J. Benda and John A. Larkin, eds. Copyright © 1967 by Harper & Row Publishers. Used with permission of John A. Larkin.

representative in India of the East India Company, which had been founded as a joint stock company in 1600. Eventually, the French were restricted to the fort at Pondicherry (pon-di-CHER-ee) and a handful of small territories on the southeastern coast.

In the meantime, Clive began to consolidate British control in Bengal, where the local ruler had attacked Fort William and imprisoned the local British population in the "Black Hole of Calcutta" (an underground prison for holding the prisoners, many of whom died in captivity). In 1757, a small British force numbering about three thousand men defeated a Mughal-led army more than ten times its size in the Battle of Plassey (PLAH-see). As part of the spoils of victory, the British East India Company received from the now-decrepit Mughal court the authority to collect taxes from lands in the area surrounding Calcutta. During the Seven Years' War (1756–1763), the British forced the French to withdraw completely from India (see Chapter 18).

China

In 1514, a Portuguese fleet dropped anchor off the coast of China. At the time, the Chinese thought little of the event. China appeared to be at the height of its power as the most magnificent civilization on earth. Its empire stretched from the steppes of Central Asia to the China Sea, from the Gobi Desert to the tropical rain forests of Southeast Asia. From the lofty perspective of the imperial throne in Beijing, the Europeans could only be seen as an unusual form of barbarian. To the Chinese ruler, the rulers of all other countries were simply "younger brothers" of the Chinese emperor, who was regarded as the Son of Heaven.

By the time the Portuguese fleet arrived off the coast of China, the Ming dynasty, which ruled from 1369 to 1644, had already begun a new era of greatness in Chinese history. Under a series of strong rulers, China extended its rule into Mongolia and Central Asia. The Ming even briefly reconquered Vietnam. Along the northern frontier, they strengthened the Great Wall and made peace with the nomadic tribesmen who had troubled China for centuries.

But the days of the Ming dynasty were numbered. After a period of prosperity and growth, the Ming gradually began to decline. During the late sixteenth century, a series of weak rulers led to a period of government corruption, and these internal problems went hand in hand with unrest along the northern frontier. The Ming had tried to come to terms with the frontier tribes by making alliances with them. One of the alliances was with the Manchus, who lived northeast of the Great Wall in the area known today as Manchuria. In 1644, the Manchus overthrew the last Ming emperor and declared the creation of a new dynasty with the reign title of the Qing (Ch'ing, "Pure"). The Qing (CHING) were blessed with a series of strong early rulers who pacified the country, corrected the most serious social and economic ills, and restored peace and prosperity. Two Qing monarchs, Kangxi (GANG-zhee) and Qianlong (CHAN-lung), ruled China for well over a century, from the middle of the seventeenth century to the end of the eighteenth, and were responsible for much of the greatness of Qing China.

WESTERN INROADS Although China was at the height of its power and glory in the mid-eighteenth century, the first signs of internal decay in the Qing dynasty were

The Qing Empire

beginning to appear. Unfortunately for China, this decline occurred just as Europe was increasing pressure for more trade. The first conflict had come from the north, where Russian traders sought skins and furs. Formal diplomatic relations between China and Russia were established in 1689 and provided for regular trade between the two countries.

Dealing with the foreigners who arrived by sea was more difficult. By the end of the seventeenth century, the English had replaced the Portuguese as the dominant force in European trade. Operating through the East India Company, which served as both a trading unit and the administrator of English territories in Asia, the English established their first trading post at Canton (modern Guangzhou) in 1699. Over the next decades, trade with China, notably the export of tea and silk to England, increased rapidly. To limit contacts between Europeans and Chinese, the Qing government confined all European traders to a small island just outside the city walls of Canton and permitted them to reside there only from October through March.

By the end of the eighteenth century, some British traders had begun to demand access to other cities along the Chinese coast and insist that the country be opened to British manufactured goods. In 1793, a British mission under Lord Macartney visited Beijing to press for liberalization of trade restrictions. But Emperor Qianlong expressed no interest in British products. The Chinese would later pay for their rejection of the British request (see Chapter 24).

Japan

At the end of the fifteenth century, Japan was at a point of near anarchy, but in the course of the sixteenth century, a number of powerful individuals achieved the unification of Japan. One of them, Tokugawa Ieyasu (toh-koo-GAH-wah ee-yeh-YAH-soo) (1543–1616), took the title of shogun ("general") in 1603, an act that initiated the most powerful and longest-lasting of all the Japanese shogunates. The Tokugawa rulers completed the restoration of central authority and remained in power until 1868.

OPENING TO THE WEST Portuguese traders had landed on the islands of Japan in 1543, and in a few years, Portuguese ships began stopping at Japanese ports on a regular basis to take part in the regional trade between Japan, China, and Southeast Asia. The first Jesuit missionary, Francis Xavier, arrived in 1549 and had some success in converting the local population to Christianity.

Initially, the Japanese welcomed the visitors. They were fascinated by tobacco, clocks, eyeglasses, and other European goods, and local nobles were interested in purchasing all types of European weapons and armaments. Japanese rulers found the new firearms especially helpful in defeating their enemies and unifying the islands.

The success of the Catholic missionaries, however, provoked a strong reaction against the Westerners. When the missionaries interfered in local politics, Tokugawa Ieyasu, newly come to power, expelled all missionaries. Japanese Christians were now persecuted.

The European merchants were the next to go. The government closed the two major foreign trading posts on the island of Hirado and at Nagasaki. Only a small Dutch community in Nagasaki was allowed to remain in Japan. The Dutch, unlike the Spanish and Portuguese, had not allowed missionary activities to interfere with their trade interests. But the conditions for staying were strict. Dutch ships were allowed to dock at Nagasaki harbor once a year and could remain for only two to three months.

The Americas

In the sixteenth century, Spain and Portugal had established large colonial empires in the Americas. Portugal continued to profit from its empire in Brazil. The Spanish also maintained an enormous South American empire, but Spain's importance as a commercial power declined rapidly in the seventeenth century because of a drop in the output of the silver mines and the poverty of the Spanish monarchy. As the seventeenth century began, both Portugal and Spain found themselves facing new challenges to their American empires from the Dutch, English, and French, who increasingly sought to create their own colonial empires in the New World.

THE WEST INDIES Both the French and English colonial empires in the New World included large parts of the West Indies. The English held Barbados, Jamaica, and Bermuda, and the French possessed Saint-Domingue, Martinique, and Guadeloupe.

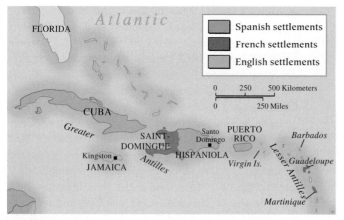

The West Indies

On these tropical islands, both the English and the French had developed plantation economies, worked by African slaves, which produced tobacco, cotton, coffee, and sugar, all products increasingly in demand in Europe.

The "sugar factories," as the sugar plantations in the Caribbean were called, played an especially prominent role. By the last two decades of the eighteenth century, the British colony of Jamaica, one of Britain's most important, was producing 50,000 tons of sugar annually with the labor of 200,000 African slaves. By the early eighteenth century, sugar was the main export from Britain's American colonies. The French colony of Saint-Domingue (later Haiti) had 500,000 slaves working on three thousand plantations at the same time. This colony produced 100,000 tons of sugar a year, but at the expense of a high death rate from the brutal treatment of the slaves.

BRITISH NORTH AMERICA The Dutch were among the first to establish settlements on the North American continent after Henry Hudson, an English explorer hired by the Dutch, in 1609 discovered the river that bears his name. Within a few years, the Dutch had established the mainland colony of New Netherland, which

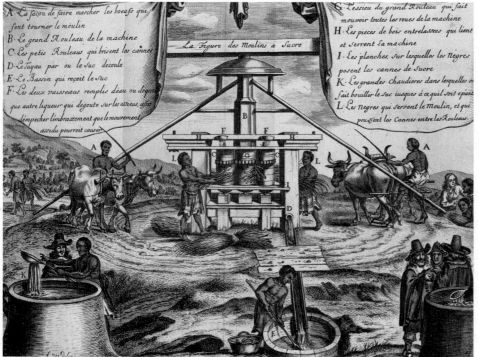

A Sugar Mill in the West Indies. Cane sugar was one of the most valuable products produced in the West Indies. By 1700, sugar was replacing honey as a sweetener for increasing numbers of Europeans. This seventeenth-century French illustration shows the operation of a sugar mill in the French West Indies.

stretched from the mouth of the Hudson River as far north as Albany, New York. In the second half of the seventeenth century, competition from the English and French and years of warfare with those rivals led to the decline of the Dutch commercial empire. In 1664, the English seized the colony of New Netherland and renamed it New York.

In the meantime, the English had begun to establish their own colonies in North America. The first permanent English settlement in America was Jamestown, founded in 1607 in modern Virginia. It barely survived, making it evident that the colonizing of American lands was not necessarily conducive to quick profits. But the desire to practice one's own religion, combined with economic interests, could lead to successful colonization, as the Massachusetts Bay Company demonstrated. The Massachusetts colony had 4,000 settlers in its early years but by 1660 had swelled to 40,000. By the end of the seventeenth century, the English had established control over most of the eastern seaboard of the present United States.

British North America came to consist of thirteen colonies. They were thickly populated, containing about 1.5 million people by 1750, and were also prosperous. Supposedly run by the British Board of Trade, the Royal Council, and Parliament, these thirteen colonies had legislatures that tended to act independently. Merchants in such port cities as Boston, Philadelphia, New York, and Charleston resented and resisted regulation by the British government.

FRENCH NORTH AMERICA The French also established a colonial empire in North America. In 1663, Canada was made the property of the French crown and administered by a French governor like a French province.

CHRONOLOGY New Rivals on the World Stage	
Portuguese traders land in Japan	1543
British East India Company formed	1600
Dutch East India Company formed	1602
English settlement at Jamestown	1607
Dutch fort established at Batavia	1619
Dutch seize Malacca from the Portuguese	1641
English seize New Netherland	1664
English establish trading post at Canton	1699
Battle of Plassey	1757
British mission to China	1793

French North America was run autocratically as a vast trading area, where valuable furs, leather, fish, and timber were acquired. The French government was unable to get people to emigrate to its Canadian possessions, however, so they remained thinly populated. By the mid-eighteenth century, there were only about fifteen thousand French Canadians, most of whom were hunters, trappers, missionaries, and explorers. The French failed to provide adequate men or money, allowing their European wars to take precedence over the conquest of the North American continent.

The Impact of European Expansion

Q FOCUS QUESTION: How did European expansion affect both the conquered and the conquerors?

Between 1500 and 1800, the Atlantic nations of Europe moved into all parts of the world. The first had been Spain and Portugal, the two great colonial powers of the sixteenth century, followed by the Dutch, who built their colonial empire in the seventeenth century as Portugal and Spain declined. The Dutch were soon challenged by the British and French, who outstripped the others in the eighteenth century while becoming involved in a bitter rivalry. By the end of the eighteenth century, it appeared that Britain would become the great European imperial power. European expansion made a great impact on both the conquered and the conquerors.

The Conquered

Different regions experienced different effects from the European expansion. The native American civilizations, which had their own unique qualities and a degree of sophistication not much appreciated by the Europeans, were virtually destroyed. In addition to devastating losses of population from European diseases, ancient social and political structures were ripped up and replaced by European institutions, religion, language, and culture. In Africa, the real demographic impact of the slave trade is uncertain due to a lack of records; however, estimates of the population in West Africa suggest that the slave trade negated any population growth, rather than causing a decline. Politically and socially, the slave trade encouraged the growth of territories in West Africa, such as Dahomey and Benin, where the leaders waged internal wars to secure more slaves to trade for guns and gunpowder. Without the slave trade in the nineteenth century, these territories became susceptible to European control. In Asia, the Portuguese trading posts had little impact on native Asian civilizations, although Dutch control of the Indonesian archipelago was more intrusive. China and Japan were still little affected by Westerners, although India was subject to ever-growing British encroachment.

In Central and South America, a new civilization arose that we have come to call Latin America. It was a multiracial society. Spanish and Portuguese settlers who arrived in the Western Hemisphere were few in number relative to the native Indians; many of the newcomers were males who not only used local females for their sexual pleasure but married them as well. Already by 1501, Spanish rulers had authorized intermarriage between Europeans and native American Indians, whose offspring became known as mestizos (mess-TEE-zohs). Another group of people brought to Latin America were the Africans. Over a period of three centuries, possibly as many as 8 million slaves were brought to Spanish and Portuguese America to work the plantations. Africans also contributed to Latin America's multiracial character. Mulattoes (muh-LAH-tohs)—the offspring of Africans and whites—joined mestizos and descendants of whites, Africans, and native Indians to produce a unique society in Latin America. Unlike both Europe and British North America, which remained a largely white offshoot of Europe, Latin America developed a multiracial society with less rigid attitudes about race.

The ecology of the conquered areas was also affected by the European presence. Europeans brought horses and cattle to the Americas, which revolutionized the life of the Indians. Cattle farming supplanted the Indian agricultural practice of growing maize (Indian corn), eventually leading to the development of large estates for raising cattle. South America would later become a great exporter of beef. Europeans also brought new crops, such as wheat and cane sugar, to be cultivated on large plantations by native or imported slave labor. In their trips to other parts of the world, Europeans also carried New World plants with them. Thus, Europeans introduced sweet potatoes and maize to Africa in the sixteenth century.

CATHOLIC MISSIONARIES Although there were some Protestant missionaries in the world outside Europe, Catholic missionaries were far more active in spreading Christianity. From the beginning of their conquest of the New World, Spanish and Portuguese rulers were determined to Christianize the native peoples. This policy gave the Catholic Church an important role to play in the New World, one that added considerably to church power. Catholic missionaries—especially the Dominicans, Franciscans, and Jesuits—fanned out to different parts of the Spanish Empire.

To facilitate their efforts, missionaries brought Indians together into villages, where they could be converted, taught trades, and encouraged to grow crops. These missions enabled the missionaries to control the lives of the Indians and helped ensure that they would remain docile members of the empire (see the box on p. 349 and the Film & History feature on p. 350). Basically, the missions benefited the missionaries more than the Indians. In frontier districts such as California and Texas, missions also served as military barriers to foreign encroachment.

The Catholic Church constructed hospitals, orphanages, and schools. Monastic schools instructed Indian students in the rudiments of reading, writing, and arithmetic. The church also provided outlets for women other than marriage. Nunneries were places of prayer and quiet contemplation, but women in religious orders, many of them of aristocratic background, often lived well and worked outside their establishments by running schools and hospitals. Indeed, one of these nuns, Sor Juana Inés de la Cruz (SAWR HWAH-nuh ee-NAYSS day lah KROOZ) (1651–1695), was one of seventeenth-century Latin America's best-known literary figures. She wrote poetry and prose and urged that women be educated.

Christian missionaries also made the long voyage to China on European merchant ships. The Jesuits were among the most active and the most effective. Many of the early Jesuit missionaries to China were highly educated men who were familiar with European philosophical and scientific developments. They brought along clocks and various other instruments that impressed Chinese officials and made them more open to Western ideas.

The Jesuits used this openness to promote Christianity. To make it easier for the Chinese to accept Christianity, the Jesuits pointed to similarities between Christian morality and Confucian ethics. The efforts of the Christian missionaries reached their height in the early eighteenth century. Several hundred Chinese officials became Catholics, as did an estimated 300,000 ordinary Chinese. But ultimately squabbling among the religious orders themselves undermined the Christian effort. To make it easier for the Chinese to convert, the Jesuits had allowed the new Catholics to continue the

The Mission

In 1609, two Jesuit priests embarked on a missionary calling with the Guaraní Indians in eastern Paraguay. Eventually, the Jesuits established more than thirty missions in the region. This description of a Jesuit mission in Paraguay was written by Felix de Azara, a Spanish soldier and scientist.

Felix de Azara, *Description and History of Paraguay and Rio de la Plata*

Having spoken of the towns founded by the Jesuit fathers, and of the manner in which they were founded, I shall discuss the government which they established in them.... In each town resided two priests, a curate and a subcurate, who had certain assigned functions. The subcurate was charged with all the spiritual tasks, and the curate with every kind of temporal responsibility....

The curate allowed no one to work for personal gain; he compelled everyone, without distinction of age or sex, to work for the community, and he himself saw to it that all were equally fed and dressed. For this purpose the curates placed in storehouses all the fruits of agriculture and the products of industry, selling in the Spanish towns their surplus of cotton, cloth, tobacco, vegetables, skins, and wood, transporting them in their own boats down the nearest rivers, and returning with implements and whatever else was required.

From the foregoing one may infer that the curate disposed of the surplus funds of the Indian towns, and that no Indian could aspire to own private property. This deprived them of any incentive to use reason or talent, since the most industrious, able, and worthy person had the same food, clothing, and pleasures as the most wicked, dull, and indolent. It also follows that although this form of government was well designed to enrich the communities it also caused the Indian to work at a languid pace, since the wealth of his community was of no concern to him.

It must be said that although the Jesuit fathers were supreme in all respects, they employed their authority with a mildness and a restraint that command admiration. They supplied everyone with abundant food and clothing. They compelled the men to work only half a day, and did not drive them to produce more. Even their labor was given a festive air, for they went in procession to the fields, to the sound of music ... and the music did not cease until they had returned in the same way they had set out. They gave them many holidays, dances, and tournaments, dressing the actors and the members of the municipal councils in gold or silver tissue and the most costly European garments, but they permitted the women to act only as spectators.

They likewise forbade the women to sew; this occupation was restricted to the musicians, sacristans, and acolytes. But they made them spin cotton; and the cloth that the Indians wove, after satisfying their own needs, they sold together with the surplus cotton in the Spanish towns.... The curate and his companion, or subcurate, had their own plain dwellings, and they never left them except to take the air in the great enclosed yard of their college. They never walked through the streets of the town or entered the house of any Indian or let themselves be seen by any woman—or indeed, by any man, except for those indispensable few through whom they issued their orders.

Q How were the missions organized to enable missionaries to control many aspects of the Indians' lives? Why was this deemed necessary?

Source: Excerpt from *Latin American Civilization* by Benjamin Keen, ed. (Boston: Houghton Mifflin, 1974), Vol. I, pp. 223–224. Reprinted by permission of the estate of Benjamin Keen.

practice of ancestor worship. Jealous Dominicans and Franciscans complained to the pope, who condemned the practice. Soon Chinese authorities began to suppress Christian activities throughout China.

The Jesuits also had some success in Japan, where they converted a number of local nobles. By the end of the sixteenth century, thousands of Japanese on the southernmost islands of Kyushu and Shikoku had become Christians. But the Jesuit practice of destroying local idols and shrines and turning some temples into Christian schools or churches caused a severe reaction. When a new group of Spanish Franciscans

FILM & HISTORY

The Mission (1986)

DIRECTED BY ROLAND JOFFÉ, *The Mission* examines religion, politics, and colonialism in Europe and South America in the mid-eighteenth century. The movie begins with a flashback as Cardinal Altamirano (Ray McAnally) is dictating a letter to the pope to discuss the fate of the Jesuit missions in Paraguay. He begins by describing the establishment of a new Jesuit mission (San Carlos) in Spanish territory in the borderlands of Paraguay and Brazil. Father Gabriel (Jeremy Irons) has been able to win over the Guaraní Indians and create a community based on communal livelihood and property (private property has been abolished). The mission includes dwellings for the Guaraní and a church where they can practice their new faith by learning the Gospel and singing hymns. This small band of Jesuits is joined by Rodrigo Mendozo (Robert De Niro), who has been a slave trader dealing in Indians and now seeks to atone for killing his brother in a fit of jealous rage by joining the community at San Carlos. Won over to Father Gabriel's perspective, he also becomes a member of the Jesuit order.

The Jesuit missionary Father Gabriel (Jeremy Irons) with the Guaraní Indians of Paraguay before their slaughter by Portuguese troops.

© Warner Brothers/Courtesy The Everett Collection, Inc.

Cardinal Altamirano now travels to the New World, sent by a pope anxious to appease the Portuguese monarch over the activities of the Jesuits. Portuguese settlers in Brazil are eager to use the native people as slaves and to confiscate their communal lands and property. In 1750, when Spain agrees to turn over the Guaraní territory in Paraguay to Portugal, they seize their opportunity. Although the cardinal visits a number of missions, including that of San Carlos, and obviously approves of their accomplishments, his hands are tied by the Portuguese king, who is threatening to disband the Jesuit order if the missions are not closed. The cardinal acquiesces, and Portuguese troops are sent to take over the missions. Although Rodrigo and the other Jesuits join the natives in fighting the Portuguese while Father Gabriel refuses to fight, all are massacred. The cardinal returns to Europe, dismayed by the murderous

activities of the Portuguese but hopeful that the Jesuit order will be spared. All is in vain, however, as the Catholic monarchs of Europe expel the Jesuits from their countries and pressure Pope Clement XIV into disbanding the Jesuit order in 1733.

In its approach to the destruction of the Jesuit missions, *The Mission* clearly exalts the dedication of the Jesuit order and praises the missionaries' devotion to the welfare of the Indians. The movie ends with a small group of Guaraní children, now all orphans, picking up a few remnants of debris left in their destroyed mission and moving off down the river back into the wilderness to escape enslavement. The final words on the screen illuminate the movie's message about the activities of the Europeans who destroyed the native civilizations in their conquest of the Americas: "The Indians of South America are still engaged in a struggle to defend their land and their culture. Many of the priests who, inspired by faith and love, continue to support the rights of the Indians, do so with their lives," a reference to the ongoing struggle in Latin America against the regimes that continue to oppress the landless masses.

continued the same policies, the government ordered the execution of nine missionaries and a number of their Japanese converts.

The Conquerors

For some Europeans, expansion abroad brought the possibility of obtaining land, riches, and social advancement. One Spaniard commented in 1572 that many "poor young men" had left Spain for Mexico, where they hoped to acquire landed estates and call themselves "gentlemen." Although some wives accompanied their husbands abroad, many ordinary European women found new opportunities for marriage in the New World because of the lack of white women. Indeed, as one commentator bluntly put it, even "a whore, if handsome, [can] make a wife for some rich planter."[6] In the violence-prone world of early Spanish America, a number of women also found themselves rich after their husbands were killed unexpectedly. In one area of Central America, women owned about 25 percent of the landed estates by 1700.

European expansion also had other economic effects on the conquerors. Wherever they went in the New World, Europeans looked for sources of gold and silver. One Aztec commented that the Spanish conquerors "longed and lusted for gold. Their bodies swelled with greed, and their hunger was ravenous; they hungered like pigs for that gold."[7] Rich silver deposits were found and exploited in Mexico and southern Peru (modern Bolivia). When the mines at Potosí in Peru were opened in 1545, the value of precious metals imported into Europe quadrupled. Between 1503 and 1650, more than 35 million pounds of silver and 400,000 pounds of gold entered the port of Seville and set off a price revolution that affected the Spanish economy.

But gold and silver were only two of the products that became part of the exchange between the New World and the Old. Historians refer to the reciprocal importation and exportation of plants and animals between Europe and the Americas as the **Columbian Exchange**. While Europeans were bringing horses, cattle, and wheat to the New World, they were taking new agricultural products such as potatoes, chocolate, corn, tomatoes, and tobacco back to Europe. Potatoes became especially popular as a basic dietary staple in some areas of Europe. High in carbohydrates and rich in vitamins A and C, potatoes could be easily stored for winter use and soon enabled more people to survive on smaller plots of land. This improvement in nutrition was soon reflected in a rapid increase in population.

The European lifestyle was greatly affected by new products from abroad. In addition to new foods, new drinks also appeared in Europe. Chocolate, which had been brought to Spain from Aztec Mexico, became a common drink by 1700. The first coffee and tea houses opened in London in the 1650s and spread rapidly to other parts of Europe. In the eighteenth century, a craze for Chinese furniture and porcelain spread among the upper classes. Chinese ideas would also make an impact on intellectual attitudes (see Chapter 17).

European expansion, which was in part a product of European rivalries, also deepened that competition and increased the tensions among European states. Bitter conflicts arose over the cargoes coming from the New World and Asia. The Anglo-Dutch trade wars and the British-French rivalry over India and North America became part of a new pattern of worldwide warfare in the eighteenth century (see Chapter 18). Bitter rivalries also led to state-sponsored piracy in which governments authorized private captains to attack enemy shipping and keep part of the proceeds for themselves.

In the course of their expansion, Europeans also came to have a new view of the world. When the travels began in the fifteenth century, Europeans were dependent on maps that were often fanciful and inaccurate. Their explorations helped them create new maps that gave a more realistic portrayal of the world, as well as new techniques called map projections that allowed them to represent the round surface of a sphere on a flat piece of paper. The most famous of these is the Mercator projection, the work of a Flemish cartographer, Gerardus Mercator (juh-RAHR-dus mur-KAY-tur) (1512–1594). A Mercator projection is what mapmakers call a conformal projection. It tries to show the true shape of landmasses, but only in a limited area. On the Mercator projection, the shapes of lands near the equator are quite accurate, but the farther away from the equator they lie, the more exaggerated their size becomes. Nevertheless, the Mercator projection was valuable to ship captains. Every straight line on a Mercator projection is a line of true direction, whether north, south, east, or west. For four centuries, ship captains were very grateful to Mercator.

The psychological impact of colonization on the colonizers is awkward to evaluate but hard to deny. Europeans were initially startled by the discovery of new peoples in the Americas. Some deemed them inhuman and thus fit to be exploited for labor. Others, however, found them to be refreshingly

A Seventeenth-Century World Map. This beautiful map was prepared in 1630 by Henricus Hondius. The portraits in the corners are of Caesar, the Roman statesman; Ptolemy, the second-century astronomer; Mercator, the Flemish cartographer whose map projection Hondius followed; and Hondius himself. By comparing this map with the map created by Ptolemy on p. 330, one can see how much Europeans had learned about the shape of the world by the seventeenth century.

natural and as yet untouched by European corruption. But even the latter group still believed that the Indians should be converted—if not forcefully, at least peacefully—to Christianity. Overall, Europeans' relatively easy success in dominating native peoples (whether Africans or Indians) reinforced Christian Europe's belief in the inherent superiority of European civilization and religion. The Scientific Revolution of the seventeenth century (see Chapter 16), the Enlightenment of the eighteenth (see Chapter 17), and the imperialism of the nineteenth (see Chapter 24) would all bolster this Eurocentric perspective, which has pervaded Western civilization's relations with the rest of the world.

Toward a World Economy

Q Focus Question: What was mercantilism, and what was its relationship to colonial empires?

During the High Middle Ages, Europeans had experienced a commercial revolution that created new opportunities for townspeople in a basically agrarian economy. Although this commercial growth was slowed by the crises of the fourteenth century, Europe's discovery of the world outside in the fifteenth century led to an even greater burst of commercial activity and the inception of a world market.

Economic Conditions in the Sixteenth Century

Inflation was a major economic problem in the sixteenth and early seventeenth centuries. This so-called **price revolution** was a Europe-wide phenomenon, although different areas were affected at different times. Foodstuffs were most subject to price increases. But wages failed to keep up with the rising prices. Wage earners, especially agricultural laborers and salaried workers in urban areas, saw their standard of living drop. At the same time, landed aristocrats, who could raise rents, managed to prosper. Commercial and industrial entrepreneurs also benefited from the price revolution because of rising prices, expanding markets, and relatively cheaper labor costs. Some historians regard this profit inflation as a valuable stimulus to investment and the growth of capitalism, helping to explain the economic expansion and prosperity of the sixteenth century. Governments were likewise affected by inflation. They borrowed heavily from bankers and imposed new tax burdens on their subjects, often arousing additional discontent.

The Growth of Commercial Capitalism

The flourishing European trade of the sixteenth century revolved around three major areas: the Mediterranean in the south, the Low Countries and the Baltic region in the north, and central Europe, whose inland trade depended on the Rhine and Danube Rivers. As overseas trade expanded, however, the Atlantic seaboard began to play a more important role, linking the Mediterranean, Baltic, and central European trading areas together and making the whole of Europe into a more integrated market that was all the more vulnerable to price shifts.

The commercial expansion of the sixteenth and seventeenth centuries was made easier by new forms of commercial organization, especially the **joint stock company**. Individuals bought shares in a company and received dividends on their investment while a board of directors ran the company and made the important business decisions. The return on investments could be spectacular. During its first ten years, investors received 30 percent on their money from the Dutch East India Company, which opened the Spice Islands and Southeast Asia to Dutch activity. The joint stock company made it easier to raise large amounts of capital for world trading ventures.

By the seventeenth century, the traditional family banking firms were no longer able to supply the numerous services needed for the expanding commercial capitalism. New institutions arose to take their place. The city of Amsterdam created the Bank of Amsterdam in 1609 as both a deposit and a transfer institution and the Amsterdam Bourse, or Exchange, where the trading of stocks replaced the exchange of goods. In the first half of the seventeenth century, the Amsterdam Exchange became the hub of the European business world, just as Amsterdam itself had replaced Antwerp as the greatest commercial and banking center of Europe.

Despite the growth of commercial capitalism, most of the European economy still depended on an agricultural system that had experienced few changes since the thirteenth century. At least 80 percent of Europeans still worked the land. Almost all of the peasants of western Europe were free of serfdom, although many still owed a variety of feudal dues to the nobility. Despite the expanding markets and rising prices, European peasants saw little or no improvement in their lot as they faced increased rents and fees and higher taxes imposed by the state.

Mercantilism

Mercantilism is the name historians use to identify a set of economic tendencies that came to dominate economic practices in the seventeenth century. Fundamental to mercantilism was the belief that the total volume of trade was unchangeable. Therefore, states protected their economies by following certain principles: hoarding precious metals, implementing protectionist trade policies, promoting colonial development, increasing shipbuilding, supporting trading companies, and encouraging the manufacturing of products to be used in trade.

According to the mercantilists, a nation's prosperity depended on a plentiful supply of bullion (gold and silver). For this reason, it was desirable to achieve a favorable balance of trade in which goods exported were of greater value than those imported, promoting an influx of gold and silver payments that would increase the quantity of bullion. Furthermore, to encourage exports, governments should stimulate and protect export industries and trade by granting trade monopolies, encouraging investment in new industries through subsidies, importing foreign artisans, and improving transportation systems by building roads, bridges, and canals. By imposing high tariffs on foreign goods, governments could keep them out of the country and prevent them from competing with domestic products. Colonies were also deemed valuable as sources of raw materials and markets for finished goods.

The mercantilists also focused on the role of the state, believing that state intervention in some aspects of the economy was desirable for the sake of the national good. Government regulations to ensure the superiority of export goods, the construction of roads and canals, and the granting of subsidies to create trade companies were all predicated on government involvement in economic affairs.

Overseas Trade and Colonies: Movement Toward Globalization

Mercantilist theory on the role of colonies was matched in practice by Europe's overseas expansion. With the development of colonies and trading posts in the Americas and the East, Europeans embarked on an adventure in international commerce in the seventeenth century. Although some historians speak of a nascent world economy, we should remember that local, regional, and intra-European trade still predominated. About one-tenth of English and Dutch exports were shipped across the Atlantic; slightly more went to the East. What made the transoceanic trade rewarding, however, was not the volume but the value of its goods. Dutch, English, and French merchants were bringing back products that were still consumed largely by the wealthy but were beginning to make their way into the lives of artisans and merchants. Pepper and spices from the Indies, West Indian and Brazilian sugar, and Asian coffee and tea were becoming more readily available to European consumers.

Trade within Europe remained strong throughout the eighteenth century, although this trade increased only slightly while overseas trade boomed. From 1716 to 1789, total French exports quadrupled; intra-European trade, which constituted 75 percent of these exports in 1716, accounted for only 50 percent of the total in 1789. This increase in overseas trade has led some historians to proclaim the emergence of a truly global economy in the eighteenth century. Trade patterns now interlocked Europe, Africa, the East, and the Americas.

Chapter Summary

At the end of the fifteenth century, Europeans sailed out into the world in all directions. Beginning in the mid-fifteenth century with the handful of Portuguese ships that ventured southward along the West African coast, bringing back slaves and gold, the process of European expansion accelerated with the epochal voyages of Christopher Columbus to the Americas and Vasco da Gama to the Indian Ocean in the 1490s. The Portuguese Empire was based on trade; Portugal's population was too small for it to establish large colonies. But Spain had greater resources. Spanish conquistadors overthrew both the Aztec and Inca Empires, and Spain created two major administrative units in New Spain and Peru that subjected the native population to Spanish control. Catholic missionaries, under the control of the Spanish crown, brought Christianity, including cathedrals and schools.

Soon a number of other European peoples, including the Dutch, British, and French, had joined in the process of expansion, and by the end of the eighteenth century, they had created a global trade network dominated by Western ships and Western power. Although originally less prized than gold and spices, slaves became a major object of trade, and by the nineteenth century 10 million African slaves had been shipped to the Americas. Slavery was common in Africa, and the African terminus of the trade was in the hands of the Africans, but the insatiable demand for slaves led to increased warfare on that unfortunate continent.

It was not until the late 1700s that slavery came under harsh criticism in Europe.

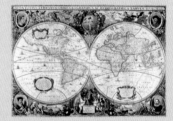

In less than three hundred years, the European age of exploration had changed the shape of the world. In some areas, such as the Americas and the Spice Islands in Asia, it led to the destruction of indigenous civilizations and the establishment of European colonies. In others, such as Africa, India, and mainland Southeast Asia, it left native regimes intact but had a strong impact on local societies and regional trade patterns. Japan and China were least affected.

At the time, many European observers viewed the process in a favorable light. They believed that it not only expanded wealth through world trade and the exchange of crops and discoveries between the Old World and the New, but also introduced "heathen peoples" to the message of Jesus. No doubt, the conquest of the Americas and expansion into the rest of the world brought out the worst and some of the best of European civilization. The greedy plundering of resources and the brutal repression and enslavement were hardly balanced by attempts to create new institutions, convert the natives to Christianity, and foster the rights of the indigenous peoples. In any event, Europeans had begun to change the face of the world and increasingly saw their culture, with its religion, languages, and technology, as a coherent force to be exported to all corners of the world.

CHAPTER TIMELINE

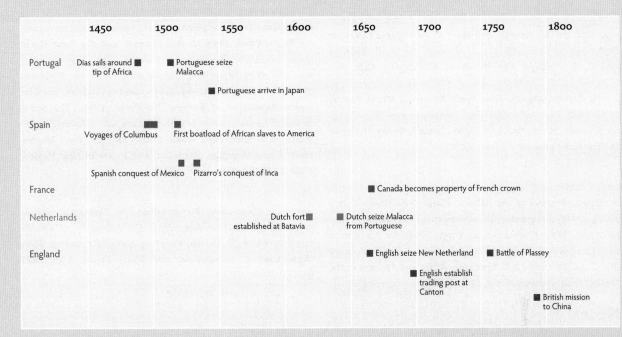

| | 1450 | 1500 | 1550 | 1600 | 1650 | 1700 | 1750 | 1800 |

Portugal — Dias sails around tip of Africa ■ — Portuguese seize Malacca ■ — Portuguese arrive in Japan ■

Spain — Voyages of Columbus ■■ — First boatload of African slaves to America ■ — Spanish conquest of Mexico ■ — Pizarro's conquest of Inca ■

France — Canada becomes property of French crown ■

Netherlands — Dutch fort ■ established at Batavia — Dutch seize Malacca from Portuguese ■

England — English seize New Netherland ■ — English establish trading post at Canton ■ — Battle of Plassey ■ — British mission to China ■

CHAPTER REVIEW

Upon Reflection

Q How did the experiences of the Spanish and Portuguese during the age of exploration differ from those of their French, Dutch, and English counterparts?

Q What role did religion play as a motivation in the age of exploration? Was it as important as the economic motive? Why or why not?

Q Why and how did Japan succeed in keeping Europeans largely away from its territory in the seventeenth century?

Key Terms

conquistadors (p. 334)
encomienda (p. 336)
viceroy (p. 337)
triangular trade (p. 338)
Middle Passage (p. 338)

Columbian Exchange (p. 339)
price revolution (p. 351)
joint stock company (p. 352)
mercantilism (p. 353)

Suggestions for Further Reading

GENERAL WORKS For general accounts of European discovery and expansion, see **G. V. Scammell, *The First Imperial*** *Age: European Overseas Expansion, c. 1400–1715* (London, 1989); **D. Arnold, *Age of Discovery,*** 2d ed. (London, 2002);

and **G. J. Ames, *The Globe Encompassed: The Age of European Discovery, 1500–1700*** (Upper Saddle River, N.J., 2007).

PORTUGUESE AND SPANISH EXPANSION On Portuguese expansion, see **M. Newitt, *A History of Portuguese Overseas Expansion*** (London, 2004). On Columbus, see **W. D. Phillips and C. R. Phillips, *The Worlds of Christopher Columbus*** (Cambridge, 1992). On the Spanish Empire in the New World, see **H. Kamen, *Empire: How Spain Became a World Power, 1492–1763*** (New York, 2003). For a revisionist view of the Spanish conquest of the Americas, see **M. Restall, *Seven Myths of the Spanish Conquest*** (Oxford, 2003).

MERCANTILE EMPIRES AND WORLDWIDE TRADE The subject of mercantile empires and worldwide trade is covered in **J. H. Elliott, *Empires of the Atlantic World*** (New Haven, Conn., 2006), and **M. J. Seymour, *Transformation of the North Atlantic World, 1492–1763*** (Westport, Conn., 2004). On the African slave trade, see **M. Rediker, *The Slave Ship: A Human History*** (New York, 2007), and **J. K. Thornton, *Africa and Africans in the Making of the Atlantic World, 1400–1800*** (Cambridge, 1998).

IMPACT OF EXPANSION The impact of expansion on European consciousness is explored in **A. Pagden, *European Encounters with the New World: From Renaissance to Romanticism*** (New Haven, Conn., 1993). On the impact of disease, see **N. D. Cook, *Born to Die: Disease and the New World*** (New York, 1998). The human and ecological effects of the interaction of New World and Old World cultures are examined thoughtfully in **A. W. Crosby, *Ecological Imperialism: The Biological Expansion of Europe*** (New York, 1986). The native American female experience with the European encounter is presented in **R. Gutierrez, *When Jesus Came the Corn Mother Went Away: Marriage, Sexuality, and Power in New Mexico, 1500–1846*** (Stanford, Calif., 1991).

ECONOMIC DIMENSIONS OF EXPANSION On mercantilism, see **L. Magnusson, *Mercantilism: The Shaping of an Economic Language*** (New York, 1994). On the concept of a world economy, see **A. K. Smith, *Creating a World Economy: Merchant Capital, Colonialism, and World Trade, 1400–1825*** (Boulder, Colo., 1991).

Notes

1. Quoted in J. R. Hale, *Renaissance Exploration* (New York, 1968), p. 32.
2. Quoted in J. H. Parry, *The Age of Reconnaissance: Discovery, Exploration, and Settlement, 1450 to 1640* (New York, 1963), p. 33.
3. Quoted in R. B. Reed, "The Expansion of Europe," in *The Meaning of the Renaissance and Reformation*, ed. R. De Molen (Boston, 1974), p. 308.
4. Quoted in B. Davidson, *Africa in History: Themes and Outlines*, rev. ed. (New York, 1991), p. 213.
5. Quoted in ibid., p. 198.
6. Quoted in G. V. Scammell, *The First Imperial Age: European Overseas Expansion, c. 1400–1715* (London, 1989), p. 62.
7. M. Leon-Portilla, ed., *The Broken Spears: The Aztec Account of the Conquest of Mexico* (Boston, 1969), p. 51.

MindTap **MindTap** is a fully online, highly personalized learning experience built upon Cengage Learning content. MindTap combines student learning tools—readings, multimedia, activities, and assessments—into a singular Learning Path that guides students through the course.

CHAPTER

15

State Building and the Search for Order in the Seventeenth Century

Nicolas-René Joallain the Elder's portrait of Louis XIV captures the king's sense of royal grandeur.

Chateaux de Versailles et de Trianon (Gérard Blot), Versailles//©RMN-Grand Palais/ Art Resource, NY

CRITICAL THINKING

Q What theories of government were proposed by Thomas Hobbes and John Locke, and how did their respective theories reflect concerns and problems of the seventeenth century?

CONNECTIONS TO TODAY

Q How does the exercise of state power in the seventeenth century compare with the exercise of state power in the twenty-first century? What, if anything, has changed?

BY THE END of the sixteenth century, Europe was beginning to experience a decline in religious passions and a growing secularization that affected both the political and intellectual worlds (for the intellectual effect, see Chapter 16). Some historians like to speak of the seventeenth century as a turning point in the evolution of the modern state system in Europe. The ideal of a united Christian Europe gave way to the practical realities of a system of secular entities in which matters of state took precedence over the salvation of subjects' souls. By the seventeenth century, the credibility of Christianity had been so weakened through religious wars that more and more Europeans came to think of politics in secular terms.

One of the responses to the religious wars and other crises of the time was a yearning for order. As the internal social and political rebellions and revolts died down, it became apparent that the privileged classes of society—the aristocrats—remained in control, although the various states exhibited important differences in political forms. The most general trend saw an extension of monarchical power as a stabilizing force. This development, which historians have called absolute monarchy or absolutism, was most evident in France during the flamboyant reign of Louis XIV, regarded by some as the perfect embodiment of an absolute monarch. In his memoirs, the duc de Saint-Simon, who had firsthand experience of French court life, said that Louis was "the very figure of a hero, so imbued with a natural but most imposing majesty that it appeared even in his most insignificant gestures and movements." The king's natural grace gave him a special charm as well: "He was as dignified and majestic in his dressing gown as when dressed in robes of state, or on horseback at the head of his troops." His life was orderly: "Nothing could be regulated with greater exactitude than were his days and hours." His self-control was impeccable: "He did not lose control of himself ten times in his whole life, and then only with inferior persons." But even absolute monarchs had imperfections, and Saint-Simon had the courage to point them out: "Louis XIV's vanity was without limit or restraint," which led to his "distaste for all merit, intelligence, education, and, most of all, for all independence of character and sentiment in others," as well as to "mistakes of judgment in matters of importance."

But absolutism was not the only response to the search for order in the seventeenth century. Other states, such as England, reacted differently to domestic crisis, and another very different system emerged in which monarchs were limited by the power of their representative assemblies. Absolute and limited monarchy were the two poles of seventeenth-century state building.

Social Crises, War, and Rebellions

Q **FOCUS QUESTION:** What economic, social, and political crises did Europe experience in the first half of the seventeenth century?

The inflation-fueled prosperity of the sixteenth century showed signs of slackening by the beginning of the seventeenth. Economic contraction was evident in some parts of Europe by the 1620s. In the 1630s and 1640s, as imports of silver from the Americas declined, economic recession intensified, especially in the Mediterranean area. Once the industrial and financial center of Europe in the Renaissance, Italy was now becoming an economic backwater. Spain's economy was also seriously failing by the 1640s.

Population trends of the sixteenth and seventeenth centuries also reveal Europe's worsening conditions. The sixteenth century was a period of expanding population, possibly related to a warmer climate and increased food supplies. It has been estimated that the population of Europe increased from 60 million in 1500 to 85 million by 1600, the first major recovery of European population since the devastation of the Black Death in the mid-fourteenth century. Records also indicate a leveling off of the population by 1620, however, and even a decline by 1650, especially in central and southern Europe.

Only the Dutch, English, and French grew in number in the first half of the seventeenth century. Europe's long-time adversaries—war, famine, and plague—continued to affect population levels, and another "little ice age," when average temperatures fell, affected harvests and gave rise to famines. These problems created social tensions that came to a boil in the witchcraft craze.

The Witchcraft Craze

Hysteria over witchcraft affected the lives of many Europeans in the sixteenth and seventeenth centuries. Witchcraft trials were held in England, Scotland, Switzerland, Germany, some parts of France and the Low Countries, and even New England in America.

Witchcraft was not a new phenomenon. Its practice had been part of traditional village culture for centuries, but it came to be viewed as both sinister and dangerous when the medieval church began to connect witches to the activities of the Devil, thereby transforming witchcraft into a heresy that had to be wiped out. After the establishment of the Inquisition in the thirteenth century, some people were accused of a variety of witchcraft practices and, following the biblical injunction "Thou shalt not suffer a witch to live," were turned over to secular authorities for burning at the stake or, in England, hanging.

THE SPREAD OF WITCHCRAFT What distinguished witchcraft in the sixteenth and seventeenth centuries from these previous developments was the increased number of trials and executions of presumed witches. Perhaps more than 100,000 people were prosecuted throughout Europe on charges of witchcraft. Although larger cities were affected first, the trials spread to smaller towns and rural areas as the hysteria persisted well into the seventeenth century (see the box on p. 360).

The accused witches usually confessed to a number of practices, most often after intense torture. Many said that they had sworn allegiance to the Devil and attended sabbats or nocturnal gatherings where they feasted, danced, and even copulated with the devil in sexual orgies. More common, however, were admissions of using evil incantations and special ointments and powders to wreak havoc on neighbors by killing their livestock, injuring their children, or raising storms to destroy their crops.

A number of contributing factors have been suggested to explain why the witchcraft frenzy became so widespread in the sixteenth and seventeenth centuries. Religious uncertainties clearly played some part. Many witchcraft trials occurred in areas where Protestantism had been recently victorious or in regions, such as southwestern Germany, where Protestant-Catholic controversies still raged. As religious passions became inflamed, accusations of being in league with the Devil became common on both sides.

Recently, however, historians have emphasized the importance of social conditions, especially the problems of a society in turmoil, in explaining the witchcraft hysteria. At a time when the old communal values that stressed working together for the good of the community were disintegrating before the onslaught of a new economic ethic that emphasized looking out for oneself, property owners became more fearful of the growing numbers of poor in their midst and transformed them psychologically into agents of the Devil. Old women were particularly susceptible to suspicion. When problems arose—and there were many in this crisis-laden period—these people were handy scapegoats.

That women should be the chief victims of witchcraft trials was hardly accidental. Nicholas Rémy, a witchcraft judge in France in the 1590s, found it "not unreasonable that this scum of humanity [witches] should be drawn chiefly from the feminine sex."[1] To another judge, it came as no surprise that witches would confess to sexual experiences with Satan: "The Devil uses them so, because he knows that women love carnal pleasures, and he means to bind them to his allegiance by such agreeable provocations."[2] Of course, witch hunters were not the only ones who held women in such low esteem. Most theologians, lawyers, and philosophers in early modern Europe believed in the natural inferiority of women and thus would have found it plausible that women would be more susceptible to witchcraft.

DECLINE By the mid-seventeenth century, the witchcraft hysteria began to subside. The destruction caused by the religious wars had forced people to accept at least a grudging toleration, tempering religious passions. Moreover, as governments began to stabilize after the period of crisis, fewer magistrates were willing to accept the unsettling and divisive conditions generated by the trials of witches. Finally, by the turn of the eighteenth century, more and more people were questioning traditional attitudes toward religion and finding it contrary to reason to believe in the old view of a world haunted by evil spirits.

The Thirty Years' War

Although many Europeans responded to the upheavals of the second half of the sixteenth century with a desire for peace and order, the first fifty years of the seventeenth century continued to be plagued by crises. A devastating war that affected much of Europe and rebellions seemingly everywhere protracted the atmosphere of disorder and violence.

Religion, especially the struggle between militant Catholicism and militant Calvinism, played an important role in the outbreak of the Thirty Years' War (1618–1648), often called the "last of the religious wars." As the war progressed, however, it became increasingly clear that secular, dynastic-nationalist considerations were far more important.

The Thirty Years' War began in the Germanic lands of the Holy Roman Empire as a struggle between Catholic forces, led by the Habsburg Holy Roman emperors, and Protestant—primarily Calvinist—nobles in Bohemia who rebelled against Habsburg authority. What began as a struggle over religious issues soon became a wider conflict determined by political motivations as

A Witchcraft Trial in France

Persecutions for witchcraft reached their high point in the sixteenth and seventeenth centuries when tens of thousands of people were brought to trial. In this excerpt from the minutes of a trial in France in 1652, we can see why the accused witch stood little chance of exonerating herself.

The Trial of Suzanne Gaudry

28 May, 1652.... Interrogation of Suzanne Gaudry,... During interrogations on May 28 and May 29, the prisoner confessed to a number of activities involving the devil.

Deliberation of the Court—June 3, 1652

The undersigned advocates of the Court ... say that the aforementioned Suzanne Gaudry confesses that she is a witch, that she had given herself to the devil, that she had renounced God, Lent, and baptism, that she has been marked on the shoulder, that she has cohabited with the devil and that she has been to the dances,...

Third Interrogation, June 27

This prisoner being led into the chamber, she was examined to know if things were not as she had said and confessed at the beginning of her imprisonment.

—Answers no, and that what she has said was done so by force....

She was placed in the hands of the officer in charge of torture, throwing herself on her knees, struggling to cry, uttering several exclamations, without being able, nevertheless, to shed a tear. Saying at every moment that she is not a witch.

The Torture

On this same day, being at the place of torture.

This prisoner, before being strapped down, was admonished to maintain herself in her first confessions....

—Says that she denies everything she has said,... Feeling herself being strapped down, says that she is not a witch, while struggling to cry ... and upon being asked why she confessed to being one, said that she was forced to say it.

Told that she was not forced, that on the contrary she declared herself to be a witch without any threat....

The mark having been probed by the officer, in the presence of Doctor Bouchain, it was adjudged by the aforesaid doctor and officer truly to be the mark of the devil.

Being more tightly stretched upon the torture rack, urged to maintain her confessions.

—Said that it was true that she is a witch and that she would maintain what she had said.

Asked how long she has been in subjugation to the devil.

—Answers that it was twenty years ago that the devil appeared to her, being in her lodgings in the form of a man dressed in a little cowhide and black breeches....

Third Verdict

July 9, 1652. In the light of the interrogations, answers, and investigations made into the charge against Suzanne Gaudry,... seeing by her own confessions that she is said to have made a pact with the devil, [and] received the mark from him,...

For expiation of which the advice of the undersigned is that the office of Rieux can legitimately condemn the aforesaid Suzanne Gaudry to death, tying her to a gallows, and strangling her to death, then burning her body and burying it here in the environs of the woods.

Q Why were women, particularly older women, especially vulnerable to accusations of witchcraft? What "proofs" are offered here that Suzanne Gaudry had consorted with the Devil? What does this account tell us about the spread of witchcraft persecutions in the seventeenth century?

Source: From *Witchcraft in Europe, 1100–1700: A Documentary History* edited by Alan C. Kors and Edward Peters. Copyright © 1972 University of Pennsylvania Press.

both minor and major European powers—Denmark, Sweden, France, and Spain—made the war a Europe-wide struggle (see Map 15.1). The struggle for European leadership between the Bourbon dynasty of France and the Habsburg dynasties of Spain and the Holy Roman Empire was an especially important factor. Nevertheless, most of the battles were fought on German soil, with devastating results for the German people.

The Peace of Westphalia, which officially ended the war in Germany in 1648, ensured that all German states, including the Calvinist ones, were free to determine their own religion. The major contenders gained new territories, and one of them, France, emerged as the dominant nation in Europe. The more than three hundred states that made up the Holy Roman Empire were recognized as virtually independent, each with the power to conduct its own foreign policy. The Habsburg emperor had been reduced to a figurehead. The Peace of Westphalia also made it clear that religion and politics were now separate in the

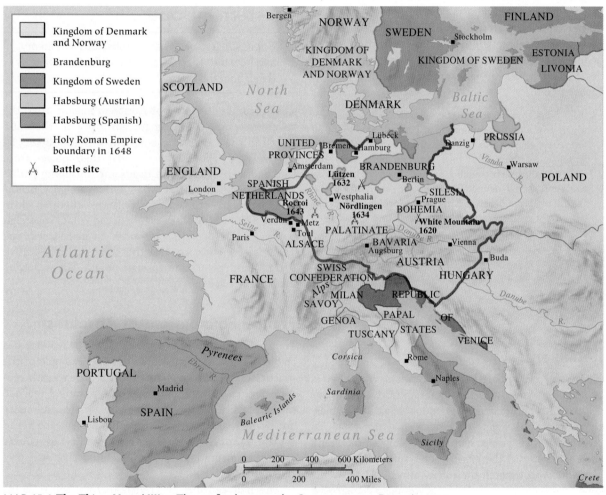

MAP 15.1 The Thirty Years' War. The conflict began in the German states as Europe's major powers backed either the northern Protestant Union or the southern Catholic League. As the war progressed, religion receded in importance, replaced by a dynastic struggle between the French Bourbons and the Spanish and Austrian Habsburgs.

Q Compare this map with Map 13.2. Which countries engaged in the war were predominantly Protestant, which were predominantly Catholic, and which were mixed?

Holy Roman Empire. Political motives became the guiding forces in public affairs as religion moved closer to becoming primarily a matter of personal conviction and individual choice. Some historians also argue that the Peace of Westphalia marks the beginning of a modern international order in which sovereign states began to operate as equals within a secular framework.

The economic and social effects of the Thirty Years' War on Germany are still debated. Some areas of Germany were completely devastated, but others remained relatively untouched. The most recent work pictures a damaged economy and a population decline of 15 to 20 percent in the Holy Roman Empire. Although historians may debate the degree of devastation, many people in Germany would have understood this description by a traveler journeying along the Main River in 1636:

> [We] came to a wretched little village called Neukirchen, which we found quite uninhabited yet with one house on fire. Here, since it was now late, we were obliged to stay all night, for the nearest town was four miles away; but we spent that night walking up and down with guns in our hands, and listening fearfully to the sound of shots in the woods around us.... Early next morning, His Excellency went to inspect the church and found it had been plundered and that the pictures and the altar had been desecrated. In the churchyard we saw a dead body, scraped out of the grave, while outside the churchyard we found another dead body.[3]

The Thirty Years' War was undoubtedly the most destructive conflict Europeans had yet experienced.

Rebellions

Before, during, and after the Thirty Years' War, a series of rebellions and civil wars stemming from the discontent of both nobles and commoners rocked the domestic stability of many European governments. To strengthen their power, monarchs attempted to extend their authority at the expense of traditional powerful elements who resisted the rulers' efforts. At the same time, to fight their battles, governments increased taxes and caused such hardships that common people also rose in opposition.

Between 1590 and 1640, peasant and lower-class revolts occurred in central and southern France, Austria, and Hungary. Portugal and Catalonia rebelled against the Spanish government in 1640. Russia, too, was rocked by urban uprisings in 1641, 1645, and

1648. Nobles rebelled in France from 1648 to 1652 to halt the growth of royal power. The northern states of Sweden, Denmark, and the United Provinces were also not immune from upheavals involving clergy, nobles, and mercantile groups. The most famous and widest-ranging struggle, however, was the civil war and rebellion in England, commonly known as the English Revolution (discussed later in this chapter).

The Practice of Absolutism: Western Europe

Q **Focus Question:** What was absolutism in theory, and how did its actual practice in France reflect or differ from the theory?

Absolute monarchy or **absolutism** meant that the sovereign power or ultimate authority in the state rested in the hands of a king who claimed to rule by divine right—that kings received their power from God and were responsible to no one (including parliaments) except God. But what did sovereignty mean? The late-sixteenth-century political theorist Jean Bodin (ZHAHN boh-DAN) believed that sovereign power consisted of the authority to make laws, tax, administer justice, control the state's administrative system, and determine foreign policy. These powers made a ruler sovereign.

France: Foundations of Absolutism

France during the reign of Louis XIV (1643–1715) has traditionally been regarded as the best example of the practice of absolute monarchy in the seventeenth century. French culture, language, and manners reached into all levels of European society. French diplomacy and wars shaped the political affairs of western and central Europe. Of course, the stability of Louis's reign was magnified by the instability that had preceded it.

The half century of French history before Louis XIV came to power was a time in which royal and ministerial governments struggled to avoid the breakdown of the state. The situation was complicated by the fact that both Louis XIII (1610–1643) and Louis XIV were only boys when they succeeded to the throne in 1610 and 1643, respectively, leaving the government dependent on royal ministers. Two especially competent ministers played crucial roles in maintaining monarchical authority.

Cardinal Richelieu (REESH-uh-lyoo), Louis XIII's chief minister from 1624 to 1642, initiated policies that eventually strengthened the power of the monarchy. By eliminating the political and military rights of the Huguenots while preserving their religious ones, Richelieu transformed the Huguenots into more reliable subjects. He acted more cautiously in "humbling the pride of the great men," the important French nobility, being well aware of their influential role in the French state. The dangerous ones were those who asserted their territorial independence when they were excluded from participating in the central government. Proceeding slowly but determinedly, Richelieu developed an efficient network of spies to uncover noble plots and then crushed the conspiracies and executed the conspirators, thereby eliminating a major threat to royal authority.

When Louis XIV succeeded to the throne in 1643 at the age of four, Cardinal Mazarin (maz-uh-RANH), the trained successor of Cardinal Richelieu, dominated the government. An Italian who had come to France as a papal legate and then became naturalized, Mazarin attempted to carry on Richelieu's policies. The most important event during Mazarin's rule was the Fronde (FROHND), a revolt led primarily by nobles who wished to curb the centralized administrative power being built up at the expense of the provincial nobility. The Fronde was crushed by 1652, and with its end, a vast number of French people concluded that the best hope for stability in France lay in the Crown. When Mazarin died in 1661, the greatest of the seventeenth-century monarchs, Louis XIV, took over supreme power.

The Reign of Louis XIV (1643–1715)

The day after Cardinal Mazarin's death, Louis XIV, age twenty-three, expressed his determination to be a real king and the sole ruler of France:

> Up to this moment I have been pleased to entrust the government of my affairs to the late Cardinal. It is now time that I govern them myself. You [secretaries and ministers of state] will assist me with your counsels when I ask for them. I request and order you to seal no orders except by my command. . . . I order you not to sign anything, not even a passport . . . without my command; to render account to me personally each day and to favor no one.[4]

His mother, who was well aware of Louis's proclivity for fun and games and getting into the beds of the maids in the royal palace, laughed aloud at these words. But Louis was quite serious.

Louis proved willing to pay the price of being a strong ruler. He established a conscientious routine from which he seldom deviated (see the box on p. 364). Eager for glory (in the French sense of achieving what was expected of one in an important position), Louis created a grand and majestic spectacle at the court of Versailles (vayr-SY). Consequently, Louis and his court came to set the standard for monarchies and aristocracies all over Europe.

Although Louis may have believed in the theory of absolute monarchy and consciously fostered the myth of himself as the Sun King, the source of light for all of his people, historians are quick to point out that the realities fell far short of the aspirations. Despite the centralizing efforts of Cardinals Richelieu and Mazarin, seventeenth-century France still possessed a bewildering system of overlapping authorities. Provinces had their own regional courts, their own local Estates (parliaments), and their own sets of laws. Members of the high nobility, with their huge estates and clients among the lesser nobility, still exercised much authority. Both towns and provinces possessed privileges and powers seemingly from time immemorial that they would not easily relinquish.

ADMINISTRATION OF THE GOVERNMENT One of the keys to Louis's power was that he was able to restructure the central policymaking machinery of government because it was part of his own court and household. The royal court located at Versailles was an elaborate structure that served different purposes: it was the personal household of the king, the location of central governmental machinery, and the place where powerful subjects came to find favors and offices for themselves and their clients as well as the main arena where rival aristocratic factions jostled for power. The greatest danger to Louis's personal rule came from the very high nobles and "princes of the blood" (the royal princes), who considered it their natural function to assert the policymaking role of royal ministers. Louis eliminated this threat by removing them from the royal council, the chief administrative body of the king and overseer of the central machinery of government, and enticing them to his court, where he could keep them preoccupied with court life and out of politics. Instead of the high nobility and royal princes, Louis relied for

The King's Day Begins

The duc de Saint-Simon (1675–1755) was one of many noble courtiers who lived at Versailles and had firsthand experience of court life there. In his *Memoirs*, he left a controversial and critical account of Louis XIV and his court. In this selection, Saint-Simon describes the scene that took place in Louis's bedroom at the beginning of each day.

——————

Duc de Saint-Simon, *Memoirs*

At eight o'clock the chief valet of the room on duty, who alone had slept in the royal chamber, and who had dressed himself, awoke the King. The chief physician, the chief surgeon, and the nurse (as long as she lived) entered at the same time. The latter kissed the King; the others rubbed and often changed his shirt, because he was in the habit of sweating a great deal. At the quarter, the grand chamberlain was called, and those who had, what was called the grandes entrées [grand entry]. The chamberlain (or chief gentleman) drew back the curtains which had been closed again, and presented the holy water from the vase, at the head of the bed. These gentlemen stayed but a moment, and that was the time to speak to the King, if any one had anything to ask of him; in which case the rest stood aside. When, contrary to custom, nobody had anything to say, they were there but for a few moments. He who had opened the curtains and presented the holy water, presented also a prayer-book. Then all passed into the

cabinet [a small room] of the council. A very short religious service being over, the King called, they reentered. The same officer gave him his dressing-gown; immediately after, other privileged courtiers entered, and then everybody, in time to find the King putting on his shoes and stockings, for he did almost everything himself and with address and grace. Every other day we saw him shave himself; and he had a little short wig in which he always appeared, even in bed, and on medicine days....

As soon as he was dressed, he prayed to God, at the side of his bed, where all the clergy present knelt, the cardinals without cushions, all the laity remaining standing; and the caption of the guards came to the balustrade during the prayer, after which the king passed into his cabinet.

He found there, or was followed by all who had the entrée, a very numerous company, for it included everybody in any office. He gave orders to each for the day; thus within a half a quarter of an hour it was known what he meant to do; and then all this crowd left directly.

——————

Q What were the message and purpose of the royal waking and dressing ceremony for both the nobles and the king? Do you think this account might be biased? Why?

——————

Source: From Bayle St. John, trans., *The Memoirs of the Duke of Saint-Simon on the Reign of Louis XIV and the Regency*, 8th ed. (London, George Allen, 1913), vol. 3, pp. 221–222.

his ministers on other nobles. His ministers were expected to be subservient; said Louis, "I had no intention of sharing my authority with them."

Louis's domination of his ministers and secretaries gave him control of the central policymaking machinery of government and thus authority over the traditional areas of monarchical power: the formulation of foreign policy, the making of war and peace, the assertion of the secular power of the Crown against any religious authority, and the ability to levy taxes to fulfill these functions. Louis had considerably less success with the internal administration of the kingdom, however. The traditional groups and institutions of French society—the nobles, officials, town councils, guilds, and

representative Estates in some provinces—were simply too powerful for the king to have direct control over the lives of his subjects. Consequently, control of the provinces and the people was achieved largely by bribing the individuals responsible for executing the king's policies.

RELIGIOUS POLICY The maintenance of religious harmony had long been considered an area of monarchical power. The desire to keep it led Louis to pursue an anti-Protestant policy, aimed at converting the Huguenots to Catholicism. In October 1685, Louis issued the Edict of Fontainebleau (fawnh-ten-BLOH). In addition to revoking the Edict of Nantes,

Interior of Versailles: The Hall of Mirrors. Pictured here is the exquisite Hall of Mirrors at Versailles. Located on the second floor, the hall overlooks the park below. Three hundred and fifty-seven mirrors were placed on the wall opposite the windows to create an illusion of even greater width. This photo shows the Hall of Mirrors after the restoration work that was completed in June 2007, a project that took three years, cost 12 million euros (more than $16 million), and included the restoration of the Bohemian crystal chandeliers.

the new edict provided for the destruction of the Huguenots' churches and the closing of Protestant schools.

FINANCIAL ISSUES The cost of building Versailles and other palaces, maintaining his court, and pursuing his wars made finances a crucial issue for Louis XIV. He was most fortunate in having the services of Jean-Baptiste Colbert (ZHAHNH-bah-TEEST kohl-BAYR) (1619–1683) as controller-general of finances. Colbert was an avid practitioner of mercantilism (see Chapter 14). To decrease the need for imports and increase exports, he founded new luxury industries and granted special privileges, including tax exemptions, loans, and subsidies, to individuals who established new industries. To improve communications and the transportation of goods internally, he built roads and canals. To decrease imports directly, Colbert raised tariffs on foreign manufactured goods and created a merchant marine to carry French goods.

THE WARS OF LOUIS XIV Both the increase in royal power that Louis pursued and his desire for military glory led the king to develop a professional army numbering 100,000 men in peacetime and 400,000 in time of war. Louis made war an almost incessant activity of his reign. To achieve the prestige and military glory befitting the Sun King as well as to ensure the domination of his Bourbon dynasty over European affairs, Louis waged four wars between 1667 and 1713. His ambitions roused much of Europe to form coalitions to prevent the destruction of the European balance of power that Bourbon hegemony would cause. Although Louis added some territory to France's northeastern frontier and established a member of his own Bourbon dynasty on the throne of Spain, he also left France impoverished and surrounded by enemies.

The Decline of Spain

At the beginning of the seventeenth century, Spain possessed the most populous empire in the world, controlling almost all of South America and a number of settlements in Asia and Africa. To most Europeans, Spain still seemed the greatest power of the age, but the reality was quite different. The treasury was empty; Philip II went bankrupt in 1596 from excessive expenditures on war, and his successor did the same in 1607 by spending a fortune on his court. The armed forces were out-of-date, the government was inefficient, and the commercial class was weak in the midst of a suppressed peasantry, a luxury-loving class of nobles, and an oversupply of priests and monks.

During the reign of Philip III (1598–1621), many of Spain's weaknesses became apparent. Interested only in court luxury and miracle-working relics, Philip III allowed his first minister, the greedy duke of Lerma, to run the country. The aristocratic Lerma's primary interest was accumulating power and wealth for himself and his family. Crucial problems went unsolved.

The reign of Philip IV (1621–1665) seemed to offer hope for a revival of Spain's energies, especially in the capable hands of his chief minister, Gaspar de Guzmán (gahs-PAR day goos-MAHN), the count of Olivares (oh-lee-BAH-rayss). This clever, hardworking, and power-hungry statesman worked to revive the interests of the monarchy. A flurry of domestic reform decrees, aimed at curtailing the power of the Catholic Church and the landed aristocracy, was soon followed by a political reform program aimed at further centralizing the government of Spain and its possessions in monarchical hands. All of these efforts met with little real success, however, because both the number (estimated at one-fifth of the population) and power of the Spanish aristocrats made them too strong to curtail in any significant fashion.

At the same time, most of the efforts of Olivares and Philip were undermined by their desire to pursue Spain's imperial glory and by a series of internal revolts. Spain's involvement in the Thirty Years' War

led to a series of frightfully expensive military campaigns that incited internal revolts and years of civil war. Unfortunately for Spain, the campaigns also failed to produce victory. As Olivares wrote to King Philip IV, "God wants us to make peace; for He is depriving us visibly and absolutely of all the means of war."[5]

The defeats in Europe and the internal revolts of the 1640s ended any illusions about Spain's greatness. The actual extent of Spain's economic difficulties is still debated, but there is no question about its foreign losses. The Peace of Westphalia formally recognized Dutch independence in 1648, and the Peace of the Pyrenees with France in 1659 meant the surrender of some border regions to France.

Absolutism in Central and Eastern Europe

Q FOCUS QUESTION: What developments enabled Brandenburg-Prussia, Austria, and Russia to emerge as major powers in the seventeenth century?

During the seventeenth century, a development of great importance for the modern Western world took place in central and eastern Europe, as three new powers made their appearance: Prussia, Austria, and Russia.

The German States

The Peace of Westphalia, which officially ended the Thirty Years' War in 1648, left each of the states in the

Holy Roman Empire virtually autonomous and sovereign. Properly speaking, there was no longer a German state but rather more than three hundred little Germanies. Of these, two emerged as great European powers in the seventeenth and eighteenth centuries.

THE RISE OF BRANDENBURG-PRUSSIA The evolution of Brandenburg into a powerful state was largely the work of the Hohenzollern (hoh-en-TSULL-urn) dynasty. By the seventeenth century, the dominions of the house of Hohenzollern, now called Brandenburg-Prussia, consisted of three disconnected masses in western, central, and eastern Germany (see Map 15.2).

Frederick William the Great Elector (1640–1688) laid the foundation for the Prussian state. Realizing that Brandenburg-Prussia was a small, open territory with no natural frontiers for defense, Frederick William built an army of 40,000 men, the fourth largest in Europe. To sustain the army and his own power, he established the General War Commissariat to levy taxes to support the army and oversee its growth and training. The Commissariat soon evolved into an agency for civil government as well. Directly responsible to the elector, the new bureaucratic machine became his chief instrument for governing the state. Many of its officials were members of the Prussian landed aristocracy, the Junkers (YOONG-kers), who also served as officers in the all-important army.

Frederick William was succeeded by his son Frederick III (1688–1713), who made one significant contribution to the development of Prussia. In return for aiding the Holy Roman emperor in a war against Spain, he was officially granted the title of king-in-Prussia in 1701. Thus was Elector Frederick III transformed into King Frederick I, ruler of an important new player on the European stage.

The Emergence of Austria

The Austrian Habsburgs had long played a significant role in European politics as Holy Roman emperors, but by the end of the Thirty Years' War, the Habsburg hopes of creating an empire in Germany had been dashed. In the seventeenth century, the house of Austria assembled a new empire in eastern and southeastern Europe.

The nucleus of the new Austrian Empire remained the traditional Austrian hereditary possessions: Lower and Upper Austria, Carinthia, Carniola, Styria, and Tyrol (see Map 15.3). To these had been added the kingdom of Bohemia and parts of northwestern Hungary in the sixteenth century. In the seventeenth century, Leopold I (1658–1705) encouraged the eastward movement of the Austrian Empire, but he was sorely challenged by the revival of Ottoman power. The Ottomans eventually pushed westward and laid siege to Vienna in 1683. A European army, led by the Austrians, counterattacked and decisively defeated the Ottomans in 1687. Austria took control of Hungary, Transylvania, Croatia, and Slovenia, thus extending its

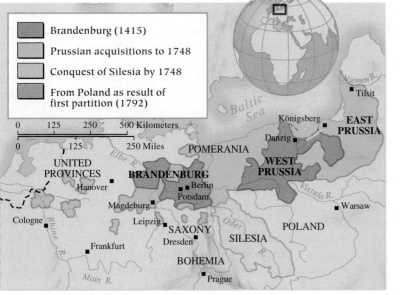

MAP 15.2 The Growth of Brandenburg-Prussia. Frederick William the Great Elector laid the foundation for a powerful state when he increased the size and efficiency of the army, raised taxes and created an efficient bureaucracy to collect them, and gained the support of the landed aristocracy. Later rulers added more territory.

Q Why were the acquisitions of Pomerania and West Prussia important for Brandenburg-Prussia's continued rise to power?

MAP 15.3 The Growth of the Austrian Empire. The Habsburgs had hoped to establish a German empire, but the results of the Thirty Years' War crushed that dream. So Austria expanded to the east and the south, primarily at the expense of the Ottoman Empire, and also gained the Spanish Netherlands and former Spanish territories in Italy.

Q In which areas did the Austrian Empire have access to the Mediterranean Sea, and why would that potentially be important?

empire in southeastern Europe. By the beginning of the eighteenth century, the house of Austria had acquired an empire of considerable size.

The Austrian monarchy, however, never became a highly centralized, absolutist state, primarily because it contained so many different national groups. The Austrian Empire remained a collection of territories held together by a personal union. The Habsburg emperor was archduke of Austria, king of Bohemia, and king of Hungary. Each of these areas, however, had its own laws, Estates-General, and political life.

Russia: From Fledgling Principality to Major Power

A new Russian state had emerged in the fifteenth century under the leadership of the principality of Moscow and its grand dukes. In the sixteenth century, Ivan IV the Terrible (1533–1584), the first ruler to take the title of tsar ("Caesar"), expanded the territories of Russia eastward. Ivan also extended the autocracy of the tsar by crushing the power of the Russian nobility, known as the **boyars**. Ivan's dynasty came to an end in 1598 and was followed by a resurgence of aristocratic power in a period of anarchy known as the Time of Troubles. It did not end until 1613, when the Zemsky Sobor (ZEM-skee suh-BOR), or national assembly, chose Michael Romanov (1613–1645) as the new tsar, beginning a dynasty that lasted until 1917.

In the seventeenth century, Muscovite society was highly stratified. At the top was the tsar, who claimed to be a divinely ordained autocratic ruler. Russian society was dominated by an upper class of landed aristocrats who, in the course of the seventeenth century, managed to bind their peasants to the land. Townspeople were also controlled. Many merchants were not allowed to move from their cities without government permission or to sell their businesses to anyone outside their class. In the seventeenth century, merchant and peasant revolts as well as a schism in the Russian

Orthodox Church created very unsettled conditions. In the midst of these political and religious upheavals, Russia was experiencing more frequent contacts with the West, and Western ideas were beginning to penetrate a few Russian circles. Nevertheless, Russia remained largely outside the framework of the West. At the end of the seventeenth century, Peter the Great (1689–1725) noticeably accelerated the westernizing process.

THE REIGN OF PETER THE GREAT (1689–1725) Peter the Great was an unusual character. A strong man, towering 6 feet 9 inches tall, Peter enjoyed a low kind of humor—belching contests and crude jokes—and vicious punishments including floggings, impalings, and roastings. He gained a firsthand view of the West when he made a trip there in 1697–1698 and returned to Russia with a firm determination to westernize or Europeanize his realm. He admired European technology and gadgets and desired to transplant these to Russia. Only this kind of modernization could give him the army and navy he needed to make Russia a great power.

As could be expected, one of his first priorities was the reorganization of the army and the creation of a navy. Employing both Russians and Europeans as officers, he conscripted peasants for twenty-five-year stints of service to build a standing army of 210,000 men. Peter has also been given credit for forming the first Russian navy.

Peter reorganized the central government, partly along Western lines. To impose the rule of the central government more effectively throughout the land, he divided Russia into eight provinces and later, in 1719, into fifty. Although he hoped to create a "police state," by which he meant a well-ordered community governed in accordance with law, few of his bureaucrats shared his concept of honest service and duty to the state. Peter hoped for a sense of civic duty, but his own forceful personality created an atmosphere of fear that prevented it.

Peter also sought to gain state control of the Russian Orthodox Church. In 1721, he abolished the position of patriarch and created a body called the Holy Synod to make decisions for the church. At its head stood a **procurator**, a layman who represented the interests of the tsar and assured Peter of effective domination of the church.

Shortly after his return from the West in 1698, Peter had begun to introduce Western customs, practices, and manners into Russia. He ordered the preparation of the first Russian book of etiquette to teach Western manners. Among other things, it pointed out that it was not polite to spit on the floor or scratch oneself at dinner. Because Europeans at that time did not wear beards or traditional long-skirted coats, Russian beards had to be shaved and coats shortened, a reform Peter personally enforced at court by shaving off his nobles' beards and cutting their coats at the knees with his own hands.

One group of Russians benefited greatly from Peter's cultural reforms—women. Having watched women mixing freely with men in Western courts, Peter shattered the seclusion of upper-class Russian women and demanded that they remove the traditional veils that covered their faces. Peter also decreed that social gatherings be held three times a week in the large houses of Saint Petersburg, where men and women could mix for conversation, card games, and dancing, which Peter had learned in the West. The tsar also now insisted that women could marry of their own free will.

The object of Peter's domestic reforms was to make Russia into a great state and a military power. His primary goal was to "open a window to the West," meaning a port easily accessible to Europe. This could only be achieved on the Baltic, but at that time the Baltic coast was controlled by Sweden, the most important power in northern Europe. Desirous of these lands, Peter attacked Sweden in the summer of 1700, believing that its young king, Charles XII (1697–1718), could easily be defeated. Charles, however, proved to be a brilliant general and, with a well-disciplined force of only 8,000 men, routed the Russian army of 40,000 at the Battle of Narva (1700). The Great Northern War (1701–1721) soon ensued.

But Peter fought back. He reorganized his army along Western lines and at the Battle of Poltava (pul-TAH-vuh) in 1709 decisively defeated Charles's army. Although the war dragged on for another twelve years, the Peace of Nystadt (NEE-shtaht) in 1721 gave formal recognition to what Peter had already achieved: the acquisition of Estonia, Livonia, and Karelia (see Map 15.4). Sweden had become a second-rate power, and Russia was now the great European state Peter had envisioned. Already in 1703, Peter had begun the construction of a new city on the Baltic, Saint Petersburg, his window to the West and a symbol that Russia was looking toward Europe. Peter realized his

attention. Advancing up the Danube, the Ottomans seized Belgrade in 1521 and Hungary by 1526, although their attempts to conquer Vienna in 1529 were repulsed. At the same time, the Ottomans extended their power into the western Mediterranean, threatening to turn it into an Ottoman lake. However, the Spanish destroyed a large Ottoman fleet at Lepanto (in modern-day Greece) in 1571. Despite the defeat, the Ottomans continued to hold nominal control over the southern shores of the Mediterranean.

By the beginning of the seventeenth century, the Ottoman Empire was being treated like any other European power by European rulers seeking alliances and trade concessions. In the first half of the century, the empire was a "sleeping giant." Occupied by domestic bloodletting and severely threatened by a challenge from Persia, the Ottomans were content with the status quo in eastern Europe. But under a new line of grand viziers in the second half of the seventeenth century, the Ottoman Empire again took the offensive. By 1683, the Ottomans had marched through the Hungarian plain and laid siege to Vienna. Repulsed by a mixed army of Austrians, Poles, Bavarians, and Saxons, the Ottomans retreated and were pushed out of Hungary by a new European coalition. Although they retained the core of their empire, the Ottoman Turks would never again be a threat to Europe.

Peter the Great as Victor. Peter the Great wished to westernize Russia, especially in the realm of technical skills. His goal was the creation of a strong army and navy and the acquisition of new territory in order to make Russia a great power. He is shown here as the victor at the Battle of Poltava in an eighteenth-century portrait attributed to Gottfried Danhauer.

dream: by the time of his death in 1725, Russia had become a great military power and an important actor on the European stage.

The Ottoman Empire

After conquering Constantinople in 1453, the Ottoman Turks tried but failed to complete their conquest of the Balkans, where they had been established since the fourteenth century (see Map 15.3). The reign of Sultan Suleiman (soo-lay-MAHN) I the Magnificent (1520–1566), however, brought the Ottomans back to Europe's

The Limits of Absolutism

In recent decades, historical studies of local institutions have challenged the traditional picture of absolute monarchs. We now recognize that their power was far from absolute, and it is misleading to think that they actually controlled the lives of their subjects. In 1700, government for most people still meant the local

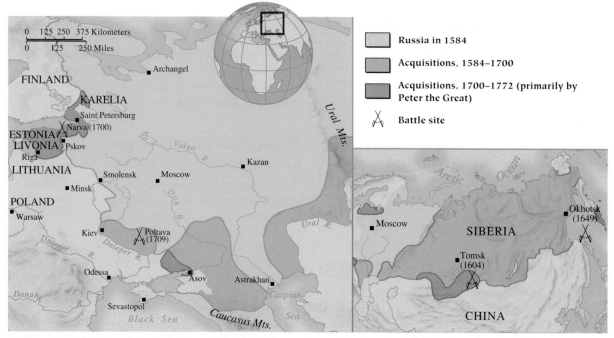

MAP 15.4 Russia: From Principality to Nation-State. Russia had expanded its territory since its emergence in the fifteenth century. Peter the Great modernized the country, instituting administrative and tax reforms and building up the military. He won territory on the Baltic from Sweden, enabling Russia to have a port at Saint Petersburg.

Q Why would the westward expansion of Russia during Peter's reign affect the international balance of power in Europe?

CHRONOLOGY	Absolutism in Central and Eastern Europe
Brandenburg-Prussia	
Frederick William the Great Elector	1640–1688
Elector Frederick III (King Frederick I)	1688–1713
Austrian Empire	
Leopold I	1658–1705
Ottoman siege of Vienna	1683
Russia	
Ivan IV the Terrible	1533–1584
Time of Troubles	1598–1613
Michael Romanov	1613–1645
Peter the Great	1689–1725
First trip to the West	1697–1698
Great Northern War	1701–1721
Battle of Poltava	1709
Holy Synod	1721
Ottoman Empire	
Suleiman I the Magnificent	1520–1566
Battle of Lepanto	1571
Ottoman defeat at Vienna	1683

institutions that affected their lives: local courts, local tax collectors, and local organizers of armed forces. Kings and ministers might determine policies and issue guidelines, but they still had to function through local agents and had no guarantee that their wishes would be carried out. A mass of urban and provincial privileges, liberties, and exemptions (including from taxation) and a whole host of corporate bodies and interest groups—provincial and national Estates, clerical officials, officeholders who had bought or inherited their positions, and provincial nobles—limited what monarchs could achieve. The most successful rulers were not those who tried to destroy the old system but rather those like Louis XIV who knew how to use the old system to their advantage. Above all other considerations stood the landholding nobility. Everywhere in the seventeenth century, the landed aristocracy played an important role in the European monarchical system. As military officers, judges, officeholders, and landowners in control of vast, untaxed estates, their power remained immense. In some places, their strength even put severe limits on how effectively monarchs could rule.

Limited Monarchy: The Dutch Republic and England

Q FOCUS QUESTION: What were the main issues in the struggle between king and Parliament in seventeenth-century England, and how were they resolved?

Almost everywhere in Europe in the seventeenth century, kings and their ministers were in control of central governments. But not all European states followed the pattern of absolute monarchy. In western Europe, two great states—the Dutch Republic and England—successfully resisted the power of hereditary monarchs.

The Golden Age of the Dutch Republic

The seventeenth century has often been called the golden age of the Dutch Republic, as the United Provinces held center stage as one of Europe's great powers. Like France and England, the United Provinces was an Atlantic power, underlining the importance of the shift of political and economic power in the seventeenth century from the Mediterranean basin to the countries on the Atlantic seaboard. As a result of the sixteenth-century revolt of the Netherlands, the seven northern provinces, which began to call themselves the United Provinces of the Netherlands in 1581, became the core of the modern Dutch state. The Peace of Westphalia officially recognized the new state in 1648.

With independence came internal dissension between two chief centers of political power. Each province had an official known as a stadholder (STAD-hohl-dur) who was responsible for leading the army and maintaining order. Beginning with William of Orange and his heirs, the house of Orange occupied the stadholderate in most provinces and favored the development of a centralized government with themselves as hereditary monarchs. The States General, an assembly of representatives from every province, opposed the Orangist ambitions and advocated a decentralized or republican form of government. For much of the seventeenth century, the republican forces were in control. But in 1672, burdened with war against both France and England, the United Provinces allowed William III (1672–1702) of the house of Orange to establish a monarchical regime. His death in 1702 without direct heirs enabled the republican forces to gain control once more, although the struggle persisted throughout the eighteenth century.

Underlying Dutch prominence in the seventeenth century was economic prosperity, fueled by the role of the Dutch as carriers of European trade (see Images of Everyday Life on p. 373). But wars with France and England placed heavy burdens on Dutch finances and manpower. English shipping began to challenge what had been Dutch commercial supremacy, and by 1715, the Dutch were experiencing a serious economic decline.

England and the Emergence of Constitutional Monarchy

One of the most prominent examples of resistance to absolute monarchy came in seventeenth-century England, where king and Parliament struggled to determine the role each should play in governing the nation.

KING JAMES I AND PARLIAMENT   On the death of Queen Elizabeth in 1603, the Tudor dynasty became extinct, and the Stuart line of rulers was inaugurated with the accession to the throne of Elizabeth's cousin, King James VI of Scotland (son of Mary, Queen of Scots), who became James I (1603–1625) of England. James espoused the divine right of kings, a viewpoint that alienated Parliament, which had grown accustomed under the Tudors to act on the premise that monarch and Parliament together ruled England as a "balanced polity." Parliament expressed its displeasure with James's claims by refusing his requests for additional monies needed by the king to meet the increased cost of government. Parliament's power of the purse proved to be its trump card in its relationship with the king.

Some members of Parliament were also alienated by James's religious policy. The Puritans—Protestants in the Anglican Church inspired by Calvinist theology—wanted James to eliminate the episcopal system of church organization used in the Church of England (in which the bishop or *episcopos* played the major administrative role) in favor of a Presbyterian model (used in Scotland and patterned after Calvin's church organization in Geneva, where ministers and elders—also called presbyters—played an important governing role). James refused because he realized that the Anglican Church, with its bishops appointed by the Crown, was a major supporter of monarchical authority. But the Puritans were not easily cowed and added to the rising chorus of opposition to the king. Many of England's **gentry**, mostly well-to-do landowners below the level of the nobility, had become Puritans, and these Puritan gentry not only formed an important and substantial part of the House of Commons, the lower house of Parliament, but also held important positions locally as justices of the peace and sheriffs. It was not wise to alienate them.

IMAGES OF EVERYDAY LIFE
Dutch Domesticity

DURING THE GOLDEN age of the Dutch Republic, Dutch painters delighted in painting scenes of domestic life, especially the lives of the wealthy burghers who prospered from trade, finance, and manufacturing. The Dutch painter Pieter de Hooch (pee-TUR duh HOHKH) specialized in painting pictures of Dutch interiors, as can be seen in three of his paintings. In *The Mother* (below left), de Hooch portrays a tranquil scene of a mother with her infant and small daughter. The spotless, polished floors reflect the sunlight streaming in through the open door. The rooms are clean and in good order. Household manuals, such as *The Experienced and Knowledgeable Hollands Householder*, provided detailed outlines of the cleaning tasks that should be performed each day of the week. In *The Linen Cupboard* (below right), a Dutch mother, assisted by her daughter, is shown storing her clean sheets in an elegant cupboard in another well-polished Dutch room. The Chinese porcelain on top of the cupboard and the antique statue indicate that this is the residence of a wealthy family. In *Two Women Teach a Child to Walk* (at the right), the artist again shows a nicely furnished and spotless interior. A small girl is learning to walk assisted by a servant holding straps attached to a band around the girl's head to keep her from falling.

CHARLES I AND THE MOVE TOWARD REVOLUTION The conflict that had begun during the reign of James came to a head during the reign of his son, Charles I (1625–1649). In 1628, Parliament passed the Petition of Right, which the king was supposed to accept before being granted any tax revenues. This petition prohibited levying taxes without Parliament's consent, arbitrary imprisonment, the quartering of soldiers in private houses, and the declaration of martial law in peacetime. Although he initially accepted it, Charles later reneged on the agreement because of its limitations on royal power. In 1629, Charles decided that since he could not work with Parliament, he would not summon it to meet. From 1629 to 1640, Charles pursued a course of personal rule, which forced him to find ways to collect taxes without the cooperation of Parliament. These expedients aroused opposition from middle-class merchants and landed gentry, who objected to the king's attempts to tax without Parliament's consent.

The king's religious policy also proved disastrous. His attempt to impose more ritual on the Anglican Church struck the Puritans as a return to Catholic popery. Charles's efforts to force them to conform to his religious policies infuriated the Puritans, thousands of whom abandoned England for the "howling wildernesses" of America.

CIVIL WAR AND A NEW GOVERNMENT

Grievances mounted until England finally slipped into a civil war (1642–1648) that was won by the parliamentary forces. Most important to Parliament's success was the creation of the New Model Army, one of whose leaders was Oliver Cromwell (1599–1658), the only real military genius of the war. The New Model Army was composed primarily of more extreme Puritans known as the Independents, who, in typical Calvinist fashion, believed they were doing battle for the Lord. As Cromwell wrote in one of his military reports, "Sir, this is none other but the hand of God; and to Him alone belongs the glory."

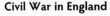

0   150   300 Kilometers

0   125   250 Miles

North Sea

SCOTLAND
  ■ Edinburgh

IRELAND   ENGLAND

        Cambridge ■
    Oxford ■ ■ London

English Channel

▨ Area supporting Parliament, 1643

▨ Area supporting Royalists, 1643

Civil War in England

Between 1648 and 1660, England faced a trying situation. After the execution of Charles I on January 30, 1649, Parliament abolished the monarchy and the House of Lords and proclaimed England a republic or commonwealth. But Cromwell and his army, unable to work effectively with Parliament, dispersed it by force.

As the members of Parliament departed in April 1653, Cromwell shouted after them, "It's you that have forced me to do this, for I have sought the Lord night and day that He would slay me rather than put upon me the doing of this work." With the certainty of one who is convinced he is right, Cromwell had destroyed both king and Parliament (see the box on p. 375). Finally, Cromwell dissolved Parliament and divided the country into eleven regions, each ruled by a major general who served as a military governor. Unable to establish a constitutional basis for a working government, Cromwell had resorted to military force to maintain the rule of the Independents.

Oliver Cromwell died in 1658. After floundering for eighteen months, the military government decided that arbitrary rule by the army was no longer feasible and reestablished the monarchy in the person of Charles II (1660–1685), the son of Charles I. The restoration of the Stuart monarchy ended England's time of troubles, but it was not long before yet another constitutional crisis arose.

RESTORATION AND A GLORIOUS REVOLUTION Charles was sympathetic to and perhaps even inclined to Catholicism. Moreover, Charles's brother James, heir to the throne, did not hide the fact that he was a Catholic. Parliament's suspicions were therefore aroused in 1672 when Charles took the audacious step of issuing the Declaration of Indulgence, which suspended the laws that Parliament had passed against Catholics and Puritans after the restoration of the Anglican Church as the official church of England. Parliament would have none of it and induced the king to suspend the declaration. Propelled by a strong anti-Catholic sentiment, Parliament then passed the Test Act of 1673, specifying that only Anglicans could hold military and civil offices.

The accession of James II (1685–1688) virtually guaranteed a new constitutional crisis for England. An open and devout Catholic, his attempt to further Catholic interests made religion once more a primary cause of conflict between king and Parliament. In 1687, James issued a new Declaration of Indulgence, which suspended all laws that excluded Catholics and Puritans from office. Parliamentary outcries against James's policies stopped short of rebellion because members knew that he was an old

OPPOSING VIEWPOINTS
Oliver Cromwell: Three Perspectives

Oliver Cromwell was a strong leader with firm religious convictions. The first selection below, taken from a letter written after the defeat of the king's forces at Naseby in 1645, reveals Cromwell's feelings about the reasons for his military victory. The next selection, also by Cromwell, is taken from his comments after his army's massacre of Catholic forces at Drogheda in Catholic Ireland. The third selection is by Edmund Ludlow, a general on Cromwell's side who broke with Cromwell after the latter dispersed Parliament in 1653. The final selection by Edward Hyde, the first earl of Clarendon, a supporter of King Charles I and later Charles II, presents a royalist view of Cromwell.

Oliver Cromwell on the Victory at Naseby

Sir, this is none other but the hand of God; and to Him alone belongs the glory, wherein none are to share with Him. The general [Fairfax] served you with all faithfulness and honor: and the best commendations I can give him is, that I dare say he attributes all to God, and would rather perish than assume to himself.

Cromwell on the Massacre at Drogheda

The next day, the other two towers were summoned, in one of which was about six or seven score; but they refused to yield themselves, and we knowing that hunger must compel them, set only good guards to secure them from running away until their stomachs were come down. From one of the said towers, notwithstanding their condition, they killed and wounded some of our men. When they submitted, their officers were knocked on the head, and every tenth man of the soldiers killed, and the rest shipped for the Barbados. The soldiers in the other tower were all spared, as to their lives only, and shipped likewise for the Barbados.

I am persuaded that this is a righteous judgment of God upon these barbarous wretches, who have imbrued their hands in so much innocent blood; and that it will tend to prevent the effusion of blood for the future.

Edmund Ludlow, *Memoirs*

Then I drew near to the council-table, where Cromwell charged me with ... endeavoring to render the officers of the army disaffected, by discoursing to them concerning new models of Government....

"You do well," said he, "to reflect on our fears.... I now require you to give assurance not to act against the Government." I desired to be excused in that particular, reminding him of the reasons I had formerly given him for my refusal, adding, that I was in his power, and that he might use me as he thought fit. "Pray then," said he, "what is it that you would have? May not every man be as good as he will? What can you desire more than you have?" "It were easy," said I, "to tell what we would have." "What is that, I pray?" said he. "That which we fought for," said I, "that the nation might be governed by its own consent." "I am," said he, "as much for a government by consent as any man; but where shall we find that consent? Amongst the Prelatical, Presbyterian, Independent, Anabaptist, or Leveling Parties?" I answered, "Amongst those of all sorts who had acted with fidelity and affection to the public."

Lord Clarendon, *The History of the Rebellion and Civil Wars in England*

He was one of those men, ... whom his very enemies could not condemn without commending him at the same time: for he could never have done half that mischief without great parts of courage, industry, and judgment. He must have had a wonderful understanding in the natures and humors of men, and as great a dexterity in applying them; who, from a private and obscure birth (though of a good family), without interest or estate, alliance or friendship, could raise himself to such a height.... [It] may very justly be said of him: he attempted those things which no good man dared have ventured on; and achieved those in which none but a valiant and great man could have succeeded. Without doubt, no man with more wickedness ever attempted any thing, or brought to pass what he desired more wickedly, more in the face and contempt

(continued)

of religion, and moral honesty; yet wickedness as great as his could never have accomplished those trophies, without the assistance of a great spirit, an admirable circumspection and sagacity, and a most magnanimous resolution.

Q What motivated Cromwell's political and military actions? What was Edmund Ludlow's criticism of Cromwell, and how did Cromwell respond? In what ways did Edward Hyde see both good and bad features in Cromwell? How do you explain the differences in these three perspectives?

Sources: Oliver Cromwell on the Victory at Naseby. Oliver Cromwell on the Massacre at Drogheda. From Thomas Carlyle, ed., *The Letters and Speeches of Oliver Cromwell*, 3 vols. (New York: G.P. Putnam's Sons, 1904), Vol. I, p. 204, Vol. II, p. 15. Edmund Ludlow, *Memoirs*. From C.H. Firth, *The Memoirs of Edmund Ludlow* (Oxford: Oxford University Press, 1894), Vol. 2, pp. 10–11. Lord Clarendon, *The History of the Rebellion and Civil Wars in England*. From Lord Clarendon, *The History of the Rebellion and Civil Wars in England* (Oxford: Oxford University Press, 1839), Vol. 6, pp. 349–350.

man and his successors were his Protestant daughters Mary and Anne, born to his first wife. But on June 10, 1688, a son was born to James II's second wife, also a Catholic. Suddenly, the specter of a Catholic hereditary monarchy loomed large.

A group of prominent English noblemen invited the Dutch chief executive, William of Orange, husband of James's daughter Mary, to invade England. William and Mary raised an army and invaded England while James, his wife, and their infant son fled to France.

CHRONOLOGY Limited Monarchy and Republics	
United Provinces of the Netherlands	
Official recognition	1648
House of Orange: William III	1672–1702
England	
James I	1603–1625
Charles I	1625–1649
Civil War	1642–1648
Commonwealth	1649–1653
Death of Cromwell	1658
Restoration of monarchy	1660
Charles II	1660–1685
Declaration of Indulgence	1672
Test Act	1673
James II	1685–1688
Declaration of Indulgence	1687
Glorious Revolution	1688
Bill of Rights	1689

With almost no bloodshed, England had embarked on a "Glorious Revolution," not over the issue of whether there would be monarchy but rather over who would be monarch.

In January 1689, Parliament offered the throne to William and Mary, who accepted it along with the provisions of a bill of rights (see the box on p. 377). The Bill of Rights affirmed Parliament's right to make laws and levy taxes and made it impossible for kings to oppose or do without Parliament by stipulating that standing armies could be raised only with the consent of Parliament. The rights of citizens to petition the sovereign, keep arms, have a jury trial, and not be subject to excessive bail were also confirmed. The Bill of Rights helped fashion a system of government based on the rule of law and a freely elected Parliament, thus laying the foundation for a constitutional monarchy.

The Bill of Rights did not settle the religious questions that had played such a large role in England's troubles in the seventeenth century. The Toleration Act of 1689 granted Puritan Dissenters the right of free public worship (Catholics were still excluded). Although the Toleration Act did not mean complete religious freedom and equality, it marked a departure in English history in that few people would ever again be persecuted for religious reasons.

Many historians have viewed the Glorious Revolution as the end of the seventeenth-century struggle between king and Parliament. By deposing one king and establishing another, Parliament had demolished the divine-right theory of kingship (William was, after all, king by grace of Parliament, not God) and confirmed its right to participate in the government. Parliament did not have complete control of the government, but it now had an unquestioned role in

The Bill of Rights

In 1688, the English experienced yet another revolution, a bloodless one in which the Stuart king James II was replaced by Mary, James's daughter, and her husband, William of Orange. After William and Mary had assumed power, Parliament passed a bill of rights that specified the rights of Parliament and laid the foundation for a constitutional monarchy.

The Bill of Rights

Whereas the said late King James II having abdicated the government, and the throne being thereby vacant, his Highness the prince of Orange (whom it has pleased Almighty God to make the glorious instrument of delivering this kingdom from popery and arbitrary power) did (by the device of the lords spiritual and temporal, and diverse principal persons of the Commons) cause letters to be written to the lords spiritual and temporal, being Protestants, and other letters to the several counties, cities, universities, boroughs, and Cinque Ports, for the choosing of such persons to represent them, as were of right to be sent to parliament, to meet and sit at Westminster upon the two and twentieth day of January, in this year 1689, in order to such an establishment as that their religion, laws, and liberties might not again be in danger of being subverted; . . .

And thereupon the said lords spiritual and temporal and Commons, . . . being now assembled in a full and free representation of this nation, taking into their most serious consideration the best means for attaining the ends aforesaid, do . . . declare:

1. That the pretended power of suspending laws, or the execution of laws, by regal authority, without consent of parliament is illegal.
2. That the pretended power of dispensing with the laws, or the execution of law by regal authority, as it has been assumed and exercised of late, is illegal. . . .

4. That levying money for or to the use of the crown by pretense of prerogative, without grant of parliament, for longer time or in other manner than the same is or shall be granted, is illegal.
5. That it is the right of the subjects to petition the king, and all commitments and prosecutions for such petitioning are illegal.
6. That the raising or keeping a standing army within the kingdom in time of peace, unless it be with consent of parliament, is against law.
7. That the subjects which are Protestants may have arms for their defense suitable to their conditions, and as allowed by law.
8. That election of members of parliament ought to be free.
9. That the freedom of speech, and debates or proceedings in parliament, ought not to be impeached or questioned in any court or place out of parliament.
10. That excessive bail ought not to be required, nor excessive fines imposed, nor cruel and unusual punishments inflicted.
11. That jurors ought to be duly impaneled and returned, and jurors which pass upon men in trials for high treason ought to be freeholders.
12. That all grants and promises of fines and forfeitures of particular persons before conviction are illegal and void.
13. And that for redress of all grievances, and for the amending, strengthening, and preserving of the laws, parliament ought to be held frequently.

Q How did the Bill of Rights lay the foundation for a constitutional monarchy in England? What key aspects of this document testify to the exceptional nature of English state politics in the seventeenth century?

Source: From *The Statutes: Revised Edition* (London: Eyre and Spottiswoode, 1871), Vol. 2, pp. 10–12.

affairs of state. Over the next century, it would gradually prove to be the real authority in the English system of constitutional monarchy.

RESPONSES TO REVOLUTION The English revolutions of the seventeenth century prompted very different responses from two English political thinkers—Thomas Hobbes and John Locke. Thomas Hobbes (1588–1679), who lived during the English Civil War, was alarmed by the revolutionary upheavals in his contemporary England. His name has since been associated with the state's claim to absolute authority over its subjects, a topic that he elaborated in his major treatise on political thought known as the *Leviathan* (luh-VY-uh-thun), published in 1651.

Hobbes claimed that in the state of nature, before society was organized, human life was "solitary, poor, nasty, brutish, and short." Humans were guided not by reason and moral ideals but by animalistic instincts and a ruthless struggle for self-preservation. To save themselves from destroying each other (the "war of every man against every man"), people contracted to form a commonwealth, which Hobbes called "that great Leviathan (or rather, to speak more reverently, that mortal god) to which we owe our peace and defense." This commonwealth placed its collective power into the hands of a sovereign authority, preferably a single ruler, who served as executor, legislator, and judge. This absolute ruler possessed unlimited power. In Hobbes's view, subjects may not rebel; if they do, they must be suppressed.

John Locke (1632–1704), author of a political work called *Two Treatises of Government*, viewed the exercise of political power quite differently from Hobbes and argued against the absolute rule of one man. Like Hobbes, Locke began with the state of nature before human existence became organized socially. But unlike Hobbes, Locke believed that humans lived then in a state of equality and freedom rather than a state of war. In this state of nature, humans had certain inalienable natural rights—to life, liberty, and property. Like Hobbes, Locke did not believe that all was well in the state of nature, and people found it difficult to protect these rights. So they mutually agreed to establish a government to ensure the protection of their rights. This agreement established mutual obligations: government would protect the rights of people, and the people would act reasonably toward their government. But if a government broke this agreement—if a king, for example, failed to live up to his obligation to protect the people's rights or claimed absolute authority and made laws without the consent of the community—the people might form a new government. For Locke, however, the community of people was primarily the landholding aristocracy who were represented in Parliament, not the landless masses. Locke was hardly an advocate of political democracy, but his ideas proved important to both the Americans and the French in the eighteenth century and were used to support demands for constitutional government, the rule of law, and the protection of rights.

The Flourishing of European Culture

Q FOCUS QUESTION: How did the artistic and literary achievements of this era reflect the political and economic developments of the period?

In the midst of religious wars and the growth of absolutism, European culture continued to flourish. The era was blessed with a number of prominent artists and writers.

The Changing Faces of Art

After the Renaissance, European art passed through a number of stylistic stages. The artistic Renaissance came to an end when a new movement called Mannerism emerged in Italy in the 1520s and 1530s.

MANNERISM The Reformation's revival of religious values brought much political turmoil. Especially in Italy, the worldly enthusiasm of the Renaissance gave way to anxiety, uncertainty, suffering, and a yearning for spiritual experience. **Mannerism** reflected this environment in its deliberate attempt to break down the High Renaissance principles of balance, harmony, and moderation. Italian Mannerist painters deliberately distorted the rules of proportion by portraying elongated figures that conveyed a sense of suffering and a strong emotional atmosphere filled with anxiety and confusion.

THE BAROQUE A new movement—the **Baroque** (buh-ROHK)—eventually replaced Mannerism. The Baroque began in Italy in the last quarter of the sixteenth century and spread to the rest of Europe, where it was most wholeheartedly embraced by the Catholic reform movement, as is evident at the Catholic courts, especially those of the Habsburgs in Madrid, Prague, Vienna, and Brussels. Eventually the Baroque style spread to all of Europe and Latin America.

Baroque artists sought to bring together the classical ideals of Renaissance art and the spiritual feelings of the sixteenth-century religious revival. In large part, though, Baroque art and architecture reflected the search for power that was such a large part of the seventeenth-century ethos. Baroque churches and palaces were magnificent and richly detailed. Kings and princes wanted other kings and princes as well as their subjects to be in awe of their power. The Catholic Church, which commissioned many new churches, wanted people to see the triumphant power of the Catholic faith.

Baroque painting was known for its use of dramatic effects to heighten emotional intensity. Perhaps the greatest figure of the Baroque was the Italian architect and sculptor Gian Lorenzo Bernini (ZHAHN loh-RENT-zoh bur-NEE-nee) (1598–1680), who completed Saint Peter's Basilica at the Vatican and designed the vast colonnade enclosing the piazza in front of it. Action, exuberance, profusion, and dramatic effects mark the work of Bernini in the interior of Saint Peter's, where his *Throne of Saint Peter* hovers in midair, held by the hands of the four great doctors of the Catholic Church. In his most striking sculptural work, the *Ecstasy of Saint Theresa*, Bernini depicts a moment of mystical experience in the life of the sixteenth-century Spanish saint.

The elegant draperies and the expression on her face create a sensuously real portrayal of physical ecstasy.

Less well known than the male artists who dominated the art world of the seventeenth century in Italy but prominent in her own right was Artemisia Gentileschi (ar-tuh-MEE-zhuh jen-tuh-LESS-kee) (1593–1653). Born in Rome, she studied painting under her father's direction. In 1616, she moved to Florence and began a successful career as a painter. At the age of twenty-three, she became the first woman to be elected to the Florentine Academy of Design. Although she was known internationally in her day as a portrait painter, her fame now rests on a series of pictures of heroines from the Old Testament, including Judith, Esther, and Bathsheba. Most famous is *Judith Beheading Holofernes*, a dramatic rendering of the biblical scene in which Judith slays the Assyrian general Holofernes to save her besieged town from the Assyrian army.

Gian Lorenzo Bernini, *Ecstasy of Saint Theresa*. One of the great artists of the Baroque period was the Italian sculptor and architect Gian Lorenzo Bernini. The *Ecstasy of Saint Theresa*, created for the Cornaro Chapel in the Church of Santa Maria della Vittoria in Rome, was one of Bernini's most famous sculptures. Bernini sought to convey visually Theresa's mystical experience when, according to her description, an angel pierced her heart repeatedly with a golden arrow.

Artemisia Gentileschi, *Judith Beheading Holofernes*. Artemisia Gentileschi painted a series of pictures portraying scenes from the lives of courageous Old Testament women. In this painting, a determined Judith, armed with her victim's sword, struggles to saw off the head of Holofernes. Gentileschi realistically and dramatically shows the gruesome nature of Judith's act.

FRENCH CLASSICISM AND DUTCH REALISM In the second half of the seventeenth century, France replaced Italy as the cultural leader of Europe. Rejecting the Baroque style as showy and overly passionate, the French remained committed to the classical values of the High Renaissance. French late Classicism, with its emphasis on clarity, simplicity, balance, and harmony of design, was a rather austere version of the High Renaissance style. Its triumph reflected the shift in seventeenth-century French society from chaos to order. Though it rejected the emotionalism and high drama of the Baroque, French Classicism continued the Baroque's conception of grandeur in the portrayal of noble subjects, especially those from classical antiquity.

A brilliant flowering of Dutch painting paralleled the supremacy of Dutch commerce in the seventeenth century. Wealthy patricians and burghers of Dutch urban society commissioned works of art for their guild halls, town halls, and private dwellings. The interests of this burgher society were reflected in the subject matter of many Dutch paintings: portraits of themselves, landscapes, seascapes, genre scenes, still lifes, and the interiors of their residences. Neither Classical nor Baroque, Dutch painters were primarily interested in the realistic portrayal of secular every-day life.

The finest product of the golden age of Dutch painting was Rembrandt van Rijn (REM-brant vahn

Rijksmuseum, Amsterdam//DEA Picture Library/Getty Images

Rembrandt van Rijn, *The Night Watch*. Dutch burghers and patricians of Dutch urban society commissioned works of art, and these quite naturally reflected the burghers' interests. This painting by Rembrandt shows the two leaders and sixteen members of a civic militia preparing for a parade in the city of Amsterdam.

RYN) (1606–1669). Although Rembrandt shared the Dutch predilection for realistic portraits, he became more introspective as he grew older. He refused to follow his contemporaries, whose pictures were largely secular; half of his own paintings depicted scenes from biblical tales. Since the Protestant tradition of hostility to religious pictures had discouraged artistic expression, Rembrandt stands out as the one great Protestant painter of the seventeenth century.

A Wondrous Age of Theater

In England and Spain, writing reached new heights between 1580 and 1640. The greatest age of English literature is often called the Elizabethan era because much of this English cultural flowering of the late sixteenth and early seventeenth centuries occurred during the reign of Queen Elizabeth I. Elizabethan literature exhibits the exuberance and pride associated with England's international exploits at the time. Of all the forms of Elizabethan literature, none expressed the energy and intellectual versatility of the era better than drama. And of all the dramatists, none is more famous than William Shakespeare (1564–1616).

WILLIAM SHAKESPEARE Shakespeare was the son of a prosperous glovemaker from Stratford-upon-Avon. When he appeared in London in 1592, Elizabethans were already addicted to the stage. In Greater London, as many as six theaters were open six afternoons a week. London theaters ranged from the Globe, which was a circular unroofed structure holding three thousand spectators, to the Blackfriars, which was roofed and held only five hundred. In the former, the admission charge of only a penny or two enabled even the lower classes to attend; the higher prices in the latter ensured an audience of the well-to-do. Elizabethan audiences varied greatly, putting pressure on playwrights to write works that pleased nobles, lawyers, merchants, and even vagabonds.

William Shakespeare was a "complete man of the theater." Although best known for writing plays, he was also an actor and a shareholder in the chief company of the time, the Lord Chamberlain's Company, which played in theaters as diverse as the Globe and the Blackfriars. Shakespeare has long been recognized as a universal genius. A master of the English language,

he was instrumental in codifying a language that was still in transition. This technical proficiency was matched by an incredible insight into human psychology. In both tragedies and comedies, Shakespeare exhibited a remarkable understanding of the human condition.

SPAIN'S GOLDEN CENTURY The theater was also one of the most creative forms of expression during Spain's golden century. The first professional theaters founded in Seville and Madrid in the 1570s were run by actors' companies, as in England. Soon a public playhouse could be found in every large town, including Mexico City in the New World. Touring companies brought the latest Spanish plays to all parts of the Spanish Empire.

Beginning in the 1580s, the agenda for playwrights was set by Lope de Vega (LOH-pay day VAY-guh) (1562–1635). Like Shakespeare, he was from a middle-class background. He was an incredibly prolific writer; almost one-third of his fifteen hundred plays survive. They have been characterized as witty, charming, action packed, and realistic. Lope de Vega made no apologies for the fact that he wrote his plays to please his audiences. In a treatise on drama written in 1609, he stated that the foremost duty of the playwright was to satisfy public demand. He remarked that if anyone thought he had written his plays for fame, "undeceive him and tell him that I wrote them for money."

FRENCH DRAMA As the great age of theater in England and Spain was drawing to a close around 1630, a new dramatic era began to dawn in France that lasted into the 1680s. Unlike Shakespeare in England and Lope de Vega in Spain, French playwrights wrote more for an elite audience and were forced to depend on royal patronage. Louis XIV used theater as he did art and architecture—to attract attention to his monarchy. French dramatists cultivated a style that emphasized the clever, polished, and correct over the emotional and imaginative. Many of the French works of this period derived their themes and plots from Greek and Roman sources.

Jean-Baptiste Molière (ZHAHNH bah-TEEST mohl-YAYR) (1622–1673) enjoyed the favor of the French court and benefited from the patronage of the Sun King. Molière wrote, produced, and acted in a series of comedies that often satirized the religious and social world of his time. In *Tartuffe*, he ridiculed religious hypocrisy. Molière's satires, however, sometimes got him into trouble. The Parisian clergy did not find *Tartuffe* funny and had it banned for five years. Only the protection of Louis XIV saved Molière from more severe harassment.

Chapter Summary

To many historians, the seventeenth century has assumed extraordinary proportions. The divisive effects of the Reformation had been assimilated, and the concept of a united Christendom, held as an ideal since the Middle Ages, had been irrevocably destroyed by the religious wars, making possible the emergence of a system of nation-states in which power politics took on an increasing significance. The growth of political thought focusing on the secular origins of state power reflected the changes that were going on in seventeenth-century society.

Within those states, there slowly emerged some of the machinery that made possible a growing centralization of power. In those states called absolutist, strong monarchs with the assistance of their aristocracies took the lead in providing the leadership for greater centralization. In this so-called age of absolutism, Louis XIV, the Sun King of France, was the model for other rulers. His palace of Versailles, where the nobles were entertained and controlled by ceremony and etiquette, symbolized his authority. Louis revoked his grandfather's Edict of Nantes and fought four costly wars, mainly to acquire lands on France's eastern borders. Strong monarchy also prevailed in central and eastern Europe, where three new powers made their appearance: Prussia, Austria, and Russia. Russia's Peter the Great attempted to westernize Russia, especially militarily, and built Saint Petersburg, a new capital city, as his window on the West.

But not all European states followed the pattern of absolute monarchy. Especially important were developments in England, where a series of struggles between king and Parliament took place in the seventeenth century. The conflict between the Stuart kings, who were advocates of divine-right monarchy, and Parliament led to civil war and the creation of a republic and then a military dictatorship under Oliver Cromwell. After his death, the Stuart monarchy was restored, but a new conflict led to the overthrow of James II and the establishment of a new order. The landed aristocracy gained power at the expense of the monarchs, thus laying the foundations for a constitutional government in which Parliament provided the focus for the institutions of centralized power. In all the major European states, a growing concern for power and dynamic expansion led to larger armies and greater conflict. War remained an endemic feature of Western civilization.

But the search for order and harmony continued, evident in art and literature. At the same time, religious preoccupations and values were losing ground to secular considerations. The seventeenth century was a period of transition toward the more secular spirit  that has characterized modern Western civilization to the present. No stronger foundation for this spirit could be found than in the new view of the universe that was ushered in by the Scientific Revolution of the seventeenth century, and it is to that story that we turn in the next chapter.

CHAPTER TIMELINE

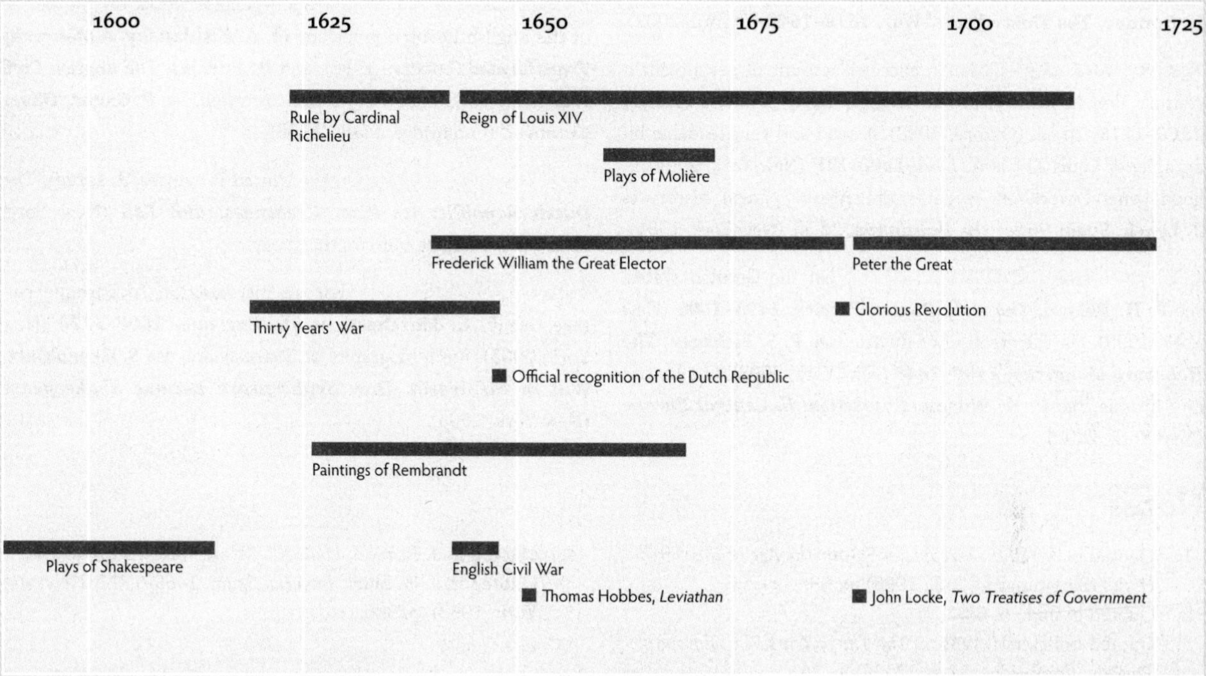

	1600	1625	1650	1675	1700	1725

Rule by Cardinal Richelieu

Reign of Louis XIV

Plays of Molière

Frederick William the Great Elector

Peter the Great

Thirty Years' War

■ Glorious Revolution

■ Official recognition of the Dutch Republic

Paintings of Rembrandt

Plays of Shakespeare

English Civil War

■ Thomas Hobbes, *Leviathan*

■ John Locke, *Two Treatises of Government*

CHAPTER REVIEW

Upon Reflection

Q What does the witchcraft craze tell us about European society in the sixteenth and seventeenth centuries?

Q What did Louis XIV hope to accomplish in his domestic and foreign policies? To what extent did he succeed?

Q What role did the nobility play in England?

Key Terms

absolutism (p. 362)
boyars (p. 368)
procurator (p. 369)

gentry (p. 372)
Mannerism (p. 378)
Baroque (p. 378)

Suggestions for Further Reading

GENERAL WORKS For general works on the seventeenth century, see **T. Munck, *Seventeenth-Century Europe, 1598–1700***, 2d ed. (London, 2005); **Q. Deakin, *Expansion, War, and Rebellion, 1598–1661*** (Cambridge, 2000); and **J. Bergin, *Seventeenth-Century Europe, 1598–1715*** (Oxford, 2001).

WITCHCRAFT CRAZE The story of the witchcraft craze can be examined in **R. Briggs, *Witches and Neighbors: The Social and Cultural Context of European Witchcraft***, 2d ed. (Oxford, 2002).

THIRTY YEARS' WAR   The fundamental study on the Thirty Years' War is **P. H. Wilson, *The Thirty Years War: Europe's Tragedy*** (Cambridge, Mass., 2009). For a brief study, see **R. Bonney, *The Thirty Years' War, 1618–1648*** (Oxford, 2002).

FRANCE AND SPAIN   For a succinct account of seventeenth-century French history, see **R. Briggs, *Early Modern France, 1560–1715,*** 2d ed. (Oxford, 1998). A solid and very readable biography of Louis XIV is **A. Levi, *Louis XIV*** (New York, 2004). A good general work on seventeenth-century Spanish history is **J. Lynch, *Spain Under the Habsburgs,*** 2d ed. (New York, 1981).

CENTRAL AND EASTERN EUROPE   On the German states, see **P. H. Wilson, *The Holy Roman Empire, 1495–1806*** (New York, 1999). On the creation of Austria, see **P. S. Fichtner, *The Habsburg Monarchy, 1490–1848*** (New York, 2003). On Austria and Prussia, see **P. H. Wilson, *Absolutism in Central Europe*** (New York, 2000).

RUSSIA   On Peter the Great, see **P. Bushkovitz, *Peter the Great*** (Oxford, 2001).

ENGLISH REVOLUTIONS   Good general works on the period of the English Revolution include **M. A. Kishlansky, *A Monarchy Transformed*** (London, 1996), and **D. Purkiss, *The English Civil War*** (New York, 2006). On Oliver Cromwell, see **P. Gaunt, *Oliver Cromwell*** (Cambridge, Mass., 1996).

UNITED PROVINCES   On the United Provinces, **J. Israel, *The Dutch Republic: Its Rise, Greatness, and Fall*** (New York, 1995), is a valuable but lengthy study.

EUROPEAN CULTURE   For an introduction to Baroque culture, see **F. C. Marchetti et al., *Baroque, 1600–1770*** (New York, 2005). For a biography of Shakespeare, see **S. Greenblatt, *Will in the World: How Shakespeare Became Shakespeare*** (New York, 2005).

Notes

1. Quoted in J. Klaits, *Servants of Satan: The Age of the Witch Hunts* (Bloomington, Ind., 1985), p. 68.
2. Quoted in ibid., p. 68.
3. Quoted in Peter H. Wilson, *The Thirty Years War: Europe's Tragedy* (Cambridge, Mass., 2009), p. 783.
4. Quoted in J. B. Wolf, *Louis XIV* (New York, 1968), p. 134.
5. Quoted in J. H. Elliot, *Imperial Spain, 1469–1716* (New York, 1963), p. 306.

MindTap   **MindTap** is a fully online, highly personalized learning experience built upon Cengage Learning content. MindTap combines student learning tools—readings, multimedia, activities, and assessments—into a singular Learning Path that guides students through the course.

Toward a New Heaven and a New Earth: The Scientific Revolution and the Emergence of Modern Science

A nineteenth-century painting of Galileo before the Holy Office in the Vatican in 1633

Louvre, Paris/Erich Lessing/Art Resource, NY

CHAPTER OUTLINE AND FOCUS QUESTIONS

> **CRITICAL THINKING**
> Q In what ways were the intellectual, political, social, and religious developments of the seventeenth century related?
>
> **CONNECTIONS TO TODAY**
> Q What scientific discoveries of the twentieth and twenty-first centuries have had as great an impact on society as those of the Scientific Revolution?

IN ADDITION TO the political, economic, social, and international crises of the seventeenth century, we need to add an intellectual one. The Scientific Revolution questioned and ultimately challenged conceptions and beliefs about the nature of the external world and reality that had crystallized into a rather strict orthodoxy by the later Middle Ages. Derived from the works of ancient Greeks and Romans and grounded in Christian thought, the medieval worldview had become formidable. But the breakdown of Christian unity during the Reformation and the subsequent religious wars had created an environment in which Europeans became more comfortable with challenging both the ecclesiastical and the political realms. Should it surprise us that a challenge to intellectual authority soon followed?

The Scientific Revolution taught Europeans to view the universe and their place in it in a new way. The shift from an earth-centered to a sun-centered cosmos had an emotional as well as an intellectual effect on those who understood it. Thus, the Scientific Revolution, popularized in the eighteenth-century Enlightenment, stands as the major force in the transition to the largely secular, rational, and materialistic perspective that has defined the modern Western mentality since its full acceptance in the nineteenth and twentieth centuries.

The transition to a new worldview was far from easy, however. In the seventeenth century, the Italian scientist Galileo Galilei (gal-li-LAY-oh GAL-li-lay), an outspoken advocate of the new worldview, found that his ideas were strongly opposed by the authorities of the Catholic Church. Galileo's position was clear: "I hold the sun to be situated motionless in the center of the revolution of the celestial bodies, while the earth rotates on its axis and revolves about the sun." Moreover, "nothing physical that sense-experience sets before our eyes … ought to be called in question (much less condemned) upon the testimony of biblical passages." But the church had a different view, and in 1633, Galileo, now sixty-eight and in ill health, was called before the dreaded Inquisition in Rome. He was kept waiting for two months before he was tried and found guilty of heresy and disobedience. Completely shattered by the experience, he denounced his errors: "With a sincere heart and unfeigned faith I curse and detest the said errors and heresies contrary to the Holy Church." Legend holds that when he left the trial room, Galileo muttered to himself: "And yet it does move!" In any case, Galileo had been silenced, but his writings remained, and they spread throughout Europe. The Inquisition had failed to stop the new ideas of the Scientific Revolution.

In one sense, the Scientific Revolution was not a revolution. It was not characterized by the explosive change and rapid overthrow of traditional authority that we normally associate with the word *revolution*. The Scientific Revolution did overturn centuries of authority, but only in a gradual and piecemeal fashion. Nevertheless, its results were truly revolutionary. The Scientific Revolution was a key factor in setting Western civilization along its modern secular and material path.

Background to the Scientific Revolution

Q **Focus Question:** What developments during the Middle Ages and the Renaissance contributed to the Scientific Revolution of the seventeenth century?

To say that the **Scientific Revolution** brought about a dissolution of the medieval worldview is not to say that the Middle Ages was a period of scientific ignorance. Many educated Europeans took an intense interest in the world around them; it was, after all, "God's handiwork" and therefore an appropriate subject for study. Late medieval scholastic philosophers had advanced mathematical and physical thinking in many ways, but the subjection of these thinkers to a strict theological framework and their unquestioning reliance on a few ancient authorities, especially Aristotle and Galen, limited where they could go. Many "natural philosophers," as medieval scientists were called, preferred refined logical analysis to systematic observations of the natural world. A number of changes and advances in the fifteenth and sixteenth centuries may have played a major role in helping the "natural philosophers" abandon their old views and develop new ones.

Ancient Authors and Renaissance Artists

The Renaissance humanists mastered both Greek and Latin and made available new works of Ptolemy and Archimedes as well as Plato. These writings made it apparent that even the unquestioned authorities of the Middle Ages, Aristotle and Galen, had been contradicted by other thinkers. The desire to discover which school of thought was correct stimulated new scientific work that sometimes led to a complete rejection of the classical authorities.

Renaissance artists have also been credited with making an impact on scientific study. Their desire to imitate nature led them to rely on a close observation of nature. Their accurate renderings of rocks, plants, animals, and human anatomy established new standards for the study of natural phenomena. At the same time, the "scientific" study of the problems of perspective and correct anatomical proportions led to new insights. "No painter," one Renaissance artist declared, "can paint well without a thorough knowledge of geometry."[1]

Technological Innovations and Mathematics

Technical problems such as accurately calculating the tonnage of ships also stimulated scientific activity because they required careful observation and precise measurements. Then, too, the invention of new instruments and machines, such as the telescope and microscope, often made new scientific discoveries possible. The printing press had an indirect but crucial role in spreading innovative ideas quickly and easily.

Mathematics, so fundamental to the scientific achievements of the sixteenth and seventeenth centuries, was promoted in the Renaissance by the rediscovery of the works of ancient mathematicians and the influence of Plato, who had emphasized the importance of mathematics in explaining the universe. Applauded as the key to navigation, military science, and geography, mathematics was also regarded as the key to understanding the nature of things. According to Leonardo da Vinci, since God eternally geometrizes, nature is inherently mathematical: "Proportion is not only found in numbers and measurements but also in sounds, weights, times, positions, and in whatsoever power there may be."[2] Copernicus, Kepler, Galileo, and Newton were all great mathematicians who believed that the secrets of nature were written in the language of mathematics.

Renaissance Magic

Another factor in the Scientific Revolution may have been magic. Renaissance magic was the preserve of an intellectual elite from all of Europe. By the end of the sixteenth century, Hermetic magic had become fused with alchemical thought into a single intellectual framework. This tradition believed that the world was a living embodiment of divinity and that humans also had that spark of divinity within and could use magic, especially mathematical magic, to understand and dominate the world of nature or employ the powers of nature for beneficial purposes. Was it Hermeticism, then, that inaugurated the shift in consciousness that made the Scientific Revolution possible, since the desire to control and dominate the natural world was a crucial motivating force in the Scientific Revolution? Scholars debate the issue, but histories of the Scientific Revolution frequently overlook the fact that the great names we associate with the revolution in cosmology—Copernicus, Kepler, Galileo, and Newton—all had a serious interest in Hermetic ideas and the fields of astrology and alchemy. The mention of these names also reminds us of one final consideration in the origins of the Scientific Revolution: it resulted largely from the work of a handful of great intellectuals.

Toward a New Heaven: A Revolution in Astronomy

Q **Focus Question:** What did Copernicus, Kepler, Galileo, and Newton contribute to a new vision of the universe, and how did it differ from the Ptolemaic conception of the universe?

The cosmological views of the later Middle Ages had been built on a synthesis of the ideas of Aristotle, Ptolemy (the greatest astronomer of antiquity, who lived in the second century C.E.), and Christian theology. In the resulting Ptolemaic (tahl-uh-MAY-ik) or **geocentric** (earth-centered) **conception**, the universe was seen as a series of concentric spheres with a fixed or motionless earth at its center. Composed of material substance, the earth was imperfect and constantly changing. The spheres that surrounded the earth were made of a crystalline, transparent substance and moved in circular orbits around the earth. Circular movement, according to Aristotle, was the most "perfect" kind of motion and hence appropriate for the "perfect" heavenly bodies thought to consist of a non-material, incorruptible "quintessence." These heavenly bodies, pure orbs of light, were embedded in the moving, concentric spheres, which in 1500 were believed to number ten. Working outward from the earth, the first eight spheres contained the moon, Mercury, Venus, the sun, Mars, Jupiter, Saturn, and the fixed stars. The ninth sphere imparted to the eighth sphere of the fixed stars its motion, and the tenth sphere was frequently described as the prime mover that moved itself and imparted motion to the other spheres. Beyond the tenth sphere was the Empyrean Heaven—the location of God and all the saved souls. This Christianized Ptolemaic universe, then, was finite. It had a fixed outer boundary in harmony with Christian thought and expectations. God and the saved souls were at one end of the universe, and humans were at the center. They had been given power over the earth, but their real purpose was to achieve salvation.

Copernicus

Shortly before his death, Nicolaus Copernicus (nee-koh-LOW-uss kuh-PURR-nuh-kuss) (1473–1543), who had

Image Select/Art Resource, NY

Medieval Conception of the Universe.
As this sixteenth-century illustration shows, the medieval cosmological view placed the earth at the center of the universe, surrounded by a series of concentric spheres. The earth was imperfect and constantly changing, whereas the heavenly bodies that surrounded it were perfect and incorruptible. Beyond the tenth and final sphere was Heaven, where God and all the saved souls were located. (The circles read, from the center outward: 1. Moon, 2. Mercury, 3. Venus, 4. Sun, 5. Mars, 6. Jupiter, 7. Saturn, 8. Firmament (of the Stars), 9. Crystalline Sphere, 10. Prime Mover; and around the outside, Empyrean Heaven—Home of God and All the Elect, that is, saved souls.)

studied mathematics and astronomy first at Krakow in his native Poland and later at the Italian universities of Bologna and Padua, published his famous book *On the Revolutions of the Heavenly Spheres.* Copernicus was not an accomplished observational astronomer and relied for his data on the records of his predecessors. But he was a mathematician who felt that Ptolemy's geocentric system was too complicated and failed to accord with the observed motions of the heavenly bodies (see the box on p. 390). Copernicus hoped that his **heliocentric** (sun-centered) **conception** would offer a more accurate explanation.

Copernicus argued that the universe consisted of eight spheres with the sun motionless at the center and the sphere of the fixed stars at rest in the eighth sphere. The planets revolved around the sun in the order of Mercury, Venus, the earth, Mars, Jupiter, and Saturn. The moon, however, revolved around the earth. Moreover, according to Copernicus, what appeared to be the movement of the sun and the fixed stars around the earth was really explained by the daily rotation of

the earth on its axis and the journey of the earth around the sun each year.

The heliocentric theory had little immediate impact; most people were not yet ready to accept Copernicus's thinking. But doubts about the Ptolemaic system were growing. The German scientist Johannes Kepler took the next step in destroying the geocentric conception and supporting the Copernican system.

Kepler

The work of Johannes Kepler (1571–1630) illustrates the narrow line that often separated magic and science in the early Scientific Revolution. An avid astrologer, Kepler possessed a keen interest in Hermetic thought and mathematical magic. In a book written in 1596, he elaborated on his theory that the universe was constructed on the basis of geometric figures, such as the pyramid and the cube. Believing that the harmony of the human soul (a divine attribute) was mirrored in

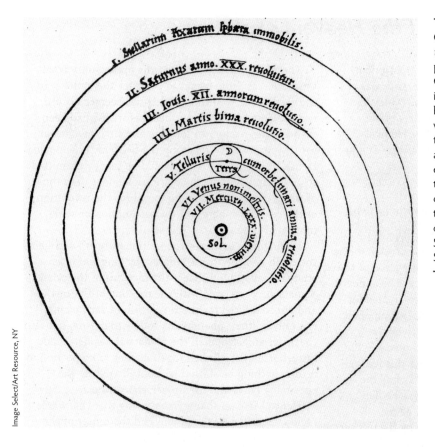

The Copernican System. The Copernican system was presented in *On the Revolutions of the Heavenly Spheres*, published in 1543 shortly before Copernicus's death. As shown in this illustration from the first edition of the book, Copernicus maintained that the sun was at the center of the universe and that the planets, including the earth, revolved around it. Moreover, the earth rotated daily on its axis. (The circles read, from the center outward: 1. Sun; 2. Mercury, orbit of 80 days; 3. Venus; 4. Earth, with the moon, orbit of 1 year; 5. Mars, orbit of 2 years; 6. Jupiter, orbit of 12 years; 7. Saturn, orbit of 30 years; 8. Immobile Sphere of the Fixed Stars.)

the numerical relationships existing between the planets, he focused much of his attention on discovering the "music of the spheres." Kepler was also a brilliant mathematician and astronomer who took a post as imperial mathematician to Emperor Rudolf II. Using the detailed astronomical data compiled by his predecessor, Kepler derived laws of planetary motion that confirmed the heliocentric theory. In his first law, he contradicted Copernicus by showing that the orbits of the planets around the sun were not circular but elliptical, with the sun at one focus of the ellipse rather than at the center.

Kepler's work effectively eliminated the idea of uniform circular motion as well as the idea of crystalline spheres revolving in circular orbits. The basic structure of the traditional Ptolemaic system had been disproved, and people had been freed to think in new ways of the paths of planets revolving around the sun. By the end of Kepler's life, the Ptolemaic system was rapidly losing ground to the new ideas. Important questions remained unanswered, however. What were the planets made of? And how could

motion in the universe be explained? It was an Italian scientist who achieved the next important breakthrough to a new cosmology by answering the first question.

Galileo

Galileo Galilei (1564–1642) taught mathematics, first at Pisa and later at Padua, one of the most prestigious universities in Europe. Galileo was the first European to make systematic observations of the heavens by means of a telescope, thereby inaugurating a new age in astronomy. He had heard of a Flemish lens grinder who had created a "spyglass" that magnified objects seen at a distance and soon constructed his own. Instead of peering at terrestrial objects, Galileo turned his telescope to the skies and made a remarkable series of discoveries: mountains and craters on the moon, four moons revolving around Jupiter, the phases of Venus, and sunspots. Galileo's observations demolished yet another aspect of the traditional cosmology in that the universe seemed to be composed of a material

On the Revolutions of the Heavenly Spheres

Nicolaus Copernicus began a revolution in astronomy when he argued that the sun and not the earth was at the center of the universe. Expecting controversy and scorn, Copernicus hesitated to publish the work in which he put forth his heliocentric theory. He finally relented, however, and managed to see a copy of it just before he died.

Nicolaus Copernicus, *On the Revolutions of the Heavenly Spheres*

For a long time, then, I reflected on this confusion in the astronomical traditions concerning the derivation of the motions of the universe's spheres. I began to be annoyed that the movements of the world machine, created for our sake by the best and most systematic Artisan of all, were not understood with greater certainty by the philosophers, who otherwise examined so precisely the most insignificant trifles of this world. For this reason I undertook the task of rereading the works of all the philosophers which I could obtain to learn whether anyone had ever proposed other motions of the universe's spheres than those expounded by the teachers of astronomy in the schools. And in fact first I found in Cicero that Hicetas supposed the earth to move. Later I also discovered in Plutarch that certain others were of this opinion. I have decided to set his words down here, so that they may be available to everybody:

> Some think that the earth remains at rest. But Philolaus the Pythagorean believes that, like the sun and moon, it revolves around the fire in an oblique circle. Heraclides of Pontus and Ecphantus the Pythagorean make the earth move, not in a progressive motion, but like a wheel in a rotation from the west to east about its own center.

Therefore, having obtained the opportunity from these sources, I too began to consider the mobility of the earth. And even though the idea seemed absurd, nevertheless I know that others before me had been granted the freedom to imagine any circles whatever for the purpose of explaining the heavenly phenomena. Hence I thought that I too would be readily permitted to ascertain whether explanations sounder than those of my predecessors could be found for the revolution of the celestial spheres on the assumption of some motion of the earth.

Having thus assumed the motions which I ascribe to the earth later on in the volume, by long and intense study I finally found that if the motions of the other planets are correlated with the orbiting of the earth, and are computed for the revolution of each planet, not only do their phenomena follow therefrom but also the order and size of all the planets and spheres, and heaven itself is so linked together that in no portion of it can anything be shifted without disrupting the remaining parts and the universe as a whole....

Hence I feel no shame in asserting that this whole region engirdled by the moon, and the center of the earth, traverse this grand circle amid the rest of the planets in an annual revolution around the sun. Near the sun is the center of the universe. Moreover, since the sun remains stationary, whatever appears as a motion of the sun is really due rather to the motion of the earth.

Q What major new ideas did Copernicus discuss in this excerpt? What was the source of these ideas? Why might one say that European astronomers finally destroyed the Middle Ages?

Source: From *The Collected Works* by Copernicus, translated by Edward Rosen. Rev. ed. published 1978 by Palgrave Macmillan. Reproduced with permission of Palgrave Macmillan.

substance similar to that of earth rather than of ethereal or perfect and unchanging substances.

Galileo's revelations, published in *The Starry Messenger* in 1610, stunned his contemporaries and probably did more to make Europeans aware of the new picture of the universe than the mathematical theories of Copernicus and Kepler. But his newfound acclaim brought Galileo under the increasing scrutiny of the Catholic Church. The Roman Inquisition (or Holy Office) of the church condemned Copernicanism and ordered Galileo to reject the Copernican thesis. The Inquisition's report insisted that "the doctrine that the sun was the center of the world and immovable was false and absurd, formally heretical and contrary to Scripture, whereas the doctrine that the earth was not the center of the world but moved, and has further a daily motion, was

The Telescope. The invention of the telescope enabled Europeans to inaugurate a new age in astronomy. Shown here is Johannes Hevelius, an eminent German-Polish astrologer (1611–1697), making an observation with his telescope. Hevelius's observations were highly regarded. He located his telescope on the roof of his own house, and by the 1660s, his celestial observatory was considered one of the best in Europe. The inset shows a photograph of Galileo's original telescope, built in 1609.

philosophically false and absurd and theologically at least erroneous."[3] Thus, the church attacked the Copernican system because it threatened not only Scripture but also the entire prevailing conception of the universe (see the box on p. 392). The heavens were no longer a spiritual world but a world of matter. Humans were no longer at the center, and God was no longer in a specific place. All this the church found intolerable. In 1633, Galileo was found guilty of teaching the condemned Copernican system and was forced to recant his "errors."

The condemnation of Galileo by the Inquisition, coming at a time of economic decline, seriously undermined further scientific work in Italy, which had been at the forefront of scientific innovation. Leadership in science now passed to the northern countries, especially England, France, and the Dutch Netherlands. By the 1630s and 1640s, no reasonable astronomer could overlook that Galileo's discoveries, combined with Kepler's mathematical laws, had made nonsense of the Ptolemaic-Aristotelian world system and clearly established the reasonableness of the Copernican model. Nevertheless, the problem of explaining motion in the universe and tying together the ideas of Copernicus, Galileo, and Kepler had not yet been solved. This would be the work of an Englishman who has long been considered the greatest genius of the Scientific Revolution.

Newton

Born in the English village of Woolsthorpe, Isaac Newton (1642–1727) at first showed little promise. Then he attended Cambridge University, and in 1669 he accepted a chair in mathematics at the university. During an intense period of creativity from 1684 to 1686, he wrote his major work, *Mathematical Principles of Natural Philosophy*, known simply as the *Principia* (prin-SIP-ee-uh), from the first word of its Latin title. In this work, Newton spelled out the mathematical proofs demonstrating his universal law of gravitation. Newton's work was the culmination of the theories of Copernicus, Kepler, and Galileo. Though each had undermined some part of the Ptolemaic-Aristotelian cosmology, no one until Newton had pieced together a coherent synthesis for a new cosmology.

A New Heaven? Faith Versus Reason

In 1614, Galileo wrote a letter to the Grand Duchess Christina of Tuscany in which he explained why his theory that the earth rotated around the sun was not necessarily contrary to Scripture. To Galileo, it made little sense for the church to determine the nature of physical reality on the basis of biblical texts that were subject to different interpretations. One year later, Cardinal Robert Bellarmine, a Jesuit and now a member of the church's Inquisition, wrote a letter to one of Galileo's followers that laid out the Roman Catholic Church's approach to the issue of Galileo's theory.

Galileo, Letter to the Grand Duchess Christina, 1614

Some years ago, as Your Serene Highness well knows, I discovered in the heavens many things that had not been seen before our own age. The novelty of these things, as well as some consequences which followed from them in contradiction to the physical notions commonly held among academic philosophers, stirred up against me no small number of professors—as if I had placed these things in the sky with my own hands in order to upset nature and overturn the sciences....

Contrary to the sense of the Bible and the intention of the holy Fathers, if I am not mistaken, they would extend such authorities until even in purely physical matters—where faith is not involved—they would have us altogether abandon reason and the evidence of our senses in favor of some biblical passage, though under the surface meaning of its words this passage may contain a different sense....

The reason produced for condemning the opinion that the earth moves and the sun stands still is that in many places in the Bible one may read that the sun moves and the earth stands still. Since the Bible cannot err, it follows as a necessary consequence that anyone takes an erroneous and heretical position who maintains that the sun is inherently motionless and the earth movable.

With regard to this argument, I think in the first place that it is very pious to say and prudent to affirm that the holy Bible can never speak untruth—whenever its true meaning is understood. But I believe nobody will deny that it is often very abstruse, and may say things which are quite different from what its bare words signify.... For the sake of those who deserve to be separated from the herd, it is necessary that wise expositors should produce the true senses of such passages, together with the special reasons for which they were set down in these words....

This being granted, I think that in discussions of physical problems we ought to begin not from the authority of scriptural passages, but from sense-experiences and necessary demonstrations.... For that reason it appears that nothing physical which sense-experience sets before our eyes, or which necessary demonstrations prove to us, ought to be called in question (much less condemned) upon the testimony of biblical passages which may have some different meaning beneath their words.

Robert Bellarmine, Letter to Paolo Foscarini, 1615

First, I say that it seems to me that Your Reverence and Galileo did prudently to content yourself with speaking hypothetically, and not absolutely, as I have always believed that Copernicus spoke. For to say that, assuming the earth moves and the sun stands still, all the appearances are saved better than with eccentrics and epicycles, is to speak well; there is no danger in this, and it is sufficient for mathematicians. But to want to affirm that the sun really is fixed in the center of the heavens and only revolves around itself (i.e., turns upon its axis) without traveling from east to west, and that the earth is situated in the third sphere and revolves with great speed around the sun, is a very dangerous thing, not only by irritating all the philosophers and scholastic theologians, but also by injuring our holy faith and rendering the Holy Scriptures false....

Second, I say that, as you know, the Council [of Trent] prohibits expounding the Scriptures contrary to the common agreement of the holy Fathers. And if Your Reverence would read not only the Fathers but also the commentaries of modern writers on Genesis,

Psalms, Ecclesiastes and Josue, you would find that all agree in explaining literally (*ad litteram*) that the sun is in the heavens and moves swiftly around the earth, and that the earth is far from the heavens and stands immobile in the center of the universe. Now consider whether in all prudence the Church could encourage giving to Scripture a sense contrary to the holy Fathers and all the Latin and Greek commentators.... Third, I say that if there were a true demonstration that the sun was in the center of the universe and the earth in the third sphere, and that the sun did not travel around the earth but the earth circled the sun, then it would be necessary to proceed with great caution in explaining the passages of Scripture which seemed contrary, and we would rather have to say that we did not understand them than to say that something was false which has been demonstrated. But I do not believe that there is any such demonstration; none has been shown to me.

Q What did Galileo think was the difference between knowledge about the natural world and knowledge about the spiritual world? What did Galileo suggest that his opponents should do before dismissing his ideas? In what ways did Cardinal Bellarmine attempt to refute Galileo's ideas? Why did Galileo's ideas represent a threat to the Catholic Church?

Sources: Galileo, Letter to the Grand Duchess Christina, 1614. From *Discoveries and Opinions of Galileo* by Galileo Galilei, translated by Stillman Drake, copyright ©1957 by Stillman Drake. Used by permission of Doubleday, a division of Random House, Inc. Robert Bellarmine, Letter to Paolo Foscarini, 1615. From *Galileo, Science, and the Church* by Jerome J. Langford (New York: Desclee, 1966).

In the first book of the *Principia*, Newton defined the basic concepts of mechanics by elaborating the three laws of motion: every object continues in a state of rest or uniform motion in a straight line unless deflected by a force; the rate of change of motion of an object is proportional to the force acting on it; and to every action there is always an equal and opposite reaction. In book 3, Newton applied his theories of mechanics to the problems of astronomy by demonstrating that these three laws of motion govern the planetary bodies as well as terrestrial objects. Integral to his whole argument was the universal law of gravitation, which explained why the planetary bodies did not go off in straight lines but continued in elliptical orbits about the sun. In mathematical terms, Newton explained that every object in the universe was attracted to every other object with a force (gravity) that is directly proportional to the product of their masses and inversely proportional to the square of the distances between them.

The implications of Newton's universal law of gravitation were enormous, even though another century would pass before they were widely recognized. Newton had demonstrated that one universal law, mathematically proved, could explain all motion in the universe, from the movements of the planets in the celestial world to an apple falling from a tree in the terrestrial world. At the same time, the Newtonian synthesis created a new cosmology in which the world was seen largely in mechanistic terms. The universe was one huge, regulated, and uniform machine that operated according to natural laws in absolute time, space, and motion. Although Newton believed that God was "everywhere present" and acted as the force that moved all bodies on the basis of the laws he had discovered, later generations dropped his spiritual assumptions. Newton's **world-machine**, conceived as operating absolutely in space, time, and motion, dominated the modern worldview until the twentieth century, when the Einsteinian revolution, based on the concept of relativity, superseded the Newtonian mechanistic concept.

Newton's ideas were soon accepted in England but were resisted on the continent, and it took much of the eighteenth century before they were generally accepted everywhere in Europe. They were also reinforced by developments in other fields, especially medicine.

Advances in Medicine and Chemistry

Q FOCUS QUESTION: What did Vesalius, Harvey, Boyle, and Lavoisier contribute to a scientific view of medicine and chemistry?

Although the Scientific Revolution of the sixteenth and seventeenth centuries is associated primarily with the dramatic changes in astronomy and mechanics that precipitated a new perception of the universe, a third field that had been dominated by Greek thought in the later Middle Ages, that of medicine, also experienced a transformation. Late medieval medicine was dominated by the teachings of the Greek physician Galen, who had lived in the second century C.E.

Galen's influence on the medieval medical world was pervasive in anatomy, physiology, and disease. Galen had relied on animal, rather than human, dissection to arrive at a picture of human anatomy that was quite inaccurate in many instances. Even when Europeans began to practice human dissection in the later Middle Ages, instruction in anatomy still relied on Galen. While a professor read a text of Galen, an assistant dissected a cadaver for illustrative purposes. Physiology, or the functioning of the body, was also dominated by Galenic hypotheses, including the belief that there were two separate blood systems. One controlled muscular activities and contained bright red blood moving upward and downward through the arteries; the other governed the digestive functions and contained dark red blood that ebbed and flowed in the veins.

Vesalius

Two major figures are associated with the changes in medicine in the sixteenth and seventeenth centuries: Andreas Vesalius and William Harvey. The new anatomy of the sixteenth century was the work of the Belgian Andreas Vesalius (ahn-DRAY-ahs vi-SAY-lee-uss) (1514–1564). After receiving a doctorate in medicine at the University of Padua in 1536, Vesalius accepted a position there as professor of surgery and in 1543 published his masterpiece, *On the Fabric of the Human Body*. This book was based on his Paduan lectures, in which he deviated from traditional practice by personally dissecting a body to illustrate what he was discussing. Vesalius's anatomical treatise, which presented a careful examination of the individual organs and general structure of the human body, would not have been feasible without the artistic advances of the Renaissance and the technical developments in the art of printing. Together, they made possible the creation of illustrations superior to any hitherto produced.

Vesalius's hands-on approach to teaching anatomy enabled him to rectify some of Galen's most glaring errors. He did not hesitate, for example, to correct Galen's assertion that the great blood vessels originated from the liver, since his own observations made it apparent that they came from the heart. Nevertheless, Vesalius still clung to a number of Galen's erroneous assertions, including the Greek physician's ideas on the ebb and flow of two kinds of blood in the veins and

arteries. It was not until William Harvey's work on the circulation of the blood nearly a century later that this Galenic misperception was corrected.

Harvey

The Englishman William Harvey (1578–1657) attended Cambridge University and later Padua, where he earned a doctorate in medicine in 1602. His reputation rests on his book *On the Motion of the Heart and Blood*, published in 1628. Although questions had been raised in the sixteenth century about Galen's physiological principles, no major challenge to his system had emerged. Harvey's work, based on meticulous observations and experiments, led him to demolish the ancient Greek's contentions. Harvey demonstrated that the heart was the beginning point of the circulation of blood in the body, that the same blood flows in both veins and arteries, and that the blood makes a complete circuit as it passes through the body. Although Harvey's work dealt a severe blow to Galen's theories, his ideas did not begin to achieve general recognition until the 1660s, when the capillaries, which explained how the blood passed from the arteries to the veins, were discovered. Harvey's theory of the circulation of the blood laid the foundation for modern physiology.

Chemistry

In the seventeenth and eighteenth centuries, a science of chemistry emerged. Robert Boyle (1627–1691), one of the first scientists to conduct controlled experiments, did pioneering work on the properties of gases. His efforts led to Boyle's law, which states that the volume of a gas varies with the pressure exerted on it. Boyle also rejected the medieval belief that all matter consisted of the same components in favor of the view that matter is composed of atoms, which he called "little particles of all shapes and sizes" and which would later be known as the chemical elements.

In the eighteenth century, the Frenchman Antoine Lavoisier (AHN-twahn lah-vwah-ZYAY) (1743–1794) invented a system of naming the chemical elements, much of which is still used today. In helping to show that water is a compound of oxygen and hydrogen, he demonstrated the fundamental rules of chemical combination. He is regarded by many as the founder of modern chemistry. Lavoisier's wife, Marie-Anne, was her husband's scientific collaborator. She learned English in order to translate the work of British chemists for her husband and made engravings to illustrate his scientific experiments. Marie-Anne Lavoisier is a reminder that women too played a role in the Scientific Revolution.

Women in the Origins of Modern Science

Q Focus Question: What role did women play in the Scientific Revolution?

During the Middle Ages, except for members of religious orders, women who sought a life of learning were severely hampered by the traditional attitude that a woman's proper role was as a daughter, wife, and mother. But in the late fourteenth and early fifteenth centuries, new opportunities for elite women emerged as enthusiasm for the new secular learning called humanism led Europe's privileged and learned men to encourage women to read and study classical and Christian texts. The ideal of a humanist education for some of the daughters of Europe's elite persisted into the seventeenth century, but only for some privileged women.

Margaret Cavendish

Much as they were drawn to humanism, women were also attracted to the Scientific Revolution. Unlike girls educated formally in humanist schools, women interested in science had to obtain a largely informal education. European nobles had the leisure and resources that gave them easy access to the world of learning. This door was also open to noblewomen, who could participate in the informal scientific networks of their fathers and brothers.

One of the most prominent female scientists of the seventeenth century, Margaret Cavendish (KAV-un-dish) (1623–1673), was not a popularizer of science for women but was able to participate in the crucial scientific debates of her time because of her aristocratic background. Despite her achievements, however, she was excluded from membership in the Royal Society (see "The Spread of Scientific Knowledge" later in this chapter), although she was once allowed to attend a meeting. She wrote a number of works on scientific matters, including *Observations upon Experimental Philosophy* and *Grounds of Natural Philosophy*. In these works, she did not hesitate to attack what she considered the defects of the rationalist and empiricist approaches to scientific knowledge and was especially critical of the growing belief that humans through science were the masters of nature: "We have no power at all over natural causes and effects ... for man is but a small part.... His powers are but particular actions of Nature, and he cannot have a supreme and absolute power."[4]

As an aristocrat, Cavendish, the duchess of Newcastle, was a good example of the women in France and England who worked in science (see the box on p. 396). Women interested in science who lived in Germany came from a different background. There the tradition of female participation in craft production enabled some women to become involved in observational science, especially astronomy. Between 1650 and 1710, one in every seven German astronomers was a woman.

Maria Winkelmann

The most famous of the female astronomers in Germany, Maria Winkelmann (VINK-ul-mahn) (1670–1720), was educated by her father and uncle and received advanced training from a local self-taught astronomer. When she married Gottfried Kirch, Germany's foremost astronomer, she became his assistant at the astronomical observatory operated in Berlin by the Academy of Science. Here she made some original contributions, including the sighting of a hitherto undiscovered comet, as her husband related:

> Early in the morning (about 2:00 A.M.) the sky was clear and starry. Some nights before, I had observed a variable star, and my wife (as I slept) wanted to find and see it for herself. In so doing, she found a comet in the sky. At which time she woke me, and I found that it was indeed a comet.... I was surprised that I had not seen it the night before.[5]

When her husband died in 1710, she applied for a position as assistant astronomer. Although highly

CHRONOLOGY Important Works of the Scientific Revolution	
Copernicus, *On the Revolutions of the Heavenly Spheres*	1543
Vesalius, *On the Fabric of the Human Body*	1543
Galileo, *The Starry Messenger*	1610
Harvey, *On the Motion of the Heart and Blood*	1628
Cavendish, *Grounds of Natural Philosophy*	1668
Newton, *Principia*	1687

Margaret Cavendish: The Education of Women

Margaret Cavendish's husband, who was thirty years her senior, encouraged her to pursue her literary interests. In addition to scientific works, she wrote plays, an autobiography, and a biography of her husband titled *The Life of the Thrice Noble, High and Puissant Prince William Cavendish, Duke, Marquess and Earl of Newcastle*. The autobiography and biography led one male literary critic to call her "a mad, conceited and ridiculous woman." In an essay titled "The Philosophical and Physical Opinions," she discussed the constraints placed upon women, including education.

Margaret Cavendish, "The Philosophical and Physical Opinions"

But to answer those objections that are made against me, as first how should I come by so much experience as I have expressed in my several books to have? I answer: I have had by relation the long and much experience of my lord, who hath lived to see and be in many changes of fortune and to converse with many men of sundry nations, ages, qualities, tempers, capacities, abilities, wits, humours, fashions and customs.

And as many others, especially wives, go from church to church, from ball to ball, . . . gossiping from house to house, so when my lord admits me to his company I listen with attention to his edifying discourse and I govern myself by his doctrine: I dance a measure with the muses, feast with sciences, or sit and discourse with the arts.

The second is that, since I am no scholar, I cannot know the names and terms of art and the divers and several opinions of several authors. I answer: that I must have been a natural fool if I had not known and learnt them, for they are customarily taught all children from the nurse's breast, being ordinarily discoursed of in every family that is of quality, and the family from whence I sprung are neither natural idiots or ignorant fools, but the contrary, for they were rational, learned, understanding and witty. . . .

But as I have said my head was so full of my own natural fantasies, as it had not room for strangers to board therein, and certainly natural reason is a better tutor than education. For though education doth help natural reason to a more sudden maturity, yet natural reason was the first educator: for natural reason did first compose commonwealths, invented arts and science, and if natural reason hath composed, invented and discovered, I know no reason but natural reason may find out what natural reason hath composed, invented and discovered with the help of education. . . .

Q What arguments does Cavendish make to defend her right and her ability to be an author?

Source: Kate Aughterson, *Renaissance Woman: A Sourcebook* (London and New York: Routledge, 1995), pp. 286–288.

---

qualified, she was a woman with no university degree, and she was denied the post by the Berlin Academy, which feared that it would establish a precedent if it hired a woman ("mouths would gape").

Winkelmann's difficulties with the Berlin Academy reflect the obstacles women faced in being accepted in scientific work, which was considered a male preserve. Although no formal statutes excluded women from membership in the new scientific societies, no woman was invited to join either the Royal Society of England or the French Academy of Sciences until the twentieth century. All of these women scientists were exceptional, since a life devoted to any kind of scholarship was still viewed as being at odds with the domestic duties women were expected to perform.

Debates on the Nature of Women

The nature and value of women had been the subject of an ongoing, centuries-long debate. Male opinions in the debate were largely a carryover from medieval times and were not favorable. Women were portrayed as inherently base, prone to vice, easily swayed, and "sexually insatiable." Hence, men needed to control them. Learned women were viewed as having overcome female liabilities to become like men. One man in praise of a woman scholar remarked that her writings

396   Chapter 16   Toward a New Heaven and a New Earth: The Scientific Revolution were so good that you "would hardly believe they were done by a woman at all."

In the seventeenth century, women joined this debate by arguing against these male images of women. They argued that women also had rational minds and could grow from education. Further, since most women were pious, chaste, and temperate, there was no need for male authority over them. These female defenders of women emphasized education as the key to women's ability to move into the world. How, then, did the Scientific Revolution affect this debate over the nature of women? As this was an era of intellectual revolution in which traditional authorities were being overthrown, we might expect significant change in men's views of women. But by and large, instead of becoming an instrument for liberation, science was used to find new support for the old, stereotypical views about a woman's "true place" in the scheme of things.

An important project in the new anatomy of the sixteenth and seventeenth centuries was the attempt to illustrate the human body and skeleton. For Vesalius, the physical differences between males and females were limited to external bodily form (the outlines of the body) and the sexual organs. Vesalius saw no differences in male and female skeletons and portrayed them as being the same. It was not until the eighteenth century, in fact, that a new anatomy finally prevailed. Drawings of female skeletons between 1730 and 1790 varied, but females tended to have a larger pelvic area, and in some instances, female skulls were portrayed as smaller than those of males. Eighteenth-century studies on the anatomy and physiology of sexual differences provided "scientific evidence" to reaffirm the traditional inferiority of women. The larger pelvic area "proved" that women were meant to be child-bearers, and men's larger skulls "demonstrated" the superiority of the male mind. Male-dominated science had been used to "prove" male social dominance.

Overall, the Scientific Revolution reaffirmed traditional ideas about women. Male scientists used the new science to spread the view that women were inferior by nature, subordinate to men, and suited by nature to play a domestic role as nurturing mothers. The widespread distribution of books—written primarily by men, of course—ensured the continuation of these ideas. Jean de La Bruyère (ZHAHNH du lah broo-YARE), the seventeenth-century French moralist, was typical when he remarked that an educated woman was like a collector's item "which one shows to the curious, but which has no use at all, any more than a carousel horse."[6]

Toward a New Earth: Descartes, Rationalism, and a New View of Humankind

Q Focus Question: Why is Descartes considered the "founder of modern rationalism"?

The fundamentally new conception of the universe contained in the cosmological revolution of the sixteenth and seventeenth centuries inevitably had an impact on the Western view of humankind. Nowhere is this more evident than in the work of the Frenchman René Descartes (ruh-NAY day-KART) (1596–1650), an extremely important figure in Western history. Descartes began by reflecting the doubt and uncertainty that seemed pervasive in the confusion of the seventeenth century and ended with a philosophy that dominated Western thought until the twentieth century.

René Descartes. René Descartes was one of the primary figures in the Scientific Revolution. Claiming to use reason as his sole guide to truth, Descartes posited a sharp distinction between mind and matter. He is shown here in a portrait by Frans Hals, one of the painters of the Dutch golden age who was famous for his portraits, especially that of Descartes.

The starting point for Descartes's new system was doubt, as he explained at the beginning of his most famous work, *Discourse on Method*, written in 1637:

> From my childhood I have been familiar with letters; and as I was given to believe that by their means a clear and assured knowledge can be acquired of all that is useful in life, I was extremely eager for instruction in them. As soon, however, as I had completed the course of study, at the close of which it is customary to be admitted into the order of the learned, I entirely changed my opinion. For I found myself entangled in so many doubts and errors that, as it seemed to me, the endeavor to instruct myself had served only to disclose to me more and more of my ignorance.[7]

Descartes decided to set aside all that he had learned and begin again. One fact seemed beyond doubt—his own existence:

> But I immediately became aware that while I was thus disposed to think that all was false, it was absolutely necessary that I who thus thought should be something; and noting that this truth *I think, therefore I am*, was so steadfast and so assured that the suppositions of the skeptics, to whatever extreme they might all be carried, could not avail to shake it, I concluded that I might without scruple accept it as being the first principle of the philosophy I was seeking.[8]

With this emphasis on the mind, Descartes asserted that he would accept only things that his reason said were true.

From his first postulate, Descartes deduced an additional principle, the separation of mind and matter. Descartes argued that since "the mind cannot be doubted but the body and material world can, the two must be radically different." From this came an absolute duality between mind and matter that has been called **Cartesian dualism**. Using mind or human reason, the path to certain knowledge, and its best instrument, mathematics, humans can understand the material world because it is pure mechanism, a machine that is governed by its own physical laws because it was created by God—the great geometrician.

Descartes's conclusions about the nature of the universe and human beings had important implications. His separation of mind and matter allowed scientists to view matter as dead or inert, as something that was totally separate from themselves and could be investigated independently by reason. The split between mind and body led Westerners to equate their identity with mind and reason rather than with the whole organism. Descartes has rightly been called the father of modern **rationalism**. The radical Cartesian split between mind and matter, and between mind and body, had devastating implications not only for traditional religious views of the universe but also for how Westerners viewed themselves.

The Spread of Scientific Knowledge

Q FOCUS QUESTION: How were the ideas of the Scientific Revolution spread, and what impact did they have on society and religion?

During the seventeenth century, scientific learning and investigation began to increase dramatically. Major universities in Europe established new chairs of science, especially in medicine, and royal and princely patronage of individual scientists became an international phenomenon. Of greater importance to the work of science, however, was the creation of a scientific method and new learned societies that enabled the new scientists to communicate their ideas to each other and to disseminate them to a wider, literate public.

The Scientific Method

In the course of the Scientific Revolution, attention was paid to the problem of establishing the proper means to examine and understand the physical realm. The development of a **scientific method** was crucial to the evolution of science in the modern world. Curiously enough, it was an Englishman with few scientific credentials who attempted to put forth a new method of acquiring knowledge that made an impact on English scientists in the seventeenth century and other European scientists in the eighteenth century. Francis Bacon (1561–1626), a lawyer and lord chancellor, rejected Copernicus and Kepler and misunderstood Galileo. And yet in his unfinished work *The Great Instauration (The Great Restoration)*, he called for his contemporaries "to commence a total reconstruction of sciences, arts, and all human knowledge, raised upon the proper foundations." Bacon did not doubt humans' ability to know the natural world, but he believed that they had proceeded incorrectly: "The entire fabric of human reason which we employ in the inquisition of nature is badly put together and built up, and like some magnificent structure without foundation."[9]

Bacon's new foundation—a correct scientific method—was to be built on inductive principles. Rather than beginning with assumed first principles from which logical conclusions could be deduced, he urged scientists to proceed from the particular to the general. From carefully organized experiments and systematic, thorough observations, correct generalizations could be developed. Bacon was clear about what he believed his method could accomplish. His concern was for practical results rather than for pure science. He stated that "the true and lawful goal of the sciences is none other than this: that human life be endowed with new discoveries and power." He wanted science to contribute to the "mechanical arts" by creating devices that would benefit industry, agriculture, and trade. Bacon was prophetic when he said that "I am laboring to lay the foundation, not of any sect or doctrine, but of human utility and power." And how would this "human power" be used? To "conquer nature in action."[10] The control and domination of nature became a central proposition of modern science and the technology that accompanied it. Only in the twentieth century did some scientists ask whether this assumption might not be at the heart of the earth's ecological crisis.

René Descartes proposed a different approach to scientific methodology by emphasizing deduction and mathematical logic. Descartes believed that one could start with self-evident truths, comparable to geometrical axioms, and deduce more complex conclusions. His emphasis on deduction and mathematical order complemented Bacon's stress on experiment and induction. It was Isaac Newton who synthesized the two approaches into a single scientific methodology by uniting Bacon's **empiricism** with Descartes's rationalism. This scientific method began with systematic observations and experiments, which were used to arrive at general concepts. New deductions derived from these general concepts could then be tested and verified by precise experiments.

The Scientific Societies

The first of the scientific societies appeared in Italy, but those of England and France were ultimately of more significance. The English Royal Society evolved out of informal gatherings of scientists at London and Oxford in the 1640s, although it did not receive a formal charter from King Charles II until 1662. The French Royal Academy of Sciences also arose out of informal scientific meetings in Paris during the 1650s and was formally recognized by Louis XIV in 1666. The French Academy received abundant state support and remained under government control, with its members being appointed and paid salaries by the state. In contrast, the Royal Society of England received little government encouragement, and its fellows simply co-opted new members.

Early on, both the English and French scientific societies formally emphasized the practical value of scientific research. The Royal Society created a committee to investigate technological improvements for industry; the French Academy collected tools and machines. This concern with the practical benefits of science proved short-lived, however, as both societies came to focus on theoretical work in mechanics and astronomy. The construction of observatories at Paris in 1667 and at

Louis XIV and Colbert Visit the Academy of Sciences. In the seventeenth century, individual scientists received royal and princely patronage, and a number of learned societies were established. In France, Louis XIV, urged on by his minister Colbert, gave formal recognition to the French Academy in 1666. In this painting by Henri Testelin, Louis XIV is shown seated, surrounded by Colbert and members of the French Royal Academy of Sciences.

Chateaux de Versailles et de Trianon (Gérard Blot), Versailles//© RMN-Grand Palais/Art Resource, NY

Greenwich, England, in 1675 greatly facilitated research in astronomy by both groups. Although both the English and French societies made useful contributions to scientific knowledge in the second half of the seventeenth century, their true significance was that they demonstrated the benefits of science proceeding as a cooperative venture.

Science and Society

The importance of science in the history of modern Western civilization is usually taken for granted. But how did science become such an integral part of Western culture in the seventeenth and early eighteenth centuries? Recent research has stressed that one cannot simply assert that people perceived that science was a rationally superior system. An important social factor, however, might help explain the relatively rapid acceptance of the new science.

It has been argued that the literate mercantile and propertied elites of Europe were attracted to the new science because it offered new ways to exploit resources for profit. Some of the early scientists made it easier for these groups to accept the new ideas by showing how they could be applied directly to specific industrial and technological needs. Galileo, for example, consciously sought an alliance between science and the material interests of the educated elite when he assured his listeners that the science of mechanics would be quite useful "when it becomes necessary to build bridges or other structures over water, something occurring mainly in affairs of great importance." Galileo also stressed that science was fit for the "minds of the wise" and not for "the shallow minds of the common people." This idea made science part of the high culture of Europe's wealthy elites at a time when that culture was being increasingly separated from the popular culture of the lower classes (see Chapter 17).

At the same time, princes and kings who were providing patronage for scientists were doing so not only for prestige but also for practical reasons, especially the military applications of the mathematical sciences. The use of gunpowder, for example, gave new importance to ballistics and metallurgy. Rulers, especially absolute ones, were also concerned about matters of belief in their realms and recognized the need to control and manage the scientific body of knowledge, as occurred with the French Academy. In appointing its members and paying their salaries, Louis XIV was also ensuring that the scientists and their work would be under his control.

Science and Religion

In Galileo's struggle with the inquisitorial Holy Office of the Catholic Church, we see the beginning of the conflict between science and religion that has marked the history of modern Western civilization. Since time immemorial, theology had seemed to be the queen of the sciences. It was natural that the churches would continue to believe that religion was the final measure of all things. The emerging scientists, however, tried to draw lines between the knowledge of religion and the knowledge of "natural philosophy" or nature. Galileo had clearly felt that it was unnecessary to pit science against religion when he wrote:

> In discussions of physical problems we ought to begin not from the authority of scriptural passages, but from sense-experiences and necessary demonstrations; for the holy Bible and the phenomena of nature proceed alike from the divine word, the former as the dictate of the Holy Ghost and the latter as the observant executrix of God's commands. It is necessary for the Bible, in order to be accommodated to the understanding of every man, to speak many things which appear to differ from the absolute truth so far as the bare meaning of the words is concerned. But Nature, on the other hand, is inexorable and immutable; she never transgresses the laws imposed upon her, or cares a whit whether her abstruse reasons and methods of operation are understandable to men.[11]

To Galileo, it made little sense for the church to determine the nature of physical reality on the basis of biblical texts that were subject to radically divergent interpretations. The church, however, decided otherwise in Galileo's case and lent its great authority to one scientific theory, the Ptolemaic-Aristotelian cosmology, no doubt because it fit so well with the church's philosophical views of reality. But the church's decision had tremendous consequences. For educated individuals, it established a dichotomy between scientific investigations and religious beliefs. As the scientific beliefs triumphed, it became almost inevitable that religious beliefs would suffer, leading to a growing secularization in European intellectual life. Many seventeenth-century intellectuals were both religious and scientific and believed that the implications of this split would be tragic. Some believed that the split was largely unnecessary, while others felt the need to combine God, humans, and a mechanistic universe into a new philosophical synthesis.

PASCAL Blaise Pascal (BLEZ pass-KAHL) (1623–1662) was a Frenchman who sought to keep science and religion united. An accomplished scientist and a brilliant mathematician, Pascal excelled at both the practical, by

Pascal: "What Is a Man in the Infinite?"

Perhaps no intellectual in the seventeenth century gave greater expression to the uncertainties generated by the cosmological revolution than Blaise Pascal, himself a scientist. Pascal's mystical vision of God's presence caused him to pursue religious truths with a passion. His work, the *Pensées*, consisted of notes for a larger, unfinished work justifying the Christian religion. In this selection, Pascal presents his musings on the human place in an infinite world.

Blaise Pascal, *Pensées*

Let man then contemplate the whole of nature in her full and exalted majesty. Let him turn his eyes from the lowly objects which surround him. Let him gaze on that brilliant light set like an eternal lamp to illumine the Universe; let the earth seem to him a dot compared with the vast orbit described by the sun, and let him wonder at the fact that this vast orbit itself is no more than a very small dot compared with that described by the stars in their revolutions around the firmament. But if our vision stops here, let the imagination pass on; it will exhaust its powers of thinking long before nature ceases to supply it with material for thought. All this visible world is no more than an imperceptible speck in nature's ample bosom. No idea approaches it. We may extend our conceptions beyond all imaginable space; yet produce only atoms in comparison with the reality of things. It is an infinite sphere, the center of which is everywhere, the circumference nowhere.

In short, it is the greatest perceptible mark of God's almighty power that our imagination should lose itself in that thought.

Returning to himself, let man consider what he is compared with all existence; let him think of himself as lost in his remote corner of nature; and from this little dungeon in which he finds himself lodged—I mean the Universe—let him learn to set a true value on the earth, its kingdoms, and cities, and upon himself. What is a man in the infinite? . . .

For, after all, what is a man in nature? A nothing in comparison with the infinite, an absolute in comparison with nothing, a central point between nothing and all. Infinitely far from understanding these extremes, the end of things and their beginning are hopelessly hidden from him in an impenetrable secret. He is equally incapable of seeing the nothingness from which he came, and the infinite in which he is engulfed. What else then will he perceive but some appearance of the middle of things, in an eternal despair of knowing either their principle or their purpose? All things emerge from nothing and are borne onward to infinity. Who can follow this marvelous process? The Author of these wonders understands them. None but He can.

Q Why did Pascal question whether human beings could achieve scientific certainty? What is the significance of Pascal's thoughts for modern science?

Source: From *Pensées* by Blaise Pascal, translated with an introduction by A. J. Krailsheimer (Penguin Classics, 1966). Copyright © A. J. Krailsheimer, 1966. Reproduced by permission of Penguin Books Ltd.

inventing a calculating machine, and the abstract, by devising a theory of chance or probability and doing work on conic sections. After a profound mystical vision on the night of November 23, 1654, which assured him that God cared for the human soul, he devoted the rest of his life to religious matters. He planned to write an "apology for the Christian religion" but died before he could do so. He did leave a set of notes for the larger work however, which in published form became known as the *Pensées* (pahn-SAY) (*Thoughts*).

In the *Pensées*, Pascal tried to convert rationalists to Christianity by appealing to both their reason and their emotions. Humans were, he argued, frail creatures, often deceived by their senses, misled by reason, and battered by their emotions. And yet they were beings whose very nature involved thinking: "Man is but a reed, the weakest in nature; but he is a thinking reed."[12]

Pascal was determined to show that the Christian religion was not contrary to reason: "If we violate the principles of reason, our religion will be absurd, and it will be laughed at."[13] To a Christian, a human being was both fallen and at the same time God's special creation. But it was not necessary to emphasize one at the expense of the other—to view humans as only rational or only hopeless. Pascal even had an answer for skeptics in his famous wager: God is a reasonable bet; it is worthwhile to assume that God exists. If he does, then we win all; if he does not, we lose nothing. Despite his own background as a scientist and mathematician, Pascal refused to rely on the scientist's world of order and rationality to attract people to God: "If we submit everything to reason, there will be no mystery and no supernatural element in our religion." In the new cosmology of the seventeenth century, "finite man," Pascal believed, was lost in the new infinite world, a realization that frightened him: "The eternal silence of those infinite spaces strikes me with terror" (see the box on p. 401).

For Pascal, then, the world of nature could never reveal God: "Because they have failed to contemplate these infinites, men have rashly plunged into the examination of nature, as though they bore some proportion to her.... Their assumption is as infinite as their object." A Christian could only rely on a God who through Jesus cared for human beings. In the final analysis, after providing reasonable arguments for Christianity, Pascal came to rest on faith. Reason, he believed, could take people only so far: "The heart has its reasons of which the reason knows nothing." As a Christian, faith was the final step: "The heart feels God, not the reason. This is what constitutes faith: God experienced by the heart, not by the reason."[14]

Chapter Summary

The Scientific Revolution represents a major turning point in modern Western civilization. In the Scientific Revolution, the Western world overthrew the medieval, Ptolemaic-Aristotelian worldview and geocentric universe and arrived at a new conception of the universe: the sun at the center, the planets as material bodies revolving around the sun in elliptical orbits, and an infinite rather than finite world. This new conception of the heavens was the work of a number of brilliant individuals: Nicolaus Copernicus, who theorized a heliocentric or sun-centered universe; Johannes Kepler, who discovered that planetary orbits were elliptical; Galileo Galilei, who, by using a telescope and observing the moon and sunspots, discovered that the universe

seemed to be composed of material substance; and Isaac Newton, who tied together all of these ideas with his universal law of gravitation. The contributions of each individual built on the contributions of the others, thus establishing one of the basic principles of the new science—cooperation in the pursuit of new knowledge.

With the changes in the conception of "heaven" came changes in the conception of "earth." The work of Bacon and Descartes left Europeans with the separation of mind and matter and the belief that by using only reason they could in fact understand and dominate the world of nature. The development of a scientific methodology furthered the work of the scientists, and the creation of scientific societies and learned journals spread its

results. The Scientific Revolution was more than merely intellectual theories. It also appealed to nonscientific elites because of its practical implications for economic progress and for maintaining the social order, including the waging of war.

Although traditional churches stubbornly resisted the new ideas and a few intellectuals pointed to some inherent flaws, nothing was able to halt the replacement of the traditional ways of thinking by new ways of thinking that created a more fundamental break with the past than that represented by the breakup of Christianity in the Reformation.

The Scientific Revolution forced Europeans to change their conception of themselves. At first, some were appalled and even frightened by its implications. Formerly, humans on earth had viewed themselves as being at the center of the universe. Now the earth was only a tiny planet revolving around a sun that was itself only a speck in a boundless universe. Most people remained optimistic despite the apparent blow to human dignity. After all, had Newton not demonstrated that the universe was a great machine governed by natural laws? Newton had found one—the universal law of gravitation. Could others not find other laws? Were there not natural laws governing every aspect of human endeavor that could be found by the new scientific method? Thus, as we shall see in the next chapter, the Scientific Revolution leads us logically to the Enlightenment in the eighteenth century.

CHAPTER TIMELINE

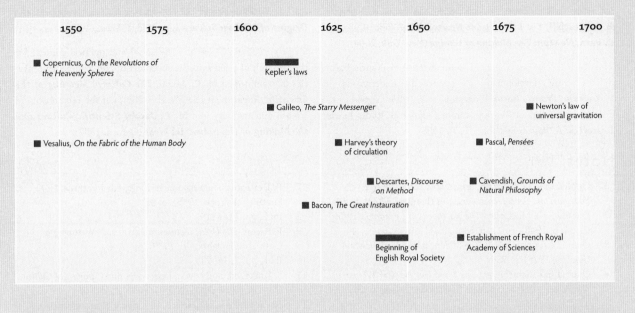

1550	1575	1600	1625	1650	1675	1700

■ Copernicus, *On the Revolutions of the Heavenly Spheres*

■ Kepler's laws

■ Galileo, *The Starry Messenger*

■ Newton's law of universal gravitation

■ Vesalius, *On the Fabric of the Human Body*

■ Harvey's theory of circulation

■ Pascal, *Pensées*

■ Descartes, *Discourse on Method*

■ Cavendish, *Grounds of Natural Philosophy*

■ Bacon, *The Great Instauration*

■ Beginning of English Royal Society

■ Establishment of French Royal Academy of Sciences

CHAPTER REVIEW

Upon Reflection

Q How do you explain the emergence of the Scientific Revolution?

Q What do we mean by the "Newtonian world-machine," and what is its significance?

Q Compare the methods used by Bacon and Descartes. Would Pascal agree with the methods and interests of these men? Why or why not?

Key Terms

Scientific Revolution (p. 386)
geocentric conception (p. 387)
heliocentric conception (p. 388)
world-machine (p. 393)

Cartesian dualism (p. 398)
rationalism (p. 398)
scientific method (p. 398)
empiricism (p. 399)

Suggestions for Further Reading

GENERAL WORKS   General surveys of the entire Scientific Revolution include **J. Henry, The Scientific Revolution and the Origins of Modern Science,** 2d ed. (London, 2002), and **J. R. Jacob, The Scientific Revolution: Aspirations and Achievements, 1500–1700** (Atlantic Highlands, N.J., 1998). See also **P. Dear, Revolutionizing the Sciences: European Knowledge and Its Ambitions, 1500–1700** (Princeton, N.J., 2001). On the relationship of magic to the beginnings of the Scientific Revolution, see the pioneering work by **F. Yates, The Rosicrucian Enlightenment** (London, 1975). On the

importance of mathematics, see **P. Dear, Discipline and Experience: The Mathematical Way in the Scientific Revolution** (Chicago, 1995). On the relationship between Renaissance artists and the Scientific Revolution, see **P. H. Smith, Body of the Artisan: Art and Experience in the Scientific Revolution** (Chicago, 2006).

A REVOLUTION IN ASTRONOMY   On the important figures of the revolution in astronomy, see **H. Margolis, It Started with Copernicus: How Turning the World Inside Out Led to the**

Scientific Revolution (New York, 2002); **M. Sharratt, *Galileo: Decisive Innovator*** (Oxford, 1994); **M. Casper, *Johannes Kepler***, trans. C. D. Hellman (London, 1959), the standard biography; **R. S. Westfall, *The Life of Isaac Newton*** (New York, 1993); and **P. Fara, *Newton: The Making of Genius*** (New York, 2004).

THE IMPACT OF SCIENCE   The importance of Francis Bacon in the early development of science is underscored in **P. Zagorin, *Francis Bacon*** (Princeton, N.J., 1998). A good introduction to the work of Descartes can be found in **G. Radis-Lewis, *Descartes: A Biography*** (Ithaca, N.Y., 1998).

WOMEN AND SCIENCE   On the subject of women and early modern science, see the comprehensive and highly informative work by **L. Schiebinger, *The Mind Has No Sex? Women in the Origins of Modern Science*** (Cambridge, Mass., 1989).

SCIENCE AND SOCIETY   The social and political context for the triumph of science in the seventeenth and eighteenth centuries is examined in **M. C. Jacob, *The Cultural Meaning of the Scientific Revolution*** (New York, 1988). On the relationship of science and industry, see **M. C. Jacob, *Scientific Culture and the Making of the Industrial West*** (Oxford, 1997).

Notes

1. Quoted in A. G. R. Smith, *Science and Society in the Sixteenth and Seventeenth Centuries* (London, 1972), p. 59.
2. Quoted in E. MacCurdy, *The Notebooks of Leonardo da Vinci* (London, 1948), vol. 1, p. 634.
3. Quoted in J. H. Randall, *The Making of the Modern Mind* (Boston, 1926), p. 234.
4. Quoted in L. Schiebinger, *The Mind Has No Sex? Women in the Origins of Modern Science* (Cambridge, Mass., 1989), pp. 52–53.
5. Quoted in ibid., p. 85.
6. Quoted in P. Stock, *Better than Rubies: A History of Women's Education* (New York, 1978), p. 16.
7. R. Descartes, *Philosophical Writings*, ed. and trans. N. K. Smith (New York, 1958), p. 95.
8. Ibid., pp. 118–119.
9. F. Bacon, *The Great Instauration*, trans. J. Weinberger (Arlington Heights, Ill., 1989), pp. 2, 8.
10. Ibid., pp. 2, 16, 21.
11. S. Drake, ed. and trans., *Discoveries and Opinions of Galileo* (New York, 1957), p. 182.
12. B. Pascal, *Pensées*, trans. J. M. Cohen (Harmondsworth, England, 1961), p. 100.
13. Ibid., p. 31.
14. Ibid., pp. 52–53, 164, 165.

MindTap   **MindTap** is a fully online, highly personalized learning experience built upon Cengage Learning content. MindTap combines student learning tools—readings, multimedia, activities, and assessments—into a singular Learning Path that guides students through the course.

The Eighteenth Century: An Age of Enlightenment

Portrait of Madame Geoffrin

Chateaux de Versailles et de Trianon (Franck Raux), Versailles// © RMN-Grand Palais/Art Resource, NY

CHAPTER OUTLINE AND FOCUS QUESTIONS

The Enlightenment

Q What intellectual developments led to the emergence of the Enlightenment? Who were the leading figures of the Enlightenment, and what were their main contributions? In what type of social environment did the philosophes thrive, and what role did women play in that environment?

Culture and Society in the Enlightenment

Q What innovations in art, music, and literature occurred in the eighteenth century? How did popular culture differ from high culture in the eighteenth century?

Religion and the Churches

Q How did popular religion differ from institutional religion in the eighteenth century?

CRITICAL THINKING

Q What was the relationship between the Scientific Revolution and the Enlightenment?

CONNECTIONS TO TODAY

Q What intellectual movements today parallel the philosophes of the Enlightenment in challenging accepted ideas about government, religion, women, and the economy?

THE EARTH-SHATTERING WORK of the "natural philosophers" in the Scientific Revolution had affected only a relatively small number of Europe's educated elite. In the eighteenth century, this changed dramatically as a group of intellectuals known as the philosophes popularized the ideas of the Scientific Revolution and used them to undertake a dramatic reexamination of all aspects of life. In Paris, the cultural capital of Europe, women took the lead in bringing together groups of men and women to discuss the new ideas of the philosophes. At her fashionable home on the Rue Saint-Honoré, Marie-Thérèse de Geoffrin (ma-REE-tay-RAYZ duh zhoh-FRANH), the wife of a wealthy merchant, held sway over gatherings that became the talk of France and even Europe. Distinguished foreigners, including a future king of Sweden and a future king of Poland, competed to receive invitations. When Madame Geoffrin made a visit to Vienna, she was so well received that she exclaimed, "I am better known here than a couple of yards from my own house!" Madame Geoffrin was an amiable but firm hostess who allowed wide-ranging discussions as long as they remained in good taste. When she found that artists and philosophers did not mix particularly well (the artists were high-strung and the philosophers talked too much), she set up separate meetings. Artists were invited only on Mondays; philosophers, on Wednesdays. These gatherings were among the many avenues for the spread of the ideas of the philosophes. And those ideas had such a widespread impact on their society that historians ever since have called the eighteenth century the Age of Enlightenment.

For most of the philosophes, "enlightenment" included the rejection of traditional Christianity. The religious wars and intolerance of the sixteenth and seventeenth centuries had so alienated intellectuals that they were open and even eager to embrace the new ideas of the Scientific Revolution. Whereas the great scientists of the seventeenth century believed that their work exalted God, the intellectuals of the eighteenth century read those scientific conclusions a different way and increasingly turned their backs on Christian orthodoxy. Consequently, European intellectual life in the eighteenth century was marked by the emergence of the secularization that has characterized the modern Western mentality ever since. Ironically, at the same time that reason and materialism were beginning to replace faith and worship, a great outburst of religious sensibility manifested itself in music and art. Clearly, the growing secularization of the eighteenth century had not yet captured the hearts and minds of all European intellectuals and artists.

The Enlightenment

Q **Focus Questions:** What intellectual developments led to the emergence of the Enlightenment? Who were the leading figures of the Enlightenment, and what were their main contributions? In what type of social environment did the philosophes thrive, and what role did women play in that environment?

In 1784, the German philosopher Immanuel Kant (i-MAHN-yoo-el KAHNT) (1724–1804) defined the **Enlightenment** as "man's leaving his self-caused immaturity." Whereas earlier periods had been handicapped by the inability to "use one's intelligence without the guidance of another," Kant proclaimed as the motto of the Enlightenment: "Dare to know! Have the courage to use your own intelligence!" The eighteenth-century Enlightenment was a movement of intellectuals who dared to know. They were greatly impressed with the accomplishments of the Scientific Revolution, and when they used the word *reason*—one of their favorite words—they were advocating the application of the scientific method to the understanding of all life. All institutions and all systems of thought were subject to the rational, scientific way of thinking if only people would free themselves from the shackles of old, worthless traditions, especially religious ones. If Isaac Newton could discover the natural laws regulating the world of nature, they too, using reason, could find the laws that governed human society. This belief in turn led them to hope that they could make progress toward a better society than the one they had inherited. *Reason, natural law, hope, progress*—these were buzzwords in the heady atmosphere of the eighteenth century.

The Paths to Enlightenment

Although the intellectuals of the eighteenth century were much influenced by the scientific ideas of the seventeenth century, they did not always acquire this knowledge directly from the original sources. After all, Newton's *Principia* was not an easy book to read or comprehend. Scientific ideas were spread to ever-widening circles of educated Europeans not so much by scientists themselves as by popularizers. Especially important as the direct link between the Scientific Revolution of the seventeenth century and the intellectuals of the eighteenth was Bernard de Fontenelle (bayr-NAHR duh fawnt-NELL) (1657–1757), secretary of the French Royal Academy of Sciences from 1691 to 1741. In his *Plurality of Worlds*, he used the form of an intimate conversation between a lady aristocrat and her lover to present a detailed account of the new mechanistic universe. Scores of the educated elite of Europe learned the new cosmology in this lighthearted fashion.

A NEW SKEPTICISM Although the Reformation had attempted to restore religion as the central focus of people's lives, it was perhaps inevitable that the dogmatic controversies, intolerance, and warfare engendered by religious differences would open the door to the questioning of religious truths and values. The overthrow of medieval cosmology and the advent of scientific ideas and rational explanations in the seventeenth century likewise affected the belief of educated men and women in the traditional teachings of Christianity. **Skepticism** toward religion and a growing secularization of thought were important factors in the emergence of the Enlightenment.

THE IMPACT OF TRAVEL LITERATURE Skepticism about both Christianity and European culture itself was nourished by travel reports. As we saw in Chapter 14, Europeans had embarked on voyages of discovery to other parts of the world in the late fifteenth and sixteenth centuries. In the course of the seventeenth century, traders, missionaries, medical practitioners, and explorers began to publish an increasing number of travel books that gave accounts of many different cultures. Then, too, the new geographic adventures of the eighteenth century, especially the discovery in the Pacific of Tahiti, New Zealand, and Australia by the British explorer James Cook, aroused much enthusiasm. Educated Europeans responded to these accounts of lands abroad in different ways.

For some intellectuals, the existence of exotic peoples, such as the natives of Tahiti, presented an image of a "natural man" who was far happier than many Europeans. One intellectual wrote:

> The life of savages is so simple, and our societies are such complicated machines! The Tahitian is close to the origin of the world, while the European is closer to its old age.... They understand nothing about our manners or our laws, and they are bound to see in them nothing but shackles disguised in a hundred different ways. Those shackles could only provoke the indignation and scorn of creatures in whom the most profound feeling is a love of liberty.[1]

To that author, the noble primitives of Tahiti were honest and simple people unencumbered by the inequality, religious hypocrisy, sexual repression, and vices of European society. The idea of the "noble savage" would play an important role in the political work of some philosophes.

The travel literature of the seventeenth and eighteenth centuries also led to the realization that there were highly developed civilizations with different customs in other parts of the world. China was especially singled out. One German university professor praised Confucian morality as superior to the intolerant attitudes of Christianity. Some European intellectuals began to evaluate their own civilization relative to others. Practices that had seemed to be grounded in reason now appeared to be merely matters of custom. Certainties about European practices gave way to **cultural relativism**.

As Europeans were exposed to growing numbers of people around the world who were different from themselves, some intellectuals began to classify people into racial groups. One group espoused polygenesis, or the belief in separate human species; others argued for monogenesis, or the belief in one human species characterized by racial variations. Both groups were especially unsympathetic to Africans and placed them in the lowest rank of humankind. In his *Encyclopedia*, the intellectual Denis Diderot (see "Diderot and the *Encyclopedia*" later in this chapter) maintained that all Africans were black and characterized the Negro as a "new species of mankind."

THE LEGACY OF LOCKE AND NEWTON A final source of inspiration for the Enlightenment came primarily from Isaac Newton and John Locke. Newton was frequently

The Popularization of Science in the Enlightenment. During the Enlightenment, the ideas of the Scientific Revolution were spread and popularized in a variety of ways. Scientific societies funded by royal and princely patronage were especially valuable in providing outlets for the spread of new scientific ideas. This illustration shows the German prince Frederick Christian visiting his Academy of Sciences in 1739. Note the many instruments of the new science around the rooms—human skeletons, globes, microscopes, telescopes, and orreries (mechanical models of the solar system). (Archivio di Stato, Bologna//Alinari/Art Resource, NY)

singled out for praise as the "greatest and rarest genius that ever rose for the ornament and instruction of the species."[2] The English poet Alexander Pope declared, "Nature and Nature's Laws lay hid in Night; God said, 'Let Newton be,' and all was Light." Enchanted by the grand design of the Newtonian world-machine, the intellectuals of the Enlightenment were convinced that by following Newton's rules of reasoning, they could discover the natural laws that governed politics, economics, justice, religion, and the arts.

John Locke's theory of knowledge had a great impact on eighteenth-century intellectuals. In his *Essay Concerning Human Understanding*, written in 1690, Locke denied Descartes's belief in innate ideas. Instead, argued Locke, every person was born with a tabula rasa, a blank mind:

> Let us then suppose the mind to be, as we say, white paper, void of all characters, without any ideas. How comes it to be furnished? Whence comes it by that vast store which the busy and boundless fancy of man has painted on it with an almost endless variety? Whence has it all the materials of reason and knowledge? To this I answer, in one word, from experience.... Our observation, employed either about external sensible objects or about the internal operations of our minds perceived and reflected on by ourselves, is that which supplies our understanding with all the materials of thinking.[3]

Our knowledge, then, is derived from our environment, not from heredity; from reason, not from faith.

Locke's philosophy implied that people were molded by their environment, by the experiences that they received through their senses from their surrounding world. If the environment was changed and people were subjected to proper influences, they could be changed and a new society created. And how should the environment be changed? Newton had already paved the way by showing how reason enabled enlightened people to discover the natural laws to which all institutions should conform. No wonder the intellectuals were enamored of Newton and Locke. Taken together, their ideas seemed to offer the hope of a "brave new world" built on reason.

The Philosophes and Their Ideas

The intellectuals of the Enlightenment were known by the French term *philosophes* (fee-loh-ZAWF), although not all of them were French and few were actually philosophers. The **philosophes** were literary people, professors, journalists, statesmen, economists, political scientists, and above all, social reformers. They came from both the nobility and the middle class, and a few even stemmed from lower origins. Although it was a truly international and **cosmopolitan** movement, the Enlightenment also enhanced the dominant role being played by French culture; Paris was its recognized capital, and most of the leaders of the Enlightenment were French (see Map 17.1). The French philosophes in turn affected intellectuals elsewhere and created a movement that engulfed the entire Western world, including the British and Spanish colonies in America.

Although the philosophes faced different political circumstances depending on the country in which they lived, they shared common bonds as part of a truly international movement. Although they were called philosophers, what did philosophy mean to them? The role of philosophy was to change the world, not just to discuss it. To the philosophes, rationalism did not mean the creation of a grandiose system of thought to explain all things. Reason was scientific method, an appeal to facts and experience. A spirit of rational criticism was to be applied to everything, including religion and politics.

Although the philosophes constituted a kind of "family circle" bound together by common intellectual bonds, they often disagreed. Spanning almost a century, the Enlightenment evolved over time, with each succeeding generation becoming more radical as it built on the contributions of the previous one. A few people, however, dominated the landscape completely, and we might best begin our survey of the ideas of the philosophes by looking at the three French giants—Montesquieu, Voltaire, and Diderot.

MONTESQUIEU AND POLITICAL THOUGHT Charles de Secondat, baron de Montesquieu (MOHN-tess-kyoo) (1689–1755), came from the French nobility. He received an education in the classics and then studied law. In his first work, the *Persian Letters*, published in 1721, he used the format of two Persians supposedly traveling in western Europe and sending their impressions back home to enable him to criticize French institutions, especially the Catholic Church and the French monarchy. Much of the program of the French Enlightenment is contained in this work: the attack on traditional religion, the advocacy of religious toleration, the denunciation of slavery, and the use of reason to liberate human beings from their prejudices.

Montesquieu's most famous work, *The Spirit of the Laws*, was published in 1748. This treatise was a comparative study of governments in which Montesquieu attempted to apply the scientific method to the social

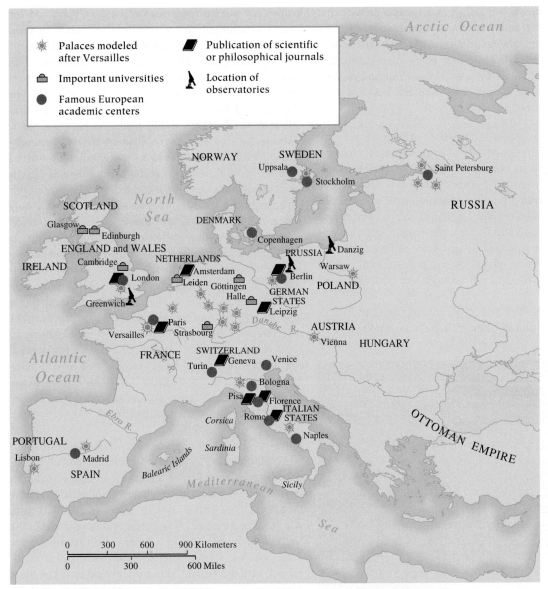

MAP 17.1 The Enlightenment in Europe. "Have the courage to use your own intelligence!" Kant's words epitomize the role of the individual in using reason to understand all aspects of life—the natural world and the sphere of human nature, behavior, and institutions.

Q Which countries or regions were at the center of the Enlightenment, and what could account for peripheral regions being less involved?

and political arena to ascertain the "natural laws" governing the social relationships of human beings. Montesquieu distinguished three basic kinds of governments: republics, suitable for small states and based on citizen involvement; monarchy, appropriate for middle-sized states and grounded in the ruling class's adherence to law; and despotism, apt for large empires and dependent on fear to inspire obedience. Montesquieu used England as an example of the second category, and it was his praise and analysis of England's constitution that led to his most far-reaching and longest-lasting contribution to political thought—the importance of checks and balances achieved through a **separation of powers**. He believed that England's system, with its separate executive, legislative, and judicial powers that served to limit and control each other, provided the greatest freedom and security for a state. The translation of his work into English two years after publication ensured that it would be read by American philosophes, who incorporated its principles into the U.S. Constitution (see Chapter 19).

VOLTAIRE AND THE ENLIGHTENMENT The greatest figure of the Enlightenment was François-Marie Arouet, known simply as Voltaire (vohl-TAYR) (1694–1778). Son of a prosperous middle-class family from Paris, Voltaire received a classical education in Jesuit schools. Although he studied law, he wished to be a writer and achieved his first success as a playwright. Voltaire was a prolific author and wrote an almost endless stream of pamphlets, novels, plays, letters, philosophical essays, and histories. His writings brought him both fame and wealth.

Although he touched on all of the themes of importance to the philosophes, Voltaire was especially well

Voltaire. François-Marie Arouet, better known as Voltaire, achieved his first success as a playwright. A philosophe, Voltaire was known for his criticism of traditional religion and his support of religious toleration. Maurice-Quentin de La Tour painted this portrait of Voltaire holding one of his books in 1736.

known for his criticism of traditional religion and his strong attachment to the ideal of religious toleration (see the box on p. 411). He lent his prestige and skills as a polemicist to fight intolerance in France. In 1763, he penned his *Treatise on Toleration*, in which he argued that religious toleration had created no problems for England and Holland and reminded governments that "all men are brothers under God." As he grew older, Voltaire became ever more strident in his denunciations. "Crush the infamous thing," he thundered repeatedly—the infamous thing being religious fanaticism, intolerance, and superstition.

Throughout his life, Voltaire championed not only religious tolerance but also **deism**, a religious outlook shared by most other philosophes. Deism was built on the Newtonian world-machine, which suggested the existence of a mechanic (God) who had created the universe. To Voltaire and most other philosophes, the universe was like a clock. God, the clockmaker, had created it, set it in motion, and allowed it to run without interference. Thus, God had no direct involvement in the world he had created and allowed it to run according to its own natural laws. God did not extend grace or answer prayers as Christians liked to believe. Jesus might be a "good fellow," as Voltaire called him, but he was not divine, as Christianity claimed.

DIDEROT AND THE *ENCYCLOPEDIA* Denis Diderot (duh-NEE DEE-droh) (1713–1784), the son of a skilled craftsman from eastern France, became a freelance writer so that he could study many subjects and read in many languages. One of his favorite topics was Christianity, which he condemned as fanatical and unreasonable. As he grew older, his literary attacks on Christianity grew more vicious. Of all religions, Christianity, he maintained, was the worst, "the most absurd and the most atrocious in its dogma." This progression reflected his own movement from deism to atheism, ending with a basic materialistic conception of life: "This world is only a mass of molecules."

Diderot's most famous contribution to the Enlightenment was the twenty-eight-volume *Encyclopedia, or Classified Dictionary of the Sciences, Arts, and Trades*, which he edited and referred to as the "great work of his life." Its purpose, according to Diderot, was to "change the general way of thinking." It did precisely that in becoming a major weapon of the philosophes' crusade against the old French society. The contributors included many philosophes, who expressed their major concerns. They attacked religious superstition and advocated toleration as well as a program for

The Attack on Religious Intolerance

Although Voltaire's attacks on religion were in no way original, his lucid prose, biting satire, and clever wit caused his works to be widely read and all the more influential. These two selections present different sides of Voltaire's attack on religious intolerance. The first is from his straightforward treatise *The Ignorant Philosopher*, and the second is from his only real literary masterpiece, the novel *Candide*, in which he uses humor to make the same fundamental point about religious intolerance.

Voltaire, *The Ignorant Philosopher*

The contagion of fanaticism then still subsists.... The author of the *Treatise upon Toleration* has not mentioned the shocking executions wherein so many unhappy victims perished in the valleys of Piedmont. He has passed over in silence the massacre of six hundred inhabitants of Valtelina, men, women, and children, who were murdered by the Catholics in the month of September, 1620. I will not say it was with the consent and assistance of the archbishop of Milan, Charles Borome, who was made a saint. Some passionate writers have averred this fact, which I am very far from believing; but I say, there is scarce any city or borough in Europe, where blood has not been spilt for religious quarrels; I say, that the human species has been perceptibly diminished, because women and girls were massacred as well as men; I say, that Europe would have had a third larger population, if there had been no theological disputes. In fine, I say, that so far from forgetting these abominable times, we should frequently take a view of them, to inspire an eternal horror for them; and that it is for our age to make reparation by toleration, for this long collection of crimes, which has taken place through the want of toleration, during sixteen barbarous centuries.

Let it not then be said, that there are no traces left of that shocking fanaticism, of the want of toleration; they are still everywhere to be met with, even in those countries that are esteemed the most humane. The Lutheran and Calvinist preachers, were they masters, would, perhaps, be as little inclined to pity, as obdurate, as insolent as they upbraid their antagonists with being.

Voltaire, *Candide*

At last [Candide] approached a man who had just been addressing a big audience for a whole hour on the subject of charity. The orator peered at him and said:

"What is your business here? Do you support the Good Old Cause?"

"There is no effect without a cause," replied Candide modestly. "All things are necessarily connected and arranged for the best. It was my fate to be driven from Lady Cunegonde's presence and made to run the gantlet, and now I have to beg my bread until I can earn it. Things should not have happened otherwise."

"Do you believe that the Pope is Antichrist, my friend?" said the minister.

"I have never heard anyone say so," replied Candide, "but whether he is or he isn't, I want some food."

"You don't deserve to eat," said the other. "Be off with you, you villain, you wretch! Don't come near me again or you'll suffer for it."

The minister's wife looked out of the window at that moment, and seeing a man who was not sure that the Pope was Antichrist, emptied over his head a chamber pot, which shows to what lengths ladies are driven by religious zeal.

Q Compare the two approaches that Voltaire uses to address the problem of religious intolerance. Do you think one is more effective? Why?

Sources: Voltaire, *The Ignorant Philosopher*. From *Candide or Optimism* by Voltaire, translated by John Butt (Penguin Classics, 1947). This edition copyright © John Butt, 1947. Voltaire, *Candide*. From *Candide or Optimism* by Voltaire, translated by John Butt (Penguin Classics, 1947). This edition copyright © John Butt, 1947. Reproduced by permission of Penguin Books, Ltd.

social, legal, and political improvements that would lead to a society that was more cosmopolitan, more tolerant, more humane, and more reasonable. In later editions, the price of the *Encyclopedia* was drastically reduced, dramatically increasing its sales and making it available to doctors, clergymen, teachers, lawyers, and even military officers. The ideas of the Enlightenment were spread even further as a result.

TOWARD A NEW "SCIENCE OF MAN" The Enlightenment belief that Newton's scientific methods could be used to discover the natural laws underlying all areas of human life led to the emergence in the eighteenth century of what the philosophes called a "science of man," or what we would call the social sciences. In a number of areas, philosophes arrived at natural laws that they believed governed human actions.

The Physiocrats and Adam Smith have been regarded as founders of the modern discipline of economics. The leader of the Physiocrats was François Quesnay (frahnn-SWAH keh-NAY) (1694–1774), a successful French court physician. Quesnay and the Physiocrats claimed they would discover the natural economic laws that governed human society. Their major "natural law" of economics was a repudiation of mercantilism, specifically its emphasis on a controlled economy for the benefit of the state. Instead, the Physiocrats stressed that the existence of the natural economic forces of supply and demand made it imperative that individuals should be left free to pursue their own economic self-interest. In doing so, all of society would ultimately benefit. Consequently, they argued that the state should in no way interrupt the free play of natural economic forces by government regulation of the economy but rather just leave it alone, a doctrine that subsequently became known by its French name, **laissez-faire** (less-ay-FAYR) (noninterference; literally, "let people do as they choose").

In 1776, a Scottish philosopher, Adam Smith (1723–1790), made the clearest statement of laissez-faire in his *Inquiry into the Nature and Causes of the Wealth of Nations*, known simply as *The Wealth of Nations*. Like the Physiocrats, Smith believed that the state should not interfere in economic matters; indeed, he assigned to government only three basic functions: to protect society from invasion (army), defend individuals from injustice and oppression (police), and keep up certain public works, such as roads and canals, that private individuals could not afford. Thus, in Smith's view, the state should stay out of the lives of individuals. In emphasizing the economic liberty of the individual, the Physiocrats and Adam Smith laid the foundation for what became known in the nineteenth century as **economic liberalism**.

THE LATER ENLIGHTENMENT By the late 1760s, a new generation of philosophes who had grown up with the worldview of the Enlightenment began to move beyond their predecessors' beliefs. Baron Paul d'Holbach (dawl-BAHK) (1723–1789), a wealthy German aristocrat who settled in Paris, preached a doctrine of strict atheism and materialism. In his *System of Nature*, written in 1770, he argued that everything in the universe consisted of matter in motion. Human beings were simply machines; God was a product of the human mind and was unnecessary for leading a moral life. People needed only reason to live in this world. Holbach shocked almost all of his fellow philosophes with his uncompromising atheism. Most intellectuals remained more comfortable with deism and feared the effect of atheism on society.

No one was more critical of the work of his predecessors than Jean-Jacques Rousseau (ZHAHNH-ZHAHK roo-SOH) (1712–1778). Almost entirely self-educated, Rousseau, born in Geneva, Switzerland, spent his youth wandering about France and Italy holding various jobs. Eventually, he made his way to Paris, where he was introduced into the circles of the philosophes.

Rousseau presented his political beliefs in two major works. In his *Discourse on the Origins of the Inequality of Mankind*, Rousseau argued that people had adopted laws and governors to protect their private property, but in the process, they had become enslaved by government. In his most celebrated treatise, *The Social Contract*, published in 1762, Rousseau tried to harmonize individual liberty with governmental authority (see the box on p. 413). The social contract was basically an agreement on the part of an entire society to be governed by its general will. If any individual wished to follow his own self-interest, he should be compelled to abide by the general will. "This means nothing less than that he will be forced to be free," said Rousseau, because the general will represented a community's highest aspirations, what was best for the entire community. Thus, liberty was achieved through being forced to follow what was best for all people because, he believed, what was best for all was best for each individual. To Rousseau, because everybody was responsible for framing the general will, the creation of laws could never be delegated to a parliamentary body:

> Thus, the people's deputies are not and could not be its representatives; they are merely its agents; and they cannot decide anything finally. Any law which the people has not ratified in person is void; it is not law at all. The English people believes itself to be free; it is gravely mistaken; it is free only during the election of Members of Parliament; as soon as the Members are elected, the people is enslaved; it is nothing.[4]

This is an extreme and idealistic statement, but it is the ultimate statement of participatory democracy.

A Social Contract

Although Jean-Jacques Rousseau was one of the French philosophes, he has also been called "the father of Romanticism." His political ideas have proved extremely controversial. While some political theorists have hailed him as the prophet of democracy, others have labeled him an apologist for totalitarianism. This selection is taken from one of his most famous books, *The Social Contract*.

Jean-Jacques Rousseau, *The Social Contract*

Book 1, Chapter 6: "The Social Pact"

"How to find a form of association which will defend the person and goods of each member with the collective force of all, and under which each individual, while uniting himself with the others, obeys no one but himself, and remains as free as before." This is the fundamental problem to which the social contract holds the solution. . . .

Book 1, Chapter 7: "The Sovereign"

Despite their common interest, subjects will not be bound by their commitment unless means are found to guarantee their fidelity.

For every individual as a man may have a private will contrary to, or different from, the general will that he has as a citizen. His private interest may he speak with a very different voice from that of the public interest; his absolute and naturally independent existence may make him regard what he owes to the common cause as a gratuitous contribution, the loss of which would be less painful for others than the payment is onerous for him; and fancying that the artificial person which constitutes the state is a mere rational entity, he might seek to enjoy the rights of a citizen without doing the duties of a subject. The growth of this kind of injustice would bring about the ruin of the body politic.

Hence, in order that the social pact shall not be an empty formula, it is tacitly implied in that commitment—which alone can give force to all others—that whoever refused to obey the general will shall be constrained to do so by the whole body, which means nothing other than that he shall be forced to be free; for this is the condition which, by giving each citizen to the nation, secures him against all personal dependence, it is the condition which shapes both the design and the working of the political machine, and which alone bestows justice on civil contracts—without it, such contracts would be absurd, tyrannical and liable to the grossest abuse.

Q What was Rousseau's concept of the social contract? What implications did it have for political thought, especially in regard to the development of democratic ideals?

Source: Extract from *A Social Contract* by Jean-Jacques Rousseau translated by Maurice Cranston (translation copyright © Estate Maurice Cranston 1968) is reproduced by permission of PFD (www.pfd.co.uk) on behalf of the Estate of Maurice Cranston.

Another influential treatise by Rousseau also appeared in 1762. Titled *Émile*, it is one of the Enlightenment's most important works on education. Written in the form of a novel, the work is really a general treatise "on the education of the natural man." Rousseau's fundamental concern was that education should foster rather than restrict children's natural instincts. Life's experiences had shown Rousseau the importance of the promptings of the heart, and what he sought was a balance between heart and mind, between sentiment and reason. This emphasis on heart and sentiment made him a precursor of the intellectual movement called **Romanticism** that dominated Europe at the beginning of the nineteenth century.

But Rousseau did not necessarily practice what he preached. His own children were sent to foundling homes, where many children died young. Rousseau also viewed women as "naturally" different from men: "to fulfill [a woman's] functions, an appropriate physical constitution is necessary to her. . . . She needs a soft sedentary life to suckle her babies. How much care and tenderness does she need to hold her family together?" In *Émile*, Sophie, who was Emile's intended wife, was educated for her role as wife and mother by learning obedience and the nurturing skills that would enable her to provide loving care for her husband and children. Not everyone in the eighteenth century, however, agreed with Rousseau, making ideas of gender an important issue in the Enlightenment.

THE "WOMAN'S QUESTION" IN THE ENLIGHTENMENT For centuries, men had dominated the debate about the nature and value of women. In general, many male intellectuals had argued that the base nature of women made them inferior to men and made male domination of women necessary (see Chapter 16). In the seventeenth and eighteenth centuries, many male thinkers reinforced this view by arguing that it was based on "natural" biological differences between men and women. Like Rousseau, they argued that the female constitution made women suitable only as mothers. Male writers, in particular, were critical of the attempts of some women in the Enlightenment to write on intellectual issues, arguing that women by nature were intellectually inferior to men. Nevertheless, some Enlightenment thinkers offered more positive views of women. Diderot, for example, maintained that men and women were not all that different, and Voltaire asserted that "women are capable of all that men are" in intellectual activity.

It was women thinkers, however, who added new perspectives to the "woman's question" by making specific suggestions for improving the conditions of women. Mary Astell (AST-ul) (1666–1731), daughter of a wealthy English coal merchant, argued in 1697 in *A Serious Proposal to the Ladies* that women needed to become better educated. Men, she believed, would resent her proposal, "but they must excuse me, if I be as partial to my own sex as they are to theirs, and think women as capable of learning as men are, and that it becomes them as well."[5]

The strongest statement for the rights of women in the eighteenth century was advanced by the English writer Mary Wollstonecraft (WULL-stun-kraft) (1759–1797), viewed by many as the founder of modern European **feminism**. In *Vindication of the Rights of Woman*, written in 1792, Wollstonecraft pointed out two contradictions in the views of women held by such Enlightenment thinkers as Rousseau. To argue that women must obey men, she said, was contrary to the beliefs of the same individuals that a system based on the arbitrary power of monarchs over their subjects or slave owners over their slaves was wrong. The subjection of women to men was equally wrong. In addition, she argued, the Enlightenment was based on the ideal that reason is innate in all human beings. If women have reason, then they are entitled to the same rights that men have. Women, Wollstonecraft declared, should have equal rights with men in education and in economic and political life as well (see the box on p. 415).

The Social Environment of the Philosophes

The social backgrounds of the philosophes varied considerably, from the aristocratic Montesquieu to the lower-middle-class Diderot and Rousseau. The Enlightenment was not the preserve of any one class, although obviously its greatest appeal was to the aristocracy and upper middle classes of the major cities. The common people, especially the peasants, were little affected by the Enlightenment.

Of great importance to the Enlightenment was the spread of its ideas to the literate elite of European society. Although the publication and sale of books and treatises were crucial to this process, the salon was also a factor. **Salons** came into being in the seventeenth century but rose to new heights in the eighteenth. These were elegant drawing rooms in the urban houses of the wealthy where philosophes and guests gathered to engage in witty, sparkling conversations that often centered on the ideas of the philosophes. In France's rigid hierarchical society, the salons were important in bringing together writers and artists with aristocrats, government officials, and wealthy members of the bourgeoisie.

As hostesses of the salons, women found themselves in a position to affect the decisions of kings, sway political opinion, and influence literary and artistic taste. Salons provided havens for people and views unwelcome in the royal court. When the *Encyclopedia* was suppressed by the French authorities, Marie-Thérèse de Geoffrin (1699–1777), a wealthy bourgeois widow whose father had been a valet, welcomed the encyclopedists to her salon and offered financial assistance to complete the work in secret. Madame Geoffrin was not

CHRONOLOGY Works of the Philosophes	
Montesquieu, *Persian Letters*	1721
Montesquieu, *The Spirit of the Laws*	1748
Diderot, *Encyclopedia*	1751–1765
Rousseau, *The Social Contract, Émile*	1762
Voltaire, *Treatise on Toleration*	1763
Beccaria, *On Crimes and Punishments*	1764
Smith, *The Wealth of Nations*	1776
Wollstonecraft, *Vindication of the Rights of Woman*	1792

OPPOSING VIEWPOINTS

Women in the Age of the Enlightenment: Rousseau and Wollstonecraft

The "woman's question"—the debate about the nature and value of women—continued to be discussed in the eighteenth century. In *Émile*, Jean-Jacques Rousseau reflected the view of many male thinkers when he argued that there were natural biological differences between men and women that predisposed women to be mothers rather than intellectuals. Some women thinkers, however, presented new perspectives.

Mary Wollstonecraft responded to an unhappy childhood in a large family by seeking to lead an independent life. Few occupations were available for middle-class women in her day, but she survived by working as a teacher, chaperone, and governess to aristocratic children. All the while, she wrote and developed her ideas on the rights of women. The selection featured here is taken from her *Vindication of the Rights of Woman*, the work that led to her reputation as the foremost British feminist thinker of the eighteenth century.

Jean-Jacques Rousseau, *Émile* (1762)

It follows that woman is made specially to please men. If man ought to please her in turn, it is due to a less direct necessity. His merit is in his power; he pleases by the sole fact of his strength. . . .

The strictness of the relative duties of the two sexes is not and cannot be the same. When woman complains on this score about unjust man-made inequality, she is wrong. This inequality is not a human institution—or, at least, it is the work not of prejudice but of reason. It is up to the sex that nature has charged with the bearing of children to be responsible for them to the other sex. Doubtless it is not permitted to anyone to violate his faith, and every unfaithful husband who deprives his wife of the only reward of the austere duties of sex is an unjust and barbarous man. But the unfaithful woman does more; she dissolves the family and breaks all the bonds of nature. . . .

The good constitution of children initially depends on that of their mothers. The first education of men depends on the care of women. . . . Thus, the whole education of women ought to relate to men. To please men, to be useful to them, to make herself loved and honored by them, to raise them when young, to care for them when grown, to counsel them, to console them, to make their lives agreeable and sweet—these are the duties of women at all times, and they ought to be taught from childhood. . . .

The quest for abstract and speculative truths, principles, and axioms in the sciences, for everything that tends to generalize ideas, is not within the competence of women. All their studies ought to be related to practice. . . . Nor do women have sufficient precision and attention to succeed at the exact sciences. And as for the physical sciences, they are for the sex which is more active, gets around more, and sees more objects, the sex which has more strength and uses it more to judge the relations of sensible beings and the laws of nature. Woman, who is weak and who sees nothing outside the house, estimates and judges the forces she can put to work to make up for her weakness.

Mary Wollstonecraft, *Vindication of the Rights of Woman* (1792)

It is a melancholy truth—yet such is the blessed effect of civilization—the most respectable women are the most oppressed; and, unless they have understandings far superior to the common run of understandings, taking in both sexes, they must, from being treated like contemptible beings, become contemptible. How many women thus waste life away the prey of discontent, who might have practiced as physicians, regulated a farm, managed a shop, and stood erect, supported by their own industry, instead of hanging their heads surcharged with the dew of sensibility, that consumes the beauty to which it at first gave luster . . . ?

Proud of their weakness, however, [women] must always be protected, guarded from care, and all the rough toils that dignify the mind. If this be the fiat of fate, if they will make themselves insignificant and contemptible, sweetly to waste "life away," let them not

(continued)

(Opposing Viewpoints continued)

expect to be valued when their beauty fades, for it is the fate of the fairest flowers to be admired and pulled to pieces by the careless hand that plucked them. In how many ways do I wish, from the purest benevolence, to impress this truth on my sex; yet I fear that they will not listen to a truth that dear-bought experience has brought home to many an agitated bosom, nor willingly resign the privileges of rank and sex for the privileges of humanity, to which those have no claim who do not discharge its duties....

Would men but generously snap our chains, and be content with the rational fellowship instead of slavish obedience, they would find us more observant daughters, more affectionate sisters, more faithful wives, and

more reasonable mothers—in a word, better citizens. We should then love them with true affection, because we should learn to respect ourselves; and the peace of mind of a worthy man would not be interrupted by the idle vanity of his wife.

Q What did Rousseau believe was the role of women, and how did he think they should be educated? What arguments did Mary Wollstonecraft make on behalf of the rights of women? What picture did she paint of the women of her day? Why did Wollstonecraft suggest that both women and men were at fault for the "slavish" situation of women?

Sources: Rousseau, *Émile* (1762). Copyright © 1979 Jean-Jacques Rousseau, Michael Wu. Reprinted by permission of Basic Books, a member of the Perseus Books Group. Mary Wollstonecraft, *Vindication of the Rights of Woman* (1792). From Mary Wollstonecraft, *A Vindication of the Rights of Woman* (1792).

without rivals, however. The marquise du Deffand (mar-KEEZ duh duh-FAHNH) (1697–1780) had abandoned her husband in the provinces and established herself in Paris, where her ornate drawing room attracted many of the Enlightenment's great figures, including Montesquieu and Voltaire.

Madame Geoffrin. As hostesses of salons, women played a pivotal role in the spread of Enlightenment ideas. Salons also offered women access to intellectual stimulus that was generally otherwise denied to them. Throughout Europe, women were barred from any other higher educational opportunities. Shown here is Madame Geoffrin (third on the right), the prominent salon hostess, surrounded by various philosophes in her home on the rue Saint-Honoré.

Although the salons were run by women, the reputation of a salon depended on the stature of the males a hostess was able to attract. Despite this male domination, however, both French and foreign observers complained that females exerted undue influence in French political affairs. Though exaggerated, this perception led to the decline of salons during the French Revolution toward the end of the century.

The salon served an important role in promoting conversation and sociability between upper-class men and women as well as spreading the ideas of the Enlightenment. But other means of spreading Enlightenment ideas were also available. Coffeehouses, cafés, reading clubs, and public lending libraries established by the state were gathering places for the exchange of ideas. Secret societies also developed. The most famous was the Freemasons, established in London in 1717, France and Italy in 1726, and Prussia in 1744. It was no secret that the Freemasons were sympathetic to the ideas of the philosophes.

Culture and Society in the Enlightenment

Q FOCUS QUESTIONS: What innovations in art, music, and literature occurred in the eighteenth century? How did popular culture differ from high culture in the eighteenth century?

The intellectual adventure fostered by the philosophes was accompanied by both traditional practices and important changes in eighteenth-century culture and society.

Innovations in Art, Music, and Literature

Although the Baroque and Neoclassical styles that had dominated the seventeenth century continued into the eighteenth century, by the 1730s a new style known as **Rococo** (ruh-KOH-koh) began to affect decoration and architecture all over Europe. Unlike the Baroque, which stressed majesty, power, and movement, Rococo emphasized grace and gentle action. Rococo rejected strict geometrical patterns and had a fondness for curves; it liked to follow the wandering lines of natural objects, such as seashells and flowers. It made much use of interlaced designs colored in gold with delicate contours and graceful curves. Highly secular, its lightness and charm spoke of the pursuit of pleasure, happiness, and love.

Some of Rococo's appeal is evident already in the work of the French painter Antoine Watteau (AHN-twahn wah-TOH) (1684–1721), whose lyrical views of aristocratic life—refined, sensual, civilized, with gentlemen and ladies in elegant dress—revealed a world of upper-class pleasure and joy. Underneath that exterior, however, was an element of sadness as the artist revealed the fragility and transitory nature of pleasure, love, and life.

Another aspect of Rococo was that its decorative work could easily be used with Baroque architecture. The palace of Versailles had made an enormous impact on Europe. "Keeping up with the Bourbons" became

Antoine Watteau, *Return from Cythera*. Antoine Watteau was one of the most gifted painters in eighteenth-century France. His portrayal of aristocratic life reveals a world of elegance, wealth, and pleasure. In this painting, which is considered his masterpiece, Watteau depicts a group of aristocratic lovers about to depart from the island of Cythera, where they have paid homage to Venus, the goddess of love. Luxuriously dressed, they move from the woodlands to a golden barge that is waiting to take them from the island.

important as the Austrian emperor, the Swedish king, German princes, Italian princes, and even a Russian tsar built grandiose palaces. While emulating Versailles's size, they were modeled less after the French classical style of Versailles than after the seventeenth-century Italian Baroque, as modified by a series of brilliant German and Austrian sculptor-architects. This Baroque-Rococo architectural style of the eighteenth century was used in both palaces and churches, and often the same architects designed both. This is evident in the work of one of the greatest architects of the eighteenth century, Balthasar Neumann (BAHL-tuh-zahr NOI-mahn) (1687–1753).

Neumann's two masterpieces are the pilgrimage church of the Vierzehnheiligen (feer-tsayn-HY-li-gen) (Fourteen Saints) in southern Germany and the palace known as the Residenz, the residential palace of the Schönborn (SHURN-bawn) prince-bishop of Würzburg (VOORTS-boork). Secular and spiritual become easily interchangeable in both buildings as the visitor is greeted by lavish and fanciful ornament; light, bright colors; and elaborate and rich detail.

THE DEVELOPMENT OF MUSIC The eighteenth century was one of the greatest in the history of European music. In the first half of the century, two composers—Bach and Handel—stand out as musical geniuses. Johann Sebastian Bach (yoh-HAHN suh-BASS-chun BAHK) (1685–1750) came from a family of musicians. Bach held the post of organist and music director at a number of small German courts before becoming director of church music at the Church of Saint Thomas in Leipzig in 1723. There Bach composed his Mass in B Minor, his *Saint Matthew's Passion*, and the cantatas and motets that have established his reputation as one of the greatest composers of all time. For Bach, music was above all a means to worship God; in his own words, his task in life was to make "well-ordered music in the honor of God."

The other great musical giant of the early eighteenth century, George Frederick Handel (HAN-dul) (1685–1759), was, like Bach, born in Saxony in Germany and in the same year. Unlike Bach, however, he was profoundly secular in temperament. After studying in Italy, where he began his career writing operas in the Italian manner, in 1712 he moved to England, where he spent most of his adult life attempting to run an operatic company. Although patronized by the English royal court, Handel wrote music for large public audiences and was not averse to writing huge, unusual-sounding pieces. The band for his *Fireworks Music*, for

Vierzehnheiligen, Germany//Erich Lessing/Art Resource, NY

Vierzehnheiligen, Interior View. Pictured here is the interior of the Vierzehnheiligen, the pilgrimage church designed by Balthasar Neumann. As this illustration shows, the Baroque-Rococo style of architecture produced lavish buildings in which secular and spiritual elements became easily interchangeable. Elaborate detail, blazing light, rich colors, and opulent decoration were blended together to create a work of stunning beauty.

example, was supposed to be accompanied by 101 cannon. Although he wrote much secular music, the worldly Handel is, ironically, probably best known for his religious music. His *Messiah* has been called "one of those rare works that appeal immediately to everyone, and yet is indisputably a masterpiece of the highest order."[6]

Bach and Handel perfected the Baroque musical style, with its monumental and elaborate musical structures. Two geniuses of the second half of the eighteenth century—Haydn and Mozart—were innovators who wrote music called classical rather than Baroque. Their renown caused the musical center of Europe to shift from Italy and Germany to the Austrian Empire.

Franz Joseph Haydn (FRAHNTS YO-zef HY-dun) (1732–1809) spent most of his adult life as musical director for wealthy Hungarian princes, the Esterhazy brothers. Haydn was incredibly prolific, composing 104 symphonies in addition to string quartets, concerti, songs, oratorios, and Masses. His visits to England in 1790 and 1794 introduced him to a world where musicians wrote for public concerts rather than for princely patrons. This "liberty," as he called it, induced him to write his two great oratorios, *The Creation* and *The Seasons*, both of which were dedicated to the common people.

Wolfgang Amadeus Mozart (VULF-gahng ah-muh-DAY-uss MOH-tsart) (1756–1791), born in Salzburg, Austria, was a child prodigy who gave his first harpsichord concert at six and wrote his first opera at twelve. He, too, sought a patron, but his discontent with the overly demanding archbishop of Salzburg forced him to move to Vienna, where his failure to find a permanent patron made his life miserable. Nevertheless, he wrote music prolifically and passionately—string quartets, sonatas, symphonies, concerti, and operas—until he died at thirty-five, a debt-ridden pauper. *The Marriage of Figaro*, *The Magic Flute*, and *Don Giovanni* are three of the world's greatest operas. Mozart composed with an ease of melody and a blend of grace and precision that arguably no one has ever surpassed.

DEVELOPMENT OF THE NOVEL The eighteenth century was also decisive in the development of the novel. The modern novel grew out of the medieval romances and the picaresque stories of the sixteenth century. The English are credited with establishing the novel as the primary form of fiction writing. With no established rules, the novel was open to much experimentation.

The High Culture of the Eighteenth Century

Historians and cultural anthropologists have grown accustomed to distinguishing between a civilization's high culture and its popular culture. **High culture** usually means the literary and artistic world of the educated and wealthy ruling classes; **popular culture** refers to the written and unwritten lore of the masses, most of which is passed down orally. By the eighteenth century, European high culture consisted of a learned world of theologians, scientists, philosophers, intellectuals, poets, and dramatists, for whom Latin remained a truly international language. Their work was supported by a wealthy and literate lay group, the most

important of whom were the landed aristocracy and the wealthier upper classes in the cities.

Especially noticeable in the eighteenth century was the expansion of both the reading public and publishing. One study revealed that French publishers were issuing about 1,600 titles yearly in the 1780s, up from 300 titles in 1750. Though many of these titles were still aimed at small groups of the educated elite, many were also directed to the new reading public of the middle classes, which included women and even urban artisans. The growth of publishing houses made it possible for authors to make money from their works and be less dependent on wealthy patrons.

An important aspect of the growth of publishing and reading in the eighteenth century was the development of magazines for the general public. Great Britain, an important center for the new magazines, saw 25 periodicals published in 1700, 103 in 1760, and 158 in 1780. Along with magazines came daily newspapers. The first was printed in London in 1702, but by 1780, thirty-seven other English towns had their own newspapers. Filled with news and special features, they were relatively cheap and were available free of charge in coffeehouses.

Popular Culture

Popular culture refers to the written and unwritten literature, and the social activities and pursuits that are fundamental to the lives of most people. The distinguishing characteristic of popular culture is its collective and public nature. Group activity was especially evident in the festival, a broad name used to cover a variety of celebrations: community festivals in Catholic Europe that celebrated the feast day of the local patron saint; annual festivals, such as Christmas and Easter, that went back to medieval Christianity; and Carnival, the most spectacular form of festival, which was celebrated in Spain, Italy, France, Germany, and Austria. All of these festivals were special occasions when people ate, drank, and celebrated to excess. In traditional societies, festival was a time for relaxation and enjoyment because much of the rest of the year was taken up with unrelieved work. As the poet Thomas Gray said of Carnival in Turin in 1739: "This Carnival lasts only from Christmas to Lent; one half of the remaining part of the year is passed in remembering the last, the other in expecting the future Carnival."[7]

Carnival was celebrated in the weeks leading up to the beginning of Lent, the forty-day period of fasting and purification preceding Easter. Because people were

Popular Culture: Carnival. Pictured here in a painting by Giovanni Signorini is a scene from the celebration of Carnival on the Piazza Santa Croce in Florence, Italy. Carnival was a period of festivities before Lent that was celebrated in most Roman Catholic countries. It became an occasion for indulgence in food, drink, games, practical jokes, and merriment, all of which are evident here.

expected to abstain from meat, sex, and most recreations during Lent, Carnival was a time of great indulgence. Hearty consumption of food, especially meat and other delicacies, and heavy drinking were the norm during Carnival; so too was intense sexual activity. Songs with double meanings that would be considered offensive at other times could be sung publicly at this time of year. A float of Florentine key makers, for example, sang this ditty to the ladies: "Our tools are fine, new and useful. / We always carry them with us. / They are good for anything. / If you want to touch them, you can." Finally, Carnival was a time of aggression, a time to release pent-up feelings. Most often this took the form of verbal aggression, since people were allowed to openly insult other people and even to criticize their social superiors and authorities.

The same sense of community evident in festival was also present in the chief gathering places of the common people, the local taverns or cabarets. Taverns functioned as a regular gathering place for neighborhood men to talk, play games, conduct small business matters, and drink. In some countries, the favorite drinks of poor people, such as gin in England and vodka in Russia, proved devastating as poor people regularly drank themselves into oblivion. Gin was cheap; the classic sign in English taverns, "Drunk for a penny, dead drunk for two pence," was literally true. In England, the consumption of gin rose from 2 million to 5 million gallons between 1714 and 1733 and declined only when complaints finally led to laws to restrict sales in the 1750s.

In the eighteenth century, the gulf between elite and poor grew ever wider. In 1500, popular culture was for everyone, including members of the aristocracy. But between 1500 and 1800, the nobility, clergy, and bourgeoisie had abandoned popular culture to the lower classes. By abandoning the popular festivals, the upper classes were also cutting themselves off from the popular worldview as well. Their new scientific outlook led them to regard such things as witchcraft, faith healing, fortune-telling, and prophecy as the beliefs of people, as one writer said, "of the weakest judgment and reason, as women, children, and ignorant and superstitious persons."

Crime and Punishment

By the eighteenth century, most European states had developed a hierarchy of courts to deal with crimes.

The Punishment of Crime

Torture and capital punishment remained common features of European judicial systems well into the eighteenth century. Public spectacles were especially gruesome, as this excerpt from the *Nocturnal Spectator* of Restif de la Bretonne demonstrates.

Restif de la Bretonne, "The Broken Man"

I went home by way of rue Saint-Antoine and the Place de Greve. Three murderers had been broken on the wheel there, the day before. I had not expected to see any such spectacle, one that I had never dared to witness. But as I crossed the square I caught sight of a poor wretch, pale, half dead, wracked by the pains of the interrogation inflicted on him twenty hours earlier; he was stumbling down from the Hotel de Ville supported by the executioner and the confessor. These two men, so completely different, inspired an inexpressible emotion in me! I watched the latter embrace a miserable man consumed by fever, filthy as the dungeons he came from, swarming with vermin!

And I said to myself, "O Religion, here is your greatest glory! . . ."

I saw a horrible sight, even though the torture had been mitigated. . . . The wretch had revealed his accomplices. He was garroted before he was put to the wheel. A winch set under the scaffold tightened a noose around the victim's neck and he was strangled; for a long while the confessor and the hangman felt his heart to see whether the artery still pulsed, and the hideous blows were dealt only after it beat no longer. . . . I left, with my hair standing on end in horror.

Q What does this selection reveal about the punishment of crime in the eighteenth century? What impact did such descriptions have on the philosophes' attitudes toward the administration of justice as it was carried out by their respective monarchical states?

Source: From *Les Nuits de Paris or Nocturnal Spectator: A Selection*, trans. L. Asher and E. Fertig, pp. 7–8. New York: Knopf, 1964.

Except in England, judicial torture remained an important means of obtaining evidence before a trial. Courts used the rack, thumbscrews, and other instruments to obtain confessions in criminal cases. Punishments for crimes were often cruel and even spectacular. Public executions were a basic part of traditional punishment and were regarded as a necessary means of deterring potential offenders in an age when a state's police forces were too weak to ensure the capture of criminals. Although nobles were executed by simple beheading, lower-class criminals condemned to death were tortured, broken on the wheel, or drawn and quartered. The death penalty was still commonly used for property crimes as well as for violent offenses (see the box above). By 1800, more than two hundred crimes were subject to the death penalty in England. In addition to executions, European states resorted to forced labor in mines, forts, and navies. England also sent criminals as indentured servants to colonies in the New World and, after the American Revolution, to Australia.

Appalled by the unjust laws and brutal punishments of their times, some philosophes sought to create a new approach to justice. The most notable effort was made by an Italian philosophe, Cesare Beccaria (CHAY-zuh-ray buh-KAH-ree-uh) (1738–1794). In his essay *On Crimes and Punishments*, written in 1764, Beccaria argued that punishments should serve only as deterrents, not as exercises in brutality: "Such punishments . . . ought to be chosen as will make the strongest and most lasting impressions on the minds of others, with the least torment to the body of the criminal."[8] Beccaria was also opposed to the use of capital punishment. It was spectacular, but it failed to stop others from committing crimes. Imprisonment—the deprivation of freedom—made a far more lasting impression. Moreover, capital punishment was harmful to society because it set an example of barbarism: "Is it not absurd, that the laws, which detest and punish homicide, should, in order to prevent murder, publicly commit murder themselves?"[9] By the end of the eighteenth century, a growing sentiment against executions and torture led to a decline in both corporal and capital punishment. A new type of prison, in which criminals were confined to cells and subjected to discipline and regular work to rehabilitate them, began to replace the public spectacle of barbarous punishments.

Religion and the Churches

Q FOCUS QUESTION: How did popular religion differ from institutional religion in the eighteenth century?

The music of Bach and the pilgrimage and monastic churches of southern Germany and Austria make us aware of a curious fact. Though much of the great art and music of the time was religious, the thought of the time was antireligious as life became increasingly secularized and men of reason attacked the established churches. And yet most Europeans were still Christians. Even many of those most critical of the churches accepted that society could not function without religious faith.

The Institutional Church

In the eighteenth century, the established Catholic and Protestant churches were basically conservative institutions that upheld society's hierarchical structure, privileged classes, and traditions. Although churches experienced change because of new state policies, they did not sustain any dramatic internal changes. In both Catholic and Protestant countries, the parish church run by priest or pastor remained the center of religious practice. In addition to providing religious services, the parish church kept records of births, deaths, and marriages; provided charity for the poor; supervised whatever primary education there was; and cared for orphans.

Toleration and Religious Minorities

One of the chief battle cries of the philosophes was a call for religious toleration. Out of political necessity, a certain level of tolerance of different creeds had occurred in the seventeenth century. Many rulers, however, still believed that there was only one path to salvation and that it was a ruler's duty not to allow subjects to be condemned to Hell by being heretics. Hence, persecution of heretics continued; the last burning of a heretic took place in 1781.

The Jews remained the despised religious minority of Europe. The largest number of Jews (known as the Ashkenazic Jews) lived in eastern Europe. Except in relatively tolerant Poland, Jews were restricted in their movements, forbidden to own land or hold certain jobs, forced to pay burdensome special taxes, and subject to periodic outbursts of popular wrath. The resulting **pogroms**, in which Jewish communities

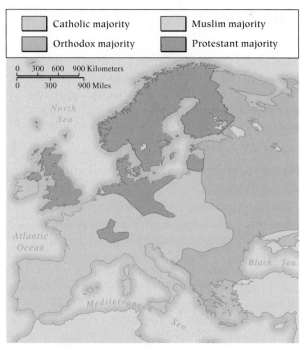

Catholic majority   Muslim majority
Orthodox majority   Protestant majority

0   300   600   900 Kilometers
0   300   900 Miles

North Sea

Atlantic Ocean

Black Sea

Mediterranean Sea

Religious Populations of Eighteenth-Century Europe

were looted and massacred, made Jewish existence precarious and dependent on the favor of their territorial rulers.

Another major group was the Sephardic Jews, who had been expelled from Spain in the fifteenth century. Although many had migrated to the Ottoman Empire, some of them had settled in cities such as Amsterdam, Venice, London, and Frankfurt, where they were relatively free to participate in the banking and commercial activities that Jews had practiced since the Middle Ages. The highly successful ones came to provide valuable services to rulers, especially in central Europe. But even these Jews were insecure because their religion set them apart from the Christian majority and served as a catalyst for social resentment.

Some Enlightenment thinkers in the eighteenth century favored a new acceptance of Jews. They argued that Jews and Muslims were human and deserved the full rights of citizenship despite their religion. Many philosophes denounced persecution of the Jews but made no attempt to hide their hostility and ridiculed Jewish customs. Diderot, for example, said that the Jews had "all the defects peculiar to an ignorant and superstitious nation." Many Europeans favored assimilation of the Jews into the mainstream of society, but only by the conversion of Jews to Christianity. This, of course, was not acceptable to most Jews.

The Austrian emperor Joseph II (1780–1790) attempted to adopt a new policy toward the Jews, although it too was limited. It freed Jews from nuisance taxes and allowed them more freedom of movement and job opportunities, but they were still restricted from owning land and worshiping in public. At the same time, Joseph encouraged Jews to learn German and to work toward greater assimilation into Austrian society.

Popular Religion in the Eighteenth Century

Despite the rise of skepticism and the intellectuals' belief in deism and natural religion, religious devotion remained strong in the eighteenth century. It is difficult to assess precisely the religiosity of Europe's Catholics. The Catholic parish church remained an important center of life for the entire community. How many people went to church regularly cannot be known exactly, but 90 to 95 percent of Catholic populations did go to Mass on Easter Sunday, one of the church's most important celebrations.

After the initial century of religious fervor that created Protestantism in the sixteenth century, Protestant churches in the seventeenth century had settled down into established patterns controlled by state authorities and served by a well-educated clergy. In the process, Protestant churches became bureaucratized and bereft of religious enthusiasm. In Germany and England, where rationalism and deism had become influential and moved some theologians to a more "rational" Christianity, the desire of ordinary Protestant churchgoers for greater depths of religious experience led to new and dynamic religious movements.

One of the most famous movements—Methodism—was the work of John Wesley (1703–1791). An ordained Anglican minister, Wesley underwent a mystical experience in which "the gift of God's grace" assured him of salvation and led him to become a missionary to the English people, bringing the "glad tidings" of salvation to all people, despite opposition from the Anglican Church, which criticized this emotional mysticism or religious enthusiasm as superstitious nonsense. To Wesley, all could be saved by experiencing God and opening the doors to his grace.

In taking the Gospel to the people, Wesley preached to the masses in open fields, appealing especially to the lower classes neglected by the socially elitist Anglican Church. He tried, he said, "to lower religion to the level of the lowest people's capacities." Wesley's charismatic preaching often provoked highly charged and even violent conversion experiences. Afterward, converts were organized into so-called Methodist societies or chapels in which they could aid each other in doing the good works that Wesley considered a component of salvation. Although Wesley sought to keep Methodism within the Anglican Church, after his death it became a separate and independent sect. Methodism was an important revival of Christianity and proved that the need for spiritual experience had not been extinguished by the eighteenth-century search for reason.

Chapter Summary

The eighteenth century was a time of change but also of tradition. The popularization of the ideas of the Scientific Revolution, the impact of travel literature, a new skepticism, and the ideas of Locke and Newton led to what historians call the Age of Enlightenment. Its leading figures were the intellectuals known as philosophes, who hoped that they could create a new society by using reason to discover the natural laws that governed it. Like the Christian humanists of the fifteenth and sixteenth centuries, they believed that education could create better human beings and a better human society. Such philosophes as Montesquieu, Voltaire, Diderot, Quesnay, Smith, Beccaria, and Rousseau attacked traditional religion as the enemy, advocated religious toleration and freedom of thought, criticized their oppressive societies, and created a new "science of man" in economics, politics, and education. In doing so, the philosophes laid the foundation for a modern worldview based on rationalism and secularism.

Although many of the philosophes continued to hold traditional views about women, female intellectuals like Mary Astell and Mary Wollstonecraft began to argue for the equality of the sexes and the right of women to be educated. The Enlightenment appealed largely to the urban middle classes and some members of the nobility, and its ideas were

discussed in salons, coffeehouses, reading clubs, lending libraries, and societies like the Freemasons.

Innovation in the arts also characterized the eighteenth century. The cultural fertility of the age is evident in Rococo painting and architecture; the achievements of Bach, Handel, Haydn, and Mozart in music; and the birth of the novel in literature.

Although the philosophes attacked the established Christian churches, many Europeans continued to practice their traditional faith. Moreover, a new wave of piety swept both Catholic and

Protestant churches, especially noticeable in Protestant Europe with the advent of John Wesley and Methodism in England.

Thus, despite the secular thought and secular ideas that began to pervade the mental world of the ruling elites, most people in eighteenth-century Europe still lived by seemingly eternal verities and practices—God, religious worship, and farming. The most brilliant architecture and music of the age were religious. And yet the forces of secularization were too strong to stop. In the midst of intellectual change, economic, political, and social transformations of great purport were taking shape and would lead, as we shall see in the next two chapters, to both political and social upheavals and even revolution before the century's end.

CHAPTER TIMELINE

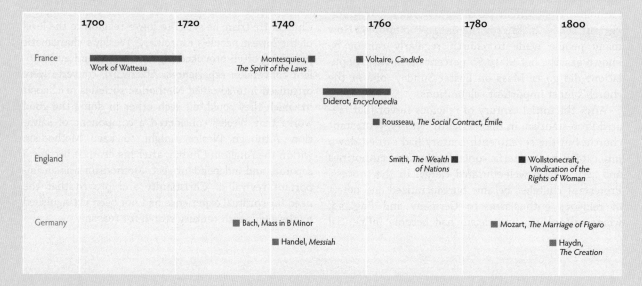

	1700	1720	1740	1760	1780	1800
France	Work of Watteau		Montesquieu, ■ *The Spirit of the Laws*	■ Voltaire, *Candide*		
			Diderot, *Encyclopedia*			
				■ Rousseau, *The Social Contract, Émile*		
England				Smith, *The Wealth* ■ of Nations	■ Wollstonecraft, *Vindication of the Rights of Woman*	
Germany			■ Bach, Mass in B Minor		■ Mozart, *The Marriage of Figaro*	
			■ Handel, *Messiah*		■ Haydn, *The Creation*	

CHAPTER REVIEW

Upon Reflection

Q What contributions did Montesquieu, Voltaire, Diderot, and Rousseau make to the Enlightenment? What did they have in common? How did they differ?

Q What is popular culture, and how was it expressed in the eighteenth century?

Q What kinds of experiences do you associate with popular religion in the eighteenth century? How do you explain the continuing growth of popular religious devotion?

Key Terms

Enlightenment (p. 406)
skepticism (p. 407)
cultural relativism (p. 407)
philosophes (p. 408)
cosmopolitan (p. 408)
separation of powers (p. 409)
deism (p. 410)
laissez-faire (p. 412)

economic liberalism (p. 412)
Romanticism (p. 413)
feminism (p. 414)
salons (p. 414)
Rococo (p. 417)
high culture (p. 419)
popular culture (p. 419)
pogroms (p. 422)

Suggestions for Further Reading

EIGHTEENTH-CENTURY EUROPE Surveys of eighteenth-century Europe include **M. S. Anderson, *Europe in the Eighteenth Century***, 4th ed. (London, 2000); **I. Woloch, *Eighteenth-Century Europe*** (New York, 1986); and **T. C. W. Blanning, ed., *The Eighteenth Century: Europe, 1689–1815*** (Oxford, 2000).

THE ENLIGHTENMENT Good introductions to the Enlightenment can be found in **U. Im Hof, *The Enlightenment*** (Oxford, 1994), and **D. Outram, *The Enlightenment***, 2d ed. (Cambridge, 2005). See also **M. Fitzpatrick et al., *The Enlightenment World*** (New York, 2004). On the social history of the Enlightenment, see **T. Munck, *The Enlightenment: A Comparative Social History, 1721–1794*** (London, 2000). Studies of the major Enlightenment intellectuals include **R. Pearson, *Voltaire Almighty: A Life in Pursuit of Freedom*** (New York, 2005); **P. N. Furbank, *Diderot: A Critical Biography*** (New York, 1992); and **L. Damrosch, *Jean-Jacques Rousseau: Restless Genius*** (Boston, 2005). On women in the eighteenth century, see **N. Z. Davis and A. Farge,** eds., ***A History of Women: Renaissance and Enlightenment Paradoxes*** (Cambridge, Mass., 1993), and **M. E. Wiesner-Hanks, *Women and Gender in Early Modern Europe*** (Cambridge, 2000).

CULTURE AND SOCIETY On Rococo art, see **E. G. Baur and I. F. Walther, *Rococo*** (New York, 2007). On the growth of literacy, see **R. A. Houston, *Literacy in Early Modern Europe: Culture and Education, 1500–1800*** (New York, 1988).

POPULAR CULTURE Important studies on popular culture include **P. Burke, *Popular Culture in Early Modern Europe*** (New York, 1978), and **J. Mullan, ed., *Eighteenth-Century Popular Culture*** (Oxford, 2000).

EIGHTEENTH-CENTURY RELIGIOUS HISTORY A good introduction to the religious history of the eighteenth century can be found in **G. R. Cragg, *The Church and the Age of Reason, 1648–1789*,** rev. ed. (London, 1990). On John Wesley, see **H. Rack, *Reasonable Enthusiast: John Wesley and the Rise of Methodism*,** 3d ed. (New York, 2002).

Notes

1. Quoted in D. Outram, *The Enlightenment* (Cambridge, 1995), p. 67.
2. D. Hume, *History of England* (London: 1754–62), vol. 8, p. 326.
3. J. Locke, *An Essay Concerning Human Understanding* (New York, 1964), pp. 89–90.
4. J. J. Rousseau, *The Social Contract*, trans. M. Cranston (Harmondsworth, England, 1968), p. 141.
5. M. Astell, *A Serious Proposal to the Ladies*, in *First Feminists: British Women Writers, 1578–1799*, ed. M. Ferguson (Bloomington, Ind., 1985), p. 190.
6. K. Clark, *Civilization* (New York, 1969), p. 231.
7. Quoted in P. Burke, *Popular Culture in Early Modern Europe* (New York, 1978), p. 179.
8. C. Beccaria, *An Essay on Crimes and Punishments*, trans. E. D. Ingraham (Philadelphia, 1819), pp. 59–60.
9. Ibid., p. 60.

MindTap **MindTap** is a fully online, highly personalized learning experience built upon Cengage Learning content. MindTap combines student learning tools—readings, multimedia, activities, and assessments—into a singular Learning Path that guides students through the course.

CHAPTER 18

The Eighteenth Century: European States, International Wars, and Social Change

A 1793 portrait of Catherine the Great of Russia by Johann Lampi

CHAPTER OUTLINE AND FOCUS QUESTIONS

The European States

Q What were the main developments in France and Great Britain in the eighteenth century? What do historians mean by the term *enlightened absolutism*, and to what degree did eighteenth-century Prussia, Austria, and Russia exhibit its characteristics?

Wars and Diplomacy

Q What were the causes and results of the Seven Years' War?

Economic Expansion and Social Change

Q What changes occurred in agriculture, finance, industry, and trade during the eighteenth century?

The Social Order of the Eighteenth Century

Q Who were the main groups making up the European social order in the eighteenth century, and how did the conditions in which they lived differ both between groups and between different parts of Europe?

CRITICAL THINKING

Q What was the relationship among intellectual, political, economic, and social changes in the eighteenth century?

CONNECTIONS TO TODAY

Q How do the benefits and consequences of the agricultural revolution of the eighteenth century compare with the benefits and consequences of the changes in agricultural production occurring in the twenty-first century?

HISTORIANS OFTEN DEFINE the eighteenth century as the years from 1715 to 1789. Politically, this makes sense, since 1715 marks the end of the age of Louis XIV and 1789 was the year in which the French Revolution erupted. This period has often been portrayed as the final phase of Europe's old order, before the violent upheaval and reordering of society associated with the French Revolution. Europe's old order—still largely agrarian, dominated by kings and landed aristocrats, and grounded in privileges for nobles, clergy, towns, and provinces—seemed to continue a basic pattern that had prevailed in Europe since medieval times. But new ideas and new practices were also beginning to emerge. Just as a new intellectual order based on rationalism and secularism was evolving from the Scientific Revolution and the Enlightenment, demographic, economic, and social patterns were beginning to change in ways that heralded the emergence of a modern new order.

The ideas of the Enlightenment seemed to proclaim a new political age as well. Catherine the Great, who ruled Russia from 1762 to 1796, wrote to Voltaire: "Since 1746 I have been under the greatest obligations to you. Before that period I read nothing but romances, but by chance your works fell into my hands, and ever since then I have never ceased to read them, and have no desire for books less well written than yours, or less instructive." The empress also invited Diderot to Russia and, when he arrived, urged him to speak frankly "as man to man." Diderot did, offering her advice for a far-ranging program of political and financial reform. But Catherine's apparent eagerness to make enlightened reforms was tempered by skepticism. She said of Diderot, "If I had believed him, everything would have been turned upside down in my kingdom; legislation, administration, finance—all would have been turned topsy-turvy to make room for impractical theories." For Catherine, enlightened reform remained more a dream than a reality, and in the end, the waging of wars to gain more power was more important.

In the eighteenth century, the process of centralization that had characterized the growth of states since the Middle Ages continued as most European states enlarged their bureaucratic machinery and consolidated their governments in order to collect the revenues and build the armies they needed to compete militarily with the other European states. International competition continued to be the favorite pastime of eighteenth-century rulers. Within the European state system, the nations that would dominate Europe until World War I—Britain, France, Austria, Prussia, and Russia—emerged as the five great powers of Europe. Their rivalries led to major wars, which some have called the first world wars because they were fought outside as well as inside Europe. In the midst of this state building and war making, dramatic demographic, economic, and social changes gave rise to a radical transformation in the way Europeans would raise food and produce goods.

The European States

Q **FOCUS QUESTIONS:** What were the main developments in France and Great Britain in the eighteenth century? What do historians mean by the term *enlightened absolutism*, and to what degree did eighteenth-century Prussia, Austria, and Russia exhibit its characteristics?

Monarchs ruled most European states in the eighteenth century. Although the seventeenth-century justification for strong monarchy on the basis of divine right continued to hold sway, divine-right assumptions were gradually superseded by influential utilitarian arguments as Europe became increasingly secularized. The Prussian king Frederick II expressed these well when he attempted to explain the services a monarch must provide for his people:

> These services consisted in the maintenance of the laws; a strict execution of justice; an employment of his whole powers to prevent any corruption of manners; and defending the state against its enemies. It is the duty of this magistrate to pay attention to agriculture; it should be his care that provisions for the nation should be in abundance, and that commerce and industry should be encouraged. He is a perpetual sentinel, who must watch the acts and the conduct of the enemies of the state.... If he be the first general, the first minister of the realm, it is not that he should remain the shadow of authority, but that he should fulfill the duties of such titles. He is only the first servant of the state.[1]

This utilitarian argument was reinforced by the praises of the philosophes.

Enlightened Absolutism?

There is no doubt that Enlightenment thought had an impact on the political development of European states in the eighteenth century. Closely related to the Enlightenment idea of **natural laws** was the belief in **natural rights**, which were thought to be fundamental privileges that must not be withheld from any person. These natural rights included equality before the law, freedom of religious worship, freedom of speech and the press, and the rights to assemble, hold property, and seek happiness. The American Declaration of Independence summarized the Enlightenment concept of natural rights in its opening paragraph: "We hold these truths to be self-evident, that all men are created equal, that they are endowed by their Creator with certain unalienable rights, that among these are Life, Liberty and the pursuit of Happiness."

But how were these natural rights to be established and preserved? In the opinion of most philosophes, people needed the direction provided by an enlightened ruler. What made rulers enlightened? They must allow religious toleration, freedom of speech and the press, and the right to hold private property. They must foster the arts, sciences, and education. Above all, they must not be arbitrary in their rule; they must obey the laws and enforce them fairly for all subjects. Only strong monarchs seemed capable of overcoming vested interests and effecting the reforms society needed. Reforms, then, should come from above—from the rulers rather than from the people. Distrustful of the masses, the philosophes believed that absolute rulers, swayed by enlightened principles, were the best hope of reforming their societies.

The extent to which rulers actually did so is frequently discussed in the political histories of Europe in the eighteenth century. Many historians once assumed that a new type of monarchy emerged in the late eighteenth century, which they called enlightened despotism or **enlightened absolutism**. Monarchs such as Frederick II of Prussia, Catherine the Great of Russia, and Joseph II of Austria supposedly followed the advice of the philosophes and ruled by enlightened principles, establishing a path to modern nationhood. Recent scholarship, however, has questioned the usefulness of the concept of enlightened absolutism. We can best determine the extent to which it can be applied by surveying the development of the European states and then making a judgment about the enlightened absolutism of the century's later years.

The Atlantic Seaboard States

As a result of the overseas voyages of the sixteenth century, the European economic axis began to shift from the Mediterranean to the Atlantic seaboard. In the seventeenth century, English and Dutch influence expanded while Spanish and Portuguese power declined. By the eighteenth century, Dutch power had waned, and it fell to the English and the French to build the commercial empires that ultimately fostered a truly global economy.

FRANCE: THE PROBLEMS OF THE FRENCH MONARCHY In the eighteenth century, France experienced an economic revival as the Enlightenment gained strength.

The French monarchy, however, was not overly influenced by the philosophes and resisted reforms even as the French aristocracy grew stronger.

Louis XIV had left France with enlarged territories, an enormous debt, an unhappy populace, and a five-year-old great-grandson as his successor. Louis XV (1715–1774) did not begin to rule in his own right until 1743. But Louis proved to be both lazy and weak, and ministers and mistresses soon began to influence the king, control the affairs of state, and undermine the prestige of the monarchy. The loss of an empire in the Seven Years' War (discussed later in this chapter), accompanied by burdensome taxes, an ever-mounting public debt, more hungry people, and a court life at Versailles that remained frivolous and carefree, forced even Louis to recognize the growing disgust with his monarchy.

The next king, Louis's twenty-year-old grandson who became Louis XVI (1774–1792), knew little about the operations of the French government and lacked the energy to deal decisively with state affairs. His wife, Marie Antoinette (ma-REE ahn-twahn-NET), was a spoiled Austrian princess who devoted much of her time to court intrigues (see the Film & History feature on p. 429). As France's financial crises worsened, neither Louis nor his queen seemed able to fathom the depths of despair and discontent that soon led to violent revolution (see Chapter 19).

GREAT BRITAIN: KING AND PARLIAMENT The success of the Glorious Revolution in England had prevented absolutism without clearly inaugurating constitutional monarchy. The eighteenth-century British political system was characterized by a sharing of power between king and Parliament, with Parliament gradually gaining the upper hand. (The United Kingdom of Great Britain came into existence in 1707 when the governments of England and Scotland were united; the term *British* came to refer to both English and Scots.) The king chose ministers responsible to himself who set policy and guided Parliament, which had the power to make laws, levy taxes, pass the budget, and indirectly influence the king's ministers. The eighteenth-century British Parliament was dominated by a landed aristocracy that historians usually divide into two groups: the peers, who sat for life in the House of Lords, and the landed gentry, who sat in the House of Commons and served as justices of the peace. The two groups had much in common: both were made up of landowners with similar economic interests, and they frequently intermarried.

FILM & HISTORY

Marie Antoinette (2006)

THE FILM *MARIE ANTOINETTE* **(2006),** directed by Sofia Coppola, is based on Antonia Fraser's interpretation of the early life of Marie Antoinette in her book, *Marie Antoinette: A Journey* (2001). The film begins with the marriage of Marie Antoinette (Kirsten Dunst), the daughter of Empress Maria Theresa of Austria (Marianne Faithfull), to the dauphin Louis (Jason Schwartzman)—heir to the French throne. Four years later, in 1774, Marie Antoinette became queen of France; in 1793, she went to the guillotine. Although the French Revolution (see Chapter 19) and financial troubles of the monarchy enter briefly, the film primarily concentrates on the experiences of a young Marie Antoinette who naively entered into the court of Versailles and was subjected to suspicion and subsequent isolation.

Marie Antoinette (Kirsten Dunst) at Versailles.

Columbia/American Zoetrope/Sony/The Kobal Collection at Art Resource, NY

Perhaps the best part of the film is the portrayal of Marie Antoinette's court life at Versailles, her days filled with courtly ceremonies, daily Mass, and attendance of the public at meals. Under intense scrutiny due to her Austrian heritage and unfamiliarity with the protocol of life at Versailles, Marie Antoinette makes several early missteps. She refuses to speak to Louis XV's mistress, the comtesse du Barry (Asia Argento), because the comtesse threatens Marie Antoinette's position as the highest-ranking woman at court. Ignoring the king's mistress, however, places the young dauphine in the precarious position of insulting the king.

In addition to her troubles at court, Marie Antoinette faces an even greater challenge: the need to secure her place by producing an heir to the French throne. Her young husband, however, has other interests, including hunting, lock making, and reading—all take precedence over the consummation of the marriage, which does not take place for seven years. During this time, Marie Antoinette faces increasing pressure from her mother, who has produced sixteen children while ruling the Austrian Empire. Bored but aware that she must remain chaste, the young dauphine turns to frivolous pursuits, including games, plays, outings in Paris, decorating,

gambling, and above all, purchasing clothing. Marie Antoinette's desire for elaborate gowns is encouraged by her role as the tastemaker for the French court. In 1782, she commissions ninety-three gowns made of silk and other expensive fabrics. Her life of frivolity and luxury is depicted beautifully in the scenes from her twenty-first birthday, where, dressed in her finery, she plays cards and eats sweets until the early hours of the morning.

After the birth of her children, the first in 1777, Marie Antoinette begins to withdraw from the scrutiny of the court. In 1783, she is given the keys to the Petit Trianon, a small palace on the grounds of Versailles, where she spends most of her days. Although she is spending more time with her children and less on the frivolity of her earlier days at Versailles, her increasing estrangement from the court only worsens her reputation with the French public.

Filmed at Versailles, the film captures the grandeur and splendor of eighteenth-century royal life. The movie received negative reviews, however, when it opened in France, in part because of its use of contemporary music by artists such as The Cure and The Strokes and its inclusion of modern products such as Converse sneakers. The flurry of costumes and music can be distracting, but it also conveys the rebelliousness of a young woman, frustrated and bored, isolated—yet always on display.

The British House of Commons. A sharing of power between king and Parliament characterized the British political system in the eighteenth century. Parliament was divided into the House of Lords and the House of Commons. This painting shows the House of Commons in session in 1793 during a debate over the possibility of war with France. William Pitt the Younger is addressing the chamber.

The deputies to the House of Commons were chosen from the boroughs and counties but not by popular voting. Who was eligible to vote in the boroughs varied widely, enabling wealthy landed aristocrats to gain support by **patronage** and bribery; the result was a number of "pocket boroughs" controlled by a single person (hence "in his pocket"). The duke of Newcastle, for example, controlled the representatives from seven boroughs. It has been estimated that out of 405 borough deputies, 293 were chosen by fewer than 500 voters. This aristocratic control also extended to the county delegates, two from each of England's forty counties. Although all holders of property worth at least 40 shillings a year could vote, members of the leading landed gentry families were elected over and over again.

In 1714, a new dynasty—the Hanoverians—was established. When the last Stuart ruler, Queen Anne (1702–1714), died without an heir, the crown was offered to the Protestant rulers of the German state of Hanover. Because the first Hanoverian king, George I (1714–1727), did not speak English and neither he nor George II (1727–1760) had much familiarity with the British system, their chief ministers were allowed to handle Parliament. Many historians believe that this exercise of ministerial power was an important step in the development of the modern cabinet system in British government.

Robert Walpole served as prime minister from 1721 to 1742 and pursued a peaceful foreign policy to avoid new land taxes. But new forces were emerging in eighteenth-century England as growing trade and industry led an ever-increasing middle class to favor expansion of trade and world empire. The exponents of empire found a spokesperson in William Pitt the Elder, who became prime minister in 1757 and furthered imperial ambitions by acquiring Canada and India in the Seven Years' War.

Despite his successes, Pitt the Elder was dismissed in 1761 by the new king, George III (1760–1820), and replaced by the king's favorite, Lord Bute. Discontent

CHRONOLOGY	France and Britain in the Eighteenth Century
France	
Louis XV	1715–1774
Louis XVI	1774–1792
Great Britain	
The Stuarts	
Anne	1702–1714
The Hanoverians	
George I	1714–1727
George II	1727–1760
Robert Walpole	1721–1742
William Pitt the Elder	1757–1761
George III	1760–1820
William Pitt the Younger	1783–1801

over the electoral system and the loss of the American colonies (see Chapter 19), however, led to public criticism of the king. In 1780, the House of Commons affirmed that "the influence of the crown has increased, is increasing, and ought to be diminished." King George III managed to avoid drastic change by appointing William Pitt the Younger (1759–1806), son of William Pitt the Elder, as prime minister in 1783. Supported by the merchants, industrial classes, and the king, Pitt managed to stay in power. George III, however, remained an uncertain supporter because of periodic bouts of insanity (he once mistook a tree in Windsor Park for the king of Prussia). Nevertheless, thanks to Pitt's successes, serious reform of the corrupt parliamentary system was avoided for another generation.

Absolutism in Central and Eastern Europe

Of the five major European powers, three were located in central and eastern Europe and came to play an increasingly important role in European international politics (see Map 18.1).

PRUSSIA: ARMY AND BUREAUCRACY Two able Prussian kings in the eighteenth century, Frederick William I and Frederick II, further developed the two major institutions—the army and the bureaucracy—that were the backbone of Prussia. Frederick William I (1713–1740) promoted the evolution of Prussia's highly efficient civil bureaucracy by establishing the General Directory, which served as the chief administrative agent of the

MAP 18.1 Europe in 1763. By the middle of the eighteenth century, five major powers dominated Europe—Prussia, Austria, Russia, Britain, and France. Each sought to enhance its power both domestically, through a bureaucracy that collected taxes and ran the military, and internationally, by capturing territory or preventing other powers from capturing territory.

Q Given the distribution of Prussian and Habsburg holdings, in what areas of Europe were they most likely to compete for land and power?

central government, supervising military, police, economic, and financial affairs. Frederick William strove to make these civil service workers into a highly efficient bureaucracy; their code stressed obedience, honor, and service to the king as the supreme values. As Frederick William asserted, "One must serve the king with life and limb, with goods and chattels, with honor and conscience, and surrender everything except salvation. The latter is reserved for God. But everything else must be mine."[2] Close personal supervision of the bureaucracy became a hallmark of the eighteenth-century Prussian rulers.

Frederick William's other major concern was the army. By the end of his reign, it had grown from 45,000 to 83,000 men. Though tenth in geographic area and thirteenth in population among the European states, Prussia had the fourth-largest army, after France, Russia, and Austria. The nobility or landed aristocracy known as Junkers, who owned large estates with many serfs, were the officers in the Prussian army. By using nobles as officers, Frederick William ensured a close bond between the nobility and the army and, in turn, the loyalty of the nobility to the absolute monarch. Prussian nobles believed in duty, obedience, and sacrifice. At the same time, because of its size and reputation as one of the finest in Europe, the Prussian army was the most important institution in the state.

Frederick the II, known as the Great (1740–1786), was one of the best-educated and most cultured monarchs in the eighteenth century. He was well versed in Enlightenment thought and even invited Voltaire to live at his court for several years. His father despised his intellectual interests and forced his intelligent son to prepare for a career as a ruler. A believer in the king as the "first servant of the state," Frederick became a conscientious ruler who made few innovations in administration. His diligence in overseeing its operation, however, made the Prussian bureaucracy well known for both efficiency and honesty.

For a time, Frederick seemed quite willing to follow the philosophes' suggestions for reform. He established a single code of laws for his territories that eliminated the use of torture except in treason and murder cases. He also granted limited freedom of speech and the press as well as complete religious toleration—no difficult task since he had no strong religious convictions anyway. Although Frederick was well aware of the philosophes' condemnation of serfdom, he was too dependent on the Prussian nobility to interfere with it or with the hierarchical structure

Frederick II. Frederick II was one of the most cultured and best-educated European monarchs. He is seen here in a portrait done five years before his death by the Swiss artist Anton Graff. The painting is regarded as Graff's masterpiece, and contemporaries considered it the best and most accurate portrait of the ruler. (bpk, Berlin /Charlottenburg Castle, Preussische Schlösser und Gärten, Berlin/Jörg P. Anders/Art Resource, NY)

of Prussian society. In fact, Frederick was a social conservative who made Prussian society even more aristocratic than it had been before. Frederick reversed his father's policy of allowing commoners to have power in the civil service and reserved the higher positions in the bureaucracy for members of the nobility. The upper ranks of the bureaucracy came close to constituting a hereditary caste.

Like his predecessors, Frederick the Great took great interest in military affairs and enlarged the Prussian army (to 200,000 men). Unlike his predecessors, he had no objection to using it. Frederick did not hesitate to take advantage of a succession crisis in the Habsburg monarchy to seize the Austrian province of Silesia for Prussia. This act aroused Austria's bitter hostility toward Prussia and embroiled Frederick in two major wars, the War of the Austrian Succession and the Seven Years' War. Although the latter war left his country exhausted, Frederick succeeded in keeping Silesia. After the wars, the first partition of Poland with Austria and Russia in 1772 won him the Polish territory between Prussia and Brandenburg and gave greater unity to the scattered lands of Prussia. By the end of his reign, Prussia was recognized as a great European power.

THE AUSTRIAN EMPIRE OF THE HABSBURGS The Austrian Empire had become one of the great European states by the beginning of the eighteenth century. The city of Vienna, center of the Habsburg monarchy, was filled with magnificent palaces and churches built in the Baroque style and became the music capital of Europe. Yet the sprawling assemblage of nationalities, languages, religions, and cultures that was Austria made it difficult to provide common laws and administrative centralization for its people. Although Empress Maria Theresa (1740–1780) managed to make administrative reforms that helped centralize the Austrian Empire, these reforms were done for practical reasons—to strengthen the power of the Habsburg state—and were accompanied by an enlargement and modernization of the armed forces. Maria Theresa remained staunchly Catholic and conservative and was not open to the wider reform calls of the philosophes. But her successor was.

Joseph II (1780–1790) was determined to make changes; at the same time, he carried on his mother's chief goal of enhancing Habsburg power within the monarchy and Europe. Joseph was an earnest man who believed in the need to sweep away anything standing in the path of reason. As he expressed it, "I have made Philosophy the lawmaker of my empire; her logical applications are going to transform Austria."

Joseph's reform program was far-reaching. He abolished serfdom and tried to give the peasants hereditary rights to their holdings. A new penal code was instituted that abrogated the death penalty and established the principle of equality of all before the law. Joseph introduced drastic religious reforms as well, including complete religious toleration and restrictions on the Catholic Church. Altogether, Joseph II issued 6,000 decrees and 11,000 laws in his effort to transform his empire.

Joseph's reform program proved overwhelming for Austria, however. He alienated the nobility by freeing the serfs and alienated the church by his attacks on the monastic establishment. Even the newly freed peasants were unhappy, unable to comprehend the drastic changes inherent in Joseph's policies. His attempt to rationalize the administration of the empire by imposing German as the official bureaucratic language alienated the non-German nationalities. As Joseph complained, there were not enough people for the kind of bureaucracy he needed. His deep sense of failure is revealed in the epitaph he wrote for his gravestone: "Here lies Joseph II, who was unfortunate in everything that he undertook." His successors undid many of his reform efforts.

RUSSIA UNDER CATHERINE THE GREAT Peter the Great of Russia was followed by six successors who were made and unmade by the palace guard. After the last of these, Peter III, was murdered by a faction of nobles in 1762, his German wife emerged as autocrat of all the Russians (see the box on p. 434). Catherine II (1762–1796) was an intelligent woman who was familiar with the works of the philosophes. She claimed that she wished to reform Russia along the lines of Enlightenment ideas, but she was always shrewd

Maria Theresa and Her Family. Maria Theresa governed the vast possessions of the Austrian Empire from 1740 to 1780. Of her ten surviving children, Joseph II (shown here in red standing beside his mother) succeeded her; Leopold became grand-duke of Tuscany and the ruler of Austria after Joseph's death; Ferdinand was made duke of Modena; and Marie Antoinette became the bride of King Louis XVI of France.

Enlightened Absolutism: Enlightened or Absolute?

Although historians have used the term *enlightened absolutism* to describe a new type of monarchy in the eighteenth century, scholars have recently questioned the usefulness of the concept. The three selections below offer an opportunity to evaluate one so-called enlightened monarch, Catherine the Great of Russia. The first selection is from a letter written by the baron de Breteuil, the French ambassador to Russia, giving his impressions of Catherine. In 1767, Catherine convened a legislative commission to prepare a new code of laws for Russia. In her *Instruction*, parts of which form the second selection, she gave the delegates a detailed guide to the principles they should follow. Although the guidelines were culled from the liberal ideas of the philosophes, the commission itself accomplished nothing. The third selection, from a Decree on Serfs (also issued in 1767), reveals Catherine's authoritarian nature.

Letter of the Baron de Breteuil

[Catherine] seems to combine every kind of ambition in her person. Everything that may add luster to her reign will have some attraction for her. Science and the arts will be encouraged to flourish in the empire, projects useful for the domestic economy will be undertaken. She will endeavor to reform the administration of justice and to invigorate the laws; but her policies will be based on Machiavellianism; and I should not be surprised if in this field she rivals the king of Prussia. She will adopt the prejudices of her entourage regarding the superiority of her power and will endeavor to win respect not by the sincerity and probity of her actions but also by an ostentatious display of her strength. Haughty as she is, she will stubbornly pursue her undertakings and will rarely retrace a false step. Cunning and falsity appear to be vices in her character; woe to him who puts too much trust in her.

Catherine II, Proposals for a New Law Code

13. What is the true End of Monarchy? Not to deprive People of their natural Liberty; but to correct their Actions, in order to attain the supreme good....

33. The Laws ought to be so framed, as to secure the Safety of every Citizen as much as possible.

34. The Equality of the Citizens consists in this; that they should all be subject to the same Laws....

123. The Usage of Torture is contrary to all the Dictates of Nature and Reason; even Mankind itself cries out against it, and demands loudly the total Abolition of it....

180. That Law, therefore, is high beneficial to the Community where it is established, which ordains that every Man be judged by his Peers and Equals. For when the Fate of a Citizen is in Question, all Prejudices arising from the Difference of Rank or Fortune should be stifled; because they ought to have no Influence between the Judges and the Parties accused....

194. No Man ought to be looked upon as guilty, before he has received his judicial Sentence; nor can the Laws deprive him of their Protection, before it is proved that he has forfeited all Right to it. What Right therefore can Power give to any to inflict Punishment upon a Citizen at a Time, when it is yet dubious, whether he is Innocent or guilty?

Catherine II, Decree on Serfs

The Governing Senate ... has deemed it necessary to make known that the landlords' serfs and peasants ... owe their landlords proper submission and absolute obedience in all matters, according to the laws that have been enacted from time immemorial by the autocratic forefathers of Her Imperial Majesty and which have not been repealed, and which provide that all persons who dare to incite serfs and peasants to disobey their landlords shall be arrested and taken to the nearest government office, there to be punished forthwith as disturbers of the public tranquility, according to the laws and without leniency. And should it so happen that even after the publication of the present decree of Her Imperial Majesty any serfs and peasants should cease to give the proper obedience to their landlords ... and should make bold to submit unlawful petitions complaining of their landlords, and especially to petition Her Imperial Majesty personally, then both those who make complaints and those who write up the petitions shall be punished by the knout and forthwith deported to Nerchinsk to penal servitude for life and shall be counted as part of the quota of recruits which their landlords must furnish to the army.

Q What impressions of Catherine do you get from the letter by the French ambassador to Russia? To what extent were the ideas expressed in the proposals for a new law code taken from the writings of the philosophes? What does the decree on serfs reveal about Catherine's view of power? Based on these documents, was Catherine an enlightened monarch? Why or why not?

Sources: Letter of the Baron de Breteuil. From G. Vernadsky, *A Source Book for Russian History* (New Haven: Yale University Press, 1972), Vol. 2, p. 451. Catherine II, Proposals for a New Law Code. From *Documents of Catherine the Great*, W. F. Reddaway. © 1931 by Cambridge University Press. Catherine II, Decree on Serfs. From G. Vernadsky, *A Source Book for Russian History* (New Haven: Yale University Press, 1972), Vol. 2 pp. 453–454.

enough to realize that her success depended on the support of the palace guard and the gentry class from which it stemmed. She could not afford to alienate the Russian nobility.

Initially, Catherine seemed eager to pursue reform. She called for the election of an assembly in 1767 to debate the details of a new law code. In her *Instruction*, written as a guide to the deliberations, Catherine questioned the institution of serfdom, torture, and capital punishment and even advocated the principle of the equality of all people in the eyes of the law. But a year and a half of negotiation produced little real change.

In fact, Catherine's subsequent policies had the effect of strengthening the landholding class at the expense of all others, especially the Russian serfs. To reorganize local government, Catherine divided Russia into fifty provinces, each of which was in turn subdivided into districts ruled by officials chosen by the nobles. In this way, the local nobility became responsible for the day-to-day governing of Russia. Moreover, the gentry were now formed into corporate groups with special legal privileges, including the right to trial by peers and exemption from personal taxation and corporal punishment. The Charter of the Nobility formalized these rights in 1785.

Catherine's policy of favoring the landed nobility led to even worse conditions for the Russian peasants and provoked a rebellion beginning in 1773. Led by an illiterate Cossack, Emelyan Pugachev (yim-yil-YAHN

Pugachev's Rebellion

poo-guh-CHAWF), the rebellion spread across southern Russia. But the insurrection soon faltered, and Pugachev was captured, tortured, and executed. Catherine responded to the failed revolt with even harsher measures against the peasantry. All rural reform was halted, and serfdom was expanded into new parts of the empire.

Catherine proved a worthy successor to Peter the Great by expanding Russia's territory westward into Poland and southward to the Black Sea. Russia gained land to the south by defeating the Ottoman Turks. In the Treaty of Kuchuk-Kainarji (koo-CHOOK-ky-NAR-jee) in 1774, the Russians also gained the privilege of protecting Greek Orthodox Christians in the Ottoman Empire. This Russian expansion westward came at the expense of neighboring Poland. In the three partitions of Poland in 1772, 1793, and 1795, Russia gained about 50 percent of Polish territory; Austria and Prussia took the rest.

Enlightened Absolutism Revisited

Of the three major rulers traditionally associated most closely with enlightened absolutism—Joseph II, Frederick II, and Catherine the Great—only Joseph sought truly radical changes based on Enlightenment ideas. Both Frederick and Catherine liked to be cast as disciples of the Enlightenment, expressed interest in enlightened reforms, and even attempted some, but neither ruler's policies seemed seriously affected by

CHRONOLOGY	Central and Eastern Europe in the Eighteenth Century	
Prussia		
Frederick William I	1713–1740	
Frederick II the Great	1740–1786	
Austrian Empire		
Maria Theresa	1740–1780	
Joseph II	1780–1790	
Russia		
Peter III	1762	
Catherine II the Great	1762–1796	
Pugachev's rebellion	1773–1775	
Charter of the Nobility	1785	
Poland		
First partition	1772	
Second partition	1793	
Third partition	1795	

Enlightenment thought. Indeed, many historians maintain that Joseph, Frederick, and Catherine were all guided primarily by a concern for the power and well-being of their states and that their policies were not all that different from those of their predecessors. In the final analysis, state power was used to build armies and wage wars to gain even more power. Nevertheless, in their desire to forge stronger state systems, these rulers did pursue such enlightened ideas as legal reform, religious toleration, and the extension of education, since these served to create more satisfied subjects and strengthened the state in significant ways.

It would be foolish, however, to overlook the fact that not only military but also political and social realities limited the ability of enlightened rulers to make reforms. Everywhere in Europe, the hereditary aristocracy was still the most powerful class in society. Enlightened reforms were often limited to changes in the administrative and judicial systems that did not seriously undermine the powerful interests of the European nobility. Although aristocrats might join the populace in opposing monarchical extension of centralizing power, as the chief beneficiaries of a system based on traditional rights and privileges for their class, they were certainly not willing to support a political ideology that trumpeted the principle of equal rights for all.

Wars and Diplomacy

Q **FOCUS QUESTION:** What were the causes and results of the Seven Years' War?

The philosophes condemned war as a foolish waste of life and resources in stupid quarrels of no value to humankind. Rulers, however, paid little attention to these comments and continued their costly struggles. By the eighteenth century, Europe consisted of a number of self-governing states guided by the self-interest of the ruler. And as Frederick the Great of Prussia said, "The fundamental rule of governments is the principle of extending their territories."

International rivalry and the continuing centralization of the European states were closely related. The need for taxes to support large armies and navies created its own imperative for more efficient and effective control of power in the hands of bureaucrats who could collect taxes and organize states for the task of winning wars. At the same time, the development of large standing armies ensured that political disputes would periodically be resolved by armed conflict rather than diplomacy. Between 1715 and 1740, it had seemed that Europe preferred peace. But in 1740, a major conflict erupted over the succession to the Austrian throne.

After the death of the Habsburg emperor Charles VI (1711–1740), King Frederick II of Prussia took advantage of the succession of Maria Theresa to the throne of Austria by invading Austrian Silesia. The vulnerability of Maria Theresa encouraged France to enter the war against its traditional enemy, Austria; in turn, Maria Theresa made an alliance with Great Britain, which feared French hegemony over continental affairs. All too quickly, the Austrian succession had set off a worldwide conflagration. The War of the Austrian Succession (1740–1748) was fought not only in Europe, where Prussia seized Silesia and France occupied the Austrian Netherlands, but also in the East, where France took Madras (now Chennai) in India from the British, and in North America, where the British captured the French fortress of Louisbourg at the entrance to the Saint Lawrence River. By 1748, all parties were exhausted and agreed to a peace that guaranteed the return of all occupied territories except Silesia to their original owners. Prussia's refusal to return Silesia guaranteed another war, at least between the two hostile central European powers of Prussia and Austria.

The Seven Years' War (1756–1763)

Maria Theresa refused to accept the loss of Silesia and prepared for its return by rebuilding her army while working diplomatically to separate Prussia from its chief ally, France. In 1756, Austria achieved what was soon labeled a diplomatic revolution. French-Austrian rivalry had been a fact of European diplomacy since the late sixteenth century. But two new rivalries made this old one seem superfluous: Britain and France over colonial empires, and Austria and Prussia over Silesia. France now abandoned Prussia and allied with Austria. Russia, which saw Prussia as a major hindrance to Russian goals in central Europe, joined the new alliance. In turn, Great Britain allied with Prussia. This diplomatic revolution of 1756 now led to another war—the Seven Years' War, which could be seen, as some historians have argued, as the first world war.

There were three major areas of conflict: Europe, India, and North America (see Map 18.2). Europe witnessed the clash of the two major alliances: the British and Prussians against the Austrians, Russians, and French. With his superb army and military prowess, Frederick the Great of Prussia was able for some time to dominate the Austrian, French, and Russian armies. Eventually, however, Frederick's forces were worn down and faced defeat until a new Russian tsar, Peter III, withdrew Russia's troops from the conflict. His withdrawal guaranteed a stalemate and resuscitated the desire for peace. The European conflict was ended by the Peace of Hubertusburg in 1763. All occupied territories were returned, and Austria officially recognized Prussia's permanent control of Silesia.

The Anglo-French struggle in the rest of the world had more decisive results. Known as the Great War for

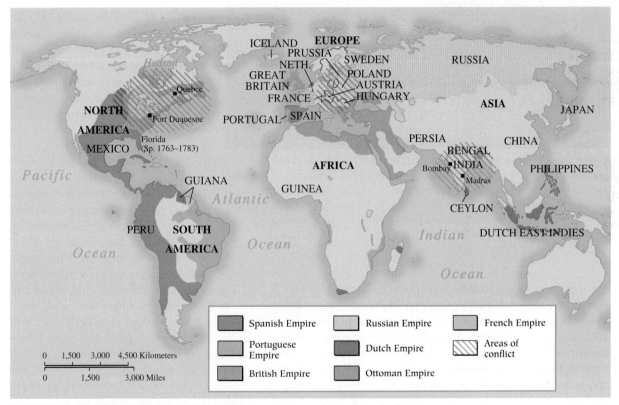

MAP 18.2 Battlefields of the Seven Years' War. A major struggle involving the five great powers, the Seven Years' War was truly a worldwide conflict. In central Europe, Prussia survived against the combined forces of France, Austria, and Russia, while Britain emerged victorious against France in the struggle for empire, gaining control of French North America and India.

Q Why were naval strength and ability important in the conflict between Britain and France?

Robert Clive in India. Robert Clive, the leader of the army of the British East India Company, had been commanded to fight the ruler of Bengal in order to gain trading privileges. After the Battle of Plassey in 1757, Clive and the East India Company took control of Bengal. In this painting by Edward Penny, Clive is shown receiving a grant of money for his injured soldiers from the local nabob or governor of Bengal.

of contention. One consisted of the waterways of the Gulf of Saint Lawrence, protected by the fortress of Louisbourg and by forts near the Great Lakes and Lake Champlain that protected French Quebec and French traders. The other was the unsettled Ohio River Valley. As the French moved south from the Great Lakes and north from their garrisons along the Mississippi, they began to establish forts from the Appalachians to the Mississippi River. To British settlers in the thirteen colonies to the east, this French activity threatened to cut off a vast area of the continent from British expansion.

Despite initial French successes, British fortunes were revived by the efforts of William Pitt the Elder, who was convinced that the destruction of the French colonial empire was a prerequisite for the survival of Britain's own colonial empire. Accordingly, Pitt decided to make a minimal effort in Europe while concentrating resources, especially the British navy, on the war in the colonies. Although the French troops were greater in number, the ability of the French to use them in the New World was contingent on naval support. The defeat of French fleets in major naval battles in 1759 gave the British an advantage because the French could no longer easily reinforce their garrisons. A se-

Empire, it was fought in India and North America. The French had returned Madras to Britain after the War of the Austrian Succession, but jockeying for power continued as the French and British supported opposing native Indian princes. The British under Robert Clive (1725–1774) ultimately won out, not because they had better forces but because they were more persistent (see the box on p. 439). By the Treaty of Paris in 1763, the French withdrew and left India to the British.

By far the greatest conflicts of the Seven Years' War took place in North America, where it was known as the French and Indian War. There were two primary areas

ries of British victories soon followed. On the night of September 13, 1759, British forces led by General James Wolfe scaled the heights outside Quebec and defeated the French under General Louis-Joseph Montcalm on the Plains of Abraham. Both generals died in the battle. The British went on to seize Montreal, the Great Lakes area, and the Ohio Valley. The French were forced to make peace. By the Treaty of Paris, they ceded Canada and the lands east of the Mississippi to Britain. Their ally Spain transferred Spanish Florida to British control; in return, the French gave their Louisiana territory to the Spanish. By 1763, Great Britain had become the world's greatest colonial power.

British Victory in India

The success of the British in defeating the French in India was due to Robert Clive. In this excerpt from one of his letters, Clive describes his famous victory at Plassey, north of Calcutta (modern Kolkata), on June 23, 1757. This battle demonstrated the inability of native Indian soldiers to compete with Europeans and signified the beginning of British control in Bengal. Clive claimed to have a thousand Europeans, two thousand sepoys (local soldiers), and eight cannon available for this battle.

Robert Clive's Account of His Victory at Plassey

At daybreak we discovered the [governor's] army moving toward us, consisting, as we since found, of about fifteen thousand horse and thirty-five thousand foot, with upwards of forty pieces of cannon. They approached apace, and by six began to attack with a number of heavy cannon, supported by the whole army, and continued to play on us very briskly for several hours, during which our situation was of the utmost service to us, being lodged in a large grove with good mud banks. To succeed in an attempt on their cannon was next to impossible, as they were planted in a manner round us and at considerable distances from each other. We therefore remained quiet in our post, in expectation of a successful attack upon their camp at night. About noon the enemy drew off their artillery and retired to their camp....

On finding them make no great effort to dislodge us, we proceeded to take possession of one or two more eminences lying very near an angle of their camp, from whence, and an adjacent eminence in their possession, they kept a smart fire of musketry upon us. They made several attempts to bring out their cannon, but our advanced fieldpieces played so warmly and so well upon them that they were always driven back. Their horse exposing themselves a good deal on this occasion, many of them were killed, and among the rest four or five officers of the first distinction; by which the whole army being visibly dispirited and thrown into some confusion, we were encouraged to storm both the eminence and the angle of their camp, which were carried at the same instant, with little or no loss; though the latter was defended (exclusively of blacks) by forty French and two pieces of cannon; and the former by a large body of blacks, both horse and foot. On this a general rout ensued, and we pursued the enemy six miles, passing upwards of forty pieces of cannon they had abandoned, with an infinite number of carts and carriages filled with baggage of all kinds.... It is computed there are killed of the enemy about five hundred. Our loss amounted to only twenty-two killed and fifty wounded, and those chiefly blacks.

Q In what ways, if any, would Clive's account likely have been different if the Battle of Plassey had occurred in Europe? According to the letter, what role did native Indians seemingly play in the battle? Why did Clive give them such little mention?

Source: From *Readings in European History*, vol. 2, by James Harvey Robinson (Lexington, Mass.: Ginn and Co., 1906).

Economic Expansion and Social Change

Q FOCUS QUESTION: What changes occurred in agriculture, finance, industry, and trade during the eighteenth century?

The eighteenth century witnessed the beginning of economic changes in Europe that ultimately had a strong impact on the rest of the world. Rapid population growth, expansion in banking and trade, an agricultural revolution (at least in Britain), the stirrings of industrialization, and an increase in worldwide trade characterized the economic patterns of the eighteenth century.

Population and Food

Europe's population began to grow around 1750 and continued a slow but steady rise, with some regional variations. It has been estimated that the total European population was around 120 million in 1700, rose to 140 million by 1750, and to 190 million by 1790; thus, the growth rate in the second half of the century was double that of the first half. These increases occurred during the same time that several million Europeans were going abroad as colonists. Perhaps the most important cause of population growth was the decline in the death rate, thanks, no doubt, to more plentiful food and better transportation of food supplies, which led to improved diets and some relief from devastating famines. Also of great significance in lowering death rates was the disappearance of bubonic plague: the last great outbreak in western Europe occurred in 1720 in southern France.

More food was in part a result of improvements in agricultural practices and methods in the eighteenth century, especially in Britain, parts of France, and the Low Countries. The increases in food production can be attributed to four interrelated factors: improved climate, more farmland, healthier and more abundant livestock, and increased yields per acre.

Climatologists believe that the "little ice age" of the seventeenth century abated in the eighteenth, especially evident in moderate summers that provided more ideal growing conditions. The amount of land under cultivation was increased by abandoning the old open-field system, in which part of the land was left to lie fallow to renew it. The formerly empty fields were now planted with new crops, such as alfalfa and clover, which stored nitrogen in their roots, restored the soil's fertility, and also provided winter fodder for livestock, enabling landlords to maintain an ever-larger number of animals. The more numerous livestock made available more animal manure, which was used to fertilize fields and produce better yields per acre.

Also important to the increased yields was the spread of new vegetables, including two important American crops, the potato and maize (Indian corn). Although they were not grown in quantity until after 1700, they had been brought to Europe from America in the sixteenth century and were part of the Columbian Exchange—the reciprocal exchange of plants and animals between Europe and America. The potato became a staple in Germany, the Low Countries, and especially Ireland, where repression by British landlords forced large numbers of poor peasants to survive on small plots of marginal land. The potato took relatively little effort to produce in large quantities, was high in carbohydrates and calories and rich in vitamins A and C, and could be easily stored for winter use.

All these new techniques of the eighteenth century have been characterized as an **agricultural revolution**. The English were the leaders in adopting them. This early modernization of English agriculture, with its noticeable increase in productivity, made possible the feeding of an expanding population about to enter a new world of industrialization and urbanization. In other parts of Europe, however, noble privileges and heavy taxes on the peasants prevented the adoption of new agricultural practices.

Family, Marriage, and Birthrate Patterns

The family, rather than the individual, was still at the heart of Europe's social organization. For the most part, people still thought of the family in traditional terms, as a patriarchal institution with the husband dominating his wife and children. The upper classes in particular were still concerned for the family as a "house," an association whose collective interests were more important than those of its individual members. In all social classes, parents, especially the fathers, still generally selected marriage partners for their children, based on the interests of the family (see the box on p. 441). One French noble responded to his son's inquiry about his upcoming marriage, "Mind your own business."

In most of Europe, newly married couples established their own households independent of their parents. This nuclear family, which had its beginning in the Middle Ages, had become a common pattern, especially in northwestern Europe. To save up what they needed to establish their own households, both men and women (outside the aristocracy) married quite late; the average age for men in northwestern Europe was between twenty-seven and twenty-eight; for women, between twenty-five and twenty-seven.

Late marriages imposed limits on the birthrate; in fact, they might be viewed as a natural form of birth control. For married couples, the first child usually appeared within one year of marriage, and additional children came at intervals of two or three years, producing an average of five births per family. It would appear, then, that the birthrate had the potential of causing a significant increase in population. This possibility was restricted, however, because 40 to 60 percent of European women of childbearing age (between fifteen and forty-four) were not married at any given time. Moreover, by the end of the eighteenth century, especially among the upper classes in France and Britain, birth control techniques were being used to limit the number of children. Among

Marital Arrangements

In the eighteenth century, upper-class parents continued to choose marriage partners for their children. This practice and the turmoil it could cause are evident in this selection from *The Rivals*, a play written in 1775 by Richard Sheridan. Sheridan was an Irish playwright who quit writing plays to pursue a political career. In this scene from *The Rivals*, a father, Sir Anthony Absolute, informs his son, Captain Jack Absolute, of the arrangements he has made for his son's marriage. Jack, in love with another woman, is dumbfounded by his father's plans.

Richard Sheridan, *The Rivals*

ABSOLUTE: Now, Jack, I am sensible that the income of your commission, and what I have hitherto allowed you, is but a small pittance for a lad of your spirit.

CAPTAIN JACK: Sir, you are very good.

ABSOLUTE: And it is my wish, while yet I live, to have my boy make some figure in the world. I have resolved, therefore, to fix you at once in a noble independence.

CAPTAIN JACK: Sir, your kindness overpowers me—such generosity makes the gratitude of reason more lively than the sensations even of filial affection.

ABSOLUTE: I am so glad you are so sensible of my attention—and you shall be master of a large estate in a few weeks.

CAPTAIN JACK: Let my future life, sir, speak my gratitude; I cannot express the sense I have of your munificence.—Yet, sir, I presume you would not wish me to quit the army?

ABSOLUTE: Oh, that shall be as your wife chooses.

CAPTAIN JACK: My wife, sir!

ABSOLUTE: Ay, ay, settle that between you—settle that between you.

CAPTAIN JACK: A wife, sir, did you say?

ABSOLUTE: Ay, a wife—why, did I not mention her before?

CAPTAIN JACK: Not a word of her, sir.

ABSOLUTE: Odd, so! I musn't forget her though.—Yes, Jack, the independence I was talking of is by marriage—the fortune is saddled with a wife—but I suppose that makes no difference.

CAPTAIN JACK: Sir! Sir! You amaze me!

ABSOLUTE: Why, what the devil's the matter with you, fool? Just now you were all gratitude and duty.

CAPTAIN JACK: I was, sir—you talked of independence and a fortune, but not a word of a wife!

ABSOLUTE: Why—what difference does that make? Odds life, sir! If you had an estate, you must take it with the livestock on it, as it stands!

CAPTAIN JACK: If my happiness is to be the price, I must beg leave to decline the purchase. Pray, sir, who is the lady?

ABSOLUTE: What's that to you, sir? Come, give me your promise to love, and to marry her directly.

CAPTAIN JACK: Sure, sir, this is not very reasonable. . . . You must excuse me, sir, if I tell you, once for all, that in this point I cannot obey you. . . .

ABSOLUTE: Sir, I won't hear a word—not one word! . . .

CAPTAIN JACK: What, sir, promise to link myself to some mass of ugliness!

ABSOLUTE: Zounds! Sirrah! The lady shall be as ugly as I choose: she shall have a hump on each shoulder; she shall be as crooked as the crescent; her one eye shall roll like the bull's in Cox's Museum; she shall have a skin like a mummy, and the beard of a Jew—she shall be all this, sirrah! Yet I will make you ogle her all day, and sit up all night to write sonnets on her beauty.

Q What point is Sheridan making about marriages among the upper classes in the eighteenth century? What social, political, and economic considerations were significant in eighteenth-century marriages?

Source: From *The Rivals* by Richard Sheridan (London, 1775).

the French aristocracy, the average number of children declined from six in the period between 1650 and 1700 to three between 1700 and 1750 and to two between 1750 and 1780. These figures are even more significant when one considers that aristocrats married at younger ages than the rest of the population. Coitus interruptus remained the most common form of birth control.

New Methods of Finance

A decline in the supply of gold and silver in the seventeenth century had created a chronic shortage of money that undermined the efforts of governments to meet their needs. In the eighteenth century, the establishment of new public and private banks and the acceptance of paper notes made possible an expansion of credit.

Perhaps the best example of this process can be observed in England, where the Bank of England was founded in 1694. Unlike other banks that mainly received deposits and exchanged foreign currencies, the Bank of England also made loans. In return for lending money to the government, the bank was allowed to issue paper "banknotes" backed by its credit. These soon became negotiable and provided a paper substitute for gold and silver currency. In addition, the issuance of government bonds created the notion of a "national debt."

European Industry

The most important product of European industry in the eighteenth century was textiles, most of which were still produced by traditional methods. In cities that were textile centers, master artisans used timeworn methods to turn out finished goods in their guild workshops. But by the eighteenth century textile production in parts of Europe was shifting to the countryside, where the so-called putting-out or domestic system was used. A merchant-capitalist entrepreneur bought the raw materials, mostly wool and flax, and "put them out" to rural workers, who spun the raw material into yarn and then wove it into cloth on simple looms. Capitalist entrepreneurs sold the finished product, made a profit, and used the profit to manufacture more.

This system became known as the **cottage industry** because spinners and weavers did their work at home, in their own cottages. It was truly a family enterprise—women and children could spin while men wove on the looms, enabling rural people to supplement their pitiful wages as agricultural laborers. The cottage system spread to many areas of rural Europe in the eighteenth century. But in the second half of the century, significant changes began to occur that would soon revolutionize industrial production (see Chapter 20).

Mercantile Empires and Worldwide Trade

As we saw in Chapter 14, the growth of commercial capitalism led to integrated markets, joint stock trading companies, and banking and stock exchange facilities. Mercantilist theory had posited that a nation should acquire as much gold and silver as possible; that there should be a favorable balance of trade, or more exports than imports; and that the state should provide subsidies to manufacturers, grant monopolies to traders, build roads and canals, and impose high tariffs to limit imports. Colonies were also seen as valuable sources of raw materials and markets for finished goods. Mercantilist theory on the role of colonies was matched in practice by Europe's overseas expansion.

With the development of colonies and trading posts in the Americas, Asia, and Africa, Europeans embarked on an adventure in international commerce that has led some historians to speak of the emergence of a truly global economy in the eighteenth century. Trade between European states and their colonies increased dramatically. In 1715, 19 percent of Britain's trade was with its American colonies; by 1785, that figure had nearly doubled to 34 percent. The growing trade of Europe with the Americas, Africa, and Asia was also visible in the growth of merchant fleets. The British, for example, had 3,300 merchant ships carrying 260,000 tons in 1700; by 1775, those numbers had increased to 9,400 ships carrying 695,000 tons.

Flourishing trade also had a significant impact on the European economy, especially visible in the growth of towns and cities. The rise of the Atlantic trade led to great prosperity for such port cities as Bordeaux, Nantes, and Marseilles in France, Bristol and Liverpool in Britain, and Lisbon and Oporto in Portugal. Trade also led to the growth of related industries, such as textile manufacturing, sugar refining, and tobacco processing, and an increase in dock workers, building tradesmen, servants, and service people of various sorts. Visitors' accounts of their visits to prosperous port cities detail the elegant buildings and affluent lifestyle they encountered.

The Social Order of the Eighteenth Century

Q FOCUS QUESTION: Who were the main groups making up the European social order in the eighteenth century, and how did the conditions in which they lived differ both between groups and between different parts of Europe?

The pattern of Europe's social organization, first established in the Middle Ages, continued well into the eighteenth century. Social status was still largely determined not by wealth and economic standing but by the division into the traditional "orders" or "estates" determined by heredity. This "divinely sanctioned" division of society was supported by Christian teaching, which emphasized the need to fulfill the responsibilities of one's estate. The ideas of the Enlightenment made some headway as reformers argued that an unchanging social order based on privilege was hostile to the progress of society. But traditional distinctions did not die easily. In the Prussian law code of 1794, marriage between noble males and middle-class females was forbidden without a government dispensation. Even without government regulation, different social groups remained easily distinguished everywhere in Europe by the distinctive, traditional clothes they wore. Not until the revolutionary upheavals at the end of the eighteenth century did the old order finally begin to crumble.

The Peasants

Because society was still mostly rural in the eighteenth century, the peasantry constituted the largest social group, making up as much as 85 percent of Europe's population. There were rather wide differences, however, between peasants in different areas. The most important distinction, at least legally, was between the free peasant and the serf. Peasants in Britain, northern Italy, the Low Countries, Spain, most of France, and some areas of western Germany were legally free, although not exempt from burdens. Some free peasants in Andalusia in Spain, southern Italy, Sicily, and Portugal lived in a poverty more desperate than that of many serfs in Russia and eastern Germany. In France, 40 percent of free peasants owned little or no land by 1789 (see the box on p. 444).

Small peasant proprietors or tenant farmers in western Europe were also not free from compulsory services. Most owed **tithes**, often one-third of their crops. Although tithes were intended for parish priests, in France only 10 percent of the priests received them. Instead they wound up in the hands of wealthy townspeople and aristocratic landowners. Moreover, peasants could still owe a variety of dues and fees. Local aristocrats claimed hunting rights on peasant land and had monopolies over the flour mills, community ovens, and wine and oil presses needed by the peasants. Hunting rights, dues, fees, and tithes were all deeply resented.

The local village remained the center of peasants' social lives. Villages, especially in western Europe, maintained public order; provided poor relief, a village church, and sometimes a schoolmaster; collected taxes for the central government; maintained roads and bridges; and established common procedures for sowing, plowing, and harvesting crops. But villages were often dominated by richer peasants and proved highly resistant to innovations, such as new agricultural practices.

The Nobility

The nobles, who constituted only 2 to 3 percent of the European population, played a dominating role in society (see Images of Everyday Life on p. 445). Being born a noble automatically guaranteed a place at the top of the social order, with all of the attendant special privileges and rights. The legal privileges of the nobility included judgment by their peers, immunity from severe punishment, and exemption from many forms of taxation. Especially in central and eastern Europe, the rights of landlords over their serfs were overwhelming.

Nobles also played important roles in military and government affairs. Since medieval times, landed aristocrats had functioned as military officers. Although commoners occasionally became officers, nobles were still considered the most natural and hence the best officers. The eighteenth-century nobility also played a significant role in the administrative machinery of state. In some countries, such as Prussia, the entire bureaucracy reflected aristocratic values. Moreover, in most of Europe, the landholding nobles controlled much of the life of their local districts.

Although the nobles clung to their privileged status and struggled to keep others out, almost everywhere the possession of money made it possible to enter the ranks of the nobility. Rights of nobility were frequently attached to certain lands, so purchasing the lands made one a noble; the acquisition of government offices also often conferred noble status.

The Inhabitants of Towns and Cities

Townspeople were still a distinct minority of the total population except in the Dutch Republic, Britain, and parts of Italy. At the end of the eighteenth century, about one-sixth of the French population lived in towns of 2,000 inhabitants or more. The biggest city in Europe was London, with 1 million inhabitants, while Paris numbered between 550,000 and 600,000. Altogether, Europe had at least twenty cities in twelve

Poverty in France

Unlike the British, who had a system of public-supported poor relief, the French responded to poverty with ad hoc policies when conditions became acute. This selection is taken from an *intendant's* report to the controller general at Paris describing his suggestions for a program to relieve the grain shortages expected for the winter months.

M. de la Bourdonnaye, *Intendant* of Bordeaux, to the Controller General, September 30, 1708

Having searched for the means of helping the people of Agen in this cruel situation and having conferred with His Eminence, the Bishop, it seems to us that three things are absolutely necessary if the people are not to starve during the winter.

Most of the inhabitants do not have seed to plant their fields. However, we decided that we would be going too far if we furnished it, because those who have seed would also apply [for more]. Moreover, we are persuaded that all the inhabitants will make strenuous efforts to find some seed, since they have every reason to expect prices to remain high next year. . . .

But this project will come to nothing if the collectors of the taille continue to be as strict in the exercise of their functions as they have been of late and continue to employ troops [to force collection]. Those inhabitants who have seed grain would sell it to be freed from an oppressive garrison, while those who must buy seed, since they have none left from their harvest and have scraped together a little money for this purchase, would prefer to give up that money [for taxes] when put under police constraint. To avoid this, I feel it is absolutely necessary that you order the receivers-general to reduce their operations during this winter, at least with respect to the poor. . . .

We are planning to import wheat for this region from Languedoc and Quercy, and we are confident that there will be enough. But there are two things to be feared: one is the greed of the merchants. When they see that general misery has put them in control of prices, they will raise them to the point where the calamity is almost as great as if there were no provisions at all. The other fear is that the artisans and the lowest classes, when they find themselves at the mercy of the merchants, will cause disorders and riots. As a protective measure, it would seem wise to establish two small storehouses. Ten thousand ecus [30,000 livres] would be sufficient for each. . . .

A third point demanding our attention is the support of beggars among the poor, as well as of those who have no other resources than their wages. Since there will be very little work, these people will soon be reduced to starvation. We should establish public workshops to provide work as was done in 1693 and 1694. I should choose the most useful kind of work, located where there are the greatest number of poor. In this manner, we should rid ourselves of those who do not want to work and assure the others a moderate subsistence. For these workshops, we would need about 40,000 livres, or altogether 100,000 livres. The receiver-general of the taille of Agen could advance this sum. The 60,000 livres for the storehouses he would get back very soon. I shall await your orders on all of the above.

Marginal Comments by the Controller General

Operations for the collection of the taille are to be suspended. The two storehouses are to be established; great care must be taken to put them to good use. The interest on the advances will be paid by the king. His Majesty has agreed to the establishment of the public workshops for the able-bodied poor and is willing to spend up to 40,000 livres on them this winter.

Q What does this document reveal about the nature of poverty in France in the eighteenth century? How would the growing ranks of the poor in Europe further destabilize this society?

Source: From *European Society in the Eighteenth Century* by Robert Forster and Elborg Forster. Copyright © 1969 by Robert and Elborg Forster. Reprinted by permission of Walker & Co.

IMAGES OF EVERYDAY LIFE
The Aristocratic Way of Life

© Collection of the Earl of Pembroke, Wilton House, Wiltshire, UK/ The Bridgeman Art Library

Louvre, Paris/Scala/Art Resource, NY

Alnwick Castle, Northumberland, UK/Erich Lessing/Art Resource, NY

Staatliche Schloesser und Gaerten, Karlsruhe/Erich Lessing/Art Resource, NY

THE EIGHTEENTH-CENTURY country house in Britain fulfilled the desire of aristocrats for both elegance and greater privacy. The painting on the top left, by Richard Wilson, shows a typical English country house of the eighteenth century surrounded by a simple, serene landscape. Thomas Gainsborough's *Conversation in the Park*, top right, captures the relaxed life of two aristocrats in the park of their country estate. The illustration on the bottom left shows the formal dining room of a great British country house. In the course of the eighteenth century, upper-class country houses came to be furnished with upholstered furniture and elaborate carpets as aristocrats sought greater comfort. Cabinets with glass windows also became fashionable as a way to display fine china and other objects. Especially desirable were objects from the East as vast amounts of Chinese and Japanese ceramics were imported into Europe in the eighteenth century. The illustration on the bottom right shows Chinese cups without handles, which became extremely fashionable. As seen in the painting, it was even acceptable to pour tea into the saucer in order to cool it.

A Market Square in Naples. Below the wealthy patrician elites who dominated the towns and cities were a number of social groups with a wide range of incomes and occupations. This eighteenth-century painting by Angelo Costa captures this remarkable diversity of peoples at a fair being held in the chief market square of the Italian city of Naples.

countries with populations over 100,000, including Naples, Lisbon, Moscow, Saint Petersburg, Vienna, Amsterdam, Berlin, Rome, and Madrid.

Although urban dwellers were vastly outnumbered by rural inhabitants, towns played an important role in Western culture. The contrasts between the city, with its education, culture, and material consumption, and the surrounding, often poverty-stricken countryside were striking, as evidenced by this British traveler's account of Russia's Saint Petersburg in 1741:

> The country about Petersburg has full as wild and desert a look as any in the Indies; you need not go above 200 paces out of the town to find yourself in a wild wood of firs, and such a low, marshy, boggy country that you would think God when he created the rest of the world for the use of mankind had created this for an inaccessible retreat for all sorts of wild beasts.[3]

Peasants often resented the prosperity of towns and their exploitation of the countryside to serve urban interests. Palermo in Sicily consumed one-third of the island's food production while paying only one-tenth of the taxes. Towns lived off the countryside not by buying the peasants' produce but by acquiring it through tithes, rents, and feudal dues.

Many cities in western and even central Europe had a long tradition of patrician oligarchies that continued to control their communities by dominating town and city councils. Despite their highly visible role, patricians constituted only a small minority of the urban population. Just below the patricians stood an upper crust of the middle classes: nonnoble officeholders, financiers and bankers, merchants, wealthy **rentiers** (rahn-TYAY) who lived off their investments, and important professionals, including lawyers. Another large urban group was the petty bourgeoisie or lower middle class, made up of master artisans, shopkeepers, and small traders. Below them were the laborers or working classes. Much urban industry was still done in small guild workshops by masters, journeymen, and apprentices. Urban communities also had a large group of unskilled workers who served as servants, maids, and cooks at pitifully low wages.

Despite an end to the ravages of plague, eighteenth-century cities still experienced high death rates, especially among children, because of unsanitary living conditions, polluted water, and a lack of sewage facilities.

One observer compared the stench of Hamburg to an open sewer that could be smelled for miles around. Overcrowding also exacerbated urban problems as cities continued to grow from an influx of rural immigrants. But cities proved no paradise for them, for unskilled workers found few employment opportunities. The result was a serious problem of poverty in the eighteenth century.

Chapter Summary

Everywhere in Europe at the beginning of the eighteenth century, the old order remained strong. Nobles, clerics, towns, and provinces all had privileges, some medieval in origin, others the result of the attempt of monarchies in the sixteenth and seventeenth centuries to gain financial support from their subjects. Everywhere in the eighteenth century, monarchs sought to enlarge their bureaucracies to raise taxes to support the new large standing armies that had originated in the seventeenth century. Royal authority was often justified by the service the monarch could give to the state and its people rather than by divine right, creating a form of monarchy labeled by some as "enlightened absolutism." Three rulers, Frederick II of Prussia, Joseph II of Austria, and Catherine the Great of Russia, are traditionally associated with the concept of enlightened absolutism, although only Joseph II of Austria truly sought radical change based on Enlightenment ideas. Joseph

abolished serfdom, reformed the laws, and granted religious toleration, but his reforms did not outlast his reign. Frederick and Catherine expressed interest in enlightened reforms, but maintenance of the existing political system took precedence over reform. Indeed, many historians believe that Frederick, Catherine, and Joseph were all guided by a policy of using state power to amass armies and wage wars to gain more power.

The existence of these armies made wars more likely. The emergence of five great powers, two of them (France and

Britain) in conflict in the East and North America, initiated a new scale of confrontation. The midcentury War of the Austrian Succession and the Seven Years' War were fought not only in Europe but also in North America and India. Frederick the Great was the instigator, desiring Austrian Silesia, but Britain was the true victor, driving France from Canada and India. Britain emerged with a worldwide empire and became the world's greatest naval and colonial power. Standing armies became the norm, and everywhere in Europe, increased demands for taxes to support these conflicts led to attacks on the privileged orders and a desire for change not met by the ruling monarchs.

At the same time, the population grew, mainly as a result of a declining death rate and improvements in agriculture; paper money began to compensate for the decline in the supply of gold and silver; institutions such as the Bank of England

mobilized the wealth of the nation through credit; and the beginnings of an industrial revolution emerged in the textile industry. This growth in population, the dramatic changes in finance, trade, and industry, and the increase in poverty created tensions that undermined the traditional foundations of European society. The inability of the old order to deal meaningfully with these changes led to a revolutionary outburst at the end of the eighteenth century that marked the beginning of the end for that old order.

CHAPTER TIMELINE

	1700	1720	1740	1760	1780	1800

France

Louis XV of France

Austria/Prussia/ Russia

Maria Theresa of Austria

Frederick the Great of Prussia

War of the Austrian Succession

Seven Years' War

Joseph II of Austria

Catherine the Great of Russia

England

Robert Walpole as prime minister

William Pitt the Younger as prime minister

Poland

■ First partition of Poland

CHAPTER REVIEW

Upon Reflection

Q If you were a philosophe serving Joseph II of Austria or Catherine the Great of Russia, what advice would you give the monarch on the best way to rule his or her country?

Q What were the characteristics of war and diplomacy in the eighteenth century, and how would you compare the nature of war and diplomacy in the eighteenth century with that of the seventeenth century?

Q How and why did the nobility play a dominating role in European society in the eighteenth century?

Key Terms

natural laws (p. 427)
natural rights (p. 427)
enlightened absolutism (p. 428)
patronage (p. 430)

agricultural revolution (p. 440)
cottage industry (p. 442)
tithes (p. 443)
rentiers (p. 446)

Suggestions for Further Reading

GENERAL WORKS For a good introduction to the political history of the eighteenth century, see the relevant chapters in the general works by **Woloch, Anderson**, and **Blanning** listed in Chapter 17. See also **G. Treasure,** *The Making of Modern Europe, 1648–1780,* rev. ed. (London, 2003), and **O. Hufton,** *Europe: Privilege and Protest, 1730–1789,* 2d ed. (London, 2001). On enlightened absolutism, see **D. Beales,** *Enlightenment and Reform in Eighteenth-Century Europe* (New York, 2005). Good biographies of some of Europe's monarchs include **G. Mac-Donough,** *Frederick the Great* (New York, 2001); **V. Rounding,**

Catherine the Great: Love, Sex, and Power (New York, 2007); **T. C. W. Blanning, *Joseph II*** (New York, 1994); and **J. Black, *George III: America's Last King*** (New Haven, Conn., 2006).

EIGHTEENTH-CENTURY WARFARE   The warfare of this period is examined in **M. S. Anderson, *War and Society in Europe of the Old Regime, 1615–1789*** (New York, 1998).

ECONOMIC AND SOCIAL CHANGE   A good introduction to European population can be found in **M. W. Flinn, *The European**

*Demographic System, 1500–1820*** (Brighton, 1981). One of the best works on family and marriage patterns is **L. Stone, *The Family, Sex, and Marriage in England, 1500–1800*** (New York, 1977). On England's agricultural revolution, see **M. Overton, *Agricultural Revolution in England*** (Cambridge, 1996).

THE SOCIAL ORDER   On the European nobility, see **J. Dewald, *The European Nobility, 1400–1800,*** 2d ed. (Cambridge, 2004). On European cities, see **J. de Vries, *European Urbanization, 1500–1800*** (Cambridge, Mass., 1984).

Notes

1. Frederick II, *Forms of Government*, in *The Western Tradition*, ed. E. Weber (Lexington, Mass., 1972), pp. 538, 544.
2. Quoted in R. A. Dorwart, *The Administrative Reforms of Frederick William I of Prussia* (Cambridge, Mass., 1953), p. 36.
3. I. Vinogradoff, "Russian Missions to London, 1711–1789: Further Extracts from the Cottrell Papers," *Oxford Slavonic Papers*, New Series, 15 (1982):76.

MindTap

MindTap is a fully online, highly personalized learning experience built upon Cengage Learning content. MindTap combines student learning tools—readings, multimedia, activities, and assessments—into a singular Learning Path that guides students through the course.

A Revolution in Politics: The Era of the French Revolution and Napoleon

The storming of the Bastille

CCI/The Art Archive at Art Resource, NY

CHAPTER OUTLINE AND FOCUS QUESTIONS

The Beginning of the Revolutionary Era: The American Revolution

Q What were the causes and results of the American Revolution, and what impact did it have on Europe?

Background to the French Revolution

Q What were the long-range and immediate causes of the French Revolution?

The French Revolution

Q What were the main events of the French Revolution between 1789 and 1799? What role did each of the following play in the French Revolution: lawyers, peasants, women, the clergy, the Jacobins, the sans-culottes, the French revolutionary army, and the Committee of Public Safety?

The Age of Napoleon

Q Which aspects of the French Revolution did Napoleon preserve, and which did he destroy?

CRITICAL THINKING

Q In what ways were the French Revolution and the English revolutions of the seventeenth century similar? In what ways were they different?

CONNECTIONS TO TODAY

Q What similarities and differences do you see between the French Revolution and contemporary revolutions?

ON THE MORNING of July 14, 1789, a Parisian mob of some eight thousand people in search of weapons streamed toward the Bastille (bass-STEEL), a royal armory filled with arms and ammunition. The Bastille was also a state prison, and although it now held only seven prisoners, in the eyes of these angry Parisians, it was a glaring symbol of the government's despotic policies. The marquis de Launay (mar-KEE duh loh-NAY) and a small garrison of 114 men were defending the armory. The attack began in earnest in the early afternoon, and after three hours of fighting, de

Launay and the garrison surrendered. Angered by the loss of ninety-eight of their members, the victorious mob beat de Launay to death, cut off his head, and carried it aloft in triumph through the streets of Paris. When King Louis XVI was informed of the fall of the Bastille by the duc de La Rochefoucauld-Liancourt (dook duh lah RUSH-foo-koh-lee-ahnh-KOOR), he exclaimed, "Why, this is a revolt." "No, Sire," replied the duc, "it is a revolution."

Historians have long held that the modern history of Europe began with two significant transformations—the French Revolution (discussed in this chapter) and the Industrial Revolution (see Chapter 20). Accordingly, the French Revolution has been portrayed as the major turning point in European political and social history when the institutions of the "old regime" were destroyed and a new order was created based on individual rights, representative institutions, and a concept of loyalty to the nation rather than the monarch. This perspective does have certain limitations, however.

France was only one of a number of places in the Western world where the assumptions of the old order were challenged. Although some historians have used the phrase "democratic revolution" to refer to the upheavals of the late eighteenth and nineteenth centuries, it is probably more appropriate to speak of a liberal movement to extend political rights and power to the bourgeoisie in possession of capital—citizens besides the aristocracy who were literate and had become wealthy through capitalist enterprises in trade, industry, and finance. The years preceding and accompanying the French Revolution included attempts at reform and revolt in the North American colonies, Britain, the Dutch Republic, some Swiss cities, and the Austrian Netherlands. The success of the American and French Revolutions makes them the center of attention for this chapter.

Not all of the decadent privileges that characterized the old European regime were destroyed in 1789, however. The revolutionary upheaval of the era, especially in France, did create new liberal and national political ideals, summarized in the French revolutionary slogan, "Liberty, Equality, Fraternity," that transformed France and were then spread to other European countries through the conquests of Napoleon. After Napoleon's defeat, however, the forces of reaction did their best to restore the old order and resist pressures for reform.

The Beginning of the Revolutionary Era: The American Revolution

Q FOCUS QUESTION: What were the causes and results of the American Revolution, and what impact did it have on Europe?

At the end of the Seven Years' War in 1763, Great Britain had become the world's greatest colonial power. In North America, Britain controlled Canada and the lands east of the Mississippi. After the Seven Years' War, British policymakers sought to obtain new revenues from the thirteen American colonies to pay for expenses the British army incurred in defending the colonists. But an attempt to levy new taxes by the Stamp Act in 1765 led to riots and the law's quick repeal.

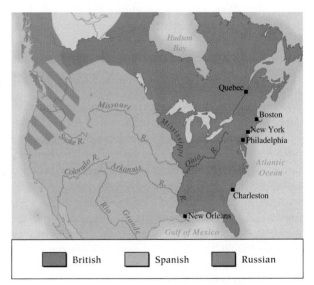

North America, 1763

The Americans and the British had different conceptions of empire. The British envisioned a single empire with Parliament as the supreme authority throughout. Only Parliament could make laws for all the people in the empire, including the American colonists. The Americans, in contrast, had their own representative assemblies. They believed that neither the king nor Parliament had any right to interfere in their internal affairs and that no tax could be levied without the consent of the people or their chosen representatives.

Crisis followed crisis in the 1770s until 1776, when the colonists decided to declare their independence from the British Empire. On July 4, 1776, the Second Continental Congress released a declaration written by Thomas Jefferson. A stirring political document, the Declaration of Independence affirmed the Enlightenment's natural rights of "life, liberty, and the pursuit of happiness" and declared the colonies to be "free and independent states absolved from all allegiance to the British crown." The war for American independence had formally begun.

The War for Independence

The war against Great Britain was a great gamble. Britain was a strong European military power with enormous financial resources. The Second Continental Congress had authorized the formation of the Continental Army under George Washington as commander in chief. Washington, who had had political experience in Virginia and military experience in the French and Indian War, was a good choice for the job. As a southerner, he brought balance to an effort that to that point had been led by New Englanders. Nevertheless, compared with the British forces, the Continental Army consisted of undisciplined amateurs whose terms of service were usually very brief.

Complicating the war effort were the internal divisions within the colonies. Though fought for independence, the Revolutionary War was also a civil war, pitting family members and neighbors against one another. The Loyalists, 15 to 30 percent of the population, questioned whether British policies justified the rebellion.

Since probably half of the people living in the colonies were apathetic at the start of the struggle, the Patriots, like the Loyalists, constituted a minority of the population. The Patriots, however, managed to win over many of the uncommitted, either by persuasion or by force. There were Patriots among the rich as well as Loyalists; Washington owned an estate with 15,000 acres and 150 slaves. But the rich Patriots joined an extensive coalition that included farmers and artisans. The wide social spectrum in this coalition had an impact on representative governments in the states after the war. In many states, the right to vote was broadened; Pennsylvania, for example, dropped all property qualifications for voting.

Of great importance to the colonists' cause was the assistance provided by foreign countries that were eager to gain revenge for earlier defeats at the hands of the British. The French supplied arms and money to the rebels from the beginning of the war, and French officers and soldiers also served in the Continental

Army. When the British army of General Cornwallis was forced to surrender to a combined American and French army and French fleet under Washington at Yorktown in 1781, the British government decided to call it quits. The Treaty of Paris, signed in 1783, recognized the independence of the American colonies and granted the Americans control of the territory from the Appalachians to the Mississippi River.

Forming a New Nation

The thirteen American colonies had gained their independence as the United States of America, but fear of concentrated power and concern for their own interests caused them to have little enthusiasm for establishing a united nation with a strong central government. The Articles of Confederation, ratified in 1781, did little to provide for a strong central government. A movement for a different form of national government soon arose. In the summer of 1787, fifty-five delegates attended a convention in Philadelphia to revise the Articles of Confederation. The convention's delegates—wealthy, politically experienced, and well educated—rejected revision and decided to devise a new constitution.

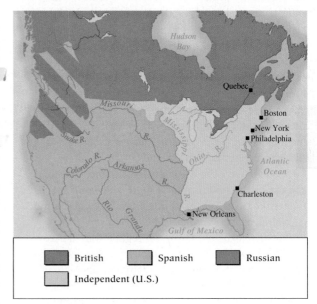

North America, 1783

The proposed constitution created a central government distinct from and superior to the governments of the individual states. The national government was given the power to levy taxes, raise a national army, regulate domestic and foreign trade, and create a national currency. The central or federal government was divided into three branches, each with some power to check the functioning of the others. A president would serve as the chief executive, with the power to execute laws, veto the legislature's acts, supervise foreign affairs, and direct military forces. Legislative power was vested in the second branch of government, a bicameral legislature composed of the Senate, elected by the state legislatures, and the House of Representatives, elected directly by the people. The Supreme Court and other courts "as deemed necessary" by Congress served as the third branch of government. They would enforce the Constitution as the "supreme law of the land."

The United States Constitution was approved by the states—by a slim margin—in 1788. Important to its success was the promise to add a "bill of rights" as the new government's first piece of business. Accordingly, in March 1789, the new Congress proposed twelve amendments to the Constitution; the ten that were ratified by the states have been known ever since as the Bill of Rights. These guaranteed freedom of religion, speech, the press, petition, and assembly, as well as the right to bear arms, be protected against unreasonable searches and arrests, trial by jury, due process of law, and the protection of property rights. Many of these rights were derived from the natural rights philosophy of the eighteenth-century philosophes, which was popular among the American colonists. Many European intellectuals saw the American Revolution as the embodiment of the Enlightenment's political dreams. And when French officers who had fought in the American War for Independence returned to France, they carried with them ideas of individual liberties and notions of republicanism and popular sovereignty that would soon play a role in the early stages of the French Revolution.

Background to the French Revolution

Q FOCUS QUESTION: What were the long-range and immediate causes of the French Revolution?

Although we associate events like the French Revolution with sudden changes, such events involve long-range problems as well as immediate precipitating forces. The causes of the French Revolution must be found in a multifaceted examination of French society and its problems in the late eighteenth century.

Social Structure of the Old Regime

The long-range or indirect causes of the French Revolution must first be sought in the condition of French society. Before the Revolution, French society was grounded in the idea of privilege or inequality of rights. The population of 27 million was divided, as it had been since the Middle Ages, into legal categories known as the three orders or estates.

THE FIRST ESTATE The First Estate consisted of the clergy and numbered about 130,000 people. The church owned approximately 10 percent of the land. Clergy were exempt from the *taille*, France's chief tax, although the church had agreed to pay a "voluntary" contribution every five years to the state. Clergy were also radically divided: the higher clergy, stemming from aristocratic families, shared the interests of the nobility, while the parish priests were often poor commoners.

THE SECOND ESTATE The Second Estate was the nobility, composed of no more than 350,000 people who nevertheless owned perhaps 30 percent of the land. The nobility had continued to play an important and even crucial role in French society in the eighteenth century, holding many of the leading positions in the government, the military, the law courts, and the higher church offices. Nobles also controlled much heavy industry in France, either through investment or by ownership of mining and metallurgical enterprises. The French nobility were also divided. The "nobility of the robe" derived their status from officeholding, a pathway that had often enabled commoners to attain noble rank. These nobles now dominated the royal law courts and important administrative offices. The "nobility of the sword" claimed to be descended from the original medieval nobility. As a group, the nobles sought to expand their privileges at the expense of the monarchy—to defend liberty by resisting the arbitrary actions of monarchy, as some nobles asserted—and to maintain their monopolistic control over positions in the military, church, and government. Moreover, the possession of privileges remained a hallmark of the nobility. Common to all nobles were tax exemptions, especially from the *taille*.

THE THIRD ESTATE The Third Estate, the commoners of French society, constituted the overwhelming majority of the population. They were divided by vast differences in occupation, level of education, and wealth. The peasants, who alone made up 75 to 80 percent of the total population, were by far the largest segment of the Third Estate. They owned about 35 to 40 percent

© Bettmann/Corbis

The Three Estates. This French political cartoon from 1789 reveals a critical view of France's privileged orders. Shown in the cartoon is a naked common man held in chains and being ridden by an aristocrat, a clergyman, and a judge. The message is clear: most ordinary French people (the Third Estate) are suffering horribly as a result of the privileges of the First and Second Estates.

consumer prices rose faster than wages, causing these urban groups to experience a decline in purchasing power. In Paris, for example, income lagged behind food prices and well behind a 140 percent rise in rents for working people in skilled and unskilled trades. Ordinary people spent one-third to one-half of their income on bread, which constituted three-fourths of their diet, so sudden increases in the price of bread immediately affected public order. The economic discontent of this segment of the Third Estate—and often simply the struggle for survival—led the common people to play an important role in the French Revolution, especially in the city of Paris.

About 8 percent of the population, or 2.3 million people, constituted the bourgeoisie or middle class, who owned about 20 to 25 percent of the land. This group included merchants, bankers, and industrialists who controlled the resources of trade, finance, and manufacturing and benefited from the economic prosperity after 1730. The bourgeoisie also included professionals—lawyers, holders of public offices, doctors, and writers. Many members of the bourgeoisie sought security and status through the purchase of land. They had their own set of grievances because they were often excluded from the social and political privileges monopolized by the nobles.

of the land, although these holdings varied from area to area and more than half the peasants had little or no land on which to support themselves. Serfdom no longer existed on any large scale in France, but French peasants still had obligations to their local landlords that they deeply resented. These "relics of feudalism," survivals from an earlier age, included the payment of fees for the use of village facilities, such as the flour mill, community oven, and winepress, as well as tithes to the clergy. The nobility also maintained the right to hunt on the peasants' land.

Another part of the Third Estate consisted of skilled artisans, shopkeepers, and other wage earners in the cities. Although the eighteenth century had been a period of rapid urban growth, 90 percent of French towns had fewer than 10,000 inhabitants, and only nine cities had more than 50,000. In the eighteenth century,

At the same time, remarkable similarities existed at the upper levels of society between the wealthier bourgeoisie and the nobility. It was still possible for wealthy middle-class individuals to enter the ranks of the nobility by obtaining public offices and entering the nobility of the robe. During this century, 6,500 new noble families were created. Moreover, the new and critical ideas of the Enlightenment proved attractive to aristocrats and bourgeoisie alike, since members of both groups shared a common world of liberal political thought. Both aristocratic and bourgeois elites, long accustomed to a new socioeconomic reality based on wealth and economic achievement, were increasingly frustrated by a monarchical system resting on privileges and an old and rigid social order based on the concept of estates. The opposition of these elites to the **old order** ultimately led them to take drastic action against the monarchical regime, although they soon split over the question of how far to proceed in eliminating traditional privileges. In a real sense, the Revolution had its origins in political grievances.

Other Problems Facing the French Monarchy

The inability of the French monarchy to deal with new social realities was exacerbated by specific problems in the 1780s. Although France had enjoyed fifty years of growth overall, periodic economic crises still occurred. Bad harvests in 1787 and 1788 and the beginnings of a manufacturing depression resulted in food shortages, rising prices for food and other necessities, and unemployment in the cities. The number of poor, estimated by some analysts at almost one-third of the population, reached crisis proportions on the eve of the Revolution.

The immediate cause of the French Revolution was the near collapse of government finances. At a time when France was experiencing economic crises, the government found itself drastically short of money. Yet governmental expenditures continued to grow due to costly wars and royal extravagance. The government responded by borrowing; in the budget of 1788, the interest on the debt constituted half of government spending. The total debt had reached 4 billion livres (roughly $40 billion). Financial lenders, fearful that they would never be repaid, were refusing to lend additional amounts. On the verge of a complete financial collapse, the government of Louis XVI was finally forced to call a meeting of the Estates-General, the French parliamentary body that had not met since 1614.

The French Revolution

Q FOCUS QUESTIONS: What were the main events of the French Revolution between 1789 and 1799? What role did each of the following play in the French Revolution: lawyers, peasants, women, the clergy, the Jacobins, the sans-culottes, the French revolutionary army, and the Committee of Public Safety?

In summoning the Estates-General, the government was merely looking for a way to solve the immediate financial crisis. The monarchy had no wish for a major reform of the government, nor did the delegates who arrived at Versailles come with plans for the revolutionary changes that ultimately emerged. Yet over the next years, through the interplay of the deputies meeting in various legislative assemblies, the common people in the streets of Paris and other cities, and the peasants in the countryside, much of the old regime would be destroyed, and Europe would have a new model for political and social change.

From Estates-General to National Assembly

The Estates-General consisted of representatives from the three orders of French society. In the elections for the Estates-General, the government had ruled that the Third Estate should get double representation (it did, after all, constitute 97 percent of the population). Consequently, while both the First Estate (the clergy) and the Second Estate (the nobility) had about 300 delegates each, the commoners had almost 600 representatives. Two-thirds of the latter were people with legal training, and three-fourths were from towns with over two thousand inhabitants, giving the Third Estate a particularly strong legal and urban representation. Most members of the Third Estate advocated a regular constitutional government that would abolish the fiscal privileges of the church and nobility as the major way to regenerate France.

The Estates-General opened at Versailles on May 5, 1789. It was divided from the start over the question of whether voting should be by order or by head (each delegate having one vote). Traditionally, each order would vote separately; each would have veto power over the other two, thus guaranteeing aristocratic control over reforms. But the Third Estate was opposed to this approach and pushed its demands for voting by head. Since it had double representation, with the assistance of liberal nobles and clerics, it could turn the three estates into a single-chamber legislature that would reform France in its own way. Most delegates still desired to make changes within a framework of respect for the authority of the king; revival or reform did not mean the overthrow of traditional institutions. But when the First Estate declared in favor of voting by order, the Third Estate felt compelled to respond in a significant fashion. On June 17, 1789, the Third Estate voted to constitute itself a "National Assembly" and decided to draw up a constitution. Three days later, on June 20, the deputies of the Third Estate arrived at their meeting place to find the door locked; thereupon they moved to a nearby indoor tennis court and swore (in what became known as the Tennis Court Oath) that they would continue to meet until they had

The Fall of the Bastille

On July 14, 1789, Parisian crowds in search of weapons attacked and captured the royal armory known as the Bastille. It had also been a state prison, and its fall marked the triumph of "liberty" over despotism. This intervention of the Parisian populace saved the Third Estate from Louis XVI's attempted counter-revolution.

A Parisian Newspaper Account of the Fall of the Bastille

First, the people tried to enter this fortress by the Rue St.-Antoine, this fortress, which no one has ever penetrated against the wishes of this frightful despotism and where the monster still resided. The treacherous governor had put out a flag of peace. So a confident advance was made; a detachment of French Guards, with perhaps five to six thousand armed bourgeois, penetrated the Bastille's outer courtyards, but as soon as some six hundred persons had passed over the first drawbridge, the bridge was raised and artillery fire mowed down several French Guards and some soldiers; the cannon fired on the town, and the people took fright; a large number of individuals were killed or wounded; but then they rallied and took shelter from the fire. . . . Meanwhile, they tried to locate some cannon; they attacked from the water's edge through the gardens of the arsenal, and from there made an orderly siege; they advanced from various directions, beneath a ceaseless round of fire. It was a terrible scene. . . . The fighting grew steadily more intense; the citizens had become hardened to the fire; from all directions they clambered onto the roofs or broke into the rooms; as soon as an enemy appeared among the turrets on the tower, he was fixed in the sights of a hundred guns and mown down in an instant; meanwhile cannon fire was hurriedly directed against the second drawbridge, which it pierced, breaking the chains; in vain did the cannon on the tower reply, for most people were sheltered from it; the fury was at its height; people bravely faced death and every danger; women, in their eagerness, helped us to the utmost; even the children, after the discharge of fire from the fortress, ran here and there picking up the bullets and shot; [and so the Bastille fell and the governor, De Launay, was captured]. . . . Serene and blessed liberty, for the first time, has at last been introduced into this abode of horrors, this frightful refuge of monstrous despotism and its crimes.

Meanwhile, they get ready to march; they leave amidst an enormous crowd; the applause, the outbursts of joy, the insults, the oaths hurled at the treacherous prisoners of war; everything is confused; cries of vengeance and of pleasure issue from every heart; the conquerors, glorious and covered in honor, carry their arms and the spoils of the conquered, the flags of victory, the militia mingling with the soldiers of the fatherland, the victory laurels offered them from every side, all this created a frightening and splendid spectacle. On arriving at the square, the people, anxious to avenge themselves, allowed neither De Launay nor the other officers to reach the place of trial; they seized them from the hands of their conquerors, and trampled them underfoot one after the other. De Launay was struck by a thousand blows, his head was cut off and hoisted on the end of a pike with blood streaming down all sides. . . . This glorious day must amaze our enemies, and finally usher in for us the triumph of justice and liberty. In the evening, there were celebrations.

Q Why did the fall of the Bastille come to mark the triumph of French "liberty" over despotism? Do you think this Parisian newspaper account might be biased? Why or why not?

Source: From *The Press in the French Revolution: a Selection of Documents Taken from the Press of the Revolution for the Years 1789–1794.* J. Gilchrist and W. J. Murray, eds. (London: Ginn, 1971).

produced a French constitution. These actions of June 17 and June 20 constitute the first step in the French Revolution, since the Third Estate had no legal right to act as the National Assembly.

This revolution, largely the work of the lawyers of the Third Estate, was soon in jeopardy, as the king sided with the First Estate and threatened to dissolve the Estates-General. Louis XVI now prepared to use force. However, his attempt to stop the Revolution was thwarted by the common people in a series of urban and rural uprisings in the summer of 1789. In the most famous of the urban risings, Parisians organized a popular force and on July 14 attacked the Bastille, a royal armory (see the box above). But the Bastille had also been a state prison, and though it now held only seven prisoners (five forgers and two insane people), its fall quickly became a popular symbol of the common people's triumph over despotism. Paris was abandoned to the insurgents, and Louis XVI was soon informed that the royal troops were unreliable. Louis's acceptance of that reality signaled the collapse of royal authority; the king could no longer enforce his will. The fall of the Bastille had saved the National Assembly.

At the same time, independent of what was going on in Paris, popular revolts broke out in numerous cities and were paralleled by peasant insurrections in the countryside. A growing resentment of the entire landholding system, with its fees and obligations, greatly exacerbated by the economic and fiscal activities of the great estate holders—noble or bourgeois—in the difficult decade of the 1780s, created the conditions for a popular uprising. The fall of the Bastille and the king's apparent capitulation to the demands of the Third Estate now encouraged peasants to take matters into their own hands. In July and August, peasant rebellions occurred throughout France. In some places peasants renounced their dues and tithes; elsewhere they burned charters listing their obligations.

The agrarian revolts served as a backdrop to the Great Fear, a vast panic that spread through the country like wildfire between July 20 and August 6. Fear of invasion by foreign troops, aided by a supposed aristocratic plot, encouraged the formation of more citizens' militias and committees. The greatest impact of the agrarian revolts and the Great Fear was on the National Assembly meeting in Versailles. We will now examine its attempt to reform France.

Destruction of the Old Regime

One of the first acts of the National Assembly was to destroy the relics of feudalism or aristocratic privileges. On the night of August 4, 1789, the National Assembly, in an astonishing session, voted to abolish seigneurial rights as well as the fiscal privileges of nobles, clergy, towns, and provinces. On August 26, it provided the ideological foundation for its actions and an educational device for the nation by adopting the Declaration of the Rights of Man and the Citizen (see the box on p. 458). This charter of basic liberties began with a ringing affirmation of "the natural and imprescriptible [unalterable] rights of man" to "liberty, property, security, and resistance to oppression." It went on to affirm the destruction of aristocratic privileges by proclaiming an end to exemptions from taxation, freedom and

equal rights for all men, and access to public office based on talent. The monarchy was restricted, and all citizens were to have the right to take part in the legislative process. Freedom of speech and the press were coupled with the outlawing of arbitrary arrests.

The Declaration also raised another important issue. Did the proclamation's ideal of equal rights for all men also include women? Many deputies insisted that it did, at least in terms of civil liberties, provided that, as one said, "women do not aspire to exercise political rights and functions." Olympe de Gouges (oh-LAMP duh GOOZH), a playwright and pamphleteer, refused to accept this exclusion of women from political rights. Echoing the words of the official declaration, she penned a Declaration of the Rights of Woman and the Female Citizen, in which she insisted that women should have all the same rights as men. The National Assembly ignored her demands (see the box on p. 458).

In the meantime, Louis XVI had remained inactive at Versailles. He did refuse, however, to promulgate the decrees on the abolition of feudalism and the Declaration of Rights. An unexpected turn of events soon forced the king to change his mind. On October 5, thousands of Parisian women, described by one eyewitness as "detachments of women coming up from every direction, armed with broomsticks, lances, pitchforks, swords, pistols and muskets," marched to Versailles, twelve miles away, and insisted that the royal family return to Paris. On October 6, the king complied. As a goodwill gesture, he brought along wagonloads of flour from the palace stores. All were escorted by women armed with pikes (some of which held the severed heads of the king's guards), singing, "We are bringing back the baker, the baker's wife, and the baker's boy" (the king, the queen, and their son). The king now accepted the National Assembly's decrees and was virtually a prisoner in Paris.

Because the Catholic Church was viewed as an important pillar of the old order, it soon felt the impact of reform. Most of the lands of the church were confiscated, and the church was secularized. In July 1790, the Civil Constitution of the Clergy was put into effect. Both bishops and priests of the Catholic Church were to be elected by the people and paid by the state, and all clergy were required to swear an oath of allegiance to the Civil Constitution. Only 54 percent of the French parish clergy took the oath, and the majority of bishops refused. The Catholic Church, still an important institution in the life of the French people, now became an enemy of the Revolution.

OPPOSING VIEWPOINTS

The Natural Rights of the French People: Two Views

One of the most important documents of the French Revolution, the Declaration of the Rights of Man and the Citizen, was adopted in August 1789 by the National Assembly. The declaration affirmed that "men are born and remain free and equal in rights," that government must protect these natural rights, and that political power is derived from the people.

Olympe de Gouges (the pen name used by Marie Gouze) was a butcher's daughter who wrote plays and pamphlets. She argued that the Declaration of the Rights of Man and the Citizen did not apply to women and composed her own Declaration of the Rights of Woman and the Female Citizen in 1791.

Declaration of the Rights of Man and the Citizen

The representatives of the French people, organized as a national assembly, considering that ignorance, neglect, and scorn of the rights of man are the sole causes of public misfortunes and of corruption of governments, have resolved to display in a solemn declaration the natural, inalienable, and sacred rights of man, so that this declaration, constantly in the presence of all members of society, will continually remind them of their rights and their duties.... Consequently, the National Assembly recognizes and declares, in the presence and under the auspices of the Supreme Being, the following rights of man and citizen:

1. Men are born and remain free and equal in rights; social distinctions can be established only for the common benefit.
2. The aim of every political association is the conservation of the natural and imprescriptible rights of man; these rights are liberty, property, security, and resistance to oppression.
3. The source of all sovereignty is located in essence in the nation; no body, no individual can exercise authority which does not emanate from it expressly.
4. Liberty consists in being able to do anything that does not harm another person....
6. The law is the expression of the general will; all citizens have the right to concur personally or through their representatives in its formation; it must be the same for all, whether it protects or punishes. All citizens being equal in its eyes are equally admissible to all honors, positions, and public employments, according to their capabilities and without other distinctions than those of their virtues and talents.
7. No man can be accused, arrested, or detained except in cases determined by the law, and according to the forms which it has prescribed....
10. No one may be disturbed because of his opinions, even religious, provided that their public demonstration does not disturb the public order established by law.
11. The free communication of thoughts and opinions is one of the most precious rights of man: every citizen can therefore freely speak, write, and print....
12. The guaranteeing of the rights of man and citizen necessitates a public force; this force is therefore instituted for the advantage of all, and not for the private use of those to whom it is entrusted....
14. Citizens have the right to determine for themselves or through their representatives the need for taxation of the public, to consent to it freely, to investigate its use, and to determine its rate, basis, collection, and duration.
15. Society has the right to demand an accounting of his administration from every public agent.
16. Any society in which guarantees of rights are not assured nor the separation of powers determined has no constitution.
17. Property being an inviolable and sacred right, no one may be deprived of it unless public necessity, legally determined, clearly requires such action, and then only on condition of a just and prior indemnity.

Declaration of the Rights of Woman and the Female Citizen

... Mothers, daughters, sisters, and representatives of the nation demand to be constituted into a national assembly. Believing that ignorance, omission, or scorn

[handwritten notes in margin: popular sovereignty? → women not included]

for the rights of woman are the only causes of public misfortunes and of the corruption of governments, the women have resolved to set forth in a solemn declaration the natural, inalienable, and sacred rights of woman in order that this declaration, constantly exposed before all the members of the society, will ceaselessly remind them of their rights and duties....

Consequently, the sex that is as superior in beauty as it is in courage during the sufferings of maternity recognizes and declares in the presence and under the auspices of the Supreme Being, the following Rights of Woman and of Female Citizens.

1. Woman is born free and lives equal to man in her rights. Social distinctions can be based only on the common utility.

2. The purpose of any political association is the conservation of the natural and imprescriptible rights of woman and man; these rights are liberty, property, security, and especially resistance to oppression.

3. The principle of all sovereignty rests essentially with the nation, which is nothing but the union of woman and man; no body and no individual can exercise any authority which does not come expressly from it [the nation].

4. Liberty and justice consist of restoring all that belongs to others; thus, the only limits on the exercise of the natural rights of woman are perpetual male tyranny; these limits are to be reformed by the laws of nature and reason....

6. The law must be the expression of the general will; all female and male citizens must contribute either personally or through their representatives to its formation; it must be the same for all: male and female citizens, being equal in the eyes of the law, must be equally admitted to all honors, positions, and public employment according to their capacity and without other distinctions besides those of their virtues and talents.

7. No woman is an exception; she is accused, arrested, and detained in cases determined by law. Women, like men, obey this rigorous law....

10. No one is to be disquieted for his very basic opinions; woman has the right to mount the scaffold; she must equally have the right to mount the rostrum, provided that her demonstrations do not disturb the legally established public order.

11. The free communication of thought and opinions is one of the most precious rights of woman, since that liberty assured the recognition of children by their fathers....

12. The guarantee of the rights of woman and the female citizen implies a major benefit; this guarantee must be instituted for the advantage of all, and not for the particular benefit of those to whom it is entrusted....

14. Female and male citizens have the right to verify, either by themselves or through their representatives, the necessity of the public contribution. This can only apply to women if they are granted an equal share, not only of wealth, but also of public administration, and in the determination of the proportion, the base, the collection, and the duration of the tax.

15. The collectivity of women, joined for tax purposes to the aggregate of men, has the right to demand an accounting of his administration from any public agent.

16. No society has a constitution without the guarantee of rights and the separation of powers; the constitution is null if the majority of individuals comprising the nation have not cooperated in drafting it.

17. Property belongs to both sexes whether united or separate; for each it is an inviolable and sacred right; no one can be deprived of it, since it is the true patrimony of nature, unless the legally determined public need obviously dictates it, and then only with a just and prior indemnity.

Q What "natural rights" does the first document proclaim? To what extent was this document influenced by the writings of the philosophes? What rights for women does the second document enunciate? Given the nature and scope of the arguments in favor of natural rights and women's rights in these two documents, what key effects on European society would you attribute to the French Revolution?

Sources: Declaration of the Rights of Man and the Citizen. From *The French Revolution* by Paul H. Beik. Copyright © 1970 by Paul H. Beik. Reprinted by permission of Walker & Co. Declaration of the Rights of Woman and the Female Citizen. From *Women in Revolutionary Paris, 1789–1795: Selected Documents Translated with Notes and Commentary.* Translated with notes and commentary by Darline Gay Levy, Harriet Branson Applewhite, and Mary Durham Johnson. Copyright 1979 by the Board of Trustees of the University of Illinois. Used with permission of the editors and the University of Illinois Press.

A NEW CONSTITUTION By 1791, the National Assembly had completed a new constitution that established a limited constitutional monarchy. There was still a monarch (now called "king of the French"), but he enjoyed few powers not subject to review by the new Legislative Assembly. The Assembly, in which sovereign power was vested, was to sit for two years and consist of 745 representatives chosen by an indirect system of election that preserved power in the hands of the more affluent members of society. Only active citizens (men over the age of twenty-five paying taxes equivalent in value to three days' unskilled labor) could vote for electors (men paying taxes equal in value to ten days' labor). This relatively small group of 50,000 electors then chose the deputies. To qualify as a deputy, one had to pay taxes equal in value to fifty-four days' labor.

OPPOSITION FROM WITHIN By 1791, France had moved into a vast reordering of the old regime that had been achieved by a revolutionary consensus that was largely the work of the wealthier members of the bourgeoisie. Soon, however, this consensus faced growing opposition from clerics angered by the Civil Constitution of the Clergy, lower classes hurt by a rise in the cost of living, peasants angry that dues had still not been abandoned, and political clubs offering more radical solutions to France's problems. The most famous were the Jacobins (JAK-uh-binz), who first emerged as a gathering of more radical deputies at the beginning of the Revolution and had grown into more than nine hundred Jacobin clubs by early 1791.

By mid-1791, the government was still facing severe financial difficulties due to massive tax evasion. Despite all of their problems, however, the bourgeois politicians in charge remained relatively unified on the basis of their trust in the king. But Louis XVI disastrously undercut them. Upset with the whole turn of revolutionary events, he attempted to flee France in disguise in June 1791 and almost succeeded before being recognized, captured, and brought back to Paris. In this unsettled situation, with a discredited and seemingly disloyal monarch, the new Legislative Assembly held its first session in October 1791. France's relations with the rest of Europe soon led to Louis's downfall.

OPPOSITION FROM ABROAD By this time, some European monarchs had become concerned about the French example and feared that revolution would spread to their countries. On August 27, 1791, Emperor Leopold II of Austria and King Frederick William II of Prussia invited other European monarchs to use force to reestablish monarchical authority in France. Insulted by this threat, the Legislative Assembly declared war on Austria on April 20, 1792.

The French fared badly in the initial fighting. A French army invaded the Austrian Netherlands (Belgium) but was routed, and Paris now feared invasion by the Austrians and Prussians. Alarmed by the turn of events, the Legislative Assembly called for 20,000 national guardsmen from the provinces to come and defend Paris. One group came from Marseilles singing a rousing war song, soon known as the "Marseillaise," that three years later was made the French national anthem:

> *Arise, children of the motherland.*
> *The day of glory has arrived.*
> *Against us, tyranny's*
> *Bloody flag is raised.*
> *Don't you hear in our countryside*
> *The roar of their ferocious soldiers?*
> *They are coming into your homes*
> *To butcher your sons and your companions.*
> *To arms, citizens! Form your battalions!*
> *We march, we march!*
> *Let their impure blood water our fields.*

As fears of invasion grew, a frantic search for scapegoats began. As one observer noted, "Everywhere you hear the cry that the king is betraying us, the generals are betraying us, that nobody is to be trusted;... that Paris will be taken in six weeks by the Austrians.... We are on a volcano ready to spout flames."[1] Defeats in war coupled with economic shortages in the spring reinvigorated popular groups that had been dormant since the previous summer and led to renewed political demonstrations, especially against the king. Radical Parisian political groups, declaring themselves an insurrectionary "commune," organized a mob attack on the royal palace and Legislative Assembly in August 1792, took the king captive, and forced the Assembly to suspend the monarchy and call for a national convention, chosen on the basis of universal male suffrage, to decide on the future form of government. The French Revolution was about to enter a more radical stage as power passed from the Assembly to the new Paris Commune, composed of many who proudly called themselves the **sans-culottes** (sahn-koo-LUT or sanz-koo-LAHTSS), ordinary patriots without fine clothes (the name literally means "without knee-breeches," the fashionable men's attire of the day). Although it has become customary to equate the more radical sans-culottes with working people or the poor, many were merchants and better-off artisans who were often the elite of their neighborhoods.

The Radical Revolution

In September 1792, the newly elected National Convention began its sessions. Although it was called to draft a new constitution, it also acted as the sovereign ruling body of France. Socially, the composition of the National Convention was similar to that of its predecessors, being dominated by lawyers, professionals, and property owners. Two-thirds of the deputies were under age forty-five, and almost all had had political experience as a result of the Revolution. Almost all were also intensely distrustful of the king and his activities. It was therefore no surprise that the Convention's first major step on September 21 was to abolish the monarchy and establish a republic. At the beginning of

Execution of the King. At the beginning of 1793, the National Convention sentenced the king to death, and Louis XVI was duly executed on January 21. As seen in this engraving by Carnavalet, the execution of the king was accomplished by a new revolutionary device, the guillotine.

1793, the National Convention found the king guilty of treason and sentenced him to death. With Louis XVI's execution on January 21, 1793, the destruction of the old regime was complete. There could be no turning back. But the execution of the king produced new challenges by creating new enemies for the Revolution both at home and abroad while strengthening groups that were already opposed to it.

In Paris, the local government, the Commune, led by the newly appointed minister of justice, Georges Danton (ZHORZH dahn-TAWNH) (1759–1794), favored drastic change and put constant pressure on the Convention, pushing it to ever more radical positions. Moreover, the National Convention still did not rule all of France. Peasants in the west and inhabitants of France's major provincial cities refused to accept the authority of the Convention. Domestic turmoil was paralleled by a foreign crisis. By the time the king was executed, most of Europe—an informal coalition of Austria, Prussia, Spain, Portugal, Britain, the Dutch Republic, and Russia—had aligned against France, and by late spring, some members of the coalition were poised to invade France in an effort to destroy the revolutionaries and reestablish the old regime.

To meet these crises, the program of the National Convention became one of curbing anarchy and counter-revolution at home while attempting to win the war by a vigorous mobilization of the people. To administer the government, the Convention gave broad powers to an executive committee of twelve known as the Committee of Public Safety, which came to be dominated by Maximilien Robespierre (mak-see-meel-YENH ROHBZ-pyayr) (1758–1794)—the leader of the Jacobins. For a twelve-month period, this committee gave the country the leadership it needed to weather the domestic and foreign crises of 1793.

A NATION IN ARMS To meet the foreign crisis and save the republic from its foreign enemies, the Committee of Public Safety decreed a universal mobilization of the nation on August 23, 1793:

> Young men will fight, young men are called to conquer. Married men will forge arms, transport military baggage and guns and prepare food supplies. Women, who at long last are to take their rightful place in the revolution and follow their true destiny, will forget their futile tasks: their delicate hands will work at making clothes for soldiers; they will make tents and they will extend their tender care to shelters where the defenders of the [nation] will receive the help that their wounds require. Children will make lint of old cloth. It is for them that we are

Citizens in the New French Army. To save the republic from its foreign enemies, the National Convention created a new revolutionary army of unprecedented size. The illustration above, from a book of paintings on the French Revolution by the Lesueur brothers, shows three citizens learning to drill, while a young volunteer is being armed and outfitted by his family. The illustration at the left, also by the Lesueur brothers, shows two volunteers joyfully going off to fight.

fighting: children, those beings destined to gather all the fruits of the revolution, will raise their pure hands toward the skies. And old men, performing their missions again, as of yore, will be guided to the public squares of the cities where they will kindle the courage of young warriors and preach the doctrines of hate for kings and the unity of the Republic.[2]

In less than a year, the French revolutionary government had raised an army of 650,000; by September 1794, it numbered 1,169,000. The republic's army—a **nation in arms**—was the largest ever seen in European history. It pushed the allies back across the Rhine and even conquered the Austrian Netherlands to the north (see Map 19.1).

Historians have focused on the importance of the French revolutionary army as an important step in the creation of modern **nationalism**. Previously, wars had been fought between governments or ruling dynasties by relatively small armies of professional soldiers. The new French army, however, was the creation of a "people's" government; its wars were now "people's" wars. The entire nation was to be involved in the war. But when dynastic wars became people's wars, warfare increased in ferocity and lack of restraint. Although innocent civilians had suffered in the earlier struggles, now the carnage became appalling at times. The wars of the French revolutionary era opened the door to the total war of the modern world.

THE COMMITTEE OF PUBLIC SAFETY AND THE REIGN OF TERROR To meet the domestic crisis, the National Convention and the Committee of Public Safety established the "Reign of Terror." Revolutionary courts were organized to protect the republic from its internal enemies (see the box on p. 464). Many victims were persons

MAP 19.1 **French Expansion During the Revolutionary Wars, 1792–1799.** The conservative rulers of Europe, appalled at the republican character of the French Revolution, took up arms to restore the power of the Bourbon monarchy. The French responded with a people's army, the largest ever seen, that pushed the invaders out of France, annexed the Austrian Netherlands and some Italian territory, and created a number of French satellite states.

Q Why would Austria desire cooperation from the German states if it wanted to wage war on France?

who had opposed the radical activities of the sans-culottes. In the course of nine months, 16,000 people were officially killed under the blade of the guillotine, a revolutionary device for the quick and efficient separation of heads from bodies. But the true number of the Terror's victims was probably closer to 50,000. The bulk of the Terror's executions took place in places that had been in open rebellion against the authority of the National Convention. The Terror demonstrated no class prejudice—victims ranged from royalists, such as Queen Marie Antoinette, to the former revolutionary Olympe de Gouges. Estimates are that the nobles constituted 8 percent of its victims; the middle classes, 25 percent; the clergy, 6 percent; and the peasant and laboring classes, 61 percent. To the Committee of Public Safety, this bloodletting was only a temporary expedient. After the wars and domestic emergencies were over, a "republic of virtue" would arise, and the Declaration of the Rights of Man and the Citizen would be fully established.

Military force in the form of revolutionary armies was used to bring recalcitrant cities and districts back under the control of the National Convention. Since Lyons (LYOHNH) was France's second city after Paris and had defied the National Convention during a time when the republic was in peril, the Committee of Public Safety decided to make an example of it. By April 1794, a total of 1,880 citizens of Lyons had been executed.

Justice in the Reign of Terror

The Reign of Terror created a repressive environment in which courts often acted quickly to condemn traitors to the revolutionary cause. In this account, an English visitor describes the court, the procession to the scene of execution, and the final execution procedure.

J. G. Milligen, *The Revolutionary Tribunal* (Paris, October 1793)

In the center of the hall, under a statue of Justice, holding scales in one hand, and a sword in the other, sat Dumas, the President, with the other judges. Under them were seated the public accuser, Fourquier-Tinville, and his scribes. . . . To the right were benches on which the accused were placed in several rows, and *gendarmes* with carbines and fixed bayonets by their sides. To the left was the jury. Never can I forget the mournful appearance of these funereal processions to the place of execution. The march was opened by a detachment of mounted *gendarmes*—the carts followed; they were the same carts as those that are used in Paris for carrying wood; four boards were placed across them for seats, and on each board sat two, and sometimes three victims; their hands were tied behind their backs, and the constant jolting of the cart made them nod their heads up and down, to the great amusement of the spectators. On the front of the cart stood Samson, the executioner, or one of his sons or assistants; *gendarmes* on foot marched by the side; then followed a hackney, in which was the reporting clerk, whose duty it was to witness the execution, and then return to the public accuser's office to report the execution of what they called the law.

The process of execution was also a sad and heartrending spectacle. In the middle of the Place de la Revolution was erected a guillotine, in front of a colossal statue of Liberty, represented seated on a rock, a cap on her head, a spear in her hand, the other reposing on a shield. On one side of the scaffold were drawn out a sufficient number of carts, with large baskets painted red, to receive the heads and bodies of the victims. Those bearing the condemned moved on slowly to the foot of the guillotine; the culprits were led out in turn, and if necessary, supported by two of the executioner's assistants, but their assistance was rarely required. Most of these unfortunates ascended the scaffold with a determined step—many of them looked up firmly on the menacing instrument of death, beholding for the last time the rays of the glorious sun, beaming on the polished axe: and I have seen some young men actually dance a few steps before they went up to be strapped to the perpendicular plane, which was then tilted to a horizontal plane in a moment, and ran on the grooves until the neck was secured and closed in by a moving board, when the head passed through what was called, in derision, "the republican toilet seat"; the weighty knife was then dropped with a heavy fall; and, with incredible dexterity and rapidity, two executioners tossed the body into the basket, while another threw the head after it.

Q How were the condemned taken to the executioner? How did this serve to inflame the crowds? How were people executed? Why?

Source: From J. M. Thompson, *English Witness of the French Revolution* (Oxford: Blackwell, 1938).

When guillotining proved too slow, cannon fire and grapeshot were used to blow condemned men into open graves. A German observed:

> Whole ranges of houses, always the most handsome, burnt. The churches, convents, and all the dwellings of the former patricians were in ruins. When I came to the guillotine, the blood of those who had been executed a few hours beforehand was still running in the street. . . . I said to a group of sans-culottes that it would be decent to clear away all this human blood. Why should it be cleared? one of them said to me. It's the blood of aristocrats and rebels. The dogs should lick it up.[3]

In western France, revolutionary armies were also brutal in defeating the rebel armies. The commander of one revolutionary army ordered that no quarter be given: "The road to Laval is strewn with corpses. Women, priests, monks, children, all have been put to death. I have spared nobody." Perhaps the most notorious act of violence occurred in Nantes, where victims were executed by sinking them in barges in the Loire River.

THE "REPUBLIC OF VIRTUE" Along with the Terror, the Committee of Public Safety took other steps both to control France and to create a new republican order and new republican citizens. By spring 1793, it was sending "representatives on mission" as agents of the central government to all parts of France to implement the laws dealing with the wartime emergency. The committee also attempted to provide some economic controls by the Law of the General Maximum, which established price limits on goods declared of first necessity, ranging from food and drink to fuel and clothing. The controls failed to work very well because the government lacked the machinery to enforce them.

Women played an active role in this radical phase of the French Revolution. As spectators at sessions of revolutionary clubs and the National Convention, women made the members and deputies aware of their demands. Nevertheless, despite the women's efforts, including founding the Society for Revolutionary Republican Women in 1793, which was largely composed of working-class women, the Paris Commune outlawed women's clubs and forbade women to be present at its meetings.

Women Patriots. Women played a variety of roles in the events of the French Revolution. This picture shows a middle-class women's patriotic club discussing the decrees of the National Convention, an indication that some women had become highly politicized by the upheavals of the Revolution. The women are also giving coins to create a fund for impoverished families.

In its attempt to create a new order, the National Convention also pursued a policy of de-Christianization. The word *saint* was removed from street names, churches were pillaged and closed by revolutionary armies, and priests were encouraged to marry. In Paris, the cathedral of Notre-Dame was designated a "temple of reason." In November 1793, in a public ceremony dedicated to the worship of Reason in the former cathedral, patriotic maidens adorned in white dresses paraded where the high altar had once stood. However, de-Christianization backfired because France was still overwhelmingly Catholic.

Yet another manifestation of de-Christianization was the adoption of a new republican calendar on October 5, 1793. Years would no longer be numbered from the birth of Jesus but from September 22, 1792, the day the French republic was proclaimed. Thus, at the time the calendar was adopted, the French were already living in year II. The months were named after the seasons, temperatures, or the state of vegetation. The new calendar also eliminated Sundays and church holidays, reinforcing its anti-Christian purpose.

EQUALITY AND SLAVERY Early in the French Revolution, the desire for equality led to a discussion of what to do about slavery. A club called Friends of the Blacks advocated the abolition of slavery, which was achieved in France in September 1791. Nevertheless, French planters in the West Indies, who profited greatly from the use of slaves on their sugar plantations, opposed the abolition of slavery in the French colonies. When the National Convention came to power, the issue was revisited, and on February 4, 1794, guided by ideals of equality, the government abolished slavery in the colonies.

In one French colony, slaves had already rebelled for their freedom. In 1791, black slaves in the French sugar colony of Saint-Domingue (the western third of the island of Hispaniola), inspired by the ideals of the revolution occurring in France, revolted against French plantation owners, killing the owners and their families and burning their buildings. White planters retaliated with equal brutality. One wealthy French settler exclaimed, "How can we stay in a country where slaves have raised their hands against their masters?"

Eventually, leadership of the revolt was taken over by Toussaint L'Ouverture (too-SANH loo-vayr-TOOR) (1746–1803), a son of African slaves, who seized control of all of Hispaniola by 1801. Although Napoleon (see "The Age of Napoleon" later in this chapter) had accepted the revolutionary ideal of equality, he did not deny the reports that the massacres of white planters by slaves demonstrated the savage nature of blacks. In 1802, he reinstated slavery in the French West Indian colonies and sent an army that captured L'Ouverture, who died in a French dungeon within a year. But the French soldiers, weakened by disease, soon succumbed to the slave forces. On January 1, 1804, the western part of Hispaniola, now called Haiti, announced its freedom and became the first independent state in Latin America. Despite Napoleon's efforts to the contrary, one of the French revolutionary ideals had triumphed abroad.

THE DECLINE OF THE COMMITTEE OF PUBLIC SAFETY Maintaining the revolutionary ideals in France, however, proved not to be easy. By the summer of 1794, the French had been successful on the battlefield against their foreign foes. The military successes meant that the Terror no longer served much purpose. But the Terror continued because Robespierre, now its dominant figure, had become obsessed with purifying the body politic of all corruption. Many deputies in the National Convention, however, feared that they were not safe while Robespierre was free to act. An anti-Robespierre coalition in the National Convention gathered enough votes to condemn him, and Robespierre was guillotined on July 28, 1794, beginning a reaction that brought an end to this radical stage of the French Revolution.

The National Convention and its Committee of Public Safety had accomplished a great deal. By creating a nation in arms, they had preserved the French Revolution and prevented it from being destroyed by its foreign enemies, who, if they had succeeded, would have reestablished the old monarchical order. Domestically, the Revolution had also been saved from the forces of counter-revolution. The committee's tactics, however, provided an example for the use of violence in domestic politics that has continued to bedevil the Western world to this day.

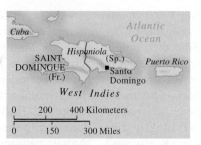

Revolt in Saint-Domingue (Haiti)

Reaction and the Directory

After the execution of Robespierre, revolutionary fervor began to give way to the Thermidorean Reaction, named after the month of Thermidor on the new French calendar. The Terror began to abate. The National Convention curtailed the power of the Committee of Public Safety, shut down the Jacobin club, and attempted to provide better protection for its deputies against the Parisian mobs. Churches were allowed to reopen for public worship. Economic regulation was dropped in favor of *laissez-faire* policies, another clear indication that moderate forces were again gaining control of the Revolution. In addition, a new constitution was adopted in August 1795 that reflected this more conservative republicanism and a desire for a stability that did not sacrifice the ideals of 1789.

To avoid the dangers of another single legislative assembly, the Constitution of 1795 established a national legislative assembly consisting of two chambers: a lower house, known as the Council of 500, that initiated legislation, and an upper house, the Council of Elders, that accepted or rejected the proposed laws. The 750 members of the two legislative bodies were chosen by electors who had to be owners or renters of property worth between 100 and 200 days' labor, a requirement that limited their number to 30,000. The Council of Elders elected five directors from a list presented by the Council of 500 to act as the executive committee, known as the Directory.

The period of the Directory was an era of materialistic reaction to the suffering and sacrifices that had been demanded during the Reign of Terror and the Republic of Virtue. Speculators made fortunes in property by taking advantage of the government's severe monetary problems. Elaborate fashions, which had gone out of style because of their identification with the nobility, were worn again. Gambling and roulette became popular once more. Groups of "gilded youth"—the sons of the wealthy, with long hair and rumpled clothes—took to the streets to insult former supporters of the Revolution.

The government of the Directory had to contend with political enemies from both ends of the political spectrum. On the right, royalists who dreamed of restoring the monarchy continued their agitation. On the left, Jacobin hopes of power were revived by the continuing economic problems. Battered by the left

CHRONOLOGY The French Revolution	
National Assembly (Constituent Assembly)	*1789–1791*
Meeting of Estates-General	May 5, 1789
Formation of National Assembly	June 17, 1789
Tennis Court Oath	June 20, 1789
Fall of the Bastille	July 14, 1789
Great Fear	Summer 1789
Abolition of feudalism	August 4, 1789
Declaration of the Rights of Man and the Citizen	August 26, 1789
Women's march to Versailles; king's return to Paris	October 5–6, 1789
Civil Constitution of the Clergy	July 12, 1790
Flight of the king	June 1791
Legislative Assembly	*1791–1792*
French declaration of war on Austria	April 20, 1792
Attack on the royal palace	August 1792
National Convention	*1792–1795*
Abolition of the monarchy	September 21, 1792
Execution of the king	January 21, 1793
Universal mobilization of the nation	August 23, 1793
Execution of Robespierre	July 28, 1794
Directory	*1795–1799*
Constitution of 1795	August 22, 1795

and right, unable to find a definitive solution to the country's economic difficulties, and still carrying on the wars inherited from the Committee of Public Safety, the Directory increasingly relied on the military to maintain its power. This led to a coup d'état in 1799 in which the successful and popular military general Napoleon Bonaparte was able to seize power.

The Age of Napoleon

Q Focus Question: Which aspects of the French Revolution did Napoleon preserve, and which did he destroy?

Napoleon dominated the history of both France and the rest of Europe from 1799 to 1815. In a sense, Napoleon brought the Revolution to an end, but he was also its product; he even called himself the "Son of the Revolution." The French Revolution had made possible his rise first in the military and then to supreme power in France. Even beyond this, Napoleon had once said, "I am the Revolution," and he never ceased to remind the French that they owed to him the preservation of all that was beneficial in the revolutionary program.

The Rise of Napoleon

Napoleon Bonaparte was born in Corsica in 1769, a few months after France had annexed the island. The son of a lawyer whose family stemmed from the Florentine nobility, the young Napoleon obtained a royal scholarship to study at a military school in France. When the Revolution broke out in 1789, Napoleon was a lieutenant, but the Revolution and the European war that followed broadened his sights and presented him with new opportunities. Napoleon rose quickly through the ranks. In 1794, when he was only twenty-five, the Committee of Public Safety promoted him to the rank of major general. Two years later, he was made commander of the French armies in Italy (see the box on p. 468), where he won a series of stunning victories and dictated peace to the Austrians in 1797. Throughout his Italian campaigns, Napoleon won the confidence of his men by his energy, charm, and ability to comprehend complex issues quickly and make decisions rapidly. These qualities, combined with his keen intelligence, ease with words, and supreme confidence in himself, enabled him throughout the rest of his life to influence people and win their firm support. Napoleon liked to see himself as a man of destiny and a great man who mastered luck. He also saw himself as a military genius who had a "touch for leading, which could not be learned from books, nor by practice."

In 1797, Napoleon was received in France as a conquering hero. Despite a disastrous expedition to Egypt in 1799, he returned to Paris, where he participated in the coup d'état that ultimately led to his virtual dictatorship of France. He was only thirty years old at the time.

With the coup of 1799, a new form of the republic was proclaimed in which, as first consul, Napoleon directly controlled the entire executive authority of government. He had overwhelming influence over the legislature, appointed members of the administrative bureaucracy, controlled the army, and conducted foreign affairs. In 1802, Napoleon was made consul for life and in 1804 returned France to monarchy when he

Napoleon and Psychological Warfare

In 1796, at the age of twenty-seven, Napoleon Bonaparte was given command of the French army in Italy, where he won a series of stunning victories. His use of speed, deception, and surprise to overwhelm his opponents is well known. In this selection from a proclamation to his troops in Italy, Napoleon also appears as a master of psychological warfare.

Napoleon Bonaparte, Proclamation to the French Troops in Italy (April 26, 1796)

Soldiers:

In a fortnight you have won six victories, taken twenty-one standards, fifty-five pieces of artillery, several strong positions, and conquered the richest part of Piedmont [in northern Italy]; you have captured 15,000 prisoners and killed or wounded more than 10,000 men.... You have won battles without cannon, crossed rivers without bridges, made forced marches without shoes, camped without brandy and often without bread. Soldiers of liberty, only republican troops could have endured what you have endured. Soldiers, you have our thanks! The grateful Patrie [nation] will owe its prosperity to you....

FLATTERY

The two armies which but recently attacked you with audacity are fleeing before you in terror; the wicked men who laughed at your misery and rejoiced at the thought of the triumphs of your enemies are confounded and trembling.

But, soldiers, as yet you have done nothing compared with what remains to be done.... Undoubtedly the greatest obstacles have been overcome; but you still have battles to fight, cities to capture, rivers to cross. Is there one among you whose courage is abating? No.... All of you are consumed with a desire to extend the glory of the French people; all of you long to humiliate those arrogant kings who dare to contemplate placing us in fetters; all of you desire to dictate a glorious peace, one which will indemnify the Patrie for the immense sacrifices it has made; all of you wish to be able to say with pride as you return to your villages, "I was with the victorious army of Italy!"

Q What themes did Napoleon use to play on the emotions of his troops and inspire them to greater efforts? Do you think Napoleon believed these words? Why or why not?

Source: From *A Documentary Survey of the French Revolution* by John Hall Stewart. Copyright © 1951 by Macmillan Publishing Company, renewed 1979 by John Hall Stewart. Reprinted with permission of Prentice-Hall, Inc., a Pearson Education Company.

---

crowned himself Emperor Napoleon I. The revolutionary era that had begun with an attempt to limit arbitrary government had ended with a government far more autocratic than the monarchy of the old regime.

The Domestic Policies of Emperor Napoleon

Napoleon once claimed that he had preserved the gains of the Revolution for the French people. The ideal of republican liberty had, of course, been destroyed by Napoleon's thinly disguised autocracy. But were revolutionary ideals maintained in other ways? An examination of his domestic policies will enable us to judge the accuracy of Napoleon's assertion.

NAPOLEON AND THE CATHOLIC CHURCH In 1801, Napoleon established peace with the oldest and most implacable enemy of the Revolution, the Catholic Church. Both sides gained from the Concordat that Napoleon arranged with the pope. Napoleon agreed to recognize Catholicism as the religion of a majority of the French people. Although the Catholic Church was permitted to hold processions again and reopen the seminaries, the pope agreed not to raise the question of the church lands confiscated during the Revolution. As a result of the Concordat, the Catholic Church was no longer an enemy of the French government. At the same time, the agreement reassured those who had acquired church property during the Revolution that they could keep it, an assurance that obviously made them supporters of the Napoleonic regime.

A NEW CODE OF LAWS Napoleon's most famous domestic achievement was his codification of the laws. Before the Revolution, France did not have a single set of laws

The Coronation of Napoleon. In 1804, Napoleon restored monarchy to France when he crowned himself emperor. In the coronation scene painted by Jacques-Louis David, Napoleon is shown crowning his wife, the empress Josephine, while the pope looks on. Shown seated in the box in the background is Napoleon's mother, even though she was not present at the ceremony.

but rather a conglomeration of three hundred legal systems. During the Revolution, efforts were made to codify the laws for the entire nation, but it remained for Napoleon to oversee the project and bring the work to completion in seven codes, of which the most important was the Civil Code (or Code Napoléon). This preserved most of the revolutionary gains by recognizing the principle of the equality of all citizens before the law, the right of the individual to choose a profession, religious toleration, and the abolition of serfdom and feudalism. Property rights continued to be carefully protected, and the interests of employers were safeguarded by outlawing trade unions and strikes. The Civil Code clearly reflected the revolutionary aspirations for a uniform legal system, legal equality, and protection of property and individuals.

But the Civil Code strictly curtailed the rights of some people. During the radical phase of the French Revolution, new laws had made divorce an easy process for both husbands and wives, restricted the rights of fathers over their children (they could no longer have their children put in prison arbitrarily), and allowed all children (including daughters) to inherit property equally. Napoleon's Civil Code undid most of this legislation. Fathers' control over their families was restored. Divorce was still allowed but was made more difficult for women to obtain. A wife caught in adultery, for example, could be divorced by her husband and even imprisoned. A husband, however, could be accused of adultery only if he moved his mistress into his home. Women were now "less equal than men" in other ways as well. When they married, their property passed into the control of their husbands. In lawsuits, they were treated as minors, and their testimony was regarded as less reliable than that of men.

THE FRENCH BUREAUCRACY Napoleon also worked on rationalizing the bureaucratic structure of France by developing a powerful centralized administrative machine. Administrative centralization required a bureaucracy of capable officials, and Napoleon worked hard to develop one. Early on, the regime showed its preference for experts and cared little whether that expertise had been acquired in royal or revolutionary bureaucracies. Promotion, in civil as well as military offices, was to be based not on rank or birth but on demonstrated abilities. This was, of course, what many bourgeois had wanted before the Revolution. Napoleon, however, also created a new aristocracy based on merit in the state service. He elevated 3,263 individuals to the nobility between 1808 and 1814; nearly 60 percent were military officers; the remainder came from the upper ranks of the civil service and other state and local officials. Socially, only 22 percent of Napoleon's aristocracy came from the nobility of the old regime; almost 60 percent were bourgeois in origin.

NAPOLEON'S GROWING DESPOTISM In his domestic policies, then, Napoleon both destroyed and retained aspects of the Revolution. Although equality was preserved in the law code and in the opening of careers to talent, the creation of a new aristocracy, the strong protection accorded to property rights, and the use of conscription for the military make it clear that much equality had been lost. Liberty had been replaced by an initially benevolent despotism that grew increasingly arbitrary. Napoleon shut down sixty of France's seventy-three newspapers and insisted that all manuscripts be subjected to government scrutiny before they were published. Government police even opened the mail.

One prominent writer, Germaine de Staël (zhayr-MEN duh STAHL) (1766–1817), refused to accept Napoleon's growing despotism. Educated in Enlightenment ideas, she set up a salon in Paris that had become a prominent intellectual center by 1800 and wrote novels and political works that denounced Napoleon's rule as tyrannical. Napoleon banned her books in France and exiled her to the German states, where she continued to write, although not without considerable homesickness for France. "The universe is in France," she once wrote; "outside it there is nothing." After the overthrow of Napoleon, Germaine de Staël returned to her beloved Paris, where she died two years later.

Napoleon's Empire and the European Response

When Napoleon became first consul in 1799, France was at war with a second European coalition of Russia, Great Britain, and Austria. Napoleon realized the need for a pause and achieved a peace treaty in 1802 that left France with new frontiers and a number of client territories from the North Sea to the Adriatic. But the peace did not last because the British and French both regarded it as temporary and had little intention of adhering to its terms.

In 1803, war was renewed with Britain, which was soon joined by Austria and Russia in the Third Coalition. At the Battle of Ulm in southern Germany in 1805, Napoleon surrounded an Austrian army of 50,000 men, which quickly surrendered. Proceeding eastward from Ulm, Napoleon attacked Austrian and Russian forces gathered at Austerlitz (AWSS-tur-litz) and devastated the combined armies. Austria sued for peace, and Tsar Alexander I took his remaining forces back to Russia.

At first, Prussia had refused to join the Third Coalition, but after Napoleon began to reorganize the German states, Prussia reversed course. Acting quickly, Napoleon crushed the Prussian forces in two battles, at Jena (YAY-nuh) and Auerstadt (OW-urr-shtaht), in October 1806 and then moved on to defeat the Russians, who had decided to reenter the fray, at Eylau (Y-low) and Friedland (FREET-lahnt) in June 1807. The Treaties of Tilsit, signed by Napoleon and the rulers of Prussia and Austria at the beginning of July, ended the fighting and gave the French the opportunity to create a new European order.

NAPOLEON'S GRAND EMPIRE The Grand Empire was composed of three major parts: the French empire, dependent states, and allied states (see Map 19.2). The French empire, the inner core of the Grand Empire, consisted of an enlarged France extending to the Rhine in the east and including the western half of Italy north of Rome. Dependent states were kingdoms under the rule of Napoleon's relatives; these included Spain, the United Provinces of the Netherlands, the kingdom of Italy, the Swiss Republic, the Grand Duchy of Warsaw, and the Confederation of the Rhine (a union of all the German states except Austria and Prussia). Allied states were those defeated by Napoleon and forced to join his struggle against Britain; they included Prussia, Austria, and Russia. Although the structure of the Grand Empire varied outside its inner core, Napoleon considered himself the leader of the whole.

MAP 19.2 **Napoleon's Grand Empire in 1810.** Napoleon's Grand Army won a series of victories against Austria, Prussia, and Russia that gave the French emperor full or partial control over much of Europe by 1807.

Q On the continent, what is the overall relationship between distance from France and degree of French control, and how can you account for this?

Within his empire, Napoleon sought acceptance everywhere of certain revolutionary principles, including legal equality, religious toleration, and economic freedom. As he explained to his brother Jerome after naming him king of the new German state of Westphalia:

> What the peoples of Germany desire most impatiently is that talented commoners should have the same right to your esteem and to public employments as the nobles, that any trace of serfdom and of an intermediate hierarchy between the sovereign and the lowest class of the people should be completely abolished. The benefits of the Code Napoléon, the publicity of judicial procedure, the creation of juries must be so many distinguishing marks of your monarchy.... What nation would wish to return under the arbitrary Prussian government once it had tasted the benefits of a wise and liberal administration? The peoples of Germany, the peoples of France, of Italy, of Spain all desire equality and liberal ideas. I have guided the affairs of Europe for many years now, and I have had occasion to convince myself that the buzzing of the privileged classes is contrary to the general opinion. Be a constitutional king.[4]

In the inner core and dependent states of his Grand Empire, Napoleon tried to destroy the old order.

Nobility and clergy everywhere in these states lost their special privileges. He decreed equality of opportunity with offices open to talent, equality before the law, and religious toleration. This spread of French revolutionary principles was an important factor in the development of liberal traditions in these countries and has led some historians to view Napoleon as the last of the enlightened absolutists.

THE PROBLEM OF GREAT BRITAIN Like Hitler 130 years later, Napoleon hoped that his Grand Empire would last for centuries; like Hitler's empire, it collapsed almost as rapidly as it had been formed. Two major reasons help explain this: the survival of Great Britain and the force of nationalism. Britain's survival was due primarily to its sea power. As long as Britain ruled the waves, it was almost invulnerable to military attack. Although Napoleon contemplated an invasion of Britain and even collected ships for it, he could not overcome the British navy's decisive defeat of a combined French-Spanish fleet at Trafalgar in 1805. Napoleon then turned to his **Continental System** to defeat Britain. Put into effect between 1806 and 1808, it attempted to prevent British goods from reaching the European continent in order to weaken Britain economically and destroy its capacity to wage war. But the Continental System failed. Allied states resented the ever-tightening French economic hegemony, and some began to cheat and others to resist, thereby opening the door to British collaboration. New markets in the Levant (Middle East) and in Latin America also provided compensation for the British. Indeed, in 1809 and 1810, British overseas exports reached near-record highs.

NATIONALISM The second important factor in the failure of Napoleon was nationalism. This political creed had arisen during the French Revolution in the French people's emphasis on brotherhood (*fraternité*) and

Museo del Prado, Madrid/Erich Lessing/Art Resource, NY

Francisco Goya, *The Third of May 1808*. After Napoleon imposed his brother Joseph on Spain as its king, the Spanish people revolted against his authority, and a series of riots broke out in Madrid. This painting by Francisco Goya shows the French response—a deliberate execution of Spanish citizens to frighten people into submission. Goya portrays the French troops as a firing squad, killing people (including a monk) reacting in terror. The peasant in the middle throws out his arms in a gesture reminiscent of crucifixion. Goya painted many scenes depicting the horrors of war in Napoleonic Spain.

solidarity against other peoples. Nationalism involved the unique cultural identity of a people based on common language, religion, and national symbols. The spirit of French nationalism had made possible the mass armies of the revolutionary and Napoleonic eras. But in spreading the principles of the French Revolution beyond France, Napoleon inadvertently brought about a spread of nationalism as well. The French aroused nationalism in two ways: by making themselves hated oppressors, and thus arousing the patriotism of others in opposition to French nationalism, and by showing the people of Europe what nationalism was and what a nation in arms could do. The lesson was not lost on other peoples and rulers. A Spanish uprising against Napoleon's rule, aided by British support, kept a French force of 200,000 pinned down for years.

Nationalist movements also arose in the German states, where a number of intellectuals advocated a cultural nationalism based on the unity of the German people. In Prussia, feeling against Napoleon led to a serious reform of the old order that had been so easily crushed by the French emperor. As one Prussian official argued, the Prussians must learn from the French example and "place their entire national energies in opposition to the enemy." Under the direction of Baron Heinrich von Stein (HYN-rikh fun SHYTN) and later Prince Karl von Hardenberg (KARL fun HAR-den-berk), Prussia embarked on a series of political and military reforms, including the abolition of serfdom, election of city councils, and creation of a larger standing army. Prussia's reforms, instituted as a response to Napoleon, enabled it to again play an important role in European affairs.

THE FALL OF NAPOLEON Napoleon once said, "If I had experienced pleasure, I might have rested; but the peril was always in front of me, and the day's victory was always forgotten in the preoccupation with the necessity of winning a new victory on the morrow."[5] Never at rest, Napoleon decided in 1812 to invade Russia. It was the beginning of his downfall, but Russia's defection from the Continental System left Napoleon with little choice. Although aware of the risks of invading such a large country, he also knew that if the Russians were allowed to challenge the Continental System unopposed, others would soon follow suit. In June 1812, a Grand Army of more than 600,000 men entered Russia. Napoleon's hopes for victory depended on quickly meeting and defeating the Russian armies, but the Russian forces refused to give battle and

retreated across hundreds of miles while torching their own villages and countryside to prevent Napoleon's army from finding food and shelter. When the Russians did stop to fight at Borodino, Napoleon's forces won an indecisive and costly victory. When the remaining troops of the Grand Army arrived in Moscow, they found the city ablaze. Lacking food and supplies, Napoleon abandoned Moscow late in October and made the "Great Retreat" across Russia in terrible winter conditions. Only one-fifth of the original army managed to straggle back to Poland in January 1813.

This military disaster then led to a war of liberation all over Europe, culminating in Napoleon's defeat in April 1814. The vanquished emperor of the French was allowed to play ruler on the island of Elba, off the coast of Tuscany, while the Bourbon monarchy was restored to France in the person of Louis XVIII, brother of the executed king. But the new king had little support, and Napoleon, bored on Elba, slipped back into France. When troops were sent to capture him, Napoleon opened his coat and addressed them: "Soldiers of the fifth regiment, I am your Emperor.... If there is a man among you would kill his Emperor, here I am!" No one fired a shot. Shouting "Vive l'Empéreur! Vive l'Empéreur," the troops went over to his side, and Napoleon entered Paris in triumph on March 20, 1815.

The powers who had defeated him pledged once more to fight this person they called the "Enemy and Disturber of the Tranquillity of the World." Having decided to strike first at his enemies, Napoleon raised yet another army and moved to attack the nearest allied forces stationed in Belgium. At Waterloo on June

CHRONOLOGY The Napoleonic Era, 1799–1815	
Napoleon as first consul	1799–1804
Concordat with Catholic Church	1801
Emperor Napoleon I	1804–1815
Battles of Austerlitz, Trafalgar, Ulm	1805
Battle of Jena	1806
Continental System	1806
Battle of Eylau	1807
Invasion of Russia	1812
War of liberation	1813–1814
Exile to Elba	1814
Battle of Waterloo; exile to Saint Helena	1815

18, Napoleon met a combined English and Prussian army under the duke of Wellington and suffered a bloody defeat. This time the victorious allies exiled him to Saint Helena, a small, forsaken island in the South Atlantic, where he died in 1821. Only Napoleon's memory would continue to haunt French political life.

Chapter Summary

The late eighteenth century was a time of dramatic political transformation. Revolutionary upheavals, beginning in North America and continuing in France, produced movements for political liberty and equality. The documents created by these revolutions, the Declaration of Independence and the Declaration of the Rights of Man and the Citizen, embodied the fundamental ideas of the Enlightenment and set forth a liberal political agenda based on a belief in popular sovereignty—the people as the source of political power—and the principles of liberty and equality. Liberty meant, in theory, freedom from arbitrary power as well as the freedom to think, write, and worship as one chose. Equality meant equality in rights and equality of opportunity based on talent rather than birth. In practice, equality remained limited; men who owned property had great opportunities for voting and officeholding, and there was certainly no equality between men and women.

The leaders of France's liberal revolution during the era of the National and Legislative Assemblies between 1789 and 1791 were men of property, both bourgeois and noble, but they were assisted by commoners, both sans-culottes and peasants. In this first phase of the Revolution, the old order was demolished as a new constitution established a limited constitutional monarchy. Yet, despite the hopes of the men of property, the liberal revolution was not the end of the Revolution. The decision of the revolutionaries to go to war with European monarchs who opposed the Revolution "revolutionized the Revolution," opening the door to a more radical, democratic, and violent stage between 1792 and 1795 under the National Convention led by the Committee of Public Safety. During this phase, revolutionary courts

persecuted those not sufficiently supportive of the revolutionary cause, creating the infamous Reign of Terror. The excesses of the Reign of Terror, however, led to a reaction and a government headed by a five-member Directory, which governed from 1795 to 1799. But it satisfied neither the radicals nor the royalists. In 1799, Napoleon Bonaparte overthrew this government and established first the Consulate and then a new monarchy with himself as emperor. Napoleon, while diminishing freedom by establishing order and centralizing the government, shrewdly preserved equality of rights and the opening of careers to talent and integrated the bourgeoisie and old nobility into a new elite of property owners.

The French Revolution defined the modern revolutionary concept. No one had foreseen or consciously planned the upheaval that began in 1789, but after 1789, "revolutionaries" knew that mass uprisings could succeed in overthrowing unwanted governments. The French Revolution became the classic political and social model for revolution. At the same time, the liberal and national political ideals created by the Revolution and spread through Europe by Napoleon's conquests dominated the political landscape of the nineteenth and early twentieth centuries.

CHAPTER TIMELINE

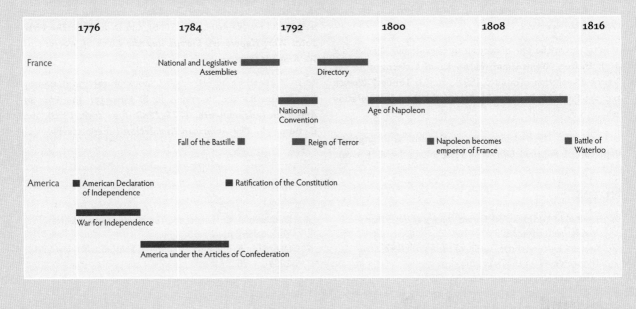

	1776	1784	1792	1800	1808	1816

France

National and Legislative Assemblies

Directory

National Convention

Age of Napoleon

Fall of the Bastille

Reign of Terror

Napoleon becomes emperor of France

Battle of Waterloo

America

American Declaration of Independence

Ratification of the Constitution

War for Independence

America under the Articles of Confederation

CHAPTER REVIEW

Upon Reflection

Q How was France changed by the revolutionary events of 1789 to 1792, and who benefited the most from these changes?

Q Why did the French Revolution enter a radical phase, and what did that radical phase accomplish?

Q In what ways did Napoleon's policies reject the accomplishments of the French Revolution? In what ways did his policies strengthen the Revolution's accomplishments?

Key Terms

old order (p. 454)
sans-culottes (p. 460)
nation in arms (p. 462)

nationalism (p. 462)
Continental System (p. 472)

Suggestions for Further Reading

GENERAL WORKS   A well-written introduction to the French Revolution can be found in **W. Doyle, *The Oxford History of the French Revolution,*** 2d ed. (Oxford, 2003). On the entire revolutionary and Napoleonic eras, see **O. Connelly, *The French Revolution and Napoleonic Era,*** 3d ed. (Fort Worth, Tex., 2000). A brief work is **J. D. Popkin et al., *A Short History of the French Revolution,*** 4th ed. (Upper Saddle River, N.J., 2005).

EARLY YEARS OF THE REVOLUTION   The origins and early years of the French Revolution are examined in **W. Doyle,** ***Origins of the French Revolution,*** 3d ed. (Oxford, 1999), and **T. Tackett, *Becoming a Revolutionary*** (Princeton, N.J., 1996). For interesting insight into Louis XVI and French society, see **T. Tackett, *When the King Took Flight*** (Cambridge, Mass., 2003).

RADICAL REVOLUTION   On the radical stage of the French Revolution, see **D. Andress, *The Terror: The Merciless War for Freedom in Revolutionary France*** (New York, 2005). For a biography of Robespierre, one of the leading figures of this period, see **R. Scurr, *Fatal Purity: Robespierre and the French***

Revolution (New York, 2006). The importance of the revolutionary wars in the radical stage of the Revolution is underscored in **T. C. W. Blanning, *The French Revolutionary Wars, 1787–1802*** (New York, 1996).

WOMEN   On the role of women in revolutionary France, see **O. J. Hufton, *Women and the Limits of Citizenship in the French Revolution*** (Toronto, 1992), and **J. Landes, *Women and the Public Sphere in the Age of the French Revolution*** (Ithaca, N.Y, 1988).

NAPOLEON   The best biography of Napoleon is **S. Englund, *Napoleon: A Political Life*** (New York, 2004). See **A. I. Grab,**

Napoleon and the Transformation of Europe (New York, 2003) on Napoleon's Grand Empire. On Napoleon's wars, see **O. Connelly, *Blundering to Glory: Napoleon's Military Campaigns,*** 3d ed. (Lanham, Md., 2006), and **D. A. Bell, *The First Total War: Napoleon's Europe and the Birth of Warfare as We Know It*** (Boston, 2007).

AMERICAN REVOLUTION   A history of the revolutionary era in America can be found in **S. Conway, *The War of American Independence, 1775–1783*** (New York, 1995), and **C. Bonwick, *The American Revolution*** (Charlottesville, Va., 1991).

Notes

1. Quoted in W. Doyle, *The Oxford History of the French Revolution* (Oxford, 1989), p. 184.
2. Quoted in L. Gershoy, *The Era of the French Revolution* (Princeton, N.J., 1957), p. 157.
3. Quoted in Doyle, *Oxford History*, p. 254.
4. Quoted in J. C. Herold, ed., *The Mind of Napoleon* (New York, 1955), pp. 74–75.
5. Quoted in S. Englund, *Napoleon: A Political Life* (New York, 2004), p. 285.

MindTap   **MindTap** is a fully online, highly personalized learning experience built upon Cengage Learning content. MindTap combines student learning tools—readings, multimedia, activities, and assessments—into a singular Learning Path that guides students through the course.

C H A P T E R 20

The Industrial Revolution and Its Impact on European Society

Power looms in an English textile factory

© World History Archive/Alamy

CHAPTER OUTLINE AND FOCUS QUESTIONS

The Industrial Revolution in Great Britain

Q Why did the Industrial Revolution occur first in Great Britain, and why did it happen when it did? What were the basic features of the new industrial system created by the Industrial Revolution?

The Spread of Industrialization

Q How did the Industrial Revolution spread from Great Britain to the European continent and the United States, and how did industrialization in those areas differ from industrialization in Britain?

The Social Impact of the Industrial Revolution

Q What effects did the Industrial Revolution have on urban life, social classes, family life, and standards of living? What were working conditions like in the early decades of the Industrial Revolution, and what efforts were made to improve them?

CRITICAL THINKING

Q What role did government and trade unions play in the industrial development of the Western world? Who helped the workers the most?

CONNECTIONS TO TODAY

Q How do the locations of the centers of industrialization today compare with those during the Industrial Revolution, and how do you account for any differences?

THE FRENCH REVOLUTION dramatically and quickly altered the political structure of France, and the Napoleonic conquests spread many of the revolutionary principles to other parts of Europe. During the late eighteenth and early nineteenth centuries, another revolution—an industrial one— was transforming the economic and social structure of Europe. Although the pace of this transformation was slower, the changes it produced were no less fundamental.

The Industrial Revolution caused a quantum leap in industrial production. New sources of energy and power, especially coal and steam, replaced wind and water to build and run machines that dramatically decreased the use of human and animal muscle power and at the same time increased productivity. This in turn called for new ways of organizing human labor to maximize the benefits and profits from the new machines; factories replaced workshops and home workrooms. Many early factories were dreadful places with difficult working conditions. Reformers, appalled at these conditions, were especially critical of the treatment of married women. One reported, "We have repeatedly seen married females, in the last stage of pregnancy, slaving from morning to night beside these never-tiring machines, and when ... they were obliged to sit down to take a moment's ease, and being seen by the manager, were fined for the offense." But there were also examples of well-run factories. William Cobbett described one in Manchester in 1830: "In this room, which is lighted in the most convenient and beautiful manner, there were five hundred pairs of looms at work, and five hundred persons attending those looms; and, owing to the goodness of the masters, the whole looking healthy and well-dressed."

During the Industrial Revolution, Europe experienced a shift from a traditional, labor-intensive economy based on farming and handicrafts to a more capital-intensive economy based on manufacturing by machines, specialized labor, and industrial factories. Although the Industrial Revolution took decades to spread, it was truly revolutionary in the way it fundamentally changed Europeans, their society, and their relationship to the rest of the world. The development of large factories encouraged mass movements of people from the countryside to urban areas where impersonal coexistence replaced the traditional intimacy of rural life. Higher levels of productivity led to a search for new sources of raw materials, new consumption patterns, and a revolution in transportation that allowed raw materials and finished products to be moved quickly around the world. The rise of a wealthy industrial middle class and a huge industrial working class (or proletariat) substantially transformed traditional social relationships.

The Industrial Revolution in Great Britain

Q FOCUS QUESTIONS: Why did the Industrial Revolution occur first in Great Britain, and why did it happen when it did? What were the basic features of the new industrial system created by the Industrial Revolution?

Although the Industrial Revolution evolved over a long period of time, historians generally agree that it began in Britain sometime after 1750. By 1850, industry had made Great Britain the wealthiest country in the world, and the revolution had spread to the European continent and the New World. In another fifty years, both Germany and the United States would surpass Britain in industrial production.

Origins of the Industrial Revolution

A number of factors or conditions came together in Britain to produce the first Industrial Revolution. One of these was the **agricultural revolution** of the eighteenth century, which led to a significant increase in food production. British agriculture could now feed more people at lower prices with less labor; even ordinary British families did not have to use most of their income to buy food, giving them the potential to purchase manufactured goods. At the same time, rapid population growth in the second half of the eighteenth century provided a substantial pool of labor for the new factories of the emerging British industry.

Britain also had a ready supply of **capital** for investment in the new industrial machines and the factories that were needed to house them. In addition to profits from trade and the cottage industry, Britain possessed an effective central bank and well-developed, flexible credit facilities. Many early factory owners were merchants and entrepreneurs who had profited from the eighteenth-century cottage industry. But capital is only part of the story; Britain also had a fair number of individuals who were interested in making profits if the opportunity presented itself. The British were a people, as one historian has said, "fascinated by wealth and commerce, collectively and individually." Undoubtedly, the English revolutions of the seventeenth century had helped create an environment in Britain, unlike that of the absolutist states on the continent, where political power rested in the hands of a progressive group of people who favored innovation in economic matters.

In addition, Britain was richly supplied with the important mineral resources, such as coal and iron ore, that were needed in the manufacturing process. Since it was also a small country, these resources needed to be transported only relatively short distances. In addition to nature's provision of abundant rivers, from the mid-seventeenth century onward, both private and public investment poured into the construction of new roads, bridges, and waterways. By 1780, roads, rivers, and canals linked the major industrial centers of the North, the Midlands, London, and the Atlantic.

Finally, a supply of markets gave British industrialists a ready outlet for their manufactured goods. British exports quadrupled from 1660 to 1760. In the course of its eighteenth-century wars and conquests, Great Britain had developed a vast colonial empire at the expense of its leading continental rivals, the Dutch Republic and France. Britain also possessed a well-developed merchant marine that was able to transport goods to any place in the world. A crucial factor in Britain's successful industrialization was the ability to cheaply produce the articles that were most in demand abroad. And the best markets abroad were not in Europe, where countries protected their own incipient industries, but in the Americas, Africa, and the East, where people wanted sturdy, inexpensive clothes rather than costly, highly finished luxury items. Britain's machine-produced textiles satisfied that demand. Nor should we overlook the British domestic market. Britain had the highest standard of living in Europe and a rapidly growing population. This demand from both domestic and foreign markets and the inability of the old system to fulfill it led entrepreneurs to seek and accept the new methods of manufacturing that a series of inventions provided. In doing so, these individuals initiated the Industrial Revolution.

Technological Changes and New Forms of Industrial Organization

In the 1770s and 1780s, the cotton textile industry took the first major revolutionary step by inventing the modern factory.

THE COTTON INDUSTRY Already in the eighteenth century, Great Britain had surged ahead in the production of cheap cotton goods using the traditional methods of the cottage industry. The development of the flying shuttle had speeded the process of weaving on a loom, enabling weavers to double their output. This caused shortages of yarn, however, until James Hargreaves's spinning jenny, perfected by 1768, allowed spinners to produce yarn in greater quantities. Edmund Cartwright's power loom, invented in 1787, allowed the weaving of cloth to catch up with the spinning of yarn and presented new opportunities to entrepreneurs. It was much more efficient to bring workers to the machines and organize their labor collectively in factories located next to rivers and streams, the sources of power for many of these early machines, than to leave the workers dispersed in their cottages. The concentration of labor in the new factories also brought the laborers and their families to live in the new towns that rapidly grew up around the factories.

THE STEAM ENGINE The steam engine revolutionized the production of cotton goods and allowed the factory system to spread to other areas of production, thereby creating whole new industries. The steam engine thus secured the triumph of the Industrial Revolution.

In the 1760s, a Scottish engineer, James Watt (1736–1819), invented an engine powered by steam that could pump water from mines three times as quickly as previous engines. In 1782, Watt enlarged those possibilities when he developed a rotary engine that could turn a shaft and thus drive machinery. Steam power could now be applied to spinning and weaving cotton, and before long, cotton mills using steam engines were multiplying across Britain. Because steam engines were fired by coal, they did not need to be located near rivers, so entrepreneurs now had greater flexibility in their choice of location.

The new boost given to cotton textile production by technological changes became readily apparent. In 1760, Britain had imported 2.5 million pounds of raw cotton, which was farmed out to cottage industries. In 1787, the British imported 22 million pounds of cotton; most of it was spun on machines, some powered by water in large mills. By 1840, fully 366 million pounds of cotton—now Britain's most important product in value—were imported. By this time, most cotton industry employees worked in factories. The cheapest labor in India could not compete in quality or quantity with Britain. British cotton goods sold everywhere in the world. And in Britain itself, cheap cotton cloth made it possible for millions of poor people to wear undergarments, long a luxury of the rich, who could afford expensive linen cloth. Cotton clothing was tough, comfortable, cheap, and easily washable.

The steam engine proved indispensable. Unlike horses, the steam engine was a tireless source of power and depended for fuel on a substance—coal—that seemed in unlimited supply. The popular saying that "steam is an Englishman" had real significance by 1850. The success of the steam engine led to a need for more coal and an expansion in coal production; between 1815 and 1850, the output of coal quadrupled. In turn, new processes using coal furthered the development of the iron industry.

THE IRON INDUSTRY The British iron industry was radically transformed during the Industrial Revolution. Britain had large resources of iron ore, but at the beginning of the eighteenth century, the basic process for producing iron had changed little since the Middle Ages and still depended heavily on charcoal. In the early eighteenth century, new methods of smelting iron ore to produce cast iron were devised using coke or "courke" that was made by slowly burning coal. Still, a better quality of iron was not possible until the 1780s, when Henry Cort developed a system called puddling, in which coke was used to burn away impurities in **pig iron** (the product of smelting iron ore with coke) to produce an iron of high quality called **wrought iron**. Wrought iron, with its lower carbon content, was malleable and able to withstand strain. A boom then ensued in the British iron industry. In 1740, Britain produced 17,000 tons of iron; by the 1840s, more than 2 million tons; and by 1852, almost 3 million tons, more than the rest of the world combined.

A REVOLUTION IN TRANSPORTATION The high-quality wrought iron produced by the Cort process encouraged the use of machinery in other industries, most noticeably in such new means of transportation as steamboats and railroads. In 1804, Richard Trevithick (TREV-uh-thik) pioneered the first steam-powered locomotive on an industrial rail line in southern Wales. It pulled ten tons of ore and seventy people at 5 miles per hour. Better locomotives soon followed. The engines built by George Stephenson and his son proved superior, and it was in their workshops in Newcastle-upon-Tyne that the locomotives for the first modern railways in Britain were built. George Stephenson's *Rocket* was used on the first public railway line, which opened in 1830, extending 32 miles from Liverpool to Manchester. *Rocket* sped along at 16 miles per hour. Within twenty years, locomotives had reached 50 miles per hour, an incredible speed to contemporary passengers. During the same period, new companies were formed to build additional railroads as the infant industry proved successful not only technically but also financially. In 1840, Britain had almost 2,000 miles of railroads; ten years later, 6,000 miles of track crisscrossed the country (see Map 20.1).

The railroad contributed significantly to the maturing of the Industrial Revolution. The railroad's demands for coal and iron furthered the growth of those industries, and railway construction created new job opportunities, especially for farm laborers and peasants who had long been accustomed to finding work outside their local villages. Perhaps most important, the availability of a cheaper and faster means of transportation had a domino effect on the growth of the industrial economy. Lower prices of goods led to the creation of larger markets, and the increased sales in turn necessitated more factories and more machinery. This self-sustaining

Time Life Pictures/Getty Images

Railroad Line from Liverpool to Manchester. The railroad line from Liverpool to Manchester, which opened in 1830, relied on steam locomotives. As is evident in this illustration, carrying passengers was the railroad's main business. First-class passengers rode in covered cars, second- and third-class passengers in open cars.

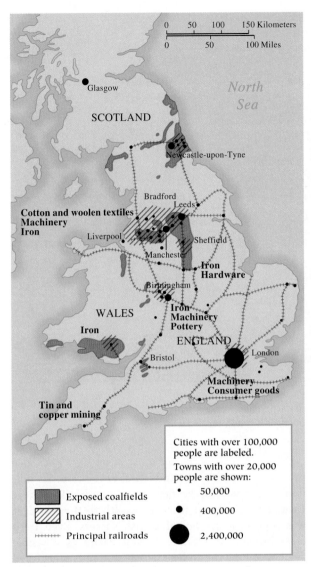

MAP 20.1 **The Industrial Revolution in Britain by 1850.**
The Industrial Revolution began in the mid-1700s. Increased food production, rapid population growth, higher incomes, plentiful capital, solid banking and financial institutions, an abundance of mineral resources, and easy transport all furthered the process, making Britain the world's wealthiest country by 1850.

Q How well did the early railroad system connect important British industrial areas?

nature of the Industrial Revolution marked a fundamental break with the traditional European economy. Its great productivity enabled entrepreneurs to reinvest their profits in new capital equipment, further expanding the capacity of the economy. Continuous, even rapid, self-sustaining economic growth came to be seen as a fundamental characteristic of the new industrial economy.

The railroad was the perfect symbol of this aspect of the Industrial Revolution. The ability to transport goods and people at hitherto unheard-of speeds also provided visible confirmation of a new sense of power. When railway builders penetrated mountains with tunnels and spanned chasms with breathtaking bridges, contemporaries experienced a sense of power over nature not felt before in Western civilization.

THE INDUSTRIAL FACTORY Another visible symbol of the Industrial Revolution was the factory, which became the chief means of organizing labor for the new machines. From its beginning, the factory system demanded a new type of discipline from its employees. Since factory owners could not afford to let their expensive machinery stand idle, workers were forced to work regular hours and in shifts to keep the machines producing at a steady pace for maximum output. This required a massive adjustment on the part of early factory laborers.

Preindustrial workers were not accustomed to a timed format. Agricultural laborers had always kept irregular hours; hectic work at harvesttime might be followed by days or weeks of inactivity. Even in the burgeoning cottage industry of the eighteenth century, weavers and spinners who worked at home might fulfill their weekly quotas by working around the clock for two or three days and then proceeding at a leisurely pace until the next week's demands forced another work spurt.

Factory owners therefore faced a formidable task. They had to create a system of time-work discipline in which employees became accustomed to working regular, unvarying hours during which they performed a set number of tasks over and over again as efficiently as possible. Such work, of course, tended to be repetitive and boring, and factory owners resorted to tough methods to accomplish their goals. Factory regulations were minute and detailed (see the box on p. 483). Adult workers were fined for a wide variety of minor infractions, such as being a few minutes late for work, and dismissed for more serious misdeeds, especially intoxication. Drunkenness was viewed as particularly offensive because it set a bad example for younger workers and also courted disaster around dangerous machinery. Employers found that dismissals and fines

© ARPL/HIP/The Image Works

A British Textile Factory. The development of the factory changed the relationship between workers and their employers, as workers were coerced by disciplinary action into working a standard workday. This 1835 illustration shows women and men working in a British textile factory.

worked well for adult employees; in a time when great population growth had produced large masses of unskilled labor, dismissal could mean not getting another job. Children were less likely to understand the implications of dismissal, so they were sometimes disciplined more directly—by beating. In one crucial sense, the early industrialists' efforts proved successful. As the nineteenth century progressed, the second and third generations of workers came to view a regular workweek as a natural way of life. It was, of course, an attitude that made possible Britain's incredible economic growth in that century.

The Great Exhibition: Britain in 1851

In 1851, the British organized the world's first industrial fair at Kensington, London, in the Crystal Palace, an enormous structure that was a tribute to British engineering skills. Made entirely of glass and iron and covering nineteen acres, it contained more than 100,000 exhibits that showed the wide variety of products created by the Industrial Revolution. Six million people visited the fair in six months. The Great Exhibition displayed Britain's wealth to the world; it was a gigantic symbol of British success. Even trees were brought inside the Crystal Palace as a visible symbol of how the Industrial Revolution had achieved human domination over nature. The Great Exhibition also represented British imperial power. Among the highlights of the exhibition were goods from India, especially a display of Indian silks, jewels, and an elephant canopy that captured the attention of the British press and visitors.

By the year of the Great Exhibition, Great Britain had become the world's first and richest industrial nation, the "workshop, banker, and trader of the world." It produced one-half of the world's coal and manufactured goods; its cotton industry alone in 1851 was equal in size to the industries of all other European countries combined. Britain's certainty about its mission in the world in the nineteenth century was grounded in its incredible material success.

Discipline in the New Factories

Workers in the new factories of the Industrial Revolution had been accustomed to a lifestyle free of overseers. Unlike the cottages, where workers spun thread and wove cloth in their own rhythm and time, the factories demanded a new, rigorous discipline geared to the requirements of the machines. This selection is taken from a set of rules for a factory in Berlin in 1844. They were typical of company rules wherever the factory system had been established.

The Foundry and Engineering Works of the Royal Overseas Trading Company, Factory Rules

In every large works, and in the co-ordination of any large number of workmen, good order and harmony must be looked upon as the fundamentals of success, and therefore the following rules shall be strictly observed.

1. The normal working day begins at all seasons at 6 A.M. precisely and ends, after the usual break of half an hour for breakfast, an hour for dinner and half an hour for tea, at 7 P.M., and it shall be strictly observed.... Workers arriving 2 minutes late shall lose half an hour's wages; whoever is more than 2 minutes late may not start work until after the next break or at least shall lose his wages until then. Any disputes about the correct time shall be settled by the clock mounted above the gatekeepers lodge....

3. No workman, whether employed by time or piece, may leave before the end of the working day, without having first received permission from the overseer and having given his name to the gate-keeper. Omission of these two actions shall lead to a fine of ten silver groschen [pennies] payable to the sick fund.

4. Repeated irregular arrival at work shall lead to dismissal. This shall also apply to those who are found idling by an official or overseer, and refused to obey their order to resume work....

6. No worker may leave his place of work otherwise than for reasons connected with his work.

7. All conversation with fellow-workers is prohibited; if any worker requires information about his work, he must turn to the overseer, or to the particular fellow-worker designated for the purpose.

8. Smoking in the workshops or in the yard is prohibited during working hours; anyone caught smoking shall be fined five silver groschen for the sick fund for every such offense....

10. Natural functions must be performed at the appropriate places, and whoever is found soiling walls, fences, squares, etc., and similarly, whoever is found washing his face and hands in the workshop and not in the places assigned for the purpose, shall be fined five silver groschen for the sick fund....

12. It goes without saying that all overseers and officials of the firm shall be obeyed without question, and shall be treated with due deference. Disobedience will be punished by dismissal.

13. Immediate dismissal shall also be the fate of anyone found drunk in any of the workshops....

14. Every workman is obliged to report to his superiors any acts of dishonesty or embezzlement on the part of his fellow workmen. If he omits to do so, and it is shown after subsequent discovery of a misdemeanor that he knew about it at the time, he shall be liable to be taken to court as an accessory after the fact and the wage due to him shall be retained as punishment.

Q What impact did factories have on the lives of workers? To what extent have such rules determined much of modern industrial life?

Source: From *Documents of European Economic History*, Vol. I by Sidney Pollard & Colin Holmes. Copyright © Sidney Pollard and Colin Holmes. Reproduced with permission of Palgrave Macmillan.

The Great Exhibition of 1851. The Great Exhibition of 1851 was a symbol of the success of Great Britain, which had become the world's first industrial nation and its richest. More than 100,000 exhibits were housed in the Crystal Palace, a giant structure of cast iron and glass. The first illustration shows the front of the palace and some of its numerous visitors. The second shows the opening day ceremonies. Queen Victoria is seen at the center with her family, surrounded by visitors from all over the world. Note the large tree inside the building, providing a visible symbol of how the Industrial Revolution had supposedly achieved human domination over nature.

The Spread of Industrialization

Q FOCUS QUESTION: How did the Industrial Revolution spread from Great Britain to the European continent and the United States, and how did industrialization in those areas differ from industrialization in Britain?

Beginning first in Great Britain, industrialization spread to the continental countries of Europe and America at different times and speeds during the nineteenth century. First to be industrialized on the continent were Belgium, France, and the German states; the first in North America was the new United States. Not until after 1850 did the Industrial Revolution spread to the rest of Europe and other parts of the world.

Industrialization on the Continent

Industrialization on the continent faced numerous hurdles, and as it proceeded in earnest after 1815, it did so along lines that were somewhat different from Britain's. Lack of technical knowledge was initially a major obstacle to industrialization. But the continental countries had an advantage here; they could simply borrow British techniques and practices. Of course, the British tried to prevent that. Until 1825, British artisans were prohibited from leaving the country; until 1842, the export of important machinery and machine parts was forbidden. Nevertheless, the British were not able to control emigration and exports by legislation. Already by 1825, there were at least two thousand skilled British mechanics on the continent, and British equipment was being sold abroad, legally or illegally.

Gradually, the continent achieved technological independence as local people learned all the skills their British teachers had to offer. By the 1840s, new generations of skilled mechanics from Belgium and France were spreading their knowledge east and south. Even more important, however, continental countries, especially France and the German states, began to establish a wide range of technical schools to train engineers and mechanics.

That government played an important role in this brings us to a second difference between British and continental industrialization. Governments in most of the continental countries were accustomed to playing a significant role in economic affairs. Furthering the development of industrialization was a logical extension of that attitude. Hence, governments provided for the costs of technical education, awarded grants to inventors and foreign entrepreneurs, exempted foreign industrial equipment from import duties, and in some places even financed factories. Of equal if not greater importance in the long run, governments actively bore much of the cost of building roads and canals, deepening and widening river channels, and constructing railroads. By 1850, a network of iron rails had spread across Europe, although only Germany and Belgium had largely completed their systems by that time.

Centers of Continental Industrialization

As noted earlier, the Industrial Revolution on the continent occurred in three major centers between 1815 and 1850—Belgium, France, and the German states (see Map 20.2). Cotton played an important role, although it was not as significant as heavy industry. The development of cotton manufacturing on the continent and Britain differed in two significant ways. Unlike Britain, where cotton manufacturing was mostly centered in Lancashire (in northwestern England) and the Glasgow area of Scotland, cotton mills in France, Germany, and to a lesser degree Belgium were dispersed through many regions. Noticeable, too, was the mixture of old and new. The old techniques of the cottage system, such as the use of hand looms, held on much longer. In the French district of Normandy, for example, in 1849, eighty-three mills were still driven by hand or animal power.

Heavy industry on the continent before 1850 was likewise a mixture of old and new. The adoption of new techniques, such as coke-smelted iron and puddling furnaces, coincided with the expansion of old-type charcoal blast furnaces. Before 1850, Germany lagged significantly behind both Belgium and France in heavy industry, and most German iron manufacturing remained based on old techniques. Not until the 1840s was coke-blast iron produced in the Rhineland. At that time, no one had yet realized the treasure of coal buried in the Ruhr Valley. A German official wrote in 1852 that "it is clearly not to be expected that Germany will ever be able to reach the level of production of coal and iron currently attained in England. This is implicit in our far more limited resource endowment." Little did he realize that although the industrial development of continental Europe was about a generation behind Britain at midcentury, after 1850 an incredibly rapid growth in continental industry would demonstrate that Britain was not, after all, destined to remain the world's greatest industrial nation.

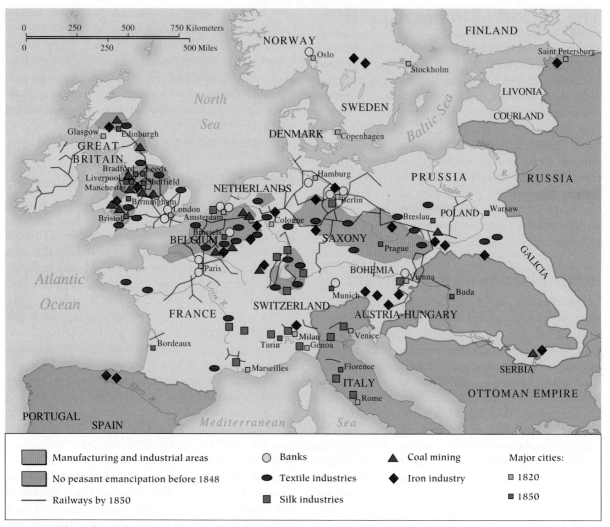

Legend:

Manufacturing and industrial areas	Banks ○
No peasant emancipation before 1848	Textile industries ●
—— Railways by 1850	Silk industries ■
	Coal mining ▲
	Iron industry ◆

Major cities:
▫ 1820
▪ 1850

MAP 20.2 The Industrialization of Europe by 1850. Great Britain was Europe's first industrialized country; by the middle of the nineteenth century, however, several regions on the continent, especially in Belgium, France, and the German states, had made significant advances in industrialization.

Q What reasons could explain why coal mining *and* iron industries are densely clustered in manufacturing and industrial areas?

The Industrial Revolution in the United States

In 1800, the United States was an agrarian society. There were no cities with populations of more than 100,000, and six out of every seven American workers were farmers. By 1860, however, the population had grown from 5 million to 30 million people, larger than Great Britain's. Almost half of them lived west of the Appalachian Mountains. The number of states had more than doubled, from sixteen to thirty-four, and nine American cities had more than 100,000 in population. Only 50 percent of American workers were farmers. In those sixty years, the United States had experienced its own Industrial Revolution and the urbanization that accompanied it.

The initial application of machinery to production was accomplished, as in continental Europe, by borrowing from Great Britain. A British immigrant, Samuel Slater, established the first textile factory using water-powered spinning machines in Rhode Island in 1790. By 1813, factories were being established with power looms copied from British versions. Soon thereafter, however, Americans began to equal or surpass British technical inventions. The Harpers Ferry arsenal, for example, built muskets with interchangeable parts. Because the individual parts of various muskets were identical (for example, all triggers were the same), the final product could be put together quickly and easily, enabling Americans to avoid the more costly system in which skilled craftspeople fitted together individual parts made separately. The so-called American system reduced costs and revolutionized production by saving labor, important to a society that had few skilled artisans.

Unlike Britain, the United States was a large country. The lack of a good system of internal transportation seemed to limit American economic development by making the transport of goods prohibitively expensive. This deficiency was gradually remedied by the introduction of the steamboat and the railroad as well as the construction of roads and canals. Thousands of miles of roads and canals were built linking east and west. The steamboat facilitated transportation on the Great Lakes, Atlantic coastal waters, and rivers and was especially important to the Mississippi River valley; by 1860, a thousand steamboats plied the Mississippi. Most important of all in the development of an American transportation system was the railroad. Beginning with 100 miles in 1830, by 1860 there were more than 27,000 miles of railroad track covering the United States. This transportation revolution turned the United States into a single massive market for the manufactured goods of the Northeast, the early center of American industrialization.

Labor for the growing number of factories in this area came primarily from rural New England. The United States did not possess a large number of craftspeople, but it did have a rapidly expanding farm population whose size in the Northeast soon outstripped the available farmland. While some of this excess population, especially men, went west, others, mostly women, found work in the new textile and shoe factories of New England. Indeed, women made up more than 80 percent of the labor force in the large textile factories. In Massachusetts mill towns, company boarding houses provided rooms for large numbers of young women who worked for several years before marriage. Outside Massachusetts, factory owners sought entire families, including children, to work in their mills; one

mill owner ran this advertisement in a newspaper in Utica, New York: "Wanted: A few sober and industrious families of at least five children each, over the age of eight years, are wanted at the Cotton Factory in Whitestown. Widows with large families would do well to attend this notice." When a decline in rural births threatened to dry up this labor pool in the 1830s and 1840s, European immigrants, especially poor and unskilled Irish, English, Scots, and Welsh, appeared in large numbers to replace American women and children in the factories. By 1860, the United States was well on its way to being an industrial nation.

Limiting the Spread of Industrialization

Before 1870, the industrialization that had developed in western and central Europe and the United States did not extend in any significant way to the rest of the world. Even in eastern Europe, industrialization lagged far behind. Russia, for example, remained largely rural and agricultural with an autocratic regime that kept the peasants in serfdom. There was not much of a middle class, and the tsarist regime, fearful of change, preferred to import industrial goods in return for the export of raw materials, such as grain and timber. Russia would not have an Industrial Revolution until the end of the nineteenth century.

THE EXAMPLE OF INDIA In other parts of the world where they had established control, newly industrialized European states pursued a deliberate policy of preventing the growth of mechanized industry. A good example is India. In the eighteenth century, India produced 85 million pounds of yarn, versus 3 million in England, becoming one of the world's greatest exporters of cotton cloth produced by hand labor. In the first half of the nineteenth century, much of India fell under the control of the British East India Company (see Chapter 24). With British control came inexpensive British factory-produced textiles, and soon thousands of Indian spinners and hand-loom weavers were unemployed. British policy encouraged Indians to export their raw materials while buying British-made goods. Although modest industrial factories for making textiles and jute (used in making rope) were opened in India in the 1850s, a lack of local capital and the advantages given to British imports limited the growth of new manufacturing operations. India, then, provides an excellent example of how some of the rapidly industrializing nations of Europe worked to deliberately thwart the spread of the Industrial Revolution to their colonial dominions.

The Social Impact of the Industrial Revolution

Q FOCUS QUESTIONS: What effects did the Industrial Revolution have on urban life, social classes, family life, and standards of living? What were working conditions like in the early decades of the Industrial Revolution, and what efforts were made to improve them?

Eventually, the Industrial Revolution radically altered the social life of Europe and the world. Although much of Europe remained bound by its traditional ways, the social impact of the Industrial Revolution was already being felt in the first half of the nineteenth century, and future avenues of growth were becoming apparent. Vast changes in the number of people and where they lived were already dramatically evident.

Population Growth

Population increases had begun in the eighteenth century, but they became dramatic in the nineteenth century. In 1750, the total European population stood at an estimated 140 million; by 1800, it had increased to 187 million and, by 1850, to 266 million, almost twice its 1750 level. The key to the expansion of population was the decline in death rates evident throughout Europe. Two major factors explain this decline: fewer premature deaths and better nutrition. There was a drop in the number of deaths from famines, epidemics, and war. Major epidemic diseases in particular, such as plague and smallpox, declined noticeably, although small-scale epidemics broke out now and then. The ordinary death rate also declined as a general increase in the food supply, already evident in the agricultural revolution of Britain in the late eighteenth century, spread to more areas. More food enabled a greater number of people to be better fed and therefore more resistant to disease. Famine largely disappeared from western Europe, although there were dramatic exceptions in isolated areas, Ireland being the most significant.

THE GREAT HUNGER Ireland was one of the most oppressed areas in western Europe. The predominantly Catholic peasant population rented land from mostly absentee British Protestant landlords whose primary concern was collecting their rents. Irish peasants lived in mud hovels in desperate poverty. The cultivation of the potato, a nutritious and relatively easy crop to grow that produced three times as much food per acre as grain, gave Irish peasants a basic staple that enabled them to survive and even expand in numbers. Between 1781 and 1845, the Irish population doubled from 4 million to 8 million. Probably half of this population depended on the potato for survival. In the summer of 1845, the potato crop in Ireland was struck by blight due to a fungus that turned the potatoes black. Between 1845 and 1861, the Great Famine decimated the Irish population (see the box on p. 489). More than a million died of starvation and disease, and almost 2 million emigrated to the United States and Britain. Of all the European nations, only Ireland lost population in the nineteenth century.

The flight of so many Irish to America reminds us that the traditional safety valve for overpopulation has always been emigration. Between 1821 and 1850, the number of emigrants from Europe averaged about 110,000 a year. Most of these emigrants came from places like Ireland and southern Germany, where the peasants' life had been reduced to a marginal existence. More often than emigrating, however, the rural masses sought a solution to their poverty by moving to towns and cities within their own countries to find work. It should not astonish us then that the first half of the nineteenth century was a period of rapid urbanization.

The Growth of Cities

Although the Western world would not become a predominantly urban society until the twentieth century, cities and towns had already grown dramatically in the first half of the nineteenth century, a phenomenon related to industrialization. Cities had traditionally been centers for princely courts, government and military offices, churches, and commerce. By 1850, especially in Great Britain and Belgium, cities were rapidly becoming places for manufacturing and industry. With the steam engine, entrepreneurs could locate their manufacturing plants in urban centers where they had ready access to transportation facilities and unemployed people from the country looking for work. In 1800, Great Britain had one major city, London, with a population of 1 million and six cities between 50,000 and 100,000. Fifty years later, London's population had swelled to 2,363,000, and there were nine cities with populations over 100,000 and eighteen with populations between 50,000 and 100,000. More than 50 percent of the British population now lived in towns

The Great Irish Potato Famine

The Great Irish Famine was one of the nineteenth century's worst natural catastrophes and resulted in the decimation of the Irish population. Nicholas Cummins, a magistrate from County Cork, visited Skibbereen, one of the areas most affected by the famine, and sent a letter to the duke of Wellington reporting what he had seen. A copy of the letter was published in the London newspaper *The Times*, on Christmas Eve in 1846, and became one of the most famous descriptions of the Irish crisis.

_____

Nicholas Cummins, "The Famine in Skibbereen"

My Lord Duke,

Without apology or preface, I presume so far to trespass on your Grace as to state to you, and by the use of your illustrious name, to present to the British public the following statement of what I have myself seen within the last three days. Having for many years been intimately connected with the western portion of the County of Cork, and possessing some small property there, I thought it right personally to investigate the truth of several lamentable accounts which had reached me, of the appalling state of misery to which that part of the country was reduced. I accordingly went to ... Skibbereen, and ... I shall state simply what I there saw.... Being aware that I should have to witness scenes of frightful hunger, I provided myself with as much bread as five men could carry, and on reaching the spot I was surprised to find the wretched hamlet apparently deserted. I entered some of the hovels to ascertain the cause, and the scenes which presented themselves were such as no tongue or pen can convey the slightest idea of. In the first, six famished and ghastly skeletons, to all appearances dead, were huddled in a corner on some filthy straw, their sole covering what seemed a ragged horsecloth, their wretched legs hanging about, naked above the knees. I approached with horror, and found by a low moaning they were alive—they were in fever, four children, a woman and what had once been a man. It is impossible to go through the detail. Suffice it to say, that in a few minutes I was surrounded by at least 200 such phantoms, such frightful spectres as no words can describe, either from famine or from fever....

In another case, decency would forbid what follows, but it must be told. My clothes were nearly torn off in my endeavor to escape from the throng of pestilence around, when my neckcloth was seized from behind by a grip which compelled me to turn, I found myself grasped by a woman with an infant just born in her arms and the remains of a filthy sack across her loins—the sole covering of herself and baby. The same morning the police opened a house on the adjoining lands, which was observed shut for many days, and two frozen corpses were found, lying upon the mud floor, half devoured by rats.

Q What was the impact of the Great Irish Famine on the Irish people and on the broader Atlantic world? Why do you think the British government failed to provide relief for the Irish during the famine?

Source: "The Famine in Skibbereen" from *The Great Hunger* by Cecil Woodham-Smith. New York: Harper Collins 1962.

and cities. Urban populations also grew on the continent, but less dramatically.

URBAN LIVING CONDITIONS IN THE EARLY INDUSTRIAL ERA The dramatic growth of cities in the first half of the nineteenth century produced miserable living conditions for many of the inhabitants. Of course, this had been true for centuries in European cities, but the rapid urbanization associated with the Industrial Revolution intensified the problems and made these wretched conditions all the more apparent. Wealthy, middle-class inhabitants, as usual, insulated themselves as best they could, often living in suburbs or the outer ring of the city where they could have individual houses and gardens. In the inner ring of the city stood the small row houses, some with gardens, of the artisans and lower middle class. Finally, located in the center of most industrial towns were the row houses of the industrial workers (see Images of Everyday Life on p. 491). This report on working-class housing in the British city of Birmingham in 1843 gives an idea of the general conditions they faced:

The courts [of working-class row houses] are extremely numerous; ... a very large portion of the poorer classes of

A New Industrial Town. Cities and towns grew dramatically in Britain in the first half of the nineteenth century, largely as a result of industrialization. Pictured here is Saltaire, a model textile factory and town founded near Bradford by Titus Salt in 1851. To facilitate the transportation of goods, the town was built on the Leeds and Liverpool canals.

Oxford Science Archive, Oxford/HIP/Art Resource, NY

the inhabitants reside in them.... The courts vary in the number of the houses which they contain, from four to twenty, and most of these houses are three stories high, and built, as it is termed, back to back. There is a wash-house, an ash-pit, and a privy at the end, or on one side of the court, and not unfrequently one or more pigsties and heaps of manure. Generally speaking, the privies in the old courts are in a most filthy condition. Many which we have inspected were in a state which renders it impossible for us to conceive how they could be used; they were without doors and overflowing with filth.[1]

Rooms were not large and were frequently overcrowded, as this government report of 1838 revealed: "I entered several of the tenements. In one of them, on the ground floor, I found six persons occupying a very small room, two in bed, ill with fever. In the room above this were two more persons in one bed, ill with fever." Another report said, "There were 63 families where there were at least five persons to one bed; and there were some in which even six were packed in one bed, lying at the top and bottom—children and adults."[2]

Sanitary conditions in these towns were appalling. Due to the lack of municipal direction, city streets were often used as sewers and open drains: "In the centre of this street is a gutter, into which potato parings, the refuse of animal and vegetable matters of all kinds, the dirty water from the washing of clothes and of the houses, are all poured, and there they

stagnate and putrefy."[3] Unable to deal with human excrement, cities in the new industrial era smelled horrible and were extraordinarily unhealthy. The burning of coal covered towns and cities with black soot, as Charles Dickens described in one of his novels: "A long suburb of red brick houses—some with patches of garden ground, where coal-dust and factory smoke darkened the shrinking leaves, and coarse rank flowers; and where the struggling vegetation sickened and sank under the hot breath of kiln and furnace."[4] Towns and cities were fundamentally death traps. As deaths outnumbered births in most large cities in the first half of the nineteenth century, only a constant flow of people from rural areas kept them alive and growing.

URBAN REFORMERS To many of the well-to-do, this situation presented a clear danger to society. Were not these masses of workers, sunk in crime, filth, disease, and immorality, a potential threat to their own well-being? Might not the masses be organized and used by unscrupulous demagogues to overthrow the established order? Some observers, however, wondered if the workers could be held responsible for their fate.

One of the best of a new breed of urban reformers was Edwin Chadwick (1800–1890). With a background in law, Chadwick became obsessed with eliminating the poverty and squalor of the metropolitan areas. As secretary of the Poor Law Commission, he

IMAGES OF EVERYDAY LIFE

Living Conditions of London's Poor

ALTHOUGH SOME ENVIRONMENTAL hazards existed before industrialization, others intensified in early industrial Britain and had a dramatic impact on living conditions. Burning coal filled the air with ash and soot, metal smelting gave off pungent fumes, and industrial plants belched clouds of smoke from the fires stoked in the steam engines. Water pollution was another problem as slaughterhouses dumped their refuse into the streams and human waste found its way there as well due to a lack of proper sewerage. Consequently, working-class tenants in London found themselves living in crowded rooms surrounded by filth and putrid smells. Many of the houses for the poor were built back to back, leaving little room for sanitation. Despite efforts to improve conditions, the plight of London's workers remained dire. In 1869, an English writer, Blanchard Jerrold, commissioned the French illustrator Gustave Doré to create illustrations for a guide to London called *London: A Pilgrimage*. The book was published in 1872 with Doré's illustrations accompanying Jerrold's textual descriptions of the living conditions of London's poor. Doré's most haunting images are of tenement housing and its inhabitants in areas such as Whitechapel. In the first illustration, he shows a London slum district overshadowed by rail viaducts. The second image depicts an open air market on Drury Lane, where men, women, and children are attempting to sell their wares. In the image at the right, children in ragged clothes play in the street.

initiated a passionate search for detailed facts about the living conditions of the working classes. After three years of investigation, Chadwick summarized the results in his *Report on the Condition of the Labouring Population of Great Britain*, published in 1842. In it, he concluded that the "various forms of epidemic, endemic, and other disease" were directly caused by the "atmospheric impurities produced by decomposing animal and vegetable substances, by damp and filth, and close overcrowded dwellings [prevailing] amongst the population in every part of the kingdom." Such conditions, he argued, could be eliminated. As to the means: "The primary and most important measures, and at the same time the most practicable, and within the recognized province of public administration, are drainage, the removal of all refuse of habitations, streets, and roads, and the improvement of the supplies of water."[5] In other words, Chadwick was advocating a system of modern sanitary reforms consisting of efficient sewers and a supply of piped water. Six years after his report and largely due to his efforts, Britain's first Public Health Act created the National Board of Health, which was empowered to form local boards that would establish modern sanitary systems.

New Social Classes: The Industrial Middle Class

The rise of industrial capitalism added a new group to the middle class. The bourgeoisie or middle class was not new; it had existed since the emergence of cities in the Middle Ages. Originally, the bourgeois was a burgher or town dweller active as a merchant, official, artisan, lawyer, or scholar, who enjoyed a special set of rights from the charter of his town. As wealthy townspeople bought land, the term *bourgeois* came to include people involved in commerce, industry, and banking as well as professionals, such as lawyers, teachers, and physicians, and government officials at varying levels. At the lower end of the economic scale were master craftspeople and shopkeepers.

Lest we make the industrial middle class too much of an abstraction, we need to look at who the new industrial entrepreneurs actually were. These were the people who constructed the factories, purchased the machines, and figured out where the markets were (see the box on p. 493). Their qualities included resourcefulness, single-mindedness,

resolution, initiative, vision, ambition, and often greed. As Jedediah Strutt, a cotton manufacturer said, "getting of money . . . is the main business of the life of men." But this was not an easy task. The early industrial entrepreneurs were called on to superintend an enormous array of functions that are handled today by teams of managers. They raised capital, determined markets, set company objectives, organized the factory and its labor, and trained supervisors who could act for them. The opportunities for making money were great, but the risks were also tremendous.

By 1850, in Britain at least, the kind of traditional entrepreneurship that had fueled the Industrial Revolution was declining and being replaced by a new business aristocracy. This new generation of entrepreneurs stemmed from the professional and industrial middle classes, especially as sons inherited successful businesses established by their fathers. Increasingly, the new industrial entrepreneurs—the bankers and owners of factories and mines—came to amass much wealth and play an important role alongside the traditional landed elites of their societies. The Industrial Revolution began at a time when the agrarian world was still largely dominated by landed elites. As the new bourgeoisie bought great estates and acquired social respectability, they also sought political power, and in the course of the nineteenth century, their wealthiest members would merge with those old elites.

New Social Classes: Workers in the Industrial Age

At the same time that the members of the industrial middle class were seeking to reduce the barriers between themselves and the landed elite, they were also trying to separate themselves from the laboring classes below them. The working class was actually a mixture of groups in the first half of the nineteenth century. Factory workers would eventually form an industrial proletariat, but in the first half of the century, they did not constitute a majority of the working class in any major city, even in Britain. According to the 1851 census in Britain, there were 1.8 million agricultural laborers and 1 million domestic servants, but only 811,000 workers in the cotton and woolen industries. And one-third of these were still working in small workshops or in their own homes.

OPPOSING VIEWPOINTS

Attitudes of the Industrial Middle Class in Britain and Japan

In the nineteenth century, a new industrial middle class in Great Britain took the lead in creating the Industrial Revolution. Japan did not begin to industrialize until after 1870. There, too, an industrial middle class emerged, although there were important differences in the attitudes of business leaders in Britain and Japan. Some of these differences can be seen in these documents. The first is an excerpt from the book *Self-Help*, first published in 1859, by Samuel Smiles, who espoused the belief that people succeed through "individual industry, energy, and uprightness." The other two selections are by Shibuzawa Eiichi, a Japanese industrialist who supervised textile factories. Although he began his business career in 1873, he did not write his autobiography, the source of his first excerpt, until 1927.

Samuel Smiles, *Self-Help*

"Heaven helps those who help themselves" is a well-worn maxim, embodying in a small compass the results of vast human experience. The spirit of self-help is the root of all genuine growth in the individual; and, exhibited in the lives of many, it constitutes the true source of national vigor and strength. Help from without is often enfeebling in its effects, but help from within invariably invigorates. Whatever is done for men or classes, to a certain extent takes away the stimulus and necessity of doing for themselves; and where men are subjected to overguidance and overgovernment, the inevitable tendency is to render them comparatively helpless....

National progress is the sum of individual industry, energy, and uprightness, as national decay is of individual idleness, selfishness, and vice. What we are accustomed to decry as great social evils, will, for the most part, be found to be only the outgrowth of our own perverted life; and though we may endeavor to cut them down and extirpate them by means of law, they will only spring up again with fresh luxuriance in some other form, unless the individual conditions of human life and character are radically improved. If this view be correct, then it follows that the highest patriotism and philanthropy consist, not so much in altering laws and modifying institutions as in helping and stimulating men to elevate and improve themselves by their own free and independent action as individuals....

Many popular books have been written for the purpose of communicating to the public the grand secret of making money. But there is no secret whatever about it, as the proverbs of every nation abundantly testify.... "A penny saved is a penny gained."— "Diligence is the mother of good-luck."—"Sloth, the Key of poverty."—"Work, and thou shalt have."—"He who will not work, neither shall he eat."—"The world his, who has patience and industry."

Shibuzawa Eiichi, *Autobiography*

I ... felt that it was necessary to raise the social standing of those who engaged in commerce and industry. By way of setting an example, I began studying and practicing the teachings of the *Analects* of Confucius. It contains teachings first enunciated more than twenty-four hundred years ago. Yet it supplies the ultimate in practical ethics for all of us to follow in our daily living. It has many golden rules for businessmen. For example, there is a saying: "Wealth and respect are what men desire, but unless a right way is followed, they cannot be obtained; poverty and lowly position are what men despise, but unless a right way is found, one cannot leave that status once reaching it." It shows very clearly how a businessman must act in this world.

Shibuzawa Eiichi on Progress

One must beware of the tendency of some to argue that it is through individualism or egoism that the State and society can progress most rapidly. They claim that under individualism, each individual competes with the others, and progress results from this competition. But this is to see merely the advantages and ignore the disadvantages, and I cannot support such a theory. Society exists, and a State has been founded. Although people desire to rise to positions of wealth and honor, the social order and the tranquillity of the State will be disrupted if this is done egoistically. Men

(continued)

should not do battle in competition with their fellow men. Therefore, I believe that in order to get along together in society and serve the State, we must by all means abandon this idea of independence and self-reliance and reject egoism completely.

Q What are the major similarities and differences between the attitudes toward business of Samuel Smiles and Shibuzawa Eiichi? How do you explain the differences, and what are their implications?

Sources: Samuel Smiles, *Self-Help*. From Samuel Smiles, *Self-Help*, 1859. Shibuzawa Eiichi, *Autobiography* and Shibuzawa Eiichi on Progress. From Shibuzawa Eiichi, *The Autobiography of Shibusawa Eiichi: From Peasant to Entrepreneur*, 1927, University of Tokyo Press, 1994.

WORKING CONDITIONS FOR THE INDUSTRIAL WORKING CLASS Workers in the new industrial factories faced wretched working conditions. Unquestionably, in the early decades of the Industrial Revolution, "places of work," as early factories were called, were dreadful. Work hours ranged from twelve to sixteen hours a day, six days a week, with a half hour for lunch and dinner. There was no security of employment and no minimum wage. Workers endured the worst conditions in the cotton mills, where temperatures were especially debilitating. One report noted that "in the cotton-spinning work, these creatures are kept, fourteen hours in each day, locked up, summer and winter, in a heat of from eighty to eighty-four degrees." Mills were also dirty, dusty, and unhealthy:

> Not only is there not a breath of sweet air in these truly infernal scenes, but ... there is the abominable and pernicious stink of the gas to assist in the murderous effects of the heat. In addition to the noxious effluvia of the gas, mixed with the steam, there are the dust, and what is called cotton-flyings or fuz, which the unfortunate creatures have to inhale; and ... the notorious fact is that well constitutioned men are rendered old and past labour at forty years of age, and that children are rendered decrepit and deformed, and thousands upon thousands of them slaughtered by consumptions [wasting away of body tissues, especially the lungs], before they arrive at the age of sixteen.[6]

Conditions in the coal mines were also harsh. The introduction of steam power in the coal mines meant only that steam-powered engines mechanically lifted coal to the top. Inside the mines, men still bore the burden of digging the coal out while horses, mules, women, and children hauled coal carts on rails to the lift. Dangers abounded in coal mines; cave-ins, explosions, and gas fumes (called "bad air") were a way of life. The cramped conditions—tunnels often did not exceed three or four feet in height—and constant dampness in the mines resulted in deformed bodies and ruined lungs.

Both children and women were employed in large numbers in early factories and mines. Children had been an important part of the family economy in preindustrial times, working in the fields or carding and spinning wool at home with the growth of the cottage industry. In the Industrial Revolution, however, child labor was exploited more than ever and in a considerably more systematic fashion (see the box on p. 496). The owners of cotton factories appreciated certain features of child labor. Children had an especially delicate touch as spinners of cotton, and their smaller size made it easier for them to crawl under machines to gather loose cotton. Moreover, children were more easily trained to factory work. Above all, children represented a cheap supply of labor. In 1821, half the British population was under twenty years of age. Hence, children made up a particularly abundant supply of labor, and they were paid only one-sixth to one-third of what a man was paid. In the cotton factories in 1838, children under eighteen made up 29 percent of the workforce; children as young as seven worked twelve to fifteen hours per day, six days a week, in cotton mills.

By 1830, women and children made up two-thirds of the cotton industry's labor. After the Factory Act of 1833 set limits on child labor, however, the number of children employed declined, and their places were taken by women, who came to dominate the labor forces of the early factories. Women made up 50 percent of the labor force in textile (cotton and woolen) factories before 1870. They were mostly unskilled labor and were paid half or less of what

Women and Children in the Mines. Women and children were often employed in the factories and mines of the early nineteenth century. This illustration shows a woman and boy in a coal mine struggling to draw and push a barrel filled with coal. In 1842, the Coal Mines Act forbade the use of boys younger than ten and women in the mines.

Universal Images Group/Getty Images

men received. Excessive working hours for women were outlawed in 1844, but only in textile factories and mines; not until 1867 were they outlawed in craft workshops.

The employment of children and women in large part represents a continuation of a preindustrial kinship pattern. The cottage industry had always involved the efforts of the entire family, and it seemed perfectly natural to continue this pattern. Men migrating from the countryside to industrial towns and cities took their wives and children with them into the factory or into the mines. Of 136 employees in Robert Peel's factory at Bury in 1801, 95 came from twenty-six families. The impetus for this family work often came from the family itself. The factory owner Jedediah Strutt was opposed to employing children under ten but was forced by parents to take children as young as seven.

The employment of large numbers of women in factories did not produce a significant transformation in female working patterns, as was once assumed. Studies of urban households in France and Britain, for example, have revealed that throughout the nineteenth century, traditional types of female labor still predominated in the women's work world. In 1851, fully 40 percent of the working women in Britain were employed as domestic servants. In France, the largest group of female workers, 40 percent, worked in

agriculture. Only 20 percent of female workers labored in Britain's factories, and only 10 percent in France. Regional and local studies have also indicated that most of the workers were single women. Few married women worked outside the home.

The laws that limited the work hours of children and women also began to break up the traditional kinship pattern of work and led to a new pattern based on a separation of work and home. Men came to be regarded as responsible for the primary work obligations while women assumed daily control of the family and performed low-paying jobs such as laundry work that could be done in the home. Domestic industry made it possible for women to continue their contributions to family survival.

Historians have also reminded us that if the treatment of children in the mines and factories seems particularly cruel and harsh, contemporary treatment of children in general was often brutal. Beatings, for example, had long been regarded, even by dedicated churchmen and churchwomen, as the best way to discipline children.

The problem of poverty among the working classes was also addressed in Britain by government action in the form of the Poor Law Act of 1834, which established workhouses where jobless poor people were forced to live. The intent of this policy, based on the assumption that the poor were responsible for their

Child Labor: Discipline in the Textile Mills

Child labor was not new, but in the early Industrial Revolution, it was exploited more systematically. These selections are taken from the *Report of Sadler's Committee*, a report that was commissioned in 1832 to inquire into the condition of child factory workers.

How They Kept the Children Awake

It is a very frequent thing at Mr. Marshall's [at Shrewsbury] where the least children were employed (for there were plenty working at six years of age), for Mr. Horseman to start the mill earlier in the morning than he formerly did; and provided a child should be drowsy, the overlooker walks round the room with a stick in his hand, and he touches that child on the shoulder, and says, "Come here." In a corner of the room there is an iron cistern; it is filled with water; he takes this boy, and takes him up by the legs, and dips him over head in the cistern, and sends him to work for the remainder of the day...

What means were taken to keep the children to their work?—Sometimes they would tap them over the head, or nip them over the nose, or give them a pinch of snuff, or throw water in their faces, or pull them off where they were, and job them about to keep them waking.

The Sadistic Overlooker

Samuel Downe, age 29, factory worker living near Leeds; at the age of about ten began work at Mr. Marshall's mills at Shrewsbury, where the customary hours when work was brisk were generally 5 A.M. to 8 P.M., sometimes from 5:30 A.M. to 8 or 9.

What means were taken to keep the children awake and vigilant, especially at the termination of such a day's labor as you have described?—There was generally a blow or a box, or a tap with a strap, or sometimes the hand.

Have you yourself been strapped?—Yes, most severely, till I could not bear to sit upon a chair without having pillows, and through that I left. I was strapped both on my own legs, and then I was put upon a man's back, and then strapped and buckled with two straps to an iron pillar, and flogged, and all by one overlooker; after that he took a piece of tow [flax fiber], and twisted it in the shape of a cord, and put it in my mouth, and tied it behind my head.

He gagged you?—Yes; and then he ordered me to run round a part of the machinery where he was overlooker, and he stood at one end, and every time I came there he struck me with a stick, which I believe was an ash plant, and which he generally carried in his hand, and sometimes he hit me, and sometimes he did not; and one of the men in the room came and begged me off, and that he let me go, and not beat me any more, and consequently he did.

You have been beaten with extraordinary severity?—Yes, I was beaten so that I had not power to cry at all, or hardly speak at one time.

What age were you at that time?—Between 10 and 11.

Q What kind of working conditions did children face in the mills during the early Industrial Revolution? Why were they beaten?

Source: From *Human Documents of the Industrial Revolution in Britain* by E. Royston Pike. London: Unwin & Hyman, 1966.

---

own pitiful conditions, was "to make the workhouses as like prisons as possible ... to establish therein a discipline so severe and repulsive as to make them a terror to the poor." Within a few years, despite sporadic opposition, more than 200,000 poor people were locked up in workhouses, where family members were separated, forced to live in dormitories, given work assignments, and fed dreadful food. Children were often recruited from parish workhouses as cheap labor in factories.

DID INDUSTRIALIZATION BRING AN IMPROVED STANDARD OF LIVING? Historians have also debated the overall effect industrialization had on the standard of living. Most historians assume that in the long run industrialization dramatically improved living standards in the form of higher capital incomes and greater consumer choices. Some historians argue, however, that wage labor made life worse for most families during the first half of the nineteenth century. They maintain that employment in the early factories was highly volatile as employers quickly dismissed workers whenever demand declined. Wages were not uniform, and inadequate housing in cities forced families to live in cramped and unsanitary conditions.

Most historians agree that what certainly did occur in the first half of the nineteenth century was a widening gap between rich and poor. In Britain, the wealthiest 1 percent of the population increased their share of the national product from 25 percent in 1801 to 35 percent in 1848. Meanwhile, in the United States, the wealthiest 10 percent of the population increased their share of the national product by 20 percent. The real gainers in the early Industrial Revolution were members of the middle class—and some skilled workers whose jobs were not eliminated by the new machines. But industrial workers themselves would have to wait until the second half of the nineteenth century to reap the benefits of industrialization.

Efforts at Change: The Workers

Before long, workers in Great Britain began to look to the formation of labor organizations as a way to gain decent wages and working conditions. Despite government opposition, new associations known as **trade unions** were formed by skilled workers in a number of industries, including the cotton spinners, ironworkers, coal miners, and shipwrights. These unions served two purposes. One was to preserve their own workers' positions by limiting entry into their trade; the other was to gain benefits from the employers. Their goals were limited. They favored a working-class struggle against employers, but only to win improvements for the members of their own trades. The largest and most successful was the Amalgamated Society of Engineers, formed in 1850. Its provision of generous unemployment benefits in return for a small weekly payment was precisely the kind of practical gains these trade unions sought.

LUDDITES Trade unionism was not the only type of collective action by workers in the early decades of the Industrial Revolution. The Luddites were skilled craftsmen in the Midlands and northern England who in 1812 physically attacked the machines that they believed threatened their livelihoods. Their actions failed to stop the industrial mechanization of Britain, but the inability of 12,000 troops to track down the culprits provides stunning evidence of the local support they received in their areas.

Trades Union Congress, London/The Bridgeman Art Library

A Trade Union Membership Card. Skilled workers in a number of industries formed trade unions in an attempt to gain higher wages, better working conditions, and special benefits. The scenes at the bottom of this membership card for the Associated Shipwrights Society illustrate some of the medical and social benefits it provided for its members.

CHARTISM A much more meaningful expression of the attempts of British workers to improve their condition developed in the movement known as Chartism, which aimed to achieve political democracy. It took its name from the People's Charter, a document drawn up in 1838 by the London Working Men's Association. The charter demanded universal male suffrage, payment for members of Parliament, the elimination of property qualifications for members of Parliament, and annual sessions of Parliament.

Two national petitions incorporating these demands gained millions of signatures and were presented to

Parliament in 1839 and 1842. Chartism attempted to encourage change through peaceful, constitutional means, although there was an underlying threat of force, as is evident in the Chartist slogan, "Peacefully if we can, forcibly if we must." In 1842, Chartist activists organized a general strike on behalf of their goals, but it had little success.

Despite the pressures exerted by Chartists, both national petitions were rejected by the members of Parliament, who were not at all ready for political democracy. As one member said, universal suffrage would be "fatal to all the purposes for which government exists" and was "utterly incompatible with the very existence of civilization." After 1848, Chartism as a movement had largely played itself out. It had never really posed a serious threat to the British establishment, but it had not been a total failure either. Its true significance stemmed from its ability to arouse and organize millions of working-class men and women, to give them a sense of working-class consciousness that they had not really possessed before. The political education of working people was important to the ultimate acceptance of all the points of the People's Charter in the future.

Efforts at Change: Reformers and Government

Efforts to improve the worst conditions of the industrial factory system also came from outside the ranks of the working classes. Reform-minded individuals, be they factory owners who felt twinges of conscience or social reformers in Parliament, campaigned against the evils of the industrial factory, especially condemning the abuse of children. Their efforts eventually met with success, especially in the reform-minded decades of the 1830s and 1840s. The Factory Act of 1833 stipulated that children between nine and thirteen could work only eight hours a day; those between thirteen and eighteen, twelve hours. Another piece of legislation in 1833 required that children between nine and thirteen have at least two hours of elementary education during the working day. In 1847, the Ten Hours Act reduced the workday for children between thirteen and eighteen to ten hours. Women were also now included in the ten-hour limitation. In 1842, the Coal Mines Act eliminated the employment of boys under ten and all women in mines. Eventually, men too would benefit from the move to restrict factory hours.

Chapter Summary

The Industrial Revolution was one of the major forces of change in the nineteenth century as it led Western civilization into the machine-dependent modern world. It began in Britain, which had an agricultural revolution that increased the quantity of foodstuffs, a population increase that created a supply of labor, capital for investment, a good supply of coal and iron ore, and a transportation revolution that created a system of canals, roads, and bridges. As the world's leading colonial power, Britain also had access to overseas markets. The cotton industry led the way as new machines such as the spinning jenny and power loom enabled the British to produce cheap cotton goods. Most important was the steam engine, which led to factories and a system of steam-powered railroads that moved people and goods effi-

ciently. The Great Exhibition of 1851 in London showed the world the achievements of Britain's Industrial Revolution. By 1860, industrialization had

spread to the continent and the United States. In the non-Western world, industrial development was much slower, in large part because European colonial powers deliberately pursued a policy of preventing the growth of mechanized industry, thus keeping the colonies as purchasers of industrial products.

The Industrial Revolution also transformed the social world of Europe. The creation of an industrial proletariat produced a whole new force for change. The work environment, especially in the new factories and mines, was

dreadful, characterized by long hours, unsafe conditions, monotonous labor, and the use of child labor. Eventually, laws were passed to improve working conditions, especially for women and children.

Trade unions were also formed to improve wages and conditions but met with limited success. Workers sometimes protested by destroying the factories and machines, as did the Luddites. The Chartist movement petitioned Parliament, calling for the right to vote and other reforms, but the members of Parliament refused their demands. The development of a wealthy industrial middle class presented a challenge to the long-term hegemony of landed wealth. Though that wealth had been threatened by the fortunes of commerce, it had never been overturned. But the new bourgeoisie became more demanding, as we shall see in the next chapter.

The Industrial Revolution seemed to prove to Europeans the underlying assumption of the Scientific Revolution of the seven-teenth century—that human beings were capable of dominating nature. By rationally manipulating the material environment for human benefit, people could attain new levels of material prosperity and produce machines not dreamed of in their wildest imaginings. Lost in the excitement of the Industrial Revolution were the voices that pointed to the dehumanization of the work-force and the alienation from one's work, one's associates, one-self, and the natural world.

CHAPTER TIMELINE

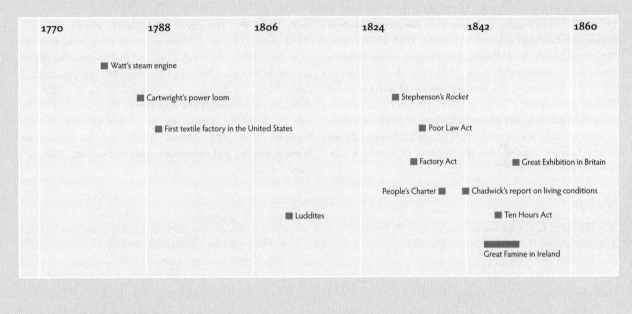

CHAPTER REVIEW

Upon Reflection

Q What made the factory system possible, and why was it such an important part of the early industrial system? What impact did it have on the lives of workers?

Q How are changes in population growth and the increase in urbanization related to the Industrial Revolution?

Q What efforts did workers make to ameliorate the harsh working conditions of the early Industrial Revolution?

Key Terms

agricultural revolution (p. 478)
capital (p. 478)
pig iron (p. 480)

wrought iron (p. 480)
trade unions (p. 497)

Suggestions for Further Reading

GENERAL WORKS   For a brief introduction to the Industrial Revolution, see **J. Horn, *The Industrial Revolution*** (Westport, Conn., 2007). A more detailed account can be found in the classic work by **D. Landes, *The Unbound Prometheus: Technological Change and Industrial Development in Western Europe from 1750 to the Present*** (Cambridge, 1969). On the "makers" of the Industrial Revolution, see **G. Wightman, *The Industrial Revolutionaries: The Making of the Modern World, 1776–1914*** (New York, 2007).

BRITAIN IN THE INDUSTRIAL REVOLUTION   On the Industrial Revolution in Britain, see **P. Mathias, *The First Industrial Nation: An Economic History of Britain, 1700–1914*,** 3d ed. (New York, 2001); **E. J. Evans, *The Forging of the Modern State: Early Industrial Britain, 1783–1870*,** 3d ed. (London, 2001); and **K. Morgan, *The Birth of Industrial Britain: Social Change, 1750–1850*** (New York, 2004). On the Crystal Palace, see **J. A. Auerbach, *The Great Exhibition of 1851: A Nation on Display*** (New Haven, Conn., 1999), and **L. Kriegel, *Grand Designs: Labor, Empire, and the Museum in Victorian Culture*** (Durham, N.C., 2007).

INDUSTRIALIZATION IN THE UNITED STATES   The early industrialization of the United States is examined in **B. Hindle** and **S. Lubar, *Engines of Change: The American Industrial Revolution, 1790–1860*** (Washington, D.C., 1986).

SOCIAL IMPACT OF INDUSTRIALIZATION   A general discussion of population growth in Europe can be found in **T. McKeown, *The Modern Rise of Population*** (London, 1976). For an examination of urban growth, see **J. G. Williamson, *Coping with City Growth During the British Industrial Revolution*** (Cambridge, 2002). On the great Irish famine, see **J. S. Donnelly, *The Great Irish Potato Famine*** (London, 2001). On city life, see **J. Merriman, *The Margins of City Life*** (New York, 1991), on French cities, and **P. Pilbeam, *The Middle Classes in Europe, 1789–1914*** (Basingstoke, England, 1990). A classic work on female labor patterns is **L. A. Tilly** and **J. W. Scott, *Women, Work, and Family*** (New York, 1978). See also **J. Rendall, *Women in an Industrializing Society: England, 1750–1880*** (Oxford, 2002), and **K. Honeyman, *Women, Gender, and Industrialization in England, 1700–1870*** (New York, 2000).

Notes

1. Quoted in E. R. Pike, *Human Documents of the Industrial Revolution in Britain* (London, 1966), p. 320.
2. Ibid., pp. 314, 343.
3. Ibid., p. 315.
4. Charles Dickens, *The Old Curiosity Shop* (New York, 2000), p. 340. Originally published in 1840–41.
5. Pike, *Human Documents*, pp. 343–344.
6. Ibid., pp. 60–61.

MindTap   **MindTap** is a fully online, highly personalized learning experience built upon Cengage Learning content. MindTap combines student learning tools—readings, multimedia, activities, and assessments—into a singular Learning Path that guides students through the course.

CHAPTER

21

Reaction, Revolution, and Romanticism, 1815–1850

A gathering of statesmen at the Congress of Vienna

CHAPTER OUTLINE AND FOCUS QUESTIONS

The Conservative Order, 1815–1830

Q What were the goals of the Congress of Vienna and the Concert of Europe, and how successful were they in achieving those goals?

The Ideologies of Change

Q What were the main tenets of conservatism, liberalism, nationalism, and utopian socialism, and what role did each ideology play in Europe in the first half of the nineteenth century?

Revolution and Reform, 1830–1850

Q What forces for change were present in France and Great Britain between 1830 and 1848, and how did each nation respond? What were the causes of the revolutions of 1848, and why did the revolutions fail?

Culture in an Age of Reaction and Revolution: The Mood of Romanticism

Q What were the characteristics of Romanticism, and how were they reflected in literature, art, and music?

CRITICAL THINKING

Q In what ways were intellectual and artistic developments related to the political and social forces of the age?

CONNECTIONS TO TODAY

Q What are the dominant ideologies today, and how do they compare with those in the first half of the nineteenth century?

IN SEPTEMBER 1814, hundreds of foreigners began to converge on Vienna, the capital city of the Austrian Empire. Many were members of European royalty—kings, princes, archdukes, and their wives—accompanied by their diplomatic advisers and scores of servants. Their congenial host was the Austrian emperor Francis I, who never tired of regaling Vienna's guests with concerts, glittering balls, sumptuous feasts, and hunting parties. One participant remembered, "Eating, fireworks, public illuminations. For eight or ten days, I haven't been able to work at all. What a life!" Of course, not every waking hour was spent in pleasure during this

501

gathering of notables, known to history as the Congress of Vienna. These people were also representatives of all the states that had fought Napoleon, and their real business was to arrange a final peace settlement after almost a decade of war. On June 8, 1815, they finally completed their task.

The forces of upheaval unleashed during the French revolutionary and Napoleonic wars were temporarily quieted in 1815 as rulers sought to restore stability by re-establishing much of the old order to a Europe ravaged by war. Kings, landed aristocrats, and bureaucratic elites regained their control over domestic governments, and internationally the forces of conservatism tried to maintain the new status quo; some states even used military force to intervene in the internal affairs of other countries in their desire to crush revolutions.

But the Western world had been changed, and it would not readily go back to the old system. New ideologies, especially liberalism and nationalism, both products of the revolutionary upheaval initiated in France, had become too powerful to be contained. Not content with the status quo, the forces of change gave rise first to the revolts and revolutions that periodically shook Europe in the 1820s and 1830s and then to the widespread revolutions of 1848. Some of the revolutions and revolutionaries were successful; most were not. Although the old order usually appeared to have prevailed, by 1850 it was apparent that its days were numbered. This perception was reinforced by the changes wrought by the Industrial Revolution. Together the forces unleashed by the dual revolutions—the French Revolution and the Industrial Revolution—made it impossible to return to prerevolutionary Europe. Nevertheless, although these events ushered in what historians like to call the modern European world, remnants of the old persisted in the midst of the new.

The Conservative Order, 1815–1830

Q FOCUS QUESTION: What were the goals of the Congress of Vienna and the Concert of Europe, and how successful were they in achieving those goals?

After the defeat of Napoleon, European rulers moved to contain revolution and the revolutionary forces by restoring much of the old order. This was the goal of

the great powers—Great Britain, Austria, Prussia, and Russia—when they met at the Congress of Vienna in September 1814 to arrange a final peace settlement. The leader of the congress was the Austrian foreign minister, Prince Klemens von Metternich (KLAY-menss fun MET-ayr-nikh) (1773–1859), who claimed that he was guided at Vienna by the **principle of legitimacy**. To keep peace and stability in Europe, he said it was necessary to restore the legitimate monarchs who would preserve traditional institutions. This had already been done in France by restoring the Bourbon monarchy.

In fact, however, the principle of legitimacy was largely ignored elsewhere. At the Congress of Vienna, the great powers all grabbed land to add to their states. They believed that they were forming a new **balance of power** that would keep any one country from dominating Europe. For example, to balance Russian gains, Prussia and Austria had been strengthened (see Map 21.1). According to Metternich, this arrangement had clearly avoided a great danger: "Prussia and Austria are completing their systems of defense; united, the two monarchies form an unconquerable barrier against the enterprises of any conquering prince who might perhaps once again occupy the throne of France or that of Russia."[1]

Conservative Domination

The peace arrangements of 1815 were the beginning of a conservative reaction determined to contain the liberal and nationalist forces unleashed by the French Revolution. Metternich and his kind were representatives of the **ideology** known as **conservatism** (see the box on p. 504). As a modern political philosophy, conservatism dates from 1790, when Edmund Burke wrote *Reflections on the Revolution in France* in reaction to the French Revolution, especially its radical republican and democratic ideas. Burke maintained that society was a contract, but "the state ought not to be considered as nothing better than a partnership agreement in a trade of pepper and coffee, to be taken up for a temporary interest and to be dissolved by the fancy of the parties."[2] No one generation has the right to destroy this partnership; each generation has the duty to preserve and transmit it to the next. Burke advised against the violent overthrow of a government by revolution, but he did not reject the possibility of change. Sudden change was unacceptable, but that did not eliminate gradual or evolutionary improvements.

Most conservatives held to a general body of beliefs. They favored obedience to political authority, believed that organized religion was crucial to social

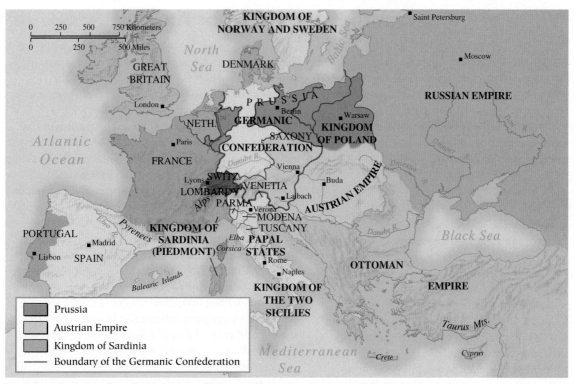

MAP 21.1 Europe After the Congress of Vienna, 1815. The Congress of Vienna imposed order on Europe based on the principles of monarchical government and a balance of power. Monarchs were restored in France, Spain, and other states recently under Napoleon's control, and much territory changed hands, often at the expense of small, weak states.

Q How did Europe's major powers manipulate territory to decrease the probability that France could again threaten the continent's stability?

order, hated revolutionary upheavals, and were unwilling to accept either the liberal demands for civil liberties and representative governments or the nationalistic aspirations generated by the French revolutionary era. The community took precedence over individual rights. After 1815, the political philosophy of conservatism was supported by hereditary monarchs, government bureaucracies, landowning aristocracies, and revived churches, be they Protestant or Catholic. The conservative forces seemed dominant after 1815, both internationally and domestically.

THE CONCERT OF EUROPE The European powers' fear of revolution and war led them to develop the Concert of Europe as a means to maintain the new status quo they had constructed. Great Britain, Russia, Prussia, and Austria (and later France) agreed to meet periodically in conferences to discuss their common interests and

examine measures that "will be judged most salutary ... for the maintenance of peace in Europe."

Eventually, the five great powers formed the Quintuple Alliance and adopted a **principle of intervention** that was based on the right of the great powers to send armies into countries where revolutions were occurring to restore legitimate monarchs to their thrones. Britain refused to agree to the principle, arguing that it had never been the intention of the alliance to interfere in the internal affairs of other states. Ignoring the British response, Austria, Prussia, Russia, and France used military intervention to defeat revolutionary movements in Spain and Italy and to restore legitimate (and conservative) monarchs to their thrones. The success of this policy of intervention came at a price, however. The Concert of Europe had broken down when the British rejected Metternich's principle of intervention, and ultimately

The Voice of Conservatism: Metternich of Austria

There was no greater symbol of conservatism in the first half of the nineteenth century than Prince Klemens von Metternich of Austria. Metternich played a crucial role at the Congress of Vienna and worked tirelessly for thirty years to repress the "revolutionary seed," as he called it, that had been spread to Europe by the "military despotism of Bonaparte."

Klemens von Metternich, *Memoirs*

We are convinced that society can no longer be saved without strong and vigorous resolutions on the part of the Governments still free in their opinions and actions.

We are also convinced that this may be, if the Governments face the truth, if they free themselves from all illusion, if they join their ranks and take their stand on a line of correct, unambiguous, and frankly announced principles.

By this course the monarchs will fulfill the duties imposed upon them by Him who, by entrusting them with power, has charged them to watch over the maintenance of justice, and the rights of all, to avoid the paths of error, and tread firmly in the way of truth....

If the same elements of destruction which are now throwing society into convulsions have existed in all ages—for every age has seen immoral and ambitious men, hypocrites, men of heated imaginations, wrong motives, and wild projects—yet ours, by the single fact of the liberty of the press, possesses more than any preceding age the means of contact, seduction, and attraction whereby to act on these different classes of men.

We are certainly not alone in questioning if society can exist with the liberty of the press, a scourge unknown to the world before the latter half of the seventeenth century, and restrained until the end of the eighteenth, with scarcely any exceptions but England—a part of Europe separated from the continent by the sea, as well as by her language and by her peculiar manners.

The first principle to be followed by the monarchs, united as they are by the coincidence of their desires and opinions, should be that of maintaining the stability of political institutions against the disorganized excitement which has taken possession of men's minds; the immutability of principles against the madness of their interpretation; and respect for laws actually in force against a desire for their destruction....

The first and greatest concern for the immense majority of every nation is the stability of the laws, and their uninterrupted action—never their change. Therefore, let the Governments govern, let them maintain the groundwork of their institutions, both ancient and modern; for if it is at all times dangerous to touch them, it certainly would not now, in the general confusion, be wise to do so....

Let them maintain religious principles in all their purity, and not allow the faith to be attacked and morality interpreted according to the social contract or the visions of foolish sectarians.

Let them suppress Secret Societies, that gangrene of society....

To every great State determined to survive the storm there still remain many chances of salvation, and a strong union between the States on the principles we have announced will overcome the storm itself.

Q Based on Metternich's discussion, how would you define conservatism? What experiences conditioned Metternich's ideas? Based on this selection, what policies do you think Metternich would have wanted his government to pursue?

Source: Reprinted from Klemens von Metternich, *Memoirs*, Alexander Napler, trans. (London: Richard Bentley & Sons, 1881).

they were able to prevent the continental powers from intervening in the revolutions in Latin America.

THE REVOLT OF LATIN AMERICA Although much of North America had been freed of European domination in the eighteenth century by the American Revolution, Latin America remained in the hands of the Spanish and Portuguese. When Napoleon Bonaparte toppled the Bourbon monarchy of Spain, however, Spanish authority in its colonial empire was weakened. By 1810, the disintegration of royal power in Argentina had led to that nation's independence. In Venezuela, Simón Bolívar (see-MOHN buh-LEE-var) (1783–1830), hailed as "the Liberator," led a bitter struggle for

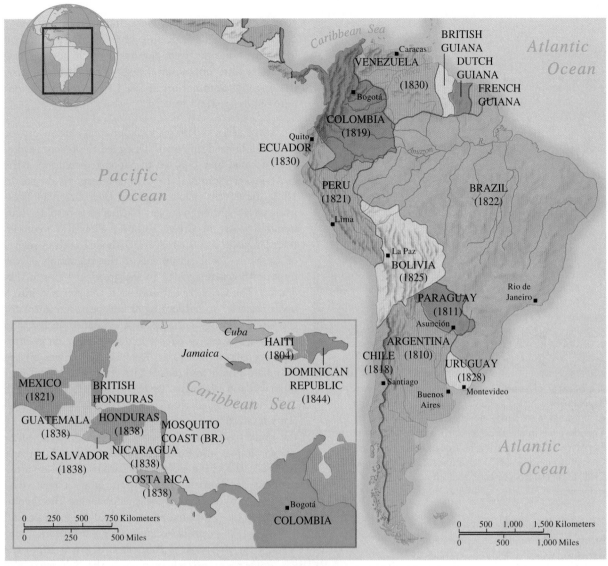

MAP 21.2 Latin America in the First Half of the Nineteenth Century. Latin American colonies took advantage of Spain's weakness during the Napoleonic wars to fight for independence, beginning with Argentina in 1810 and spreading throughout the region over the next decade with the help of leaders like Simón Bolívar and José de San Martín. The dates in parentheses show the years in which the countries received formal recognition.

Q How many South American countries are sources of rivers that feed the Amazon, and roughly what percentage of the continent is contained within the Amazon's watershed?

independence. His forces freed Colombia in 1819 and Venezuela in 1821. A second liberator was José de San Martín (hoh-SAY day san mar-TEEN) (1778–1850) who freed Chile in 1817 and then in 1821 moved on to Lima, Peru, the center of Spanish authority. He was soon joined by Bolívar, who assumed the task of crushing the last significant Spanish army in 1824. Mexico and the Central American provinces also achieved their freedom, and by 1825, after Portugal had recognized the independence of Brazil, almost all of Latin America had been freed of colonial domination (see Map 21.2).

A Liberator of South America. José de San Martín of Argentina was hailed as one of the leaders of the Latin American independence movement. In this portrait by Theodore Géricault (zhay-rih-KOH), a French Romantic artist, San Martin is shown leading his troops at the Battle of Chacabuco in Chile in 1817. His forces liberated Argentina, Chile, and Peru from Spanish authority.

Although political independence brought economic independence, old patterns were quickly reestablished. Instead of Spain and Portugal, Great Britain now dominated the Latin American economy. British merchants moved into the region in large numbers while British investors poured in funds, especially in the mining industry. Old trade patterns soon re-emerged. Because Latin America served as a source of raw materials and foodstuffs for the industrializing nations of Europe and the United States, exports—especially of wheat, tobacco, wool, sugar, coffee, and hides—to the North Atlantic countries increased noticeably. At the same time, finished consumer

The Balkans by 1830

goods, especially textiles, were imported in increasing quantities, causing a decline in industrial production in Latin America. The emphasis on exporting raw materials and importing finished products ensured the ongoing domination of the Latin American economy by foreigners.

THE GREEK REVOLT The principle of intervention proved to be a double-edged sword. Designed to prevent revolution, it could also be used to support revolution if the great powers found it in their interests to do so. In 1821, the Greeks revolted against their Ottoman Turkish masters. Although subject to Muslim control for four hundred years, the Greeks had been allowed to maintain their language and their Greek Orthodox faith. A revival of Greek national sentiment at the beginning of the nineteenth century added to the growing desire for liberation. The Greek revolt was soon transformed into a noble cause by an outpouring of European sentiment for the Greeks' struggle. In 1827, a combined British and French fleet went to Greece and defeated a large Ottoman armada. A year later, Russia declared war on the Ottoman Empire and invaded its European provinces of Moldavia and Wallachia. By the Treaty of Adrianople in 1829, which ended the Russian-Turkish war, the Russians received a protectorate over the two provinces. By the same treaty, the Ottoman Empire agreed to allow Russia, France, and Britain to decide the fate of Greece. In 1830, the three powers declared Greece an independent kingdom, and two years later, a new royal dynasty was established. The revolution in Greece had been successful only because the great powers themselves supported it. Until 1830, the Greek revolt was the only successful one in Europe; the conservative domination was still largely intact.

Conservatives in the European States

Between 1815 and 1830, the conservative domination of Europe evident in the Concert of Europe was also apparent in domestic affairs as conservative governments throughout Europe worked to preserve the old order.

GREAT BRITAIN In 1815, Great Britain was governed by the aristocratic landowning classes that controlled both houses of Parliament. Within Parliament, there were two political factions, the Tories and the Whigs. Both were still dominated by members of the landed classes, although the Whigs were beginning to gain support from the new industrial middle class. Tory ministers largely ran the government until 1830 and had little desire to change the existing political and electoral system.

Popular discontent grew after 1815 as the poor experienced increased economic difficulties. In response to falling agricultural prices, the Tory government enacted the Corn Law of 1815, which imposed high tariffs on imports of foreign grain. Though the tariffs benefited the landowners, the price of bread rose substantially, making conditions more difficult for the working classes. In 1819, mass protest meetings took a nasty turn when a squadron of cavalry attacked a crowd of 60,000, killing 11 people. Parliament responded by restricting large public meetings and the dissemination of pamphlets among the poor. The Tories managed to avoid meeting the demands for electoral reforms—at least until 1830—by making minor reforms.

RESTORATION IN FRANCE In 1814, the Bourbon family was restored to the throne of France in the person of Louis XVIII (1814–1824). Louis understood the need to accept some of the changes brought to France by the Revolution and the Napoleonic era. He accepted Napoleon's Civil Code, with its recognition of the principle of equality before the law. The property rights of individuals who had purchased confiscated lands during the Revolution were also preserved. In 1824, Louis died and was succeeded by his brother, who became Charles X (1824–1830). Charles's attempt to restore as much of the old regime as possible led to public outrage. By 1830, France was on the brink of another revolution.

THE ITALIAN STATES The Congress of Vienna had established nine states in Italy, including the kingdom of Sardinia in the north, ruled by the house of Savoy; the kingdom of the Two Sicilies (Naples and Sicily); the Papal States; a handful of small duchies ruled by relatives of the Austrian emperor; and the important northern provinces of Lombardy and Venetia, which were now part of the Austrian

Empire. Italy was largely under Austria's thumb, and all the states had extremely reactionary governments eager to smother any liberal or nationalist sentiment.

REPRESSION IN CENTRAL EUROPE After 1815, the forces of repression were particularly successful in central Europe. The Habsburg empire and its chief agent, Prince Klemens von Metternich, played an important role. Metternich boasted, "You see in me the chief Minister of Police in Europe. I keep an eye on everything. My contacts are such that nothing escapes me."[3] Metternich's spies were everywhere, searching for evidence of liberal or nationalist plots. But Metternich worried too much in 1815. Although both liberalism and nationalism emerged in the German states and the Austrian Empire, they were initially weak, as central Europe tended to remain under the domination of the aristocratic landowning classes and autocratic, centralized monarchies.

The Vienna settlement in 1815 had recognized the existence of thirty-eight sovereign states in what had once been the Holy Roman Empire. Austria and Prussia were the two major powers, and the other states varied considerably in size. Together these states formed the Germanic Confederation, but the confederation had little real power. It had no true executive, and its only central organ was the federal diet, which needed the consent of all member states to take action.

The Austrian Empire was a multinational state, a collection of different peoples under the Habsburg emperor, who provided a common bond. The empire contained people of eleven ethnicities, including Germans, Czechs, Slovaks, Magyars (Hungarians), Romanians, Slovenes, Poles, Serbs, and Italians. The Germans, though only a quarter of the population, were economically the most advanced and played a leading role in governing Austria. Despite the growing belief that each national group had the right to its own system of government, Metternich managed to repress the nationalist forces and hold the empire together.

RUSSIA: AUTOCRACY OF THE TSARS At the beginning of the nineteenth century, Russia was overwhelmingly rural, agricultural, and autocratic. The Russian tsar was still regarded

Italy, 1815

as a divine-right monarch. Alexander I (1801–1825) had been raised in the ideas of the Enlightenment and initially seemed willing to make reforms. He relaxed censorship, freed political prisoners, and reformed the educational system. But after the defeat of Napoleon, Alexander became a reactionary, and his government reverted to strict and arbitrary censorship. His brother Nicholas I (1825–1855), who succeeded him, became a strict reactionary after a military revolt at the beginning of his reign led him to strengthen both the bureaucracy and the secret police to maintain order. There would be no revolutions in Russia during the rest of his reign; if he could help it, there would be none in Europe either. Contemporaries called him the Policeman of Europe because of his willingness to use Russian troops to crush uprisings.

Private Collection/The Bridgeman Art Library

Portrait of Nicholas I. Tsar Nicholas I was a reactionary ruler who sought to prevent rebellion in Russia by strengthening the government bureaucracy, increasing censorship, and suppressing individual freedom by the use of political police. One of his enemies remarked about his facial characteristics: "The sharply retreating forehead and the lower jaw were expressive of iron will and feeble intelligence."

The Ideologies of Change

Q FOCUS QUESTION: What were the main tenets of conservatism, liberalism, nationalism, and utopian socialism, and what role did each ideology play in Europe in the first half of the nineteenth century?

Although the conservative forces were in the ascendancy from 1815 to 1830, powerful movements for change were also at work. These depended on ideas embodied in a series of political philosophies or ideologies that came into their own in the first half of the nineteenth century.

Liberalism

One of these ideologies was **liberalism**, which owed much to the Enlightenment of the eighteenth century and the American and French Revolutions. It was based on the belief that people should be as free from restraint as possible. This opinion is evident in both economic and political liberalism.

ECONOMIC LIBERALISM Also called classical economics, economic liberalism has as its primary tenet the concept of *laissez faire*, the belief that the state should not interrupt the free play of natural economic forces, especially supply and demand. Government should not interfere with the economic liberty of the individual and should restrict itself to only three primary functions: defense of the country, police protection of individuals, and the construction and maintenance of public works too expensive for individuals to undertake.

POLITICAL LIBERALISM Politically, liberals came to hold a common set of beliefs. Chief among them was the protection of civil liberties or the basic rights of all people, which included equality before the law; freedom of assembly, speech, and press; and freedom from arbitrary arrest. All of these freedoms should be guaranteed by a written document, such as the American Bill of Rights or the French Declaration of the Rights of Man and the Citizen. In addition to religious toleration for all, most liberals advocated separation of church and state. The right of peaceful opposition to the government in and out of parliament and the making of laws by a representative assembly (legislature) elected by qualified voters constituted two other liberal demands. Many liberals believed, then, in a constitutional monarchy or constitutional state with limits on the powers of government in order to prevent despotism and in written constitutions that would also help guarantee these rights.

Many liberals also advocated **ministerial responsibility**, a system in which ministers of the king were responsible to the legislature rather than to the king, giving the legislative branch a check on the power of the executive. Liberals in the first half of the nineteenth century also believed in a limited suffrage. Although all people were entitled to equal civil rights, they should not have equal political rights. The right to vote and hold office should be open only to men who met certain property qualifications. As a political philosophy, liberalism was tied to middle-class and especially industrial middle-class men who favored the extension of voting rights so that they could share power with the landowning classes. They had little desire to let the lower classes share that power. Liberals were not democrats.

One of the most prominent advocates of liberalism in the nineteenth century was the English philosopher John Stuart Mill (1806–1873). *On Liberty* (1859), his most famous work, has long been regarded as a classic statement on the liberty of the individual (see the box on p. 510). Mill argued for an "absolute freedom of opinion and sentiment on all subjects" that needed to be protected from both government censorship and the tyranny of the majority.

Mill was also instrumental in expanding the meaning of liberalism by becoming an enthusiastic supporter of women's rights. When his attempt to include women in the voting reform bill of 1867 failed, Mill published an essay titled *On the Subjection of Women*, which he had written earlier with his wife, Harriet Taylor. He argued that "the legal subordination of one sex to the other" was wrong. Differences between women and men, he claimed, were due not to different natures but simply to social practices. With equal education, women could achieve as much as men. *On the Subjection of Women* would become an important work in the nineteenth-century movement for women's rights.

Nationalism

Nationalism was an even more powerful ideology for change in the nineteenth century. Nationalism arose out of an awareness of being part of a community that has common institutions, traditions, language, and customs. This community constitutes a "nation," and it, rather than a dynasty, city-state, or other political unit, becomes the focus of the individual's primary political loyalty. Nationalism did not become a popular force for change until the French Revolution. From

then on, nationalists came to believe that each nationality should have its own government. Thus, a divided people such as the Germans wanted national unity in a German nation-state with one central government. Subject peoples, such as the Hungarians, wanted the right to establish their own autonomy, rather than be subject to a German minority in a multinational empire.

Because nationalism threatened to upset the existing political order (see Map 21.3), it was fundamentally radical. A united Germany or united Italy would upset the balance of power established in 1815. By the same token, an independent Hungarian state would mean the breakup of the Austrian Empire. Because many European states were multinational, conservatives tried hard to repress the radical threat of nationalism.

At the same time, in the first half of the nineteenth century, nationalism and liberalism became strong allies. Most liberals believed that only peoples who ruled themselves could realize freedom. One British liberal said, "It is in general a necessary condition of free institutions that the boundaries of government should coincide in the main with those of nationalities." Many nationalists believed that once each people obtained its own state, all nations could be linked into a broader community of all humanity.

Early Socialism

In the first half of the nineteenth century, the pitiful conditions found in the slums, mines, and factories of the Industrial Revolution gave rise to another ideology for change known as **socialism**. The term eventually became associated with a Marxist analysis of human society (see Chapter 22), but early socialism was largely the product of political theorists or intellectuals who wanted to introduce equality into social conditions and believed that human cooperation was superior to the competition that characterized early industrial capitalism. To later Marxists, such ideas were impractical dreams, and they contemptuously labeled the theorists **utopian socialists**. The term has endured to this day.

The utopian socialists were against private property and the competitive spirit of early industrial capitalism. By eliminating these things and creating new systems of social organization, they thought, a better environment for humanity could be achieved. One prominent utopian socialist was Robert Owen (1771–1858), a British cotton manufacturer who believed that humans would reveal their true natural goodness if they lived in a cooperative environment. At New Lanark in

The Voice of Liberalism: John Stuart Mill on Liberty

John Stuart Mill was one of Britain's most famous philosophers of liberalism. Mill's *On Liberty* is viewed as a classic statement of the liberal belief in the unfettered freedom of the individual. In this excerpt, Mill defends freedom of opinion from both government and the coercion of the majority.

John Stuart Mill, *On Liberty*

The object of this Essay is to assert one very simple principle, as entitled to govern absolutely the dealings of society with the individual in the way of compulsion and control, whether the means used be physical force in the form of legal penalties, or the moral coercion of public opinion. That principle is, that the sole end for which mankind are warranted, individually or collectively, interfering with the liberty of action of any of their number, is self-protection. That the only purpose for which power can be rightfully exercised over any member of a civilized community, against his will, is to prevent harm to others. His own good, either physical or moral, is not a sufficient warrant.... These are good reasons for remonstrating with him, or reasoning with him, or persuading him, or entreating him, but not for compelling him, or visiting him with any evil in case he do otherwise....

Society can and does execute its own mandates: and if it issues wrong mandates instead of right, or any mandates at all in things with which it ought not to meddle, it practices a social tyranny more formidable than many kinds of political oppression, since, though not usually upheld by such extreme penalties, it leaves fewer means of escape, penetrating more deeply into the details of life, and enslaving the soul itself. Protection, therefore, against the tyranny of the magistrate is not enough: there needs protection also against the tyranny of prevailing opinion and feeling, against the tendency of society to impose, by other means than civil penalties, its own ideas and practices as rules of conduct on those who dissent from them....

But there is a sphere of action in which society, as distinguished from the individual, has, if any, only an indirect interest; comprehending all that portion of a person's life and conduct which affects only himself, or if it also affects others, only with their free, voluntary and undeceived consent and participation.... This then is the appropriate region of human liberty. It comprises, first, the inward domain of consciousness; demanding liberty of conscience in the most comprehensive sense; liberty of thought and feeling; absolute freedom of opinion and sentiment on all subjects, practical or speculative, scientific, moral, or theological....

Let us suppose, therefore, that the government is entirely at one with the people, and never thinks of exerting any power of coercion unless in agreement with what it conceives to be their voice. But I deny the right of the people to exercise such coercion, either by themselves or by their government. The power itself is illegitimate. The best government has no more title to it than the worst. It is as noxious, or more noxious, when exerted in accordance with public opinion, than when in opposition to it. If all mankind minus one were of one opinion, and only one person were of the contrary opinion, mankind would be no more justified in silencing that one person, than he, if he had the power, would be justified in silencing mankind.... The peculiar evil of silencing the expression of an opinion is, that it is robbing the human race; posterity as well as the existing generation; those who dissent from the opinion, still more than those who hold it. If the opinion is right, they are deprived of the opportunity of exchanging error for truth: if wrong, they lose, what is almost as great a benefit, the clearer perception and livelier impression of truth, produced by its collision with error.

Q Based on the principles outlined here, how would you define liberalism? How do Mill's ideas fit into the concept of democracy? What is more important in his thought: the individual or society?

Source: From *Utilitarianism, On Liberty,* and *Representative Government* by John Stuart Mill. Published by Viking Press, 1914.

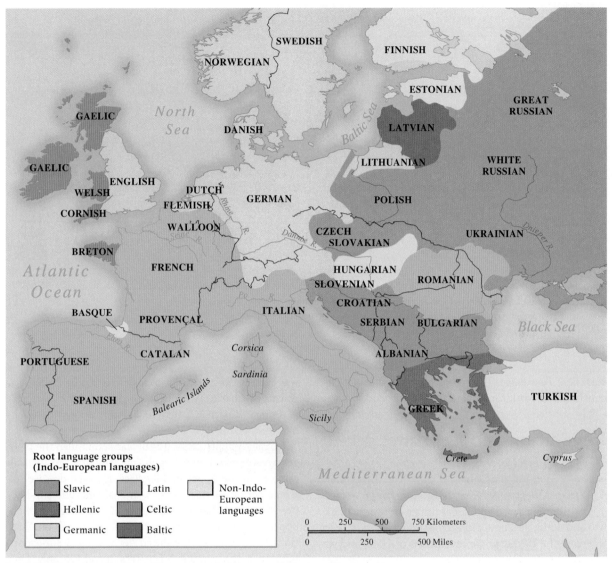

MAP 21.3 The Distribution of Languages in Nineteenth-Century Europe. Numerous languages were spoken in Europe. People who used the same language often had a shared history and culture, which laid the seeds for growing nationalism in the nineteenth century. Such nationalism eventually led to unification for Germany and Italy but spelled trouble for the polyglot Habsburg empire.

Q Look at the distribution of Germanic, Latin, and Slavic languages. What patterns emerge, and how can you explain them?

Scotland, he was successful in transforming a squalid factory town into a flourishing, healthy community. But when he attempted to create a self-contained cooperative community at New Harmony, Indiana, in the United States in the 1820s, bickering within the community eventually destroyed his dream.

The utopian socialists' plans for the reconstruction of society attracted a number of female supporters who believed that only a reordering of society would help women. One of Owen's disciples, a wealthy woman named Frances Wright, bought slaves in order to set up a model community at

The Ideologies of Change **511**

Children at New Lanark. Robert Owen created an early experiment in utopian socialism by establishing a model industrial community at New Lanark, Scotland. In this illustration, the children of factory workers are shown dancing the quadrille.

Nashoba, Tennessee. The community failed, but Wright continued to work for women's rights.

Revolution and Reform, 1830–1850

Q Focus Questions: What forces for change were present in France and Great Britain between 1830 and 1848, and how did each nation respond? What were the causes of the revolutions of 1848, and why did the revolutions fail?

Beginning in 1830, the forces of change began to break through the conservative domination of Europe, more successfully in some places than in others.

The Revolutions of 1830

In France, the Bourbon monarch Charles X and the ultraroyalists attempted to restore much of the old regime by issuing a set of edicts that imposed rigid censorship on the press, dissolved the legislative assembly, and reduced the electorate in preparation for new elections. Charles's actions produced an immediate rebellion by liberals in 1830 known as the July Revolution. Barricades went up in Paris as a provisional government led by a group of moderate, propertied liberals

was hastily formed and appealed to Louis-Philippe, a cousin of Charles X, to become the constitutional king of France. Charles X fled to Britain; a new monarchy had been born.

Louis-Philippe (1830–1848) was soon called the bourgeois monarch because political support for his rule came from the upper middle class. He even dressed like a member of the middle class, in business suits and hats. Constitutional changes that favored the interests of the upper bourgeoisie were instituted. Financial qualifications for voting were reduced yet remained sufficiently high that the number of voters increased only from 100,000 to barely 200,000, guaranteeing that only the wealthiest men would vote. To the upper middle class, the bourgeois monarchy represented the stopping place for political progress.

Supporters of liberalism played a primary role in the revolution in France, but nationalism was the crucial force in three other revolutionary outbursts in 1830. In an effort to create a stronger, larger state on France's northern border, the Congress of Vienna had added the area once known as the Austrian Netherlands (modern-day Belgium) to the Dutch Republic. The merger of Catholic Belgium into the Protestant Dutch Republic never sat well with the Belgians, however, and in 1830, they rose up against the Dutch and succeeded in convincing the major European powers to accept their independence. The revolutionary scenarios in Poland and

The Revolution of 1830. In 1830, the forces of change began to undo the conservative domination of Europe. In France, the reactionary Charles X was overthrown and replaced by the constitutional monarch Louis-Philippe, a liberal and former revolutionary soldier. In this painting by Horace Vernet, Louis-Philippe is seen riding to the Hôtel de Ville, the city hall, preceded by a man holding the French revolutionary tricolor flag, which had not been seen in France since 1815.

Italy were much less successful. Russian forces crushed the attempt of the Poles to liberate themselves from foreign domination, and Metternich sent Austrian troops to crush revolts in three Italian states.

The successful July Revolution in France served to catalyze change in Britain. The Industrial Revolution had led to an expanding group of industrial leaders who objected to the corrupt British electoral system, which excluded them from political power. The Whigs, who gained power in 1830 following new parliamentary elections, were members of the landed classes. Nevertheless, they realized that concessions to reform were superior to revolution; the demands of the wealthy industrial middle class could no longer be ignored (see the box on p. 514). In 1832, Parliament passed the Reform Act, which increased the number of voters but primarily benefited the upper middle class; the lower middle class, artisans, and industrial workers still had no vote. Nevertheless, a significant step had been taken. The "monied, manufacturing, and educated elite" had been joined to the landed interests in ruling Britain. As a result of the reforms, Britain would be immune to the revolutionary disturbances of 1848.

The Revolutions of 1848

Despite the successful revolutions in France, Belgium, and Greece, the conservative order remained in control of much of Europe. But liberalism and nationalism continued to grow. In 1848, these forces of change erupted once more. Yet again, revolution in France provided the spark for other countries, and soon most of central and southern Europe was ablaze with revolutionary fires. Tsar Nicholas I of Russia lamented to Britain's Queen Victoria in April 1848, "What remains standing in Europe? Great Britain and Russia."

ANOTHER FRENCH REVOLUTION A severe industrial and agricultural depression beginning in 1846 brought great hardship to the lower middle class, workers, and peasants in France. One-third of the workers in Paris were unemployed by the end of 1847. Scandals, graft, and corruption were rife, and the government's persistent refusal to extend the suffrage angered the disenfranchised members of the middle class. As Louis-Philippe's government continued to refuse to make changes, opposition grew and finally overthrew the monarchy on February 24, 1848. A group of moderate and radical republicans established a provisional government and called for the election by universal male suffrage of a "constituent assembly" that would draw up a new constitution.

The provisional government also established national workshops, which were supposed to be cooperative factories run by the workers. In fact, the workshops came to provide jobs for unemployed workers, consisting primarily of leaf raking and ditch digging. The cost of

OPPOSING VIEWPOINTS

Response to Revolution: Two Perspectives

Based on their political beliefs, Europeans responded differently to the specter of revolution that haunted Europe in the first half of the nineteenth century. The first excerpt is taken from a speech given by Thomas Babington Macaulay (muh-KAH-lee) (1800–1859), a historian and a Whig member of Parliament. Macaulay spoke in Parliament on behalf of the Reform Act of 1832, which extended the right to vote to the industrial middle classes of Britain. The revolution of 1830 in France had influenced his belief that reform was better than revolution.

The second excerpt is taken from the *Reminiscences* of Carl Schurz (1829–1906). Like many liberals and nationalists in Germany, Schurz received the news of the February Revolution of 1848 in France with much excitement and great expectations for revolutionary change in the German states. After the failure of the German revolution, Schurz made his way to the United States and eventually became a U.S. senator.

Thomas Babington Macaulay, Speech of March 2, 1831

My hon. friend the member of the University of Oxford tells us that, if we pass this law, England will soon be a Republic. The reformed House of Commons will, according to him, before it has sat ten years, depose the King, and expel the Lords from their House. Sir, if my hon. friend could prove this, he would have succeeded in bringing an argument for democracy infinitely stronger than any that is to be found in the works of Paine. His proposition is, in fact, this—that our monarchical and aristocratical institutions have no hold on the public mind of England; that these institutions are regarded with aversion by a decided majority of the middle class.... Now, sir, if I were convinced that the great body of the middle class in England look with aversion on monarchy and aristocracy, I should be forced, much against my will, to come to this conclusion, that monarchical and aristocratical institutions are unsuited to this country. Monarchy and aristocracy, valuable and useful as I think them, are still valuable and useful as means, and not as ends. The end of government is the happiness of the people; and I do not conceive that, in a country like this, the happiness of the people can be promoted by a form of government in which the middle classes place no confidence, and which exists only because the middle classes have no organ by which to make their sentiments known. But, sir, I am fully convinced that the middle classes sincerely wish to uphold the royal prerogatives, and the constitutional rights of the Peers....

But let us know our interest and our duty better. Turn where we may—within, around—the voice of great events is proclaiming to us, "Reform, that you may preserve." Now, therefore, while everything at home and abroad forebodes ruin to those who persist in a hopeless struggle against the spirit of the age; now ... take counsel, not of prejudice, not of party spirit, not of the ignominious pride of a fatal consistency, but of history, of reason, of the ages which are past, of the signs of this most portentous time.... Save property divided against itself. Save the multitude, endangered by their own ungovernable passions. Save the aristocracy, endangered by its own unpopular power. Save the greatest, and fairest, and most highly civilized community that ever existed, from calamities which may in a few days sweep away all the rich heritage of so many ages of wisdom and glory. The danger is terrible. The time is short. If this Bill should be rejected, I pray to God that none of those who concur in rejecting it may ever remember their votes with unavailing regret, amidst the wreck of laws, the confusion of ranks, the spoliation of property, and the dissolution of social order.

Carl Schurz, *Reminiscences*

One morning, toward the end of February, 1848, I sat quietly in my attic-chamber, working hard at my tragedy of "Ulrich von Hutten" [a sixteenth-century German knight] when suddenly a friend rushed breathlessly into the room, exclaiming: "What, you sitting here! Do you not know what has happened?"

"No; what?"

"The French have driven away Louis Philippe and proclaimed the republic."

I threw down my pen—and that was the end of "Ulrich von Hutten." I never touched the manuscript again. We tore down the stairs, into the street, to the market-square, the accustomed meeting-place for all the student societies after their midday dinner. Although it was still forenoon, the market was already crowded with young men talking excitedly. There was no shouting, no noise, only agitated conversation. What did we want there? This probably no one knew. But since the French had driven away Louis Philippe and proclaimed the republic, something of course must happen here, too....

The next morning there were the usual lectures to be attended. But how profitless! The voice of the professor sounded like a monotonous drone coming from far away. What he had to say did not seem to concern us. The pen that should have taken notes remained idle. At last we closed with a sigh the notebook and went away, impelled by a feeling that now we had something more important to do—to devote ourselves to the affairs of the fatherland. And this we did by seeking as quickly as possible again the company of our friends, in order to discuss what had happened and what was to come. In these conversations, excited as they were, certain ideas and catchwords worked themselves to the surface, which expressed more or less the feelings of the people. Now had arrived in Germany the day for the establishment of "German Unity," and the founding of a great, powerful national German Empire. In the first line the convocation of a national parliament. Then the demands for civil rights and liberties, free speech, free press, the right of free assembly,

equality before the law, a freely elected representation of the people with legislative power, responsibility of ministers, self-government of the communes, the right of the people to carry arms, the formation of a civic guard with elective officers, and so on—in short, that which was called a "constitutional form of government on a broad democratic basis." Republican ideas were at first only sparingly expressed. But the word *democracy* was soon on all tongues, and many, too, thought it a matter of course that if the princes should try to withhold from the people the rights and liberties demanded, force would take the place of mere petition. Of course the regeneration of the fatherland must, if possible, be accomplished by peaceable means.... Like many of my friends, I was dominated by the feeling that at last the great opportunity had arrived for giving to the German people the liberty which was their birthright and to the German fatherland its unity and greatness, and that it was now the first duty of every German to do and to sacrifice everything for this sacred object.

Q What arguments did Macaulay use to support the Reform Act of 1832? Was he correct? Why or why not? Why was Carl Schurz so excited when he heard the news about the revolution in France? Do you think being a university student helps explain his reaction? Why or why not? What differences do you see in the approaches of these two writers? What do these selections tell you about the development of politics in the German states and Britain in the nineteenth century?

Sources: Thomas Babington Macaulay, Speech of March 2, 1831. From *Speeches, Parliamentary and Miscellaneous* by Thomas B. Macauley (New York: Hurst Co., 1853), vol. 1, pp. 20–21, 25–26. Carl Schurz, *Reminiscences*. From *The Reminiscence of Carl Schurz* by Carl Schurz (New York: The McClure Co., 1907), vol. I, pp. 112–13.

the program became increasingly burdensome to the government.

The result was a growing split between the moderate republicans, who had the support of most of France, and the radical republicans, whose main support came from the Parisian working class. From March to June, the number of unemployed enrolled in the national workshops rose from 10,000 to almost 120,000, emptying the treasury and frightening the moderates, who responded by closing the workshops on June 23. The workers refused to accept this decision and poured into the streets. Four days of bitter and bloody fighting by

government forces crushed the working-class revolt. Thousands were killed, and four thousand prisoners were deported to the French colony of Algeria in northern Africa.

The new constitution, ratified in November, established a republic (the Second Republic) with a one-house legislature of 750 members elected by universal male suffrage for three years and a president, also elected by universal male suffrage, for four years. In the elections for the presidency held in December 1848, Charles Louis Napoleon Bonaparte, the nephew of the famous French ruler, won a resounding victory.

REVOLUTION IN THE GERMANIC STATES News of the revolution in Paris in February 1848 triggered upheavals in central Europe as well (see the box on p. 514). Revolutionary cries for change caused many German rulers to promise constitutions, a free press, jury trials, and other liberal reforms. Concessions to appease the revolutionaries were also made in Prussia. King Frederick William IV (1840–1861) agreed to abolish censorship, establish a new constitution, and work for a united Germany. This last promise had its counterpart throughout all the German states as governments allowed elections by universal male suffrage for deputies to an all-German parliament. Its purpose was to fulfill a liberal and nationalist dream—the preparation of a constitution for a new united Germany.

But the Frankfurt Assembly, as the parliament was called, failed to achieve its goals. Although some members spoke of using force, they had no real means of compelling the German rulers to accept the constitution they had drawn up. The attempt of the German liberals at Frankfurt to create a German state had failed.

UPHEAVAL IN THE AUSTRIAN EMPIRE The subjects of the Austrian Empire also had their social, political, and nationalist grievances and needed only the news of the revolution in Paris to encourage them to erupt in March 1848. The Hungarian liberals under Louis Kossuth (KAWSS-uth or KAW-shoot) agitated for "commonwealth" status; they were willing to keep the Habsburg monarch but wanted their own legislature. In March, demonstrations in Buda, Prague, and Vienna led to Metternich's dismissal, and the archsymbol of the conservative order fled abroad. In Vienna, revolutionary forces, carefully guided by the educated and propertied classes, took control of the capital and insisted that a constituent assembly be summoned to draw up a liberal constitution. Hungary was granted its wish for its own legislature, a separate national army, and control over foreign policy and budget. In Bohemia, the Czechs began to demand their own government as well.

Although Emperor Ferdinand I (1835–1848) and Austrian officials had made concessions to appease the revolutionaries, they awaited an opportunity to re-establish their firm control. As in the German states, they were increasingly encouraged by the divisions between radical and moderate revolutionaries and played on the middle-class fear of a working-class social revolution. Their first success came in June 1848 when Austrian military forces under General Alfred Windischgrätz (VIN-dish-grets) ruthlessly suppressed the Czech rebels in Prague. By the end of October,

radical rebels had been crushed in Vienna. In December, the feebleminded Ferdinand agreed to abdicate in favor of his nephew, Francis Joseph I (1848–1916), who worked vigorously to restore the imperial government in Hungary. The Austrian armies, however, were unable to defeat Kossuth's forces, and it was only through the intervention of Nicholas I, who sent a Russian army of 140,000 men to aid the Austrians, that the Hungarian revolution was finally crushed in 1849. The revolutions in the Austrian Empire had also failed. Autocratic government was restored, emperor and propertied classes remained in control, and the numerous nationalities were still subject to the Austrian government.

REVOLTS IN THE ITALIAN STATES The failure of revolutionary uprisings in Italy in 1830 and 1831 had encouraged the Italian movement for unification to take a new direction. The leadership of Italy's resurgence passed into the hands of Giuseppe Mazzini (joo-ZEP-pay maht-SEE-nee) (1805–1872), a dedicated Italian nationalist who founded an organization known as Young Italy in 1831. This group set as its goal the creation of a united Italian republic. In *The Duties of Man*, Mazzini urged Italians to dedicate their lives to the Italian nation: "O my Brother! Love your country. Our Country is our home." A number of Italian women also took up Mazzini's call. Especially notable was Cristina Belgioioso (bell-joh-YOH-soh) (1808–1871), a wealthy aristocrat who worked to bring about Italian unification. Pursued by the Austrian authorities, she fled to Paris and started a newspaper to espouse the Italian cause.

The dreams of Mazzini and Belgioioso seemed on the verge of fulfillment when a number of Italian states rose in revolt in 1848. Beginning in Sicily, rebellions spread northward as ruler after ruler granted a constitution to his people. Citizens in Lombardy and Venetia also rebelled against their Austrian overlords. The Venetians declared a republic in Venice. The king of the northern Italian state of Piedmont, Charles Albert (1831–1849), took up the call and assumed the leadership for a war of liberation from Austrian domination. His invasion of Lombardy proved unsuccessful, however, and by 1849 the Austrians had re-established complete control over Lombardy and Venetia. Counterrevolutionary forces also prevailed throughout Italy as Italian rulers managed to recover power on their own. Only Piedmont was able to keep its liberal constitution.

THE FAILURES OF 1848 Throughout Europe in 1848, popular revolts had initiated revolutionary upheavals that had led to the formation of liberal constitutions and liberal governments. But the failure of the revolutionaries to remain united soon led to the re-establishment of the old regimes. Nationalities everywhere had also revolted in pursuit of self-government. But here too, frightfully little was achieved as divisions among nationalities proved utterly disastrous. Though the Hungarians demanded autonomy from the Austrians, at the same time they refused the same to their minorities—the Slovenes, Croats, and Serbs. Instead of joining together against the old empire, minorities fought each other.

The Maturing of the United States

The United States Constitution, ratified in 1789, committed the nation to two of the major forces of the first half of the nineteenth century, liberalism and nationalism. Initially, divisions over the power of the federal government vis-à-vis the individual states challenged this constitutional commitment to national unity. Bitter conflict erupted between the Federalists and the Republicans. Led by Alexander Hamilton (1757–1804), the Federalists favored a financial program that would establish a strong central government. The Republicans, guided by Thomas Jefferson (1743–1826) and James Madison (1751–1836), feared centralization and its consequences for popular liberties. European rivalries intensified these divisions because the Federalists were pro-British and the Republicans pro-French. The successful conclusion of the War of 1812 against the British brought an end to the Federalists, who had opposed the war, while the surge of national feeling generated by the war served to heal the nation's divisions.

Another strong force for national unity came from the Supreme Court under the leadership of John Marshall (1755–1835) as chief justice from 1801 to 1835. Marshall made the Supreme Court into an important national institution by asserting the right of the Court to overrule an act of Congress if the Court found it to be in violation of the Constitution. Under Marshall, the Supreme Court contributed further to establishing the supremacy of the national government by curbing the actions of state courts and legislatures.

The election of Andrew Jackson (1767–1845) as president in 1828 opened a new era in American politics, the era of mass democracy. The electorate was expanded by dropping traditional property qualifications; by the end of Jackson's presidency, suffrage had been extended to almost all adult white males.

CHRONOLOGY	Reaction, Reform, and Revolution: The European States, 1815–1850
Great Britain	
Reform Act	1832
France	
Louis XVIII	1814–1824
Charles X	1824–1830
July Revolution	1830
Louis-Philippe	1830–1848
Abdication of Louis-Philippe; formation of provisional government	1848 (February 22–24)
Workers' revolt in Paris	1848 (June)
Establishment of Second Republic	1848 (November)
Election of Louis Napoleon as French president	1848 (December)
Low Countries	
Union of Netherlands and Belgium	1815
Belgian revolt and independence	1830
German States	
Germanic Confederation	1815
Frederick William IV of Prussia	1840–1861
Revolution in Germany	1848
Frankfurt Assembly	1848–1849
Austrian Empire	
Emperor Ferdinand I	1835–1848
Revolt in Austrian Empire; dismissal of Metternich	1848 (March)
Suppression of Czech rebels	1848 (June)
Suppression of Viennese rebels	1848 (October)
Francis Joseph I	1848–1916
Defeat of Hungarians with help of Russian troops	1849
Italian States	
King Charles Albert of Piedmont	1831–1849
Revolutions in Italy	1848
Attack on Austria	1848
Restoration of Austrian control in Lombardy and Venetia	1849
Russia	
Tsar Alexander I	1801–1825
Tsar Nicholas I	1825–1855
Suppression of Polish revolt	1831

Culture in an Age of Reaction and Revolution: The Mood of Romanticism

Q FOCUS QUESTION: What were the characteristics of Romanticism, and how were they reflected in literature, art, and music?

At the end of the eighteenth century, a new intellectual movement known as **Romanticism** emerged to challenge the Enlightenment's preoccupation with using reason to discover truth. The Romantics tried to balance the use of reason by stressing the importance of feeling, emotion, and imagination as sources of knowing. As one German Romantic put it, "It was my heart that counseled me to do it, and my heart cannot err."

The Characteristics of Romanticism

Romantic writers emphasized emotion, sentiment, and inner feelings in their works, rejecting the rationalist ideals of the Enlightenment. An important model for Romantics was the tragic figure in *The Sorrows of Young Werther*, a novel by the great German writer Johann Wolfgang von Goethe (yoh-HAHN VULF-gahnk fun GUR-tuh) (1749–1832), who later rejected Romanticism in favor of Classicism. Werther was a Romantic figure who sought freedom in order to fulfill himself. Misunderstood and rejected by society, he continued to believe in his own worth through his inner feelings, but his deep love for a girl who did not love him finally led him to commit suicide. After Goethe's *Sorrows of Young Werther*, numerous novels and plays appeared whose plots revolved around young maidens tragically carried off at an early age (twenty-three was most common) by disease (usually tuberculosis, at that time a protracted disease that was usually fatal) to the sorrow and despair of their male lovers.

Another important characteristic of Romanticism was **individualism**, an interest in the unique traits of each person. The Romantics' desire to follow their inner drives led them to rebel against middle-class conventions. Long hair, beards, and outrageous clothes served to reinforce the individualism that young Romantics were trying to express. Moreover, sentiment and individualism came together in the Romantics' stress on the heroic. The Romantic hero was a solitary genius who was ready to defy the world and sacrifice his life for a great cause. Some writers stressed that the deeds of such heroes largely determined the course of historical events.

Many Romantics possessed a passionate interest in the past. In Germany, the brothers Jacob and Wilhelm Grimm collected and published local fairy tales, as did Hans Christian Andersen in Denmark. A revival of Gothic architecture left European countrysides adorned with pseudo-medieval castles and cities bedecked with grandiose neo-Gothic cathedrals, city halls, parliamentary buildings, and even railway stations. Literature, too, reflected this historical consciousness. The novels of Walter Scott (1771–1832) became European best-sellers in the first half of the nineteenth century. *Ivanhoe*, in which Scott evoked the clash between Saxon and Norman knights in medieval England, became one of his most popular works.

To the historical-mindedness of the Romantics could be added an attraction to the bizarre and unusual. In an exaggerated form, this preoccupation gave rise to so-called **Gothic literature** (see the box on p. 519), chillingly evident in short stories of horror by the American Edgar Allan Poe (1808–1849) and in *Frankenstein* by Mary Wollstonecraft Shelley (1797–1851). Shelley's novel was the story of a mad scientist who brings into being a humanlike monster who goes berserk. Some Romantics even sought the unusual in their own lives by experimenting with cocaine, opium, and hashish to achieve altered states of consciousness.

Romantic Poets and the Love of Nature

To the Romantics, poetry ranked above all other literary forms because they believed it was the direct expression of one's soul. The Romantic poets were viewed as seers who could reveal the invisible world to others. Their incredible sense of drama made some of them the most colorful figures of their era, living intense but short lives. Percy Bysshe Shelley (1792–1822), expelled from school for advocating atheism, set out to reform the world. His *Prometheus Unbound*, completed in 1820, is a portrait of the revolt of human beings against the laws and customs that oppress them. He drowned in a storm in the Mediterranean. Lord Byron (1788–1824) dramatized himself as the melancholy Romantic hero that he had described in his own work, *Childe Harold's Pilgrimage*. He participated in the movement for Greek independence and died in Greece fighting the Ottomans.

Romantic poetry gave full expression to one of the most important characteristics of Romanticism: love of nature, especially evident in the works of William Wordsworth (1770–1850). His experience of nature

Gothic Literature: Edgar Allan Poe

American writers and poets made significant contributions to Romanticism. Although Edgar Allan Poe was influenced by the German Romantic school of mystery and horror, many literary historians credit him with pioneering the modern short story. This selection from the conclusion of "The Fall of the House of Usher" gives a sense of the nature of so-called Gothic literature.

Edgar Allan Poe, "The Fall of the House of Usher"

No sooner had these syllables passed my lips, than—as if a shield of brass had indeed, at the moment, fallen heavily upon a floor of silver—I became aware of a distinct, hollow, metallic, and clangorous, yet apparently muffled, reverberation. Completely unnerved, I leaped to my feet; but the measured rocking movement of Usher was undisturbed. I rushed to the chair in which he sat. His eyes were bent fixedly before him, and throughout his whole countenance there reigned a stony rigidity. But, as I placed my hand upon his shoulder, there came a strong shudder over his whole person; a sickly smile quivered about his lips and I saw that he spoke in a low, hurried, and gibbering murmur, as if unconscious of my presence. Bending closely over him, I at length drank in the hideous import of his words.

"Not hear it?—yes, I hear it, and *have* heard it. Long-long-long-many minutes, many hours, many days, have I heard it—yet I dared not—oh, pity me, miserable wretch that I am!—I dared not—I *dared* not speak! *We have put her living in the tomb!* Said I not that my senses were acute? I now tell you that I heard her first feeble movements in the hollow coffin.

I heard them—many, many days ago—yet I dared not—I *dared not speak!* And now—tonight . . . the rending of her coffin, and the grating of the iron hinges of her prison, and her struggles within the coppered archway of the vault! Oh whither shall I fly? Will she not be here anon? Is she not hurrying to upbraid me for my haste? Have I not heard her footstep on the stair? Do I not distinguish that heavy and horrible beating of her heart? MADMAN!"—here he sprang furiously to his feet, and shrieked out his syllables, as if in the effort he were giving up his soul—"MADMAN! I TELL YOU THAT SHE NOW STANDS WITHOUT THE DOOR!"

As if in the superhuman energy of his utterance there had been found the potency of a spell, the huge antique panels to which the speaker pointed threw slowly back, upon the instant, their ponderous and ebony jaws. It was the work of the rushing gust—but then without those doors there DID stand the lofty and enshrouded figure of the lady Madeline of Usher. There was blood upon her white robes, and the evidence of some bitter struggle upon every portion of her emaciated frame. For a moment she remained trembling and reeling to and fro upon the threshold, then, with a low moaning cry, fell heavily inward upon the person of her brother, and in her violent and now final death-agonies, bore him to the floor a corpse, and a victim to the terrors he had anticipated.

Q What characteristics of Romanticism are revealed in Poe's tale? In what ways did Romanticism offer alternatives to the reigning influences of rationalism and industrialization?

Source: From *Selected Prose and Poetry*, Edgar Allan Poe. New York: Holt, Rinehart, and Winston, 1950.

---

was almost mystical as he claimed to receive "authentic tidings of invisible things":

> One impulse from a vernal wood
> May teach you more of man,
> Of Moral Evil and of good,
> Than all the sages can.[4]

To Wordsworth, nature contained a mysterious force that the poet could perceive and learn from. Nature served as a mirror into which humans could look to learn about themselves. Nature was, in fact, alive and sacred:

> To every natural form, rock, fruit or flower,
> Even the loose stones that cover the high-way,
> I gave a moral life, I saw them feel,
> Or link'd them to some feeling: the great mass
> Lay bedded in a quickening soul, and all
> That I beheld, respired with inward meaning.[5]

Other Romantics carried this worship of nature further into **pantheism** by identifying the great force in nature with God. As the German Romantic poet Friedrich Novalis (FREED-rikh noh-VAH-lis) said, "Anyone seeking God will find him anywhere."

Romanticism in Art

Like the literary arts, the visual arts were also deeply affected by Romanticism. To Romantic artists, all artistic expression was a reflection of the artist's inner feelings; a painting should mirror the artist's vision of the world and be the instrument of his own imagination. Moreover, Romantic artists deliberately rejected the classical principles of austerity and geometry. Beauty was not a timeless thing; its expression depended on one's culture and one's age. The Romantics abandoned classical restraint for warmth, emotion, and movement.

The early life experiences of the German painter Caspar David Friedrich (kass-PAR dah-VEET FREED-rikh) (1774–1840) left him with a lifelong preoccupation with God and nature. Friedrich painted landscapes, but with an interest that transcended the mere presentation of natural details. His portrayal of mountains shrouded in mist, gnarled trees bathed in moonlight, and the stark ruins of monasteries surrounded by withered trees all conveyed a feeling of mystery and mysticism. For Friedrich, nature was a manifestation of divine life, as is evident in *The Wanderer Above the Sea of Fog*. To Friedrich, the artistic process depended on the use of an unrestricted imagination that could only be achieved through inner vision. He advised artists, "Shut your physical eye and look first at your picture with your spiritual eye, then bring to the light of day what you have seen in the darkness."

Eugène Delacroix (oo-ZHEN duh-lah-KRWAH) (1798–1863) was one of the most famous French exponents of the Romantic school of painting. Delacroix's paintings exhibited a fascination with the exotic and a passion for color, exemplified by *Death of Sardanapalus*. In Delacroix, theatricality and movement combined with a daring color palette. Many of his works reflect his belief that "a painting should be a feast to the eye."

Romanticism in Music

To many Romantics, music was the most Romantic of the arts because it enabled the composer to probe deeply into human emotions. Music historians have called the eighteenth century the age of Classicism and the nineteenth the era of Romanticism. One of

© The Art Gallery Collection/Alamy

Casper David Friedrich, *The Wanderer Above the Sea of Fog*. The German artist Caspar David Friedrich sought to express in painting his own mystical view of nature. "The divine is everywhere," he once wrote, "even in a grain of sand." In this painting, a solitary wanderer is shown from the back gazing at mountains covered in fog. Overwhelmed by the all-pervasive presence of nature, the figure expresses the human longing for infinity.

the greatest composers of all time, Ludwig van Beethoven, served as a bridge between Classicism and Romanticism.

Beethoven (1770–1827) was born in Bonn, Germany, but soon made his way to Vienna, then the musical capital of Europe. During his first major period of composing, from 1792 to 1802, his work was still largely within the classical framework of the eighteenth century, and the influences of Mozart and Haydn were paramount. But with the composition of the Third Symphony (1804), the *Eroica*, originally intended for Napoleon, Beethoven broke through to Romanticism in his use of uncontrolled rhythms to create dramatic struggle and uplifted resolutions. E. T. A. Hoffman, a contemporary composer and writer, said, "Beethoven's music opens the flood gates of fear, of terror, of horror, of pain, and arouses that longing for the eternal

Eugène Delacroix, _Death of Sardanapalus._ Delacroix's _Death of Sardanapalus_ was based on Lord Byron's verse account of the decadent Assyrian king's dramatic last moments. Besieged by enemy troops and with little hope of survival, Sardanapalus orders that his harem women and prize horses go to their death with him. At the right, a guard stabs one of the women as the king looks on.

which is the essence of Romanticism. He is thus a pure Romantic composer."[6] Beethoven went on to write a vast quantity of works, but in the midst of this productivity and growing fame, he was more and more burdened by his growing deafness. One of the most moving pieces of music of all time, the chorale finale of his Ninth Symphony, was composed when Beethoven was totally deaf.

Chapter Summary

In 1815, a conservative order was re-established throughout Europe at the Congress of Vienna, which made peace at the end of the Napoleonic wars and tried to restore Europe's "legitimate" rulers. The great powers, whose cooperation was embodied in the Concert of Europe, attempted to ensure the durability of the new conservative order by intervening to uphold conservative govern-

ments. Great Britain, however, seeking new markets, opposed intervention when the Latin American colonies of Spain and Portugal declared their independence. Within the European countries, conservative rulers worked to re-establish the old order.

But the revolutionary waves of the 1820s and 1830s made it clear that the ideologies of liberalism and nationalism, first unleashed by the French Revolution

and now reinforced by the spread of the Industrial Revolution, were still alive and active. Liberalism favored freedom both in politics and in economics. Natural rights and representative government were essential, but most liberals favored limiting voting rights to male property owners. Nationalism, with its belief in a community with common traditions, language, and customs, threatened the status quo in divided Germany and Italy and the multiethnic Austrian Empire. The forces of liberalism and nationalism, however, faced enormous difficulties. as failed revolutions in Poland, Russia, Italy, and Germany all testify. At the same time, reform legislation in Britain and successful revolutions in Greece, France, and Belgium demonstrated the continuing strength of these forces of change. In 1848, they erupted once more as revolutions broke out all across Europe. A republic with universal manhood suffrage was established in France, but conflict emerged between socialist demands and the republican political agenda. The

Frankfurt Assembly worked to create a unified Germany, but it failed. In Austria, the liberal demands of Hungarians and other nationalities were eventually put down. In Italy, too, uprisings against Austrian rule failed when conservatives regained control. Although they had failed, both liberalism and nationalism would succeed in the second half of the nineteenth century, but in ways not foreseen by the idealistic liberals and nationalists.

Efforts at reform had a cultural side as well in the movement of Romanticism. Romantics reacted against what they viewed as the Enlightenment's emphasis on reason. They favored intuition, feeling, and emotion, which became evident in the medieval fantasies of Walter Scott, the poetry of William Wordsworth and Percy Bysshe Shelley, the Gothic literature of Mary Shelley and Edgar Allan Poe, the paintings of Caspar David Friedrich and Eugène Delacroix, and the music of Ludwig van Beethoven.

CHAPTER TIMELINE

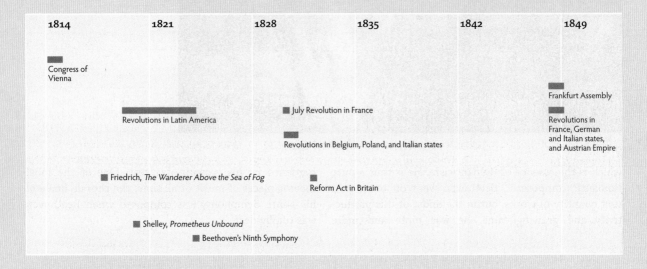

1814	1821	1828	1835	1842	1849

Congress of Vienna

Revolutions in Latin America

July Revolution in France

Revolutions in Belgium, Poland, and Italian states

Frankfurt Assembly

Revolutions in France, German and Italian states, and Austrian Empire

Friedrich, *The Wanderer Above the Sea of Fog*

Reform Act in Britain

Shelley, *Prometheus Unbound*

Beethoven's Ninth Symphony

CHAPTER REVIEW

Upon Reflection

Q What were the chief ideas associated with the ideology of conservatism, and how were these ideas put into practice in the first half of the nineteenth century?

Q What were the chief ideas associated with the ideologies of liberalism and nationalism, and how were these ideas put into practice in the first half of the nineteenth century?

Q How was Great Britain able to avoid revolution in the 1830s and the 1840s?

Key Terms

principle of legitimacy (p. 502)
balance of power (p. 502)
ideology (p. 502)
conservatism (p. 502)

principle of intervention (p. 503)
liberalism (p. 508)
ministerial responsibility (p. 509)
socialism (p. 509)

utopian socialists (p. 509)
Romanticism (p. 518)
individualism (p. 518)

Gothic literature (p. 518)
pantheism (p. 520)

Suggestions for Further Reading

GENERAL WORKS For a good survey of the entire nineteenth century, see **R. Gildea**, *Barricades and Borders: Europe, 1800–1914*, 3d ed. (Oxford, 2003), in the Short Oxford History of the Modern World series. Also valuable is **T. C. W. Blanning**, ed., *Nineteenth Century: Europe, 1789–1914* (Oxford, 2000). For surveys of the period covered in this chapter, see **M. Lyons**, *Postrevolutionary Europe, 1815–1856* (New York, 2006), and **C. Breunig** and **M. Levinger**, *The Age of Revolution and Reaction, 1789–1850*, 3d ed. (New York, 2002). There are also some useful books on individual countries that cover more than the subject of this chapter. These include **R. Magraw**, *France, 1815–1914: The Bourgeois Century*, rev. ed. (Oxford, 2006); **D. Saunders**, *Russia in the Age of Reaction and Reform, 1801–1881* (London, 1992); **D. Blackbourn**, *The Long Nineteenth Century: A History of Germany, 1789–1918* (New York, 1998); **A. Sked**, *The Decline and Fall of the Habsburg Empire, 1815–1918*, 2d ed. (London, 2001); and **J. A. David**, *Italy in the Nineteenth Century, 1796–1900* (Oxford, 2001).

EUROPE, 1815–1830 On the peace settlement of 1814–1815, see **T. Chapman**, *The Congress of Vienna* (London, 1998). A concise summary of the international events of the entire nineteenth century can be found in **R. Bullen** and **F. R. Bridge**, *The Great Powers and the European States System, 1815–1914*, rev. ed. (London, 2004). On the revolutions in Europe in 1830, see **C. Church**, *Europe in 1830: Revolution and Political Change* (Chapel Hill, N.C., 1983). On Great Britain's reform legislation, see **E. J. Evans**, *Great Reform Act of 1832*, 2d ed. (London, 1994). The Greek revolt is examined in detail in **D. Brewer**, *Greek War of Independence* (New York, 2001).

REVOLUTIONS OF 1848 The best introduction to the revolutions of 1848 is **J. Sperber**, *The European Revolutions, 1848–1851*, 2d ed. (New York, 2005).

ROMANTICISM On the ideas of the Romantics, see **M. Cranston**, *The Romantic Movement* (Oxford, 1994). For an introduction to the arts, see **I. Ciseri**, *Romanticism, 1780–1860: The Birth of a New Sensibility* (New York, 2003).

Notes

1. Quoted in M. S. Anderson, *The Ascendancy of Europe 1815–1914*, 2d ed. (London, 1985), p. 1.
2. Quoted in P. Viereck, *Conservatism* (Princeton, N.J., 1956), p. 27.
3. Quoted in G. de Berthier de Sauvigny, *Metternich and His Times* (London, 1962), p. 105.
4. W. Wordsworth, "The Tables Turned," in *Poems of Wordsworth*, ed. M. Arnold (London, 1963), p. 138.
5. W. Wordsworth, *The Prelude* (Harmondsworth, England, 1971), p. 109.
6. Quoted in S. Prawer, ed., *The Romantic Period in Germany* (London, 1970), p. 285.

MindTap **MindTap** is a fully online, highly personalized learning experience built upon Cengage Learning content. MindTap combines student learning tools—readings, multimedia, activities, and assessments—into a singular Learning Path that guides students through the course.

CHAPTER 22

An Age of Nationalism and Realism, 1850–1871

Proclamation of the German Empire in the Hall of Mirrors in the palace of Versailles

Schloss Friedrichsruhe, Germany/The Bridgeman Art Library

CHAPTER OUTLINE AND FOCUS QUESTIONS

The France of Napoleon III

Q What were the characteristics of Napoleon III's government, and how did his foreign policy contribute to the unification of Italy and Germany?

National Unification: Italy and Germany

Q What actions did Cavour and Bismarck take to bring about unification in Italy and Germany, respectively, and what role did war play in their efforts?

Nation Building and Reform: The National State in Midcentury

Q What efforts for reform occurred in the Austrian Empire, Russia, and Great Britain between 1850 and 1870, and how successful were they in alleviating each nation's problems?

Industrialization and the Marxist Response

Q What were the main ideas of Karl Marx?

Science and Culture in an Age of Realism

Q How did the belief that the world should be viewed realistically manifest itself in science, literature, and art in the second half of the nineteenth century?

CRITICAL THINKING

Q What was the relationship between nationalism and reform between 1850 and 1871?

CONNECTIONS TO TODAY

Q How do we define classes in society today, and in what ways are our definitions different from or similar to those that Marx and Engels used in *The Communist Manifesto* for the classes emerging in the wake of the Industrial Revolution?

ACROSS THE CONTINENT, the revolutions of 1848 had failed. The forces of liberalism and nationalism appeared to have been decisively defeated as authoritarian governments reestablished their control almost everywhere in

Europe by 1850. And yet within twenty-five years, many of the goals sought by the liberals and nationalists during the first half of the century seemed to have been achieved. National unity became a reality in Italy and Germany, and many European states were governed by constitutional monarchies, even though the constitutional-parliamentary features were frequently facades.

All the same, these goals were not achieved by liberal nationalist leaders but by a new generation of conservative leaders who were proud of being practitioners of *Realpolitik* (ray-AHL-poh-lee-teek), the "politics of reality." One reaction to the failure of the revolutions of 1848 had been a new toughness of mind in which people prided themselves on being realistic in their handling of power. The new conservative leaders used armies and power politics to achieve their foreign policy goals. And they did not hesitate to manipulate liberal means to achieve conservative ends at home. Nationalism had failed as a revolutionary movement in 1848–1849, but in the ensuing decades, these new leaders found a variety of ways to pursue nation building. Winning wars was, however, only one means of nation building, as rulers also sought to improve the economy and foster cultural policies that led the citizens of their states to a greater sense of national identity.

One of the most successful of these leaders was the Prussian Otto von Bismarck, who used both astute diplomacy and war to achieve the unification of Germany. On January 18, 1871, Bismarck and six hundred German princes, nobles, and generals filled the Hall of Mirrors in the palace of Versailles, outside Paris. The Prussian army had defeated the French, and the assembled notables were gathered for the proclamation of the Prussian king as the new emperor of a united German state. When the words "Long live His Imperial Majesty, the Emperor William!" rang out, the assembled guests took up the cry. One participant wrote, "A thundering cheer, repeated at least six times, thrilled through the room while the flags and standards waved over the head of the new emperor of Germany." European rulers who feared the power of the new German state were not so cheerful. "The balance of power has been entirely destroyed," declared the British prime minister.

The France of Napoleon III

Q FOCUS QUESTION: What were the characteristics of Napoleon III's government, and how did his foreign policy contribute to the unification of Italy and Germany?

After 1850, a new generation of conservative leaders came to power in Europe. Foremost among them was Napoleon III (1852–1870) of France, who taught his contemporaries how authoritarian governments could use liberal and nationalistic forces to bolster their own power. It was a lesson others quickly learned.

Chateaux de Versailles et de Trianon, Versailles//©RMN-Grand Palais/Art Resource, NY

Emperor Napoleon III. On December 2, 1852, Louis Napoleon of France took the title of Napoleon III and then proceeded to create an authoritarian monarchy. As opposition to his policies intensified in the 1860s, Napoleon III began to liberalize his government. A disastrous military defeat at the hands of Prussia in 1870–1871, however, brought the collapse of his regime.

Louis Napoleon: Toward the Second Empire

Even after his election as the president of the French Republic in 1848, many of his contemporaries dismissed "Napoleon the Small" as a nonentity whose success was due only to his name. But Louis Napoleon was a clever politician who was especially astute at understanding the popular forces of his day. After his election, he was clear about his desire to have personal power. He wrote, "I shall never submit to any attempt to influence me.... I follow only the promptings of my mind and heart.... Nothing, nothing shall trouble the clear vision of my judgment or the strength of my resolution."[1]

Louis Napoleon was a patient man. For three years, he persevered in winning the support of the French people, and when the National Assembly rejected his wish to be allowed to stand for re-election, Louis used troops to seize control of the government on December 1, 1851. After restoring universal male suffrage, Louis Napoleon asked the French people to restructure the government by electing him president for ten years (see the box on p. 527). Ninety-seven percent responded affirmatively, and on December 2, 1852, Louis Napoleon assumed the title of Napoleon III (the first Napoleon had abdicated in favor of his son, Napoleon II, on April 6, 1814). The Second Empire had begun.

The Second Napoleonic Empire

The government of Napoleon III was clearly authoritarian in a Bonapartist sense. As chief of state, Napoleon III controlled the armed forces, police, and civil service. Only he could introduce legislation and declare war. The Legislative Corps gave an appearance of representative government since its members were elected by universal male suffrage to six-year terms, but they could neither initiate legislation nor affect the budget.

The first five years of Napoleon III's reign were a spectacular success as he reaped the benefits of worldwide economic prosperity as well as some of his own economic policies. Napoleon believed in using the resources of government to stimulate the national economy and took many steps to expand industrial growth. Government subsidies were used to foster the construction of railroads, harbors, roads, and canals. The major French railway lines were completed during Napoleon's reign, and industrial expansion was evident in the tripling of iron production. Napoleon III also undertook a vast reconstruction of the city of Paris. A modern Paris of broad boulevards, spacious buildings, circular plazas, public squares, an underground sewage system, a new public water supply, and gaslights replaced the medieval Paris of narrow streets and old city walls. The new Paris served a military as well as an aesthetic purpose. Broad streets made it more difficult for would-be insurrectionists to throw up barricades and easier for troops to move rapidly through the city to put down revolts.

In the 1860s, as opposition to some of the emperor's policies began to mount, Napoleon III liberalized his regime. He reached out to the working class by legalizing trade unions and granting them the right to strike. He also began to open up the political process. The Legislative Corps was permitted more say in affairs of state, including debate over the budget. Napoleon's liberalization policies did serve initially to strengthen the hand of the government. In a plebiscite in May 1870 on whether to accept a new constitution that might have inaugurated a parliamentary regime, the French people gave Napoleon another resounding victory. This triumph was short-lived, however. Foreign policy failures led to growing criticism, and war with Prussia in 1870 turned out to be the death blow for Napoleon III's regime (see "The Franco-Prussian War" later in this chapter). Napoleon was ousted, and the Third Republic was proclaimed.

Foreign Policy: The Mexican Adventure

The most flagrant of Napoleon III's foreign policy failures was his imperialistic adventure in Mexico. Seeking to dominate Mexican markets for French goods, the emperor sent French troops to Mexico in 1861 to join British and Spanish forces in protecting their interests in the midst of the upheaval caused by a struggle between liberal and conservative Mexican factions. Although the British and Spanish withdrew their troops after order had been restored, French forces remained, and in 1864, Napoleon III installed Archduke Maximilian of Austria, his handpicked choice, as the new emperor of Mexico. When the French troops were needed in Europe, however, Maximilian became an emperor without an army. He surrendered to Mexican forces in May 1867 and was executed in June. His execution was a blow to the prestige of the French emperor.

Foreign Policy: The Crimean War

Napoleon III's participation in the Crimean War (1854–1856) had been more rewarding. As heir to the Napoleonic empire, Napoleon III was motivated by the desire to free France from the restrictions of the

OPPOSING VIEWPOINTS

The Practice of *Realpolitik*: Two Approaches

During the mid-nineteenth century, a new generation of conservative leaders emerged who were proud of being practitioners of *Realpolitik*, the "politics of reality." Two of the most prominent were Louis Napoleon of France and Otto von Bismarck of Prussia. The first selection is taken from Louis Napoleon's proclamation to the French people in 1851, asking them to approve his actions after his coup d'état on December 1, 1851. The second and third selections are excerpts from Bismarck's famous "iron and blood" speech to a committee of the Prussian Reichstag and his 1888 speech to the German Reichstag on Germany's need for military preparation.

Louis Napoleon, Proclamation to the People, 1851

Frenchmen! The present situation cannot last much longer. Each passing day increases the danger to the country. The [National] Assembly, which ought to be the firmest supporter of order, has become a center of conspiracies.... It attacks the authority that I hold directly from the people; it encourages all evil passions; it jeopardizes the peace of France: I have dissolved it and I make the whole people judge between it and me....

I therefore make a loyal appeal to the whole nation, and I say to you: If you wish to continue this state of uneasiness which degrades us and makes our future uncertain, choose another in my place, for I no longer wish an authority which is powerless to do good, makes me responsible for acts I cannot prevent, and chains me to the helm when I see the vessel speeding toward the abyss....

Persuaded that the instability of authority and the preponderance of a single Assembly are permanent causes of trouble and discord, I submit to you the following fundamental bases of a constitution which the Assemblies will develop later.

1. A responsible chief elected for ten years.
2. Ministers dependent upon the executive power alone.

3. A Council of State composed of the most distinguished men to prepare the laws and discuss them before the legislative body.
4. A legislative body to discuss and vote the laws, elected by universal [male] suffrage....

This system, created by the First Consul [Napoleon I] at the beginning of the century, has already given France calm and prosperity; it will guarantee them to her again.

Such is my profound conviction. If you share it, declare that fact by your votes. If, on the contrary, you prefer a government without force, monarchical or republican, borrowed from I know not what past or from which chimerical future, reply in the negative....

If I do not obtain a majority of your votes, I shall then convoke a new assembly, and I shall resign to it the mandate that I received from you. But if you believe that the cause of which my name is the symbol, that is, France regenerated by the revolution of 1789 and organized by the Emperor, is forever yours, proclaim it by sanctioning the powers that I ask from you. Then France and Europe will be saved from anarchy, obstacles will be removed, rivalries will disappear, for all will respect the decree of Providence in the decision of the people.

Bismarck, Speech to the Prussian Reichstag, 1862

It is true that we can hardly escape complications in Germany, although we do not seek them. Germany does not look to Prussia's liberalism, but to her power. The south German States—Bavaria, Württemberg, and Baden—would like to indulge in liberalism, and because of that no one will assign Prussia's role to them! Prussia must collect her forces and hold them in reserve for an opportune moment, which has already come and gone several times. Since the Treaty of Vienna, our frontiers have not been favorably designed for a healthy body politic. Not by speeches and majorities will the great questions of the day be decided— that was the mistake of 1848 and 1849—but by iron and blood.

(continued)

(Opposing Viewpoints continued)

Bismarck, Speech to the German Reichstag, 1888

When I say that it is our duty to endeavor to be ready at all times and for all emergencies, I imply that we must make greater exertions than other people for the same purpose, because of our geographical position. We are situated in the heart of Europe, and have at least three fronts open to an attack. France has only her eastern, and Russia only her western frontier where they may be attacked. We are also more exposed to the dangers of a coalition than any other nation, as is proved by the whole development of history, by our geographical position, and the lesser degree of cohesiveness, which until now has characterized the German nation in comparison with others. God has placed us where we are prevented, thanks to our neighbors, from growing lazy and dull. He has placed by our side the most warlike and restless of all nations, the French, and He has permitted warlike inclinations to grow strong in Russia, where formerly they existed to a lesser degree. Thus we are given the spur, so to speak, from both sides, and are compelled to exertions which we should perhaps not be making otherwise.

Q Why did Louis Napoleon's argument to the French people have such a strong popular appeal? What are the similarities in the practice of *Realpolitik* by these two leaders? What are the noticeable differences in their approaches? Are the similarities more important than the differences? Why or why not? What can you learn about *Realpolitik* from these three selections?

Sources: Louis Napoleon, Proclamation to the People, 1851. From *The Constitutions and Other Select Documents Illustrative of the History of France 1789–1907*, by Frank Maloy Anderson (Minneapolis: H. W. Wilson, 1904). Bismarck, Speech to the Prussian Reichstag, 1862. From Louis L. Snyder, *Documents of German History*, Rutgers University Press, 1958, p. 202. Bismarck, Speech to the German Reichstag, 1888. From Brian Tierney and Joan Scott, eds., *Western Societies: A Documentary History*, Vol. 2 (Alfred A. Knopf, 1984), p. 366.

peace settlements of 1814–1815 and to make France the chief arbiter of Europe. In the decline of the Ottoman Empire, he saw an opportunity to take steps toward these goals.

THE OTTOMAN EMPIRE The Crimean War was yet another attempt to answer the Eastern Question: Who would be the chief beneficiaries of the disintegration of the Ottoman Empire? In the seventeenth century, the Ottoman Empire had controlled southeastern Europe, but in 1699 it had lost Hungary, Transylvania, Croatia, and Slovenia to the expanding Austrian Empire. The Russian empire to its north also encroached on the Ottoman Empire by seizing the Crimea in 1783 and Bessarabia in 1812.

By the beginning of the nineteenth century, the Ottoman Empire had entered a fresh period of decline. A nationalist revolt had gained independence for Greece in 1830. Serbia claimed autonomy in 1827,

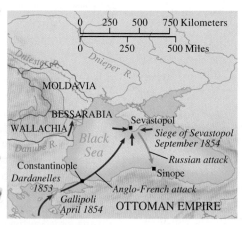

The Crimean War

which was recognized by the Ottoman Empire in 1830. The Russians had obtained a protectorate over the Danubian provinces of Moldavia and Wallachia in 1829.

WAR IN THE CRIMEA As Ottoman authority over the outlying territories in southeastern Europe waned, European governments began to take an active interest in the empire's apparent demise. Russia's proximity to the Ottoman Empire naturally gave it special opportunities to enlarge its sphere of influence. In 1853, the Russians demanded the right to protect Christian shrines in Palestine, a privilege that had already been extended to the French. When the Ottomans refused, the Russians invaded Ottoman Moldavia and Wallachia. Failure to resolve the dispute by negotiations led the Turks to declare war on Russia on October 4, 1853. Other European powers not only feared Russian ambitions but also had objectives of their own in the area. Austria craved more land in the Balkans, a desire that inevitably meant conflict with Russia, and France and Britain were interested in commercial opportunities and naval bases in the eastern Mediterranean. The following year, on March 28, Great Britain and France, fearful of Russian gains at the expense of the disintegrating Ottoman Empire, declared war on Russia.

The Crimean War was poorly planned and poorly fought. Britain and France decided to attack Russia's Crimean peninsula in the Black Sea. After a long siege and at a terrible cost in lives for all combatants, the main Russian fortress of Sevastopol fell in September 1855, and the Russians soon sued for peace. By the Treaty of Paris, signed in March 1856, Russia was forced to give up Bessarabia and accept the neutrality of the Black Sea. In addition, Moldavia and Wallachia were placed under the protection of all five Great Powers.

The Crimean War proved costly to both sides. More than 250,000 soldiers died in the war; 60 percent of the deaths were from disease (especially cholera). Even more would have died on the British side had it not been for the efforts of the nurse Florence Nightingale (1820–1910). Her insistence on strict sanitary conditions saved many lives and helped make nursing a profession of trained, middle-class women.

The Crimean War broke up long-standing European power relationships and effectively destroyed the Concert of Europe. Austria and Russia, the two chief powers maintaining the status quo in the first half of the nineteenth century, were now enemies because of Austria's unwillingness to support Russia in the war. Russia, defeated, humiliated, and weakened by the obvious failure of its armies, withdrew from European affairs for the next two decades to set its house in order. Great Britain, disillusioned by its role in the war, also pulled back from continental affairs. Austria, paying the price for its neutrality, was now without friends. Not until the 1870s were new combinations formed, and in the meantime, the European international situation remained fluid. Leaders who were willing to pursue the "politics of reality" found themselves in a situation rife with opportunity. It was this new international situation that made possible the unification of Italy and Germany.

Florence Nightingale. Florence Nightingale is shown caring for wounded soldiers in the military hospital at Scutari in Turkey. After a British journalist, W. H. Russell, published a scathing denunciation of the quality of medical care provided to wounded British soldiers, the British government allowed Nightingale to take a group of nurses to the Crimean warfront. Through her efforts in the Crimean War, Nightingale established high standards for battlefield medical care and helped make nursing an admirable profession for middle-class women. At the right is a photograph of Nightingale. (Right: Private Collection/The Bridgeman Art Library)

National Unification: Italy and Germany

Q FOCUS QUESTION: What actions did Cavour and Bismarck take to bring about unification in Italy and Germany, respectively, and what role did war play in their efforts?

The breakdown of the Concert of Europe opened the way for the Italians and the Germans to establish national states, and their successful unification transformed the power structure of the European continent. Europe would be dealing with the consequences well into the twentieth century.

The Unification of Italy

In 1850, Austria was still the dominant power on the Italian peninsula. After the failure of the revolution of 1848–1849, a growing number of advocates for Italian unification focused on the northern Italian state of Piedmont as their best hope to achieve their goal. The royal house of Savoy ruled the kingdom of Piedmont, which also included the island of Sardinia (see Map 22.1). The little state seemed unlikely to supply the needed leadership to unify Italy, however, until King Victor Emmanuel II (1849–1878) selected Count Camillo di Cavour (kuh-MEEL-oh dee kuh-VOOR) (1810–1861) as his prime minister in 1852.

THE LEADERSHIP OF CAVOUR Cavour was a liberal-minded nobleman who had made a fortune in agriculture. A moderate who favored constitutional government, he was a consummate politician with the ability to persuade others of the rightness of his own convictions. As prime minister, he pursued a policy of economic expansion that increased government revenues and enabled him to pour money into equipping a large army. Cavour, however, had no illusions about Piedmont's military strength and was well aware that he could not challenge Austria directly. Consequently, in

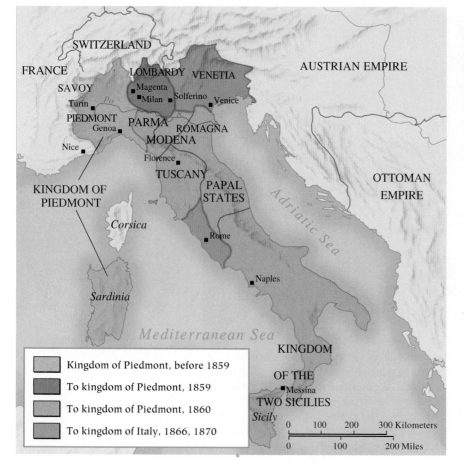

MAP 22.1 The Unification of Italy. Piedmont, under the able guidance of Count Camillo di Cavour, provided the nucleus for Italian unification. Alliances with France and Prussia, combined with the military actions of republican nationalists like Giuseppe Garibaldi, led to complete unification in 1870.

Q Considering geographic location and size of population, which of the countries shown on this map would likely have posed the greatest military threat to the new Italian state?

1858 he made an alliance with the French emperor Napoleon III and then provoked the Austrians into invading Piedmont in 1859. In the initial stages of fighting, it was the French who were largely responsible for defeating the Austrians in two major battles. A peace settlement gave the French Nice and Savoy and awarded Lombardy to Piedmont. More important, however, Cavour's success caused nationalists in the northern Italian states of Parma, Modena, and Tuscany to overthrow their governments and join their states to Piedmont after holding plebiscites in 1860.

THE EFFORTS OF GARIBALDI Meanwhile, in southern Italy, a new leader of Italian unification had come to the fore. Giuseppe Garibaldi (joo-ZEP-pay gar-uh-BAHL-dee) (1807–1882), a dedicated Italian patriot, raised an army of a thousand Red Shirts, as his volunteers were called because of their distinctive dress, and landed in Sicily, where a revolt had broken out against the Bourbon king of the Two Sicilies. By the end of July 1860, most of Sicily had been pacified under Garibaldi's control. In August, Garibaldi and his forces crossed over to the mainland and began a victorious march up the Italian peninsula. Naples and the Two Sicilies fell in early September. Ever the patriot, Garibaldi chose to turn over his conquests to Cavour's Piedmontese forces. On March 17, 1861, the new kingdom of Italy was proclaimed under a centralized government subordinated to the control of Piedmont and King Victor Emmanuel II of the house of Savoy. Worn out by his efforts, Cavour died three months later.

Despite the proclamation of the new kingdom, unification was not yet complete because Venetia in the north was still held by Austria and Rome remained under papal control, supported by French troops. To attack either one meant war with a major European state, which the Italian army was not prepared to handle. It was the Prussian army that indirectly completed the task of Italian unification. In the Austro-Prussian War of 1866, the new Italian state became an ally of Prussia. Although the Austrians defeated the Italian army, Prussia's victory left the Italians with Venetia. In 1870, the Franco-Prussian War resulted in the withdrawal of French troops from Rome. The Italian army then annexed the city on September 20, 1870, and Rome became the new capital of the united Italian state.

The Unification of Germany

After the failure of the Frankfurt Assembly to achieve German unification in 1848–1849, German nationalists

CHRONOLOGY The Unification of Italy	
Victor Emmanuel II	1849–1878
Count Cavour as prime minister of Piedmont	1852
Austrian War	1859
Plebiscites in the northern Italian states	1860
Garibaldi's invasion of the Two Sicilies	1860
Kingdom of Italy is proclaimed	1861
Italy's annexation of Venetia	1866
Italy's annexation of Rome	1870

focused on Austria and Prussia as the only two states powerful enough to unify Germany. But Austria, a large multinational empire, feared the creation of a strong German state in central Europe, and more and more Germans began to look to Prussia for leadership in the cause of German unification.

BISMARCK In the 1860s, King William I (1861–1888) attempted to enlarge and strengthen the Prussian army. When the Prussian legislature refused to levy new taxes for the proposed military changes in March 1862, William appointed a new prime minister, Count Otto von Bismarck (1815–1898). Bismarck ignored the legislative opposition to the military reforms, arguing that "Germany does not look to Prussia's liberalism but to her power. . . . Not by speeches and majorities will the great questions of the day be decided—that was the mistake of 1848–1849—but by iron and blood."[2] Bismarck collected the taxes and reorganized the army anyway. From 1862 to 1866, Bismarck governed Prussia by simply ignoring parliament. Unwilling to revolt, parliament did nothing. In the meantime, opposition to his domestic policy set Bismarck on an active foreign policy, which led to war and German unification.

Because Bismarck succeeded in guiding Prussia's unification of Germany, it is often assumed that he had determined on a course of action that led precisely to that goal. That is hardly the case. Bismarck was a consummate politician and opportunist. He was not a political gambler but rather a moderate who waged war only when all other diplomatic alternatives had been exhausted and when he was reasonably sure that all the military and diplomatic advantages were on his side. Bismarck has often been portrayed as the ultimate realist, the foremost nineteenth-century practitioner of *Realpolitik*. He was also quite open about his strong dislike of anyone who opposed him. He said one morning to his wife, "I could not sleep the whole night; I hated throughout the whole night."

THE DANISH WAR (1864) Bismarck's first war was against Denmark, fought over the duchies of Schleswig (SHLESS-vik) and Holstein (HOHL-shtyn). Bismarck persuaded the Austrians to join Prussia in declaring war on Denmark on February 1, 1864. The Danes were quickly defeated and surrendered Schleswig and Holstein to the victors (see Map 22.2). Austria and Prussia then agreed to divide the administration of the two duchies; Prussia took Schleswig while Austria administered Holstein. But Bismarck used the joint administration of the two duchies to create friction with the Austrians and goad them into a war on June 14, 1866.

THE AUSTRO-PRUSSIAN WAR (1866) Many Europeans expected a quick Austrian victory, but they overlooked the effectiveness of the Prussian military reforms of the 1860s. The Prussian breech-loading needle gun had a much faster rate of fire than the Austrian muzzle-loader, and a superior network of railroads enabled the Prussians to mass troops quickly. At Königgrätz

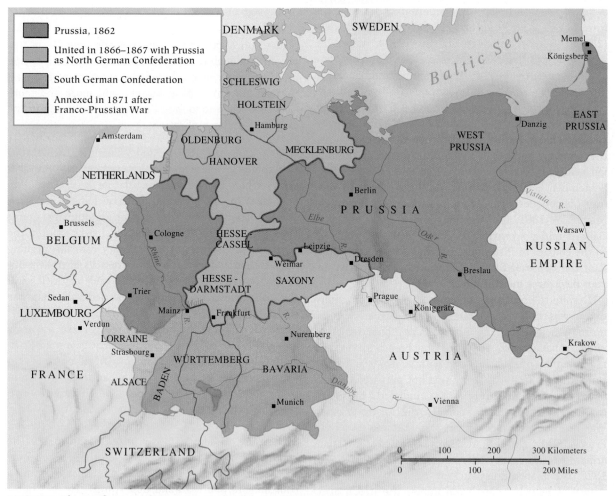

MAP 22.2 **The Unification of Germany.** Count Otto von Bismarck, the Prussian prime minister, skillfully combined domestic policies with wars with Denmark, Austria, and France to achieve the creation of the German Empire in 1871.

Q In terms of increasing Prussia's military power and ability to rule all parts of its lands, which was more important: the formation of the North German Confederation or the absorption of the South German Confederation?

(kurnig-GRETS) (Sadowa) on July 3, the Austrian army was defeated. Austria was now excluded from German affairs, and the German states north of the Main River were organized into the North German Confederation, controlled by Prussia. The southern German states, largely Catholic in contrast to the Protestant north, remained independent but were coerced into signing military agreements with Prussia.

THE FRANCO-PRUSSIAN WAR (1870–1871)   Bismarck and William I had achieved a major goal by 1866. Prussia now dominated all of northern Germany, and Austria had been excluded from any significant role in German affairs. Nevertheless, unsettled business led to new international complications and further change. Bismarck realized that France would never be content with a strong German state to its east because of the potential threat to French security. At the same time, after a series of setbacks, Napoleon III, the French ruler, needed a diplomatic triumph to offset his serious domestic problems. The French were not happy with the turn of events in Germany and looked for opportunities to humiliate the Prussians.

In 1870, Prussia and France became embroiled in a dispute over the candidacy of a Hohenzollern relative of the Prussian king for the throne of Spain. Bismarck manipulated the misunderstandings between the French and Prussians to goad the French into declaring war on Prussia on July 15, 1870. The French proved no match for the better-led and better-organized Prussian forces. The southern German states honored their military alliances with Prussia and joined the war effort against the French. The Prussian armies advanced into France, and at Sedan, on September 2, 1870, an entire French army and Napoleon III himself were captured. After four months of bitter resistance, Paris finally capitulated on January 28, 1871, and an official peace treaty was signed in May. France had to pay an indemnity of 5 billion francs (about $1 billion) and give up the provinces of Alsace and Lorraine to the new German state, a loss that angered the French and left them burning for revenge.

Even before the war had ended, the southern German states had agreed to enter the North German Confederation. On January 18, 1871, in the Hall of Mirrors in Louis XIV's palace at Versailles, William I, with Bismarck standing at the foot of the throne, was proclaimed kaiser or emperor of the Second German Empire (the first was the medieval Holy Roman Empire). German unity had been achieved by the Prussian monarchy and the Prussian army. In a real sense,

CHRONOLOGY   The Unification of Germany

King William I of Prussia	1861–1888
Bismarck as minister-president of Prussia	1862
Danish War	1864
Austro-Prussian War	1866
Battle of Königgrätz	1866 (July 3)
Franco-Prussian War	1870–1871
Battle of Sedan	1870 (September 2)
Fall of Paris	1871 (January 28)
German Empire proclaimed	1871 (January 18)

Germany had been merged into Prussia, not Prussia into Germany. German liberals also rejoiced. They had dreamed of unity and freedom, but the achievement of unity now seemed much more important. One old liberal proclaimed:

> I cannot shake off the impression of this hour. I am no devotee of Mars; I feel more attached to the goddess of beauty and the mother of graces than to the powerful god of war, but the trophies of war exercise a magic charm even upon the child of peace. One's view is involuntarily chained and one's spirit goes along with the boundless row of men who acclaim the god of the moment—success.[3]

The Prussian leadership of German unification meant the triumph of authoritarian, militaristic values over liberal, constitutional sentiments in the development of the new German state. With its industrial resources and military might, the new state had become the strongest power on the continent. A new European balance of power was at hand.

Nation Building and Reform: The National State in Midcentury

Q FOCUS QUESTION: What efforts for reform occurred in the Austrian Empire, Russia, and Great Britain between 1850 and 1870, and how successful were they in alleviating each nation's problems?

While European affairs were dominated by the unification of Italy and Germany, other states in the Western world were also undergoing transformations (see Map 22.3). War, civil war, and changing political alignments served as catalysts for domestic reforms.

MAP 22.3 Europe in 1871. By 1871, most of the small states of Europe had been absorbed into larger ones, leaving the major powers uncomfortably rubbing shoulders with one another. Meanwhile, the power equation was shifting: the German Empire increased in power while Austria-Hungary and the Ottoman Empire declined.

Q Of the Great Powers, which had the greatest overall exposure to the others in terms of shared borders and access to the sea?

The Austrian Empire: Toward a Dual Monarchy

After crushing the revolutions of 1848–1849, the Habsburgs restored centralized, autocratic government to their empire. But failure in war led to severe internal consequences for Austria. Defeat at the hands of the Prussians in 1866 forced the Austrians to deal with the fiercely nationalistic Hungarians. The result was

the negotiated *Ausgleich* (OWSS-glykh), or Compromise, of 1867, which created the Dual Monarchy of Austria-Hungary. Each part of the empire now had its own constitution, its own bicameral legislature, its own governmental machinery for domestic affairs, and its own capital (Vienna for Austria and Buda, which soon merged with the city of Pest to become Budapest, for Hungary). Holding the two states together were a single monarch (Francis Joseph was emperor of Austria and king of Hungary) and a common army, foreign policy, and system of finances. In domestic affairs, the Hungarians had become an independent nation. But the Ausgleich did not satisfy the other nationalities that made up the multinational Austro-Hungarian Empire (see Map 22.4). The Dual Monarchy simply enabled the German-speaking Austrians and Hungarian Magyars to dominate the minorities, especially the Slavic peoples (Poles, Croats, Czechs, Serbs, Slovaks, Slovenes, and Little Russians) in their respective states. As the Hungarian nationalist Louis Kossuth remarked, "Dualism is the alliance of the conservative, reactionary and any apparently liberal elements in Hungary with those of the Austrian Germans who despise liberty, for the oppression of the other nationalities and races."[4]

Imperial Russia

Russia's defeat in the Crimean War at the hands of the British and French revealed the blatant deficiencies behind the facade of absolute power and made it clear even to staunch conservatives that Russia was falling hopelessly behind the western European powers. Tsar Alexander II (1855–1881) turned his energies to a serious overhaul of the Russian system.

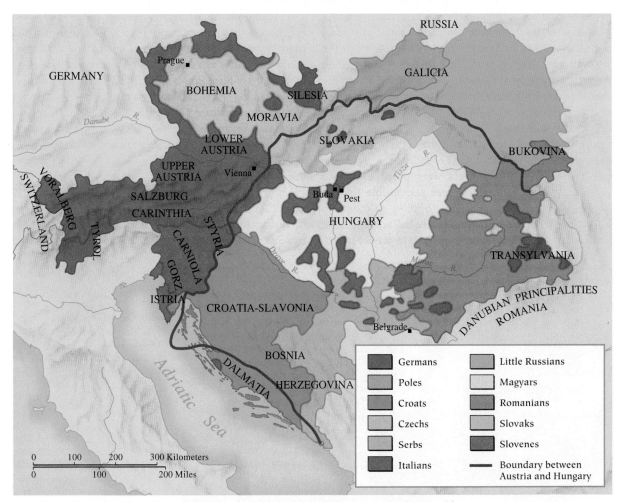

MAP 22.4 Ethnic Groups in the Dual Monarchy, 1867. Nationalism continued to be a problem in the Austrian Empire after the suppression of the 1848–1849 revolutions. Military defeats led Emperor Francis Joseph to create the Dual Monarchy, giving Hungary power over its domestic affairs. The demands of other ethnic minorities went largely unmet, however.

Q Which ethnic group was most widely dispersed throughout the Dual Monarchy?

Serfdom was the most burdensome problem in tsarist Russia. The continuing subjugation of millions of peasants to the land and their landlords was an obviously corrupt and failing system. On March 3, 1861, Alexander issued his emancipation edict (see the box on p. 537). Peasants could now own property, marry as they chose, and bring suits in the law courts. Nevertheless, the benefits of emancipation were limited. The government provided land for the peasants by purchasing it from the landlords, but the landowners often chose to keep the best parcels. The Russian peasants soon found that they had inadequate amounts of good arable land to support themselves, a situation that worsened as the peasant population increased rapidly in the second half of the nineteenth century.

Nor were the peasants completely free. The state compensated the landowners for the land given to the peasants, but the peasants, in turn, were expected to repay the state in long-term installments. To ensure that the payments were made, peasants were subjected to the authority of their *mir*, or village commune, which was collectively responsible for the land payments to the government. In a very real sense, then, the village commune, not the individual peasants, owned the land the peasants were purchasing. And since the village communes were responsible for the payments, they were reluctant to allow peasants to leave their land. Emancipation, then, led not to a free, landowning peasantry along the Western model but to

an unhappy, land-starved peasantry that largely followed the old ways of farming.

Alexander II also attempted other reforms. In 1864, he instituted a system of **zemstvos** (ZEMPST-vohz), or local assemblies, that provided a moderate degree of self-government. Zemstvos were given limited power to provide public services, such as education, famine relief, and road and bridge maintenance. They could levy taxes for these services, but their efforts were frequently disrupted by bureaucrats who feared any hint of self-government. The legal reforms of 1864, which created a regular system of local and provincial courts and a judicial code that accepted the principle of equality before the law, proved successful, however.

Even the autocratic tsar was unable to control the forces he unleashed by his reform program. Reformers wanted more and rapid change; conservatives opposed what they perceived as the tsar's attempts to undermine the basic institutions of Russian society. By 1870, Russia was witnessing increasing levels of dissatisfaction. When one group of radicals assassinated Alexander II in 1881, his son and successor, Alexander III (1881–1894), turned against reform and returned to the traditional methods of repression.

Great Britain: The Victorian Age

Like Russia, Britain was not troubled by revolutionary disturbances during 1848, although for quite different reasons. The Reform Act of 1832 had opened the door

Emancipation of the Serfs. On March 3, 1861, Tsar Alexander II issued an edict emancipating the Russian serfs. This watercolor by Alexei Kivshenko shows the tsar proclaiming the emancipation.

State Central Navy Museum, St. Petersburg, Russia/© culture-images/Lebrecht

Emancipation: Serfs and Slaves

Although overall their histories have been quite different, Russia and the United States shared a common feature in the 1860s. They were the only states in the Western world that still had large enslaved populations (the Russian serfs were virtually slaves). The leaders of both countries issued emancipation proclamations within two years of each other. The first excerpt is taken from Tsar Alexander II's Imperial Decree of March 3, 1861, which freed the Russian serfs. The second excerpt is from Abraham Lincoln's Emancipation Proclamation, issued on January 1, 1863.

Tsar Alexander II, Imperial Decree, March 3, 1861

By the grace of God, we, Alexander II, Emperor and Autocrat of all the Russias, King of Poland, Grand Duke of Finland, etc., to all our faithful subjects, make known:

Called by Divine Providence and by the sacred right of inheritance to the throne of our ancestors, we took a vow in our innermost heart to respond to the mission which is intrusted to us as to surround with our affection and our Imperial solicitude all our faithful subjects of every rank and of every condition, from the warrior, who nobly bears arms for the defense of the country to the humble artisan devoted to the works of industry; from the official in the career of the high offices of the State to the laborer whose plow furrows the soil....

We thus came to the conviction that the work of a serious improvement of the condition of the peasants was a sacred inheritance bequeathed to us by our ancestors, a mission which, in the course of events, Divine providence called upon us to fulfill....

In virtue of the new dispositions above mentioned, the peasants attached to the soil will be invested within a term fixed by the law with all the rights of free cultivators....

At the same time, they are granted the right of purchasing their close, and, with the consent of the proprietors, they may acquire in full property the arable lands and other appurtenances which are allotted to them as a permanent holding. By the acquisition in full property of the quantity of land fixed, the peasants are free from their obligations toward the proprietors for land thus purchased, and they enter definitely into the condition of free peasants-landholders.

President Abraham Lincoln, Emancipation Proclamation, January 1, 1863

Now therefore, I, Abraham Lincoln, President of the United States, by virtue of the power in me vested as Commander-in-Chief of the Army and Navy of the United States in time of actual armed rebellion against the authority and government of the United States, and as a fit and necessary war measure for suppressing such rebellion, do, on this 1st day of January, A.D. 1863, and in accordance with my purpose to do so, ... order and designate as the States and parts of States wherein the people thereof, respectively, are this day in rebellion against the United States the following, to wit:

Arkansas, Texas, Louisiana, ... Mississippi, Alabama, Florida, Georgia, South Carolina, North Carolina, and Virginia....

And by virtue of the power for the purpose aforesaid, I do order and declare that all persons held as slaves within said designated States and parts of States are, and henceforward shall be free; and that the Executive Government of the United States, including the military and naval authorities thereof, will recognize and maintain the freedom of said persons.

Q What changes did Tsar Alexander's emancipation of the serfs initiate in Russia? What effect did Lincoln's Emancipation Proclamation have on the southern "armed rebellion"? What reason did each leader give for his actions? Were their actions equally effective?

Sources: Tsar Alexander II, Imperial Decree, March 3, 1861. From *Annual Register* (New York: Longmans, Green, 1861), p. 207. President Abraham Lincoln, Emancipation Proclamation, January 1, 1863. From *U.S. Statutes at Large* (Washington, D.C., Government Printing Office, 1875), vol. 12, pp. 1268–69.

to political representation for the industrial middle class, ushering in a period of general contentment and stability, and in the 1860s, Britain's liberal parliamentary system demonstrated once again its ability to make both social and political reforms that kept the country stable and prosperous.

One of the reasons for Britain's stability was its continuing economic growth. After 1850, middle-class prosperity was at last coupled with some improvements for the working classes. Real wages for laborers increased more than 25 percent between 1850 and 1870. The British feeling of national pride was well reflected in Queen Victoria, whose reign from 1837 to 1901 was the longest in English history. Victoria had nine children and, when she died at age eighty-one, thirty-seven great-grandchildren. Her sense of duty and moral respectability reflected the attitudes of her age, which has ever since been known as the Victorian Age (see the Film & History feature on p. 539).

Politically, this was an era of somewhat uneasy stability as the aristocratic and upper-middle-class representatives who dominated Parliament blurred party lines by their internal strife and shifting positions. One important issue was the extension of voting rights. The Tory (Conservative Party) leader in Parliament, Benjamin Disraeli (diz-RAY-lee) (1804–1881), became a supporter of voting reform, primarily because he thought he could win over the newly enfranchised groups to his party. The Reform Act of 1867 was an important step toward the democratization of Britain. By lowering the monetary requirements for voting (taxes paid or income earned), it enfranchised many male urban workers. The number of voters increased from about 1 million to slightly over 2 million (see Table 22.1). Although Disraeli believed that this would benefit the Conservatives, industrial workers helped produce a huge Liberal victory in 1868.

The United States: Slavery and War

By the mid-nineteenth century, the issue of slavery increasingly threatened American national unity. Both North and South had grown dramatically in population during the first half of the nineteenth century, but their development was quite different. The cotton economy and social structure of the South were based on the exploitation of enslaved black Africans and their descendants. The importance of cotton is evident from production figures. In 1810, the South produced a raw cotton crop of 178,000 bales worth $10 million. By

TABLE 22.1   Expansion of the British Electorate

YEAR	NUMBER OF VOTERS	PERCENTAGE OF TOTAL POPULATION
1831 (Reform Act of 1832)	516,000	2.1
1833	812,000	3.4
1866 (Reform Act of 1867)	1,364,000	4.7
1868	2,418,000	8.4
1883 (Reform Act of 1884)	3,152,000	9.0
1885	5,669,000	16.3

SOURCE: Chris Cook and Brendan Keith, *British Historical Facts*, 1830–1900 (London, 1975), pp. 115, 232–233.

1860, it was generating 4.5 million bales of cotton with a value of $249 million. Fully 93 percent of southern cotton in 1850 was produced by a slave population that had grown dramatically in fifty years. Although new slave imports had been barred in 1808, there were 4 million Afro-American slaves in the South by 1860—four times the number in 1800. The cotton economy and plantation-based slavery were intimately related, and the attempt to maintain them in the first half of the nineteenth century led the South to become increasingly defensive, monolithic, and isolated. At the same time, the growth of an abolitionist movement in the North challenged the southern order and created an "emotional chain reaction" that led to civil war.

As polarization over the issue of slavery intensified, compromise became less feasible. When Abraham Lincoln, the man who had said in a speech in Illinois in 1858 that "this government cannot endure permanently half slave and half free," was elected president in November 1860, the die was cast. Lincoln carried only 2 of the 1,109 counties in the South; the Republicans were not even on the ballot in ten southern states. On December 20, 1860, a South Carolina convention voted to repeal the state's ratification of the U.S. Constitution. In February 1861, six more southern states did the same, and a rival nation—the Confederate States of America—was formed. In March, fighting erupted between North and South.

THE CIVIL WAR The American Civil War (1861–1865) was an extraordinarily bloody struggle. More than 600,000 soldiers died, either in battle or from deadly infectious diseases spawned by filthy camp conditions. Over a period of four years, the Union states of the North mobilized their superior assets and gradually

FILM & HISTORY

The Young Victoria (2009)

DIRECTED BY JEAN-MARC VALLÉE, *The Young Victoria* is an imaginative and yet relatively realistic portrayal of the early struggles of the young woman who became Britain's longest-reigning monarch. The film begins in 1836 when the seventeen-year-old Victoria (Emily Blunt) is the heir to the throne. Her controlling mother, the duchess of Kent (Miranda Richardson), schemes to prevent her daughter from ascending the throne by trying to create a regency for herself and her close adviser and paramour, Sir John Conroy (Mark Strong). Conroy is accurately shown trying to force the young Victoria to sign a paper establishing a regency. The mother and Conroy fail, and Victoria succeeds to the throne after the death of her uncle, King William IV (Jim Broadbent), on June 20, 1837, about one month after Victoria turns eighteen. The movie also shows the impact that Lord Melbourne (Paul Bettany), the prime minister, had on the young queen as her private secretary and adviser. Indeed, Victoria's attachment to Melbourne led to considerable discontent among her subjects. Central to the film, however, is the romantic portrayal of the wooing of Victoria by her young German cousin, Prince Albert of Saxe-Coburg-Gotha (Rupert Friend), the nephew of the king of Belgium. The film accurately conveys the close bond and the deep and abiding love that developed between Victoria and Albert.

The film is a visual treat, re-creating the life of young Victoria in a number of castle and cathedral settings. As a romantic dramatization of some of the main events before and after the coronation of Victoria, the film also contains some noticeable flaws. Victoria is shown painting with her right hand, although she was actually left-handed. The facts are also embellished at times in order to dramatize the story. Although there was an assassination attempt on the queen, Prince Albert was not shot while trying to protect her. Both shots fired by Edward Oxford, her would-be assassin, went wide of the mark. The character of Victoria's other uncle, King Leopold I of Belgium (Thomas Kretschmann), is also not quite accurate. He was not as selfish as he is portrayed in pushing Albert to marry Victoria. The banquet scene in which King William IV insults the duchess of Kent is quite accurate (it actually uses many of the exact words the king uttered), but its consequences are not. The duchess did not leave the room, and Victoria did not remain calm, but broke into tears. Finally, except for a passing reference to Victoria's concern for workers' housing conditions, this romantic movie makes no attempt to understand the political and social issues that troubled the British Empire of Victoria's time.

The coronation of Victoria (Emily Blunt) as the queen of England.

GK Films/The Kobal Collection at Art Resource, NY

wore down the Confederate forces of the South. As the war dragged on, it had the effect of radicalizing public opinion in the North. What began as a war to save the Union became a war against slavery. On January 1, 1863, Lincoln's Emancipation Proclamation made most of the nation's slaves "forever free" (see the box on p. 537). An increasingly effective Union blockade of the South combined with a shortage of fighting men made the Confederate cause desperate by the end of 1864. The final push of Union troops under General Ulysses

S. Grant forced General Robert E. Lee's Confederate army to surrender on April 9, 1865. Although problems lay ahead, the Union victory confirmed that the United States would be "one nation, indivisible."

The Emergence of a Canadian Nation

Nation building was also taking place to the north of the United States. By the Treaty of Paris in 1763, Canada—or New France, as it was called—passed into the hands of the British. By 1800, most Canadians favored more independence, although the colonists disagreed on the form this autonomy should take. Upper Canada (now Ontario) was predominantly English-speaking, whereas Lower Canada (now Quebec) was dominated by French Canadians. Increased immigration to Canada after 1815 also fueled the desire for self-government.

In 1837, a number of Canadian groups rose in rebellion against British authority. Rebels in Lower Canada demanded separation from Britain, creation of a republic, universal male suffrage, and freedom of the press. Although the rebellions were crushed by the following year, the British government now began to seek ways to satisfy some of the Canadian demands. The American Civil War proved to be a turning point. Fearful of U.S. designs on Canada during the war and eager to reduce the costs of maintaining the colonies, the British government finally capitulated to Canadian demands. In 1867, Parliament established the Canadian nation—the Dominion of Canada—with its own constitution. Canada now possessed a parliamentary system and ruled itself, although foreign affairs still remained under the control of the British government.

Industrialization and the Marxist Response

Q **Focus Question:** What were the main ideas of Karl Marx?

Between 1850 and 1871, continental industrialization came of age. The innovations of the British Industrial Revolution—mechanized factory production, the use of coal, the steam engine, and the transportation revolution—all became regular features of economic expansion. Although marred periodically by economic depression (1857–1858) or recession (1866–1867), this was an age of considerable economic prosperity, particularly evident in the growth of domestic and foreign markets.

CHRONOLOGY The National State

France	
Louis Napoleon's election as president	1848
Creation of the Second Empire	1852
Emperor Napoleon III	1852–1870
"Authoritarian empire"	1852–1860
Crimean War	1854–1856
"Liberal empire"	1860–1870
Austrian Empire	
Ausgleich: Dual Monarchy	1867
Russia	
Tsar Alexander II	1855–1881
Emancipation edict	1861 (March 3)
Creation of zemstvos and legal reforms	1864
Great Britain	
Queen Victoria	1837–1901
Reform Act	1867
United States	
Election of Lincoln and secession of South Carolina	1860
Outbreak of Civil War	1861
Surrender of Lee	1865 (April 9)
Canada	
Formation of Dominion of Canada	1867

Before 1870, capitalist factory owners remained largely free to hire labor on their own terms based on market forces. Although workers formed trade unions in an effort to fight for improved working conditions and reasonable wages, the unions tended to represent only a small part of the industrial working class and proved largely ineffective. Real change for the industrial proletariat would come only with the development of socialist parties and socialist trade unions. These emerged after 1870, but the theory that made them possible had already been developed by midcentury in the work of Karl Marx.

Marx and Marxism

The beginnings of **Marxism** can be traced to the 1848 publication of *The Communist Manifesto*, a short treatise written by two Germans, Karl Marx (1818–1883)

Karl Marx. Karl Marx was a radical journalist who joined with Friedrich Engels to write *The Communist Manifesto*, which proclaimed the ideas of a revolutionary socialism. After the failure of the 1848 revolution in Germany, Marx fled to Britain, where he continued to write and became involved in the work of the first International Working Men's Association.

and Friedrich Engels (1820–1895). It became one of the most influential political treatises in world history.

Marx and Engels began their treatise with the statement that "the history of all hitherto existing society is the history of class struggles." Throughout history, oppressed and oppressor have "stood in constant opposition to one another." In an earlier struggle, the feudal classes of the Middle Ages were forced to accede to the emerging middle class or bourgeoisie. As the bourgeoisie took control in turn, its ideas became the dominant views of the era, and government became its instrument. Marx and Engels declared, "The executive of the modern State is but a committee for managing the common affairs of the whole bourgeoisie."[5] In other words, the government of the state reflected and defended the interests of the industrial middle class and its allies.

Although bourgeois society had emerged victorious out of the ruins of feudal society, Marx and Engels insisted that it had not triumphed completely. Now once again the bourgeoisie were antagonists in an emerging class struggle, but this time they faced the **proletariat**, or the industrial working class. The struggle would be fierce, but eventually, so Marx and Engels predicted, the workers would overthrow their bourgeois masters. After their victory, the proletariat would form a dictatorship to reorganize the means of production. Then a classless society would emerge, and the state—itself an instrument of the bourgeoisie—would wither away since it no longer represented the interests of a particular class. Class struggles would be over (see the box on p. 542). Marx believed that the emergence of a classless society would lead to progress in science, technology, and industry and to greater wealth for all.

After the failure of the revolutions of 1848, Marx went to London, where he spent the rest of his life. He continued his writing on political economy, especially his famous work *Das Kapital* (Capital), of which he completed only one volume. In *The Communist Manifesto*, Marx had defined the communists as "the most advanced and resolute section of the working-class parties of every country." Their advantage was their ability to understand "the line of march, the conditions, and the ultimate general results of the proletarian movement."[6] Marx viewed his role in this light and participated enthusiastically in the activities of the International Working Men's Association. Formed in 1864 by British and French trade unionists, this "First International" served as an umbrella organization for working-class interests. Marx was the dominant personality on the International's General Council and devoted much time to its activities. But internal dissension within the ranks soon damaged the organization, and it failed in 1872. Although it would be revived in 1889, the fate of socialism by that time was in the hands of national socialist parties.

Science and Culture in an Age of Realism

Q FOCUS QUESTION: How did the belief that the world should be viewed realistically manifest itself in science, literature, and art in the second half of the nineteenth century?

Between 1850 and 1870, two major intellectual developments were evident: the growth of scientific knowledge,

The Classless Society

In *The Communist Manifesto*, Karl Marx and Friedrich Engels projected the creation of a classless society as the end product of the struggle between the bourgeoisie and the proletariat. In this selection, they discuss the steps by which that classless society would be reached.

———————

Karl Marx and Friedrich Engels, *The Communist Manifesto*

The first step in the revolution by the working class is to raise the proletariat to the position of ruling class.... The proletariat will use its political supremacy to wrest, by degrees, all capital from the bourgeoisie; to centralize all instruments of production in the hands of the State, i.e., of the proletariat organized as the ruling class; and to increase the total of productive forces as rapidly as possible.

Of course, in the beginning, this cannot be effected except by means of despotic inroads on the rights of property, and on the conditions of bourgeois production; by means of measures, therefore, which ... necessitate further inroads upon the old social order, and are unavoidable as a means of entirely revolutionizing the mode of production.

These measures will of course be different in different countries.

Nevertheless, in the most advanced countries, the following will be pretty generally applicable:

1. Abolition of property in land and application of all rents of land to public purposes.
2. A heavy progressive or graduated income tax.
3. Abolition of all right of inheritance....
5. Centralization of credit in the hands of the State, by means of a national bank with State capital and an exclusive monopoly.
6. Centralization of the means of communication and transport in the hands of the State.
7. Extension of factories and instruments of production owned by the State....
8. Equal liability of all to labor. Establishment of industrial armies, especially for agriculture.
9. Combination of agriculture with manufacturing industries; gradual abolition of the distinction between town and country, by a more equable distribution of the population over the country.
10. Free education for all children in public schools. Abolition of children's factory labor in its present form....

When, in the course of development, class distinctions have disappeared, and all production has been concentrated in the whole nation, the public power will lose its political character. Political power, properly so called, is merely the organized power of one class for oppressing another. If the proletariat during its contest with the bourgeoisie is compelled, by the force of circumstances, to organize itself as a class, if, by means of a revolution, it makes itself the ruling class, and, as such, sweeps away by force the old conditions of production, then it will, along with these conditions, have swept away the conditions for the existence of class antagonisms and of classes generally, and will thereby have abolished its own supremacy as a class.

In place of the old bourgeois society, with its classes and class antagonisms, we shall have an association, in which the free development of each is the condition for the free development of all.

———————

Q How did Marx and Engels define the proletariat? The bourgeoisie? Why did Marxists come to believe that this distinction was paramount for understanding history? What steps did Marx and Engels believe would lead to a classless society? Considering that Marx criticized early socialists as utopian and regarded his own socialism as scientific, does his socialism also seem utopian? If so, in what ways?

———————

Source: From *The Communist Manifesto* by Karl Marx and Frederick Engels, trans. Samuel Moore, 1888.

with its rapidly increasing impact on the Western world-view, and the shift from Romanticism, with its emphasis on the inner world of reality, to Realism, with its focus on the outer, material world.

A New Age of Science

By the mid-nineteenth century, science was having an ever-greater impact on European life. The Scientific Revolution of the sixteenth and seventeenth centuries had fundamentally transformed the Western worldview and fostered a modern, rational approach to the study of the natural world. Even in the eighteenth century, however, these intellectual developments had remained the preserve of an educated elite and resulted in few practical benefits. Moreover, the technical advances of the early Industrial Revolution had depended little on pure science and much more on the practical experiments of technologically oriented amateur inventors. Advances in industrial technology, however, fed an interest in basic scientific research, which from the 1830s on resulted in a rash of basic scientific discoveries that were soon transformed into technological improvements that affected all Europeans.

The development of the steam engine was important in encouraging scientists to work out its theoretical foundations, a preoccupation that led to the study of thermodynamics, the science of the relationship between heat and mechanical energy. The laws of thermodynamics were at the core of nineteenth-century physics. In biology, the Frenchman Louis Pasteur (LWEE pas-TOOR) (1822–1895) formulated the germ theory of disease, which had enormous practical applications in the development of modern scientific medical practices. The German physician Robert Koch (1843–1910) took the study of bacteriology even further with his work on bacteria and tuberculosis. In chemistry, in the 1860s the Russian Dmitri Mendeleyev (di-MEE-tree men-duh-LAY-ef) (1834–1907) classified all the material elements then known on the basis of their atomic weights and provided the systematic foundation for the periodic law. The Englishman Michael Faraday (1791–1867) discovered the phenomenon of electromagnetic induction and put together a primitive generator that laid the groundwork for the use of electricity, although economically efficient generators were not built until the 1870s.

The steadily increasing and often dramatic material gains generated by science and technology led to a growing faith in the benefits of science. The popularity of scientific and technological achievements produced a widespread acceptance of the scientific method, based on observation, experiment, and logical analysis, as the only path to objective truth and objective reality. This, in turn, undermined the faith of many people in religious revelation and truth. It is no accident that the nineteenth century was an age of increasing secularization, particularly evident in the growth of **materialism**, the belief that everything mental, spiritual, or ideal was simply a result of physical forces. Truth was to be found in the concrete material existence of human beings, not, as the Romantics imagined, in revelations gained by feeling or intuitive flashes. The importance of materialism was strikingly evident in the most important scientific event of the nineteenth century, the development of the theory of organic evolution according to natural selection. On the theories of Charles Darwin could be built a picture of humans as material beings that were simply part of the natural world.

Charles Darwin and the Theory of Organic Evolution

In 1859, Charles Darwin (1809–1882) published his celebrated book *On the Origin of Species by Means of Natural Selection*. The basic idea of this book was that all plants and animals had evolved over a long period of time from earlier and simpler forms of life, a principle known as **organic evolution**. Darwin was important in explaining how this natural process worked. In every species, he argued, "many more individuals of each species are born than can possibly survive." This results in a "struggle for existence." Darwin believed that "as more individuals are produced than can possibly survive, there must in every case be a struggle for existence, either one individual with another of the same species, or with the individuals of distinct species, or with the physical conditions of life." Those who succeeded in this struggle for existence had adapted better to their environment, a process made possible by the appearance of "variants." Chance variations that occurred in the process of inheritance enabled some organisms to be more adaptable to the environment than others, a process that Darwin called **natural selection**: "Owing to this struggle [for existence], variations, however slight ... if they be in any degree profitable to the individuals of a species, in their infinitely complex relations to other organic beings and to their physical conditions of life, will tend to the preservation of such individuals, and will generally be inherited by the offspring."[7] Those that were naturally selected for survival ("survival of the fit") survived. The unfit did not and became extinct. The fit who survived, in turn, propagated and passed on the variations that enabled them to survive until, from Darwin's point of view, a separate species emerged.

In *On the Origin of Species*, Darwin discussed plant and animal species only. He was not concerned with human beings and only later applied his theory of natural selection to humans. In *The Descent of Man*, published in 1871, he argued for the animal origins of human beings: "Man is the co-descendant with other mammals of a common progenitor." Humans were not an exception to the rule governing other species.

Darwin's ideas were controversial at first. Some people fretted that his theory made humans ordinary products of nature rather than unique beings. Others were disturbed by the implications of life as a struggle for survival, of "nature red in tooth and claw." Was there a place in the Darwinian world for moral values? For those who believed in a rational order in the world, Darwin's theory seemed to eliminate purpose and design from the universe. Gradually, however, scientists and other intellectuals accepted Darwin's theory. As Darwin's ideas became more generally accepted, some people even tried to apply them to society, yet another example of the increasing prestige of the scientific approach.

Realism in Literature

The belief that the world should be viewed realistically, frequently expressed after 1850, was closely related to the materialistic outlook. The term **Realism** was first employed in 1850 to describe a new style of painting and soon spread to literature.

The literary Realists of the mid-nineteenth century were distinguished by their deliberate rejection of Romanticism, the desire to deal with ordinary characters from actual life rather than Romantic heroes in unusual settings. They also sought to avoid flowery and sentimental language by using careful observation and accurate description, an approach that led them to eschew poetry in favor of prose, primarily in the form of the novel. Realists often combined their interest in everyday life with a searching examination of social questions.

The leading novelist of the 1850s and 1860s, the Frenchman Gustave Flaubert (goo-STAHV floh-BAYR) (1821–1880), perfected the Realist novel in his *Madame Bovary* (1857), a straightforward description of barren and sordid small-town life in France. Emma Bovary, a woman of some vitality, is trapped in a marriage to a drab provincial doctor (see the box on p. 545). Impelled by the images of romantic love she has read about in novels, she seeks the same thing for herself in adulterous affairs. Unfulfilled, she is ultimately driven to suicide, unrepentant to the end for her lifestyle. Flaubert's contempt for bourgeois society was evident in his portrayal of middle-class hypocrisy and smugness.

William Thackeray (1811–1863), who wrote Britain's prototypical Realist novel, *Vanity Fair: A Novel Without a Hero*, deliberately flouted Romantic conventions. A novel, Thackeray said, should "convey as strongly as possible the sentiment of reality as opposed to a tragedy or poem, which may be heroical." Perhaps the greatest of the Victorian novelists was Charles Dickens (1812–1870), whose realistic novels focusing on the lower and middle classes in Britain's early industrial age became extraordinarily popular. His descriptions of the urban poor and the brutalization of human life were vividly realistic.

Realism in Art

In art, Realism became dominant after 1850, although Romanticism was by no means dead. Among the most important characteristics of Realism are a desire to depict the everyday life of ordinary people, whether peasants, workers, or prostitutes; an attempt at photographic realism; and an interest in the natural environment. The French became leaders in Realist painting.

Gustave Courbet (goo-STAHV koor-BAY) (1819–1877) was the most famous artist of the Realist school. In fact, the term *Realism* was first applied to one of his paintings. Courbet reveled in a straightforward portrayal of everyday life. His subjects were factory workers, peasants, and the wives of saloon keepers. "I have never seen either angels or goddesses, so I am not interested in painting them," he exclaimed. One of his famous works, *The Stonebreakers*, painted in 1849, shows two men engaged in the exhausting work of breaking stones to build a road. This representation of human misery was a scandal to those who objected to his "cult of ugliness." To Courbet, no subject was too ordinary, too harsh, or too ugly to be of interest.

Jean-François Millet (ZHAHNH-frahnh-SWAH mi-YEH) (1814–1875) was preoccupied with scenes from

Flaubert and an Image of Bourgeois Marriage

In *Madame Bovary*, Gustave Flaubert portrays the tragic life of Emma Rouault, a farm girl whose hopes of escape from provincial life fail after she marries a doctor, Charles Bovary. After she grows disillusioned by her domestic life, Emma seeks refuge in extramarital affairs and extravagant shopping. In this excerpt, Emma expresses her restlessness and growing boredom with her new husband. Flaubert's detailed descriptions of everyday life make *Madame Bovary* one of the seminal works of Realism.

Gustave Flaubert, *Madame Bovary*

If Charles only suspected, if his gaze had even once penetrated her thought, it seemed to her that a sudden abundance would have broken away from her heart, as the fruit falls from a tree when you shake it. But as their life together brought increased physical intimacy, she built up an inner emotional detachment that separated her from him.

Charles's conversation was as flat as a sidewalk, with everyone's ideas walking through it in ordinary dress, arousing neither emotion, nor laughter, nor dreams. He had never been curious, he said, the whole time he was living in Rouen to go see a touring company of Paris actors at the theater. He couldn't swim, or fence, or shoot, and once he couldn't even explain to Emma a term about horseback riding she had come across in a novel.

But a man should know everything, shouldn't he? Excel in many activities, initiate you into the excitements of passion, into life's refinements, into all its mysteries? Yet this man taught nothing, knew nothing, hoped for nothing. He thought she was happy, and she was angry at him for this placid stolidity, for this leaden serenity, for the very happiness she gave to him.

Sometimes she would draw. Charles was always happy watching her lean over her drawing board, squinting in order to see her work better, or rolling little bread pellets between her fingers. As for the piano, the faster her fingers flew over it, the more he marveled. She struck the keys with aplomb and ran from one end of the keyboard to the other without a stop. . . .

On the other hand, Emma did know how to run the house. She sent patients statements of their visits in well-written letters that didn't look like bills. When some neighbor came to dine on Sundays, she managed to offer some tasty dish, would arrange handsome pyramids of greengages on vine leaves, serve fruit preserves on a dish, and even spoke of buying finger bowls for dessert. All this reflected favorably on Bovary.

Charles ended up thinking all the more highly of himself for possessing such a wife. In the living room he pointed with pride to her two small pencil sketches that he had mounted in very large frames and hung against the wallpaper on long green cords. People returning from Mass would see him at his door wearing handsome needlepoint slippers.

He would come home late, at ten o'clock, sometimes at midnight. Then he would want something to eat and Emma would serve him because the maid was asleep. He would remove his coat in order to eat more comfortably. He would report on all the people he had met one after the other, the villages he had been to, the prescriptions he had written, and, content with himself, would eat the remainder of the stew, peel his cheese, bite into an apple, empty the decanter, then go to sleep, lying on his back and snoring. . . .

And yet, in line with the theories she admired, she wanted to give herself up to love. In the moonlight of the garden she would recite all the passionate poetry she knew by heart and would sing melancholy adagios to him with sighs, but she found herself as calm afterward as before and Charles didn't appear more amorous or moved because of it.

After she had several times struck the flint on her heart without eliciting a single spark, incapable as she was of understanding that which she did not feel or of believing things that didn't manifest themselves in conventional forms, she convinced herself without difficulty that Charles's passion no longer offered anything extravagant. His effusions had become routine; he embraced her at certain hours. It was one habit among others, like the established custom of eating dessert after the monotony of dinner.

Q What does this passage reveal about bourgeois life in France during the mid-nineteenth century? What does this tell us about the roles of women during this time? How did Charles fail to live up to Emma's expectations of romantic love?

Source: Gustave Flaubert, *Madame Bovary*, trans. by Mildred Marmur (New York: Penguin Press), 39–43.

Gustave Courbet, *The Stonebreakers.* Realism, largely developed by French painters, aimed at a lifelike portrayal of the daily activities of ordinary people. Gustave Courbet was the most famous of the Realist artists. As is evident in *The Stonebreakers*, he sought to portray things as they really appear. He shows an old road builder and his young assistant in their tattered clothes, engrossed in their dreary work of breaking stones to construct a road. The use of browns and grays helps communicate the drudgery of their task.

Jean-François Millet, *The Gleaners.* Jean-François Millet, another prominent French Realist painter, took a special interest in the daily activities of French peasants, although he tended to transform his peasants into heroic figures who dominated their environment. In *The Gleaners*, for example, the three peasant women engaged in the backbreaking work of gathering grain left after the harvest still appear as powerful figures, symbolizing the union of humans with the earth.

rural life, especially peasants laboring in the fields, although his Realism still contained an element of Romantic sentimentality. In *The Gleaners*, Millet's most famous work, three peasant women gather grain in a field, a centuries-old practice that for Millet showed the symbiotic relationship between humans and nature. Millet made landscapes and country life important subjects for French artists, but he too was criticized by his contemporaries for crude subject matter and unorthodox technique.

Chapter Summary

Between 1850 and 1871, the national state became the focus of people's loyalty, and the nations of Europe spent their energies in achieving unification or reform. France attempted to relive its memories of Napoleonic greatness with the election of Louis Napoleon, Napoleon's nephew, as president and later Emperor Napoleon III. Louis Napoleon was one of a new generation of conservative political leaders who were practitioners of *Realpolitik*.

Unification to achieve a national state preoccupied leaders in Italy and Germany. The dreams of Mazzini became a reality when the combined activities of Count Cavour and Giuseppe Garibaldi finally led to the unification of Italy in 1870. Under the guidance of Otto von Bismarck, Prussia engaged in wars with Denmark, Austria, and France before it finally achieved the goal of national unification in 1871.

Reform characterized developments in other Western states. Austria compromised with Hungarian nationalists and created the Dual Monarchy of Austria-Hungary. Russia's defeat in the Crimean War led to reforms under Alexander II, which included the freeing of the Russian serfs. In Great Britain, the pressures of industrialization led to a series of reforms that made the realm of Queen Victoria more democratic. The American Civil War ended with the union of the states preserved and slavery abolished. Canada achieved dominion status from Britain, which included the right to rule itself in domestic affairs.

Political nationalism had emerged during the French revolutionary era and had become a powerful force of change during the first half of the nineteenth century, but its triumph came only after 1850. Associated initially with middle-class liberals, it would have great appeal to the broad masses as well by the end of the nineteenth century as people created their national "imagined communities." In 1871, however, the political transformations stimulated by the force of nationalism were by no means complete. Significantly large minorities, especially in the multiethnic empires controlled by the Austrians, Turks, and Russians, had not achieved the goal of their own national states. Moreover, the nationalism that had triumphed by 1871 was no longer the nationalism that had been closely identified with liberalism. Liberal nationalists had believed that unified nation-states would preserve individual rights and lead to a greater community of European peoples. Rather than unifying people, however, the new, loud, and chauvinistic nationalism of the late nineteenth century divided them as the new national states became embroiled in bitter competition after 1871.

The emergence of Marxian socialism, new advances in science, including the laws of thermodynamics and Darwin's theory of evolution, also characterized the period between 1850 and 1871. In the arts, Realism prevailed, evident in the writers and artists who were only too willing to portray realistically the grim world in which they lived.

CHAPTER TIMELINE

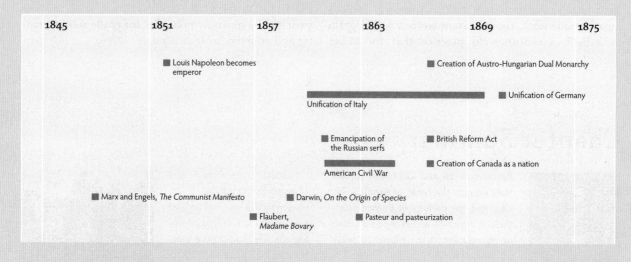

1845	1851	1857	1863	1869	1875

- Louis Napoleon becomes emperor
- Creation of Austro-Hungarian Dual Monarchy
- Unification of Italy
- Unification of Germany
- Emancipation of the Russian serfs
- British Reform Act
- American Civil War
- Creation of Canada as a nation
- Marx and Engels, *The Communist Manifesto*
- Darwin, *On the Origin of Species*
- Flaubert, *Madame Bovary*
- Pasteur and pasteurization

CHAPTER REVIEW

Upon Reflection

Q Despite the defeat of the revolutions of 1848, the forces of liberalism and nationalism triumphed after 1850. To what extent was this true in the Austrian Empire, Russia, and Great Britain between 1850 and 1871?

Q Despite Marx's claim for its scientific basis, why can Marxism be viewed primarily as a product of its age?

Q How did Realism differ from Romanticism, and how did Realism reflect the economic and social realities of Europe during the middle decades of the nineteenth century?

Key Terms

Realpolitik (p. 531)
Ausgleich (p. 534)
mir (p. 536)
zemstvos (p. 536)
Marxism (p. 540)

proletariat (p. 541)
materialism (p. 543)
organic evolution (p. 543)
natural selection (p. 543)
Realism (p. 544)

Suggestions for Further Reading

GENERAL WORKS   In addition to the general works on nineteenth-century Europe cited in Chapter 21, see two general surveys of the mid-century decades: **N. Rich, *The Age of Nationalism and Reform, 1850–1890,*** 2d ed. (New York, 1980), and **J. A. S. Grenville, *Europe Reshaped, 1848–1878,*** 2d ed. (London, 2000).

THE FRENCH SECOND EMPIRE   For a good introduction to the French Second Empire, see **A. Plessis, *The Rise and Fall of the Second Empire, 1852–1871,*** trans. **J. Mandelbaum** (New York, 1985). The Crimean War and its impact are examined in **C. Ponting, *The Crimean War*** (New York, 2004).

UNIFICATION OF ITALY AND GERMANY The unification of Italy can be examined in **B. Derek** and **E. F. Biagini,** *The Risorgimento and the Unification of Italy,* 2d ed. (London, 2002). The unification of Germany can be pursued in **W. Carr,** *The Origins of the Wars of German Unification* (New York, 1991). On Bismarck, see **E. Feuchtwanger,** *Bismarck* (London, 2002). On the Franco-Prussian War, see **G. Wawro,** *The Franco-Prussian War* (Cambridge, 2003).

THE NATIONAL STATE For a background discussion of the impact and character of nationalism, see **B. Anderson,** *Imagined Communities: Reflections on the Origins and Spread of Nationalism,* rev. ed. (New York, 2006). On the Austrian Empire, see **R. Okey,** *The Habsburg Monarchy* (New York, 2001). Imperial Russia is covered in **T. Chapman,** *Imperial Russia, 1801–1905* (London, 2001). On Victorian Britain, see **W. L. Arnstein,** *Queen Victoria* (New York, 2005). The definitive

one-volume history of the American Civil War is **J. M. McPherson,** *Battle Cry of Freedom: The Civil War Era,* in the Oxford History of the United States series (New York, 2003).

ECONOMIC DEVELOPMENTS AND THOUGHT See the general works on economic development listed in Chapters 20 and 21. On Marx, a standard work is **D. McLellan,** *Karl Marx: A Biography,* 4th ed. (New York, 2006). See also **F. Wheen,** *Karl Marx: A Life* (New York, 2001).

SCIENCE AND CULTURE For an introduction to the intellectual changes of the nineteenth century, see **O. Chadwick,** *The Secularization of the European Mind in the Nineteenth Century* (Cambridge, 1975). A detailed biography of Darwin can be found in **J. Bowlby,** *Charles Darwin: A Biography* (London, 1990). On Realism, **J. Malpas,** *Realism* (Cambridge, 1997), is a good introduction.

Notes

1. Quoted in J. F. McMillan, *Napoleon III* (New York, 1991), p. 37.
2. L. L. Snyder, ed., *Documents of German History* (New Brunswick, N.J., 1958), p. 202.
3. Quoted in O. Pflanze, *Bismarck and the Development of Germany: The Period of Unification, 1815–1871* (Princeton, N.J., 1963), p. 327.
4. Quoted in G. Szabad, *Hungarian Political Trends Between the Revolution and the Compromise, 1849–1867* (Budapest, 1977), p. 163.
5. K. Marx and F. Engels, *The Communist Manifesto* (Harmondsworth, England, 1967), pp. 79, 81, 82. Originally published in 1848.
6. Ibid., p. 95.
7. C. Darwin, *On the Origin of Species* (New York, 1872), vol. 1, pp. 77, 79.

MindTap **MindTap** is a fully online, highly personalized learning experience built upon Cengage Learning content. MindTap combines student learning tools—readings, multimedia, activities, and assessments—into a singular Learning Path that guides students through the course.

CHAPTER 23

Mass Society in an "Age of Progress," 1871–1894

Coney Island fun

The Museum of the City of New York/Art Resource, NY

CHAPTER OUTLINE AND FOCUS QUESTIONS

The Growth of Industrial Prosperity

Q What was the Second Industrial Revolution, and what effects did it have on European economic and social life? What roles did socialist parties and trade unions play in improving conditions for the working classes?

The Emergence of a Mass Society

Q What is a mass society, and what were its main characteristics? What role were women expected to play in society and family life in the latter part of the nineteenth century, and how closely did patterns of family life correspond to this ideal?

The National State

Q What general political trends were evident in the nations of western Europe in the last decades of the nineteenth century, and how did these trends differ from the policies pursued in Germany, Austria-Hungary, and Russia?

CRITICAL THINKING

Q What was the relationship among economic, social, and political developments between 1871 and 1894?

CONNECTIONS TO TODAY

Q In the late nineteenth century, new work opportunities for women emerged, but many middle-and upper-class women were still expected to remain in the home. What are the new opportunities and challenges for women today, and how do they compare with those in the nineteenth century?

IN THE LATE 1800s, Europe was enjoying a dynamic age of material prosperity. Bringing with it new industries, new sources of energy, and new goods, a Second Industrial Revolution transformed the environment, dazzled Europeans, and led them to believe that their material progress meant human progress. Scientific and technological achievements, many naively believed, would improve the human condition and solve all problems. The doctrine of progress became an article of faith.

The new urban and industrial world created by the rapid economic changes of the nineteenth century led to the emergence of a mass society by the late nineteenth century. Mass society meant improvements for the lower classes, who benefited from the extension of voting rights, a better standard of living, and education. It also brought mass leisure and mass consumption. New work patterns established the "weekend" as a distinct time of recreation and fun, and new forms of mass transportation—railroads and streetcars—enabled even ordinary workers to make brief excursions to beaches and amusement parks. Coney Island was only 8 miles from central New York City; Blackpool in England was a short train ride from nearby industrial towns. With their Ferris wheels and other daring rides that threw young men and women together, amusement parks offered a whole new world of entertainment. Thanks to the railroad, seaside resorts, once the preserve of the wealthy, became accessible to more people for weekend visits, much to the disgust of one upper-class regular who described the new "day-trippers": "They swarm upon the beach, wandering listlessly about with apparently no other aim than to get a mouthful of fresh air." Entrepreneurs in resort areas, however, welcomed the masses of new visitors and built piers laden with food, drink, and entertainment to serve them.

The coming of mass society also created new roles for the governments of Europe's nation-states. In the early nineteenth century, "nations" functioned as communities of people bound together by common language, traditions, customs, and institutions. By the mid-nineteenth century, however, the "state"—the organized institutions of government—had come to dominate European lives. By 1871, the national states promoted economic growth and mass education, amassed national armies by conscription, and took more responsibility for public health and housing in their cities. By taking these steps, the governments of the national states hoped to foster national unity and national loyalty.

Within many of these national states, the growth of the middle class had led to the triumph of liberal practices: constitutional governments, parliaments, and principles of equality. The period after 1871 also witnessed the growth of political democracy as the right to vote was extended to all adult males; women, though, would still have to fight for their political rights. With political democracy came a new mass politics and a new mass press. Both would become standard features of the twentieth century.

The Growth of Industrial Prosperity

Q FOCUS QUESTIONS: What was the Second Industrial Revolution, and what effects did it have on European economic and social life? What roles did socialist parties and trade unions play in improving conditions for the working classes?

At the heart of Europeans' belief in progress after 1871 was the stunning material growth produced by what historians have called the Second Industrial Revolution. The First Industrial Revolution had given rise to textiles, railroads, iron, and coal. In the second revolution, steel, chemicals, electricity, and petroleum led the way to new industrial frontiers.

New Products

The first major change in industrial development after 1870 was the substitution of steel for iron. New methods of rolling and shaping steel made it useful in the construction of lighter, smaller, and faster machines and engines, as well as railways, ships, and armaments. In 1860, Great Britain, France, Germany, and Belgium produced 125,000 tons of steel; by 1913, the total was 32 million tons. By 1910, German steel production was double that of Great Britain, and both had been surpassed by the United States in 1890.

Electricity was a major new form of energy that proved to be of great value because it could be easily converted into other forms of energy, such as heat, light, and motion, and moved relatively effortlessly through wires. In the 1870s, the first commercially practical generators of electrical current were developed. By 1910, hydroelectric power stations and coal-fired steam-generating plants enabled entire districts to be tied into a single power distribution system that provided a common source of power for homes, shops, and industrial enterprises.

Electricity spawned a whole new series of inventions. The invention of the lightbulb by the American Thomas Edison (1847–1931) and the Briton Joseph Swan (1828–1914) opened homes and cities to illumination by electric lights. A revolution in communications was fostered when the American inventor Alexander Graham Bell (1847–1922) invented the telephone in 1876 and the Italian physicist Guglielmo Marconi (goo-LYEL-moh mar-KOH-nee) (1874–1937) sent the first radio waves across the Atlantic in 1901.

Photo courtesy of private collection

An Age of Progress. Between 1871 and 1914, the Second Industrial Revolution led many Europeans to believe that they were living in an age of progress when most human problems would be solved by scientific achievements. This illustration is taken from a special issue of the *Illustrated London News* celebrating the Diamond Jubilee of Queen Victoria in 1897. On the left are scenes from 1837, when Victoria came to the British throne; on the right are scenes from 1897. The vivid contrast underscored the magazine's conclusion: "The most striking ... evidence of progress during the reign is the ever increasing speed which the discoveries of physical science have forced into everyday life. Steam and electricity have conquered time and space to a greater extent during the last sixty years than all the preceding six hundred years witnessed."

Although most electricity was initially used for lighting, it was eventually put to use in transportation. By the 1880s, electric streetcars and subways had appeared in major European cities. Electricity also transformed the factory. Conveyor belts, cranes, machines, and machine tools could all be powered by electricity and located anywhere. Thanks to electricity, all countries could now enter the industrial age.

The development of the internal combustion engine had a similar effect. The processing of oil and gasoline made possible the widespread use of the internal combustion engine as a source of power in transportation. An oil-fired engine was made in 1897, and by 1902, the Hamburg-Amerika Line had switched from coal to oil on its new ocean liners. By the end of the nineteenth century, some naval fleets had been converted to oil burners as well.

The development of the internal combustion engine gave rise to the automobile and the airplane. In 1900, world production stood at 9,000 cars; by 1906, Americans had overtaken the initial lead of the French. It was an American, Henry Ford, who revolutionized the auto industry with the mass production of the affordable Model T. By 1916, Ford's factories were producing 735,000 cars a year. In the meantime, air transportation began with the Zeppelin airship in 1900. In 1903, at Kitty Hawk, North Carolina, the Wright brothers, Orville and Wilbur, made the first flight in a fixed-wing plane powered by a gasoline engine. It took World War I to stimulate the aircraft industry, however, and regular passenger air service did not begin until 1919.

New Markets

The growth of industrial production depended on the development of markets for the sale of manufactured goods. After 1870, the best foreign markets were already heavily saturated, forcing Europeans to take a renewed look at their domestic markets. As Europeans were the richest consumers in the world, those markets offered abundant possibilities. Between 1850 and 1900, real wages increased by two-thirds in Britain and by one-third in Germany. As the prices of both food and manufactured goods declined due to lower transportation costs, Europeans could spend more on consumer products. Businesses soon perceived the value of using new techniques of mass marketing to sell the consumer goods made possible by the development of the steel and electrical industries. Bringing together a vast array of new products in one place, they created the department store (see the box on p. 554). The desire to own sewing machines, clocks, bicycles, electric lights, and typewriters created a new consumer ethic that rapidly became a crucial part of the modern economy (see "Mass Consumption" later in this chapter).

Meanwhile, increased competition for foreign markets and the growing importance of domestic demand led to a reaction against the free trade that had characterized much of the European economy between 1820 and 1870. To many industrial and political leaders, protective **tariffs** guaranteed domestic markets for the products of their own industries. By the 1870s, Europeans were returning to tariff protection. During this same period, **cartels** were being formed to decrease competition internally. In a cartel, independent enterprises worked together to control prices and fix production quotas, thereby restraining the kind of competition that led to reduced prices.

The formation of cartels was paralleled by a move toward ever-larger factories, especially in the iron and steel, machine, heavy electrical equipment, and chemical industries. This growth in the size of industrial plants led to pressure for greater efficiency in factory production at the same time that competition led to demands for greater economy. The result was a desire to streamline or rationalize production as much as possible. The development of precision tools enabled manufacturers to produce interchangeable parts, which in turn led to the creation of the assembly line for production. First used in the United States for small arms and clocks, the assembly line had moved to Europe by 1850. In the second half of the nineteenth century, it was primarily used in manufacturing nonmilitary goods, such as sewing machines, typewriters, bicycles, and eventually automobiles.

New Patterns in an Industrial Economy

The Second Industrial Revolution played a role in the emergence of basic economic patterns that have characterized much of modern European economic life.

Although the period after 1871 has been characterized as an age of material prosperity, recessions and crises were still very much a part of economic life. From 1873 to 1895, Europeans experienced a series of economic crises in which prices, especially those of agricultural products, fell dramatically. After 1895, however, until World War I, Europe overall experienced an economic boom and achieved a level of prosperity that encouraged people later to look back to that era as *la belle époque* (la BEL ay-PUK)—a golden age in European civilization.

After 1870, Germany replaced Great Britain as the industrial leader of Europe. Already in the 1890s, Germany's superiority was evident in new areas of manufacturing, such as organic chemicals and electrical equipment, and was increasingly apparent in its ever-greater share of worldwide trade. But the struggle for economic (and political) supremacy between Great Britain and Germany should not cause us to overlook the other great polarization of the age. By 1900, Europe was divided into two economic zones. Great Britain, Belgium, France, the Netherlands, Germany, the western part of the Austro-Hungarian Empire, and northern Italy constituted an advanced industrialized core that had a high standard of living, decent systems of transportation, and relatively healthy and educated populations (see Map 23.1). The backward and little industrialized areas to the south and east, consisting of southern Italy, most of Austria-Hungary, Spain, Portugal, the Balkan kingdoms, and Russia, were still largely agricultural and relegated by the industrial countries to the function of providing food and raw materials. The presence of Romanian oil, Greek olive oil, and Serbian pigs and prunes in western Europe served as reminders of an economic division of Europe that continued well into the twentieth century.

THE SPREAD OF INDUSTRIALIZATION After 1870, industrialization began to spread beyond western and central Europe and North America. Especially noticeable was its rapid development in Japan and Russia (see Chapter 24). In Japan, the imperial government took the lead in promoting industry. The government financed industries, built railroads, brought foreign experts to train Japanese employees in new industrial techniques, and instituted a universal educational system based on applied science. By the end of the nineteenth century, Japan had developed key industries in tea, silk, armaments, and shipbuilding. Workers for these industries came from the large number of people who had abandoned their farms due to severe hardships in the countryside and fled to the cities, where they provided an abundant source of cheap labor.

The Department Store and the Beginnings of Mass Consumerism

Domestic markets were especially important for the sale of the goods being turned out by Europe's increasing number of industrial plants. New techniques of mass marketing arose to encourage people to purchase the new consumer goods. The Parisians pioneered the development of the department store, and this selection is taken from a 1907 account of the growth of these stores in the French capital city.

E. Lavasseur, "On Parisian Department Stores"

It was in the reign of Louis-Philippe that department stores for fashion goods and dresses, extending to material and other clothing, began to be distinguished. The type was already one of the notable developments of the Second Empire; it became one of the most important ones of the Third Republic. These stores have increased in number and several of them have become extremely large. Combining in their different departments all articles of clothing, toilet articles, furniture and many other ranges of goods, it is their special object so to combine all commodities as to attract and satisfy customers who will find conveniently together an assortment of a mass of articles corresponding to all their various needs. They attract customers by permanent display, by free entry into the shops, by periodic exhibitions, by special sales, by fixed prices, and by their ability to deliver the goods purchased to customers' homes, in Paris and to the provinces. Turning themselves into direct intermediaries between the producer and the consumer, even producing sometimes some of their articles in their own workshops, buying at lowest prices because of their large orders and because they are in a position to profit from bargains, working with large sums, and selling to most of their customers for cash only, they can transmit these benefits in lowered selling prices. They can even decide to sell at a loss, as an advertisement or to get rid of out-of-date fashions. Taking 5–6 percent on 100 million [francs] brings them in more than 20 percent would bring to a firm doing a turnover of 50,000 francs.

The success of these department stores is only possible thanks to the volume of their business and this volume needs considerable capital and a very large turnover. Now capital, having become abundant, is freely combined nowadays in large enterprises, although French capital has the reputation of being more wary of the risks of industry than of State or railway securities. On the other hand, the large urban agglomerations, the ease with which goods can be transported by the railways, the diffusion of some comforts to strata below the middle classes, have all favored these developments.

As example we may cite some figures relating to these stores. . . . *Le Louvre*, dating to the time of the extension of the rue de Rivoli under the Second Empire, did in 1893 a business of 120 million at a profit of 6.4 percent. *Le Bon Marché*, which was a small shop when Mr. Boucicaut entered it in 1852, already did a business of 20 million at the end of the Empire. During the republic its new buildings were erected; Mme. Boucicaut turned it by her will into a kind of cooperative society, with shares and an ingenious organization; turnover reached 150 million in 1893, leaving a profit of 5 percent. . . .

According to the tax records of 1891, these stores in Paris, numbering 12, employed 1,708 persons and were rated on their site values at 2,159,000 francs; the largest had then 542 employees. These same stores had, in 1901, 9,784 employees; one of them over 2,000 and another over 1,600; their site value has doubled (4,089,000 francs).

Q Did the invention of department stores respond to or create the new "consumer ethic" in industrialized societies? What was this new turn-of-the-century ethic? According to Lavasseur, what were the positive effects of department stores for Parisian society?

Source: From *Documents of European Economic History*, Vol. I, by Sidney Pollard & Colin Holmes. Copyright © Sidney Pollard and Colin Holmes. Reproduced with permission of Palgrave Macmillan.

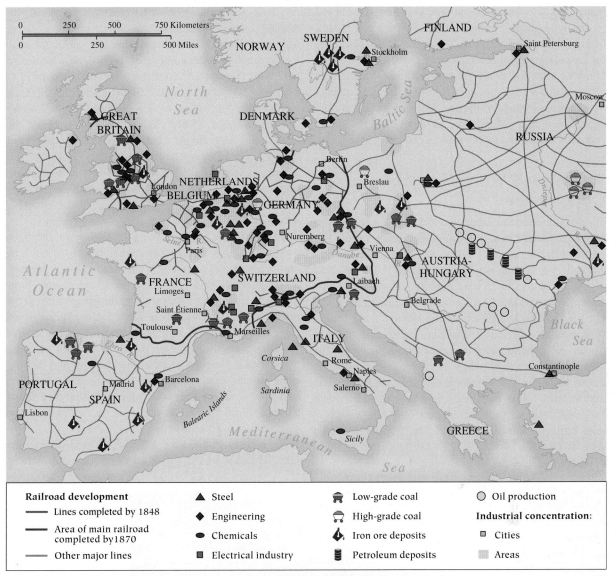

MAP 23.1 The Industrial Regions of Europe at the End of the Nineteenth Century. By the end of the nineteenth century, the Second Industrial Revolution—in steelmaking, electricity, petroleum, and chemicals—had spurred substantial economic growth and prosperity in western and central Europe; it also sparked economic and political competition between Great Britain and Germany.

Q Look back at Map 20.2. What parts of Europe not industrialized in 1850 had become industrialized in the ensuing decades?

As in Europe during the early decades of the Industrial Revolution, workers toiled for long hours in the coal mines and textile mills, often under horrendous conditions. Reportedly, coal miners employed on a small island in Nagasaki harbor worked naked in temperatures up to 130 degrees Fahrenheit. If they tried to escape, they were shot.

A WORLD ECONOMY The economic developments of the late nineteenth century, combined with the transportation revolution that saw the growth of marine transport and railroads, also fostered a true world economy. By 1900, Europeans were importing beef and wool from Argentina and Australia, coffee from Brazil, nitrates from Chile, iron ore from Algeria, and sugar from Java. European capital was also invested abroad to develop railways, mines, electrical power plants, and banks. High rates of return, upwards of 11.3 percent on Latin American banking shares that were floated in London, provided plenty of incentive. Of course, foreign countries also provided markets for the surplus manufactured goods of Europe. With its capital, industries, and military might, Europe dominated the world economy by the end of the nineteenth century.

Women and Work: New Job Opportunities

The Second Industrial Revolution had an enormous impact on the position of women in the labor market. During the course of the nineteenth century, considerable controversy erupted over a woman's "right to work." Working-class organizations tended to reinforce the underlying ideal of domesticity: women should remain at home to bear and nurture children and should not be allowed in the industrial workforce. Working-class men argued that keeping women out of industrial work would ensure the moral and physical well-being of families. In reality, keeping women out of the industrial workforce simply made it easier to exploit them when they needed income to supplement their husbands' wages or to support their families when their husbands were unemployed. The desperate need to work at times forced women to do marginal work at home or labor as pieceworkers in sweatshops.

After 1870, however, new job opportunities for women became available. The development of larger industrial plants and the expansion of government services created a large number of service or white-collar jobs. The increased demand for white-collar workers at relatively low wages coupled with a shortage of male workers led employers to hire women. Big businesses and retail shops needed clerks, typists, secretaries, file clerks, and sales-clerks. The expansion of government services created opportunities for women to be secretaries and telephone operators and to take jobs in health and social services. Compulsory education necessitated more teachers, and the development of modern hospital services opened opportunities to serve as nurses.

Many of the new white-collar jobs were far from exciting. The work was routine and, except for teaching and nursing, required few skills beyond basic literacy. Although there was little hope for advancement, these jobs had distinct advantages for the daughters of the middle classes and especially the upward-aspiring working classes. For some middle-class women, they offered freedom from the domestic patterns expected of them. Nevertheless, because middle-class women did not receive an education comparable to men's, they were limited in the careers they could pursue. Thus, they found it easier to fill the jobs at the lower end of middle-class occupations, such as teaching and civil service jobs, especially in the postal service. Most of the new white-collar jobs, however, were filled by working-class women who

New Jobs for Women: The Telephone Exchange. The invention of the telephone in 1876 soon led to its widespread use. As is evident from the illustration of a telephone exchange in New York, most of the telephone operators were women. This was but one of a number of new job opportunities for women created by the Second Industrial Revolution.

Museum of the City of New York/The Art Archive at Art Resource, NY saw them as an opportunity to escape from the physical labor of the lower-class world.

Organizing the Working Classes

In the first half of the nineteenth century, many workers had formed trade unions that had functioned primarily as mutual aid societies (see Chapter 20). In return for a small weekly payment, benefits were provided to assist unemployed workers. In the late nineteenth century, the desire to improve their working and living conditions led many industrial workers to form political parties and labor unions, often based on the ideas of Karl Marx (see Chapter 22). One of the most important of the working-class or socialist parties was formed in Germany in 1875.

SOCIALIST PARTIES Under the direction of its two Marxist leaders, Wilhelm Liebknecht (VIL-helm LEEP-knekht) (1826–1900) and August Bebel (ow-GOOST BAY-bul) (1840–1913), the German Social Democratic Party (SPD) espoused revolutionary Marxist rhetoric while organizing itself as a mass political party competing in elections for the Reichstag (RYKHSS-tahk), the German parliament. Once in the Reichstag, SPD delegates worked to enact legislation to improve the condition of the working class. As Bebel explained, "Pure negation would not be accepted by the voters. The masses demand that something should be done for today irrespective of what will happen on the morrow."[1] Despite government efforts to destroy it, the SPD continued to grow. In 1890, it received 1.5 million votes and thirty-five seats in the Reichstag. When it won 4 million votes in the 1912 elections, it became the largest single party in Germany.

Socialist parties also emerged in other European states, although none proved as successful as the German Social Democrats. As the socialist parties gained adherents, agitation for an international organization that would strengthen their position against international capitalism grew. In 1889, leaders of the various socialist parties formed the Second International, which was organized as a loose association of national groups. Although the Second International took some coordinated actions—May Day (May 1), for example, was made an international labor day to be marked by strikes and mass labor demonstrations—differences of opinion often wreaked havoc at the congresses of the organization. Two issues proved particularly divisive: nationalism and revisionism.

Despite the belief of Karl Marx and Friedrich Engels that "the working men have no country," in truth socialist parties varied from country to country and focused on national concerns and issues. Thus, nationalism remained a much more powerful force than socialism.

EVOLUTIONARY SOCIALISM Marxist parties also divided over the issue of **evolutionary socialism**, also known as **revisionism**. Some Marxists believed in a pure Marxism that accepted the imminent collapse of capitalism and the need for socialist ownership of the means of production. But others rejected the revolutionary approach and argued in a revisionist direction that the workers must continue to organize in mass political parties and even work with other progressive elements in a nation to gain reform. With the extension of the right to vote, workers were in a better position than ever to achieve their aims through democratic channels. As the most prominent revisionist, Eduard Bernstein (1850–1932), argued in his book *Evolutionary Socialism*, evolution by democratic means, not revolution, would achieve the desired goal of socialism. Many socialist parties, including the German Social Democrats, while spouting revolutionary slogans, followed Bernstein's gradualist approach.

TRADE UNIONS Workers also formed trade unions to improve their working conditions, but attempts to organize the workers did not come until after unions had won the right to strike in the 1870s. Strikes proved necessary to achieve the workers' goals. Walkouts by female workers in the match industry in 1888 and by dockworkers in London the following year led to the establishment of trade union organizations for both groups. By 1900, 2 million workers were enrolled in British trade unions, and by the outbreak of World War I in 1914, the number had risen to between 3 million and 4 million, although this was still less than one-fifth of the total workforce. By 1914, the German trade union movement with 3 million members was the largest in Europe after Great Britain's.

The Emergence of a Mass Society

Q FOCUS QUESTIONS: What is a mass society, and what were its main characteristics? What role were women expected to play in society and family life in the latter part of the nineteenth century, and how closely did patterns of family life correspond to this ideal?

The new patterns of industrial production, mass consumption, and working-class organization that we identify with the Second Industrial Revolution were only one aspect of the new **mass society** that emerged in Europe after 1870. A larger and vastly improved urban environment, new patterns of social structure, gender issues, mass education, and mass leisure were also important features of Europe's mass society.

Population Growth

The European population increased dramatically between 1850 and 1910, rising from 270 million to more than 460 million (see Table 23.1). Between 1850 and 1880, the main cause of the population increase was a rising birthrate, but after 1880, a noticeable decline in death rates largely explains the increase. Although the causes of this decline have been debated, two major factors—medical discoveries and environmental conditions—stand out. Some historians have stressed the importance of developments in medical science. Smallpox vaccinations, for example, were compulsory in many European countries by the mid-1850s. More important were improvements in the urban environment in the second half of the nineteenth century that greatly decreased fatalities from such infectious

diseases as diarrhea, dysentery, typhoid fever, and cholera, which had been spread through contaminated water supplies and improper elimination of sewage. Improved nutrition also made a significant difference in the health of the population. The increase in agricultural productivity combined with improvements in transportation facilitated the shipment of food supplies from areas of surplus to regions with poor harvests. Better nutrition and food hygiene were especially instrumental in the decline in infant mortality by 1900. The pasteurization of milk reduced intestinal disorders that had been a major cause of infant deaths.

Emigration

Although agricultural and industrial prosperity supported an increase in population, it could not do so indefinitely, especially in areas that had little industrialization and severe overpopulation. Some of the excess labor from underdeveloped areas migrated to the industrial regions of Europe (see Map 23.2). By 1913, more than 400,000 Poles were working in the heavily industrialized Ruhr region of western Germany. But a booming American economy and cheap shipping fares after 1898 led to substantial emigration from southern and eastern Europe to America. In 1880, about 500,000 people left Europe each year on average; between 1906 and 1910, annual departures increased to 1.3 million, many of them from southern and eastern Europe.

Transformation of the Urban Environment

One of the most important consequences of industrialization and the population explosion of the nineteenth century was urbanization. In 1800, city dwellers constituted 40 percent of the population in Britain, 25 percent in France and Germany, and only 10 percent in eastern Europe. By 1914, urban inhabitants had increased to 80 percent of the population in Britain, 45 percent in France, 60 percent in Germany, and 30 percent in eastern Europe. The size of cities also expanded dramatically, especially in industrialized countries. Between 1800 and 1900, London's population grew from 960,000 to 6.5 million and Berlin's from 172,000 to 2.7 million.

Urban populations grew faster than the general population primarily because of the vast migration from rural areas to cities. People were driven from the countryside to the city by sheer economic necessity—unemployment, land hunger, and physical want. Urban

TABLE 23.1 European Populations, 1851–1911

	1851	1881	1911
England and Wales	17,928,000	25,974,000	36,070,000
Scotland	2,889,000	3,736,000	4,761,000
Ireland	6,552,000	5,175,000	4,390,000
France	35,783,000	37,406,000	39,192,000
Germany	33,413,000	45,234,000	64,926,000
Belgium	4,530,000	5,520,000	7,424,000
Netherlands	3,309,000	4,013,000	5,858,000
Denmark	1,415,000	1,969,000	2,757,000
Norway	1,490,000	1,819,000	2,392,000
Sweden	3,471,000	4,169,000	5,522,000
Spain	15,455,000	16,622,000	19,927,000
Portugal	3,844,000	4,551,000	5,958,000
Italy	24,351,000	28,460,000	34,671,000
Switzerland	2,393,000	2,846,000	3,753,000
Austria	17,535,000	22,144,000	28,572,000
Hungary	18,192,000	15,739,000	20,886,000
Russia	68,500,000	97,700,000	160,700,000
Romania	N.A.	4,600,000	7,000,000
Bulgaria	N.A.	2,800,000	4,338,000
Greece	N.A.	1,679,000	2,632,000
Serbia	N.A.	1,700,000	2,912,000

NOTE: N.A. = not available.

SOURCE: Data from B. R. Mitchell, *European Historical Statistics*, 1750–1970 (New York, 1975).

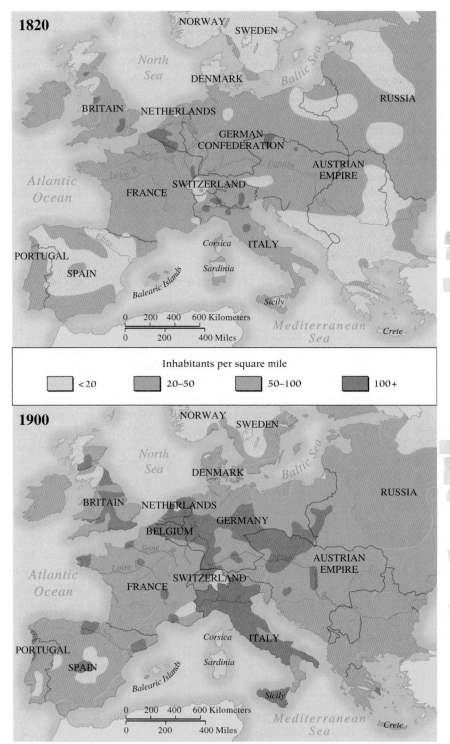

MAP 23.2 Population Growth in Europe, 1820–1900. European population increased steadily throughout the nineteenth century. Advances in medical science, hygiene, nutrition, living conditions, and standards of living help account for the population increase, even though emigration to the United States, South America, and other regions reduced the total growth numbers.

Q Which regions experienced the greatest population growth between 1820 and 1900, and how can you account for this?

centers offered something positive as well, usually ample opportunities for employment in factories and later in service trades and professions. But cities also grew faster in the second half of the nineteenth century because health and living conditions in them were improving.

IMPROVING LIVING CONDITIONS In the 1840s, a number of urban reformers, such as Edwin Chadwick in England and Rudolf Virchow (ROO-dulf FEER-khoh) and Solomon Neumann (NOI-mahn) in Germany, had pointed to filthy living conditions as the primary cause of epidemic diseases and urged sanitary reforms to correct the problem. Soon legislation created boards of health that brought governmental action to bear on public health issues. Urban medical officers and building inspectors were authorized to inspect dwellings for public health hazards. New building regulations made it more difficult for private contractors to build shoddy housing. The Public Health Act of 1875 in Britain, for example, required that all new buildings have running water and an internal drainage system. For the first time in Western history, the role of municipal governments had been expanded to include detailed regulations for the improvement of the living conditions of urban dwellers.

Essential to the public health of the modern European city was the ability to bring clean water into the city and to expel sewage from it. The problem of fresh water was solved by a system of dams and reservoirs that stored the water and aqueducts and tunnels that carried it from the countryside to the city and into individual dwellings. Regular private baths became accessible to more people as gas heaters in the 1860s and later electric heaters made hot baths possible. The treatment of wastewater was also improved by building underground pipes that carried raw sewage far from the city for disposal. Unfortunately, in many places the new underground sewers simply continued to discharge their raw sewage into what soon became highly polluted lakes and rivers. Nevertheless, the development of pure water and sewerage systems dramatically improved the public health of European cities.

HOUSING NEEDS Middle-class reformers who denounced the unsanitary living conditions of the working classes also focused on their housing needs. Overcrowded, disease-ridden slums were viewed as dangerous not only to physical health but also to the political and moral health of the entire nation. Victor Huber, the foremost early German housing reformer, wrote in 1861, "Certainly it would not be too much to say that the home is the communal embodiment of family life. Thus the purity of the dwelling is almost as important for the family as is the cleanliness of the body for the individual."[2] To Huber, good housing was a prerequisite for a stable family life, and hence a stable society.

Early efforts to attack the housing problem emphasized the middle-class, liberal belief in the efficacy of private enterprise. Reformers such as Huber believed that the construction of model dwellings renting at a reasonable price would force other private landlords to elevate their housing standards. A fine example of this approach was the work of Octavia Hill (see the box on p. 561). With the financial assistance of a friend, she rehabilitated some old dwellings and constructed new ones to create housing for 3,500 tenants.

As the number and size of cities continued to mushroom, governments by the 1880s came to the conclusion—reluctantly—that private enterprise could not solve the housing crisis. In 1890, a British law empowered local town councils to collect new taxes and construct cheap housing for the working classes. London and Liverpool were the first communities to take advantage of their new powers. Similar activity had been set in motion in Germany by 1900. Everywhere, however, these lukewarm measures failed to do much to meet the real housing needs of the working classes. In housing as in so many other areas of life in the late nineteenth and early twentieth centuries, the liberal principle that the government that governs least governs best had simply proved untrue. More and more, governments were stepping into areas of activity that they would never have touched earlier.

Housing was but one area of urban reconstruction after 1870. Many European urban centers were redesigned during the second half of the nineteenth century. The reconstruction of Paris after 1850 was perhaps the most famous project and provided a model for other cities. The old residential districts in the central city, many of them working-class slums, were demolished and replaced with town halls, government office buildings, retail stores including the new department stores, museums, cafés, and theaters, all of which provided for the shopping and recreational pleasures of the middle classes.

Social Structure of the Mass Society

Despite the improvements in living standards for many people in the last decades of the nineteenth century, wide disparities in wealth continued to exist. At the top of European society stood a wealthy elite, constituting only 5 percent of the population but controlling 30 to 40 percent of its wealth. In the course of the nineteenth century, aristocrats coalesced with the most successful industrialists, bankers, and merchants (the wealthy upper middle class) to form this new elite. The growth of big business had produced this group of wealthy **plutocrats**, while aristocrats, whose income from landed estates declined, invested in railway shares, public utilities, government bonds, and even businesses.

THE UPPER CLASSES Increasingly, aristocrats and plutocrats fused as the wealthy upper middle class purchased landed estates to join the aristocrats in the pleasures of country living and the aristocrats bought lavish town houses for part-time urban life. Common bonds were also forged when the sons of wealthy middle-class families were admitted to the elite schools dominated by the children of the aristocracy. This educated elite, whether aristocratic or middle class in background, assumed leadership roles in government bureaucracies and military hierarchies. Marriage also served to unite the two groups. Daughters of tycoons acquired titles, and aristocratic heirs gained new sources of cash. Wealthy American heiresses were in special demand. When Consuelo Vanderbilt married the duke of Marlborough, the new duchess brought £2 million (approximately $10 million) to her husband.

The Housing Venture of Octavia Hill

Octavia Hill was a practical-minded British housing reformer who believed that workers and their families were entitled to happy homes. At the same time, she was convinced that the poor needed guidance and encouragement, not charity. In this selection, she describes her housing venture.

Octavia Hill, *Homes of the London Poor*

About four years ago I was put in possession of three houses in one of the worst [blocks] of Marylebone. Six other houses were bought subsequently. All were crowded with [residents].

The first thing to be done was to put them in decent tenantable order. The set last purchased was a row of cottages facing a bit of desolate ground, occupied with wretched, dilapidated cow-sheds, manure heaps, old timber, and rubbish of every description. The houses were in a most deplorable condition—the plaster was dropping from the walls; on one staircase a pail was placed to catch the rain that fell through the roof. All the staircases were perfectly dark; the banisters were gone, having been burnt as firewood by tenants. The grates, with large holes in them, were falling forward into the rooms. The washhouse, full of lumber belonging to the landlord, was locked up; thus, the inhabitants had to wash clothes, as well as to cook eat and sleep, in their small rooms. The dustbin, standing in the front part of the houses, was accessible to the whole neighbourhood, and boys often dragged from it quantities of unseemly objects and spread them over the court. The state of the drainage was in keeping with everything else. The pavement of the back-yard was all broken up, and great puddles stood in it, so that the damp crept up the outer walls....

As soon as I entered into possession, each family had an opportunity of doing better: those who would not pay, or who led clearly immoral lives, were ejected. The rooms they vacated were cleansed; the tenants who showed signs of improvement moved into them, and thus, in turn, an opportunity was obtained for having each room distempered [painted] and papered. The drains were put in order, a large slate cistern was fixed, the washhouse was cleared of its lumber, and thrown open on stated days to each tenant in turn. The roof, the plaster, the woodwork were repaired; the staircase walls were distempered; new grates were fixed; the layers of paper and rag (black with age) were torn from the windows, and glass put in; out of 192 panes only eight were found unbroken. The yard and footpath were paved.

The rooms, as a rule, were re-let at the same prices at which they had been let before; but tenants with large families were counseled to take two rooms, and for these much less was charged than if let singly: this plan I continue to pursue. In-coming tenants are not allowed to take a decidedly insufficient quantity of room, and no subletting is permitted....

The pecuniary result has been very satisfactory. Five percent has been paid on all the capital invested. A fund for the repayment of capital is accumulating. A liberal allowance has been made for repairs....

My tenants are mostly of a class far below that of mechanics. They are, indeed, of the very poor. And yet, although the gifts they have received have been next to nothing, none of the families who have passed under my care during the whole four years have continued in what is called "distress," except such as have been unwilling to exert themselves. Those who will not exert the necessary self-control cannot avail themselves of the means of livelihood held out to them. But, for those who are willing, some small assistance in the form of work has, from time to time, been provided— not much, but sufficient to keep them from want or despair.

Q Did Octavia Hill's housing venture generate financial returns on her initial investment? What benefits did her tenants receive in turn? What feelings and beliefs about the lower classes are evident in Hill's account?

Source: From Octavia Hill, *Homes of the London Poor* (New York: Macmillan, 1875), pp. 15–16, 17–18, 23.

Paris Transformed. These two photographs, both of L'avenue de l'Opéra, show the degree of destruction that was needed to create the grand boulevards and monuments of late-nineteenth-century Paris. The first photograph was taken in 1865, and the second is from the 1880s. Evident in the second photograph are the new uniform buildings, gas street lamps, and broad boulevards that linked the city's great cultural sites, such as the Opéra, shown in the background, the most expensive building constructed during the Second Empire.

THE MIDDLE CLASSES The middle classes consisted of a variety of groups. Below the upper middle class was a level that included such traditional groups as professionals in law, medicine, and the civil service as well as moderately well-to-do industrialists and merchants. The industrial expansion of the nineteenth century also added new groups to this segment of the middle class.

These included business managers and new professionals, such as the engineers, architects, accountants, and chemists who formed professional associations as the symbols of their newfound importance. A lower middle class of small shopkeepers, traders, manufacturers, and prosperous peasants provided goods and services for the classes above them.

Standing between the lower middle class and the lower classes were new groups of white-collar workers who were the product of the Second Industrial Revolution. They were the bookkeepers, bank tellers, telephone operators, department store clerks, secretaries, and traveling salespeople. Although largely propertyless and often paid only marginally more than skilled laborers, these white-collar workers were often committed to middle-class ideals and optimistic about improving their status.

The moderately prosperous and successful middle classes shared a common lifestyle, and their values came to dominate much of late-nineteenth-century society. Members of the middle classes were especially active in preaching their worldview to their children and to the upper and lower classes of their society. This was especially evident in Victorian Britain, often considered a model of middle-class society. The European middle classes embraced and promoted the importance of progress and science. They believed in hard work, which they viewed as the primary human good, open to everyone and guaranteed to have positive results. They were also regular churchgoers who believed in the good conduct associated with traditional Christian morality. The middle classes were concerned with propriety, the right way of doing things. This concern gave rise to an endless succession of books aimed at the middle-class market with such titles as *The Habits of Good Society* and *Don't: A Manual of Mistakes and Improprieties More or Less Prevalent in Conduct and Speech*.

THE LOWER CLASSES Almost 80 percent of Europeans belonged to the lower classes. Many of the members of these classes were landholding peasants, farm laborers, and sharecroppers, especially in eastern Europe. The urban working class consisted of many different groups, including skilled artisans in such trades as cabinetmaking, printing, and jewelry making. Semiskilled laborers, who included such people as carpenters, bricklayers, and many factory workers, earned wages that were about two-thirds of those of highly skilled workers. At the bottom of the urban working class stood the largest group of workers, the unskilled laborers. They included day laborers and large numbers of domestic servants. One out of every seven employed persons in Great Britain in 1900 was a domestic servant. Most of these were women.

Urban workers did experience a real betterment in the material conditions of their lives after 1871. For one thing, urban improvements meant better living conditions. A rise in real wages, accompanied by a decline in many consumer costs, especially in the 1880s and 1890s, made it possible for workers to afford more than just food and housing. Workers' budgets now provided money for more clothes and even leisure at the same time that strikes and labor agitation were providing shorter (ten-hour) workdays and Saturday afternoons off (see "Mass Leisure" later in this chapter).

The "Woman Question": The Role of Women

The "woman question" was the term used to refer to the debate over the role of women in society. In the nineteenth century, women remained legally inferior, economically dependent, and largely defined by family and household roles. Many women still aspired to the ideal of femininity popularized by writers and poets. Alfred Lord Tennyson's poem *The Princess* expressed it well:

> Man for the field and woman for the hearth:
> Man for the sword and for the needle she:
> Man with the head and woman with the heart:
> Man to command and woman to obey;
> All else confusion.

This traditional characterization of the sexes, based on gender-defined social roles, was elevated to the status of universal male and female attributes in the nineteenth century, due largely to the impact of the Industrial Revolution on the family. As the chief family wage earners, men worked outside the home while women were left with the care of the family, for which they were paid nothing. Of course, the ideal did not always match reality, especially for the lower classes, where the need for supplemental income drove women to do sweatwork.

Throughout most of the nineteenth century, marriage was viewed as the only honorable and available career for most women. While the middle classes glorified the ideal of domesticity (see the box on p. 564), for most women marriage was a matter of economic necessity. The lack of meaningful work and the lower wages paid to women made it difficult for single women to earn a living. Most women chose to marry, which was reflected in an increase in marriage rates and a decline in illegitimacy rates in the course of the nineteenth century.

Birthrates also dropped significantly at this time. A very important factor in the evolution of the modern family was the decline in the number of offspring born to the average woman. The change was not necessarily due to new technological products. Although the invention of vulcanized rubber in the 1840s made possible the production of condoms and diaphragms, they were not widely used as contraceptive devices until the era of World War I. Some historians maintain that the change in attitude that led parents to deliberately limit the number of offspring was more important than the method used. Although some historians attribute increased birth control to more widespread use of coitus interruptus, or male withdrawal before ejaculation, others have emphasized the ability of women to restrict family size through abortion and even infanticide or abandonment. A change in attitude was apparent in the emergence of a movement to increase awareness of birth control methods. In 1882 in Amsterdam, Dr. Aletta Jacob founded Europe's first birth control clinic.

THE MIDDLE-CLASS FAMILY The family was the central institution of middle-class life. Men provided the family income, while women focused on household and child care. The use of domestic servants in many middle-class homes, made possible by an abundant supply of cheap labor, reduced the amount of time middle-class women had to spend on household work. At the same time, by reducing the number of children in the family, mothers could devote more time to child care and domestic leisure.

Advice to Women: Two Views

Industrialization had a strong impact on middle-class women as gender-based social roles became the norm. Men worked outside the home to support the family, while women provided for the needs of their children and husband at home. In the first selection, *Woman in Her Social and Domestic Character* (1842), Elizabeth Poole Sanford gives advice to middle-class women on their proper role and behavior.

Although a majority of women probably followed the nineteenth-century middle-class ideal of women as keepers of the household and nurturers of husband and children, an increasing number of women fought for the rights of women. The second selection is taken from the third act of Henrik Ibsen's 1879 play *A Doll's House*, in which the character Nora Helmer declares her independence from her husband's control.

Elizabeth Poole Sanford, *Woman in Her Social and Domestic Character*

The changes wrought by Time are many. It influences the opinions of men as familiarity does their feelings; it has a tendency to do away with superstition, and to reduce every thing to its real worth.

It is thus that the sentiment for woman has undergone a change. The romantic passion which once almost deified her is on the decline; and it is by intrinsic qualities that she must now inspire respect. She is no longer the queen of song and the star of chivalry. But if there is less of enthusiasm entertained for her, the sentiment is more rational, and, perhaps, equally sincere; for it is in relation to happiness that she is chiefly appreciated.

And in this respect it is, we must confess, that she is most useful and most important. Domestic life is the chief source of her influence; and the greatest debt society can owe to her is domestic comfort; for happiness is almost an element of virtue; and nothing conduces more to improve the character of men than domestic peace. A woman may make a man's home delightful, and may thus increase his motives for virtuous exertion. She may refine and tranquilize his mind,—may turn away his anger or allay his grief. Her smile may be

the happy influence to gladden his heart, and to disperse the cloud that gathers on his brow. And in proportion to her endeavors to make those around her happy, she will be esteemed and loved. She will secure by her excellence that interest and that regard which she might formerly claim as the privilege of her sex, and will really merit the deference which was then conceded to her as a matter of course. . . .

Perhaps one of the first secrets of her influence is adaptation to the tastes, and sympathy in the feelings, of those around her. This holds true in lesser as well as in graver points. It is in the former, indeed, that the absence of interest in a companion is frequently most disappointing. Where want of congeniality impairs domestic comfort, the fault is generally chargeable on the female side. It is for woman, not for man, to make the sacrifice, especially in indifferent matters. She must, in a certain degree, be plastic herself if she would mold others. . . .

Nothing is so likely to conciliate the affections of the other sex as a feeling that woman looks to them for support and guidance. In proportion as men are themselves superior, they are accessible to this appeal. On the contrary, they never feel interested in one who seems disposed rather to offer than to ask assistance. There is, indeed, something unfeminine in independence. It is contrary to nature, and therefore it offends. We do not like to see a woman affecting tremors, but still less do we like to see her acting the amazon. A really sensible woman feels her dependence. She does what she can; but she is conscious of inferiority, and therefore grateful for support. She knows that she is the weaker vessel, and that as such she should receive honor. In this view, her weakness is an attraction, not a blemish.

In every thing, therefore, that women attempt, they should show their consciousness of dependence. If they are learners, let them evince a teachable spirit; if they give an opinion, let them do it in an unassuming manner. There is something so unpleasant in female self-sufficiency that it not unfrequently deters instead of persuading, and prevents the adoption of advice which the judgment even approves.

Henrik Ibsen, *A Doll's House*

NORA (*Pause*): Does anything strike you as we sit here?

HELMER: What should strike me?

NORA: We've been married eight years; does it not strike you that this is the first time we two, you and I, man and wife, have talked together seriously?

HELMER: Seriously? What do you mean, *seriously*?

NORA: For eight whole years, and more—ever since the day we first met—we have never exchanged one serious word about serious things. . . .

HELMER: Why, my dearest Nora, what have you to do with serious things?

NORA: There we have it! You have never understood me. I've had great injustice done to me, Torvald; first by Father, then by you.

HELMER: What! Your father *and* me? We, who have loved you more than all the world!

NORA (*Shaking her head*): You have never loved me. You just found it amusing to think you were in love with me.

HELMER: Nora! What a thing to say!

NORA: Yes, it's true, Torvald. When I was living at home with Father, he told me his opinions and mine were the same. If I had different opinions, I said nothing about them, because he would not have liked it. He used to call me his doll-child and played with me as I played with my dolls. Then I came to live in your house.

HELMER: What a way to speak of our marriage!

NORA (*Undisturbed*): I mean that I passed from Father's hands into yours. You arranged everything to your taste and I got the same tastes as you; or pretended to—I don't know which—both, perhaps; sometimes one, sometimes the other. When I look back on it now, I seem to have been living here like a beggar, on handouts. I lived by performing tricks for you, Torvald. But that was how you wanted it. You and Father have done me a great wrong. It is your fault that my life has come to naught.

HELMER: Why, Nora, how unreasonable and ungrateful! Haven't you been happy here?

NORA: No, never. I thought I was, but I never was.

HELMER: Not—not happy! . . .

NORA: I must stand quite alone if I am ever to know myself and my surroundings; so I cannot stay with you.

HELMER: Nora! Nora!

NORA: I am going at once. I daresay [my friend] Christina will take me in for tonight.

HELMER: YOU are mad! I shall not allow it! I forbid it!

NORA: It's no use your forbidding me anything now. I shall take with me only what belongs to me; from you I will accept nothing, either now or later.

HELMER: This is madness!

NORA: Tomorrow I shall go home—I mean to what was my home. It will be easier for me to find a job there.

HELMER: On, in your blind inexperience—

NORA: I must try to gain experience, Torvald.

HELMER: Forsake your home, your husband, your children! And you don't consider what the world will say.

NORA: I can't pay attention to that. I only know that I must do it.

HELMER: This is monstrous! Can you forsake your holiest duties?

NORA: What do you consider my holiest duties?

HELMER: Need I tell you that? Your duties to your husband and children.

NORA: I have other duties equally sacred.

HELMER: Impossible! What do you mean?

NORA: My duties toward myself.

HELMER: Before all else you are a wife and a mother.

NORA: That I no longer believe. Before all else I believe I am a human being just as much as you are—or at least that I should try to become one. I know that

(continued)

most people agree with you, Torvald, and that they say so in books. But I can no longer be satisfied with what most people say and what is in books. I must think things out for myself and try to get clear about them.

Q According to Elizabeth Sanford, what is the proper role of women? What forces in nineteenth-century European society merged to shape Sanford's understanding of "proper" gender roles? In Ibsen's play, what challenges does Nora Helmer make to Sanford's view of the proper role and behavior of wives? Why is her husband so shocked? Why did Ibsen title this play *A Doll's House*?

Sources: Elizabeth Poole Sanford, *Woman in Her Social and Domestic Character*. From Elizabeth Poole Sanford, *Woman in Her Social and Domestic Character* (Boston: Otis, Broaders & Co., 1842), pp. 5–7, 15–16. Henrik Ibsen, *A Doll's House*. Excerpt as appeared in *Roots of Western Civilization* by Wesley D. Camp (Wiley, 1983).

The middle-class family fostered an ideal of togetherness (see Images of Everyday Life on p. 567). The Victorians created the family Christmas, with its yule log, Christmas tree, songs, and exchange of gifts. In the United States, Fourth of July celebrations changed from drunken revels to family picnics by the 1850s. The education of middle-class females in domestic crafts, singing, and piano playing prepared them for their function of providing a proper environment for home recreation.

THE WORKING-CLASS FAMILY Women in working-class families were more accustomed to hard work. Daughters were expected to work until they married; even after marriage, they often did piecework at home to support the family. For the children of the working class, childhood was over by the age of nine or ten when they became apprentices or were employed in odd jobs.

Between 1890 and 1914, however, family patterns among the working class began to change. High-paying jobs in heavy industry and improvements in the standard of living made it possible for working-class families to depend on the income of husbands and the wages of grown children. By the early twentieth century, some working-class mothers could afford to stay at home, following the pattern of middle-class women. At the same time, new consumer products, such as sewing machines, clocks, bicycles, and cast-iron stoves, created a new mass consumer society whose focus was on higher levels of consumption.

These working-class families also followed the middle classes in limiting the size of their families. Children began to be viewed as dependents rather than wage earners as child labor laws and compulsory

education took children out of the workforce and into schools. Improvements in public health as well as advances in medicine and a better diet resulted in a decline in infant mortality rates for the lower classes and made it easier for working-class families to choose to have fewer children. At the same time, strikes and labor agitation led to laws that reduced work hours to ten per day by 1900 and eliminated work on Saturday afternoons, which enabled working-class parents to devote more attention to their children and develop deeper emotional ties with them.

Education in the Mass Society

Being "educated" in the early nineteenth century meant attending a secondary school or possibly even a university. Secondary schools mostly emphasized a classical education based on the study of Greek and Latin. Secondary and university education was primarily for the elite, the sons of government officials, nobles, or the wealthier members of the middle classes. After 1850, secondary education was expanded as more middle-class families sought employment in public service and the professions or entry into elite scientific and technical schools.

UNIVERSAL ELEMENTARY EDUCATION **Mass education** was a product of the mass society of the late nineteenth century. In the decades after 1870, the functions of the state were extended to include the development of mass education in state-run systems. Between 1870 and 1914, most Western governments began to offer at least primary education to both boys and girls between the ages of six and twelve. States also

IMAGES OF EVERYDAY LIFE
The Middle-Class Family

NINETEENTH-CENTURY MIDDLE-CLASS MORALISTS considered the family the fundamental pillar of a healthy society. The family was a crucial institution in middle-class life, and togetherness constituted one of the important ideals of the middle-class family. The painting below by William P. Frith, titled *Many Happy Returns of the Day*, shows grandparents, parents, and children taking part in a family birthday celebration for a little girl. The servant at the left holds the presents for the little girl. New games and toys also appeared for middle-class children. The illustration on the bottom left is taken from a book of games of 1889 and shows young girls playing a game called battledore and shuttlecock, which is described in the book as "a most convenient game because one solitary individual can find amusement as well as any number, provided there is a bat for each player. The object of the game is to keep the shuttlecock going as long as possible." The final illustration shows the cover of *The Scout*, a magazine of the scouting movement founded by Robert Baden-Powell. The cover shows one of the new scouts wearing his uniform and watching a ship at sea.

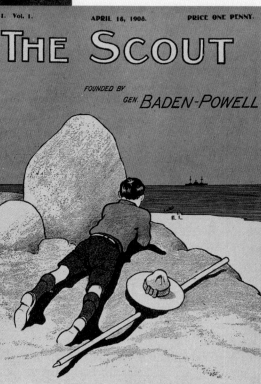

assumed responsibility for the quality of teachers by establishing teacher-training schools. By 1900, many European states, especially in northern and western Europe, were providing state-financed primary schools, salaried and trained teachers, and free, compulsory mass elementary education.

Why did European states make this commitment to mass education? Liberals believed that education was important to personal and social improvement and sought in Catholic countries to supplant Catholic education with moral and civic training based on secular values. Even conservatives were attracted to mass education as a means of improving the quality of military recruits and training people in social discipline. In 1875, a German military journal stated, "We in Germany consider education to be one of the principal ways of promoting the strength of the nation and above all military strength."[3]

Another incentive for mass education came from industrialization. In the early Industrial Revolution, unskilled labor was sufficient to meet factory needs, but the new firms of the Second Industrial Revolution demanded skilled labor. Both boys and girls with an elementary education had new possibilities of jobs beyond their villages or small towns, including white-collar jobs in railway and subway stations, post offices, banking and shipping firms, teaching, and nursing. To industrialists, then, mass education furnished the trained workers they needed.

Nevertheless, the chief motive for mass education was political. The expansion of voting rights necessitated a more educated electorate. Even more important, mass compulsory education instilled patriotism and nationalized the masses, providing an opportunity for even greater national integration. As people lost their ties to local regions and even to religion, nationalism supplied a new faith. The use of a single common language created greater national unity than loyalty to a ruler ever did.

A nation's motives for universal elementary education largely determined what was taught in its elementary schools. Indoctrination in national values took on great importance. At the core of the academic curriculum were reading, writing, arithmetic, national history (especially geared to a patriotic view), geography, literature, and some singing and drawing. The education of boys and girls differed, however. Where possible, the sexes were separated. Girls studied less math and no science but concentrated on such domestic skills as sewing, washing, ironing, and cooking, all prerequisites for providing a good home for husband and children.

Boys were taught some practical skills, such as carpentry, and even some military drill. Most of the elementary schools also inculcated the middle-class virtues of hard work, thrift, sobriety, cleanliness, and respect for the family. For most students, elementary education led to an apprenticeship and a job.

FEMALE TEACHERS   The development of compulsory elementary education created a demand for teachers, and most of them were female. In the United States, for example, women constituted two-thirds of all teachers by the 1880s. Many men viewed the teaching of children as an extension of women's "natural role" as nurturers of children. Moreover, females were paid lower salaries, in itself a considerable incentive for governments to encourage the establishment of teacher-training institutes for women. The first colleges for women were teacher-training schools; not until the beginning of the twentieth century were women permitted to enter the male-dominated universities. In France, 3 percent of university students in 1902 were women; by 1914, their number had increased to 10 percent of the total.

LITERACY AND THE MASS NEWSPAPER   The most immediate result of mass education was an increase in literacy. In Germany, Great Britain, France, and the Scandinavian countries, adult illiteracy was virtually eliminated by 1900. Where there was less schooling, the story is very different. Adult illiteracy rates were 79 percent in Serbia, 78 percent in Romania, and 79 percent in Russia. All of these countries had made only a minimal investment in mass education.

With the dramatic increase in literacy after 1871 came the rise of mass newspapers, such as the *Evening News* (1881) and *Daily Mail* (1896) in London, which sold millions of copies a day. These newspapers were written in an easily understood style and tended toward the sensational. Unlike eighteenth-century newspapers, which were full of serious editorials and lengthy political analysis, these tabloids provided lurid details of crimes, jingoistic diatribes, gossip, and sports news. There were other forms of cheap literature as well. Specialty magazines, such as the *Family Herald* for the entire family, and women's magazines began to appear in the 1860s. Pulp fiction for adults included the extremely popular westerns with their innumerable variations on conflicts between cowboys and Indians. Literature for the masses was but one feature of the new mass culture; another was the emergence of new forms of mass leisure.

Mass Leisure

In the preindustrial centuries, play or leisure activities had been closely connected to work patterns based on the seasonal or daily cycles typical of the life of peasants and artisans. The process of industrialization in the nineteenth century had an enormous impact on that traditional pattern. The factory imposed new work patterns that were determined by the rhythms of machines and clocks and removed work time completely from the family environment of farms and workshops. Work and leisure became opposites as leisure came to be defined as what people did for fun when they were not at work. In fact, the new leisure hours created by the industrial system—evening hours after work, weekends, and later a week or two in the summer—largely determined the contours of the new **mass leisure**.

New technology also determined the forms of mass leisure pursuits. New technology created novelties such as the Ferris wheel at amusement parks. The mechanized urban transportation systems of the 1880s meant that even the working classes were no longer dependent on neighborhood bars but could make their way to athletic games, amusement parks, and dance halls. Railroads could take people to the beaches on weekends.

The upper and middle classes had created the first market for tourism, but as wages increased and workers were given paid vacations, tourism became another form of mass leisure. Thomas Cook (1808–1892) was a British pioneer of mass tourism. Secretary to a British temperance group, Cook had been responsible for organizing a railroad trip to temperance gatherings in 1841. This experience led him to offer trips on a regular basis after he found that he could make substantial profits by renting special trains, lowering prices, and increasing the number of passengers.

By the late nineteenth century, team sports had developed into yet another focus of mass leisure. Unlike the old rural games, however, they were no longer chaotic and spontaneous activities but became strictly organized with formal rules and officials to enforce them. These rules were the products of organized athletic groups, such as the English Football Association (1863) and the American Bowling Congress (1895).

The new team sports rapidly became professionalized. In Britain, soccer had its Football Association in 1863 and rugby its Rugby Football Union in 1871. In the United States, the first national association to recognize professional baseball players was formed in 1863.

Soccer Moments. Until 1863, football (soccer) in Britain was an aggressive sport with few set rules. One of the first things the new English Football Association did after it was established on October 26, 1863, was to set up fourteen rules of play. In this sketch from a magazine called *The Graphic*, two players are depicted with the rose of England on their jerseys playing in an international soccer match in 1872.

By 1900, the National League and American League had a monopoly over professional baseball. The development of urban transportation systems made possible the construction of stadiums where thousands could attend, making mass spectator sports a big business.

Standardized forms of amusement drew mass audiences. Although some theorists argued that the new amusements were important for improving people, they served primarily to provide entertainment and distract people from the realities of their work lives. The new mass leisure also represented a significant change from earlier forms of popular culture. Festivals and fairs had been based on active and spontaneous community participation, whereas the new forms of mass leisure were businesses, standardized for largely passive mass audiences and organized to make profits.

Mass Consumption

Amusement parks, dance halls, organized tourist trips, and athletic events all offered new forms of leisure for masses of people, but they also quickly became part of the new mass consumption of the late nineteenth century. Earlier most people's purchases had been limited: some kitchen utensils, bedding, furniture, and a few select pieces of tailor-made clothing. Now middle- and upper-class Europeans were able to purchase and enjoy a wide variety of material goods. The new mass consumption was made possible by improvements in the standard of living, the factory system, population growth, expanded transportation systems, urbanization, and the modernization of retailing in which standardized merchandise was sold in large volumes.

When European cities were reconstructed in the late nineteenth century, space was allotted for department stores. Constructed of new industrial materials—iron columns and plate-glass windows—department stores such as Paris's Le Bon Marché (luh BAHN mar-SHAY) offered consumers an endless variety of goods in large spaces; Le Bon Marché covered 52,000 square meters of surface space (see the box on p. 554). In 1860, its merchandise included shawls, cloaks, bedding, and fabrics; by the 1880s, its stock had expanded to include women's, men's, and children's clothing, accessories, furniture, rugs, umbrellas, toothbrushes, stationery, toys, perfume, shoes, and cutlery. Sales at Le Bon Marché in 1877 registered 73 million francs. The use of gas and electricity made it possible to illuminate the wares in large spaces and extend opening hours. Omnibuses transported people throughout Paris, enabling them to travel beyond their neighborhoods to shop at the new stores. Advertising in mass newspapers introduced Europeans to the new products, while department store catalogs enabled people living outside the cities to also purchase the new goods.

Although most advertisements were directed toward women, men also took part in the new consumer culture of the late nineteenth century. Not only did men consume goods such as alcohol and tobacco, but they were also the chief purchasers of ready-made clothing in the late nineteenth century. Men also consumed such goods as shaving soaps, aftershave lotions, hair dyes, and sporting goods.

The National State

Q FOCUS QUESTION: What general political trends were evident in the nations of western Europe in the last decades of the nineteenth century, and how did these trends differ from the policies pursued in Germany, Austria-Hungary, and Russia?

Within the major European states, considerable progress was made in achieving such liberal practices as constitutions and parliaments, but it was largely in western Europe that **mass politics** became a reality. Reforms encouraged the expansion of political democracy through voting rights for men and the creation of mass political parties. At the same time, however, these developments were strongly resisted in parts of Europe where the old political forces remained strong.

Western Europe: The Growth of Political Democracy

In general, parliamentary government was most firmly rooted in the western European states. Both Britain and France saw an expansion of the right to vote, but liberal reforms proved less successful in Italy.

REFORM IN BRITAIN By 1871, Great Britain had a functioning two-party parliamentary system, and the growth of political democracy became one of the preoccupations of British politics. Its cause was pushed along by the expansion of suffrage. Much advanced by the Reform Act of 1867 (see Chapter 22), the right to vote was further extended during the second ministry of William Gladstone (1880–1885) with the passage of the Reform Act of 1884. It gave the vote to all men who paid regular rents or taxes, thus largely enfranchising agricultural workers, a group previously excluded (see Table 22.1 on p. 558). The following year, the Redistribution Act eliminated traditional boroughs and counties and established constituencies with approximately equal populations and one representative each. The payment of salaries to members of the House of Commons beginning in 1911 further democratized that institution by opening the door to people other than the wealthy. Gradual reform through parliamentary institutions had become the way of British political life.

THE THIRD REPUBLIC IN FRANCE The defeat of France by the Prussian army in 1870 brought the downfall of Louis Napoleon's Second Empire. In new elections based on universal male suffrage, the French people rejected the republicans and overwhelmingly favored the monarchists, who won two-thirds of the seats in the new National Assembly. In response, on March 26, 1871, radical republicans formed an independent republican government in Paris known as the Commune.

But the National Assembly refused to give up its power and decided to crush the renegade Commune. Vicious fighting broke out in April. Many working-class men and women stepped forth to defend the Commune. At first, women's activities were the traditional ones: caring for the wounded soldiers and feeding the troops. Gradually, however, women expanded their activities to include taking care of weapons, working as scouts, and even setting up their own fighting brigades. Louise Michel (mee-SHEL) (1830–1905), a schoolteacher who emerged as one of the leaders of the Paris Commune, proved tireless in forming committees for the defense of the Commune.

All of these efforts were in vain, however. In the last week of May, government troops massacred thousands of the Commune's defenders. Estimates are that 20,000 were shot; another 10,000 (including Louise Michel) were shipped to the French penal colony of New Caledonia, in the South Pacific. The brutal repression of the Commune bequeathed a legacy of hatred that continued to plague French politics for decades. The harsh punishment of women who participated in antigovernment activities also served to discourage any future action by working-class women to improve their conditions.

Although a majority of the members of the monarchist-dominated National Assembly wished to restore a monarchy in France, their inability to agree on who should be king caused the monarchists to miss their opportunity and led in 1875 to an improvised constitution that established a republican form of government as the least divisive compromise. This constitution established a **bicameral legislature** with an upper house, the Senate, elected indirectly and a lower house, the Chamber of Deputies, chosen by universal male suffrage; a president, selected by the legislature for a term of seven years, served as executive of the government. The Constitution of 1875, though intended only as a stopgap measure, solidified the republic—the Third Republic—which lasted sixty-five years. New elections in 1876 and 1877 strengthened the hands of the republicans, who managed by 1879 to institute ministerial responsibility and establish the power of the Chamber of Deputies. The prime minister or premier and his ministers were now responsible not to the president but to the Chamber of Deputies.

ITALY By 1870, Italy had emerged as a geographically united state with pretensions to Great Power status. Its internal weaknesses, however, gave that claim a particularly hollow ring. One Italian leader said after unification, "We have made Italy; now we must make Italians." But many Italians continued to put loyalty to their families, towns, and regions above their loyalty to the new state.

Sectional differences—a poverty-stricken south and an industrializing north—also weakened any sense of unity. Most of the Italian leaders were northerners who treated southern Italians with contempt. The Catholic Church, which had lost control of the Papal States as a result of unification, even refused to accept the existence of the new state. Chronic turmoil between workers and industrialists undermined the social fabric. And few Italians felt empowered in the new Italy: only 2.5 percent of the people could vote for the legislative body. In 1882, the number was increased, but only to 10 percent. The Italian government was unable to deal effectively with these problems because of extensive corruption among government officials and a lack of stability resulting from ever-changing government coalitions. The granting of universal male suffrage in 1912 did little to correct the corruption and weak government. Even the Italians' pretensions to Great Power status came up empty when Italy became the first modern European nation to be defeated in battle by an African state, Ethiopia.

Central and Eastern Europe: Persistence of the Old Order

Germany, Austria-Hungary, and Russia pursued political policies that were quite different from those of the western European nations. Germany and Austria-Hungary had the trappings of parliamentary government, including legislative bodies and elections by universal male suffrage, but authoritarian forces, especially powerful monarchies and conservative social groups, remained strong. In eastern Europe, especially Russia, the old system of autocracy was barely touched by the winds of change.

GERMANY The constitution of the new imperial Germany begun by Bismarck in 1871 provided for a federal system with a bicameral legislature. The lower house of the German parliament, the Reichstag, was elected on the basis of universal male suffrage, but it did not have ministerial responsibility. Ministers of government, the most important of which was the chancellor, were responsible not to the parliament but to the emperor. The emperor also commanded the armed forces and controlled foreign policy and internal administration. Although the creation of a parliament elected by universal male suffrage presented opportunities for the growth of a real political democracy, it failed to develop in Germany before World War I. The army and Bismarck were two major reasons why it did not.

The German (largely Prussian) army viewed itself as the defender of monarchy and aristocracy and sought to escape control by the Reichstag by operating under a general staff responsible only to the emperor. Prussian military tradition was strong, and military officers took steps to ensure the loyalty of their subordinates to the emperor.

The policies of Otto von Bismarck, who served as chancellor of the new German state until 1890, often prevented the growth of more democratic institutions. At first, Bismarck worked with the liberals, especially in launching an attack on the Catholic Church, the so-called *Kulturkampf* (kool-TOOR-kahmf) or "struggle for civilization." Like Bismarck, middle-class liberals distrusted Catholics' loyalty to the new Germany. But Bismarck's tactics proved counterproductive, and he soon abandoned the attack on Catholicism by making an abrupt shift in policy.

In 1878, Bismarck abandoned the liberals and, alarmed by the growth of the Social Democratic Party, began to mount an attack on the socialists. He genuinely believed that the socialists' antinationalistic, anticapitalistic, and antimonarchical stance represented a danger to the empire. In 1878, Bismarck got the parliament to pass a law that limited socialist meetings and publications while still allowing socialist candidates to run for the Reichstag. Bismarck also attempted to woo workers away from socialism by enacting social welfare legislation (see the box on p. 573). Between 1883 and 1889, the Reichstag passed laws that provided sickness, accident, and disability benefits as well as old-age pensions, financed by compulsory contributions from workers, employers, and the state. Bismarck's **social security** system was the most progressive the world had yet seen. Nevertheless, both the repressive and the social welfare measures failed to stop the growth of socialism. In his frustration, Bismarck planned still more antisocialist measures in 1890, but before he could carry them out, the new emperor, William II (1888–1918), eager to pursue his own policies, cashiered the aged chancellor.

AUSTRIA-HUNGARY   After the creation of the Dual Monarchy of Austria-Hungary in 1867, the Austrian part received a constitution that established a parliamentary system with the principle of ministerial responsibility. But Emperor Francis Joseph (1848–1916) largely ignored ministerial responsibility and proceeded to personally appoint and dismiss his ministers and rule by decree when parliament was not in session.

The problem of the minorities continued to trouble the empire. The ethnic Germans, who made up only one-third of Austria's population, governed Austria but

Bismarck and William II. In 1890, Bismarck sought to undertake new repressive measures against the Social Democrats. Disagreeing with this policy, Emperor William II forced him to resign. This political cartoon shows William II reclining on a throne made of artillery and cannonballs and holding a doll labeled "socialism." Bismarck bids farewell while Germany, personified as a woman, looks on with grave concern.

© Bettmann/Corbis

Bismarck and the Welfare of the Workers

In his attempt to win workers away from socialism, Bismarck favored an extensive program of social welfare benefits, including old-age pensions and compensation for absence from work due to sickness, accident, or disability. This selection is taken from Bismarck's address to the Reichstag on March 10, 1884, in which he explained his motives for social welfare legislation.

Bismarck, Address to the Reichstag

The positive efforts began really only in the year ... 1881 ... with the imperial message ... in which His Majesty William I said: "Already in February of this year, we have expressed our conviction that the healing of social ills is not to be sought exclusively by means of repression of Social Democratic excesses, but equally in the positive promotion of the welfare of the workers."

In consequence of this, first of all the insurance law against accidents was submitted.... And it reads ... "But those who have, through age or disability, become incapable of working have a confirmed claim on all for a higher degree of state care than could have been their share heretofore...."

The worker's real sore point is the insecurity of his existence. He is not always sure he will always have work. He is not sure he will always be healthy, and he foresees some day he will be old and incapable of work. But also if he falls into poverty as a result of long illness, he is completely helpless with his own powers, and society hitherto does not recognize relief, even when he has worked ever so faithfully and diligently before. But ordinary poor relief leaves much to be desired, especially in the great cities where it is extraordinarily much worse than in the country.... We read in Berlin newspapers of suicide because of difficulty in making both ends meet, of people who died from direct hunger and have hanged themselves because they have nothing to eat, of people who announce in the paper they were tossed out homeless and have no income.... For the worker it is always a fact that falling into poverty and onto poor relief in a great city is synonymous with misery, and this insecurity makes him hostile and mistrustful of society. That is humanly not unnatural, and as long as the state does not meet him halfway, just as long will this trust in the state's honesty be taken from him by accusations against the government, which he will find where he wills; always running back again to the socialist quacks ... and, without great reflection, letting himself be promised things, which will not be fulfilled. On this account, I believe that accident insurance, with which we show the way, ... will still work on the anxieties and ill-feeling of the working class.

Q What arguments did Bismarck advance for social welfare legislation? How did Bismarck benefit politically from these moves toward state protection of workers' interests? To what broader forces in nineteenth-century European social and political life was Bismarck responding when he formulated these policies?

Source: From *Bismarck*, edited by Frederick B. M. Hollyday, pp. 60, 63, 65. Copyright © 1970 by Prentice-Hall, Inc.

---

felt increasingly threatened by the Czechs, Poles, and other Slavic groups within the empire.

What held the Austro-Hungarian Empire together was a combination of forces. Francis Joseph, the emperor, was one unifying factor. Although strongly anti-Hungarian, the cautious emperor made an effort to take a position above national differences. Loyalty to the Catholic Church also helped maintain support for the Catholic Habsburg dynasty among such national groups as the Czechs, Slovaks, and Poles. Finally, although dominated by German-speaking officials, the large imperial bureaucracy served as a unifying force for the empire.

RUSSIA In Russia, the government made no concession whatever to liberal and democratic reforms, eliminating altogether any possibility of a mass politics. The assassination of Alexander II in 1881 convinced his son and successor, Alexander III (1881–1894), that reform had been a mistake, and he quickly instituted what he said were "exceptional measures." The powers of the secret police were expanded. Advocates of constitutional monarchy and social reform, along with revolutionary groups, were persecuted. Entire districts of Russia were placed under martial law if the government suspected the inhabitants of treason. The powers of the zemstvos, created by the reforms of Alexander II, were sharply curtailed.

Alexander also pursued a radical Russification program among the numerous nationalities that made up the Russian empire. Russians themselves constituted only 40 percent of the population, which did not stop the tsar from banning the use of all languages except Russian in schools. The Russification policy angered national groups and created new sources of opposition to tsarist policies.

When Alexander III died, his weak son and successor, Nicholas II (1894–1917), adopted his father's conviction that the absolute power of the tsars should be preserved: "I shall maintain the principle of autocracy just as firmly and unflinchingly as did my unforgettable father."[4] But conditions were changing, especially with the spread of industrialization, and the tsar's approach was not realistic in view of the new circumstances he faced.

CHRONOLOGY The National States, 1871–1894	
Great Britain	
Second ministry of William Gladstone	1880–1885
Reform Act	1884
Redistribution Act	1885
France	
Paris Commune	1871 (March–May)
Republican constitution (Third Republic)	1875
Germany	
Bismarck as chancellor	1871–1890
Antisocialist law	1878
Social welfare legislation	1883–1889
Austria-Hungary	
Emperor Francis Joseph	1848–1916
Imperial Russia	
Tsar Alexander III	1881–1894

Chapter Summary

The Second Industrial Revolution helped create a new material prosperity that led Europeans to believe they had ushered in a new age of progress. In this second revolution, steel, chemicals, electricity, petroleum, and the internal combustion engine led the way to new industrial frontiers. Europe became divided into an industrialized north and a poorer south and east, while European manufactured goods and investment capital were exported abroad in exchange for raw materials, creating a true world economy. New jobs provided work opportunities for many women. Working-class socialist parties, such as Germany's Social Democratic Party, began working for change by forming trade unions and electing representatives to legislative bodies.

A major feature of this "new age of progress" was the emergence of a mass society. Better sanitation and improved diets led to a dramatic population increase, while emigration enabled Europe to avoid overcrowding. Class divisions continued to dictate styles of living, and industrialism reinforced traditional gender patterns: women stayed at home while men went out to work. Nevertheless, some women began to espouse birth control as an avenue for change. The lower classes benefited from the right to vote, a higher standard of living, and a modicum of education from new schools as most states assumed responsibility for mass compulsory education for children. New forms of mass transportation, combined with new work patterns, enabled large numbers of people to participate in mass leisure activities, including weekend excursions to amusement parks and seaside resorts, dance halls, and sporting events. Patterns of mass consumption arose that encouraged people to accumulate more material possessions.

By 1871, the national state had become the focus of people's lives. Especially in western Europe, liberal and democratic reforms brought new possibilities for greater participation in the political process, although women were still largely excluded from political rights. After 1871, the national state also began to expand its functions beyond all previous limits by adopting social insurance measures as protection against accidents, illness, and old age and by enacting public health and housing measures designed to curb the worst ills of urban living.

This extension of state functions took place in an atmosphere of growing national loyalty. After 1871, Western national states increasingly sought to solidify the social order and win the active loyalty and support of their citizens by deliberately cultivating national feelings. Yet this policy contained potentially great dangers. As we shall see in the next chapter, nations had discovered once again that imperialistic adventures and military successes could arouse nationalistic passions, but they also found that nationalistic feelings could lead to intense international rivalries that made war almost inevitable.

CHAPTER TIMELINE

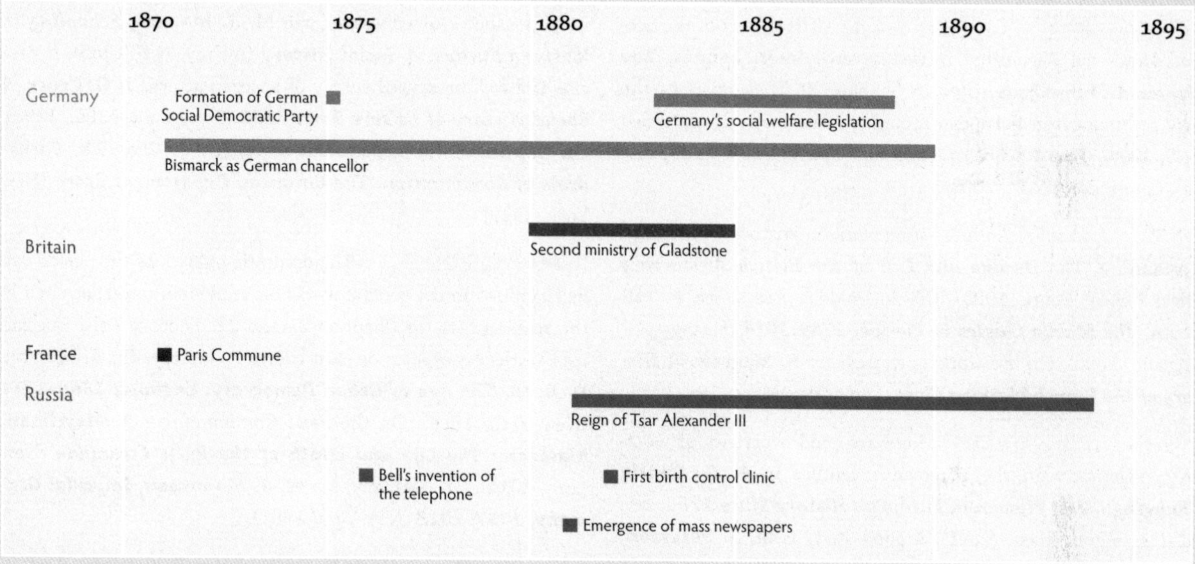

	1870	1875	1880	1885	1890	1895
Germany	Formation of German Social Democratic Party			Germany's social welfare legislation		
	Bismarck as German chancellor					
Britain			Second ministry of Gladstone			
France	■ Paris Commune					
Russia			Reign of Tsar Alexander III			
		■ Bell's invention of the telephone		■ First birth control clinic		
			■ Emergence of mass newspapers			

CHAPTER REVIEW

Upon Reflection

Q To what extent did the emergence and development of socialist parties and trade unions meet the needs of the working classes between 1871 and 1894?

Q How were the promises and problems of the new mass society reflected in education, leisure, and consumption?

Q Between 1871 and 1894, two major domestic political issues involved the achievement of liberal practices and the growth of political democracy. To what extent were these realized in Great Britain, France, Germany, Austria-Hungary, and Russia?

Key Terms

tariffs (p. 553)
cartels (p. 553)
evolutionary socialism (p. 557)

revisionism (p. 557)
mass society (p. 558)
plutocrats (p. 560)

mass education (p. 566)
mass leisure (p. 569)
mass politics (p. 570)

bicameral legislature (p. 571)
Kulturkampf (p. 572)
social security (p. 572)

Suggestions for Further Reading

GENERAL WORKS In addition to the general works on the nineteenth century and individual European countries cited in Chapters 21 and 22, a more specialized work on the subject matter of this chapter is available in **F. Gilbert** and **D. C. Large, *The End of the European Era, 1890 to the Present,*** 5th ed. (New York, 2002).

SECOND INDUSTRIAL REVOLUTION The subject of the Second Industrial Revolution is well covered in **D. Landes, *The Unbound Prometheus,*** cited in Chapter 20. The impact of the new technology on European thought is imaginatively discussed in **S. Kern, *The Culture of Time and Space, 1880–1918,*** rev. ed. (Cambridge, Mass., 2003).

SOCIAL CLASSES An interesting work on aristocratic life is **D. Cannadine, *The Decline and Fall of the British Aristocracy*** (New Haven, Conn., 1990). On the middle classes, see **P. Pilbeam, *The Middle Classes in Europe, 1789–1914*** (Basingstoke, England, 1990). On the working classes, see **R. Magraw, *A History of the French Working Class*** (Cambridge, Mass., 1992).

WOMEN'S EXPERIENCES There are good overviews of women's experiences in the nineteenth century in **B. G. Smith, *Changing Lives: Women in European History Since 1700,*** rev. ed. (Lexington, Mass., 2005). A good study is **M. J. Peterson,** *Family, Love, and Work in the Lives of Victorian Gentlewomen* (Bloomington, Ind., 1989). For a new perspective on domestic life, see **J. Flanders, *Inside the Victorian Home: A Portrait of Domestic Life in Victorian England*** (New York, 2004).

MASS EDUCATION, LEISURE, AND CONSUMPTION On various aspects of education, see **M. J. Maynes, *Schooling in Western Europe: A Social History*** (Albany, N.Y, 1985). A concise and well-presented survey of leisure patterns is **G. Cross, *A Social History of Leisure Since 1600*** (State College, Pa., 1990). On the rise of the department store, see **G. Crossick, *Cathedrals of Consumption: The European Department Store*** (New York, 1999).

DOMESTIC POLITICS The domestic politics of the period can be examined in the general works on individual countries cited in the reading lists for Chapters 21 and 22. There are also specialized works on aspects of each country's history. On Britain, see **D. Read, *The Age of Urban Democracy: England, 1868–1914*** (New York, 1994). On the Paris Commune, see **J. Merriman, *Massacre: The Life and Death of the Paris Commune*** (New York, 2014). On Germany, see **W. J. Mommsen, *Imperial Germany, 1867–1918*** (New York, 1995).

Notes

1. Quoted in W. L. Guttsman, *The German Social Democratic Party, 1875–1933* (London, 1981), p. 63.
2. Quoted in N. Bullock and J. Read, *The Movement for Housing Reform in Germany and France, 1840–1914* (Cambridge, 1985), p. 42.
3. Quoted in R. Gildea, *Barricades and Borders: Europe, 1800–1914, 2d ed.* (Oxford, 1996), pp. 240–241.
4. Quoted in S. Galai, *The Liberation Movement in Russia, 1900–1905* (Cambridge, 1973), p. 26.

MindTap **MindTap** is a fully online, highly personalized learning experience built upon Cengage Learning content. MindTap combines student learning tools—readings, multimedia, activities, and assessments—into a singular Learning Path that guides students through the course.

CHAPTER 24

An Age of Modernity, Anxiety, and Imperialism, 1894–1914

The Eiffel Tower at the World's Fair of 1900 in Paris

CHAPTER OUTLINE AND FOCUS QUESTIONS

Toward the Modern Consciousness: Intellectual and Cultural Developments

Q What developments in science, intellectual affairs, and the arts in the late nineteenth and early twentieth centuries "opened the way to a modern consciousness," and how did this consciousness differ from earlier worldviews?

Politics: New Directions and New Uncertainties

Q What gains did women make in their movement for women's rights? How did a new right-wing politics affect the Jews in different parts of Europe? What political problems did Great Britain, France, Austria-Hungary, Germany, and Russia face between 1894 and 1914, and how did they solve those problems?

The New Imperialism

Q What were the causes of the new imperialism that took place after 1880, and what effects did the European quest for colonies have on Africa and Asia?

International Rivalry and the Coming of War

Q What was the Bismarckian system of alliances, and how successful was it at keeping the peace? What issues lay behind the international crises that Europe faced in the late nineteenth and early twentieth centuries?

CRITICAL THINKING

Q What is the connection between the new imperialism of the late nineteenth century and the causes of World War I?

CONNECTIONS TO TODAY

Q What scientific discoveries of the past twenty years have challenged the modern consciousness that emerged in the late nineteenth and early twentieth centuries?

IN 1889, THE EIFFEL TOWER stood above Paris as a beacon of progress, a symbol of what technology and industrialization could accomplish. Constructed from iron to mark the entrance to the World's Fair, it was the tallest structure in the

577

world, extending one thousand feet above the city. Over a period of five months, 3.5 million visitors paid to ascend the tower and overlook the grounds teeming with throngs of people. Almost 175,000 people a day came to visit the fair's 60,000 exhibits, which included an Algerian bazaar, Swedish chalet, Indian palace, and Japanese garden. Guidebooks for the fair posited that a visitor would need ten to twenty days to see all of the displays. One awestruck visitor declared, "There is only one cry; this is the most grandiose, the most dazzling, the most marvelous spectacle ever seen." For most in attendance, the modern era was indeed an age of progress that was providing more opportunities, higher standards of living, better cities, more goods to consume, and greater democratization.

The optimism found at the World's Fair and throughout Europe's cities was not unchallenged, however. Some were still struggling to achieve progress. Many workers continued to endure pitiful housing conditions and low wages, while many women fought for the right to vote. Beneath the apparent calm, political tensions were also building, fueled by imperialist adventures, international rivalries, and cultural uncertainties. After 1880, Europeans engaged in a great race for colonies around the world. This competition for lands abroad greatly intensified existing antagonisms among European states.

Ultimately, Europeans proved incapable of finding constructive ways to cope with their international rivalries. The development of two large alliance systems—the Triple Alliance and the Triple Entente—may have helped preserve peace for a time, but eventually the alliances made it easier for the European nations to be drawn into the catastrophic carnage of World War I.

The cultural life of Europe in the decades before 1914 reflects similar dynamic tensions. The advent of mass education produced better-informed citizens but also made it easier for governments to stir up the masses by nationalistic appeals through the new mass journalism. At the same time, despite the appearance of progress, European philosophers, writers, and artists were advancing cultural expressions that questioned traditional ideas and values and undermined public confidence. Before 1914, many intellectuals had a sense of unease about the direction in which society was heading and a feeling of imminent catastrophe. They proved remarkably prophetic.

Toward the Modern Consciousness: Intellectual and Cultural Developments

Q FOCUS QUESTION: What developments in science, intellectual affairs, and the arts in the late nineteenth and early twentieth centuries "opened the way to a modern consciousness," and how did this consciousness differ from earlier worldviews?

Before 1914, most Westerners continued to believe in the values and ideals that had been generated by the Scientific Revolution and the Enlightenment. The ability of human beings to improve themselves and achieve a better society seemed well demonstrated by the rising standard of living, urban improvements, and mass education. Such products of modern technology as electric lights, phonographs, and automobiles reinforced the popular prestige of science and the belief in the ability of the human mind to comprehend the universe through the use of reason. Near the end of the nineteenth century, however, a dramatic transformation in the realm of ideas and culture challenged many of these assumptions. A new view of the physical universe, alternative views of human nature, and radically innovative forms of literary and artistic expression shattered old beliefs and opened the way to a modern consciousness. These new ideas called forth a sense of confusion and anxiety that would become even more pronounced after World War I.

Developments in the Sciences: The Emergence of a New Physics

Science was one of the chief pillars supporting the optimistic and rationalistic view of the world that many Westerners shared in the nineteenth century. Supposedly based on hard facts and cold reason, science offered a certainty of belief in the orderliness of nature that was comforting to many people for whom traditional religious beliefs no longer had much meaning. Many naively believed that the application of already known scientific laws would give humanity a complete understanding of the physical world and an accurate picture of reality. The new physics dramatically altered that perspective.

Throughout much of the nineteenth century, Westerners adhered to the mechanical conception of the universe postulated by the classical physics of Isaac

Newton. In this perspective, the universe was viewed as a giant machine in which time, space, and matter were objective realities that existed independent of the individuals observing them. Matter was thought to be composed of indivisible, solid material bodies called atoms.

These views were first seriously questioned at the end of the nineteenth century. The French scientist Marie Curie (kyoo-REE) (1867–1934) and her husband Pierre (1859–1906) discovered that an element called radium gave off rays of radiation that apparently came from within the atom itself. Atoms were not simply hard, material bodies but small worlds containing such subatomic particles as electrons and protons that behaved in a seemingly random and inexplicable fashion.

Building on this work, in 1900 a Berlin physicist, Max Planck (PLAHNK) (1858–1947), rejected the belief that a heated body radiates energy in a steady stream but maintained instead that energy is radiated discontinuously, in irregular packets of energy that he called "quanta." The quantum theory raised fundamental questions about the subatomic realm of the atom. By 1900, the old view of atoms as the basic building blocks of the material world was being seriously questioned, and Newtonian physics was in trouble.

THE WORK OF EINSTEIN Albert Einstein (YN-styn *or* YN-shtyn) (1879–1955), a German-born patent officer working in Switzerland, pushed these theories into new terrain. In 1905, Einstein published a paper titled "The Electro-Dynamics of Moving Bodies" that presented his special theory of relativity. According to **relativity theory**, space and time are not absolute but relative to the observer, and both are interwoven into what Einstein called a four-dimensional space-time continuum. Neither space nor time had an existence independent of human experience. As Einstein later explained simply to a journalist, "It was formerly believed that if all material things disappeared out of the universe, time and space would be left. According to the relativity theory, however, time and space disappear together with the things."[1] Moreover, Einstein concluded that matter was nothing but another form of energy. His epochal formula $E = mc^2$—each particle of matter is equivalent to its mass times the square of the velocity of light—was the key to explaining the vast energies contained within the atom. It led to the atomic age.

Toward a New Understanding of the Irrational: Nietzsche

Intellectually, the decades before 1914 witnessed a combination of contradictory developments. Thanks to the influence of science, confidence in human reason and progress still remained a dominant thread. At the same time, however, a small group of intellectuals attacked the idea of optimistic progress, dethroned reason, and glorified the irrational.

Friedrich Nietzsche (FREED-rikh NEE-chuh *or* NEE-chee) (1844–1900) was one of the intellectuals who glorified the irrational. According to Nietzsche, Western bourgeois society was decadent and incapable of any real cultural creativity, primarily because of its excessive emphasis on the rational faculty at the expense of emotions, passions, and instincts. Reason, claimed Nietzsche, actually played little role in human life because humans were at the mercy of irrational life forces.

Science Source/Getty Images

Marie Curie. Marie Curie was born in Warsaw, Poland, but studied at the University of Paris, where she received degrees in both physics and mathematics. She was the first woman to win two Noble Prizes, one in 1903 in physics and another in 1911 in chemistry. The photograph above was taken in her Paris laboratory in 1912. She died of leukemia in 1934, as a result of her laboratory work with radioactivity.

How, then, could Western society be renewed? First, said Nietzsche, one must recognize that "God is dead." Europeans had killed God, he said, and it was no longer possible to believe in some kind of cosmic order. Eliminating God and hence Christian morality had liberated human beings and made it possible to create a higher kind of being Nietzsche called the superman: "I teach you the Superman. Man is something that is to be surpassed."[2] Superior intellectuals must free themselves from the ordinary thinking of the masses, create their own values, and lead the masses. Nietzsche rejected and condemned political democracy, social reform, and universal suffrage.

Sigmund Freud and Psychoanalysis

At the turn of the twentieth century, a Viennese doctor Sigmund Freud (SIG-mund *or* ZIG-munt FROID) (1856–1939) put forth a series of theories that undermined optimism about the rational nature of the human mind. Freud's thought, like the new physics and the irrationalism of Nietzsche, added to the uncertainties of the age. His major ideas were published in 1900 in *The Interpretation of Dreams*, which contained the basic foundation of what came to be known as **psychoanalysis**.

According to Freud, human behavior was strongly determined by the unconscious, by earlier experiences and inner forces of which people were largely unaware. But why did some experiences whose influence persisted in controlling an individual's life remain unconscious? According to Freud, the answer was repression (see the box on p. 581), a process by which unsettling experiences were blotted from conscious awareness but still continued to influence behavior because they had become part of the unconscious. To explain how repression worked, Freud elaborated an intricate theory of the inner life of human beings.

According to Freud, a human being's inner life was a battleground of three contending forces: the id, the ego, and the superego. The id was the center of unconscious drives and was ruled by what Freud termed the pleasure principle. As creatures of desire, human beings directed their energy toward pleasure and away from pain. The id contained all kinds of lustful drives and desires and crude appetites and impulses. The ego was the seat of reason and hence the coordinator of the inner life. It was governed by the reality principle. Although humans were dominated by the pleasure principle, a true pursuit of pleasure was not feasible. The reality principle meant that people rejected pleasure so that they might live together in society. The superego was the locus of conscience and represented the inhibitions and moral values that society in general and parents in particular imposed on people. The superego served to force the ego to curb the unsatisfactory drives of the id.

The human being was thus a battleground among id, ego, and superego. Ego and superego exerted restraining influences on the unconscious id and repressed or kept out of consciousness what they wanted to. Repression began in childhood, and psychoanalysis was accomplished through a dialogue between psychotherapist and patient in which the therapist probed deeply into memory in order to retrace the chain of repression all the way back to its childhood origins. By making the conscious mind aware of the unconscious and its repressed contents, the psychotherapist could resolve the patient's psychic conflict.

The Impact of Darwin: Social Darwinism and Racism

In the second half of the nineteenth century, scientific theories were sometimes wrongly applied to achieve other ends. The application of Darwin's principle of organic evolution to the social order came to be known as **Social Darwinism**. Using Darwin's terminology, Social Darwinists argued that societies were organisms that evolved through time from a struggle with their environment. Progress came from the "struggle for survival," as the "fit"—the strong—advanced while the weak declined.

Rabid nationalists and racists also applied Darwin's ideas to human society in an even more radical way. In their pursuit of national greatness, extreme nationalists argued that nations, too, were engaged in a "struggle for existence" in which only the fittest survived. The German general Friedrich von Bernhardi (FREED-rikh fun bayrn-HAR-dee) argued in 1907 that "war is a biological necessity of the first importance, a regulative element in the life of mankind which cannot be dispensed with, since without it an unhealthy development will follow, which excludes every advancement of the race, and therefore all real civilization. 'War is the father of all things.'"[3] Numerous nationalist organizations preached the same doctrine as Bernhardi.

Racism, too, was dramatically revived and strengthened by new biological arguments. Perhaps nowhere was the combination of extreme nationalism and racism more evident and more dangerous than in Germany. One of the chief propagandists for German racism at the turn of the twentieth century was

Freud and the Concept of Repression

Freud's psychoanalytical theories resulted from his attempt to understand the world of the unconscious. This excerpt is taken from a lecture given in 1909 in which Freud described how he arrived at his theory of the role of repression.

Sigmund Freud, *Five Lectures on Psychoanalysis*

I did not abandon it [his technique of encouraging patients to reveal forgotten experiences], however, before the observations I made during my use of it afforded me decisive evidence. I found confirmation of the fact that the forgotten memories were not lost. They were in the patient's possession and were ready to emerge in association to what was still unconscious. The existence of this force could be assumed with certainty, since one became aware of an effort corresponding to it if, in opposition to it, one tried to introduce the unconscious memories into the patient's consciousness. The force which was maintaining the pathological condition became apparent in the form of resistance on the part of the patient.

It was on this idea of resistance, then, that I based my view of the course of physical events in hysteria. In order to effect a recovery, it had proved necessary to remove these resistances. Starting out from the mechanism of cure, it now became possible to construct quite definite ideas of the origin of the illness. The same forces which, in the form of resistance, were now offering opposition to the forgotten material's being made conscious, must formerly have brought about the forgetting and must have pushed the pathogenic experiences in question out of consciousness. I gave the name of "repression"

to this hypothetical process, and I considered that it was proved by the undeniable existence of resistance.

The further question could then be raised as to what these forces were and what the determinants were of the repression in which we now recognized the pathogenic mechanism of hysteria. A comparative study of the pathogenic situations which we had come to know through the cathartic procedure made it possible to answer this question. All these experiences had involved the emergence of a wishful impulse which was in sharp contrast to the subject's other wishes and which proved incompatible with the ethical and aesthetic standards of his personality. There had been a short conflict, and the end of this internal struggle was that the idea which had appeared before consciousness as the vehicle of this irreconcilable wish fell a victim to repression, was pushed out of consciousness with all its attached memories, and was forgotten. Thus, the incompatibility of the wish in question with the patient's ego was the motive for the repression; the subject's ethical and other standards were the repressing forces. An acceptance of the incompatible wishful impulse or a prolongation of the conflict would have produced a high degree of unpleasure; this unpleasure was avoided by means of repression, which was thus revealed as one of the devices serving to protect the mental personality.

Q According to Freud, how did he discover the existence of repression? What function does repression perform? What forces in modern European society might have contributed to forcing individuals into repressive modes of thinking and acting?

Source: From *Five Lectures on Psycho-analysis* by Sigmund Freud, translated by James Strachey. Copyright © 1961 by James Strachey. Used by permission of W. W. Norton & Company, Inc. and Sigmund Freud Copyrights Ltd.

Houston Stewart Chamberlain (1855–1927), an Englishman who became a German citizen. His book, *The Foundations of the Nineteenth Century*, published in 1899, made a special impact on Germany. Modern-day Germans, according to Chamberlain, were the only pure successors of the "Aryans," who were portrayed as the true and original creators of Western culture. The Aryan (AR-ee-un) race, under German leadership, must be prepared to fight for Western civilization and save it from the destructive assaults of such "lower" races as Jews, Negroes, and Orientals. Increasingly, Jews were singled out as the racial enemy who wanted to destroy the Aryan race (see "Jews in the European Nation-State" later in this chapter).

The Culture of Modernity

The revolution in physics and psychology was paralleled by a revolution in literature and the arts. Before 1914, writers and artists self-consciously rejected the traditional literary and artistic styles that had dominated European cultural life since the Renaissance. The changes that they produced have since been called **Modernism**.

NATURALISM AND SYMBOLISM IN LITERATURE Throughout much of the late nineteenth century, literature was dominated by Naturalism. Naturalists accepted the material world as real and felt that literature should be realistic. By addressing social problems, writers could contribute to an objective understanding of the world. Although Naturalism was a continuation of Realism, it lacked the underlying note of liberal optimism about people and society that had been prevalent in the 1850s. The Naturalists often portrayed characters caught in the grip of forces beyond their control.

The novels of the French writer Émile Zola (ay-MEEL ZOH-lah) (1840–1902) provide a good example of Naturalism. Against a backdrop of the urban slums and coalfields of northern France, Zola showed how alcoholism and different environments affected people's lives. He had read Darwin's *Origin of Species* and had been impressed by its emphasis on the struggle for survival and the importance of environment and heredity. These themes were central to his *Rougon-Macquart*, a twenty-volume series of novels on the "natural and social history of a family." Zola maintained that the artist must analyze and dissect life as a biologist would a living organism. He said, "I have simply done on living bodies the work of analysis which surgeons perform on corpses."

At the turn of the century, a new group of writers, known as the Symbolists, reacted against Realism. Primarily interested in writing poetry, the Symbolists believed that objective knowledge of the world was impossible. The external world was not real but only a collection of symbols that reflected the true reality of the individual human mind. Art, they believed, should function for its own sake instead of serving, criticizing, or seeking to understand society. In the works of such Symbolist poets as William Butler Yeats (YAYTS) (1865–1939) and Rainer Maria Rilke (RY-nuh mah-REE-uh RILL-kuh) (1875–1926), poetry ceased to be part of popular culture because only through a knowledge of the poet's personal language could one hope to understand what the poem was saying.

MODERNISM IN THE ARTS Since the Renaissance, artists had largely tried to represent reality as accurately as possible, carefully applying brushstrokes and employing perspective to produce realistic portrayals of their subjects. By the late nineteenth century, however, artists were seeking new forms of expression. The preamble to modern painting can be found in **Impressionism**, a movement that originated in France in the 1870s when a group of artists rejected the studios and museums and went out into the countryside to paint nature directly. But the Impressionists did not just paint scenes from nature. Their subjects included streets and cabarets, rivers, and busy boulevards—wherever people congregated for work and leisure. In this sense, Impressionist subject matter reflected the pastimes of the new upper-middle class. Instead of adhering to the conventional modes of painting and subject matter, the Impressionists sought originality and distinction from the past. Their artworks utilized bright colors, dynamic brushstrokes, and a smaller, more private scale than their predecessors. Camille Pissarro (kah-MEEL pee-SAH-roh) (1830–1903), one of Impressionism's founders, described their approach:

> Precise drawing is dry and hampers the impression of the whole, it destroys all sensations. Do not define too closely the outlines of things; it is the brushstroke of the right value and color which should produce the drawing.... Work at the same time upon sky, water, branches, ground, keeping everything going on an equal basis and unceasingly rework until you have got it.... Don't proceed according to rules and principles, but paint what you observe and feel. Paint generously and unhesitatingly, for it is best not to lose the first impression.[4]

Impressionists like Pissarro tried to put into painting their impressions of the changing effects of light on objects in nature.

An important Impressionist painter was Berthe Morisot (BAYRT mor-ee-ZOH) (1841–1895), who broke with the practice of women being only amateur artists and became a professional painter. One of the three women to exhibit with the original Impressionists, her work fetched the highest price at the first Impressionist auction. Her dedication to the new style of painting won her the disfavor of the traditional French academic artists. Morisot believed that women had a special vision that was, as she said, "more delicate than that of men." Her special touch is evident in *Young Girl by the Window*, in which she makes use of soft colors and flowing brushstrokes. Near the end of her life, she lamented the

Berthe Morisot, *Young Girl by the Window.* Berthe Morisot came from a wealthy French family that settled in Paris when she was seven. The first female Impressionist painter, she developed her own unique style. Her gentle colors and strong use of pastels are evident in *Young Girl by the Window*, painted in 1878. Many of her paintings focus on women and domestic scenes.

refusal of men to take her work seriously: "I don't think there has ever been a man who treated a woman as an equal, and that's all I would have asked, for I know I'm worth as much as they."[5]

By the 1880s, a new movement known as **Post-Impressionism** had emerged in France and soon spread to other European countries. Post-Impressionism retained the Impressionist emphasis on light and color but revolutionized it even further by paying more attention to structure and form. Post-Impressionists sought to use both color and line to express inner feelings and produce a personal statement of reality rather than an imitation of objects. Impressionist paintings had retained a sense of realism, but the Post-Impressionists shifted from objective reality to subjective reality and in so doing began to withdraw from the artist's traditional task of depicting the external world. The works of the Post-Impressionists were the real forerunners of modern art.

A famous Post-Impressionist was the tortured and tragic figure Vincent van Gogh (von GOH *or* vahn GOK) (1853–1890). For van Gogh, art was a spiritual experience. He was especially interested in color and believed that it could act as its own form of language. Van Gogh maintained that artists should paint what they feel.

By the beginning of the twentieth century, the belief that the task of art was to "represent reality" had lost much of its meaning. By that time, the new psychology and the new physics had made it evident that many people were not sure what constituted reality anyway. Then, too, the development of photography gave artists another reason to reject visual realism. Invented in the 1830s, photography became popular and widespread after George Eastman produced the first Kodak camera for the mass market in 1888. What was the point of an artist doing what the camera did better? Unlike the camera, which could only mirror reality, artists could create reality. In modern art, as in literature, individual consciousness became the source of meaning. Between 1905 and 1914, this search for individual expression produced a wide variety of schools of painting, all of which had their greatest impact after World War I.

In 1905, one of the most important figures in modern art was just beginning his career. Pablo Picasso (pi-KAH-soh) (1881–1973) was from Spain but settled in Paris in 1904. Extremely versatile and capable of painting in a remarkable variety of styles, Picasso was instrumental in the development of a new style called **Cubism** that used geometric designs as visual stimuli to re-create reality in the viewer's mind. Picasso's 1907 work *Les Demoiselles d'Avignon* (lay dem-wah-ZEL dah-vee-NYONH) has been called the first Cubist painting.

The modern artist's flight from "visual reality" reached a high point in 1910 with the beginning of **abstract painting**. Wassily Kandinsky (vus-YEEL-yee kan-DIN-skee) (1866–1944), a Russian who worked in Germany, was one of its originators. As is evident in his *Painting with White Border*, Kandinsky sought to avoid representation altogether. He believed that art should speak directly to the soul. To do so, it

Vincent van Gogh, *The Starry Night*. The Dutch painter Vincent van Gogh was a major figure among the Post-Impressionists. His originality and power of expression made a strong impact on his artistic successors. In *The Starry Night*, painted in 1889, van Gogh's subjective vision was given full play as the dynamic swirling forms of the heavens above overwhelm the village below. The heavens seem alive with a mysterious spiritual force. Van Gogh painted this work in an asylum one year before he committed suicide.

must avoid any reference to visual reality and concentrate on color.

At the start of the twentieth century, developments in music paralleled those in painting. Expressionism in music was a Russian creation, the product of the composer Igor Stravinsky (EE-gor struh-VIN-skee) (1882–1971) and the Ballet Russe, the dance company of Sergei Diaghilev (syir-GYAY DYAHG-yuh-lif) (1872–1929). Together they revolutionized the world of music with *The Rite of Spring*, a ballet staged by Diaghilev to music by Stravinsky. At the premiere on May 29, 1913, the pulsating rhythms, sharp dissonances, and unusual dancing overwhelmed the Paris audience and caused a riot at the theater.

Politics: New Directions and New Uncertainties

Q FOCUS QUESTIONS: What gains did women make in their movement for women's rights? How did a new right-wing politics affect the Jews in different parts of Europe? What political problems did Great Britain, France, Austria-Hungary, Germany, and Russia face between 1894 and 1914, and how did they solve those problems?

Growing anxieties in European political life also paralleled the uncertainties in European intellectual and

Pablo Picasso, *Les Demoiselles d'Avignon*. Pablo Picasso, a major pioneer of modern art, experimented with a remarkable variety of styles. *Les Demoiselles d'Avignon* (1907) was the first great example of Cubism, which one art historian has called "the first style of [the twentieth] century to break radically with the past." Geometric shapes replace traditional forms, forcing the viewer to re-create reality in his or her own mind. Picasso said of this painting, "I paint forms as I think them, not as I see them."

cultural life. The seemingly steady progress in the growth of liberal principles and **political democracy** after 1871 soon slowed or even ceased altogether after 1894. The new mass politics had opened the door to changes that many nineteenth-century liberals found unacceptable, and liberals themselves were forced to move in new directions. The appearance of a new right-wing politics based on racism added an ugly note to the existing anxieties. With their newfound voting rights, workers elected socialists who demanded new reforms when they took their places in legislative bodies. Women, too, made demands, insisting on the right to vote and using new tactics to gain it. In central and eastern Europe, tensions grew as authoritarian governments refused to meet the demands of reformers. And outside Europe, a new giant appeared in the Western world as the United States emerged as a great industrial power with immense potential.

The Movement for Women's Rights

In the 1830s, a number of women in the United States and Europe who worked together in several reform movements argued for the right of women to divorce and own property. These early efforts were not

particularly successful, however. For example, women did not gain the right to their own property until 1870 in Britain, 1900 in Germany, and 1907 in France.

NEW PROFESSIONS Divorce and property rights were only a beginning for the women's movement, however. Some middle- and upper-middle-class women gained access to higher education while others sought entry into occupations dominated by men. The first field to open was teaching. Since medical training was largely closed to women, they sought alternatives in the development of nursing. One nursing pioneer was Amalie Sieveking (uh-MAHL-yuh SEE-vuh-king) (1794–1859), who founded the Female Association for the Care of the Poor and Sick in Hamburg, Germany. As she explained, "To me, at least as important were the benefits which [work with the poor] seemed to promise for those of my sisters who would join me in such a work of charity. The higher interests of my sex were close to my heart."[6] Sieveking's work was followed by that of the more famous British nurse Florence Nightingale (1820–1910), whose efforts during the Crimean War, like those of Clara Barton (1821–1912) in the American Civil War, transformed nursing into a profession of trained, middle-class "women in white."

THE RIGHT TO VOTE By the 1840s and 1850s, the movement for women's rights had entered the political arena with the call for equal political rights. Many feminists believed that the right to vote was the key to all other reforms to improve the position of women.

Suffragists had one basic aim: women's full citizenship in the nation-state. The British women's movement was the most vocal and most active in Europe. Emmeline Pankhurst (PANK-hurst) (1858–1928) and her daughters, Christabel and Sylvia, founded the Women's Social and Political Union, which enrolled mostly middle- and upper-class women, in 1903. The members of Pankhurst's organization realized the value of the media and used unusual publicity stunts to call attention to their demands (see the box on p. 587 and Images of Everyday Life on p. 588). Derisively labeled "suffragettes" by male politicians, they pelted government officials with eggs, chained themselves to lampposts, smashed the windows of department stores on fashionable shopping streets, burned railroad cars, and went on hunger strikes in jail.

Although demands for women's rights were heard throughout Europe and the United States before World War I, only in Finland, Norway, and a few American states did women actually receive the right to vote. It would take the dramatic upheaval of World War I before male-dominated governments capitulated on this basic issue.

Women reformers also took on issues besides suffrage. In many countries, women supported peace movements. Bertha von Suttner (ZOOT-nuh) (1843–1914) became head of the Austrian Peace Society and protested against the growing arms race of the 1890s. Her novel *Lay Down Your Arms* became a bestseller and brought her the Nobel Peace Prize in 1905. Lower-class women also took up the cause of peace. A group of women workers marched in Vienna in 1911 and demanded, "We want an end to armaments, to the means of murder, and we want these millions to be spent on the needs of the people."[7]

THE NEW WOMAN Bertha von Suttner was but one example of the "new women" who were becoming more prominent at the turn of the twentieth century. These women rejected traditional feminine roles. Although some of them supported political ideologies that flew in the face of the ruling classes such as socialism, others simply sought new freedom outside the household and new roles other than those of wives and mothers. Maria Montessori (mahn-tuh-SOR-ee) (1870–1952) was a good example of the "new woman." Breaking with tradition, she attended medical school at the University of Rome and in 1896 became the first Italian woman to receive a medical degree. Three years later, she began a lecture tour in Italy on the subject of the "new woman," whom she characterized as a woman who followed a rational, scientific perspective. In keeping with this ideal, Montessori put her medical background to work in a school for mentally handicapped children. She devised new teaching materials that enabled these children to read and write and became convinced, as she later wrote, "that similar methods applied to normal students would develop or set free their personality in a marvelous and surprising way." Subsequently, she established a system of childhood education based on natural and spontaneous activities in which students learned at their own pace. By the 1930s, hundreds of Montessori schools had been established in Europe and the United States. As a professional woman and an unwed mother, Montessori also embodied some of the freedoms of the "new woman."

Jews in the European Nation-State

Near the end of the nineteenth century, a revival of racism combined with extreme nationalism to produce a new right-wing politics directed against the Jews. Of course, anti-Semitism had a long history in Europe, but in the nineteenth century, as a result of the ideals of the Enlightenment and the French Revolution, Jews had increasingly been granted legal equality in many European countries, enabling many Jews to leave the ghetto and assimilate into the cultures around them. They became successful bankers, lawyers, scientists, scholars, journalists, and stage performers. In 1880, for example, Jews made up 10 percent of the population of the city of Vienna but 39 percent of its medical students and 23 percent of its law students.

These achievements represent only one side of the picture, however. In Germany and Austria during the 1880s and 1890s, conservatives founded right-wing anti-Semitic parties that used anti-Semitism to win the votes of traditional lower-middle-class groups who felt threatened by the economic forces of the times. The worst treatment of Jews at the turn of the century occurred in eastern Europe, where 72 percent of the world's Jewish population lived. Russian Jews were admitted to secondary schools and universities only under a quota system and were forced to live in certain regions of the country. Persecutions and pogroms (organized massacres) were widespread.

Consequently, hundreds of thousands of Jews decided to emigrate. Many went to the United States, but some (perhaps 25,000 in all) moved to Palestine,

The Struggle for the Right to Vote

Emmeline Pankhurst, with the help of her daughters, was the leader of the women's movement for the right to vote in Britain at the end of the nineteenth century and the beginning of the twentieth century. Believing that peaceful requests were having little effect on the members of Parliament, Pankhurst came to advocate more forceful methods, as is evident in this selection from *My Own Story*, her autobiography published in 1914. Although this confrontational approach was abandoned during World War I, the British government granted women the right to vote in 1918 at the end of the war.

Emmeline Pankhurst, *My Own Story*

I had called upon women to join me in striking at the Government through the only thing that governments are really very much concerned about—property—and the response was immediate. Within a few days the newspapers rang with the story of the attack made on letter boxes in London, Liverpool, Birmingham, Bristol, and half a dozen other cities. In some cases the boxes, when opened by postmen, mysteriously burst into flame; in others the letters were destroyed by corrosive chemicals; in still others the addresses were rendered illegible by black fluids. Altogether it was estimated that over 5,000 letters were completely destroyed and many thousands more were delayed in transit.

It was with a deep sense of their gravity that these letter-burning protests were undertaken, but we felt that something drastic must be done in order to destroy the apathy of the men of England who view with indifference the suffering of women oppressed by unjust laws. As we pointed out, letters, precious though they may be, are less precious than human bodies and souls.... And so, in order to call attention to greater crimes against human beings, our letter burnings continued.

In only a few cases were the offenders apprehended, and one of the few women arrested was a helpless cripple, a woman who could move about only in a wheeled chair. She received a sentence of eight months in the first division, and, resolutely hunger striking, was forcibly fed with unusual brutality, the prison doctor deliberately breaking one of her teeth in order to insert a gag. In spite of her disabilities and her weakness the crippled girl persisted in her hunger strike and her

resistance to prison rules, and within a short time had to be released. The excessive sentences of the other pillar box destroyers resolved themselves into very short terms because of the resistance of the prisoners, every one of whom adopted the hunger strike.

It was at this time, February, 1913, less than two years ago as I write these words, that militancy, as it is now generally understood by the public began—militancy in the sense of continued, destructive, guerrilla warfare against the Government through injury to private property. Some property had been destroyed before this time, but the attacks were sporadic, and were meant to be in the nature of a warning as to what might become a settled policy. Now we indeed lighted the torch, and we did it with the absolute conviction that no other course was open to us. We had tried every other measure, as I am sure that I have demonstrated to my readers, and our years of work and suffering and sacrifice had taught us that the Government would not yield to right and justice, what the majority of members of the House of Commons admitted was right and justice, but that the Government would, as other governments invariably do, yield to expediency. Now our task was to show the Government that it was expedient to yield to the women's just demands. In order to do that we had to make England and every department of English life insecure and unsafe. We had to make English law a failure and the courts farce comedy theatres; we had to discredit the Government and Parliament in the eyes of the world; we had to spoil English sports, hurt business, destroy valuable property, demoralize the world of society, shame the churches, upset the whole orderly conduct of life.

That is, we had to do as much of this guerrilla warfare as the people of England would tolerate. When they came to the point of saying to the Government: "Stop this, in the only way it can be stopped, by giving the women of England representation," then we should extinguish our torch.

Q What methods did Emmeline Pankhurst advocate be used to achieve the right to vote for women? Why did she feel justified in using these methods? Do you think she was justified? Why or why not?

Source: From Emmeline Pankhurst, *My Own Story* (New York: Hearst International Library, 1914).

IMAGES OF EVERYDAY LIFE

The Struggle for the Right to Vote

FOR MANY FEMINISTS, the right to vote came to represent the key to other reforms that would benefit women. In Britain, suffragists attracted attention to their cause by carrying out various protest acts. The photograph at the left shows the arrest of a suffragist who had chained herself to the fence outside Buckingham Palace in London. The photograph at the right shows police preventing Emmeline Pankhurst and her two daughters from entering Buckingham Palace to present a petition to the king. At the bottom is a photograph of Emily Davison throwing herself under the king's horse at the Epsom Derby horse race. Shortly before her sacrificial action, she had written, "The glorious and indomitable Spirit of Liberty has but one further penalty within its power, the surrender of life itself, the supreme consummation of sacrifice."

Central Press/Getty Images

© Bettmann/Corbis

Arthur Barrett/Getty Images

the biblical homeland of the Jews, which soon became the focus of a Jewish nationalist movement called **Zionism**.

A key figure in the growth of Zionism was Theodor Herzl (TAY-oh-dor HAYRT-sul) (1860–1904). In 1896, he published a book called *The Jewish State* in which he maintained that "the Jews who wish it will have their state." Settlement in Palestine was difficult, however, because it was then part of the Ottoman Empire, which was opposed to Jewish immigration. Despite the problems, the First Zionist Congress, which met in Switzerland in 1897, proclaimed as its aim the creation of a "home in Palestine secured by public law" for the Jewish people. Although about a thousand Jews migrated to Palestine in 1900 and three thousand more each year after that, on the eve of World War I the Zionist dream remained only a dream.

The Transformation of Liberalism: Great Britain

In dealing with the problems created by the new mass politics, liberal governments often followed policies that undermined the basic tenets of liberalism. This was particularly true in Great Britain, where the demands of the working-class movement caused Liberals to move away from their ideals. Liberals were forced to adopt significant social reforms due to the pressure of two new working-class organizations: trade unions and the Labour Party.

Frustrated by the government's failure to enact social reform, trade unions began to advocate more radical change of the economic system, calling for "collective ownership and control over production, distribution and exchange." At the same time, a movement for laborers emerged among a group of intellectuals known as the Fabian Socialists. Neither the Fabian Socialists nor the British trade unions were Marxist. They did not advocate class struggle and revolution but instead favored evolution toward a socialist state by democratic means. In 1900, representatives of the trade unions and Fabian Socialists coalesced to form the Labour Party. By 1906, they had managed to elect twenty-nine members to the House of Commons.

The Liberals, who led the government from 1906 to 1914, perceived that they would have to enact a program of social welfare or lose the support of the workers. Under the leadership of David Lloyd George

Palestine

(1863–1945), the Liberals abandoned the classic principles of *laissez faire* and voted for a series of social reforms. The National Insurance Act of 1911 provided benefits for workers in case of sickness and unemployment, to be paid for by compulsory contributions from workers, employers, and the state. Additional legislation provided a small pension for retirees over seventy and compensation for workers injured on the job. Though both the benefits of the program and the tax increases were modest, they were the first hesitant steps toward the future British welfare state.

In the effort to achieve social reform, Lloyd George was also forced to confront the power of the House of Lords. Composed of hereditary aristocrats, the House of Lords took a strong stance against Lloyd George's effort to pay for social reform measures by taxes, however modest, on the wealthy. The prime minister then pushed through a law in 1911 that restricted the ability of the House of Lords to impede legislation enacted by the House of Commons. After 1911, the House of Lords became largely a debating society.

France: Travails of the Third Republic

In the 1890s, France's fragile Third Republic experienced a crisis that was an outgrowth of the renewed anti-Semitism in Europe in the late nineteenth century. Early in 1895, Alfred Dreyfus (DRY-fuss), a Jew and a captain on the French general staff, was found guilty of selling army secrets by a secret military court and condemned to life imprisonment. Evidence soon emerged that pointed to his innocence. Another officer, a Catholic aristocrat, was more obviously the traitor, but the army, a stronghold of aristocratic and Catholic officers, refused to grant Dreyfus a new trial. Some right-wing journalists even used the case to push their own anti-Semitic views. After a wave of public outrage, however, republic leaders insisted on a new trial. Although the second trial failed to set aside the guilty verdict, the government pardoned Dreyfus in 1899, and in 1906, he was fully exonerated.

One result of the Dreyfus affair was a change in government. Moderate republicans lost control to radical republicans who were determined to make greater progress toward a more democratic society by breaking the power of the republic's enemies, especially the army and the Catholic Church. The army was purged of all high-ranking officers who had antirepublican reputations. Moreover, church and state were officially separated in 1905, and during the next two years, the government seized church property and stopped paying clerical salaries. These changes ended the political threat from the right to the Third Republic, which by now commanded the loyalty of most French people.

Growing Tensions in Germany

During the reign of Emperor William II (1888–1918), the new imperial Germany begun by Bismarck continued as an "authoritarian, conservative, military-bureaucratic power state." By 1914, Germany had become the strongest military and industrial power on the continent. New social configurations had emerged as more than 50 percent of German workers had jobs in industry, while only 30 percent of the workforce was still in agriculture. Urban centers had mushroomed in number and size. These rapid changes in William's Germany helped produce a society torn between modernization and traditionalism.

With the expansion of industry and cities came demands for more political participation and growing sentiment for reforms that would produce greater democratization. Conservative forces, especially two of the powerful ruling groups in Germany—the landowning nobility and representatives of heavy industry—tried to block reforms by supporting William II's activist foreign policy of finding Germany's "place in the sun." Expansionism, they believed, would divert people from further democratization.

The tensions in German society created by the conflict between modernization and traditionalism were also manifested in a new, radicalized, right-wing politics. A number of pressure groups arose to support nationalistic goals. Such groups as the Pan-German League stressed strong German nationalism and advocated imperialism as a tool to overcome social divisions and unite all classes. They were also anti-Semitic and denounced Jews as the destroyers of national community.

Austria-Hungary: The Problem of the Nationalities

At the beginning of the 1890s, Austria-Hungary remained troubled by the problem of its numerous nationalities (see Chapter 23). The granting of universal male suffrage in 1907 only exacerbated the problem as nationalities that had previously played no role in the government now agitated in parliament for autonomy. This led prime ministers after 1900 to ignore parliament and rely increasingly on imperial emergency decrees to govern. Parliament itself became a bizarre forum in which, in the words of one incredulous observer, "about a score of men, all decently clad, were seated or standing, each at his little desk. Some made an infernal noise violently opening and shutting the lids of their desks. Others emitted a blaring sound from little toy trumpets; . . . still others beat snare drums."[8]

The numerous nationalities threatened the position of the dominant German minority in Austria, producing a backlash in the form of virulent German nationalism. As Austria industrialized in the 1870s and 1880s, two working-class parties came into existence, both strongly influenced by nationalism. The Social Democrats, though a Marxist party, supported the Austrian government, fearful that the autonomy of the various nationalities would hinder industrial development and prevent improvements for workers. Even more nationalistic were the Christian Socialists, who combined agitation for workers with a virulent anti-Semitism.

Industrialization and Revolution in Imperial Russia

Although industrialization came late to Russia, it progressed rapidly after 1890, especially with the assistance of foreign investment capital. By 1900, Russia had become the fourth-largest producer of steel, behind the United States, Germany, and Great Britain. With industrialization came factories, an industrial working class, and the development of socialist parties, although repression in Russia soon forced these parties to go underground and become revolutionary. The Marxist Social Democratic Party, for example, held its first congress in Minsk in 1898, but the arrest of its leaders caused the next one to be held in Brussels in 1903, attended by Russian émigrés. The Social Revolutionaries worked to overthrow the tsarist autocracy and establish peasant socialism. Having no other outlet for opposition to the regime, they advocated political terrorism and attempted to assassinate government officials and members of the ruling dynasty. The growing opposition to the tsarist regime finally exploded into revolution in 1905.

The defeat of the Russians by the Japanese in 1904–1905 encouraged antigovernment groups to rebel against the tsarist regime. After a general strike in October 1905, the government capitulated. Nicholas II (1894–1917) granted civil liberties and agreed to create a legislative assembly, the Duma (DOO-muh), elected directly by a broad franchise. But real

Private Collection/The Bridgeman Art Library

Nicholas II. The last tsar of Russia hoped to preserve the traditional autocratic ways of his predecessors. In this photograph, Nicholas II and his wife, Alexandra, are shown in 1913 with their family in front of the Kremlin at the celebration of the three-hundredth anniversary of the founding of the Romanov dynasty.

constitutional monarchy proved short-lived. Already by 1907, the tsar had curtailed the power of the Duma, and he fell back on the army and bureaucracy to rule Russia.

The Rise of the United States

Between 1860 and 1914, the United States made the shift from an agrarian to a mighty industrial nation. American heavy industry stood unchallenged in 1900. In that year, the Carnegie Steel Company alone produced more steel than Great Britain's entire steel industry. Industrialization also led to urbanization. While established cities, such as New York, Philadelphia, and Boston, grew even larger, other moderate-size cities, such as Pittsburgh, grew by leaps and

bounds because of industrialization. Whereas 20 percent of Americans lived in cities in 1860, more than 40 percent did in 1900.

The United States had become the world's richest nation and greatest industrial power. Yet serious questions remained about the quality of American life. In 1890, the richest 9 percent of Americans owned an incredible 71 percent of all the wealth. Labor unrest over unsafe working conditions, strict work discipline, and periodic cycles of devastating unemployment led workers to organize. By the turn of the century, one national organization, the American Federation of Labor, emerged as labor's dominant voice. In 1900, however, it included only 8.4 percent of the American industrial labor force.

During the so-called Progressive era after 1900, a wave of reform swept across the United States. The Meat Inspection Act (1906) and the Pure Food and Drug Act (1905) provided for a limited degree of federal regulation of corrupt industrial practices. The presidency of Woodrow Wilson (1913–1921) witnessed the imposition of a graduated federal income tax and the establishment of the Federal Reserve System, which permitted the federal government to play a role in important economic decisions formerly made by bankers. Like European nations, the United States was slowly adopting policies that extended the functions of the state.

The Growth of Canada

Canada faced problems of national unity at the end of the nineteenth century. In 1870, the Dominion of Canada had four provinces: Quebec, Ontario, Nova Scotia, and New Brunswick. With the addition of two more—Manitoba and British Columbia—the following year, Canada stretched from the Atlantic to the Pacific.

Real unity was difficult to achieve, however, because of the distrust between the English-speaking majority and the French-speaking Canadians living primarily in Quebec. Wilfred Laurier (LOR-ee-ay) (1841–1919), who became the first French Canadian prime minister in

Reign of Emperor William II	1888–1918
Reign of Tsar Nicholas II	1894–1917
Dreyfus affair in France	1895–1899
Theodor Herzl, *The Jewish State*	1896
First congress of Social Democratic Party in Russia	1898
Beginning of Progressive era in the United States	1900
Formation of Labour Party in Britain	1900
Pankhursts establish Women's Social and Political Union	1903
Russo-Japanese War	1904–1905
Revolution in Russia	1905
National Insurance Act in Britain	1911

1896, was able to reconcile the two groups. During his administration, industrialization boomed, especially in production of textiles, furniture, and railway equipment. Hundreds of thousands of immigrants, most of them from Europe, also flowed into Canada. Many settled on lands in the west, thus helping populate Canada's vast territories.

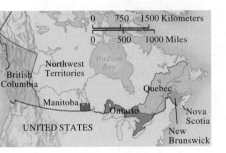

Canada, 1871

The New Imperialism

Q FOCUS QUESTION: What were the causes of the new imperialism that took place after 1880, and what effects did the European quest for colonies have on Africa and Asia?

Beginning in the 1880s, European states engaged in an intense scramble for overseas territory. This "**new imperialism**," as some have called it, led Europeans to carve up the continents of Asia and Africa. What were the reasons for this mad scramble for colonies?

Impetus for the New Imperialism

The existence of competitive nation-states after 1870 was undoubtedly a major factor in the emergence of the new imperialism. As European affairs grew tense,

competition led European states to acquire colonies abroad to provide ports and coaling stations for their navies. Great Britain, for example, often expanded into new regions not for economic reasons but to keep the French, Germans, or Russians from setting up bases that could harm British interests. Colonies were also a source of international prestige. Once the dash for colonies began, failure to enter the race was perceived as a sign of weakness, totally unacceptable to an aspiring Great Power. As a British foreign minister wrote, "When I left the Foreign Office in 1880, nobody thought about Africa. When I returned to it in 1885, the nations of Europe were almost quarreling with each other as to the various portions of Africa which they should obtain."[9] Late-nineteenth-century imperialism was closely tied to nationalism.

It was also tied to social Darwinism and racism. Social Darwinists believed that in the struggle between nations, the fit are victorious and survive. Superior races must dominate inferior races by military force to show how strong and virile they are. As one Englishman wrote, "To the development of the White Man, the Black Man and the Yellow must ever remain inferior, and as the former raised itself higher and yet higher, so did these latter seem to shrink out of humanity and appear nearer and nearer to the brutes."[10]

Some Europeans gave a more religious or humanitarian justification for imperialism by arguing that they had a "moral responsibility" to civilize "ignorant" peoples. This notion of the "white man's burden" (see the box on p. 593) helped the more idealistic individuals rationalize imperialism in their own minds. One British official declared that the British Empire was, "under Providence, the greatest instrument for good that the world has seen." Thousands of Catholic and Protestant missionaries went abroad to seek converts to their faith. Nevertheless, the belief among Europeans that the superiority of their civilization obliged them to impose it on supposedly primitive nonwhites, even if the primitives suffered or died in the process, was yet another manifestation of racism.

Some historians have emphasized an economic motivation for imperialism. There was a great demand for natural resources and products not found in Western countries, such as rubber, oil, and tin. Instead of trading for these products, European investors advocated direct control of the areas where the raw

OPPOSING VIEWPOINTS
White Man's Burden, Black Man's Burden

One of the justifications for European imperialism was the notion that superior white peoples had the moral responsibility to raise ignorant native peoples to a higher level of civilization. The British poet Rudyard Kipling (1865–1936) captured this notion in his poem *The White Man's Burden*. The Western attempt to justify imperialism on the basis of moral responsibility, evident in Kipling's poem, was often hypocritical. Edward Morel, a British journalist who spent time in the Congo, pointed out the destructive effects of Western imperialism on Africans in his book *The Black Man's Burden*.

Rudyard Kipling, *The White Man's Burden*

Take up the White Man's burden—
Send forth the best ye breed—
Go bind your sons to exile
to serve your captives' needs;
To wait in heavy harness,
On fluttered folk and wild—
Your new-caught sullen peoples,
Half-devil and half-child. . . .

Take up the White Man's burden—
The savage wars of peace—
Fill full the mouth of Famine
And bid the sickness cease;
And when your goal is nearest
The end for others sought,
Watch sloth and heathen Folly
Bring all your hopes to nought. . . .

Take up the White Man's burden—
And reap his old reward:
The blame of those ye better,
The hate of those ye guard—
The cry of hosts ye humour
(Ah, slowly!) toward the light—

"Why brought ye us from bondage,
Our loved Egyptian night?" . . .

Edward Morel, *The Black Man's Burden*

It is [the Africans] who carry the "Black man's burden." They have not withered away before the white man's occupation. Indeed . . . Africa has ultimately absorbed within itself every Caucasian and, for that matter, every Semitic invader, too. In hewing out for himself a fixed abode in Africa, the white man has massacred the African in heaps. The African has survived, and it is well for the white settlers that he has. . . .

What the partial occupation of his soil by the white man has failed to do; what the mapping out of European political "spheres of influence" has failed to do; what the Maxim [machine gun] and the rifle, the slave gang, labor in the bowels of the earth and the lash, have failed to do; what imported measles, smallpox and syphilis have failed to do; whatever the overseas slave trade failed to do; the power of modern capitalistic exploitation, assisted by modern engines of destruction, may yet succeed in accomplishing.

For from the evils of the latter, scientifically applied and enforced, there is no escape for the African. Its destructive effects are not spasmodic: they are permanent. In its permanence resides its fatal consequences. It kills not the body merely, but the soul. It breaks the spirit. It attacks the African at every turn, from every point of vantage. It wrecks his polity, uproots him from the land, invades his family life, destroys his natural pursuits and occupations, claims his whole time, enslaves him in his own home.

Q What arguments did Kipling make to justify European expansion in Africa and Asia? How does the selection by Edward Morel challenge or undermine Kipling's beliefs?

Sources: Rudyard Kipling, *The White Man's Burden*. From *Rudyard Kipling's Verse* (Garden City, NY: Doubleday, 1919), pp. 371–72. Edward Morel, *The Black Man's Burden*. From E. D. Morel, *The Black Man's Burden: The White Man in Africa from the Fifteenth Century to World War I* (London: National Labour Press, 1920).

materials were found. The large surpluses of capital that were being accumulated by bankers and industrialists often encouraged them to seek higher rates of profit in underdeveloped areas. All of these factors combined to form an **economic imperialism** whereby European finance dominated the economic activity of a large part of the world.

The Creation of Empires

Whatever the reasons for the new imperialism, it had a dramatic effect on Africa and Asia as European powers competed for control of the two continents.

THE SCRAMBLE FOR AFRICA Europeans controlled relatively little of the African continent before 1880. In 1875, they controlled 11 percent of Africa, although by 1902 that percentage had grown to 90 percent. During the Napoleonic wars, the British had established themselves in southern Africa by taking control of Cape Town, originally founded by the Dutch. After the wars, the British encouraged settlers to come to what they called the Cape Colony. British policies disgusted the Boers (BOORS *or* BORS) or Afrikaners (ah-fri-KAH-nurz), as the descendants of the Dutch colonists were called, and led them in 1835 to migrate north on the Great Trek to the region between the Orange and Vaal Rivers (later known as the Orange Free State) and north of the Vaal (the Transvaal). Hostilities between the British and the Boers continued.

In the 1880s, Cecil Rhodes (1853–1902) largely determined British policy in southern Africa. Rhodes founded diamond- and gold-mining companies that enabled him to gain control of a territory north of the Transvaal that he named Rhodesia, after himself. Rhodes was a great champion of British expansion. He once said, "If there be a God, I think what he would like me to do is to paint as much of Africa British red as possible." His imperialist ambitions led to his downfall in 1896, however, when the British government forced him to resign as prime minister of Rhodesia after he conspired to overthrow the neighboring Boer government without British approval.

Although the British government had hoped to avoid war with the Boers, it could not stop extremists on both sides from precipitating a conflict. The Boer War dragged on from 1899 to 1902 as the Boers proved to be an effective opponent. Due to the Boers' use of guerrilla tactics, the British sustained high casualties and immense expenses in securing victory. After the war, British policy toward the Boers was remarkably conciliatory. Transvaal and the Orange Free State had representative governments by 1907, and the Union of South Africa was created in 1910. Like Canada, Australia, and New Zealand, it became a self-governing dominion within the British Empire.

Before 1880, the French and Portuguese had established the only other European settlements in Africa. The Portuguese had held on to their settlements in Angola on the west coast and Mozambique on the east coast. The French had started the conquest of Algeria in Muslim North Africa in 1830, although it was not until 1879 that French civilian rule was established there. The next year, 1880, the European scramble for possession of Africa began in earnest. By 1900, the French had added the huge area of French West Africa and Tunisia to their African empire. In 1912, they established a protectorate over much of Morocco; the rest was left to Spain.

After the Suez Canal was opened by the French in 1869, the British took an active interest in Egypt and sought to control the canal area, considering the canal their lifeline to India. They landed an expeditionary force in 1882 and soon established a protectorate over Egypt. From there, the British moved south into the Sudan and seized it after narrowly averting a war with France. Not to be outdone, Italy joined in the imperialist scramble. Their humiliating defeat by the Ethiopians in 1896 only led the Italians to try again in 1911 by invading and seizing Ottoman Tripoli, which they renamed Libya.

Central Africa was also added to the list of European colonies. Popular interest in the forbiddingly dense tropical jungles of Central Africa was first aroused in the 1860s and 1870s by explorers such as the Scottish missionary David Livingstone and the British American journalist Henry M. Stanley. But the real driving force for the colonization of Central Africa was King Leopold II (1865–1909) of Belgium, who had rushed enthusiastically into pursuit of empire in Africa: "To open to civilization," he said, "the only part of our globe where it has not yet penetrated, to pierce the darkness which envelops whole populations, is a crusade, if I may say so, a crusade worthy of this century of progress." Profit, however, was far more important to Leopold than progress. In 1876, Leopold engaged Stanley to establish Belgian settlements in the Congo.

Between 1884 and 1900, the European powers had carved up most of the rest of Africa. At this time Germany also entered the ranks of the imperialist powers. Initially, Bismarck had downplayed the significance of colonies, but as domestic political pressures for a

Does Germany Need Colonies?

After its unification in 1871, Germany sought to join the other great European powers in establishing a colonial empire. Among the supporters of German colonial expansion was Friedrich Fabri, a colonial administrator in Southwest Africa, who argued that colonization would encourage national growth and the spread of German culture. This excerpt is from Fabri's popular book, *Does Germany Need Colonies?*, published in Germany in 1879.

Friedrich Fabri, *Does Germany Need Colonies?*

Above all we need to regain ample, rewarding, and reliable sources of employment; we need new and reliable export markets; in short we need a well-designed and firmly implemented commercial and labor policy. Any far-reaching and perceptive attempt to execute such a policy will necessarily lead to the irrefutable conclusion that the German State needs colonial possessions. . . .

For us, the colonial question is not at all a question of political power. Whoever is guided by the desire for expanding German power has a poor understanding of it. It is rather a question of culture. Economic needs linked to broad national perspectives point to practical action. In looking for colonial possessions Germany is not prompted by the desire for expanding its power; it wants only to fulfill a national, we may even say a moral duty. . . .

In looking for commercial colonies the question is WHERE? German participation seems most important in the colonial exploitation of newly opened Central Africa. . . . The significance of Central Africa is much greater in every respect than has been assumed since antiquity. Should not Germany in its needs for colonies participate energetically in the competition for this massive territory? . . .

What matters above all is to raise our understanding about the significance and necessity of colonial possessions and thereby forcefully arouse the will of the nation in that direction. When we have overcome all opposition and turn to effective action, our first attempts with their inevitable troubles and difficulties will justify our effort. The German nation has long experience on the oceans, is skilled in industry and commerce, more capable than others in agricultural colonization, and furnished with an ample manpower like no other modern highly cultured nation. Should it not also enter successfully upon this new venture? The more we are convinced that the colonial question has become now a question of life and death for Germany, the fewer doubts we have. Well-planned and powerfully handled, it will have the most beneficial consequences for our economic situation, and for our entire national development. . . .

Even more important is the consideration that a people at the height of their political power can successfully maintain their historic position only as long as they recognize and prove themselves as the bearers of a cultural mission. . . .

It would be well if we Germans began to learn from the colonial destiny of our Anglo-Saxon cousins and emulate them in peaceful competition. When, centuries ago, the German empire stood at the head of the European states, it was the foremost commercial and maritime power. If the new Germany wants to restore and preserve its traditional powerful position in future, it will conceive of it as a cultural mission and no longer hesitate to practice its colonizing vocation.

Q What were Fabri's justifications for colonization?

Source: From Marvin Perry, Joseph R. Peden, and Theodore H. von Laue, *Sources of the Western Tradition*, vol. 2 (New York: Houghton Mifflin, 2008), pp. 249–250.

German empire increased, Bismarck became a political convert to colonialism (see the box above). As he expressed it, "All this colonial business is a sham, but we need it for the elections." The Germans established colonies in South West Africa, Cameroons, Togoland, and East Africa.

By 1914, Britain, France, Germany, Belgium, Spain, and Portugal had divided Africa (see Map 24.1). Only Liberia, founded by emancipated American slaves, and Ethiopia remained free states. Despite the humanitarian rationalizations about the "white man's burden," Africa had been conquered by European states determined to

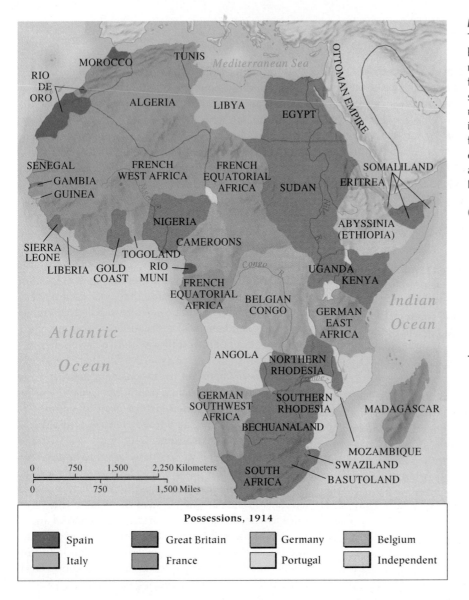

MAP 24.1 Africa in 1914.
The rush to acquire colonies by Europe's major powers was motivated by a combination of factors: ports and fueling stations for navies, sources of raw materials, enhancement of international prestige, outlets for nationalist feelings, expression of social Darwinism, and a desire to "civilize" non-Europeans.

Q Of the two countries with the largest amount of territory in Africa, which one's colonies were more geographically concentrated, and what could be the benefits of this?

Possessions, 1914

Spain
Italy
Great Britain
France
Germany
Portugal
Belgium
Independent

create colonial empires. With the exception of the Ethiopians, who defeated the Italians, any peoples who dared to resist were swiftly crushed by the superior military force of the Europeans.

IMPERIALISM IN ASIA Although Asia had been open to Western influence since the sixteenth century, not much of its immense territory had fallen under direct European control. The Dutch were established in the East Indies, the Spanish were in the Philippines, and the French and Portuguese had trading posts on the Indian coast.

It was not until the explorations of Australia by Captain James Cook between 1768 and 1771 that

CHRONOLOGY The New Imperialism: Africa	
Opening of the Suez Canal	1869
Leopold II of Belgium's settlements in the Congo	1876
French conquest of Algeria	1879
British expeditionary force in Egypt	1882
Defeat of Italians by Ethiopians	1896
Boer War	1899–1902
Union of South Africa	1910
Italian seizure of Tripoli	1911

Britain took an active interest in the East. The availability of land for grazing sheep and the discovery of gold led to an influx of free settlers, who slaughtered many of the indigenous inhabitants. In 1850, the British government granted the various Australian colonies virtually complete self-government, and fifty years later, on January 1, 1901, all the colonies were unified into the Commonwealth of Australia. Nearby New Zealand, which the British had declared a colony in 1840, was granted dominion status in 1907.

A private trading company known as the British East India Company had been responsible for subjugating much of India. In 1858, however, after a revolt of the sepoys, or Indian troops of the East India Company's army, had been crushed, the British Parliament transferred the company's powers directly to the government in London. In 1876, the title of empress of India was bestowed on Queen Victoria; Indians were now her colonial subjects.

Russian expansion in Asia was a logical outgrowth of its traditional territorial aggrandizement. Gradually, Russian settlers moved into cold and forbidding Siberia. They also moved south, attracted by the crumbling Ottoman Empire. By 1830, the Russians had established control over the entire northern coast of the Black Sea; from there, they pressed on into Central Asia, securing the trans-Caspian region by 1881. These advances brought the Russians to the borders of Persia and Afghanistan, where the British also had interests because of their desire to protect their holdings in India. In 1907, the Russians and British agreed to make Afghanistan a buffer state between Russian Turkestan and British India and divide Persia into two spheres of influence. Halted by the British in their expansion to the south, the Russians then moved east in Asia. But their occupation of Manchuria and their attempt to move into Korea brought war with Japan. After losing the Russo-Japanese War in 1905, the Russians agreed to a Japanese protectorate in Korea, and their Asian expansion was brought to a temporary halt (see Map 24.2).

The thrust of imperialism after 1880 led Westerners to move into new areas of Asia hitherto largely free of Western influence. By the nineteenth century, the ruling Manchu dynasty of the Chinese empire was showing signs of decline. In 1842, the British had obtained (through war) the island of Hong Kong and rights to trade in a number of Chinese cities. Other Western nations soon rushed in to gain similar trading privileges. Eventually, Britain, France, Germany, Russia, the United States, and Japan established spheres of influence and long-term leases on Chinese territory.

Japan avoided Western intrusion until 1853–1854, when American naval forces under Commodore Matthew Perry forced the Japanese to grant the United States trading and diplomatic privileges. Japan, however, managed to avoid China's fate. By absorbing and adopting Western military and industrial methods, the Japanese developed a modern commercial and industrial system as well as a powerful military state. They established their own sphere of influence in China, and five years after they defeated the Russians in 1905, the Japanese formally annexed Korea.

In Southeast Asia, Britain established control over Burma (modern Myanmar) and the Malay States while France played an active role in subjugating Indochina. In the 1880s, the French extended "protection" over Cambodia, Annam, Tonkin, and Laos and organized them into the Union of French Indo-China. Only Siam (Thailand) remained free as a buffer state because of British-French rivalry.

The Pacific was also the scene of great power struggles and witnessed the entry of the United States onto the imperialist stage. Soon after Americans had made Hawaii's Pearl Harbor into a naval station in 1887, American settlers gained control of the sugar industry on the islands. When Hawaiian natives tried to reassert their authority, the U.S. Marines were brought in to "protect" American lives. Hawaii was annexed by the United States in 1898 during the era of American nationalistic fervor generated by the Spanish-American War. The American defeat of Spain also encouraged Americans to extend their empire by acquiring Cuba, Puerto Rico, Guam, and the Philippine Islands. Although

CHRONOLOGY The New Imperialism: Asia	
Hong Kong to Britain, along with trading rights in cities in China	1842
Commodore Perry's mission to Japan	1853–1854
Rebellion of sepoys in India	1857–1858
Queen Victoria proclaimed empress of India	1876
Russians in Central Asia	1881
Spanish-American War; U.S. annexation of the Philippines	1898
Commonwealth of Australia	1901
Commonwealth of New Zealand	1907
Russian-British agreement over Afghanistan and Persia	1907
Japanese annexation of Korea	1910

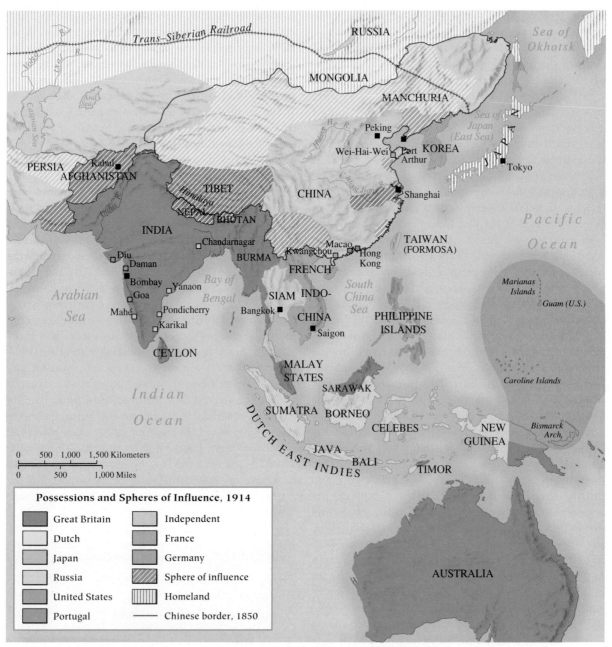

MAP 24.2 **Asia in 1914.** Asia became an important arena of international competition in the nineteenth and early twentieth centuries. Beset by economic stagnation and an inability to modernize, a weak China was unable to withstand the demands of the United States, European powers, and a Westernizing Japan. Britain, France, Russia, Japan, and the United States had direct or indirect control of nearly all of Asia by 1914.

Q Why would both Russia and Japan covet Manchuria?

the Filipinos hoped for independence, the Americans refused to grant it. As President McKinley said, the United States had the duty "to educate the Filipinos and uplift and Christianize them," a remarkable statement in view of the fact that most of them had been Roman Catholics for centuries. It took three years and sixty thousand troops to pacify the Philippines and establish American control.

Responses to Imperialism

When Europeans imposed their culture on peoples they considered inferior, how did the conquered peoples respond? Initial attempts to expel the foreigners led to devastating defeats at the hands of Westerners, whose industrial technology gave them far superior weapons of war. Most of the indigenous peoples, accustomed to rule by small elites, simply accepted their new governors, making the imposition of Western rule relatively easy. The conquered peoples subsequently adjusted to the rule of foreigners in different ways. Some sought to maintain their cultural traditions, but others believed that adoption of Western ways would enable them to reform their societies and eventually challenge Western rule. Most people probably stood somewhere between the two extremes. Four examples illustrate different responses to foreign rule.

AFRICA   By the beginning of the twentieth century, a new class of African leaders had emerged. Educated in colonial schools and some even in the West, they were the first generation of Africans to know a great deal about the West and to write in the language of their colonial masters. Although this "new class" admired Western culture and even disliked the ways of their own countries, many came to resent the foreigners and their arrogant contempt for colonial peoples. Equally important, the economic prosperity of the West never extended to the colonies. To many Africans, colonialism meant the loss of their farmlands or terrible jobs on plantations or in sweatshops and factories run by foreigners.

Although middle-class Africans did not suffer to the extent that poor peasants or workers on plantations did, they too had complaints. They usually qualified only for menial jobs in the government or business. Segregated clubs, schools, and churches were set up as more European officials brought their wives and began to raise families. Europeans also had a habit of addressing natives by their first names or calling an adult male "boy."

Such conditions led many members of the new urban educated class to harbor mixed feelings toward their colonial masters and the civilization they represented. Though willing to admit the superiority of many aspects of Western culture, these new intellectuals fiercely hated colonial rule and were determined to assert their own nationality and cultural destiny. Out of this mixture of hopes and resentments emerged the first stirrings of modern nationalism in Africa. During the first quarter of the twentieth century, in colonial societies across Africa, educated native peoples began to organize political parties and movements seeking the end of foreign rule.

CHINA   The humiliation of China by the Western powers led to much antiforeign violence, but the Westerners used this lawlessness as an excuse to extort further concessions from the Chinese. A major outburst of violence against foreigners occurred in the Boxer Rebellion in 1900–1901. "Boxers" was the popular name given to Chinese who belonged to a secret organization called the Society of Harmonious Fists, whose aim was to push the foreigners out of China. The Boxers murdered foreign missionaries, Chinese who had converted to Christianity, railroad workers, foreign businessmen, and even the German envoy to Beijing. Response to the killings was immediate and overwhelming. An allied army consisting of British, French, German, Russian, American, and Japanese troops attacked Beijing, restored order, and demanded more concessions from the Chinese government. The imperial government was so weakened that the forces of the revolutionary leader Sun Yat-sen (SOON yaht-SEN) (1866–1925), who adopted a program of "nationalism, democracy, and socialism," overthrew the Manchu dynasty in 1912. The new Republic of China remained weak and ineffective, and China's travails were far from over.

JAPAN   In the late 1850s and early 1860s, it looked as if Japan would follow China's fate and be carved up into spheres of influence by aggressive Western powers. A remarkably rapid transformation, however, produced a very different result. Before 1868, the shogun, a powerful hereditary military governor assisted by a warrior nobility known as the samurai, exercised real power in Japan. The emperor's functions had become primarily religious. After the shogun's concessions to the Western nations, antiforeign sentiment led to a samurai revolt in 1867 and the restoration of the emperor as the rightful head of the government. The new emperor was the astute, dynamic, young Mutsuhito (moo-tsoo-HEE-toh) (1867–1912), who called his reign the Meiji (MAY-jee) ("enlightened government"). The new leaders who controlled the emperor now inaugurated a remarkable transformation of Japan that has since been known as the Meiji Restoration.

Recognizing the obvious military and industrial superiority of the West, the new leaders decided to modernize Japan by absorbing and adopting Western methods. Thousands of young Japanese were sent abroad to receive Western educations, especially in the social and natural sciences. A German-style army and a British-style navy were established. The Japanese copied the industrial and financial methods of the United States and developed a modern commercial and industrial system. A highly centralized administrative system copied from the French replaced the old system. Initially, the Japanese adopted the French principles of social and legal equality, but by 1890, they had created a political system that was democratic in form but authoritarian in practice. In imitating the West, Japan also developed a powerful military state.

INDIA The British government had been in control of India since the mid-nineteenth century. Under Parliament's supervision, a small group of British civil servants directed the affairs of India's almost 300 million people.

The British brought order to a society that had been divided by civil wars for some time and implemented a relatively honest and efficient government. They also brought Western technology—railroads, banks, mines, industry, medical knowledge, and hospitals. The British introduced Western-style secondary schools and colleges where the Indian upper and middle classes and professional classes were educated so that they could serve as trained subordinates in the government and the army. British legislation also affected the legal status of Indian women. In 1829, the British banned the practice of sati, which called for a widow to immolate herself on her husband's funeral pyre. Female infanticide was also discouraged. Although women's position in Indian society was not significantly altered, the recognition of women by the law did afford some protection against these practices.

However, the Indian people paid a high price for the peace and stability brought by British rule. Due to population growth in the nineteenth century, extreme poverty was a way of life for most Indians; almost two-thirds of the population was malnourished in 1901. British industrialization brought little improvement for the masses. British manufactured goods destroyed local industries, and Indian wealth was used to pay British officials and the large army. The system of education served only the elite, upper-class Indians, and it was conducted only in the rulers' English language, while 90 percent of the population remained illiterate. Even for the Indians who benefited the most from their Western educations, British rule was degrading. The best jobs and the best housing were reserved for Britons. Despite their education, the Indians were never considered equals of the British, whose racial attitudes were made quite clear by Lord Kitchener, one of Britain's foremost military commanders in India, when he said, "It is this consciousness of the inherent superiority of the European which has won for us India.

However well educated and clever a native may be, and however brave he may prove himself, I believe that no rank we can bestow on him would cause him to be considered an equal of the British officer."[11] Such smug racial attitudes made it difficult for British rule, no matter how beneficent, ever to be ultimately accepted and led to the rise of an Indian nationalist movement. By 1883, when the Indian National Congress was formed, moderate, educated Indians were beginning to seek self-government. By 1919, in response to British violence and British insensitivity, Indians were demanding complete independence.

Results of the New Imperialism

By 1900, almost all the societies of Africa and Asia were either under full colonial rule or, as in the case of China and the Ottoman Empire, at a point of virtual collapse. Only a handful of states, such as Japan in East Asia, Thailand in Southeast Asia, Afghanistan and Persia in the Middle East, and mountainous Ethiopia in East Africa, managed to escape internal disintegration or subjection to colonial rule. For the most part, the exceptions were the result of good fortune rather than design. Thailand escaped subjugation primarily because officials in Britain and France found it more convenient to transform the country into a buffer state than to fight over it. Ethiopia and Afghanistan survived due to their remote location and mountainous terrain. Only Japan managed to avoid the common fate through a concerted strategy of political and economic reform. With the coming of imperialism, a global economy was finally established, and the domination of Western civilization over the cultures of Africa and Asia appeared to be complete. At the same time, the competition for lands abroad exacerbated the rivalry among European states.

International Rivalry and the Coming of War

Q FOCUS QUESTIONS: What was the Bismarckian system of alliances, and how successful was it at keeping the peace? What issues lay behind the international crises that Europe faced in the late nineteenth and early twentieth centuries?

Before 1914, Europeans had experienced almost fifty years of peace. There had been wars (including wars of conquest in the non-Western world), but none had involved the Great Powers. A series of crises occurred that might easily have led to general war. One reason they did not is that until 1890, Bismarck of Germany exercised a restraining influence on the Europeans.

Bismarck knew that the emergence of a unified Germany in 1871 had upset the balance of power established at Vienna in 1815. Fearing a possible anti-German alliance between France and Russia, and possibly even Austria, Bismarck made a defensive alliance with Austria in 1879 that was joined by Italy in 1882. The Triple Alliance of 1882 committed Germany, Austria-Hungary, and Italy to support the existing political order while providing a defense against France. At the same time, Bismarck maintained a separate treaty with Russia, hoping to prevent a French-Russian alliance that would threaten Germany with the possibility of a two-front war. The Bismarckian system of alliances, geared to preserving peace and the status quo, had worked, but in 1890, Emperor William II dismissed Bismarck and began to chart a new direction for Germany's foreign policy.

New Directions and New Crises

Emperor William II embarked on an activist foreign policy dedicated to enhancing German power by finding, as he put it, Germany's rightful "place in the sun." One of his changes in Bismarck's foreign policy was to drop the treaty with Russia, which the emperor viewed as being at odds with Germany's alliance with Austria. The ending of the pact achieved what Bismarck had feared: it brought France and Russia together. Republican France leaped at the chance to draw closer to tsarist Russia, and in 1894, the two powers concluded a military alliance.

During the next ten years, German policies abroad caused the British to draw closer to France. By 1907, a loose confederation of Great Britain, France, and Russia—known as the Triple Entente (ahn-TAHNT)—stood opposed to the Triple Alliance of Germany, Austria-Hungary, and Italy. Europe was divided into two opposing camps that became more and more inflexible and unwilling to compromise. When the members of the two alliances became involved in a new series of crises between 1908 and 1913 over control of the remnants of the Ottoman Empire in the Balkans (see Map 24.3), the stage was set for World War I.

Crises in the Balkans, 1908–1913

The Bosnian Crisis of 1908–1909 initiated a chain of events that eventually spun out of control. Since 1878, Bosnia and Herzegovina (HAYRT-suh-guh-VEE-nuh) had

been under the protection of Austria, but in 1908, Austria took the drastic step of annexing these two Slavic-speaking territories. Serbia became outraged at this action because it dashed the Serbs' hopes of creating a large Serbian kingdom that would include most of the southern Slavs. But this possibility was why the Austrians had annexed Bosnia and Herzegovina. A large Serbia would be a threat to the unity of their empire with its large Slavic population. The Russians, as protectors of their fellow Slavs and with their own desire to increase their authority in the Balkans, supported the Serbs and opposed the Austrian action. Backed by the Russians, the Serbs prepared for war against Austria. At this point, William II intervened and demanded that the Russians accept Austria's annexation of Bosnia and Herzegovina or face war with Germany. Weakened from their defeat in the Russo-Japanese War in 1904–1905, the Russians backed down. Humiliated, they vowed revenge.

European attention returned to the Balkans in 1912 when Serbia, Bulgaria, Montenegro (mahn-tuh-NEE-groh), and Greece organized the Balkan League and defeated the Ottomans in the First Balkan War. When the victorious allies were unable to agree on how to divide the conquered Ottoman territory, the Second Balkan War erupted in 1913, in which Greece, Serbia, Romania, and the Ottoman Empire attacked and defeated Bulgaria. As a result, Bulgaria obtained only a small part of Macedonia, and most of the rest was divided between Serbia and Greece. Yet Serbia's aspirations remained unfulfilled. The two Balkan wars left the inhabitants embittered and created more tensions among the Great Powers.

One of Serbia's major ambitions had been to acquire Albanian territory that would give it a port on the Adriatic. At the London Conference, arranged by Austria at the end of the Balkan wars, the Austrians had blocked Serbia's wishes by creating an independent Albania. The Germans, as Austrian allies, had supported this move. In their frustration, Serbian nationalists increasingly portrayed the Austrians as monsters who were keeping the Serbs from becoming a great nation. As Serbia's chief supporters, the Russians were also upset by the turn of events in the Balkans. The feeling was growing among Russian leaders that they could not back down again in the event of a confrontation with Austria or Germany in the Balkans.

Austria-Hungary had achieved another of its aims, but it was still convinced that Serbia was a mortal threat to its empire and must at some point be crushed. Meanwhile, the French and Russian governments renewed

MAP 24.3 **The Balkans in 1913.**
The First Balkan War (1912) liberated most of the region from Ottoman control; the Second Balkan War (1913) increased the size of Greece and Serbia at Bulgaria's expense. Russia supported the ambitions of fellow Slavs in Serbia, who sought to create a large Slavic kingdom in the Balkans. Austria and its ally Germany opposed Serbia's ambitions.

Q What territories had the Ottomans lost by the end of 1913?

their alliance and promised each other that they would not back down at the next crisis. Britain drew closer to France. By the beginning of 1914, two armed camps viewed each other with suspicion. The European "age of progress" was about to come to an inglorious and bloody end.

Chapter Summary

What many Europeans liked to call their "age of progress" in the decades before 1914 was also an era of anxiety. Driven by national rivalry, Social Darwinism, religious and humanitarian concerns, and economic demands for raw materials and overseas investment, Western nations at the end of the nineteenth century began a renewed frenzy of imperialist expansion around the world. By 1914, European nations had carved up most of Africa into colonies and created spheres of influence in Asia. Western imperialism also affected both China and Japan. The opening of China to Western trade concessions ultimately led to a revolution and the overthrow of the Manchu dynasty. Japan adopted Western military, educational, and governmental ways, even becoming an imperialist power in its own right. At the same time, Western treatment of non-Western peoples as racial inferiors caused educated, non-Western elites in these colonies to initiate movements for national independence. Before these movements could be successful, however, the power that Europeans had achieved through their mass armies and technological superiority had to be weakened. The Europeans soon inadvertently accomplished this task by demolishing their own civilization on the battlegrounds of Europe in World War I.

This war was a result of the growing tensions created by national rivalries. In competing with and fearing each other, the European nations formed defensive alliances that helped maintain a balance of power but also led to the creation of large armies, enormous military establishments, and immense arsenals. The alliances also generated tensions that were unleashed when Europeans were unable to resolve a series of crises, especially in the Balkans, and rushed into the catastrophic carnage of World War I.

The cultural revolutions before 1914 had also produced anxiety and a crisis of confidence in European civilization. Albert Einstein showed that time and space were relative to the observer, that matter was simply another form of energy, and that the old Newtonian view of the universe was no longer valid. Adding to the uncertainties of the age, Sigmund Freud argued that human behavior was governed not by reason but by the unconscious. Some intellectuals used the ideas of Charles Darwin to argue that in the struggle of races and nations, the fittest survive. Collectively, these new ideas helped create a modern consciousness that questioned most Europeans' optimistic faith in reason, the rational structure of nature, and the certainty of progress. As we shall see in the next two chapters, the devastating experiences of World War I would turn this culture of uncertainty into a way of life after 1918.

CHAPTER TIMELINE

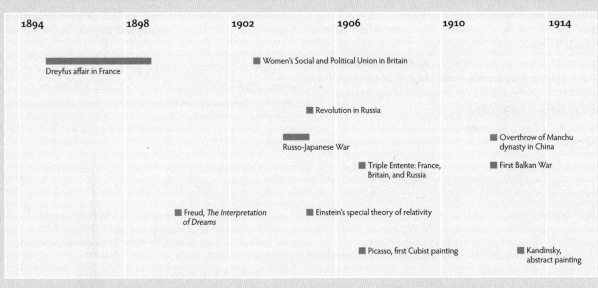

| 1894 | 1898 | 1902 | 1906 | 1910 | 1914 |

- Dreyfus affair in France
- Women's Social and Political Union in Britain
- Revolution in Russia
- Russo-Japanese War
- Overthrow of Manchu dynasty in China
- Triple Entente: France, Britain, and Russia
- First Balkan War
- Freud, *The Interpretation of Dreams*
- Einstein's special theory of relativity
- Picasso, first Cubist painting
- Kandinsky, abstract painting

CHAPTER REVIEW

Upon Reflection

Q How is Modernism evident in literature and the arts between 1894 and 1914? How do these literary and artistic products reflect the political and social developments of the age?

Q One historian has written that the history of colonial expansion was "one of long-range schemes that appear almost accidental when viewed singly." Does the practice of imperialism in Africa and Asia substantiate this statement? Why or why not?

Q What might European diplomats have done between 1894 and 1914 to avoid war?

Key Terms

relativity theory (p. 579)
psychoanalysis (p. 580)
Social Darwinism (p. 580)
Modernism (p. 582)
Impressionism (p. 582)
Post-Impressionism (p. 583)
Cubism (p. 583)

abstract painting (p. 583)
political democracy (p. 585)
suffragists (p. 585)
Zionism (p. 589)
new imperialism (p. 592)
economic imperialism (p. 594)

Suggestions for Further Reading

INTELLECTUAL AND CULTURAL DEVELOPMENTS On Modernism, see **P. Gay, *Modernism: The Lure of Heresy*** (New York, 2007). On Freud, see **P. Gay, *Freud: A Life for Our Time*,** rev. ed. (New York, 2006). Nietzsche is examined in **L. Spinks, *Friedrich Nietzsche*** (London, 2003). Very valuable on modern art are **M. Powell-Jones, *Impressionism*** (London, 1994); **G. Crepaldi, *The Impressionists*** (New York, 2002); and **B. Denvir, *Post-Impressionism*** (New York, 1992).

POLITICS: NEW DIRECTIONS The rise of feminism is examined in **J. Rendall, *The Origins of Modern Feminism: Women in Britain, France and the United States*** (London, 1985). On the "new woman," see **M. L. Roberts, *Disruptive Acts: The New Woman in Fin-de-Siècle France*** (Chicago, 2002). The subject of modern anti-Semitism is covered in **A. S. Lindemann, *Esau's Tears: Modern Anti-Semitism and the Rise of the Jews*** (New York, 1997). European racism is analyzed in **N. MacMaster, *Racism in Europe, 1870–2000*** (New York, 2001). The beginnings of the Labour Party are examined in **R. J. H. Stewart, *Origins of the British Labour Party*** (New York, 2003). A good introduction to the political world of William II's Germany can be found in **C. Clark, *Kaiser Wilhelm II*** (London, 2000). On Russia, see **A. Ascher, *Revolution of 1905: A Short History*** (Stanford, Calif., 2004).

THE NEW IMPERIALISM For broad perspectives on imperialism, see **M. W. Doyle, *Empires*** (Ithaca, N.Y, 1986), and **P. Curtin, *The World and the West: The European Challenge and the Overseas Response in the Age of Empire*** (New York, 2000). Aspects of imperialism are covered in **T. Pakhenham, *The Scramble for Africa*** (New York, 1991). On gender and imperialism, see **P. Levine, *Gender and Empire*** (Oxford, 2004).

INTERNATIONAL RIVALRY Two valuable works on the diplomatic history of the period are **N. Rich, *Great Power Diplomacy: 1814–1914*** (New York, 1991), and **C. J. Bartlett, *Peace, War and European Powers,*** rev. ed. (New York, 1996).

Notes

1. Quoted in A. E. E. McKenzie, *The Major Achievements of Science* (New York, 1960), vol. 1, p. 310.
2. F. Nietzsche, *Thus Spake Zarathustra*, in *The Philosophy of Nietzsche* (New York, 1954), p. 6.
3. F. von Bernhardi, *Germany and the Next War*, trans. A. H. Powles (New York, 1914), pp. 18–19.
4. Quoted in J. Rewald, *History of Impressionism* (New York, 1961), pp. 456–458.
5. Quoted in A. Higonnet, *Berthe Morisot's Images of Women* (Cambridge, Mass., 1992), p. 19.
6. Quoted in C. M. Prelinger, "Prelude to Consciousness: Amalie Sieveking and the Female Association for the Care of the Poor and the Sick," in *German Women in the Nineteenth Century: A Social History*, ed. J. C. Fout (New York, 1984), p. 119.
7. Quoted in B. Smith, *Changing Lives: Women in European History Since 1700* (Lexington, Mass., 1989), p. 379.
8. Quoted in J. Merriman, *A History of Modern Europe* (New York, 1996), p. 953.
9. Quoted in ibid., p. 965.
10. Quoted in J. Ellis, *The Social History of the Machine Gun* (New York, 1975), p. 80.
11. Quoted in K. M. Panikkar, *Asia and Western Dominance* (London, 1959), p. 116.

MindTap **MindTap** is a fully online, highly personalized learning experience built upon Cengage Learning content. MindTap combines student learning tools—readings, multimedia, activities, and assessments—into a singular Learning Path that guides students through the course.

CHAPTER 25

The Beginning of the Twentieth-Century Crisis: War and Revolution

British infantrymen prepare to advance during the Battle of the Somme.

© UK History/Alamy

CHAPTER OUTLINE AND FOCUS QUESTIONS

The Road to World War I

Q What were the long-range and immediate causes of World War I?

The Great War

Q What did the belligerents expect at the beginning of World War I, and why did the course of the war turn out to be so different from their expectations? How did World War I affect the belligerents' governmental and political institutions, economic affairs, and social life?

War and Revolution

Q What were the causes of the Russian Revolution of 1917, and why did the Bolsheviks prevail in the civil war and gain control of Russia?

The Peace Settlement

Q What were the objectives of the chief participants at the Paris Peace Conference of 1919, and how closely did the final settlement reflect these objectives?

CRITICAL THINKING

Q What was the relationship between World War I and the Russian Revolution?

CONNECTIONS TO TODAY

Q What lessons from the outbreak of World War I are of value in considering international relations today?

ON JULY 1, 1916, British and French infantry forces attacked German defensive lines along a twenty-five-mile front near the Somme (SUHM) River in France. Each soldier carried almost seventy pounds of equipment, making it "impossible to move much quicker than a slow walk." German machine guns soon opened fire: "We were able to see our comrades move forward in an attempt to cross No-Man's Land, only to be mown down like meadow grass," recalled one British soldier. "I felt sick at the sight of this carnage and remember weeping."[1] In one day, more than twenty-one thousand British soldiers died. After six months of fighting, the British had advanced five miles; 1 million British, French, and German soldiers had been killed or wounded.

Philip Gibbs, an English war correspondent, described what he saw in the German trenches that the British forces overran: "Victory! ... Some of the German dead were young boys, too young to be killed for old men's crimes, and others might have been old or young. One could not tell because they had no faces, and were just masses of raw flesh in rags of uniforms. Legs and arms lay separate without any bodies thereabout."[2]

World War I (1914–1918) was the defining event of the twentieth century. It devastated the prewar economic, social, and political order of Europe, and its uncertain outcome prepared the way for an even more destructive war. Overwhelmed by the size of its battles, the extent of its casualties, and its effects on all facets of life, contemporaries referred to it simply as the "Great War."

The Great War was all the more disturbing to Europeans because it came after what many considered an age of progress. There had been international crises before 1914, but somehow Europeans had managed to avoid serious and prolonged military confrontations. Material prosperity and a fervid belief in scientific and technological progress had convinced many people that Europe stood on the verge of creating the utopia that humans had dreamed of for centuries. The historian Arnold Toynbee expressed what the era before the war had meant to his generation:

> [We had expected] that life throughout the World would become more rational, more humane, and more democratic and that, slowly, but surely, political democracy would produce greater social justice. We had also expected that the progress of science and technology would make mankind richer, and that this increasing wealth would gradually spread from a minority to a majority. We had expected that all this would happen peacefully. In fact we thought that mankind's course was set for an earthly paradise.[3]

After 1918, it was no longer possible to maintain naive illusions about the progress of Western civilization. As World War I was followed by the destructiveness of World War II and the mass murder machines of totalitarian regimes, it became all too apparent that instead of a utopia, European civilization had become a nightmare. The Great War resulted not only in great loss of life and property but also in the annihilation of one of the basic intellectual precepts on which Western civilization was thought to be founded—the belief in progress. World War I and the revolutions it spawned can properly be seen as the first stage in the crisis of the twentieth century.

The Road to World War I

Q **FOCUS QUESTION:** What were the long-range and immediate causes of World War I?

On June 28, 1914, the heir to the Austrian throne, Archduke Francis Ferdinand, was assassinated in the Bosnian city of Sarajevo (sar-uh-YAY-voh). Although this event precipitated the confrontation between Austria and Serbia that led to World War I, there were also long-range underlying forces that were propelling Europeans toward armed conflict.

Nationalism and Internal Dissent

In the first half of the nineteenth century, liberals had maintained that the organization of European states along national lines would lead to a peaceful Europe based on a sense of international fraternity. They had been very wrong. The system of nation-states that had emerged in Europe in the second half of the nineteenth century led not to cooperation but to competition. Rivalries over colonial and commercial interests intensified during an era of frenzied imperialist expansion, and the division of Europe's Great Powers into two loose alliances—Germany, Austria, and Italy versus France, Great Britain, and Russia—only added to the tensions (see Map 25.1). The series of crises that tested these alliances in the early years of the new century had left European states with the belief that their allies were important and that their security depended on supporting those allies, even when they took foolish risks.

The growth of nationalism in the nineteenth century had yet another serious consequence. Not all ethnic groups had achieved the goal of nationhood. Slavic minorities in the Balkans and the Austrian Empire, for example, still dreamed of creating their own national states. So did the Irish in the British Empire and the Poles in the Russian empire.

National aspirations, however, were not the only source of internal strife at the beginning of the twentieth century. Socialist labor movements had grown more powerful and were increasingly inclined to use strikes, even violent ones, to achieve their goals. Some conservative leaders, alarmed at the increase in labor strife and class division, even feared that European nations were on the verge of revolution. Did these statesmen opt for war in 1914 because they believed that "prosecuting an active foreign policy," as one leader expressed it, would smother "internal troubles"? Some historians have argued that the desire to suppress internal disorder may

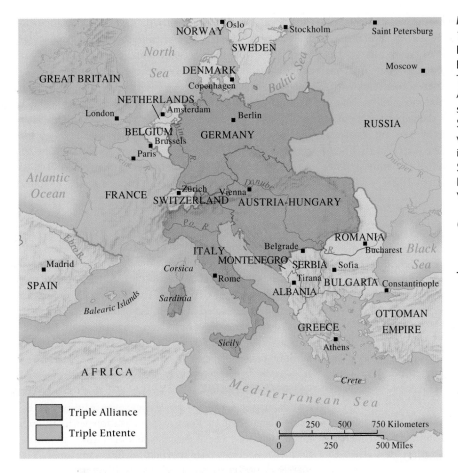

MAP 25.1 Europe in 1914. By 1914, two alliances dominated Europe: the Triple Entente of Britain, France, and Russia and the Triple Alliance of Germany, Austria-Hungary, and Italy. Russia sought to bolster fellow Slavs in Serbia, whereas Austria-Hungary was intent on increasing its power in the Balkans and thwarting Serbia's ambitions. Thus, the Balkans became the flash point for World War I.

Q Which nonaligned nations were positioned between the two alliances?

have encouraged some leaders to take the plunge into war in 1914.

Militarism

The growth of large mass armies after 1900 not only heightened the existing tensions in Europe but also made it inevitable that if war did come, it would be highly destructive. **Conscription** (obligatory military service) had been established as a regular practice in most Western countries before 1914 (the United States and Britain were major exceptions). European military machines had doubled in size between 1890 and 1914. With its 1.3 million men, the Russian army had grown to be the largest, while the French and Germans were not far behind with 900,000 each. The British, Italian, and Austrian armies numbered between 250,000 and 500,000 soldiers.

Militarism, however, involved more than just large armies. As armies grew, so did the influence of military leaders, who drew up vast and complex plans for quickly mobilizing millions of men and enormous quantities of supplies in the event of war. Fearful that changes in these plans would cause chaos in the armed forces, military leaders insisted that their plans could not be altered. In the crises during the summer of 1914, the generals' lack of flexibility forced European political leaders to make decisions for military instead of political reasons.

The Outbreak of War: The Summer of 1914

Militarism, nationalism, and the desire to stifle internal dissent may all have played a role in the coming of World War I, but the decisions made by European leaders in the summer of 1914 directly precipitated the conflict. It was another crisis in the Balkans that forced this predicament on European statesmen.

ANOTHER CRISIS IN THE BALKANS States in southeastern Europe had struggled to free themselves of Ottoman rule in the course of the nineteenth and early twentieth centuries. But the rivalry between Austria-Hungary and Russia for domination of these new states created serious tensions in the region. By 1914, Serbia, supported by Russia, was determined to create a large, independent Slavic state in the Balkans, but Austria, which had its own Slavic minorities to contend with, was equally set on preventing that possibility. Many Europeans perceived the inherent dangers in this combination of Serbian ambition bolstered by Russian opposition to Austria and Austria's conviction that Serbia's success would mean the end of its empire. The British ambassador to Vienna wrote in 1913:

> Serbia will some day set Europe by the ears, and bring about a universal war on the Continent.... I cannot tell you how exasperated people are getting here at the continual worry which that little country causes to Austria under encouragement from Russia.... It will be lucky if Europe succeeds in avoiding war as a result of the present crisis. The next time a Serbian crisis arises ..., I feel sure that Austria-Hungary will refuse to admit of any Russian interference in the dispute and that she will proceed to settle her differences with her little neighbor by herself.[4]

It was against this backdrop of mutual distrust and hatred that the events of the summer of 1914 played out.

THE ASSASSINATION OF FRANCIS FERDINAND: A "BLANK CHECK"?

A Bosnian activist who worked for the Black Hand, a Serbian terrorist organization dedicated to the creation of a pan-Slavic kingdom, carried out the assassination of the Austrian Archduke Francis Ferdinand and his wife, Sophia, on June 28, 1914. Although the Austrian government did not know whether the Serbian government had been directly involved in the archduke's assassination, it saw an opportunity to "render Serbia innocuous once and for all by a display of force," as the Austrian foreign minister put it. Fearful of Russian intervention on Serbia's behalf, Austrian leaders sought the backing of their German allies. Emperor William II and his chancellor responded with the infamous "blank check," their assurance that Austria-Hungary could rely on Germany's "full support," even if "matters went to the length of a war between Austria-Hungary and Russia." Much historical debate has focused on this "blank check" of

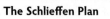

The Schlieffen Plan

July 5 extended to the Austrians. Did the Germans realize that an Austrian-Serbian war could lead to a wider war? If so, did they actually want one? Historians are still divided on the answers to these questions.

Strengthened by German support, Austrian leaders issued an ultimatum to Serbia on July 23 in which they made such extreme demands that Serbia had little choice but to reject some of them to preserve its sovereignty. Austria then declared war on Serbia on July 28. Although Austria had hoped to keep the war limited to Serbia and Austria to ensure its success in the Balkans, these hopes soon vanished.

DECLARATIONS OF WAR Still smarting from its humiliation in the Bosnian crisis of 1908, Russia was determined to support Serbia. On July 28, Tsar Nicholas II ordered partial **mobilization** of the Russian army against Austria. At this point, the Russian General Staff informed the tsar that their mobilization plans were based on a war against both Germany and Austria simultaneously. They could not execute partial mobilization without creating chaos in the army. Consequently, the Russian government ordered full mobilization of the Russian army on July 29, knowing that the Germans would consider this an act of war against them. Germany responded to Russian mobilization with its own ultimatum that the Russians must halt their mobilization within twelve hours. When the Russians ignored it, Germany declared war on Russia on August 1.

At this stage of the conflict, German war plans determined whether France would become involved in the war. Under the guidance of General Alfred von Schlieffen (SHLEE-fun), chief of staff from 1891 to 1905, the German General Staff had devised a military plan based on the assumption of a two-front war with France and Russia, since the two powers had formed a military alliance in 1894. The Schlieffen Plan called for a minimal troop deployment against Russia while most of the German army would rapidly invade western France by way of neutral Belgium. After the planned quick defeat of the French, the German army expected to redeploy to the east against Russia. Under the Schlieffen Plan, Germany could not mobilize its troops solely against Russia and therefore declared war on France on August 3

	1914
Assassination of Archduke Francis Ferdinand	June 28
Austria's ultimatum to Serbia	July 23
Austria declares war on Serbia	July 28
Russia mobilizes	July 29
Germany's ultimatum to Russia	July 31
Germany declares war on Russia	August 1
Germany declares war on France	August 3
German troops invade Belgium	August 4
Great Britain declares war on Germany	August 4

after issuing an ultimatum to Belgium on August 2 demanding the right of German troops to pass through Belgian territory. On August 4, Great Britain declared war on Germany, officially over this violation of Belgian neutrality but in fact over the British desire to maintain world power. As one British diplomat argued, if Germany and Austria won the war, "what would be the position of a friendless England?" By August 4, all the great powers of Europe were at war.

The Great War

Q **FOCUS QUESTIONS:** What did the belligerents expect at the beginning of World War I, and why did the course of the war turn out to be so different from their expectations? How did World War I affect the belligerents' governmental and political institutions, economic affairs, and social life?

Before 1914, many political leaders had become convinced that war involved so many political and economic risks that it was not worth fighting. Others had believed that "rational" diplomats could control any situation and prevent the outbreak of war. At the beginning of August 1914, both of these prewar illusions were shattered, but the new illusions that replaced them soon proved to be equally foolish.

1914–1915: Illusions and Stalemate

Many Europeans went to war in 1914 with remarkable enthusiasm. Government propaganda had been successful in stirring up national antagonisms before the war. Now, in August 1914, the urgent pleas of governments for defense against aggressors fell on receptive ears in every belligerent nation. Middle-class crowds, often composed of young students, were especially enthusiastic, but workers in the cities and peasants in the countryside were considerably less eager for war. Once the war began, however, most people seemed genuinely convinced that their nation's cause was just.

A new set of illusions also fed the enthusiasm for war. Almost everyone in August 1914 believed that the war would be over in a few weeks. People were reminded that the major battles in European wars since 1815 had in fact ended in a matter of weeks, conveniently overlooking the American Civil War (1861–1865), which was the true prototype for World War I. Both the soldiers who exuberantly boarded the trains for the war front in August 1914 and the jubilant citizens who bombarded them with flowers when they departed believed that the warriors would be home by Christmas.

German hopes for a quick end to the war rested on a military gamble. The Schlieffen Plan had called for the German army to proceed through Belgium into northern France with a vast encircling movement that would sweep around Paris and surround most of the French army. But the German advance was halted only twenty miles east of Paris at the First Battle of the Marne (September 6–10). The war quickly turned into a stalemate as neither the Germans nor the French could dislodge each other from the trenches they had begun to dig for shelter. Two lines of trenches soon extended from the English Channel to the frontiers of Switzerland (see Map 25.2). The western front had become bogged down in **trench warfare** that kept both sides immobilized in virtually the same positions for four years.

In contrast to the west, the war in the east was marked by much more mobility, although the cost in lives was equally enormous. At the beginning of the war, the Russian army moved into eastern Germany but was decisively defeated at the Battles of Tannenberg on August 26–30 and the Masurian Lakes on September 15 (see Map 25.3). The Russians were no longer a threat to German territory.

The Austrians, Germany's allies, fared less well initially. They had been defeated by the Russians in Galicia and thrown out of Serbia as well. To make matters worse, the Italians broke their alliance with the Germans and Austrians and entered the war on the Allied side by attacking Austria in May 1915. By this time, the Germans had come to the aid of the Austrians. A German-Austrian army defeated and routed the Russian army in Galicia and pushed the Russians back

The Excitement of War. The outbreak of World War I was greeted with incredible enthusiasm. Each of the major belligerents was convinced of the rightness of its cause. Everywhere in Europe, jubilant civilians sent their troops off to war with joyous fervor, as is evident in the photograph at the top, showing French troops marching off to war. The photograph below shows a group of German soldiers marching off to battle with civilian support. The belief that the soldiers would be home by Christmas proved to be a pathetic illusion.

three hundred miles into their own territory. Russian casualties stood at 2.5 million killed, captured, or wounded; the Russians had almost been knocked out of the war. Buoyed by their success, the Germans and Austrians, joined by the Bulgarians in September 1915, attacked and eliminated Serbia from the war.

1916–1917: The Great Slaughter

The successes in the east enabled the Germans to move back to the offensive in the west. The early trenches dug in 1914 had by now become elaborate systems of defense. Both lines of trenches were protected by barbed-wire entanglements three to five feet high and thirty yards wide, concrete machine-gun nests, and mortar batteries, supported further back by heavy artillery. Troops lived in holes in the ground, separated from each other by a "no-man's land."

The unexpected development of trench warfare baffled military leaders, who had been trained to fight wars of movement and maneuver. Periodically, the high command on either side would order an offensive that would begin with an artillery barrage to flatten the enemy's barbed wire and leave the enemy in a state of shock. After "softening up" the enemy in this fashion, a mass of soldiers would climb out of their trenches with fixed bayonets and hope to work their way toward the enemy trenches. The attacks rarely worked; the machine gun put hordes of men advancing unprotected across open fields at a severe disadvantage. In 1916 and 1917, millions of young men were killed in the search for the elusive breakthrough. In the German offensive at Verdun (ver-DUN) in 1916, 700,000 men lost their lives over a few miles of terrain. At the Battle of the Somme, the British suffered 57,000 casualties, including 21,000 dead, on the first day of the battle, the heaviest one-day loss in World War I.

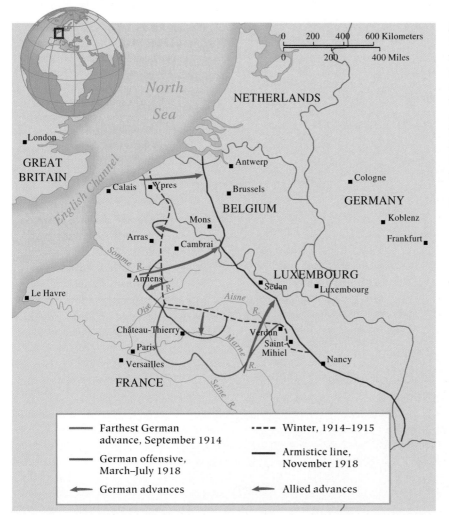

MAP 25.2 The Western Front, 1914–1918. The western front was the site of massive carnage: millions of soldiers died in offensives and counteroffensives as they moved battle lines a few miles at a time in France and Belgium from 1914 to 1917. The rotting bodies of dead comrades often surrounded soldiers in the trenches.

Q What is the approximate distance between the armistice line near Sedan and the closest approach of the Germans to Paris?

Legend:

— Farthest German advance, September 1914

— German offensive, March–July 1918

◄— German advances

---- Winter, 1914–1915

— Armistice line, November 1918

◄— Allied advances

General Photographic Agency/Getty Images

Impact of the Machine Gun. Trench warfare on the western front stymied military leaders, who had expected to fight a war based on movement and maneuver. Their efforts to effect a breakthrough by sending masses of men against enemy lines were the height of folly in view of the brutal efficiency of the machine gun. This photograph shows French soldiers moving across a rocky terrain, all open targets for their enemies armed with the new weapons.

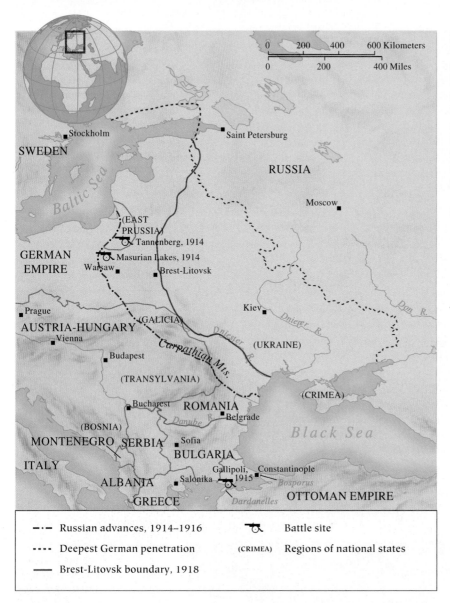

MAP 25.3 The Eastern Front, 1914–1918. The Russians made early gains but then were pushed far back into their own territory by the German army. After the Bolsheviks seized power, they negotiated the Treaty of Brest-Litovsk, which extracted Russia from the war at the cost of substantial Russian territory (see Map 25.4).

Q What is the approximate average distance between the farthest advances of Russia into Germany and the farthest advances of Germany into Russia?

Warfare in the trenches of the western front produced unimaginable horrors (see Images of Everyday Life on p. 613). Battlefields were hellish landscapes of barbed wire, shell holes, mud, and injured and dying men. The introduction of poison gas in 1915 produced new forms of injuries, as one British writer described:

> I wish those people who write so glibly about this being a holy war could see a case of mustard gas ... could see the poor things burnt and blistered all over with great mustard-coloured suppurating blisters with blind eyes all sticky ... and stuck together, and always fighting for breath, with voices a mere whisper, saying that their throats are closing and they know they will choke.[5]

Soldiers in the trenches also lived with the persistent presence of death (see the box on p. 614). Because combat went on for months, they had to carry on in the midst of countless bodies of dead men or the remains of men dismembered by artillery barrages (see the Film & History feature on p. 615). Many soldiers remembered the stench of decomposing bodies and the swarms of rats that grew fat in the trenches.

This horror was endured for one week out of every month. Soldiers on the western front did not spend all of their time on the frontline or in combat when they were on the frontline. An infantryman spent one week out of every month in the frontline

IMAGES OF EVERYDAY LIFE

Life in the Trenches

THE SLAUGHTER OF MILLIONS of men in the trenches of World War I created unimaginable horrors for the participants. For the sake of survival, many soldiers learned to harden themselves against the stench of decomposing bodies and the sight of bodies horribly dismembered by artillery barrages, as is evident in the photograph immediately below. Life in the trenches could also be boring as soldiers whiled away the time as best they could when they were not fighting. Shown in the photograph to the right below is a group of German soldiers in their trench reading and writing letters during a lull in the fighting. The introduction of poison gas in 1915 led quickly to the use of protective masks. The photograph on the bottom left shows Austrian soldiers in their trench demonstrating how to use the gas masks.

Hulton Archive/Getty Images

Three Lions/Getty Images

Hulton Archive/Getty Image

The Reality of War: Trench Warfare

The romantic illusions about the excitement and adventure of war that filled the minds of so many young men who marched off to battle quickly evaporated after a short time in the trenches on the western front. This description of trench warfare is taken from the most famous novel that emerged from World War I, Erich Maria Remarque's *All Quiet on the Western Front*, published in 1929. Remarque had served in the German army in the trenches in France.

Erich Maria Remarque, *All Quiet on the Western Front*

We wake up in the middle of the night. The earth booms. Heavy fire is falling on us. We crouch into corners. We distinguish shells of every calibre.

Each man lays hold of his things and looks again every minute to reassure himself that they are still there. The dug-out heaves, the night roars and flashes. We look at each other in the momentary flashes of light, and with pale faces and pressed lips shake our heads.

Every man is aware of the heavy shells tearing down the parapet, rooting up the embankment and demolishing the upper layers of concrete.... Already by morning a few of the recruits are green and vomiting. They are too inexperienced....

The attack does not come, but the bombardment continues. Slowly we become mute. Hardly a man speaks. We cannot make ourselves understood.

Our trench is almost gone. At many places it is only eighteen inches high, it is broken by holes, and craters, and mountains of earth. A shell lands square in front of our post. At once it is dark. We are buried and must dig ourselves out....

Towards morning, while it is still dark there is some excitement. Through the entrance rushes in a swarm of fleeing rats that try to storm the walls. Torches light up the confusion. Everyone yells and curses and slaughters....

Suddenly it howls and flashes terrifically, the dugout cracks in all its joints under a direct hit, fortunately only a light one that the concrete blocks are able to withstand. It rings metallically, the walls reel, rifles, helmets, earth, mud, and dust fly everywhere. Sulphur fumes pour in.... The recruit starts to rave again and two others follow suit. One jumps up and rushes out,

we have trouble with the other two. I start after the one who escapes and wonder whether to shoot him in the leg—then it shrieks again, I fling myself down and when I stand up the wall of the trench is plastered with smoking splinters, lumps of flesh, and bits of uniform. I scramble back....

Suddenly the nearer explosions cease. The shelling continues but it has lifted and falls behind us; our trench is free. We seize the hand-grenades, pitch them out in front of the dug-out and jump after them. The bombardment has stopped and a heavy barrage now falls behind us. The attack has come.

No one would believe that in this howling waste there could still be men; but steel helmets now appear on all sides out of the trench, and fifty yards from us a machine-gun is already in position and barking.

The wire-entanglements are torn to pieces. Yet they offer some obstacle. We see the storm-troops coming. Our artillery opens fire. Machine-guns rattle, rifles crack. The charge works its way across. Haie and Kropp begin with the hand-grenades. They throw as fast as they can, others pass them, the handles with the strings already pulled. Haie throws seventy-five yards, Kropp sixty, it has been measured, the distance is important. The enemy as they run cannot do much before they are within forty yards.

We recognize the distorted faces, the smooth helmets: they are French. They have already suffered heavily when they reach the remnants of the barbed-wire entanglements. A whole line has gone down before our machine-guns; then we have a lot of stoppages and they come nearer.

I see one of them, his face upturned, fall into a wire cradle. His body collapses, his hands remain suspended as though he were praying. Then his body drops clean away and only his hands with the stumps of his arms, shot off, now hang in the wire.

Source: Reproduced by permission of the Estate of the Late Paulette Goddard Remarque.

Q What does this excerpt reveal about the realities of trench warfare? Would the surviving frontline victims of the war have been able to describe or explain their experiences to those left behind on the home front? What effect would that have on postwar European society?

FILM & HISTORY

Paths of Glory (1957)

PATHS OF GLORY, directed by Stanley Kubrick, is a powerful antiwar film made in 1957 and based on the novel of the same name by Humphrey Cobb. Set in France in 1916, the film deals with the time during World War I when the western front had become bogged down in brutal trench warfare. The novel was based loosely on a true story of five French soldiers who were executed for mutiny. In the film, General George Broulard (Adolphe Menjou) of the French General Staff suggests to his subordinate, General Mireau (George Macready), that he launch what would amount to a suicidal attack on the well-defended Ant Hill. Mireau refuses until Broulard mentions the possibility of a promotion, at which point Mireau abruptly changes his mind and accepts the challenge. He walks through the trenches preparing his men with the stock question: "Hello there, soldier; are you ready to kill more Germans?" Mireau persuades Colonel Dax (Kirk Douglas) to mount the attack, despite Dax's protest that it will be a disaster. Dax proves to be right. None of the French soldiers reach the German lines, and one-third of the troops are not even able to leave their trenches because of enemy fire. To avoid blame for the failure, Mireau accuses his men of cowardice, and three of them (one from each company, chosen in purely arbitrary fashion) are brought before a hastily arranged court-martial. Dax defends his men but to no avail. The decision has already been made, and the three men are shot in front of the assembled troops. "One way to maintain discipline is to shoot a man now and then," Broulard cynically comments. After the execution, when Broulard offers Dax a promotion, Dax responds, "Would you like me to suggest what you can do with that promotion?" Replies Broulard, "You're an idealist; I pity you." But Dax has the last word: "I pity you for not seeing the wrongs you have done." The film ends with the troops being ordered back to the front.

The film realistically portrays the horrors of trench warfare in World War I—the senseless and suicidal attacks through no-man's land against well-entrenched machine-gun batteries. The film is also scathing in its portrayal of military leaders. The generals are shown drinking cognac in the palaces they requisitioned for their headquarters while the troops live in the mud and filth of the trenches. Both generals are portrayed as arrogant, ego-driven individuals who think nothing of the slaughter of their men in battle. The men condemned to die for cowardice are scapegoats sacrificed to cover up the mistakes of their superior officers, who are determined to pursue "paths of glory" to advance themselves. The film's portrayal of the military executions was not accurate, however. The French army did not choose individuals at random for punishment, although it did execute some soldiers on charges of cowardice, as did the armies of the other belligerents.

This realistic indictment of war and the military elites offended some countries. French authorities saw the film as an insult to the honor of the army and did not allow it to be shown in France until 1975. The military regime of Francisco Franco in Spain also banned the film for its antimilitary content. Kubrick himself went on to make two other antiwar films, capturing the Vietnam War in *Full Metal Jacket* and the Cold War in *Dr. Strangelove or: How I Learned to Stop Worrying and Love the Bomb.*

Colonel Dax (Kirk Douglas) begins to lead his mean out of the trenches to attack Ant Hill.

trenches, one week in the reserve lines, and the remaining two weeks somewhere behind the lines.

The Widening of the War

As another response to the stalemate on the western front, both sides sought to gain new allies who might provide a winning advantage. The Ottoman Empire had already come into the war on Germany's side in the autumn of 1914. Russia, Great Britain, and France declared war on the Ottoman Empire in November. Although the Allies attempted to open a Balkan front by landing forces at Gallipoli (gah-LIP-poh-lee), southwest of Constantinople, in April 1915, the entry of Bulgaria into the war on the side of the Central Powers (as Germany, Austria-Hungary, and the Ottoman Empire were called) and a disastrous campaign at Gallipoli caused them to withdraw. The Italians, as we have seen, entered the war on the Allied side after France and Britain promised to further their acquisition of Austrian territory. In the long run, however, Italian military incompetence forced the Allies to come to the assistance of Italy.

A GLOBAL CONFLICT Because the major European powers controlled colonial empires in other parts of the world, the war in Europe rapidly spiraled into a world war. In the Middle East, the British officer T. E. Lawrence (1888–1935), who came to be known as Lawrence of Arabia, incited

Arab princes to revolt against their Ottoman overlords in 1917. In 1918, British forces from Egypt and Mesopotamia destroyed the rest of the Ottoman Empire in the Middle East. For their Middle East campaigns, the British mobilized forces from India, Australia, and New Zealand.

The Allies also took advantage of Germany's preoccupation in Europe and lack of naval strength to seize German colonies in Africa. But there too the war did not end quickly. The first British shots of World War I were actually fired in Africa when British African troops moved into the German colony of Togoland near the end of August 1914. But in East Africa, the German commander Colonel Paul von Lettow-Vorbeck (POWL fun LEH-toh-FOR-bek) managed to keep his African troops fighting one campaign after another for four years; he did not surrender until two weeks after an armistice ended the war in Europe.

In the battles in Africa, Allied governments drew mainly on African soldiers, but some states, especially France, also recruited African troops to fight in Europe. The French drafted more than 170,000 West African soldiers, many of whom fought in the trenches on the western front. African troops were also used as occupation forces in the German Rhineland at the end of the war. About 80,000 Africans were killed or injured in Europe, where they were often at a distinct disadvantage due to the unfamiliar terrain and climate.

Private Collection/Archives Charmet/The Bridgeman Art Library

French African Troops. The French drafted more than 170,000 West African soldiers to fight in Europe. Shown in this photograph are French Senegalese troops arriving in France in 1915; they would later fight in the Marne campaign on the western front. The French army set up a photographic service to record various aspects of the war.

Hundreds of thousands of Africans were also used for labor, especially for carrying supplies and building roads and bridges. In East Africa, both sides drafted African laborers as carriers for their armies. More than 100,000 of these laborers died from disease and starvation caused by neglect.

The immediate impact of World War I was the extension of colonial rule, since Germany's African colonies were simply transferred to the winning powers, especially the British and the French. But the war also had unintended consequences for the Europeans. African soldiers who had gone to war for the Allies, especially those who left Africa and fought in Europe, became politically aware and began to advocate political and social equality. As one African who had fought for the French said, "We were not fighting for the French, we were fighting for ourselves [to become] French citizens."[6] Moreover, educated African elites, who had aided their colonial overlords in enlisting local peoples to fight, did so in the belief that they would be rewarded with citizenship and new political possibilities after the war. When their hopes were frustrated, they soon became involved in anticolonial movements (see Chapter 26).

In East Asia and the Pacific, Japan joined the Allies on August 23, 1914, primarily to seize control of German territories in China and the Pacific. As one Japanese statesman declared, the war in Europe was "divine aid ... for the development of the destiny of Japan."[7] The Japanese took possession of German territories in China, as well as the German-occupied islands in the Pacific. New Zealand and Australia quickly joined the Japanese in conquering the German-held parts of New Guinea.

ENTRY OF THE UNITED STATES Most important to the Allied cause was the entry of the United States into the war. At first, the United States tried to remain neutral in the Great War but found it more difficult to do so as the war dragged on. The immediate cause of American involvement grew out of the naval conflict between Germany and Great Britain. Britain used its superior naval power to maximum effect by imposing a naval blockade on Germany. Germany retaliated with a counter-blockade enforced by the use of unrestricted submarine warfare. However, strong American protests over the German sinking of passenger liners, especially the British ship *Lusitania* on May 7, 1915, when more than one hundred Americans lost their lives, forced the German government to modify its policy of unrestricted submarine warfare starting in September 1915 and to briefly suspend unrestricted submarine warfare a year later.

In January 1917, however, eager to break the deadlock in the war, the Germans decided on another military gamble. German naval officers convinced Emperor William II that use of unrestricted submarine warfare could starve the British into submission within five months, before the Americans could act. This renewed aggression brought the United States into the war on April 6, 1917. Although American troops did not arrive in large numbers in Europe until 1918, the entry of the United States into the war in 1917 gave the Allied Powers a psychological boost when they needed it. The year 1917 was not a good year for them. Allied offensives on the western front were disastrously defeated. The Italian armies were smashed in October, and in November, the Bolshevik Revolution (see "The Russian Revolution" later in this chapter) led to Russia's withdrawal from the war. The cause of the Central Powers looked favorable, although war weariness in the Ottoman Empire, Bulgaria, Austria-Hungary, and Germany was beginning to take its toll. The home front was rapidly becoming a cause for as much concern as the war front.

The Home Front: The Impact of Total War

The prolongation of World War I made it a **total war** that affected the lives of all citizens, however remote they might be from the battlefields. The need to organize masses of men and matériel for years of combat (Germany alone had 5.5 million men in active units in 1916) led to increased centralization of government powers, economic regimentation, and manipulation of public opinion to keep the war effort going.

POLITICAL AND ECONOMIC REPERCUSSIONS Because the war was expected to be short, little thought had been given to economic problems and long-term wartime needs. Governments had to respond quickly, however, when the war machines failed to achieve their knockout blows and made ever-greater demands for men and matériel. The extension of government power was a logical outgrowth of these needs. Most European countries had already devised some system of mass conscription or military draft. It was now carried to unprecedented heights as countries mobilized millions of young men for that elusive breakthrough to victory. Even countries that traditionally relied on volunteers

(Great Britain had the largest volunteer army in modern history—1 million men—in 1914 and 1915) were forced to resort to conscription, especially to ensure that skilled workers did not enlist but remained in factories that were crucial to the production of munitions. In 1916, despite widespread resistance to this extension of government power, compulsory military service was introduced in Great Britain.

Throughout Europe, wartime governments expanded their powers over their economies. Free-market capitalistic systems were temporarily shelved as governments experimented with price, wage, and rent controls, the rationing of food supplies and materials, the regulation of imports and exports, the **nationalization** of transportation systems and industries, and compulsory labor employment. In effect, to mobilize the entire resources of their nations for the war effort, European nations had moved toward planned economies directed by government agencies. Under total war mobilization, the distinction between soldiers at war and civilians at home was narrowed. In the view of political leaders, all citizens constituted a national army dedicated to victory. As the American president Woodrow Wilson expressed it, the men and women "who remain to till the soil and man the factories are no less a part of the army than the men beneath the battle flags."

PUBLIC ORDER AND PUBLIC OPINION As the Great War dragged on and both casualties and privations worsened, internal dissatisfaction replaced the patriotic enthusiasm that had marked the early stages of the war. By 1916, there were numerous signs that civilian morale was beginning to crack under the pressure of total war. War governments, however, fought back against the growing opposition to the war. Authoritarian regimes, such as those of Germany, Russia, and Austria-Hungary, had always relied on force to subdue their populations. Under the pressures of the war, however, even parliamentary regimes resorted to an expansion of police powers to stifle internal dissent. At the very beginning of the war, the British Parliament passed the Defence of the Realm Act (DORA), which allowed the public authorities to arrest dissenters as traitors. The act was later extended to authorize public officials to censor newspapers by deleting objectionable material and even to suspend newspaper publication. In France, government authorities had initially been lenient about public opposition to the war. But when Georges Clemenceau (ZHORZH kluh-mahn-SOH) (1841–1929) became premier near the end of 1917, the lenient French policies came to an end, and basic civil liberties were suppressed

for the duration of the war. The editor of an antiwar newspaper was even executed on a charge of treason.

Wartime governments also made active use of propaganda to arouse enthusiasm for the war. At the beginning, public officials needed to do little to achieve this goal. The British and French, for example, exaggerated German atrocities in Belgium and found that their citizens were only too willing to believe these accounts. But as the war dragged on and morale sagged, governments were forced to devise new techniques to stimulate flagging enthusiasm. In one British recruiting poster, for example, a small daughter asked her father, "Daddy, what did you do in the Great War?" while her younger brother played with toy soldiers and cannon.

THE SOCIAL IMPACT OF TOTAL WAR Total war made a significant impact on European society, most visibly by bringing an end to unemployment. The withdrawal of millions of men from the labor market to fight, combined with the heightened demand for wartime products, led to jobs for everyone able to work, including women.

World War I also created new roles for women. With so many men off fighting at the front, women were called on to take over jobs and responsibilities that had not been open to them before. These included certain clerical jobs that only small numbers of women had held earlier. In Britain, for example, the number of women who worked in banking rose from 9,500 to almost 64,000 in the course of the war. Overall, 1,345,000 women in Britain obtained new jobs or replaced men during the war. Women were also now employed in jobs that had been considered "beyond the capacity of women." These included such occupations as chimney sweeps, truck drivers, farm laborers, and, above all, factory workers in heavy industry (see the box on p. 620). Thirty-eight percent of the workers in the Krupp (KROOP) Armaments works in Germany in 1918 were women.

While male workers expressed concern that the employment of females at lower wages would depress their own wages, women began to demand equal-pay legislation. The French government passed a law in July 1915 that established a minimum wage for women home-workers in textiles, an industry that had grown dramatically because of the need for military uniforms. In 1917, the government decreed that men and women should receive equal rates for piecework. But despite the noticeable increase in women's wages that resulted from government regulations, women's industrial wages were still not equal to men's wages by the end of the war.

Women Munition Workers in a British Factory. World War I created new opportunities for women. They were now employed in jobs that had earlier been considered beyond their capacity. The picture at the left shows British women, dressed in caps and smocks, making munitions in an armaments factory. As the recruitment poster at the right shows, the British government encouraged women to work in the munitions factories to aid the war effort. Women working in these factories were often nicknamed "munitionettes."

Even worse, women had achieved little real security about their place in the workforce. Both men and women seemed to think that many of the new jobs for women were only temporary, an expectation quite evident in the British poem "War Girls," written in 1916:

> There's the girl who clips your ticket for the train.
> And the girl who speeds the lift from floor to floor.
> There's the girl who does a milk-round in the rain,
> And the girl who calls for orders at your door.
> Strong, sensible, and fit,
> They're out to show their grit,
> And tackle jobs with energy and knack.
> No longer caged and penned up,
> They're going to keep their end up
> Till the khaki soldier boys come marching back.[8]

At the end of the war, governments moved quickly to remove women from the jobs they had been encouraged to take earlier. By 1919, there were 650,000 unemployed women in Britain, and wages for women

who were still employed were also lowered. The work benefits for women from World War I seemed to be short-lived.

Nevertheless, in some countries, the role played by women in the wartime economies did have a positive impact on the movement for women's social and political emancipation. The most obvious gain was the right to vote, given to women in Germany and Austria immediately after the war (already in Britain in January 1918). The Nineteenth Amendment to the U.S. Constitution gave women in the United States the right to vote in 1920. Contemporary media, however, tended to focus on the more noticeable yet in some ways more superficial social emancipation of upper- and middle-class women. In ever-larger numbers, these young women took jobs, had their own apartments, and showed their new independence by smoking in public and wearing shorter dresses, cosmetics, and boyish hairstyles.

Women in the Factories

During World War I, women were called on to assume new job responsibilities, including factory work. In this selection, Naomi Loughnan, a young, upper-middle-class woman, describes the experiences in a munitions plant that considerably broadened her perspective on life.

Naomi Loughnan, "Munition Work"

We little thought when we first put on our overalls and caps and enlisted in the Munition Army how much more inspiring our life was to be than we had dared to hope.... Our long days are filled with interest, and with the zest of doing work for our country in the grand cause of Freedom. As we handle the weapons of war we are learning great lessons of life. In the busy, noisy workshops we come face to face with every kind of class, and each one of these classes has something to learn from the others....

Engineering mankind is possessed of the unshakable opinion that no woman can have the mechanical sense. If one of us asks humbly why such and such an alteration is not made to prevent this or that drawback to a machine, she is told, with a superior smile, that a man has worked her machine before her for years, and that therefore if there were any improvement possible it would have been made. As long as we do exactly what we are told and do not attempt to use our brains, we give entire satisfaction, and are treated as nice, good children. Any swerving from the easy path prepared for us by our males arouses the most scathing contempt in their manly bosoms.... Women have, however, proved that their entry into the munition world has increased the output. Employers who forget things personal in their patriotic desire for large results are enthusiastic over the success of women in the shops. But their workmen have to be handled with the utmost tenderness and caution lest they should actually imagine it was being suggested that women could do their work equally well, given equal conditions of training—at least where muscle is not the driving force....

The coming of the mixed classes of women into the factory is slowly but surely having an educative effect upon the men. "Language" is almost unconsciously becoming subdued. There are fiery exceptions who make our hair stand up on end under our close-fitting caps, but a sharp rebuke or a look of horror will often straighten out the most savage.... It is grievous to hear the girls also swearing and using disgusting language. Shoulder to shoulder with the children of the slums, the upper classes are having their eyes opened at last to the awful conditions among which their sisters have dwelt. Foul language, immorality, and many other evils are but the natural outcome of overcrowding and bitter poverty.... Sometimes disgust will overcome us, but we are learning with painful clarity that the fault is not theirs whose actions disgust us, but must be placed to the discredit of those other classes who have allowed the continued existence of conditions which generate the things from which we shrink appalled.

Q What did Naomi Loughnan learn about men and lower-class women while working in the munitions factory? What did she learn about herself? What can one conclude about the effects of total war on European women?

Source: From "Munition Work" by Naomi Loughnan, in *Women War Workers*, edited by Gilbert Stone (London: George Harrap and Company, 1917), pp. 25, 35–38.

War and Revolution

Q FOCUS QUESTION: What were the causes of the Russian Revolution of 1917, and why did the Bolsheviks prevail in the civil war and gain control of Russia?

By 1917, total war was creating serious domestic turmoil in all of the European belligerent states. Only one, however, experienced the kind of complete collapse in 1917 that others were predicting might happen throughout Europe. Out of Russia's collapse came the Russian Revolution.

The Russian Revolution

Tsar Nicholas II was an autocratic ruler who relied on the army and bureaucracy to prop up his regime. Russia was unprepared both militarily and technologically for the total war of World War I. Competent military leadership was lacking, and Russian industry was unable to produce the weapons needed for the army. Ill-led and ill-armed, Russian armies suffered incredible losses. Between 1914 and 1916, 2 million soldiers were killed, and another 4 to 6 million were wounded or captured.

In the meantime, the tsar was increasingly insulated from events by his German-born wife, Alexandra, a well-educated woman who had fallen under the influence of Rasputin (rass-PYOO-tin), a Siberian peasant whom the tsarina regarded as a holy man because he alone seemed able to stop the bleeding of her hemophiliac son, Alexis. Rasputin's influence made him a power behind the throne, and he did not hesitate to interfere in government affairs. As the leadership at the top experienced a series of military and economic disasters, the middle class, aristocrats, peasants, soldiers, and workers grew more and more disenchanted with the tsarist regime. Even conservative aristocrats who supported the monarchy felt the need to do something to reverse the deteriorating situation. For a start, they assassinated Rasputin in December 1916. By then it was too late to save the monarchy, and its fall came quickly in the first weeks of March 1917.

THE MARCH REVOLUTION At the beginning of March, a series of strikes broke out in the capital city of Petrograd (formerly St. Petersburg). Here the actions of working-class women helped change the course of Russian history. Weeks earlier, the government had introduced bread rationing in the city after the price of bread skyrocketed. Many of the women who stood in line waiting for bread were also factory workers who put in twelve-hour days. The Russian government had become aware of the volatile situation in the capital from police reports, one of which stated:

> Mothers of families, exhausted by endless standing in line at stores, distraught over their half-starving and sick children, are today perhaps closer to revolution than [the liberal opposition leaders,] and of course they are a great deal more dangerous because they are the combustible material for which only a single spark is needed to burst into flame.[9]

On March 8, about ten thousand women marched through Petrograd chanting "Peace and bread" and "Down with autocracy." Soon other workers joined the women, and together they called for a general strike that succeeded in shutting down all the factories in the city on March 10. Nicholas ordered the troops to disperse the crowds by shooting them if necessary, but soon significant numbers of the soldiers joined the demonstrators. The Duma, the legislative body that the tsar had tried to dissolve, met anyway and on March 12 declared that it was assuming governmental responsibility. It established a provisional government on March 15; the tsar abdicated the same day.

In just one week, the tsarist regime had fallen apart. Although no particular group had been responsible for the outburst, the moderate Constitutional Democrats, who represented primarily a middle-class and liberal aristocratic minority, were responsible for establishing the provisional government. Their program consisted of a liberal agenda that included working toward a parliamentary democracy and passing reforms that provided universal suffrage, civil equality, and an eight-hour workday.

The provisional government also faced another authority, the soviets, or councils of workers' and soldiers' deputies. **Soviets** sprang up spontaneously in cities, factory towns, army units, and rural areas. The soviets represented the more radical interests of the lower classes and were largely composed of socialists of different kinds. One group, the Bolsheviks, came to play a crucial role.

THE BOLSHEVIK REVOLUTION The **Bolsheviks** (BOHL-shuh-viks) were a small faction of Marxist Social Democrats who had come under the leadership of Vladimir Ulianov, known to the world as V. I. Lenin (1870–1924). Arrested for his revolutionary activity, Lenin was shipped to Siberia. After his release, he chose to go into exile in Switzerland and eventually assumed the leadership of the Bolshevik wing of the Russian Social Democratic Party.

Under Lenin's direction, the Bolsheviks became a party dedicated to a violent revolution that would destroy the capitalist system. He believed that this would be accomplished by a "vanguard" of activists consisting of a small group of well-disciplined professional revolutionaries. Between 1900 and 1917, Lenin spent most of his time in Switzerland. When the provisional government was formed in March 1917, he believed that the Bolsheviks' opportunity to seize power in Russia had come. A few weeks later, with the connivance of the German High Command, who hoped to create disorder in Russia, Lenin, his wife, and a small group of his followers were shipped to Russia in a "sealed train" by way of Finland.

Lenin's arrival in Russia on April 3 opened a new stage in the Russian Revolution. Lenin maintained that the soviets of soldiers, workers, and peasants were ready-made instruments of power. The Bolsheviks must work to gain control of these groups and then use them to overthrow the provisional government. At the same time, the Bolsheviks articulated the discontent and aspirations of the people, promising an end to the war, the redistribution of all land to the peasants, the transfer of factories and industries from capitalists to committees of workers, and the relegation of government power from the provisional government to the soviets. Three simple slogans summed up the Bolshevik program: "Peace, land, bread," "Worker control of production," and "All power to the soviets."

By the end of October, the Bolsheviks had achieved a slight majority in the Petrograd and Moscow soviets. The number of party members had also grown from 50,000 to 240,000. With Leon Trotsky (TRAHT-skee) (1877–1940), a fervid revolutionary, as chairman of the Petrograd soviet, the Bolsheviks were in a position to seize power in the name of the soviets. During the night of November 6, pro-soviet and pro-Bolshevik forces took control of Petrograd under the immensely popular slogan "All power to

the soviets." The provisional government quickly collapsed with little bloodshed. The following night, the all-Russian Congress of Soviets, representing local soviets from all over the country, affirmed the transfer of power. At the second session, on the night of November 8, Lenin announced the new Soviet government, the Council of People's Commissars, with himself as its head.

But the Bolsheviks (soon renamed the Communists) still had a long way to go (see the box on p. 623). Lenin had promised peace, but that, he realized, was not an easy task because of the humiliating losses of Russian territory that it would entail. There was no real choice, however. On March 3, 1918, Lenin signed the Treaty of Brest-Litovsk (BREST-li-TUFFSK) with Germany and gave up eastern Poland, Ukraine, Finland, and the Baltic provinces. To his critics, Lenin argued that it made no difference because the spread of socialist revolution throughout Europe would soon make the treaty largely irrelevant. In any case, he had promised peace to the Russian people; but real peace did not come, for the country soon sank into civil war.

Lenin and Trotsky. V. I. Lenin and Leon Trotsky were important figures in the Bolsheviks' successful seizure of power in Russia. On the left, Lenin is seen addressing a rally in Moscow in 1917. On the right, Trotsky, who became commissar of war in the new regime, is shown haranguing his troops.

Keystone/Getty Images

© Underwood & Underwood/Corbis

Soldier and Peasant Voices

In 1917, Russia experienced a cataclysmic upheaval as two revolutions overthrew first the tsarist regime and then the provisional government that replaced it. Peasants, workers, and soldiers poured out their thoughts and feelings on these events, some of them supporting the Bolsheviks and others denouncing the Bolsheviks for betraying their socialist revolution. These selections are taken from two letters, the first from a soldier and the second from a peasant. Both are addressed to Bolshevik leaders.

Letter from a Soldier in Leningrad to Lenin, January 6, 1918

Bastard! What the hell are you doing? How long are you going to keep on degrading the Russian people? After all, it's because of you they killed the former minister . . . and so many other innocent victims. Because of you, they might kill even other former ministers belonging to the [Socialist Revolutionary] party because you call them counterrevolutionaries and even monarchists. . . . And you, you Bolshevik gang leader hired either by Nicholas II or by Wilhelm II, are waging this pogrom propaganda against men who may have done time with you in exile.

Scoundrel! A curse on you from the politically conscious Russian proletariat, the conscious ones and not the kind who are following you—that is, the Red Guards, the tally clerks, who, when they are called to military service, all hide at the factories and now are killing . . . practically their own father, the way the soldiers did in 1905 when they killed their own, or the way the police and gendarmes did in [1917]. That's who they're more like. They're not pursuing the ideas of socialism because they don't understand them (if they did they wouldn't act this way) but because they get paid a good salary both at the factory and in the Red Guards. But not all the workers are like that—there are very politically aware ones—and the soldiers—again not all of them—are like that but only former policemen, constables, gendarmes and the very ignorant ones who under the old regime . . . couldn't tell their right foot from their left and they are pursuing not the ideas of socialism that you advocate but to be able to lie on their cots in the barracks and do absolutely nothing not even be asked to sweep the floor, . . . And so the entire proletariat of Russia is following you, by count fewer than are against you, but they are only physically or rather technically stronger than the majority, and that is what you're abusing when you disbanded the Constituent Assembly the way Nicholas II disbanded the Duma. You point out that counterrevolutionaries gathered there. You lie, scoundrel, there wasn't a single counterrevolutionary and if there was then it was you, the Bolsheviks, which you proved by your actions when you encroached on the gains of the revolution: you are shutting down newspapers, even socialist ones, arresting socialists, committing violence and deceiving the people; you promised loads but did none of it.

Letter from a Peasant to the Bolshevik Leaders, January 10, 1918

TO YOU!

Rulers, plunderers, rapists, destroyers, usurpers, oppressors of Mother Russia, citizens Lenin, Trotsky, . . . [and other leaders of the Bolshevik party]:

Allow me to ask you how long you are going to go on degrading Russia's millions, its tormented and exhausted people. Instead of peace, you signed an armistice with the enemy, and this gave our opponent a painful advantage, and you declared war on Russia. You moved the troops you had tricked to the Russian front and started a fratricidal war. Your mercenary Red Guards are looting, murdering, and raping everywhere they go. A fire has consumed all our dear Mother Russia. Rail transport is idle, as are the plants and factories; the entire population has woken up to find itself in the most pathetic situation, without bread or kerosene or any of the other essentials, unclothed and unshod in unheated houses. In short: hungry and cold. . . . You have strangled the entire press, and freedom with it, you have wiped out the best freedom fighters, you have destroyed all Russia. Think it over, you butchers, you hirelings of the Kaiser [William II]. Isn't your turn about up, too? . . . May you be damned, you accursed one, you bloodthirsty butchers, you hirelings of the Kaiser—don't think you're in the clear, because the Russian people will sober up and that will be the end of you.

Q What arguments do the writers of these letters use against Lenin and the Bolsheviks? Why do they feel so betrayed by the Bolsheviks?

Source: From *Voices of Revolution, 1917* by Mark D. Steinberg. Copyright © 2001 Yale University Press. Reprinted by permission.

CIVIL WAR   There was great opposition to the new Bolshevik or Communist regime, not only from groups loyal to the tsar but also from bourgeois and aristocratic liberals and anti-Leninist socialists. In addition, thousands of Allied troops were eventually sent to different parts of Russia in the hope of bringing Russia back into the Great War.

Between 1918 and 1921, the Bolshevik (Red) Army was forced to fight on many fronts. The first serious threat to the Bolsheviks came from Siberia, where an anti-Bolshevik (White) force attacked westward and advanced almost to the Volga River before being stopped. Attacks also came from the Ukrainians in the southeast and from the Baltic regions. In mid-1919, White forces swept through Ukraine and advanced almost to Moscow. At one point in late 1919, three separate White armies seemed to be closing in on the Bolsheviks but were eventually pushed back. By 1920, the major White forces had been defeated, and Ukraine was retaken. The next year, the Communist regime regained control over the independent nationalist governments in the Caucasus: Georgia, Russian Armenia, and Azerbaijan.

The royal family was yet another victim of the civil war. After the tsar had abdicated, he, his wife, and their five children had been taken into custody. They were moved in August 1917 to Tobolsk in Siberia and in April 1918 to Ekaterinburg (i-kat-tuh-RIN-burk), a mining town in the Urals. On the night of July 16, members of the local soviet murdered the tsar and his family and burned their bodies in a nearby mine shaft.

How had Lenin and the Bolsheviks triumphed over what seemed at one time to be overwhelming forces? For one thing, the Red Army became a well-disciplined and formidable fighting force, thanks largely to the organizational genius of Leon Trotsky. As commissar of war, Trotsky reinstated the draft and insisted on rigid discipline; soldiers who deserted or refused to obey orders were summarily executed.

The disunity of the anti-Communist forces seriously weakened their efforts. Political differences created distrust among the Whites and prevented them from cooperating effectively with each other. Some Whites insisted on restoring the tsarist regime, but others understood that only a more liberal and democratic program had any chance of success. It was difficult enough to achieve military cooperation; political differences made it virtually impossible. The lack of a common goal on the part of the Whites contrasted sharply with the Communists' single-minded clear sense of purpose. Inspired by their vision of a new socialist order, the Communists had the advantage of possessing the determination that comes from revolutionary fervor and strong convictions.

The Communists also succeeded in translating their revolutionary faith into practical instruments of power. A policy of **war communism**, for example, was used to ensure regular supplies for the Red Army. War communism included the nationalization of banks and most industries, the forcible requisition of grain from peasants, and the centralization of state administration under Bolshevik control. Another Bolshevik instrument was "revolutionary terror." Although the old tsarist secret police had been abolished, a new Red secret police—known as the Cheka (CHEK-uh)—replaced it. The Red Terror instituted by the Cheka aimed at nothing less than the destruction of all opponents of the new regime.

Finally, the intervention of foreign armies enabled the Communists to appeal to the powerful force of Russian patriotism. Although the Allied powers had initially intervened in Russia to encourage the Russians to remain in the war, the end of the war on November 11, 1918, had made that purpose inconsequential. Nevertheless, Allied troops remained, and even more were sent because Allied countries did not hide their

CHRONOLOGY The Russian Revolution	
	1916
Murder of Rasputin	December
	1917
March of women in Petrograd	March 8
General strike in Petrograd	March 10
Establishment of the provisional government	March 15
Abdication of the tsar	March 15
Formation of the Petrograd soviet	March
Arrival of Lenin in Russia	April 3
Bolshevik majority in the Petrograd soviet	October
Bolshevik overthrow of the provisional government	November 6–7
	1918
Treaty of Brest-Litovsk	March 3
Civil war	1918–1921

anti-Bolshevik feelings. At one point, more than 100,000 foreign troops, mostly Japanese, British, French, and American, were stationed on Russian soil. Although these forces rarely engaged in pitched battles and did not pursue a common strategy, they did give material assistance to anti-Bolshevik forces. This intervention by the Allies enabled the Communist government to appeal to patriotic Russians to fight the attempts of foreigners to control their country.

By 1921, the Communists had succeeded in retaining control of Russia. In the course of the civil war, the Bolshevik regime had also transformed Russia into a bureaucratically centralized state dominated by a single party. It was also a state that was largely hostile to the Allied Powers that had sought to assist the Bolsheviks' enemies in the civil war.

The Last Year of the War

For Germany, the withdrawal of the Russians from the war in March 1918 offered renewed hope for a favorable outcome. The victory over Russia persuaded General Erich Ludendorff (LOO-dun-dorf), who guided German military operations, and most German leaders to make one final military gamble—a grand offensive in the west to break the military stalemate. The German attack was launched in March and lasted into July, but an Allied counterattack, supported by the arrival of 140,000 fresh American troops, defeated the Germans at the Second Battle of the Marne on July 18. Ludendorff's gamble had failed. With the arrival of 1 million more American troops on the continent, Allied forces began making a steady advance toward Germany.

On September 29, 1918, General Ludendorff informed German leaders that the war was lost and demanded that the government sue for peace at once. When German officials discovered that the Allies were unwilling to make peace with the autocratic imperial government, they instituted reforms to set up a liberal government. But these constitutional reforms came too late for the exhausted and angry German people. On November 3, naval units in Kiel mutinied, and within days, councils of workers and soldiers were forming throughout northern Germany and taking over the supervision of civilian and military administrations. William II capitulated to public pressure and abdicated on November 9, while the Socialists under Friedrich Ebert (FREED-rikh AY-bert) announced the establishment of a republic. Two days

later, on November 11, 1918, an armistice agreed to by the new German government went into effect. The war was over.

THE CASUALTIES OF THE WAR World War I devastated European civilization. Between 8 and 9 million soldiers died on the battlefields; another 22 million were wounded. Many of those who survived later died from war injuries or suffered the loss of arms or legs or other forms of mutilation. The birthrate in many European countries declined noticeably as a result of the death or maiming of so many young men. World War I also created a "lost generation" of war veterans who had become accustomed to violence and who would form the postwar bands of fighters who supported Mussolini and Hitler in their bids for power (see Chapter 26).

Nor did the killing affect only soldiers. Untold numbers of civilians died from war, civil war, or starvation. In 1915, using the excuse of a rebellion by the Armenian minority and their supposed collaboration with the Russians, the Turkish government began systematically to kill Armenian men and expel women and children. Within seven months, 600,000 Armenians had been killed, and 500,000 had been deported. Of the latter, 400,000 died while marching through the deserts and swamps of Syria and Iraq. By September 1915, as many as 1 million, and possibly more, Armenians were dead, the victims of **genocide**.

The Peace Settlement

Q FOCUS QUESTION: What were the objectives of the chief participants at the Paris Peace Conference of 1919, and how closely did the final settlement reflect these objectives?

In January 1919, the delegations of the victorious Allied nations gathered in Paris to conclude a final settlement of the Great War. By that time, the reasons for fighting World War I had been transformed from selfish national interests to idealistic principles. No one expressed the latter better than the American president Woodrow Wilson. Wilson's proposals for a truly just and lasting peace included "open covenants of peace, openly arrived at" instead of secret diplomacy; the reduction of national armaments to a "point consistent with domestic safety"; and the self-determination of people so that "all well-defined

CHRONOLOGY World War I

1914	
Battle of Tannenberg	August 26–30
First Battle of the Marne	September 6–10
Battle of the Masurian Lakes	September 15
Russia, Britain, and France declare war on Ottoman Empire	November
1915	
Battle of Gallipoli begins	April 25
Italy declares war on Austria-Hungary	May 23
Bulgaria enters the war	September
1916	
Battle of Verdun	February 21–December 18
1917	
Germany resumes unrestricted submarine warfare	January
United States enters the war	April 6
1918	
Last German offensive	March 21–July 18
Second Battle of the Marne	July 18
Allied counteroffensive	July 18–November 10
Armistice between the Allies and Germany	November 11
1919	
Paris Peace Conference begins	January 18
Peace of Versailles	June 28

the colonial world and was influential in inspiring anticolonial nationalist movements in Africa, Asia, and the Middle East (see Chapter 26).

Wilson soon found, however, that other states at the Paris Peace Conference were guided by considerably more pragmatic motives. The secret treaties and agreements that had been made before the war could not be totally ignored, even if they did conflict with the principle of **self-determination** enunciated by Wilson. National interests also complicated the deliberations of the conference. David Lloyd George, prime minister of Great Britain, had won a decisive electoral victory in December 1918 on a platform of making the Germans pay for this dreadful war.

France's approach to peace was determined primarily by considerations of national security. Georges Clemenceau, the feisty premier of France who had led his country to victory, believed that the French people had borne the brunt of German aggression and deserved revenge and security against future German aggression (see the box on p. 627). Clemenceau wanted a demilitarized Germany, vast German reparations to pay for the costs of the war, and a separate Rhineland as a buffer state between France and Germany—demands that Wilson viewed as vindictive and contrary to the principle of national self-determination.

Wilson, Clemenceau, and Lloyd George made the most important decisions at the Paris Peace Conference. Italy was considered one of the so-called Big Four powers but played a much less important role than the other three countries. Germany, of course, was not invited to attend, and Russia could not because of civil war, although the Allies were also unwilling to negotiate with the Communist regime that was then fighting for power in Russia.

In view of the many conflicting demands at Versailles, it was inevitable that the Big Three would quarrel. Wilson was determined to create a "league of nations" to prevent future wars. Clemenceau and Lloyd George were equally determined to punish Germany. In the end, only compromise made it possible to achieve a peace settlement. On January 25, 1919, the conference adopted the principle of the League of Nations, and Wilson agreed to make compromises on territorial arrangements. Clemenceau also compromised to obtain some guarantees for French security. He renounced France's desire for a separate Rhineland and instead accepted a defensive alliance with Great Britain and the United States. Both states pledged to help France if it was attacked by Germany.

national aspirations shall be accorded the utmost satisfaction." Wilson characterized World War I as a people's war waged against "absolutism and militarism," two scourges of liberty that could be eliminated only by creating democratic governments and a "general association of nations" that would guarantee the "political independence and territorial integrity to great and small states alike" (see the box on p. 627). As the spokesman for a new world order based on democracy and international cooperation, Wilson was enthusiastically cheered by many Europeans when he arrived in Europe for the peace conference. His rhetoric on self-determination was also heard by peoples in

OPPOSING VIEWPOINTS

Three Voices of Peacemaking

When the Allied powers met in Paris in January 1919, it soon became apparent that the victors had different opinions on the kind of peace they expected. The first selection is an excerpt from a speech by Woodrow Wilson in which the American president presented his idealistic goals for a peace based on justice and reconciliation.

The French leader Georges Clemenceau had a vision of peacemaking quite different from Wilson's. The French sought revenge and security. In this selection from his book *Grandeur and Misery of Victory*, Clemenceau revealed his fundamental dislike and distrust of Germany.

Yet a third voice of peacemaking was heard in Paris in 1919, although not at the peace conference. W. E. B. Du Bois (doo BOYZ), an African American writer and activist, had organized the Pan-African Congress to meet in Paris during the sessions of the Paris Peace Conference. The goal of the Pan-African Congress was to present a series of resolutions that promoted the cause of Africans and people of African descent. As can be seen in the selection presented here, the resolutions did not call for immediate independence for African nations.

Woodrow Wilson, Speech, May 26, 1917

We are fighting for the liberty, the self-government, and the undictated development of all peoples, and every feature of the settlement that concludes this war must be conceived and executed for that purpose. Wrongs must first be righted and then adequate safeguards must be created to prevent their being committed again. . . .

No people must be forced under sovereignty under which it does not wish to live. No territory must change hands except for the purpose of securing those who inhabit it a fair chance of life and liberty. No indemnities must be insisted on except those that constitute payment for manifest wrongs done. No readjustments of power must be made except such as will tend to secure the future peace of the world and the future welfare and happiness of its peoples.

And then the free peoples of the world must draw together in some common covenant, some genuine and practical cooperation that will in effect combine their force to secure peace and justice in the dealings of nations with one another.

Georges Clemenceau, *Grandeur and Misery of Victory*

For the catastrophe of 1914 the Germans are responsible. Only a professional liar would deny this. . . .

What after all is this war, prepared, undertaken, and waged by the German people, who flung aside every scruple of conscience to let it loose, hoping for a peace of enslavement under the yoke of a militarism, destructive of all human dignity? It is simply the continuance, the recrudescence, of those never-ending acts of violence by which the first savage tribes carried out their depredations with all the resources of barbarism. . . .

I have sometimes penetrated into the sacred cave of the Germanic cult, which is, as every one knows, the *Bierhaus* [beer hall]. A great aisle of massive humanity where there accumulate, amid the fumes of tobacco and beer, the popular rumblings of a nationalism upheld by the sonorous brasses blaring to the heavens the supreme voice of Germany, *Deutschland über alles! Germany above everything!* Men, women, and children, all petrified in reverence before the divine stoneware pot, brows furrowed with irrepressible power, eyes lost in a dream of infinity, mouths twisted by the intensity of willpower, drink in long draughts the celestial hope of vague expectations.

Pan-African Congress

Resolved

That the Allied and Associated Powers establish a code of law for the international protection of the natives of Africa. . . .

The Negroes of the world demand that hereafter the natives of Africa and the peoples of African descent be governed according to the following principles:

1. The Land: the land and its natural resources shall be held in trust for the natives and at all times they shall have effective ownership of as much land as they can profitably develop. . . .

(continued)

3. Labor: slavery and corporal punishment shall be abolished and forced labor except in punishment for crime....

5. The State: the natives of Africa must have the right to participate in the government as fast as their development permits, in conformity with the principle that the government exists for the natives, and not the natives for the government.

Q How did the peacemaking aims of Wilson and Clemenceau differ? How did their different views affect the deliberations of the Paris Peace Conference and the nature of the final peace settlement? How and why did the views of the Pan-African Congress differ from those of Wilson and Clemenceau?

Sources: Woodrow Wilson, Speech, May 26, 1917. Georges Clemenceau, *Grandeur and Misery of Victory*. From Georges Clemenceau, *Grandeur and Misery of Victory* (New York: Harcourt, 1930), pp. 105, 107, 280. Pan-African Congress. Excerpts from Resolution from the Pan-African Congress, Paris, 1919.

The Treaty of Versailles

The final peace settlement of Paris consisted of five separate treaties with the defeated nations—Germany, Austria and Hungary (now separate nations), Bulgaria, and Turkey (see Map 25.4). The Treaty of Versailles with Germany, signed on June 28, 1919, was by far the most important. The Germans considered it a harsh peace and were particularly unhappy with Article 231, the so-called **War Guilt Clause**, which declared Germany (and Austria) responsible for starting the war and ordered Germany to pay **reparations** for all the damage the Allied governments and their people suffered as a result of the war.

The military and territorial provisions of the treaty also rankled the Germans, although they were by no means as harsh as the Germans claimed. Germany had to reduce its army to 100,000 men, cut back its navy, and eliminate its air force. German territorial losses included the cession of Alsace and Lorraine to France and sections of Prussia to the new Polish state (known as the Polish Corridor). German land west and as far as thirty miles east of the Rhine was established as a demilitarized zone and stripped of all armaments or fortifications to serve as a barrier to any future German military moves westward against France. Outraged by the "dictated peace," the new German government complained but accepted the treaty.

The Other Peace Treaties

The separate peace treaties made with the other Central Powers (Austria, Hungary, Bulgaria, and the Ottoman Empire) extensively redrew the map of eastern Europe. Many of these changes merely ratified what the war had already accomplished. Both the German and Russian empires lost considerable territory in eastern Europe, and the Austro-Hungarian Empire disappeared altogether. New nation-states emerged from the lands of these three empires: Finland, Latvia, Estonia, Lithuania, Poland, Czechoslovakia, Austria, and Hungary. Territorial rearrangements were also made in the Balkans. Romania acquired additional lands from Russia, Hungary, and Bulgaria. Serbia formed the nucleus of a new southern Slav state, the kingdom of the Serbs, Croats, and Slovenes (renamed Yugoslavia in 1929).

Although the Paris Peace Conference was supposedly guided by the principle of self-determination, the mixtures of peoples in eastern Europe made it impossible to draw boundaries along neat ethnic lines. As a result of compromises, virtually every eastern European state was left with a minorities problem that could lead to future conflicts. Germans in Poland; Hungarians, Poles, and Germans in Czechoslovakia; and Serbs, Croats, Slovenes, Macedonians, and Albanians in Yugoslavia all became sources of later conflict.

Yet another centuries-old empire—the Ottoman Empire—was dismembered by the peace settlement after the war. To gain Arab support against the Ottomans during the war, the Allies had promised to recognize the independence of Arab states in the Middle Eastern lands of the Ottoman Empire. But the imperialist habits of Europeans died hard. After the war, France took control of Lebanon and Syria, and Britain received Iraq and Palestine. Officially, both acquisitions were called **mandates**. Since Woodrow

MAP 25.4 Europe in 1919. The victorious Allies met to determine the shape and nature of postwar Europe. At the urging of U.S. president Woodrow Wilson, many nationalist aspirations of former imperial subjects were realized with the creation of several new countries from the prewar territory of Austria-Hungary, Germany, and Russia.

Q What new countries emerged, and what countries gained territory when Austria-Hungary was dismembered?

Wilson had opposed the outright annexation of colonial territories by the Allies, the peace settlement had created a system of mandates whereby a nation officially administered a territory on behalf of the League of Nations. The system of mandates could not hide the fact that the principle of national self-determination at the Paris Peace Conference was largely for Europeans.

Successful enforcement of the peace necessitated the active involvement of its principal architects, especially in helping the new German state develop a peaceful and democratic republic. The failure of the U.S. Senate to ratify the Treaty of Versailles, however, meant that the United States never joined the League of Nations. The Senate also rejected Wilson's defensive alliance with Great Britain and France. Already by the end of 1919, the United States was pursuing policies intended to limit its direct involvement in future European wars.

French mandates
British mandates

Constantinople (Istanbul)

TURKEY

Mediterranean Sea
LEBANON Beirut
Damascus
PALESTINE
Jerusalem
Cairo
EGYPT
TRANS-JORDAN

SYRIA
PERSIA
Baghdad
IRAQ
KUWAIT
SAUDI ARABIA

Caspian Sea

0   250   500   750 Kilometers
0   250   500 Miles

The Middle East in 1919

This retreat had dire consequences. American withdrawal from the defensive alliance with Britain and France led Britain to withdraw as well. By removing itself from European affairs, the United States forced France to stand alone facing its old enemy, leading the embittered nation to take strong actions against Germany that only intensified German resentment. By the end of 1919, it appeared that the peace established mere months earlier was already beginning to unravel.

Chapter Summary

The assassination of Archduke Francis Ferdinand of Austria-Hungary in the Bosnian capital of Sarajevo in the summer of 1914 led within six weeks to a major war among the major powers of Europe. The Germans drove the Russians back in the east, but a stalemate developed in the west, where trenches extending from the Swiss border to the English Channel were defended by barbed wire and machine guns. The Ottoman Empire joined Germany, and Italy became one of the Allies. After

German submarine attacks, the United States entered the war in 1917, but even from the beginning of the war, battles also took place in the African colonies of the Great Powers as well as in the East, making this a truly global war.

Unprepared for war, Russia soon faltered and collapsed, leading to a revolution against the tsar. But the new provisional government in Russia also soon failed, enabling the revolutionary Bolsheviks of V. I. Lenin to seize power. Lenin established a dictatorship and made a costly peace with Germany. After Russia's withdrawal from the war, Germany launched a massive attack in the west, but it had been severely weakened by the war. In the fall of 1918, after American troops entered the conflict, the German government collapsed, leading to the armistice on November 11, 1918.

World War I was the defining event of the twentieth century. It shattered the liberal and rational assumptions of late-nineteenth- and early-twentieth-century European society. The

incredible destruction and the deaths of almost 10 million people undermined the whole idea of progress. New propaganda techniques had manipulated entire populations into sustaining their involvement in a meaningless slaughter.

World War I was a total war that required extensive mobilization of resources and populations. As a result, government centralization increased, as did the power of the state over the lives of its citizens. Civil liberties, such as freedom of the press, speech, assembly, and movement, were circumscribed in the name of national security. Governments' need to plan the production and distribution of goods and to ration consumer goods restricted economic freedom. Although the late nineteenth and early twentieth centuries had witnessed the extension of government authority into such areas as mass education, social welfare legislation, and mass conscription, World War I made the practice of strong central authority a way of life.

Finally, World War I ended the age of European hegemony over world affairs. In 1917, the Russian Revolution had laid the foundation for the creation of a new Eurasian power, the Soviet Union, and the United States had entered the war. The waning of the European age was not evident to all, however, for it was clouded by American isolationism and the withdrawal of the Soviets from world affairs while they nurtured the growth of their own socialist system. These developments, though temporary, created a political vacuum in Europe that all too soon was filled by the revival of German power.

CHAPTER TIMELINE

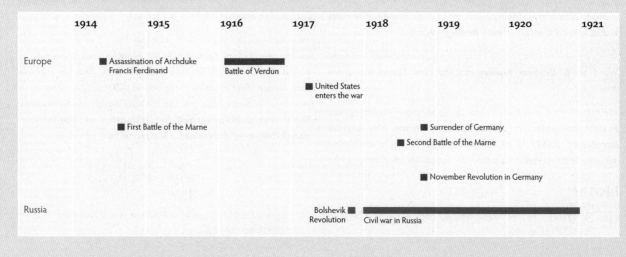

CHAPTER REVIEW

Upon Reflection

Q Which nation, if any, was most responsible for causing World War I? Why?

Q Why can 1917 be viewed as the year that witnessed the decisive turning point of World War I?

Q How did Lenin and the Bolsheviks manage to seize and hold power despite their small numbers?

Key Terms

conscription (p. 607)
militarism (p. 607)
mobilization (p. 608)
trench warfare (p. 609)
total war (p. 618)
nationalization (p. 618)
soviets (p. 621)

Bolsheviks (p. 621)
war communism (p. 623)
genocide (p. 625)
self-determination (p. 626)
War Guilt Clause (p. 628)
reparations (p. 628)
mandates (p. 630)

Suggestions for Further Reading

GENERAL WORKS ON TWENTIETH-CENTURY EUROPE A number of general works on European history in the twentieth century provide a context for understanding both World War I and the Russian Revolution. Especially valuable is **N. Ferguson, The War of the World: Twentieth-Century Conflict and the Descent of the West** (New York, 2006). See also **R. Paxton, Europe in the Twentieth Century**, 4th ed. (New York, 2004), and **H. James, Europe Reborn: A History, 1914–2000** (London, 2003).

CAUSES OF WORLD WAR I The historical literature on the causes of World War I is enormous. Good starting points are **J. Joll** and **G. Martel, The Origins of the First World War,** 3d ed. (London, 2006), and **A. Mombauer, The Origins of the First World War: Controversies and Consensus** (London, 2002).

WORLD WAR I The best brief account of World War I is **H. Strachan, The First World War** (New York, 2003). See also **S. Audoin-Rouzeau** and **A. Becker, 14–18: Understanding the**

Great War (New York, 2002). On the global nature of World War I, see **M. S. Neiberg, *Fighting the Great War: A Global History*** (Cambridge, Mass., 2005), and **W. K. Storey, *The First World War: A Concise Global History*** (New York, 2009).

WOMEN IN WORLD WAR I   On the role of women in World War I, see **S. Grayzel, *Women and the First World War*** (London, 2002).

THE RUSSIAN REVOLUTION   A good introduction to the Russian Revolution can be found in **R. A. Wade, *The Russian Revolution, 1917,*** 2d ed. (Cambridge, 2005). For a study that puts the Russian Revolution into the context of World War I, see

P. Holquist, *Making War, Forging Revolution* (Cambridge, Mass., 2002). On Lenin, see **R. Service, *Lenin: A Biography*** (Cambridge, Mass., 2000).

THE PEACE SETTLEMENT   On the Paris Peace Conference, see **M. MacMillan, *Paris 1919: Six Months That Changed the World*** (New York, 2002), and **E. Goldstein, *The First World War Peace Settlements*** (London, 2002). On the impact of Woodrow Wilson's ideas on the colonial world, see **E. Manela, *The Wilsonian Moment: Self-Determination and the International Origins of Anticolonial Nationalism*** (Oxford, 2007).

Notes

1. M. Gilbert, *The First World War: A Complete History* (New York, 1994), p. 259.
2. Quoted in ibid., p. 264.
3. A. Toynbee, *Surviving the Future* (New York, 1971), pp. 106–107.
4. Quoted in J. Remak, "1914—The Third Balkan War: Origins Reconsidered," *Journal of Modern History* 43 (1971): 364–365.
5. Quoted in J. M. Winter, *The Experience of World War I* (New York, 1989), p. 142.
6. Quoted in Hew Strachan, *The First World War* (New York, 2004), pp. 94–95.
7. Quoted in ibid., p. 72.
8. Quoted in C. W. Reilly, ed., *Scars upon My Heart: Women's Poetry and Verse of the First World War* (London, 1981), p. 90.
9. Quoted in W. M. Mandel, *Soviet Women* (Garden City, N.Y., 1975), p. 43.

MindTap   **MindTap** is a fully online, highly personalized learning experience built upon Cengage Learning content. MindTap combines student learning tools—readings, multimedia, activities, and assessments—into a singular Learning Path that guides students through the course.

CHAPTER

26

The Futile Search for Stability: Europe Between the Wars, 1919–1939

A "Hooverville" on the streets of the United States

© SuperStock, Inc./Getty Images

CHAPTER OUTLINE AND FOCUS QUESTIONS

An Uncertain Peace

Q What problems did European countries face immediately after World War I, and what impact did the Great Depression have on those problems?

The Democratic States

Q How did Great Britain, France, and the United States respond to the various crises, including the Great Depression, that they faced in the interwar years? How did World War I affect Europe's colonies in Asia and Africa?

The Authoritarian and Totalitarian States

Q Why did many European states experience a retreat from democracy in the interwar years? What are the characteristics of totalitarian states, and to what degree were these characteristics present in Fascist Italy, Nazi Germany, and Stalinist Russia?

The Expansion of Mass Culture and Mass Leisure

Q What new dimensions in mass culture and mass leisure emerged during the interwar years, and

what role did these activities play in the totalitarian states?

Cultural and Intellectual Trends in the Interwar Years

Q What were the main cultural and intellectual trends in the interwar years?

CRITICAL THINKING

Q Why have some historians called the 1920s both an age of anxiety and a period of hope?

CONNECTIONS TO TODAY

Q What lessons for dealing with the Western world's current economic crises can you learn from the responses of European states to the Great Depression?

ONLY TWENTY YEARS after the Treaty of Versailles, Europeans were again at war. Yet in the 1920s, many people assumed that the world was about to enter a new era of international peace, economic growth, and political democracy. In all of these areas, the optimistic hopes of the 1920s failed to be realized. After 1919, most people wanted peace but were unsure how to maintain it. The League of Nations, conceived as a new instrument to provide for collective security, failed to work well. New treaties that renounced the use of war looked good on paper but had no means of enforcement. Then, too, virtually everyone favored disarmament, but few could agree on how to achieve it.

Europe faced severe economic and social challenges after World War I. The European economy did not begin to recover from the war until 1922, and even then it was beset by financial problems left over from the war and, most devastating of all, the severe depression that began at the end of 1929. The Great Depression brought misery to millions of people. Begging for food on the streets became widespread, especially when soup kitchens were unable to keep up with the demand. Larger and larger numbers of people were homeless and moved from place to place looking for work and shelter. In the United States, the homeless set up shantytowns they derisively named "Hoovervilles" after the U.S. president, Herbert Hoover. Some of the destitute saw but one solution; as one unemployed person expressed it: "Today, when I am experiencing this for the first time, I think that I should prefer to do away with myself, to take gas, to jump into the river, or leap from some high place.... Would I really come to such a decision? I do not know. Animals die, plants wither, but men always go on living." Social unrest spread rapidly, and some unemployed staged hunger marches to get attention. In democratic countries, more and more people began to listen to and vote for radical voices calling for extreme measures.

According to the U.S. president Woodrow Wilson, World War I had been fought to make the world safe for democracy, and for a while after 1919, political democracy seemed well established. But hope soon faded as authoritarian regimes spread into Italy and Germany and across eastern Europe.

An Uncertain Peace

Q **Focus Question:** What problems did European countries face immediately after World War I, and what impact did the Great Depression have on those problems?

Woodrow Wilson had recognized that the peace treaties ending World War I contained unwise provisions that could serve as new causes for conflicts and had put many of his hopes for the future in the League of Nations. Although it had some success in guaranteeing protection for the rights of the many ethnic and religious minorities that remained in some of the newly formed states, the League was not particularly effective at maintaining the peace. The failure of the United States to join the League and the subsequent American determination to be less involved in European affairs undermined the League's effectiveness from the very start. Moreover, the League's sole weapon for halting aggression was economic sanctions, which often failed to work.

The French Policy of Coercion, 1919–1924

The weakness of the League of Nations and the failure of both the United States and Great Britain to honor their promises to form defensive military alliances with France left the French feeling embittered and alone. Unable to secure military support through the League of Nations, France sought security between 1919 and 1924 by relying primarily on a strict enforcement of the Treaty of Versailles. This tough policy toward Germany began with the issue of reparations, the payments that the Germans were supposed to make to compensate for the "damage done to the civilian population of the Allied and Associated Powers and to their property," as the treaty asserted. In April 1921, the Allied Reparations Commission settled on a sum of 132 billion marks ($33 billion) for German reparations, payable in annual installments of 2.5 billion (gold) marks. The new German republic made its first payment in 1921, but the following year, facing financial problems, it announced that it was unable to pay any more. Outraged by what it considered Germany's violation of the peace settlement, the French government sent troops to occupy the Ruhr Valley, Germany's chief industrial and mining center. If the Germans would not pay reparations, the French would collect reparations in kind by operating and using the Ruhr mines and factories.

Both Germany and France suffered from the French occupation of the Ruhr. The German government adopted a policy of passive resistance that was largely financed by printing more paper money, but this only intensified the inflationary pressures that had already appeared in Germany by the end of the war. The German mark soon became worthless. In 1914, one dollar was worth 4.2 marks; by the end of November 1923, the rate had reached an incredible 4.2 trillion marks to the dollar. Germany faced economic disaster. The formation of new governments in both Great Britain and France opened the door to conciliatory approaches to Germany and the reparations problem. At the same time, a new German government led by Gustav Stresemann (GOOS-tahf SHTRAY-zuh-mahn) (1878–1929) ended the policy of passive resistance and committed Germany to seek a new settlement of the reparations question.

The Hopeful Years, 1924–1929

In August 1924, an international commission produced a new plan for reparations. Named the Dawes Plan after the American banker who chaired the commission, it reduced reparations and stabilized Germany's payments on the basis of its ability to pay. The Dawes Plan also granted an initial $200 million loan for German recovery, which opened the door to heavy American investments in Europe that helped usher in a new era of European prosperity between 1924 and 1929.

With prosperity came new efforts at European diplomacy. The foreign ministers of Germany and France, Gustav Stresemann and Aristide Briand (ah-ruh-STEED bree-AHNH) (1862–1932), fostered a spirit of cooperation by concluding the Treaty of Locarno in 1925. This guaranteed Germany's new western borders with France and Belgium. Although Germany's new eastern borders with Poland were conspicuously absent from the agreement, the Locarno pact was viewed by many as the beginning of a new era of European peace. On the day after the pact was concluded, the headlines in the *New York Times* read "France and Germany Ban War Forever," and the *London Times* declared "Peace at Last."[1]

The spirit of Locarno was based on little real substance, however. Germany lacked the military power to alter its western borders even if it wanted to. And the issue of disarmament soon proved that even the spirit of Locarno could not induce nations to cut back on their weapons. The League of Nations Covenant had suggested the "reduction of national armaments to the lowest point consistent with national safety." Germany, of course, had been disarmed with the expectation that other states would do likewise. Numerous disarmament conferences, however, failed to achieve anything substantial as states proved unwilling to trust their security to anyone but their own military forces.

The Great Depression

Two factors played a major role in the coming of the Great Depression: a downturn in domestic economies and an international financial crisis precipitated by the collapse of the American stock market in 1929. In the mid-1920s, prices for agricultural goods were beginning to decline rapidly due to overproduction of basic commodities, such as wheat. During the war, farmers in Argentina, Australia, Canada, and the United States expanded food production to meet the demands of the warring European nations. Following the war, production was not curtailed, in the expectation that Europe would not recover from the devastation of its fields and the loss of farmers. By 1927, however, European production returned to prewar levels, causing a sharp decline in commodity prices. Prices fell by 30 percent between 1924 and 1929. Meanwhile, an increase in the use of oil and hydroelectricity led to a slump in the coal industry.

Furthermore, much of Europe's prosperity between 1924 and 1929 had been built on American bank loans to Germany. Already in 1928 and 1929, American investors had begun to pull money out of Germany in order to invest in the booming New York stock market. The crash of the American stock market in October 1929 led panicky American investors to withdraw even more of their funds from Germany and other European markets. The withdrawal of funds seriously weakened the banks of Germany and other central European states. The Credit-Anstalt, Vienna's most prestigious bank, collapsed on May 31, 1931. By that time, trade was slowing down, industrialists were cutting back production, and unemployment was increasing as the ripple effects of international bank failures had a devastating impact on domestic economies.

Economic depression was by no means a new phenomenon in European history. But the depth of the economic downturn after 1929 fully justifies calling it the Great Depression. During 1932, the worst year of the depression, one British worker in four was unemployed, and 6 million Germans—40 percent of the German labor force—were out of work. Between 1929 and 1932, industrial production plummeted almost 50 percent in the United States and nearly as much in Germany. The unemployed and homeless filled the streets of the cities throughout the industrialized countries (see the box on p. 637).

The economic crisis also had unexpected social repercussions. Women were often able to secure low-paying jobs as servants, housecleaners, or laundresses while many men remained unemployed, either begging on the streets or staying at home to do household tasks. Many unemployed men, resenting this reversal of traditional gender roles, were open to the shrill cries of demagogues

The Great Depression: Bread Lines in Paris. The Great Depression devastated the European economy and had serious political repercussions. Because of its more balanced economy, France did not feel the effects of the depression as quickly as other European countries. By 1931, however, even France was experiencing lines of unemployed people at free-food centers. Shown in this photograph is a soup kitchen on the Rue Réaumur that gave out free hot soup from 11 to 12 o'clock in the morning and from 6 to 7 in the evening.

with simple solutions to the economic crisis. High unemployment rates among young males often led them to join gangs that gathered in parks or other public places, arousing fear among local residents.

Governments seemed powerless to deal with the crisis. The classical liberal remedy for depression, a deflationary policy of balanced budgets, which involved cutting costs by lowering wages and raising tariffs to exclude other countries' goods from home markets, only served to worsen the economic crisis and create even greater mass discontent. This in turn led to serious political repercussions. Increased government activity in the economy was one reaction, even in countries like the United States that had a strong *laissez-faire* tradition. Another effect was a renewed interest in Marxist doctrines, since Marx had predicted that capitalism would destroy itself through overproduction. Communism took on new popularity, especially among workers and intellectuals. Finally the Great Depression increased the attractiveness of simplistic dictatorial solutions, especially from a new authoritarian movement known as **fascism**. Everywhere, democracy seemed on the defensive in the 1930s.

The Democratic States

Q FOCUS QUESTIONS: How did Great Britain, France, and the United States respond to the various crises, including the Great Depression, that they faced in the interwar years? How did World War I affect Europe's colonies in Asia and Africa?

After World War I, Great Britain went through a period of serious economic difficulties. During the war, Britain had lost many of the markets for its industrial products, especially to the United States and Japan. The postwar decline of such staple industries as coal, steel, and textiles led to a rise in unemployment, which reached the 2 million mark in 1921. Britain soon rebounded, however, and from 1925 to 1929 experienced renewed prosperity.

But Britain was not immune to the effects of the Great Depression. The Labour Party, now the largest party in Britain, failed to solve the nation's economic problems and fell from power in 1931. A National Government (a coalition of Liberals and Conservatives) claimed credit for bringing Britain out of the worst stages of the depression, primarily by using the

The Great Depression: Unemployed and Homeless in Germany

In 1932, Germany had 6 million unemployed workers, many of them wandering aimlessly through the country, begging for food and seeking shelter in city lodgings for the homeless. The Great Depression was an important factor in the rise to power of Adolf Hitler and the Nazis. This selection presents a description of the unemployed homeless in 1932.

———

Heinrich Hauser, "With Germany's Unemployed"

An almost unbroken chain of homeless men extends the whole length of the great Hamburg-Berlin highway.... All the highways in Germany over which I have traveled this year presented the same aspect....

Most of the hikers paid no attention to me. They walked separately or in small groups, with their eyes on the ground. And they had the queer, stumbling gait of barefooted people, for their shoes were slung over their shoulders.... [Most of them were] unskilled young people, for the most part, who had been unable to find a place for themselves in any city or town in Germany, and who had never had a job and never expected to have one. There was something else that had never been seen before—whole families that had piled all their goods into baby carriages and wheelbarrows that they were pushing along as they plodded forward in dumb despair. It was a whole nation on the march.

I saw them—and this was the strongest impression that the year 1932 left with me—I saw them, gathered into groups of fifty or a hundred men, attacking fields of potatoes. I saw them digging up the potatoes and throwing them into sacks while the farmer who owned the field watched them in despair and the local policeman looked on gloomily from the distance. I saw them staggering toward the lights of the city as night fell, with their sacks on their backs. What did it remind me of? Of the War, of the worst periods of starvation in 1917 and 1918, but even then people paid for the potatoes....

I know what it is to be a tramp. I know what cold and hunger are.... But there are two things that I have only recently experienced—begging and spending the night in a municipal lodging house.

Source: From *Living Age*, Vol. 344, no. 4398 (March 1933), pp. 27–31, 34–38.

I entered the huge Berlin municipal lodging house in a northern quarter of the city....

Distribution of spoons, distribution of enameled-ware bowls with the words "Property of the City of Berlin" written on their sides. Then the meal itself. A big kettle is carried. Men with yellow smocks have brought it in and men with yellow smocks ladle out the food. These men, too, are homeless and they have been expressly picked by the establishment and given free food and lodging and a little pocket money in exchange for their work about the house.

Where have I seen this kind of food distribution before? In a prison that I once helped to guard in the winter of 1919 during the German civil war. There was the same hunger then, the same trembling, anxious expectation of rations. Now the men are standing in a long row, dressed in their plain nightshirts that reach to the ground, and the noise of their shuffling feet is like the noise of big wild animals walking up and down the stone floor of their cages before feeding time. The men lean far over the kettle so that the warm steam from the food envelops them and they hold out their bowls as if begging and whisper to the attendant, "Give me a real helping. Give me a little more." A piece of bread is handed out with every bowl.

My next recollection is sitting at a table in another room on a crowded bench that is like a seat in a fourth-class railway carriage. Hundreds of hungry mouths make an enormous noise eating their food. The men sit bent over their food like animals who feel that someone is going to take it away from them. They hold their bowl with their left arm part way around it, so that nobody can take it away, and they also protect it with their other elbow and with their head and mouth, while they move the spoon as fast as they can between their mouth and the bowl.

Q Why did Hauser compare the scene he describes from 1932 with conditions in the years 1917 and 1918? How did the growing misery of many ordinary Germans promote the rise of extremist political parties like the Nazis?

traditional policies of balanced budgets and protective tariffs. British politicians largely ignored the new ideas of a Cambridge economist, John Maynard Keynes (KAYNZ) (1883–1946), who published *A General Theory of Employment, Interest and Money* in 1936. He condemned the traditional view that in a free economy, depressions should be left to work themselves out. Instead, Keynes argued that unemployment stemmed not from overproduction but from a decline in demand and that demand could be increased by public works, financed, if necessary, through deficit spending to stimulate production.

After the defeat of Germany, France had become the strongest power on the European continent. Its greatest need was to rebuild the devastated areas of northern and eastern France. But no French government seemed capable of solving France's financial problems between 1921 and 1926. Like other European countries, though, France did experience a period of relative prosperity between 1926 and 1929. By 1932, France began to feel the full effects of the Great Depression, and economic instability soon had political repercussions. During a nineteen-month period in 1932 and 1933, six different cabinets were formed as France faced political chaos. Finally, in 1936, fearful that rightists intended to seize power, a coalition of leftist parties—Socialists and Radicals—formed a Popular Front government.

Although the Popular Front succeeded in initiating a program for workers that established the right of collective bargaining, a forty-hour workweek, two-week paid vacations, and minimum wages, its policies failed to solve the problems of the depression. By 1938, the French were experiencing a serious decline of confidence in their political system that left them unprepared to deal with their aggressive Nazi enemy to the east.

After Germany, no Western nation was more affected by the Great Depression than the United States. By the end of 1932, industrial production had fallen to 50 percent of its 1929 level. Soon there were 15 million unemployed. Under these circumstances, the Democrat Franklin Delano Roosevelt (1882–1945) won the 1932 presidential election by a landslide. He and his advisers pursued a policy of active government intervention in the economy that came to be known as the New Deal. To support the nation's banks, they established the Federal Deposit Insurance Corporation, which insured the safety of bank deposits up to $5,000. A key feature of the New Deal was a stepped-up program of public works undertaken by new government agencies such as the Works Progress Administration (WPA), established in 1935; this agency put between 2 and 3 million people to work building bridges, roads, post offices, and airports. The Roosevelt administration was also responsible for social legislation that launched the American welfare state. In 1935, the Social Security Act created a system of old-age pensions and unemployment insurance.

The New Deal provided some social reform measures that perhaps averted the possibility of social revolution in the United States. It did not, however, solve the unemployment problems of the Great Depression. In May 1937, during what was considered a period of full recovery, American unemployment still stood at 7 million; by the following year, it had increased to 11 million. Only World War II and the subsequent growth of armament-related industries brought American workers back to full employment.

European States and the World: The Colonial Empires

World War I and the Great Depression also had an impact on Europe's colonial empires. Despite the war, the Allied nations had managed to keep their colonial empires intact. Great Britain and France had even added to their empires by dividing up many of Germany's colonial possessions and, as we have seen, taking control of large parts of the Middle East through a system of mandates. Although Europe had emerged from World War I relatively intact, its political and social foundations and its self-confidence had been severely undermined. In Asia and Africa, a rising tide of unrest against European political domination began to emerge and led to movements for change.

THE MIDDLE EAST For the countries of the Middle East, the period between the two world wars was a time of transition. With the fall of the Ottoman and Persian Empires, new modernizing regimes emerged in Turkey and Iran. A fiercely independent government was established in Saudi Arabia in 1932. Iraq, too, gained its independence from Britain in the same year. Elsewhere in the Middle East, European influence remained strong: the British maintained their mandates in Jordan and Palestine, the French in Syria and Lebanon.

Although Britain and France had made plans to divide up Ottoman territories in the Middle East, General Mustafa Kemal (MOOS-tah-fah kuh-MAHL) (1881–1938) led Turkish forces in creating the new republic of Turkey in 1923. Kemal wanted to modernize Turkey along Western lines. The trappings of a democratic system were put in place, although the new president did not tolerate opposition. Kemal, who adopted the name Atatürk (ah-tah-TIRK), meaning "Father Turk," made Turkey a secular republic and broke the power of the Islamic religion. New laws gave women equal rights with men in all aspects of marriage and inheritance, and in 1934, women received the right to vote. By and large, the Turkish republic was the product of Atatürk's determined efforts to use nationalism and Western ways to create a modern Turkish nation from the Ottoman remnants in Asia Minor.

INDIA By the time of World War I, the Indian people had already begun to refer to Mohandas Gandhi (moh-HAHN-dus GAHN-dee) as India's "Great Soul," or Mahatma (mah-HAHT-muh). Gandhi (1869–1948) set up a movement based on nonviolent resistance, whose aim was to force the British to improve the lot of the poor and grant independence to India. When the British tried to suppress Indian calls for independence, Gandhi called on his followers to pursue a peaceful policy of **civil disobedience** by refusing to obey British regulations. Although the British resisted Gandhi's movement, in 1935 they granted India internal self-government to be implemented through a gradual program. Legislative councils at the local level were enlarged and given responsibility for education, local affairs, and public health, and Indian participation in government slowly increased. Responsibility for law and order, land revenue, and famine relief remained under the control of the British, however. Complete independence would have to wait until after World War II.

AFRICA Black Africans who fought in World War I in the armies of the British and the French hoped for independence after the war. As one newspaper in the Gold Coast put it, if African volunteers who fought on European battlefields were "good enough to fight and die in the Empire's cause, they were good enough to have a share in the government of their countries." Many shared this feeling. The peace settlement after World War I turned out to be a great disappointment. Germany was stripped of its African colonies, but they were awarded to the British and the French to administer as mandates for the League of Nations.

After World War I, Africans became more active politically. Africans who had fought in the war had learned new ideas in the West about freedom and nationalism. Even in Africa itself, missionary schools had often taught their African pupils ideas about liberty and equality. As more Africans became aware of

the enormous gulf between Western ideals and practices, they decided to seek reform. As yet, though, independence remained only a dream.

Although the colonial powers responded to protest movements with force, they also began to make some reforms in the hope of satisfying indigenous peoples. Reforms, however, were too few and too late, and by the 1930s, an increasing number of African leaders were calling for independence. The clearest calls came from a new generation of young African leaders who had been educated in Europe and the United States.

The Authoritarian and Totalitarian States

Q FOCUS QUESTIONS: Why did many European states experience a retreat from democracy in the interwar years? What are the characteristics of totalitarian states, and to what degree were these characteristics present in Fascist Italy, Nazi Germany, and Stalinist Russia?

The apparent triumph of liberal democracy in 1919 proved extremely short-lived. By 1939, only two major states (Great Britain and France) and several minor ones (the Low Countries, the Scandinavian states, Switzerland, and Czechoslovakia) remained democratic. What had happened to Woodrow Wilson's claim that World War I had been fought to make the world safe for democracy? Actually, World War I turned out to have had the opposite effect.

The Retreat from Democracy: Did Europe Have Totalitarian States?

The postwar expansion of the electorate made mass politics a reality and seemed to enhance the spread of democracy in Europe. But the war itself had created conditions that led the new mass electorate to distrust democracy and move toward a more radicalized politics.

Many postwar societies were badly divided, especially along class lines. During the war, to maintain war production, governments had been forced to make concessions to trade unions and socialist parties, which strengthened the working class after the war. At the same time, the position of many middle-class people had declined as consumer industries had been curtailed during the war and war bonds, which had been purchased by the middle classes as their patriotic contribution to the war effort, sank in value and even became worthless in some countries.

Gender divisions also weakened social cohesion. After the war, as soldiers returned home, women were forced out of jobs they had taken during the war, jobs that many newly independent women wanted to retain. The loss of so many men during the war had also left many younger women with no marital prospects and widows with no choice but to find jobs in the labor force. At the same time, fears about a declining population because of the war led many male political leaders to encourage women to return to their traditional roles as wives and mothers. Many European countries outlawed abortions and curtailed the sale of birth control devices while providing increased welfare benefits to entice women to remain at home and bear children.

The Great Depression served to deepen social conflict. Larger and larger numbers of people felt victimized, first by the war and now by socioeconomic conditions that seemed beyond their control. Postwar politics became more and more polarized as people reverted to the wartime practice of dividing into friends and enemies, downplaying compromise and emphasizing conflict. Moderate centrist parties that supported democracy soon found themselves with fewer and fewer allies as people became increasingly radicalized politically, supporting the extremes of left-wing communism or right-wing fascism. In the 1920s, Italy had become the first fascist state, while the newborn Soviet Union moved toward a repressive communist state. In the 1930s, a host of other European nations adopted authoritarian structures of various kinds. Is it justified to call any of them **totalitarian states**?

The word *totalitarian* was first used by Benito Mussolini (buh-NEE-toh moos-suh-LEE-nee) in Italy to describe his new Fascist state: "Fascism is totalitarian," he declared. A number of historians eventually applied the term to both Nazi Germany and the Soviet Union (Fascist Italy, Nazi Germany, and the Soviet Union are discussed later in the chapter). Especially during the Cold War between the United States and the Soviet Union that followed World War II in the 1950s and 1960s, Western leaders were inclined to apply the term *totalitarian* to both the Soviet Union and the eastern European states that had been brought under Soviet control.

What did the historians who used the term think were the characteristics of a totalitarian state? Totalitarian regimes, it was argued, extended the functions and power of the central state far beyond what they had in the past. The totalitarian state expected the active loyalty and commitment of its citizens to the regime's goals and used modern mass **propaganda** techniques and high-speed modern communications to conquer the minds and hearts of its subjects. The total state aimed to control not only the economic, political, and social aspects of life but the intellectual and cultural aspects as well. The purpose of that control was the active involvement of the masses in the achievement of the regime's goal, whether it be war, a socialist state, or a thousand-year Reich (RYKH).

Moreover, the so-called totalitarian state was to be led by a single leader and a single party and would ruthlessly reject the liberal ideal of limited government power and constitutional guarantees of individual freedoms. Indeed, individual freedom was to be subordinated to the collective will of the masses, organized and determined for them by a leader. It was also believed that modern technology gave these states unprecedented ability to use police controls to enforce their wishes on their subjects.

By the 1970s and 1980s, however, revisionist historians were questioning the usefulness of the term *totalitarian* and regarded it as crude and imprecise. Certainly, some regimes, such as Fascist Italy, Nazi Germany, and the Soviet Union, sought total control, but these states exhibited significant differences, and none of them was successful in establishing total control of its society.

Fascist Italy

In the early 1920s, Benito Mussolini (buh-NEE-toh moos-suh-LEE-nee) burst onto the Italian scene with the first fascist movement in Europe. Mussolini (1883–1945) began his political career as a socialist, but in 1919, he established a new political group, the *Fascio di Combattimento* (FASH-ee-oh dee com-bat-ee-MEN-toh), or League of Combat. It received little attention in the elections of 1919, but political stalemate in Italy's parliamentary system and strong nationalist sentiment gave Mussolini and the Fascists the opportunity to rise to power.

The new parliament elected in November quickly proved incapable of governing Italy. The three major parties were unable to form an effective governmental coalition, and the Socialists, now the largest party, spoke theoretically of the need for revolution and alarmed conservatives, who quickly associated them with the Bolsheviks (Communists) in Russia. Thousands of industrial and agricultural strikes in 1919 and 1920 created a climate of class warfare and continual violence. In 1920 and 1921, bands of armed Fascists called **squadristi**

Mussolini, the Iron Duce. One of Mussolini's favorite images of himself was that of the Iron Duce—the strong leader who is always right. Consequently, he was often seen in military-style uniforms and military poses. This photograph shows Mussolini in one of his numerous uniforms with his Blackshirt bodyguards giving the Fascist salute.

(skwah-DREES-tee) were formed and turned loose to attack Socialist offices and newspapers. Strikes by trade unionists and Socialist workers and peasant leagues were broken up by force. Mussolini's Fascist movement began to gain support from middle-class industrialists fearful of working-class agitation and large landowners who objected to the agricultural strikes. Mussolini also perceived that Italians were angry over Italy's failure to receive more territorial acquisitions after World War I.

By 1922, the movement began to mushroom as Mussolini's nationalist rhetoric and the middle-class fear of socialism, Communist revolution, and disorder made the Fascists seem attractive. On October 29, 1922, after Mussolini and the Fascists threatened to march on Rome if they were not given power, King Victor Emmanuel III (1900–1946) capitulated and made Mussolini prime minister of Italy.

MUSSOLINI AND THE ITALIAN FASCIST STATE By 1926, Mussolini had established a Fascist dictatorship. Press laws gave the government the right to suspend any publications that fostered disrespect for the Catholic Church, the monarchy, or the state. The prime minister was made "head of government," with the power to legislate by decree. A police law empowered the police to arrest and confine anybody for political or nonpolitical crimes without due process of law. In 1926, all anti-Fascist parties were outlawed, and a secret police force, known as the OVRA, was established. By the end of 1926, Mussolini ruled Italy as *Il Duce* (eel DOO-chay), "the leader."

Mussolini conceived of the Fascist state as totalitarian: "Fascism is totalitarian, and the Fascist State, the synthesis and unity of all values, interprets, develops and gives strength to the whole life of the people."[2] Mussolini did try to create a police state, but police activities in Italy were never as repressive, efficient, or savage as those of Nazi Germany. Likewise, the Italian Fascists' attempt to exercise control over all forms of mass media, including newspapers, radio, and cinema, so that they could use propaganda as an instrument to integrate the masses into the state, failed to achieve its major goals. Most commonly, Fascist propaganda was disseminated through simple slogans, such as "Mussolini is always right," plastered on walls all over Italy.

Mussolini and the Fascists also attempted to mold Italians into a single-minded community by developing Fascist organizations. Because the secondary schools maintained considerable freedom from Fascist control, the regime relied more and more on the activities of youth organizations, known as the Young Fascists, to indoctrinate the young people of the nation in Fascist ideals. By 1939, nearly 7 million children and young adults of both sexes—two-thirds of the population between eight and eighteen—were enrolled in some kind of Fascist youth group. Activities for these groups included Saturday afternoon marching drills and calisthenics, seaside and mountain summer camps, and contests. Beginning in the 1930s, all male groups were given military exercises to develop discipline and provide training for war. Results were mixed. Italian teenagers, who liked neither military training nor routine discipline of any kind, simply refused to attend Fascist youth group meetings on a regular basis.

The Fascists portrayed the family as the pillar of the state and women as the basic foundation of the family. "Woman into the home" became the Fascist slogan. Women were to be homemakers and baby producers, "their natural and fundamental mission in life," according to Mussolini, who viewed population growth as an indicator of national strength. Employment outside the home distracted women from reproduction. "It forms an independence and consequent physical and moral habits contrary to child bearing."[3] A practical consideration also underlay the Fascist attitude toward women: eliminating women from the job market reduced male unemployment in the depression economy of the 1930s.

Despite the instruments of repression, the use of propaganda, and the creation of numerous Fascist organizations, Mussolini failed to attain the degree of totalitarian control achieved in Hitler's Germany or Stalin's Soviet Union. Mussolini and the Fascist Party never really destroyed the old power structure. Some institutions, including the armed forces and the monarchy, were never absorbed into the Fascist state and managed to maintain their independence. Mussolini had boasted that he would help workers and peasants, but instead he generally allied himself with the interests of industrialists and large landowners at the expense of the lower classes.

Even more indicative of Mussolini's compromise with the traditional institutions of Italy was his attempt to gain the support of the Catholic Church. In the Lateran Accords of February 1929, Mussolini's regime recognized the sovereign independence of a small enclave of 109 acres in Rome, known as Vatican City, which had remained in the church's possession since the unification of Italy in 1870; in return, the papacy

CHRONOLOGY Fascist Italy	
Creation of *Fascio di Combattimento*	1919
Squadristi violence	1920–1921
Mussolini is made prime minister	1922 (October 29)
Establishment of Fascist dictatorship	1925–1926
Lateran Accords with Catholic Church	1929

recognized the Italian state. The Lateran Accords also guaranteed the church a large grant of money and recognized Catholicism as the "sole religion of the state." In return, the Catholic Church urged Italians to support the Fascist regime.

In all areas of Italian life under Mussolini and the Fascists, there was a dichotomy between Fascist ideals and practice. The Italian Fascists promised much but actually delivered considerably less, and they were soon overshadowed by a much more powerful fascist movement to the north.

Hitler and Nazi Germany

In 1923, a small rightist party known as the Nazis, led by an obscure Austrian rabble-rouser named Adolf Hitler (1889–1945), tried to seize power in southern Germany. Although the attempt failed, Hitler and the Nazis achieved sudden national prominence. Within ten years, they had taken over complete power.

WEIMAR GERMANY After Germany's defeat in World War I, a German democratic state known as the Weimar (VY-mar) Republic had been established. Formed by a coalition of Social Democrats, the Catholic Center Party, and German Democrats, the fragmented republic had no outstanding political leader and proved to be unstable. In 1925, Paul von Hindenburg (1847–1934), a World War I military hero, was elected president. Hindenburg was a traditional military man, monarchist in sentiment, who at heart was not in favor of the republic. The young republic also suffered politically from attempted uprisings and attacks from both the left and the right.

The Weimar Republic also faced serious economic difficulties. As Germany experienced runaway inflation in 1922 and 1923, middle-class Germans and others who lived on fixed incomes watched their monthly stipends become worthless and their savings evaporate. These economic losses increasingly pushed the middle class toward rightist parties that were hostile to the republic. To make matters worse, after a short recovery between 1924 and 1929, Germany faced the Great Depression, and unemployment increased to nearly 4.4 million people by December 1930. The depression paved the way for social discontent, fear, and extremist parties. The political, economic, and social problems of the Weimar Republic provided an environment in which Hitler and the Nazis were able to seize power.

RISE OF THE NAZIS Born in 1889, Adolf Hitler was the son of an Austrian customs official. He was a total failure in secondary school and eventually made his way to Vienna to become an artist. In Vienna, Hitler established the basic ideas of an ideology from which he never deviated for the rest of his life. At the core of Hitler's ideas was racism, especially anti-Semitism. Hitler had also become an extreme German nationalist who had learned from the mass politics of Vienna how political parties could effectively use propaganda and terror. Finally, in his Viennese years, Hitler also came to a firm belief in the need for struggle, which he saw as the "granite foundation of the world."

At the end of World War I, after four years of service on the western front, Hitler went to Munich and decided to enter politics. He joined the obscure German Workers' Party, one of a number of right-wing extreme nationalist parties in Munich. By the summer of 1921, Hitler had assumed control of the party, which he renamed the National Socialist German Workers' Party (NSDAP), or Nazi Party for short. His idea was that the party's name would distinguish the Nazis from the socialist parties while gaining support from both working-class and nationalist circles. Hitler worked assiduously to develop the party into a mass political movement with flags, badges, uniforms, its own newspaper, and its own police force or party militia known as the SA, the *Sturmabteilung* (SHTOORM-ap-ty-loonk), or Storm Troops. The SA was used to defend the party in meeting halls and to break up the meetings of other parties. Hitler's own oratorical skills were largely responsible for attracting an increasing number of followers. By 1923, the party's membership had grown from its early hundreds to 55,000, with 15,000 in the SA.

Overconfident, Hitler staged an armed uprising against the government in Munich in November 1923. The so-called Beer Hall Putsch was quickly crushed, and Hitler was sentenced to prison. During his brief stay in jail, Hitler wrote *Mein Kampf* (myn KAHMPF) (*My Struggle*), an autobiographical account of his movement and its underlying ideology. Extreme German nationalism, virulent anti-Semitism, and vicious anti-communism are linked by a Social Darwinian theory of struggle that stresses the right of superior nations to **Lebensraum** (LAY-benz-rowm) (living space) through expansion and the right of "superior" individuals to secure authoritarian leadership over the masses.

THE NAZI SEIZURE OF POWER During his imprisonment, Hitler also came to the realization that the Nazis would have to acquire power by constitutional means, not by overthrowing the Weimar Republic. This implied the formation of a mass political party that would actively compete for votes with the other political parties. After his release from prison, Hitler reorganized the Nazi Party on a regional basis and expanded it to all parts of Germany. By 1929, the Nazis had a national party organization whose membership had grown from 27,000 in 1925 to 178,000 by the end of 1929. Especially noticeable was the youthfulness of the regional, district, and branch leaders of the Nazi organization. Many were under thirty and were fiercely committed to Hitler because he gave them the kind of active politics they sought. Rather than democratic debate, they wanted brawls in beer halls, enthusiastic speeches, and comradeship in the building of a new Germany. One new, young Nazi member expressed his excitement about the party:

> For me this was the start of a completely new life. There was only one thing in the world for me and that was service in the movement. All my thoughts were centered on the movement. I could talk only politics. I was no longer aware of anything else. At the time I was a promising athlete; I was very keen on sport, and it was going to be my career. But I had to give this up too. My only interest was agitation and propaganda.[4]

Such youthful enthusiasm gave the Nazi movement an aura of a "young man's movement" and a sense of dynamism that the other parties could not match.

By 1932, the Nazi Party had 800,000 members and had become the largest party in the Reichstag. No doubt Germany's economic difficulties were a crucial factor in the Nazi rise to power. Unemployment increased dramatically, from 4.4 million at the start of 1931 to 6 million by the winter of 1932. The economic and psychological impact of the Great Depression made extremist parties more attractive. The Nazis were especially effective in developing modern electioneering techniques. In their campaigns, party members pitched their themes to the needs and fears of different social groups. But even as they were making blatant appeals to class interests, the Nazis were denouncing conflicts of interest and maintaining that they stood above classes and parties. Hitler, in particular, claimed to transcend all differences and promised to create a new Germany free of class differences and party infighting. His appeal to national pride, national honor, and traditional militarism struck chords of emotion in his listeners.

Increasingly, the right-wing elites of Germany—the industrial magnates, landed aristocrats, military establishment, and higher bureaucrats—began to see Hitler as the man who had the mass support to establish an authoritarian regime that would save Germany and their privileged positions from a communist takeover. Under pressure, President Hindenburg agreed to allow Hitler to become chancellor (on January 30, 1933) and form a new government.

Within two months, Hitler had laid the foundations for the Nazis' complete control of Germany. The day after a fire broke out in the Reichstag building (February 27), supposedly set by the Communists, Hitler convinced President Hindenburg to issue a decree that gave the government emergency powers. It suspended all basic rights of citizens for the duration of the emergency, thus enabling the Nazis to arrest and imprison anyone without redress. The final step in Hitler's "legal seizure" of power came on March 23 when a two-thirds majority of the Reichstag passed the Enabling Act, which empowered the government to dispense with constitutional forms for four years while it issued laws that would deal with the country's problems. In effect, Hitler became a dictator appointed by parliament.

With their new source of power, the Nazis acted quickly to enforce *Gleichschaltung* (glykh-SHAHL-toonk), the coordination of all institutions under Nazi control. The civil service was purged of Jews and democratic elements, concentration camps were established for opponents of the new regime, the autonomy of the federal states was eliminated, trade unions were dissolved, and all political parties except the Nazis were abolished. By the end of the summer of 1933, within seven months of being appointed chancellor, Hitler and the Nazis had established the foundations for a totalitarian state. When Hindenburg died on August 2, 1934, the office of president was abolished, and Hitler became the sole ruler of Germany. Public officials and soldiers were all required to take a personal oath of loyalty to Hitler as the "Führer (FYOOR-ur) (leader) of the German Reich and people."

THE NAZI STATE, 1933–1939 Having demolished the parliamentary republic, Hitler now felt that the real task was at hand: to develop the "total state." Hitler's aims had not been simply power for power's sake; he had larger ideological goals. The development of an "Aryan" racial state that would dominate Europe and possibly the world for generations to come required a movement in which the German people would be actively involved, not passively cowed by force. Hitler stated:

> We must develop organizations in which an individual's entire life can take place. Then every activity and every need of every individual will be regulated by the collectivity represented by the party. There is no longer any arbitrary will, there are no longer any free realms in which the individual belongs to himself.... The time of personal happiness is over.[5]

The Nazis pursued the creation of this total state in a variety of ways. Mass demonstrations and spectacles were employed to integrate the German nation into a collective fellowship and to mobilize it as an instrument for Hitler's policies (see the box on p. 646). These mass demonstrations, especially the Nuremberg party rallies that were held every September, combined the symbolism of a religious service with the merriment of a popular amusement. They had great appeal and usually evoked mass enthusiasm and excitement.

Some features of Hitler's total state seem contradictory. One usually thinks of Nazi Germany as having an all-powerful government that maintained absolute control and order. In truth, Nazi Germany was the scene of almost constant personal and institutional conflict, which resulted in administrative chaos. Incessant struggle characterized relationships within the party, within the state, and between party and state. By fostering rivalry within the party and between party and state, Hitler became the ultimate decision maker.

Hitler and the Nazis also aimed to establish control in the economic sphere. Although the regime pursued the use of public works projects and "pump-priming" grants to private construction firms to foster employment and end the depression, there is little doubt that rearmament did far more to solve the unemployment problem. Unemployment dropped to 2.6 million in 1934 and less than half a million in 1937. The regime claimed full credit for solving Germany's economic woes, and the improved economy was an important factor in convincing many Germans to accept the new regime, despite its excesses.

For those who needed coercion, the Nazi total state had its instruments of terror and repression. Especially important was the *Schutzstaffel* (SHOOTS-shtah-fuhl), or SS. Originally created as Hitler's personal bodyguard, the SS, under the direction of Heinrich Himmler (1900-1945), came to control all of the regular and

The Nazi Mass Spectacle. Hitler and the Nazis made clever use of mass spectacles to rally the German people behind the Nazi regime. These mass demonstrations evoked intense enthusiasm, as is evident in this photograph of Hitler arriving at the Bückeberg near Hamelin for the Harvest Festival in 1937. Almost 1 million people were present for the celebration.

secret police forces. Himmler and the SS functioned on the basis of two principles: terror and ideology. Terror included the instruments of repression and murder: secret police, criminal police, concentration camps, and later execution squads and death camps for the extermination of the Jews. For Himmler, the primary goal of the SS was to ensure the dominance of the Aryan "master race."

Other institutions, such as the Catholic and Protestant churches, primary and secondary schools, and universities, were also brought under the control of the Nazi total state. Nazi professional organizations and leagues were formed for civil servants, teachers, women, farmers, doctors, and lawyers. Because the early indoctrination of youth would lay the foundation for a strong totalitarian state for the future, youth organizations, the *Hitler Jugend* (HIT-luh YOO-gunt) (Hitler Youth) and its female counterpart, the *Bund Deutscher Mädel* (BOONT DOIT-chuh MAY-dul) (League of German Girls), were given special attention. The oath required of Hitler Youth members demonstrates the degree of dedication expected of youth in the Nazi state: "In the presence of this blood banner, which represents our Führer, I swear to devote all my energies and my strength to the savior of our country, Adolf Hitler. I am willing and ready to give up my life for him, so help me God."

Women played a crucial role in the Aryan racial state as bearers of the children who would bring about the triumph of the Aryan race. To the Nazis, the differences between men and women were quite natural. Men were warriors and political leaders; women were destined to be wives and mothers. Motherhood was also exalted in an annual ceremony on August 12, Hitler's mother's birthday, when Hitler awarded the German Mother's Cross to a select group of German mothers. Those with four children received a bronze cross, those with six a silver cross, and those with eight or more a gold cross.

Nazi ideas determined employment opportunities for women. The Nazis hoped to drive women out of heavy industry or other jobs that might hinder them from bearing healthy children, as well as certain professions, including university teaching, law, and medicine, which were considered inappropriate for women, especially married women. The Nazis encouraged women to pursue professional occupations that had direct practical application, such as social work and nursing. In addition to using restrictive legislation against females, the Nazi regime pushed its campaign against working women with such poster slogans as "Get hold of pots and pans and broom and sooner you will find a groom!"

The Nazi total state was intended to be an Aryan racial state. From its beginning, the Nazi Party embraced Hitler's strong anti-Semitic beliefs. Once in power, the Nazis translated these ideas into anti-Semitic policies. In

Propaganda and Mass Meetings in Nazi Germany

Propaganda and mass rallies were two of the instruments that Hitler used to prepare the German people for the tasks he set before them. In the first selection, taken from a speech to a crowd at Nuremberg, Hitler describes the kind of mystical bond he hoped to create through his mass rallies. In the second excerpt, a Hamburg schoolteacher provides her impression of a Hitler rally.

Adolf Hitler, Speech at the Nuremberg Party Rally, 1936

Do we not feel once again in this hour the miracle that brought us together? Once you heard the voice of a man, and it struck deep into your hearts; it awakened you, and you followed this voice. Year after year you went after it, though him who had spoken you never even saw. You heard only a voice, and you followed it. When we meet each other here, the wonder of our coming together fills us all. Not every one of you sees me, and I do not see every one of you. But I feel you, and you feel me. It is the belief in our people that has made us small men great, that has made us poor men rich, that has made brave and courageous men out of us wavering, spiritless, timid folk; this belief made us see our road when we were astray; it joined us together into one whole! . . . You come, that . . . you may, once in a while, gain the feeling that now we are together; we are with him and he with us, and we are now Germany!

A Teacher's Impression of a Hitler Rally

The April sun shone hot like in summer and turned everything into a picture of gay expectation. There was immaculate order and discipline, although the police left the whole square to the stewards and stood on the sidelines. Nobody spoke of "Hitler," always just "the Fuhrer," "the Fuhrer says," "the Fuhrer wants," and what he said and wanted seemed right and good. The hours passed, the sun shone, expectations rose. In the background, at the edge of the track there were columns of carriers like ammunition carriers. . . . Aeroplanes above us. Testing of the loudspeakers, buzzing of the cinecameras. It was nearly 3 P.M. "The Fuhrer is coming!" A ripple went through the crowds. Around the speaker's platform one could see hands raised in the Hitler salute. A speaker opened the meeting, abused the "system," nobody listened to him. A second speaker welcomed Hitler and made way for the man who had drawn 120,000 people of all classes and ages. There stood Hitler in a simple black coat and looked over the crowd, waiting—a forest of swastika pennants swished up, the jubilation of this moment was given vent in a roaring salute. Main theme: Out of parties shall grow a nation, the German nation. He censured the "system" ("I want to know what there is left to be ruined in this state!"). "On the way here," [he said,] "Socialists confronted me with a poster, 'Turn back, Adolf Hitler.' Thirteen years ago I was a simple unknown soldier. I went my way. I never turned back. Nor shall I turn back now." Otherwise he made no personal attacks, nor any promises, vague or definite. His voice was hoarse after all his speaking during the previous days. When the speech was over, there was roaring enthusiasm and applause. Hitler saluted, gave his thanks, the Horst Wessel song sounded out across the course. Hitler was helped into his coat. Then he went.—How many look up to him with touching faith! as their helper, their savior, their deliverer from unbearable distress—to him who rescues the Prussian prince, the scholar, the clergyman, the farmer, the worker, the unemployed, who rescues them from the parties back into the nation.

Q In Hitler's view, what would mass meetings accomplish for his movement? How do mass rallies further the development of nationalism?

Source: From Adolf Hitler, Speech at the Nuremberg Party Rally, 1936. A Teacher's Impression of a Hitler Rally, 1932. From Louise Solmitz, "Diary," trans. and quoted in Jeremy Noakes and Geoffrey Pridham, *Documents on Nazism, 1919–45* (New York: Viking, 1974), p. 161. Reprinted by permission of Peters Fraser and Dunlop on behalf of Jeremy Noakes and Geoffrey Pridham.

September 1935, the Nazis announced new racial laws at the annual party rally in Nuremberg. These "Nuremberg laws" excluded German Jews from German citizenship, forbade marriages and extramarital relations between Jews and German citizens, and essentially separated Jews from the Germans politically, socially, and legally. They were a codification of Hitler's belief in the superiority of the "pure Aryan race."

Another considerably more violent phase of anti-Jewish activity took place in 1938 and 1939; it was initiated on November 9–10, 1938, the infamous *Kristallnacht* (kri-STAHL-nahkht), or Night of Shattered Glass. The assassination of a low-ranking secretary in the German embassy in Paris by a Polish Jew became the excuse for a Nazi-led destructive rampage against the Jews in Germany in which synagogues were burned, seven thousand Jewish businesses were destroyed, and at least one hundred Jews were killed. Moreover, thirty thousand Jewish males were rounded up and sent to concentration camps. Further drastic steps followed: Jews were barred from all public buildings and prohibited from owning, managing, or working in any retail store. Finally, under the direction of the SS, Jews were encouraged to "emigrate from Germany." After the outbreak of World War II, the policy of emigration was replaced by a more gruesome one.

The Soviet Union

Yet another example of totalitarianism was to be found in the Soviet Union. The civil war in Russia had taken an enormous toll of life. In addition, drought caused a great famine that claimed as many as 5 million lives between 1920 and 1922. Industrial collapse paralleled the agricultural disaster. By 1921, industrial output was only 20 percent of its 1913 level. Russia was exhausted. As Leon Trotsky said, "The collapse of the productive forces surpassed anything of the kind that history had ever seen. The country, and the government with it, were at the very edge of the abyss."[6]

LENIN'S POLICIES In March 1921, Lenin pulled Russia back from the abyss by establishing his **New Economic**

Policy (NEP), a modified version of the old capitalist system. Peasants were now allowed to sell their produce openly, and retail stores and small industries with fewer than twenty employees could now operate under private ownership; heavy industry, banking, and mines remained in the hands of the government. In 1922, Lenin and the Communists merged Russia with several smaller adjacent states to form the Union of Soviet Socialist Republics, known by its initials as the USSR and commonly called the Soviet Union. Already in that year, a revived market and a good harvest had brought the famine to an end; Soviet agricultural production climbed to 75 percent of its prewar level. Industry, especially state-owned heavy industry, fared less well and continued to stagnate. Overall, the NEP had saved the Soviet Union from complete economic disaster even though Lenin and other leading Communists intended it to be only a temporary, tactical retreat from the goals of communism.

In the meantime, Lenin and the Communists were strengthening their one-party authoritarian state. The number of bureaucrats increased dramatically and soon constituted a new elite with the best jobs, food, and dwellings. Even Lenin issued warnings about the widening power of the bureaucracy that he had helped create.

THE STRUGGLE FOR POWER Lenin's death in 1924 provoked a struggle for power among the seven members of the Politburo (POL-it-byoor-oh), the institution that had become the leading organ of the party. The Politburo was severely divided over the future direction of the Soviet Union. The Left, led by Leon Trotsky, wanted to end the NEP and launch the Soviet Union on the path of rapid industrialization. This group also believed that survival of the revolutionary vision depended on spreading communism abroad. The Right rejected the cause of world revolution and wanted instead to concentrate on constructing a socialist state at home.

These ideological divisions were underscored by an intense personal rivalry between Leon Trotsky and Joseph Stalin. In 1924, Trotsky held the post of commissar of war and was the leading spokesman for the Left in the Politburo. Joseph Stalin (1879–1953) was content to hold the dull bureaucratic job of party general secretary. But Stalin was a good organizer (his fellow Bolsheviks called him "Comrade Card-Index"), and the other members of the Politburo soon found that the position of party secretary was really the most important in the party hierarchy. Stalin used his post to gain control of the Communist Party. Trotsky was expelled

CHRONOLOGY Nazi Germany	
Hitler as Munich politician	1919–1923
Beer Hall Putsch	1923 (November)
Election of Hindenburg as president	1925
Hitler is made chancellor	1933 (January 30)
Reichstag fire	1933 (February 27)
Enabling Act	1933 (March 23)
Death of Hindenburg; Hitler as sole ruler	1934 (August 2)
Nuremberg laws	1935
Kristallnacht	1938 (November 9–10)

from the party in 1927. By 1929, Stalin had succeeded in eliminating the Old Bolsheviks of the revolutionary era from the Politburo and establishing a dictatorship so powerful that the Russian tsars of old would have been envious.

THE STALIN ERA, 1929–1939   Stalin made a significant shift in economic policy in 1928 when he launched his first five-year plan. Its real goal was nothing less than the transformation of the Soviet Union from an agricultural country into an industrial state virtually overnight. Instead of consumer goods, the first five-year plan emphasized maximum production of capital goods and armaments and succeeded in quadrupling the production of heavy machinery and doubling oil production. Between 1928 and 1937, during the first two five-year plans, steel production increased from 4 to 18 million tons per year and hard coal output went from 36 to 128 million tons.

The social and political costs of industrialization were enormous. While the industrial labor force increased by millions between 1932 and 1940, total investment in housing actually declined after 1929, with the result that millions of workers and their families lived in pitiful conditions. Real wages in industry also declined by 43 percent between 1928 and 1940, and strict laws limited workers' freedom of movement. To inspire and pacify the workers, government propaganda stressed the need for sacrifice to build the new socialist state.

Rapid industrialization was accompanied by an equally rapid collectivization of agriculture. Stalin believed that the capital needed for industrial growth could be obtained by creating agricultural surpluses through eliminating private farms and pushing people onto **collective farms** (see the box on p. 649). The elimination of private property would achieve the communist ideal.

By 1930, some 10 million peasant households had been collectivized; by 1934, the Soviet Union's 26 million family farms had been reorganized into 250,000 collective units. This was done at tremendous cost, since Stalin did not hesitate to starve the peasants, especially in Ukraine, to gain their compliance with the policy of collectivization. Stalin himself supposedly told Winston Churchill during World War II that 10 million peasants died in the artificially created famines of 1932 and 1933. The only concession Stalin made to the peasants was to allow each household to have one tiny, privately owned garden plot.

Stalin's program of rapid industrialization entailed additional costs as well. To achieve his goals, Stalin

Stalin and the First Five-Year Plan. After establishing his dictatorship, Stalin sought to achieve the rapid industrialization of the Soviet Union as well as the collectivization of agriculture with his first five-year plan. This poster, published in 1932 with a photograph of Stalin, celebrates the achievements of that plan. It reads, "At the end of the Plan, the basis of collectivization must be completed."

strengthened the party bureaucracy under his control. Those who resisted were sent to forced-labor camps in Siberia. Stalin's desire for sole control of decision making also led to purges of the Old Bolsheviks, army officers, diplomats, union officials, party members, intellectuals, and numerous ordinary citizens. One old woman was sent to Siberia for saying, "If people prayed, they would work better." Estimates are that between 1936 and 1938, 8 million Soviets were arrested; millions died in Siberian labor camps. This gave Stalin the distinction of being one of the greatest mass murderers in human history.

Disturbed by a rapidly declining birthrate, Stalin also reversed much of the permissive social legislation of the early 1920s. Advocating complete equality of rights for women, the Communists had made divorce

The Formation of Collective Farms

Accompanying the rapid industrialization of the Soviet Union was the collectivization of agriculture, a feat that involved nothing less than transforming Russia's 26 million family farms into 250,000 collective farms called *kolkhozes* (kuhl-KAHZ-zuhz). This selection provides a firsthand account of how the process worked.

Max Belov, *The History of a Collective Farm*

General collectivization in our village was brought about in the following manner: Two representatives of the [Communist] Party arrived in the village. All the inhabitants were summoned by the ringing of the church bell to a meeting at which the policy of general collectivization was announced.... The upshot was that although the meeting lasted two days, from the viewpoint of the Party representatives nothing was accomplished.

After this setback the Party representatives divided the village into two sections and worked each one separately. Two more officials were sent to reinforce the first two. A meeting of our section of the village was held in a stable which had previously belonged to a kulak [wealthy farmer]. The meeting dragged on until dark. Suddenly someone threw a brick at the lamp, and in the dark the peasants began to beat the Party representatives who jumped out the window and escaped from the village barely alive. The following day seven people were arrested. The militia was called in and stayed in the village until the peasants, realizing their helplessness, calmed down....

By the end of 1930 there were two kolkhozes in our village. Though at first these collectives embraced at most only 70 percent of the peasant households, in the months that followed they gradually absorbed more and more of them.

In these kolkhozes the great bulk of the land was held and worked communally, but each peasant household owned a house of some sort, a small plot of ground and perhaps some livestock. All the members of the kolkhoz were required to work on the kolkhoz a certain number of days each month; the rest of the time they were allowed to work on their own holdings.

They derived their income partly from what they grew on their garden strips and partly from their work in the kolkhoz.

When the harvest was over, and after the farm had met its obligations to the state and to various special funds (for instance, seed, etc.) and had sold on the market whatever undesignated produce was left, the remaining produce and the farm's monetary income were divided among the kolkhoz members according to the number of "labor days" each one had contributed to the farm's work.... It was in 1930 that the kolkhoz members first received their portions out of the "communal kettle." After they had received their earnings, at the rate of 1 kilogram of grain and 55 kopecks per labor day, one of them remarked, "You will live, but you will be very, very thin."

In the spring of 1931 a tractor worked the fields of the kolkhoz for the first time. The tractor was "capable of plowing every kind of hard soil and virgin soil," as Party representatives told us at the meeting in celebration of its arrival. The peasants did not then know that these "steel horses" would carry away a good part of the harvest in return for their work....

By late 1932 more than 80 percent of the peasant households ... had been collectivized.... That year the peasants harvested a good crop and had hopes that the calculations would work out to their advantage and would help strengthen them economically. These hopes were in vain. The kolkhoz workers received only 200 grams of flour per labor day for the first half of the year; the remaining grain, including the seed fund, was taken by the government. The peasants were told that industrialization of the country, then in full swing, demanded grain and sacrifices from them.

Q What was the purpose of collectivizing Soviet agriculture? According to Belov, why did the peasants of his village assault the Communist Party representatives? What was the result of their protest?

Source: From Fedor Belov, *The History of a Soviet Collective Farm*. Copyright © 1955 by Frederick A. Praeger, Inc. Reproduced with permission of ABC-CLIO, LLC.

and abortion easy to obtain while also encouraging women to work outside the home and liberate themselves sexually. After Stalin came to power, the family was praised as a miniature collective in which parents were responsible for inculcating values of duty, discipline, and hard work. Abortion was outlawed, and divorced fathers who did not support their children were fined heavily. The regime now praised motherhood and urged women to have large families as a patriotic duty. But by this time, many Soviet women worked in factories and spent many additional hours waiting in line to purchase increasingly scarce consumer goods. Despite the change in policy, no dramatic increase in the birthrate occurred.

The Stalinist era did witness some positive changes in the everyday lives of Soviet citizens. To create leaders for the new Communist society, Stalin began a program to enable workers, peasants, and young Communists to receive higher education, especially in engineering. There was also tremendous growth in part-time schools where large numbers of adults took courses to become literate so that they could advance to technical school or college. Increasing numbers of people saw education as the key to better jobs and upward mobility in Soviet society. One woman of peasant background recounted, "In Moscow I had a burning desire to study. Where or what wasn't important; I wanted to study." For what purpose? "We had a saying at work: 'Without that piece of paper [the diploma] you are an insect; with it, a human being.'

My lack of higher education prevented me from getting decent wages."[7]

Authoritarian States

A number of other states in Europe were not totalitarian but did have conservative authoritarian governments. These states adopted some of the trappings of totalitarian states, especially wide police powers, but their greatest concern was not the creation of a mass movement aimed at the establishment of a new kind of society but rather the defense of the existing social order. Consequently, the **authoritarian states** tended to limit the participation of the masses and were content with passive obedience rather than insisting on active involvement in the goals of the regime.

EASTERN EUROPE Nowhere had the map of Europe been more drastically altered by World War I than in eastern Europe. The new states of Austria, Poland, Czechoslovakia, and Yugoslavia adopted parliamentary systems, and the pre-existing kingdoms of Romania and Bulgaria gained new parliamentary constitutions in 1920. Greece became a republic in 1924. Hungary's government was parliamentary in form but was controlled by its landed aristocrats. At the beginning of the 1920s, political democracy seemed well established, but almost everywhere in eastern Europe, parliamentary governments soon gave way to authoritarian regimes.

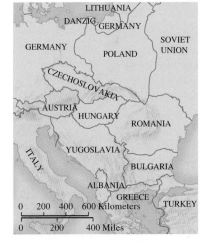

Eastern Europe in the 1920s

Several problems helped create this situation. Eastern European states had little tradition of liberalism or parliamentary politics and no substantial middle class to support them. Then, too, these states were largely rural and agrarian. Much of the land was still dominated by large landowners who feared the growth of agrarian peasant parties with their schemes for land redistribution. Ethnic conflicts also threatened to tear these countries apart. Fearful of land reform, communist agrarian upheaval, and ethnic conflict, powerful landowners, the churches, and even some members of the small middle class looked to authoritarian governments to maintain the old system. In eastern Europe, only Czechoslovakia, with its substantial middle class, liberal tradition, and strong industrial base, maintained its political democracy.

CHRONOLOGY The Soviet Union	
New Economic Policy begins in Russia	1921
Formation of the Soviet Union	1922
Death of Lenin	1924
Trotsky's expulsion from the Communist Party	1927
First five-year plan	1928–1932
Start of Stalin's dictatorship	1929
Second five-year plan	1933–1937
Stalin's purges	1936–1938

FRANCO'S SPAIN Elsewhere on the continent, the failure of political democracy was particularly dramatic in Spain. Led by General Francisco Franco (1892–1975), Spanish military forces revolted against the democratic government in 1936 and inaugurated a brutal and bloody civil war that lasted three years. The war split the country between left and right. On the left were the Republicans who supported the Popular Front government. They were concentrated in urban areas such as Madrid and Barcelona and favored modernization, workers' rights, a civilian army, and secularization. On the right were the Nationalists who supported Franco's military coup, the monarchy, the military, an agrarian economy, and the Catholic Church.

Foreign intervention complicated the Spanish Civil War. Arms, money, and men from the fascist regimes of Italy and Germany aided Franco's forces, while the government was assisted by 40,000 foreign volunteers and trucks, planes, tanks, and military advisers from the Soviet Union. After Franco's forces captured Madrid on March 28, 1939, the Spanish Civil War finally came to an end. The war had been a brutal one. Probably 400,000 people died, only one-fourth of them on the battlefield. Civilians died from air raids, disease, and bloody reprisals by both sides against their enemies and their supporters. Franco soon established a dictatorship that favored large landowners, businessmen, and the Catholic clergy—yet another traditional, conservative, authoritarian regime.

The Expansion of Mass Culture and Mass Leisure

Q FOCUS QUESTION: What new dimensions in mass culture and mass leisure emerged during the interwar years, and what role did these activities play in the totalitarian states?

The decade of the 1920s came to be known as the Roaring Twenties for the exuberance of its popular culture. Berlin, the capital of Germany, became the entertainment center of Europe, with its theaters, cabarets, cinemas, and jazz clubs. The Roaring Twenties were especially known for dance crazes. People danced in clubs and dance halls, at home, and in the streets, doing the Charleston, the Bunny Hug, and a variety of other dances. Josephine Baker (1906–1975), an American singer and dancer, became especially well known in Europe, appearing at European clubs featuring American "Negro" jazz music. One critic said, "She dances for hours without the slightest trace of tiredness." She became a wonderful symbol of the popular "flapper," the unconventional and lively young woman of the 1920s.

So popular was jazz, a musical form that had originated with African American musicians in the United States, that the 1920s were also known as the Jazz Age. Admired for its improvised qualities and forceful rhythms, jazz spread throughout the Western world as King Oliver, Bix Beider-becke (BIKS BY-der-bek), Jelly Roll Morton, and others wrote and played some of the greatest jazz music of the time.

Radio and Movies

A series of technological inventions in the late nineteenth century had prepared the way for a revolution in mass communications. Especially important was Guglielmo Marconi's discovery of "wireless" radio waves. But it was not until June 16, 1920, that a radio broadcast (of a concert by soprano Nellie Melba from London) for a mass audience was attempted. Permanent broadcasting facilities were then constructed in the United States, Europe, and Japan during 1921 and 1922, and mass production of radios (receiving sets) also began. In 1926, when the British Broadcasting Corporation (BBC) was made into a public corporation, there were 2.2 million radios in Great Britain. By the end of the 1930s, there were 9 million.

The technical foundation for motion pictures had already been developed in the 1890s when short movies were produced as novelties for music halls. Shortly before World War I, full-length features, such as the Italian film Quo Vadis and the American film Birth of a Nation, were released, and it quickly became apparent that cinema was a new form of entertainment for the masses.

Mass forms of communication and entertainment were not new, but the increased size of audiences and the ability of radio and cinema, unlike the printed word, to provide an immediate shared experience added new dimensions to mass culture. Favorite film actors and actresses became stars whose lives then became subject to public adoration and scrutiny. Sensuous actresses such as Marlene Dietrich, whose appearance in the early sound film The Blue Angel catapulted her to fame, popularized new images of women's sexuality.

Of course, radio and movies could also be used for political purposes. Film, for example, had propaganda potential, a possibility not lost on Joseph Goebbels (GUR-bulz) (1897–1945), the propaganda minister of Nazi Germany. Believing that film constituted one of the "most modern and scientific means of influencing the masses," Goebbels created a special film section in his Propaganda Ministry and encouraged the production of both documentaries and popular feature films that carried the Nazi message. *Triumph of the Will*, for example, was a documentary of the 1934 Nuremberg party rally that forcefully conveyed the power of Nazism to viewers (see the Film & History feature on p. 653).

Mass Leisure

Mass leisure activities had developed at the turn of the century, but new work patterns after World War I dramatically expanded the amount of free time available to take advantage of them. By 1920, the eight-hour day had become the norm for many office and factory workers in northern and western Europe.

Professional sporting events for mass audiences became an especially important aspect of mass leisure. Attendance at association football (soccer) games soared, and the inauguration of the World Cup contest in 1930 intensified the nationalistic rivalries that came to surround mass sporting events. Increased attendance also made the 1920s and 1930s a great era of stadium building. The Germans built a stadium in Berlin for the 1936 Olympics that held 140,000 people.

Travel opportunities also added new dimensions to mass leisure activities. The military use of aircraft during World War I helped improve planes and make civilian air travel a reality. The first regular international airmail service began in 1919, and regular passenger service soon followed. Although air travel remained the preserve of the wealthy or the adventurous, trains, buses, and private cars made excursions to beaches or holiday resorts more popular and more affordable.

Mass leisure provided the fascist and Nazi regimes with new ways to control their populations. The Nazi regime instituted a program known as *Kraft durch Freude* (KRAHFT doorkh FROI-duh) (Strength Through Joy) to coordinate the free time of the working class by offering a variety of activities, including concerts, operas, films, guided tours, and sporting events.

Especially popular were inexpensive vacations, much like modern package tours, such as cruises to Scandinavia or the Mediterranean or, more likely for workers, shorter trips to various sites in Germany. Essentially, *Kraft durch Freude* enabled the German government to supervise recreational activities. In doing so, the state imposed new rules and regulations on previously spontaneous activities, thus breaking down old group solidarities and allowing these groups to be guided by the goals of the state.

Cultural and Intellectual Trends in the Interwar Years

Q **Focus Question:** What were the main cultural and intellectual trends in the interwar years?

The artistic and intellectual innovations of the pre–World War I period, which had shocked many Europeans, had been the preserve primarily of a small group of avant-garde artists and intellectuals. In the 1920s and 1930s, these trends became more widespread as artists and intellectuals continued to work out the implications of the ideas developed before 1914. But what made the prewar avant-garde culture acceptable in the 1920s and the 1930s? Perhaps the most important factor was the impact of World War I.

Four years of devastating war left many Europeans with a profound sense of despair and disillusionment. To many people, the experiences of World War I seemed to confirm the prewar avant-garde belief that human beings were really violent and irrational animals who were incapable of creating a sane and rational world. The Great Depression of the late 1920s and early 1930s, as well as the growth of fascist movements based on violence and the degradation of individual rights, only added to the uncertainties generated by World War I.

Political and economic uncertainties were paralleled by social insecurities. The war had served to break down many traditional middle-class attitudes, especially toward sexuality. In the 1920s, women's physical appearance changed dramatically. Short skirts, short hair, the use of cosmetics once thought suitable only for prostitutes, and the new practice of suntanning gave women a new image. This change in physical appearance, which stressed more exposure of a woman's body, was also accompanied by frank discussions

FILM & HISTORY

Triumph of the Will (1934)

PROBABLY THE BEST-KNOWN films of Nazi Germany today are the documentaries, in particular those of Leni Riefenstahl (LAY-nee REE-fun-shtahl), an actress who turned to directing in 1932. Adolf Hitler liked her work and invited her to make a film about the 1934 Nuremberg party rally. In filming this party day of unity—as it was called—Hitler was trying to demonstrate, in the wake of a purge of the SA on June 30, that the Nazi Party was strongly united behind its leader. Hitler provided the film's title, *Triumph des Willens* (*Triumph of the Will*).

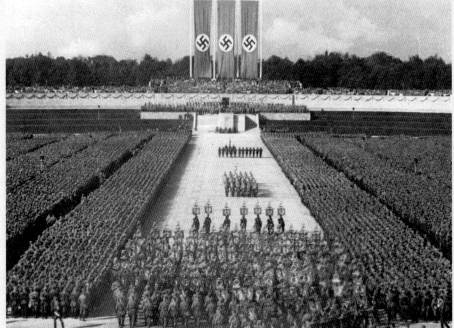

A scene from *Triumph of the Will* showing one of the many mass rallies at Nuremberg.

NSDAP/The Kobal Collection at Art Resource, NY

Much of the film's success was due to careful preparation. A crew of 172 people assisted Riefenstahl. Good camera work was coordinated with the physical arrangements for the rally to produce a spectacle that was manipulated for cinematic purposes from beginning to end. As one critic remarked, "The Rally was planned not only as a spectacular mass meeting, but as a spectacular propaganda film." To add to the dramatic effect, Riefenstahl used a number of techniques, including moving cameras (one was even mounted on Hitler's Mercedes), telephoto lenses for unusual perspectives, aerial photographs, and music carefully synchronized with each scene. The result is an effective piece of propaganda aimed at conveying to viewers the power of National Socialism.

The movie begins with introductory titles that are almost religious in character:

> *Twenty years after the outbreak of the World War,*
> *Sixteen years after the beginning of Germany's suffering,*
> *Nineteen months after the beginning of the rebirth of Germany,*
> *Adolf Hitler flew to Nuremberg to review his faithful followers.*

The rest of the film is devoted to scenes from the six days of the party rally: the dramatic opening when Hitler is greeted with thunderous applause; the major speeches of party leaders; an outdoor rally of Labor Service men who perform pseudo-military drills with their shovels; a Hitler Youth rally in which Hitler tells thousands of German boys, "in you Germany will live"; military exercises; and massive ceremonies with thousands of parading SA and SS men. The film ends with Hitler's closing speech in which he reviews the struggle of the Nazi Party to take control of Germany. The screen fades to black as the crowd sings "Das Horst Wessel Lied," a famous Nazi anthem.

Throughout the film, Hitler is depicted in messianic ways, including a descent from the clouds at the beginning, motorcades with him standing like a god in an open car as thousands of people cheer, and appearances at the rally where he commands the complete adulation of the masses assembled before him. In his speeches, Hitler emphasized the power of the new German state: "It is our will that

(continued)

this state shall endure for a thousand years." He also stressed the need for unity: "We want to be one people, one nation, and with one leader." As Rudolf Hess, Hitler's deputy, summed up at the end of the film: "The Party is Hitler. Hitler is Germany just as Germany is Hitler."

Considerable controversy has surrounded the film. Riefenstahl was accused by many of using art to promote a murderous and morally corrupt regime. In Germany, under postwar denazification laws, the film can be shown only for educational purposes. Riefenstahl always maintained, against all the evidence, that it was "a pure historical film." To a viewer today, however, the film is obviously a propaganda piece. The speeches seem tedious and the ideas simplistic, but to watch thousands of people responding the way they did is a terrible reminder of how effectively Hitler used mass spectacles to get the German people to support the goals of his new authoritarian state.

---

of sexual matters. In 1926, the Dutch physician Theodor van de Velde (TAY-oh-dor vahn duh VELL-duh) published *Ideal Marriage: Its Physiology and Technique*, which described female and male anatomy, discussed birth control techniques, and glorified sexual pleasure in marriage. Translated into a number of languages, it became an international bestseller. New ideas on sexuality and birth control were also spread to the working classes by family planning clinics, such as those of Margaret Sanger in the United States and Marie Stopes in Britain.

Nightmares and New Visions: Art and Music

Uncertainty also pervaded the cultural and intellectual achievements of the interwar years. Postwar artistic trends were largely a working out of the implications of prewar developments. Abstract painting, for example, became ever more popular as many pioneering artists of the early twentieth century matured between the two world wars. In addition, prewar fascination with the absurd and the unconscious contents of the mind seemed even more appropriate after the nightmarish landscapes of World War I battlefronts. This gave rise to both the Dada (DAH-duh) movement and Surrealism, although it was German Expressionist artists who best captured directly the disturbingly destructive effects of World War I.

GERMAN EXPRESSIONISTS   Although Expressionism as a movement began before World War I, the war itself had a devastating impact on a group of German Expressionist artists who focused on the suffering and shattered lives caused by the war. George Grosz (GROHS) (1893–1958), one of these artists, expressed his anger in this way: "Of course, there was a kind of mass enthusiasm at the start.... And then after a few years when everything bogged down, when we were defeated, when everything went to pieces, all that remained, at least of me and most of my friends, were disgust and horror."[8] Another German artist who gave visual expression to the horrors of World War I was Otto Dix (1891–1959), who had also served in the war and was well versed in its effects. In *The War*, he gave a graphic presentation of the devastating effects of the Great War.

DADAISM   **Dadaism** attempted to enshrine the purposelessness of life. Tristan Tzara (TRISS-tun TSAHR-rah) (1896–1945), a Romanian-French poet and one of the founders of Dadaism, expressed the Dadaist contempt for the Western tradition in a lecture in 1922: "The acts of life have no beginning or end. Everything happens in a completely idiotic way.... Like everything in life, Dada is useless."[9] Revolted by the insanity of life, the Dadaists tried to give it expression by creating anti-art. In the hands of Hannah Höch (HEKH) (1889–1978), however, Dada became an instrument to comment on women's roles in the new mass culture.

SURREALISM   Perhaps more important as an artistic movement was **Surrealism**, which sought a reality beyond the material, sensible world and found it in the unconscious through the portrayal of fantasies,

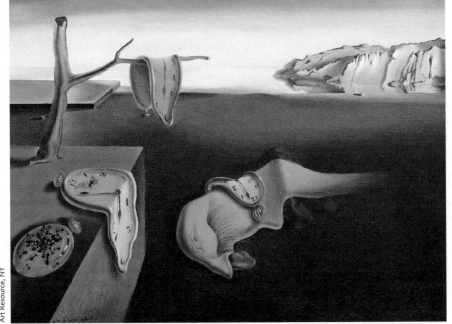

Salvador Dalí, *The Persistence of Memory*. Surrealism was another important artistic movement between the wars. Influenced by the theories of Freudian psychology, Surrealists sought to reveal the world of the unconscious, or the "greater reality" that they believed existed beyond the world of physical appearances. As is evident in this 1931 painting, Salvador Dalí sought to portray the world of dreams by painting recognizable objects in unrecognizable relationships.

dreams, or nightmares. Employing logic to portray the illogical, the Surrealists created disturbing and evocative images. The Spaniard Salvador Dalí (dah-LEE *or* DAH-lee) (1904–1989) became the high priest of Surrealism and in his mature phase became a master of representational Surrealism. In *The Persistence of Memory*, Dalí pictured recognizable objects divorced from their normal context. By placing these objects into unrecognizable relationships, Dalí created a disturbing world in which the irrational had become tangible, forcing viewers to question the rational.

FUNCTIONALISM IN ARCHITECTURE The move to **functionalism** in modern architecture also became more widespread in the 1920s and 1930s. First conceived near the end of the nineteenth century, functionalism meant that buildings, like the products of machines, should be "functional" or useful, fulfilling the purpose for which they were constructed. Art and engineering were to be unified, and all unnecessary ornamentation was to be stripped away. Functionalism was based on the architects' belief that art had a social function and could help create a new civilization.

Especially important in the spread of functionalism was the Bauhaus (BOW-howss) School of art,

Walter Gropius, The Bauhaus. Walter Gropius was one of Europe's pioneers in modern architecture. When the Bauhaus moved to Dessau in 1925, Gropius designed a building for its activities. His straightforward use of steel, reinforced concrete, and rows of windows reflects the move to functionalism in modern architecture.

architecture, and design, founded in 1919 at Weimar, Germany, by the Berlin architect Walter Gropius

(VAHL-tuh GROH-pee-uss) (1883–1969). The Bauhaus teaching staff included architects, artists, and designers who worked together to combine the study of fine arts (painting and sculpture) with the applied arts (printing, weaving, and furniture making).

ART IN NAZI GERMANY The postwar acceptance of modern art forms was by no means universal. Many traditionalists denounced what they considered degeneracy and decadence in the arts. This was especially evident in Nazi Germany. In the 1920s, Weimar Germany was one of the chief European centers for modern arts and sciences. Hitler and the Nazis rejected modern art as "degenerate" or "Jewish" art. In 1937, Hitler said, "The people regarded this art as the outcome of an impudent and unashamed arrogance or of a simply shocking lack of skill; ... these achievements which might have been produced by untalented children of from eight to ten years old could never be valued as an expression of our own times or of the German future."[10] He preferred artworks that "draw the true picture of life" and that were "clear and simple in style and manner." No longer was art an expression of individual freedom but a form of propaganda. Consequently, German artists now mostly created landscape and still life paintings, portraits, and allegorical statues with themes that included animals and nature, motherhood, sports, peasant life, military life, and battle scenes.

A NEW STYLE IN MUSIC At the beginning of the twentieth century, a revolution in music parallel to the revolution in art had begun with the work of Igor Stravinsky (see Chapter 24). But Stravinsky still wrote music in a definite key. The Viennese composer Arnold Schönberg (AR-nawlt SHURN-bayrk) (1874–1951) began to experiment with a radically new style by creating musical pieces devoid of tonality, a system that he called atonal music.

The Search for the Unconscious in Literature

The interest in the unconscious, heightened by the impact of World War I and evident in Surrealism, was also apparent in the development of new literary techniques that emerged in the 1920s. One of its most visible manifestations was the "stream of consciousness" technique in which the writer presented an interior

monologue or a report of the innermost thoughts of each character. The most famous example of this genre was written by the Irish exile James Joyce (1882–1941). His *Ulysses*, published in 1922, told the story of one day in the life of ordinary people in Dublin by following the flow of their inner thoughts.

The German writer Hermann Hesse (HESS-uh) (1877–1962) dealt with the unconscious in a different fashion. His novels reflected the influence of new psychological theories and Eastern religions and focused on, among other things, the spiritual loneliness of modern human beings in a mechanized urban society. Both *Demian* and *Steppenwolf* mirrored the psychological confusion of modern existence. Hesse's novels made a large impact on German youth in the 1920s (see the box on p. 657). He won the Nobel Prize for literature in 1946.

The Unconscious in Psychology

The growing concern with the unconscious also led to greater popular interest in psychology. The full impact of Sigmund Freud's thought was not felt until after World War I. The 1920s witnessed a worldwide acceptance of his ideas. Freudian terms such as *unconscious, repression, id,* and *ego* entered the common vocabulary. Popularization of Freud's ideas led to the widespread misconception that an uninhibited sex life was necessary for mental health. Despite such misconception, psychoanalysis did develop into a major profession, especially in the United States. But Freud's ideas did not go unchallenged, even by his own pupils. One of the most prominent challenges came from Carl Jung (YOONG).

A disciple of Freud, Carl Jung (1875–1961) came to believe that Freud's theories were too narrow and reflected Freud's own personal biases. Jung's study of dreams—his own and those of others—led him to diverge sharply from Freud. Whereas for Freud the unconscious was the seat of repressed desires or appetites, for Jung it was an opening to deep spiritual needs and ever-greater vistas for humans.

Jung viewed the unconscious as twofold: a "personal unconscious" and a deeper "collective unconscious." The collective unconscious was the repository of memories that all human beings share and consisted of archetypes, mental forms or images that appear in dreams. The archetypes are common to all people and have a special energy that creates myths, religions, and

Hesse and the Unconscious

The novels of Hermann Hesse made a strong impact on young people, first in Germany in the 1920s and then in the United States in the 1960s after they had been translated into English. Many of these young people shared Hesse's fascination with the unconscious and his dislike of modern industrial civilization. This excerpt from *Demian* spoke directly to many of them.

Hermann Hesse, *Demian*

The following spring I was to leave the preparatory school and enter a university. I was still undecided, however, as to where and what I was to study. I had grown a thin mustache, I was a full-grown man, and yet I was completely helpless and without a goal in life. Only one thing was certain: the voice within me, the dream image. I felt the duty to follow this voice blindly wherever it might lead me. But it was difficult and each day I rebelled against it anew. Perhaps I was mad, as I thought at moments; perhaps I was not like other men? But I was able to do the same things the others did; with a little effort and industry I could read Plato,

Source: From *Demian* by Hermann Hesse (New York: Bantam Books, 1966), p. 30.

was able to solve problems in trigonometry or follow a chemical analysis. There was only one thing I could not do: wrest the dark secret goal from myself and keep it before me as others did who knew exactly what they wanted to be—professors, lawyers, doctors, artists, however long this would take them and whatever difficulties and advantages this decision would bear in its wake. This I could not do. Perhaps I would become something similar, but how was I to know? Perhaps I would have to continue my search for years on end and would not become anything, and would not reach a goal. Perhaps I would reach this goal but it would turn out to be an evil, dangerous, horrible one?

I wanted only to try to live in accord with the promptings which came from my true self. Why was that so very difficult?

Q How does Hesse's interest in the unconscious appear in this excerpt? Why was a dislike of mechanized society particularly intense after World War I?

---

philosophies. To Jung, the archetypes proved that mind was only in part personal or individual because their origin was buried so far in the past that they seemed to have no human source. Their function was to bring the original mind of humans into a new, higher state of consciousness.

The "Heroic Age of Physics"

The prewar revolution in physics initiated by Max Planck and Albert Einstein continued in the interwar period. In fact, Ernest Rutherford (1871–1937), one of the physicists responsible for demonstrating that the atom could be split, dubbed the 1920s the "heroic age of physics."

The new picture of the universe that was unfolding continued to undermine the old scientific certainties

of classical physics. Classical physics had rested on the fundamental belief that all phenomena could be predicted if they could be completely understood; thus, the weather could be accurately predicted if we knew everything about the wind, sun, and water. In 1927, the German physicist Werner Heisenberg (VAYR-nur HY-zun-bayrk) (1901–1976) upset this belief when he posited the **uncertainty principle**. In essence, Heisenberg suggested that no one could determine the path of an electron because the very act of observing the electron by illuminating it with light affected the electron's location. The uncertainty principle was more than an explanation for the path of an electron, however; it was a new worldview. Heisenberg shattered confidence in predictability and dared to propose that uncertainty was at the root of all the physical laws.

Chapter Summary

The devastation wrought by World War I destroyed the liberal optimism of the prewar era. Yet many in the 1920s still hoped that the progress of Western civilization, so seemingly evident before 1914, could somehow be restored. These hopes proved largely unfounded. France, feeling vulnerable to another invasion, sought to weaken Germany by occupying the Ruhr when Germany failed to pay reparations, but it gained little. European recovery, largely the result of American loans and investments, ended with the Great Depression at the end of the 1920s.

The democratic states—Great Britain, France, the Scandinavian countries, and the United States—spent much of the 1930s trying to recover from the Great Depression. New authoritarian governments that required the active commitment and loyalty of their citizens came to power in Italy, Germany, and the Soviet Union. Italian Fascism resulted from Italy's losses in World War I, economic problems, and incompetent politicians. Mussolini organized the Fascist movement in 1919 and, after threatening to march on Rome, was chosen as prime minister in 1922. Rival parties were outlawed, and Mussolini used repression and propaganda to create a fascist state. Mussolini failed, however, to attain the degree of totalitarian control achieved in Hitler's Germany. Heading the Nazi Party, Adolf Hitler became chancellor in 1933 and within six months had seized dictatorial control. Hitler rearmed Germany, abolished all other political parties and the labor unions, and created a police state under the direction of the SS. Nazi Germany excluded Jews from citizenship and, beginning in 1938 with *Kristallnacht*, often persecuted and encouraged them to leave Germany.

After assuming leadership of the Soviet Union, Joseph Stalin followed his own path to establish total control. Five-year plans were instituted to turn the Soviet Union into an industrial society, while opponents were sent to Siberia, sentenced to labor camps, or liquidated. With the exception of Czechoslovakia, authoritarian governments appeared in eastern Europe as well as in Spain. In the Spanish Civil War, the fascist states aided Francisco Franco, and the Soviet Union backed the Popular Front.

The new authoritarian governments not only restricted individual freedoms and the rule of law but, especially in Germany and the Soviet Union, sought even greater control over the lives of their subjects in order to manipulate and guide them to achieve the goals of their regimes. For many people, despite the loss of personal freedom, these mass movements offered some sense of security in a world that seemed fraught with uncertainty, an uncertainty that was also evident in popular culture, the arts, literature, and even physics. But the seeming security of these mass movements gave rise to even great uncertainty as Europeans, after a brief twenty-year interlude of peace, again plunged into war.

CHAPTER TIMELINE

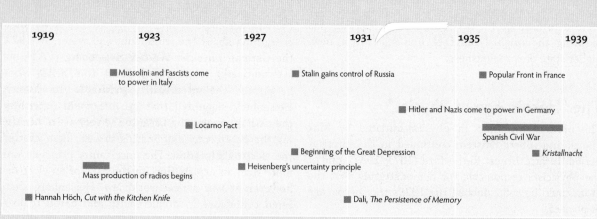

1919	1923	1927	1931	1935	1939

■ Mussolini and Fascists come to power in Italy

■ Stalin gains control of Russia

■ Popular Front in France

■ Hitler and Nazis come to power in Germany

■ Locarno Pact

Spanish Civil War

■ Beginning of the Great Depression

■ *Kristallnacht*

■ Heisenberg's uncertainty principle

Mass production of radios begins

■ Hannah Höch, *Cut with the Kitchen Knife*

■ Dali, *The Persistence of Memory*

CHAPTER REVIEW

Upon Reflection

Q What were the causes of the Great Depression, and how did European states respond to it?

Q What were Hitler's ideas, and how did he implement them once he and the Nazis had established the Nazi state in Germany?

Q How do the cultural and intellectual trends of the 1920s and 1930s reflect a crisis of confidence in Western civilization?

Key Terms

fascism (p. 636)
civil disobedience (p. 639)
totalitarian state (p. 640)
propaganda (p. 640)
squadristi (p. 640)
Lebensraum (p. 643)
New Economic Policy (p. 647)

collective farms (p. 648)
authoritarian states (p. 650)
Dadaism (p. 654)
Surrealism (p. 654)
functionalism (p. 655)
uncertainty principle (p. 657)

Suggestions for Further Reading

GENERAL WORKS   For a general introduction to the interwar period, see **M. Kitchen, *Europe Between the Wars: A Political History,*** 2d ed. (London, 2006). On the Great Depression, see **C. P. Kindleberger, *The World in Depression, 1929–39,*** rev. ed. (Berkeley, Calif., 1986).

THE DEMOCRATIC STATES   On Great Britain, see **R. Overy, *The Twilight Years: The Paradox of Britain Between the War*** (New York, 2009). France is covered in **A. P. Adamthwaite, *Grandeur and Misery: France's Bid for Power in Europe, 1914–1940*** (London, 1995).

FASCISM AND FASCIST ITALY   For general studies of fascist movements, see **R. O. Paxton, *The Anatomy of Fascism*** (New York, 2004). The best biography of Mussolini is **R. J. B. Bosworth, *Mussolini*** (London, 2002). On Fascist Italy, see **R. J. B. Bosworth, *Mussolini's Italy: Life Under the Fascist Dictatorship*** (New York, 2006).

NAZI GERMANY   A brief but sound survey of Nazi Germany is **J. J. Spielvogel** and **D. Redles, *Hitler and Nazi Germany: A History,*** 7th ed. (Upper Saddle River, N.J., 2014). A more detailed examination can be found in the three-volume history of Nazi Germany by **R. J. Evans, *The Coming of the Third Reich*** (New York, 2004), ***The Third Reich in Power: 1933–1939*** (New York, 2005), and ***The Third Reich at War*** (New York, 2009). The best biography of Hitler is **I. Kershaw, *Hitler, 1889–1936: Hubris*** (New York, 1999), and ***Hitler: Nemesis*** (New York, 2000).

AUTHORITARIAN STATES   Starting points for the study of eastern Europe are **J. Rothschild, *East Central Europe Between the Two World Wars,*** rev. ed. (New York, 1993), and **J. R. Lampe, *Balkans into Southeastern Europe: A Century of War and Transition*** (London, 2006).

THE STALINIST ERA   On Stalin, see **R. Service, *Stalin: A Biography*** (Cambridge, Mass., 2006). On everyday life in the Stalinist era, see **S. Fitzpatrick, *Everyday Stalinism*** (Oxford, 1999).

SOCIETY AND CULTURE   The use of cinema for propaganda purposes is well examined in **D. Welch, *Propaganda and the German Cinema*** (New York, 1985). Gender issues are discussed in **S. Pedersen, *Family, Dependence, and the Origins of the Welfare State: Britain and France, 1914–1945*** (New York, 1994). On the cultural and intellectual environment of Weimar Germany, see **R. Metzger** and **C. Brandstetter, *Berlin: The Twenties*** (New York, 2007).

Notes

1. R. O. Paxton, *Europe in the Twentieth Century*, 2d ed. (San Diego, Calif., 1985), p. 237.
2. B. Mussolini, "The Doctrine of Fascism," in *Italian Fascisms from Pareto to Gentile*, ed. A. Lyttleton (London, 1973), p. 42.
3. Quoted in A. De Grand, "Women Under Italian Fascism," *Historical Journal* 19 (1976): 958–959.
4. Quoted in J. Noakes and G. Pridham, eds., *Nazism, 1919–1945* (Exeter, England, 1983), vol. 1, pp. 50–51.
5. Quoted in J. Fest, *Hitler*, trans. R. Winston and C. Winston (New York, 1974), p. 418.
6. I. Howe, ed., *The Basic Writings of Trotsky* (London, 1963), p. 162.
7. Quoted in S. Fitzpatrick, *Everyday Stalinism—Ordinary Life in Extraordinary Times: Soviet Russia in the 1930s* (New York, 1999), p. 87.
8. Quoted in M. Eberle, *World War I and the Weimar Artists: Dix, Grosz, Beckmann, Schlemmer* (New Haven, Conn., 1985), p. 54.
9. T. Tzara, "Lecture on Dada," in *The Dada Painters and Poets*, ed. R. Motherwell (New York, 1951), p. 52.
10. N. H. Baynes, ed., *The Speeches of Adolf Hitler, 1922–1939* (Oxford, 1942), vol. 1, p. 591.

MindTap is a fully online, highly personalized learning experience built upon Cengage Learning content. MindTap combines student learning tools—readings, multimedia, activities, and assessments—into a singular Learning Path that guides students through the course.

CHAPTER
27

The Deepening of the European Crisis: World War II

Adolf Hitler salutes soldiers marching in Nuremberg during the party rally in 1938.

Hugo Jaeger/Time Life Pictures/Getty Images

CHAPTER OUTLINE AND FOCUS QUESTIONS

Prelude to War

Q What were Hitler's foreign policy goals, and what steps did he take to achieve them between 1933 and 1939? How did Japan's policies lead to war in Asia?

The Course of World War II

Q What were the major events of World War II in Europe and in Asia, and why were the Allies ultimately victorious?

The New Order

Q How was the Nazi empire organized? What was the Holocaust, and what was the relationship between Hitler's worldview, his foreign policy, and the Holocaust?

The Home Front

Q What were conditions like on the home front for the Soviet Union, the United States, Germany, and Japan in World War II?

Aftermath of the War

Q What were the costs of World War II? How did the Allies' visions of postwar Europe differ, and how did these differences contribute to the emergence of the Cold War?

CRITICAL THINKING

Q What was the relationship between World War I and World War II, and how did the ways in which the wars were fought differ?

CONNECTIONS TO TODAY

Q In what ways are the results of World War II still having an impact today?

ON FEBRUARY 3, 1933, only four days after he had been appointed chancellor of Germany, Adolf Hitler met secretly with Germany's leading generals. He revealed to them his desire to remove the "cancer of democracy," create a new authoritarian leadership, and forge a new domestic unity. All Germans would need to realize that "only a struggle can save us and that everything else must be subordinated to this idea." Youth especially must be trained and their will strengthened "to fight with all means." Since Germany's living space was too small for its people, Hitler said, Germany must rearm and prepare for "the conquest of new living space in the east and its ruthless Germanization." Even before he had consolidated his power, Hitler had a clear vision of his goals, and their implementation meant another European war. World War II was clearly Hitler's war. Although other countries may have helped make the war possible by not resisting Hitler's Germany earlier, Nazi Germany's actions made World War II inevitable.

World War II was more than just Hitler's war, however. This chapter will focus on the European theater of war, but both European and American armies were involved in fighting around the world. World War II consisted of two conflicts, one provoked by the ambitions of Germany in Europe, the other by the ambitions of Japan in Asia. By 1941, with the involvement of the United States in both wars, the two had merged into one global conflict.

Although World War I has been described as a total war, World War II was even more so and was fought on a scale unknown in history. Almost everyone in the warring countries was involved in one way or another: as soldiers; as workers in wartime industries; as ordinary citizens subject to invading armies, military occupation, or bombing raids; as refugees; or as victims of mass extermination. The world had never witnessed such widespread willful death and destruction.

Prelude to War

Q FOCUS QUESTIONS: What were Hitler's foreign policy goals, and what steps did he take to achieve them between 1933 and 1939? How did Japan's policies lead to war in Asia?

Only twenty years after the "war to end war," the world plunged back into the nightmare of total war. The efforts at collective security in the 1920s—the League of Nations, the attempts at disarmament, the pacts and treaties—all proved meaningless in light of the growth of Nazi Germany and its deliberate scrapping of the postwar settlement in the 1930s.

The "Diplomatic Revolution," 1933–1937

World War II in Europe began in the mind of Adolf Hitler, who believed that only the "Aryans" were capable of building a great civilization. But to Hitler, the Germans, in his view the leading group of Aryans, were threatened from the east by a large mass of inferior peoples, the Slavs, who had learned to use German weapons and technology. Germany needed more land to support a larger population and be a great power. Already in the 1920s, in the second volume of *Mein Kampf*, Hitler had indicated where a National Socialist regime would find this land: "And so we National Socialists ... take up where we broke off six hundred years ago. We stop the endless German movement to the south and west, and turn our gaze toward the land in the east.... If we speak of soil in Europe today, we can primarily have in mind only Russia and her vassal border states."[1] Once it had been conquered, the land of Russia could be resettled by German peasants, and the Slavic population could be used as slave labor to build the Aryan racial state that would dominate Europe for the next thousand years. Hitler's conclusion was clear: Germany must prepare for its inevitable war with the Soviet Union.

When Hitler became chancellor of Germany on January 30, 1933, Germany's situation in Europe seemed weak. The Treaty of Versailles had created a demilitarized zone on Germany's western border that would allow the French to move into the heavily industrialized parts of Germany in the event of war. To Germany's east, the smaller states, such as Poland and Czechoslovakia, had defensive treaties with France. The Versailles treaty had also limited Germany's army to 100,000 troops with no air force and minimal naval forces.

Posing as a man of peace in his public speeches, Hitler emphasized that Germany wished only to revise the unfair provisions of Versailles by peaceful means and achieve Germany's rightful place among the European states. On March 9, 1935, Hitler announced the creation of a new air force and one week later the introduction of a military draft that would expand Germany's army from 100,000 to 550,000 troops. This unilateral repudiation of the Versailles treaty brought a swift reaction as France, Great Britain, and Italy condemned Germany's action and warned against future aggressive steps. But nothing concrete was done.

On March 7, 1936, buoyed by his conviction that the Western democracies had no intention of using force to maintain the Treaty of Versailles, Hitler sent German troops into the demilitarized Rhineland. According to the Versailles treaty, the French had the right to use force against any violation of the demilitarized Rhineland. But France would not act without British support, and the British viewed the occupation of German territory by German troops as a reasonable action by a dissatisfied power. The *London Times* noted that the Germans were only "going into their own back garden."

Meanwhile, Hitler gained new allies. In October 1935, Benito Mussolini had committed Fascist Italy to imperial expansion by invading Ethiopia. Angered by French and British opposition to his invasion, Mussolini welcomed Hitler's support and began to draw closer to the German dictator he had once called a buffoon. In October 1936, Mussolini and Hitler concluded an agreement that recognized their common political and economic interests, and one month later, Mussolini referred publicly to the new Rome-Berlin Axis. Also in November, Germany and Japan (the rising military power in the East) concluded the Anti-Comintern Pact and agreed to maintain a common front against communism. By the beginning of 1937, Hitler and Nazi Germany had achieved a "diplomatic revolution" in Europe. The Treaty of Versailles had been virtually scrapped, and Germany was once more a "world power," as Hitler proclaimed.

The Path to War in Europe, 1938–1939

By the beginning of 1938, Hitler was convinced that neither the French nor the British would provide much opposition to his plans and decided to move on Austria. By threatening Austria with invasion, Hitler coerced the Austrian chancellor, Kurt von Schuschnigg (SHOOSH-nik) (1897–1977), into putting an Austrian Nazi in charge of the government. When German troops marched unopposed into Austria on March 12, they did so on the "legal basis" of the new Austrian chancellor's request for German troops to assist in establishing law and order. One day later, on March 13, after his triumphal return to his native land, Hitler formally annexed Austria to Germany. Great Britain's ready acknowledgment of Hitler's proclamation only increased the German dictator's contempt for Western weakness.

CZECHOSLOVAKIA The annexation of Austria improved Germany's strategic position in central Europe and put Germany in position for Hitler's next objective—the destruction of Czechoslovakia (see Map 27.1). This goal might have seemed unrealistic, since democratic Czechoslovakia was quite prepared to defend itself and was well supported by pacts with France and the Soviet Union. Nevertheless, Hitler believed that France and Britain would not use force to defend Czechoslovakia.

Hitler Arrives in Vienna. By threatening to invade Austria, Hitler forced the Austrian government to capitulate to his wishes. Austria was annexed to Germany. Shown here is the triumphal arrival of Hitler in Vienna on March 13, 1938. Sitting in the car beside Hitler is Arthur Seyss-Inquart, Hitler's new handpicked governor of Austria.

bpk, Berlin/Art Resource, NY

Germany

German advances:

Reoccupied Rhineland, March 1936

Annexed Austria, March 1938

Annexed Sudetenland, October 1938

Occupied Bohemia and Moravia, March 1939

Annexed Memel, March 1939

Italy

Annexed Albania, April 1939

Poland and Hungary Annexed Czech territory, 1938 and 1939

( ) Former independent nations: Albania, Austria, and Czechoslovakia

MAP 27.1 Changes in Central Europe, 1936–1939. Hitler's main objectives in the late 1930s were the reoccupation of the Rhineland, incorporation into a greater Germany of lands that contained German people (Austria and the Sudetenland), and the acquisition of *Lebensraum* (living space) in eastern Europe for the expansion of the German people.

Q What aspects of Czechoslovakia's location would have made it difficult for France and Britain to come directly to its aid in 1938?

He was right again. When on September 15, 1938, Hitler demanded the cession to Germany of the Sudetenland (soo-DAY-tun-land), the mountainous northwestern border area of Czechoslovakia that was home to 3.5 million ethnic Germans, and expressed his willingness to risk "world war" to achieve his objective, the British,

OPPOSING VIEWPOINTS

The Munich Conference: Two Views

At the Munich Conference, the leaders of France and Great Britain capitulated to Hitler's demands on Czechoslovakia. Although the British prime minister, Neville Chamberlain, defended his actions at Munich as necessary for peace, another British statesman, Winston Churchill, characterized the settlement at Munich as "a disaster of the first magnitude."

Winston Churchill, Speech to the House of Commons, October 5, 1938

I will begin by saying what everybody would like to ignore or forget but which must nevertheless be stated, namely, that we have sustained a total and unmitigated defeat, and that France has suffered even more than we have.... The utmost my right honorable friend the Prime Minister ... has been able to gain for Czechoslovakia and in the matters which were in dispute has been that the German dictator, instead of snatching his victuals from the table, has been content to have them served to him course by course.... And I will say this, that I believe the Czechs, left to themselves and told they were going to get no help from the Western Powers, would have been able to make better terms than they have got....

We are in the presence of a disaster of the first magnitude which has befallen Great Britain and France. Do not let us blind ourselves to that....

And do not suppose that this is the end. This is only the beginning of the reckoning. This is only the first sip, the first foretaste of a bitter cup which will be proffered to us year by year unless by a supreme recovery of moral health and martial vigor, we arise again and take our stand for freedom as in the olden time.

Neville Chamberlain, Speech to the House of Commons, October 6, 1938

That is my answer to those who say that we should have told Germany weeks ago that, if her army crossed the border of Czechoslovakia, we should be at war with her. We had no treaty obligations and no legal obligations to Czechoslovakia.... When we were convinced, as we became convinced, that nothing any longer would keep the Sudetenland within the Czechoslovakian State, we urged the Czech Government as strongly as we could to agree to the cession of territory, and to agree promptly.... It was a hard decision for anyone who loved his country to take, but to accuse us of having by that advice betrayed the Czechoslovakian State is simply preposterous. What we did was to save her from annihilation and give her a chance of new life as a new State, which involves the loss of territory and fortifications, but may perhaps enable her to enjoy in the future and develop a national existence under a neutrality and security comparable to that which we see in Switzerland today. Therefore, I think the Government deserve the approval of this House for their conduct of affairs in this recent crisis which has saved Czechoslovakia from destruction and Europe from Armageddon.

Q What were the opposing views of Churchill and Chamberlain on the Munich Conference? Why did they disagree so much? With whom do you agree? Why?

Sources: Winston Churchill, Speech to the House of Commons, October 5, 1938. From *Parliamentary Debates, House of Commons* (London: His Majesty's Stationery Office, 1938), vol. 339, pp. 361–369. Neville Chamberlain, Speech to the House of Commons, October 6, 1938. From Neville Chamberlain, *In Search of Peace* (New York: Putnam, 1939), pp. 213–215, 217.

French, Germans, and Italians—at a hastily arranged conference at Munich—reached an agreement that essentially met all of Hitler's demands. German troops were allowed to occupy the Sudetenland as the Czechs, abandoned by their Western allies, stood by helplessly. The Munich Conference was the high point of Western **appeasement** of Hitler. When Neville Chamberlain (1869–1940), the British prime minister, returned to England from Munich, he boasted that the Munich agreement meant "peace in our time." Hitler had promised Chamberlain that he had made his last demand. Like many German politicians, Chamberlain had believed Hitler's assurances (see the box above).

In fact, Munich confirmed Hitler's perception that the Western democracies were weak and would not fight. Increasingly, Hitler was convinced of his own infallibility, and he had by no means been satisfied at Munich. In March 1939, Hitler occupied the Czech lands (Bohemia and Moravia), while the Slovaks, with Hitler's encouragement, declared their independence of the Czechs and became a puppet state (Slovakia) of Nazi Germany. On the evening of March 15, 1939, Hitler triumphantly declared in Prague that he would be known as the greatest German of them all.

POLAND At long last, the Western states reacted to Hitler's threat. Hitler's naked aggression made clear that his promises were utterly worthless. When Hitler began to demand the return to Germany of Danzig (which had been made a free city by the Treaty of Versailles to serve as a seaport for Poland), Britain recognized the danger and offered to protect Poland in the event of war. At the same time, both France and Britain realized that only the Soviet Union was powerful enough to help contain Nazi aggression and began political and military negotiations with Joseph Stalin and the Soviets. The West's distrust of Soviet communism, however, made an alliance unlikely.

Meanwhile, Hitler pressed on in the belief that the West would not really fight over Poland. To preclude an alliance between the West and the Soviet Union, which would create the danger of a two-front war, Hitler, ever the opportunist, negotiated his own nonaggression pact with Stalin and shocked the world with its announcement on August 23, 1939. A secret protocol to the treaty created German and Soviet spheres of influence in eastern Europe: Finland, the Baltic states of Estonia and Latvia, and eastern Poland would go to the Soviet Union, while Germany would acquire western Poland. The treaty with the Soviet Union gave Hitler the freedom to attack Poland. He told his generals, "Now Poland is in the position in which I wanted her.... I am only afraid that at the last moment some swine or other will yet submit to me a plan for mediation."[2] He need not have worried. On September 1, German forces invaded Poland; two days later, Britain and France declared war on Germany. Two weeks later, on September 17, Germany's newfound ally, the Soviet Union, sent its troops into eastern Poland. Europe was again at war.

The Path to War in Asia

The war in Asia arose from the ambitions of Japan, whose rise to the status of world power had been swift.

Economic crises in the 1930s had stifled the growth of democracy and allowed right-wing militant elements connected with the government and the armed forces to control Japanese politics and push a program of expansion. In September 1931, Japanese soldiers had seized Manchuria, an area of northeastern China that had natural resources Japan needed. During the next several years, Japan consolidated its hold on Manchuria, which it renamed Manchukuo (man-CHOO-kwoh), and then began to expand its control in north China. As Japan moved steadily southward, popular protests in Chinese cities against Japanese aggression intensified. In July 1937, Chinese and Japanese forces clashed at the Marco Polo Bridge, south of Beijing, and hostilities spread.

Japan had not planned to declare war on China, but neither side would compromise, and the 1937 incident eventually turned into a major conflict. The Japanese advanced up the Yangtze Valley and seized the Chinese capital of Nanjing (nan-JING), raping and killing thousands of innocent civilians in the process. But the Chinese Nationalist leader Chiang Kai-shek (CHANG ky-SHEK) (1887–1975) refused to capitulate and moved his government upriver to Hankou (HAHN-kow). Japanese strategists had hoped to force Chiang to join a Japanese-dominated new order in East Asia, comprising Japan, Manchuria, and China. This aim was part of a larger plan to seize Soviet Siberia with its rich resources and create a new power structure in Asia, in which Japan would guide its Asian neighbors on the path to development and prosperity.

During the late 1930s, Japan began to cooperate with Nazi Germany on the assumption that the two countries would ultimately launch a joint attack on the Soviet Union and divide up its resources between them. But when Germany surprised the world by signing a nonaggression pact with the Soviets in August 1939, Japanese strategists were compelled to re-evaluate their long-term objectives. Japan was not strong enough to defeat the Soviet Union alone, so the Japanese began to shift their gaze southward to the vast resources of Southeast Asia—the oil of the Dutch East Indies, the rubber and tin of Malaya, and the rice of Burma and Indochina.

A move southward, of course, would risk war with the European colonial powers, especially Britain and France, as well as with the other rising power in the Pacific, the United States. When the Japanese occupied Indochina in July 1941, the Americans responded by cutting off sales of vital scrap iron and oil to Japan. Japan's military leaders decided to preempt any further American response by attacking the American naval fleet in the Pacific.

Japan seizes Manchuria	September 1931
Hitler becomes chancellor	January 30, 1933
Hitler announces military conscription	March 16, 1935
Mussolini invades Ethiopia	October 1935
Hitler occupies the demilitarized Rhineland	March 7, 1936
Rome-Berlin Axis	October 1936
Anti-Comintern Pact (Japan and Germany)	November 1936
Japan invades China	1937
Germany annexes Austria	March 13, 1938
Munich Conference: Germany occupies the Sudetenland	September 29, 1938
Germany occupies the rest of Czechoslovakia	March 1939
German-Soviet Nonaggression Pact	August 23, 1939
Germany invades Poland	September 1, 1939
Britain and France declare war on Germany	September 3, 1939

The Course of World War II

Q FOCUS QUESTION: What were the major events of World War II in Europe and in Asia, and why were the Allies ultimately victorious?

Unleashing an early form of **Blitzkrieg** (BLITZ-kreeg), or "lightning war," Hitler stunned Europe with the speed and efficiency of the German attack. Moving into Poland with about 1.5 million troops on two fronts, German forces used armored columns or panzer divisions (a **panzer division** was a strike force of about three hundred tanks and accompanying forces and supplies) supported by airplanes to break quickly through Polish lines and encircle the outnumbered and poorly equipped Polish armies. The coordinated air and ground assaults included the use of Stuka dive bombers; as they descended from the skies, their sirens emitted a blood-curdling shriek, adding a frighteningly destructive element to the German attack. Regular infantry units, still on foot with their supplies drawn by horses, then marched in to hold the newly conquered territory. Soon after, Soviet military forces attacked eastern Poland. Within four weeks, Poland had surrendered. On September 28, 1939, Germany and the Soviet Union officially divided Poland between them.

Victory and Stalemate

Although Hitler's hopes to avoid a war in the west were dashed when France and Britain declared war on September 3, he was confident that he could control the situation. After a winter of waiting (called the "phony war"), Hitler resumed the fight on April 9, 1940, with another Blitzkrieg, this time against Denmark and Norway. One month later, on May 10, the Germans launched their attack on the Netherlands, Belgium, and France. The main assault through Luxembourg and the Ardennes forest was completely unexpected by the French and British forces. German panzer divisions broke through the weak French defensive positions there and raced across northern France, splitting the Allied armies and trapping French troops and the entire British army on the beaches of Dunkirk. Only by heroic efforts did the British succeed in evacuating 330,000 Allied (mostly British) troops. The French surrendered on June 22. German armies occupied about three-fifths of France while the French hero of World War I, Marshal Henri Petain (AHN-ree pay-TANH) (1856–1951), established an authoritarian regime—known as Vichy (VISH-ee) France—over the remainder. Germany was now in control of western and central Europe, but Britain had still not been defeated.

THE PROBLEM OF BRITAIN As Hitler realized, an amphibious invasion of Britain would be possible only if Germany gained control of the air. At the beginning of August 1940, the German air force, or Luftwaffe (LOOFT-vahf-uh), launched a major offensive against British air and naval bases, harbors, communication centers, and war industries. Led by the stubbornly determined Winston Churchill (1874–1965), now prime minister of Britain, the British fought back doggedly, supported by an effective radar system that gave them early warning of German attacks. Nevertheless, the British air force suffered critical losses by the end of August and was probably saved by Hitler's change of strategy. In September, in retaliation for a British attack on Berlin, Hitler ordered a shift from military targets to massive bombing of British cities to break British morale. The British rebuilt their air strength quickly and were soon inflicting major losses on Luftwaffe bombers. By the end of September, Germany had lost the Battle of Britain, and the invasion of the island nation had to be postponed.

At this point, Hitler pursued the possibility of a Mediterranean strategy, which would involve capturing Egypt and the Suez Canal and closing the Mediterranean to British ships, thereby shutting off Britain's supply of oil. Hitler's commitment to the Mediterranean was never wholehearted, however. His initial plan was to let the Italians defeat the British in North Africa, but this strategy failed when the British routed the Italian army. Although Hitler then sent German troops to the North African theater of war, his primary concern lay elsewhere; he had already reached the decision to fulfill his lifelong obsession with the acquisition of living space in the east.

INVASION OF THE SOVIET UNION Although he had no desire for a two-front war, Hitler became convinced that Britain was remaining in the war only because it expected Russian support. If Russia were smashed, Britain's last hope would be eliminated. Moreover, Hitler had convinced himself that the Soviet Union, with its Jewish-Bolshevik leadership and a pitiful army, could be defeated quickly and decisively. Although he scheduled the invasion of the Soviet Union for spring 1941, problems in the Balkans delayed the attack. Hitler had already obtained the political cooperation of Hungary, Bulgaria, and Romania, but Mussolini's disastrous invasion of Greece in October 1940 exposed Hitler's southern flank to British air bases in Greece. To secure his Balkan position, German troops seized both Yugoslavia and Greece in April. Now reassured, Hitler turned to the east and invaded the Soviet Union on June 22, 1941, in the belief that the Russians could still be decisively defeated before winter arrived.

The massive attack stretched out along an 1,800-mile front (see Map 27.2). German troops advanced rapidly, capturing 2 million Soviet soldiers. By November, one German army group had swept through Ukraine while a second was besieging Leningrad; a third approached within twenty-five miles of Moscow, the Soviet capital. An early winter and unexpected Soviet resistance, however, brought the German advance to a halt. Temperatures of 30 below zero stalled armor and transport vehicles. Hitler's commanders wished to withdraw and regroup for the following spring, but Hitler refused. Fearing the disintegration of his lines, he insisted that there would be no retreat. A Soviet counterattack in December 1941 by an army supposedly exhausted

by Nazi victories came as an ominous ending to the year. Although the Germans managed to hold on and reestablish their lines, a war diary kept by a member of Panzer Group Three described their desperate situation: "Discipline is breaking down. More and more soldiers are heading west on foot without weapons. . . . The road is under constant air attack. Those killed by bombs are no longer being buried. All the hangers-on (cargo troops, Luftwaffe, supply trains) are pouring to the rear in full flight."[3] By December 1941, another of Hitler's decisions—the declaration of war on the United States—had probably made his defeat inevitable and again turned a European conflict into a global war.

German Troops in the Soviet Union. At first, the German attack on the Soviet Union—known as Operation Barbarossa—was enormously successful, leading one German general to remark in his diary: "It is probably no overstatement to say that the Russian campaign has been won in the space of two weeks." This photo shows German troops advancing by foot through a cornfield.

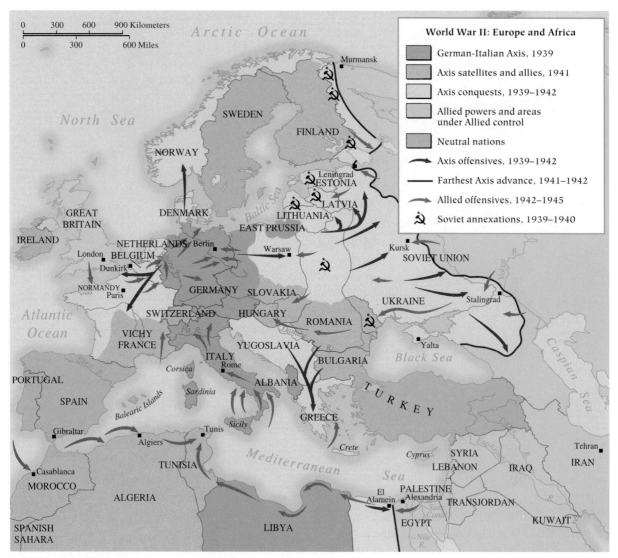

MAP 27.2 World War II in Europe and North Africa. With its fast and effective military, Germany quickly overwhelmed much of western Europe. Hitler had overestimated his country's capabilities, however, and underestimated those of his foes. By late 1942, his invasion of the Soviet Union was failing, and the United States had become a major factor in the war. The Allies successfully invaded Italy in 1943 and France in 1944.

Q Which countries were neutral, and how did geography help make their neutrality an option?

The War in Asia

On December 7, 1941, Japanese carrier-based aircraft attacked the United States naval base at Pearl Harbor in the Hawaiian Islands. The same day, other units launched additional assaults on the Philippines and began advancing toward the British colony of Malaya. Shortly thereafter, Japanese forces invaded the Dutch East Indies and occupied a number of islands in the Pacific Ocean (see Map 27.3). In some cases, as on the Bataan (buh-TAN *or* buh-THAN) peninsula and the island of Corregidor (kuh-REG-ih-dor) in the Philippines, resistance was fierce, but by the spring of 1942, almost all of Southeast Asia and much of the western Pacific had fallen into

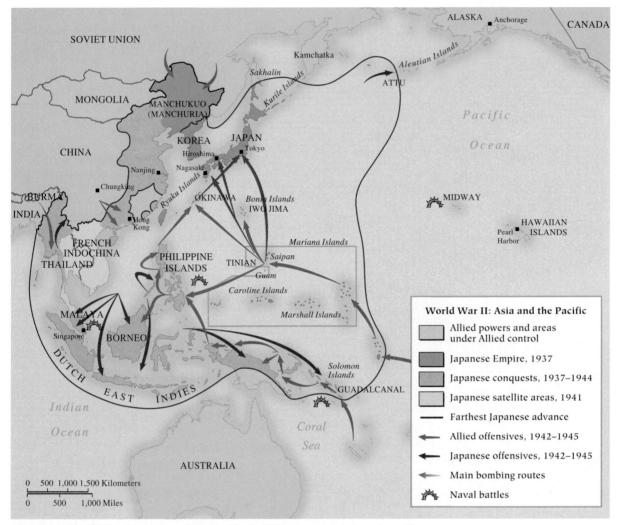

MAP 27.3 World War II in Asia and the Pacific. In 1937, Japan invaded northern China, beginning its effort to create a "Great East Asia Co-Prosperity Sphere." Further expansion caused the United States to end iron and oil sales to Japan. Deciding that war with the United States was inevitable, Japan engineered a surprise attack on Pearl Harbor.

Q Why was control of the islands in the western Pacific of great importance both to the Japanese and to the Allies?

Japanese hands. Japan then announced its intention to liberate the colonial areas of Southeast Asia from Western colonial rule and create the Great East Asia Co-Prosperity Sphere, bringing the entire region under Japanese tutelage. For the moment, however, Japan needed the resources of the region for its war machine and placed the countries under its rule on a wartime basis.

Japanese leaders had hoped that their strike at American bases would destroy the U.S. Pacific Fleet and persuade President Franklin D. Roosevelt and his administration to accept Japanese domination of the Pacific. In the eyes of Japanese leaders, material indulgence had made the American people soft. But Tokyo had miscalculated. The attack on Pearl Harbor galvanized American opinion and won broad support for Roosevelt's war policy. The United States now joined with European nations and Nationalist China in a combined effort to defeat Japan and bring to an end its hegemony in the Pacific.

The Turning Point of the War, 1942–1943

The entry of the United States into the war created a coalition (the Grand Alliance) that ultimately defeated the Axis powers (Germany, Italy, Japan). Nevertheless, the three major Allies—Britain, the United States, and the Soviet Union—had to overcome mutual suspicions before they could operate as an effective team. Two factors aided that process. First, Hitler's declaration of war on the United States made it easier for the United States to accept the British and Russian contention that the defeat of Germany should be the Americans' first priority. For that reason, the United States increased the quantity of trucks, planes, and other arms that it sent to the British and the Soviets. Also important to the alliance was the tacit agreement of the three chief Allies to stress military operations while ignoring political differences. At the beginning of 1943, the Allies agreed to fight until the Axis powers surrendered unconditionally. This principle of **unconditional surrender** had the effect of cementing the Grand Alliance by making it nearly impossible for Hitler to divide his foes.

Defeat was far from Hitler's mind at the beginning of 1942, however. As Japanese forces advanced into Southeast Asia and the Pacific, Hitler and his European allies continued the war in Europe against Britain and the Soviet Union. Until the fall of 1942, it appeared that the Germans might still prevail on the battlefield. Reinforcements in North Africa enabled the Afrika Korps under General Erwin Rommel (RAHM-ul) to break through the British defenses in Egypt and advance toward Alexandria. In the spring of 1942, a renewed German offensive in Russia led to the capture of the entire Crimea, causing Hitler to boast in August 1942:

> As the next step, we are going to advance south of the Caucasus and then help the rebels in Iran and Iraq against the English. Another thrust will be directed along the Caspian Sea toward Afghanistan and India. Then the English will run out of oil. In two years we'll be on the borders of India. Twenty to thirty elite German divisions will do. Then the British Empire will collapse.[4]

But this would be Hitler's last optimistic outburst. By the fall of 1942, the war had turned against the Germans.

In North Africa, British forces had stopped Rommel's troops at El Alamein (ell ah-lah-MAYN) in the summer of 1942 and then forced them back across the desert. In November 1942, British and American forces invaded French North Africa and forced the German and Italian troops to surrender in May 1943.

On the eastern front, the turning point of the war occurred at Stalingrad. After the capture of the Crimea, Hitler's generals wanted him to concentrate on the Caucasus and its oil fields, but Hitler decided that Stalingrad, a major industrial center on the Volga, should be taken first. The German advance on Stalingrad encountered fierce resistance, but Hitler was determined to capture the city named after the Soviet dictator. Although the Germans destroyed much of the city, the Soviet troops used the bombed-out buildings and factories as well-fortified defensive positions. A deadly and brutal street-by-street conflict evolved in which both sides took severe losses. Between November 1942 and February 1943, German troops were stopped, then encircled, and finally forced to surrender on February 2, 1943 (see the box on p. 673). The entire German Sixth Army of 300,000 men was lost. By February 1943, German forces in Russia were back to their positions of June 1942.

The tide of battle in Asia also turned dramatically in 1942. In the Battle of the Coral Sea on May 7–8, 1942, American naval forces stopped the Japanese advance and temporarily relieved Australia of the threat of invasion. On June 4, at the Battle of Midway Island, American planes destroyed all four of the attacking Japanese aircraft carriers and established American naval superiority in the Pacific. The victory came at a high cost; about two-fifths of the American planes were shot down in the encounter. By the fall of 1942, Allied forces were beginning to gather for offensive operations in three areas: from bases in north Burma and India into the rest of Burma; in the Solomon Islands and on New Guinea, with forces under the direction of American general Douglas MacArthur moving toward the Philippines; and across the Pacific, where combined U.S. Army, Marine, and Navy forces would mount attacks against Japanese-held islands. After a series of bitter engagements in the waters off the Solomon Islands from August to November 1942, Japanese fortunes began to fade.

The Last Years of the War

By the beginning of 1943, the tide of battle had turned against Germany, Italy, and Japan. After the Axis forces had surrendered in Tunisia on May 13, 1943, the Allies crossed the Mediterranean and carried the war to Italy. After taking Sicily, Allied troops began the invasion of mainland Italy in September. In the meantime, after the ouster and arrest of Benito Mussolini, a

state in northern Italy; German troops then moved in and occupied much of the peninsula. The new defensive lines established by the Germans in the hills south of Rome were so effective that the Allied advance up the Italian peninsula was a painstaking affair accompanied by heavy casualties. Rome did not fall to the Allies until June 4, 1944. By that time, the Italian war had assumed a secondary role anyway, as the Allies opened their long-awaited "second front" in western Europe two days later.

ALLIED ADVANCES IN THE WEST Since the autumn of 1943, the Allies had been planning a cross-channel invasion of France from Britain. On June 6, 1944, under the direction of the American general Dwight D. Eisenhower (1890–1969), the Allies landed five assault divisions on the beaches of Normandy in history's greatest amphibious invasion. The Germans' initially indecisive response enabled the Allied forces to establish a beachhead. Within three months, they had landed 2 million men and a half-million vehicles that pushed inland and broke through the German defensive lines.

After the breakout, Allied troops moved south and east and liberated Paris by the end of August. By March 1945, they had crossed the Rhine River and advanced farther into Germany. At the end of April, Allied forces in northern Germany moved toward the Elbe River, where they finally linked up with the Soviets.

SOVIET OFFENSIVE IN THE EAST The Soviets had come a long way since the Battle of Stalingrad in 1943. In the summer of 1943, Hitler

The Battle of Stalingrad. The Battle of Stalingrad was a major turning point on the eastern front. Shown in the first illustration is a German infantry platoon in the ruins of a tractor factory they had captured in the northern part of Stalingrad. This victory took place on October 15, 1942, at a time when Hitler still believed he was winning the battle for Stalingrad. That belief was soon dashed as a Soviet counteroffensive in November led to a total defeat for the Germans. The second illustration shows thousands of captured soldiers being marched across frozen Soviet soil to prison camps. The soldiers in white fur hats are Romanian. Fewer than 6,000 captured soldiers survived to go home; the remainder—almost 85,000 prisoners—died in captivity.

new Italian government offered to surrender to Allied forces. But the Germans liberated Mussolini in a daring raid and set him up as the head of a puppet German

gambled on taking the offensive by making use of newly developed heavy tanks. The Soviets soundly defeated the German forces at the Battle of Kursk

A German Soldier at Stalingrad

The Soviet victory at Stalingrad was a major turning point in World War II. This excerpt comes from the diary of a German soldier who fought and died in the Battle of Stalingrad. His dreams of victory and a return home with medals were soon dashed by the realities of Soviet resistance.

Diary of a German Soldier

Today, after we'd had a bath, the company commander told us that if our future operations are as successful, we'll soon reach the Volga, take Stalingrad and then the war will inevitably soon be over. Perhaps we'll be home by Christmas.

July 29. The company commander says the Russian troops are completely broken, and cannot hold out any longer. To reach the Volga and take Stalingrad is not so difficult for us. The Führer knows where the Russians' weak point is. Victory is not far away....

August 10. The Führer's orders were read out to us. He expects victory of us. We are all convinced that they can't stop us.

August 12. This morning outstanding soldiers were presented with decorations.... Will I really go back to Elsa without a decoration? I believe that for Stalingrad the Führer will decorate even me....

September 4. We are being sent northward along the front toward Stalingrad. We marched all night and by dawn had reached Voroponovo Station. We can already see the smoking town. It's a happy thought that the end of the war is getting nearer. That's what everyone is saying....

September 8. Two days of non-stop fighting. The Russians are defending themselves with insane stubbornness. Our regiment has lost many men....

September 16. Our battalion, plus tanks, is attacking the [grain storage] elevator, from which smoke is pouring—the grain in it is burning, the Russians seem to have set light to it themselves. Barbarism. The battalion is suffering heavy losses....

Source: From Vaili Chuikov, *The Battle for Stalingrad* (Grafton Books / HarperCollins), 1964.

October 10. The Russians are so close to us that our planes cannot bomb them. We are preparing for a decisive attack. The Führer has ordered the whole of Stalingrad to be taken as rapidly as possible....

October 22. Our regiment has failed to break into the factory. We have lost many men; every time you move you have to jump over bodies....

November 10. A letter from Elsa today. Everyone expects us home for Christmas. In Germany everyone believes we already hold Stalingrad. How wrong they are. If they could only see what Stalingrad has done to our army....

November 21. The Russians have gone over to the offensive along the whole front. Fierce fighting is going on. So, there it is—the Volga, victory and soon home to our families! We shall obviously be seeing them next in the other world.

November 29. We are encircled. It was announced this morning that the Führer has said: "The army can trust me to do everything necessary to ensure supplies and rapidly break the encirclement."

December 3. We are on hunger rations and waiting for the rescue that the Führer promised....

December 14. Everybody is racked with hunger. Frozen potatoes are the best meal, but to get them out of the ice-covered ground under fire from Russian bullets is not so easy....

December 26. The horses have already been eaten. I would eat a cat; they say its meat is also tasty. The soldiers look like corpses or lunatics, looking for something to put in their mouths. They no longer take cover from Russian shells; they haven't the strength to walk, run away and hide. A curse on this war!

Q What did this soldier believe about the Führer? Why? What was the source of his information? Why is the battle for Stalingrad considered a major turning point in World War II?

(KOORSK) (July 5–12), the greatest tank battle of World War II. Soviet forces now began a relentless advance westward. The Soviets had reoccupied Ukraine by the end of 1943 and lifted the siege of Leningrad and moved into the Baltic States by the beginning of 1944. Advancing along a northern front,

Crossing the Rhine. After landing at Normandy, Allied forces liberated France and prepared to move into Germany. Makeshift bridges enabled the Allies to cross the Rhine in some areas and advance deeper into Germany. Units of the U.S. Seventh Army of General Patch are shown here crossing the Rhine at Worms on a pontoon bridge constructed by battalions of engineers alongside the ruins of the old bridge.

Soviet troops occupied Warsaw in January 1945 and entered Berlin in April. Meanwhile, Soviet troops swept along a southern front through Hungary, Romania, and Bulgaria.

In January 1945, Adolf Hitler had moved into a bunker fifty-five feet under Berlin to direct the final stages of the war. In his final political testament, Hitler, consistent to the end in his rabid anti-Semitism, blamed the Jews for the war: "Above all I charge the leaders of the nation and those under them to scrupulous observance of the laws of race and to merciless opposition to the universal poisoner of all peoples, international Jewry."[5] Hitler committed suicide in his bunker on April 30, two days after Mussolini had been shot by partisan Italian forces. On May 7, German commanders surrendered. The war in Europe was over.

The war in Asia continued. Beginning in 1943, American forces had gone on the offensive and advanced their way, slowly at times, across the Pacific, taking an increasing toll of enemy resources, especially at sea and in the air. When President Harry Truman (Roosevelt had died on April 12, 1945) and his advisers became convinced that American troops might suffer heavy casualties in an invasion of the Japanese homeland, they made the decision to drop the newly developed atomic bomb on Hiroshima (hee-roh-SHEE-muh) and Nagasaki (nah-gah-SAH-kee). The resulting devastation was horrific; the Japanese surrendered unconditionally on August 14. World War II was finally over.

CHRONOLOGY The Course of World War II	
Division of Poland by Germany and the Soviet Union	September 1939
Blitzkrieg against Denmark and Norway	April 1940
Blitzkrieg against Belgium, Netherlands, and France	May 1940
Churchill as British prime minister	May 10, 1940
Surrender of France	June 22, 1940
Battle of Britain	Fall 1940
Nazi seizure of Yugoslavia and Greece	April 1941
German invasion of the Soviet Union	June 22, 1941
Japanese attack on Pearl Harbor	December 7, 1941
Battle of the Coral Sea	May 7–8, 1942
Battle of Midway Island	June 4, 1942
Allied invasion of North Africa	November 1942
German surrender at Stalingrad	February 2, 1943
Axis forces surrender in North Africa	May 1943
Battle of Kursk	July 5–12, 1943
Allied invasion of mainland Italy	September 1943
Allied invasion of France	June 6, 1944
Hitler's suicide	April 30, 1945
Surrender of Germany	May 7, 1945
Atomic bomb dropped on Hiroshima	August 6, 1945
Surrender of Japan	August 14, 1945

The New Order

Q FOCUS QUESTIONS: How was the Nazi empire organized? What was the Holocaust, and what was the relationship between Hitler's worldview, his foreign policy, and the Holocaust?

The initial victories of the Germans and the Japanese gave them the opportunity to create new orders in Europe and Asia. Although both countries presented positive images of these new orders for publicity purposes, in practice both followed policies of ruthless domination of their subject peoples.

The Nazi Empire

After the German victories in Europe between 1939 and 1941, Nazi propagandists painted glowing images of a new European order based on "equal chances" for all nations and an integrated economic community. This was not Hitler's conception of a European New Order. He saw the Europe he had conquered simply as subject to German domination. Only the Germans, he once said, "can really organize Europe."

The Nazi empire stretched across continental Europe from the English Channel in the west to the outskirts of Moscow in the east. In no way was this empire structured systematically or governed efficiently. Some areas, such as western Poland, were annexed by Nazi Germany and made into German provinces. Most of occupied Europe, however, was administered by German military or civilian officials, combined with different degrees of indirect control from collaborationist regimes.

Racial considerations played an important role in how conquered peoples were treated in the **Nazi New Order**. The Germans established civil administrations in Norway, Denmark, and the Netherlands because the Nazis considered these populations Aryan, racially akin to the Germans and hence worthy of more lenient treatment. "Inferior" Latin peoples, such as the occupied French, were given military administrations. By 1943, however, as Nazi losses continued to mount, all the occupied territories of northern and western Europe were ruthlessly exploited for material goods and manpower for Germany's war needs.

PLANS FOR AN ARYAN RACIAL EMPIRE Because the conquered lands in the east contained the living space for German expansion and were populated in Nazi eyes by racially inferior Slavic peoples, Nazi administration there was considerably more ruthless. Hitler's racial

ideology and his plans for an Aryan racial empire were so important to him that he and the Nazis began to implement their racial program soon after the conquest of Poland. Heinrich Himmler, a strong believer in Nazi racial ideology and the leader of the SS, was put in charge of German resettlement plans in the east. Himmler's task was to evacuate the inferior Slavic peoples and replace them with Germans, a policy first applied to the new German provinces created from the lands of western Poland. One million Poles were uprooted and dumped in southern Poland. Hundreds of thousands of ethnic Germans (descendants of Germans who had migrated years earlier from Germany to different parts of southern and eastern Europe) were encouraged to colonize the designated areas in Poland. By 1942, 2 million ethnic Germans had been settled in Poland.

The invasion of the Soviet Union inflated Nazi visions of German colonization in the east. Hitler spoke to his intimate circle of a colossal project of social engineering after the war, in which Poles, Ukrainians, and Russians would become slave labor while German peasants settled on the abandoned lands and Germanized them. Nazis involved in this kind of planning were well aware of the human costs. Himmler told a gathering of SS officers that although the destruction of 30 million Slavs was a prerequisite for German plans in the east, "whether nations live in prosperity or starve to death interests me only insofar as we need them as slaves for our culture. Otherwise it is of no interest."[6]

USE OF FOREIGN WORKERS Labor shortages in Germany led to a policy of ruthless mobilization of foreign labor. In 1942, a special office was created to recruit labor for German farms and industries. By the summer of 1944, 7 million foreign workers were laboring in Germany and constituted 20 percent of Germany's labor force. At the same time, another 7 million workers were supplying forced labor in their own countries on farms, in industries, and in military camps. Forced labor often proved counterproductive, however, because the brutal character of Germany's recruitment policies often caused more and more people to resist the Nazi occupation forces.

The Holocaust

There was no more terrifying aspect of the Nazi New Order than the deliberate attempt to exterminate the Jews of Europe. Racial struggle was a key element in Hitler's ideology and meant to him a clearly defined conflict of opposites: the Aryans, creators of human cultural development, against the Jews, parasites who were trying to destroy the Aryans. By the beginning of 1939, Nazi policy focused on promoting the "emigration" of German Jews from Germany. Once the war began in September 1939, however, the so-called Jewish problem took on new dimensions. For a while, there was discussion of the Madagascar plan, which aspired to the mass shipment of Jews to the African island of Madagascar. When war contingencies made this plan impractical, an even more drastic policy was conceived.

THE SS AND THE *EINSATZGRUPPEN* Heinrich Himmler and the SS organization shared Adolf Hitler's racial ideology. The SS was given responsibility for what the Nazis called their **Final Solution** to the Jewish problem—the annihilation of the Jews. Reinhard Heydrich (RYN-hart HY-drikh) (1904–1942), head of the SS's Security Service, was given administrative responsibility for the Final Solution. After the defeat of Poland, Heydrich ordered the special strike forces—**Einsatzgruppen** (YN-zahtz-groop-un)—that he had created to round up all Polish Jews and concentrate them in ghettos established in a number of Polish cities.

In June 1941, the *Einsatzgruppen* were given new responsibilities as mobile killing units. These SS death squads followed the regular army's advance into Russia. Their job was to round up Jews in their villages and execute and bury them in mass graves, often giant pits dug by the victims themselves before they were shot. Such regular killing led to morale problems among the

SS executioners. The leader of one of these death squads described the mode of operation:

> The unit selected for this task would enter a village or city and order the prominent Jewish citizens to call together all Jews for the purpose of resettlement. They were requested to hand over their valuables to the leaders of the unit, and shortly before the execution to surrender their outer clothing. The men, women, and children were led to a place of execution which in most cases was located

MAP 27.4 The Holocaust. Hitler used the fiction of the Aryan race, to which Germans supposedly belonged, to help radicalize the German people and justify his hatred of Jews. Hitler's "Final Solution" to the "Jewish problem" was the mass execution of Europe's Jews in death camps.

Q Which region lost the largest number of Jews in the camps, and what helps explain this?

next to a more deeply excavated anti-tank ditch. Then they were shot, kneeling or standing, and the corpses thrown into the ditch.[7]

THE DEATH CAMPS Although it has been estimated that the *Einsatzgruppen* killed as many as a million Jews, this approach to solving the Jewish problem was soon perceived as inadequate. Instead, the Nazis opted for the systematic annihilation of the European Jewish population in specially built death camps. The plan was simple. Jews from countries occupied by Germany or sympathetic to Germany would be rounded up, packed like cattle into freight trains, and shipped to Poland, where six extermination centers were built for this purpose (see Map 27.4). The largest and most infamous was Auschwitz-Birkenau (OWSH-vitz-BEER-kuh-now). Medical technicians chose Zyklon B (the commercial name for hydrogen cyanide) as the most effective gas for quickly killing large numbers of people in gas chambers designed to look like "shower rooms" to facilitate the cooperation of the victims. After gassing, the corpses would be burned in specially built crematoria.

By the spring of 1942, the death camps were in operation. Although initial priority was given to the elimination of the ghettos in Poland, by the summer of 1942, Jews were also being shipped from France, Belgium, and the Netherlands. Even as the Allies were making important advances in 1944, Jews were being shipped from Greece and Hungary. These shipments depended on the cooperation of Germany's Transport Ministry, and despite desperate military needs, the Final Solution had priority in using railroad cars for the transportation of Jews to death camps.

A harrowing experience awaited the Jews when they arrived at one of the six death camps. Rudolf Höss (HESS), commandant at Auschwitz-Birkenau, described it:

> We had two SS doctors on duty at Auschwitz to examine the incoming transports of prisoners. The prisoners would be marched by one of the doctors who would make spot decisions as they walked by. Those who were fit for work were sent into the camp. Others were sent immediately to the extermination plants. Children of tender years were

The Holocaust: The Extermination Camp at Auschwitz. After their initial successes in the east, Hitler and the Nazis set in motion the machinery for the physical annihilation of Europe's Jews. Shown here is a group of Jews arriving at Auschwitz. It is estimated that 1.1 million people (90 percent of them Jews) were killed there.

Heinrich Himmler: "We Had the Moral Right"

Although Nazi leaders were reluctant to talk openly about their attempted destruction of the Jews of Europe, when they did, they had no qualms about justifying it. Heinrich Himmler, the leader of the SS, assumed responsibility for executing the Holocaust and in 1943 gave a remarkable speech to the leaders of the SS in Poznan, Poland.

Heinrich Himmler, Speech to SS Leaders

I also want to talk to you, quite frankly, on a very grave matter. Among yourselves it should be mentioned quite frankly, and yet we will never speak of it publicly. I mean the clearing out of the Jews, extermination of the Jewish race. It's one of those things it is easy to talk about—"The Jewish race is being exterminated," says one party member, "that's quite clear, it's in our program—elimination of the Jews, and we're doing it, exterminating them." And then they come, 80 million worthy Germans, and each one had his decent Jew. Of course, the others are vermin, but this one is an A-1 Jew. Not one of those who talk this way has witnessed it, not one of those who talk this way has witnessed it, not one of them has been through it. Most of you must know what it means when 100 corpses are lying side by side, or 500

or 1000. To have stuck it out and at the same time . . . to have remained decent fellows, that is what has made us hard. This is a page of glory in our history which has never been written and is never to be written, . . . We have taken from them what wealth they had. I have issued a strict order, . . . that this wealth should, as a matter of course, be handed over to [Germany] without reserve. We have taken none of it for ourselves. . . . We had the moral right, we had the duty to our people, to destroy this people which wanted to destroy us. But we have not the right to enrich ourselves with so much as a fur, a watch, a mark, or a cigarette or anything else. Because we have exterminated a bacterium we do not want, in the end, to be infected by the bacterium and die of it. I will not see so much as a small area of sepsis appear here or gain a hold. Wherever it may form, we will cauterize it. But altogether we can say that we have fulfilled this most difficult duty for the love of our people. And our spirit, our soul, our character has not suffered injury from it.

Q How does Himmler justify the Holocaust? What is wrong with his argument, and how does it demonstrate the danger of ideological rigidity?

Source: *Nazi Conspiracy and Aggression* (Washington, D.C., 1946), 4: 563–564.

invariably exterminated since by reason of their youth they were unable to work. . . . At Auschwitz we endeavored to fool the victims into thinking that they were to go through a delousing process. Of course, frequently they realized our true intentions and we sometimes had riots and difficulties due to that fact.[8]

About 30 percent of the arrivals at Auschwitz were sent to a labor camp; the remainder went to the gas chambers. After they had been gassed, the bodies were burned in the crematoria. The victims' goods and even their bodies were used for economic gain. Women's hair was cut off, collected, and turned into mattresses or cloth. Some inmates were also subjected to cruel and painful "medical" experiments. The Germans killed between 5 and 6 million Jews, more than 3 million of them in the death camps. Virtually 90 percent of the Jewish populations of Poland, the Baltic countries, and Germany were exterminated. Overall, the **Holocaust**

was responsible for the death of nearly two out of every three European Jews (see the box above).

THE OTHER HOLOCAUST The Nazis were also responsible for the deliberate death by shooting, starvation, or overwork of at least another 9 to 10 million people. Because the Nazis also considered the Gypsies of Europe (like the Jews) a race containing alien blood, they were systematically rounded up for extermination. About 40 percent of Europe's 1 million Gypsies were killed in the death camps. The leading elements of the "subhuman" Slavic peoples—the clergy, intelligentsia, civil leaders, judges, and lawyers—were arrested and murdered. Probably an additional 4 million Poles, Ukrainians, and White Russians lost their lives as slave laborers for Nazi Germany, and 3 to 4 million Soviet prisoners of war were killed in captivity. The Nazis also singled out homosexuals for persecution, and thousands lost their lives in concentration camps.

The New Order in Asia

Once Japan's takeover was completed, Japanese war policy in the occupied areas in Asia became essentially defensive, as Japan hoped to use its new possessions to meet its needs for raw materials, such as tin, oil, and rubber, as well as to serve as an outlet for Japanese manufactured goods. To provide a structure for the arrangement, Japanese leaders set up the Great East Asia Co-Prosperity Sphere as a self-sufficient community designed to provide mutual benefits to the occupied areas and the home country.

The Japanese conquest of Southeast Asia had been accomplished under the slogan "Asia for the Asians." Japanese officials in occupied territories quickly promised that independent government would be established under Japanese tutelage. Such governments were eventually established in Burma, the Dutch East Indies, Vietnam, and the Philippines.

In fact, however, real power rested with Japanese military authorities in each territory, and the local Japanese military command was directly subordinated to the army general staff in Tokyo. The economic resources of the colonies were exploited for the benefit of the Japanese war machine, while local peoples were recruited to serve in local military units or were conscripted to work on public works projects. In some cases, the people living in the occupied areas were subjected to severe hardships.

Like German soldiers in occupied Europe, Japanese military forces often had little respect for the lives of their subject peoples. In their conquest of Nanjing, China, in 1937, Japanese soldiers had spent several days killing, raping, and looting. Almost 800,000 Koreans were sent overseas, most of them as forced laborers, to Japan. Tens of thousands of Korean women were forced to serve as "comfort women" (prostitutes) for Japanese troops. Both prisoners of war and local peoples were also used extensively on construction projects to help the Japanese war effort.

The Home Front

Q FOCUS QUESTION: What were conditions like on the home front for the Soviet Union, the United States, Germany, and Japan in World War II?

World War II was even more of a total war than World War I. Fighting was much more widespread and covered most of the globe. Economic mobilization was more extensive; so was the mobilization of women. The number of civilians killed was far higher: almost 20 million died as a result of bombing raids, mass extermination policies, and attacks by invading armies.

The Mobilization of Peoples

The home fronts of the major belligerents varied considerably, based on national circumstances.

THE SOVIET UNION World War II had an enormous impact on the Soviet Union. Known to the Soviets as the Great Patriotic War, the German-Soviet war witnessed the greatest land battles in history as well as incredible ruthlessness. Two out of every five persons killed in World War II were Soviet citizens.

The Soviets' initial defeats led to drastic emergency mobilization measures that affected the civilian population. Leningrad, for example, spent nine hundred days under siege; its inhabitants became so desperate for food that they ate dogs, cats, and mice. As the German army made its rapid advance into Soviet territory, the factories in the western part of the Soviet Union were dismantled and shipped to the interior—to the Urals, western Siberia, and the Volga regions. Machines were placed on the bare ground, and walls went up around them as workers began factory operations.

Stalin called this widespread military, industrial, and economic mobilization a "battle of machines," and the Soviets won, producing 78,000 tanks and 98,000 artillery pieces. Fifty-five percent of Soviet national income went for war matériel, compared to 15 percent in 1940. As a result of the emphasis on military goods, Soviet citizens experienced dire shortages of both food and housing.

Soviet women played a major role in the war effort. Women and girls worked in industries, mines, and railroads. Overall, the number of women working in industry increased almost 60 percent. Soviet women were also expected to dig antitank ditches and work as air-raid wardens. In addition, the Soviet Union was the only country in World War II to use women as combatants. Soviet women functioned as snipers and also as crews in bomber squadrons. The female pilots who helped defeat the Germans at Stalingrad were known as the "Night Witches."

THE UNITED STATES The home front in the United States was quite different from those of the other major belligerents, largely because the United States faced no threat of war on its own soil. Although the economy and labor force were slow to mobilize, eventually the United States became the arsenal of the Allied powers, producing the military equipment they needed. During the high point of war production in the United States in November 1943, the country was constructing six ships a day and $6 billion worth of war-related goods a month.

The mobilization of the American economy caused social problems, however. The construction of new factories created boomtowns where thousands came to work but then faced a shortage of houses, health facilities, and schools. The dramatic expansion of small towns into large cities often brought a breakdown in traditional social mores, especially evident in the growth of teenage prostitution. Economic mobilization also led to a widespread movement of people, which in turn created new social tensions. Sixteen million men and women were enrolled in the military, and another 16 million, mostly wives and sweethearts of the servicemen or workers looking for jobs, also relocated. More than a million African Americans migrated from the rural South to the industrial cities of the North and West, looking for jobs in industry. The presence of blacks in areas where they had not lived before led to racial tensions and sometimes even riots. In Detroit in June 1943, white mobs roamed the streets attacking blacks.

Japanese Americans were treated even more shabbily. On the West Coast, 110,000 Japanese Americans, 65 percent of whom had been born in the United States, were removed to inland camps encircled by barbed wire and required to take loyalty oaths. Although public officials claimed that this policy was necessary for security reasons, no similar treatment of German Americans or Italian Americans ever took place. The racism inherent in this treatment of Japanese Americans was evident when the governor of California, Culbert Olson, said, "You know, when I look out at a group of Americans of German or Italian descent, I can tell whether they're loyal or not. I can tell how they think and even perhaps what they are thinking. But it is impossible for me to do this with inscrutable orientals, and particularly the Japanese."[9]

GERMANY In August 1914, Germans had enthusiastically cheered their soldiers marching off to war. In September 1939, the streets were quiet. Many Germans were apathetic or, even worse for the Nazi regime, had a foreboding of disaster. Hitler was very aware of the importance of the home front. He believed that the collapse of the home front in World War I had caused Germany's defeat, and in his determination to avoid a repetition of that experience, he adopted economic policies that may have cost Germany the war.

To maintain the morale of the home front during the first two years of the war, Hitler refused to convert production from consumer goods to armaments. The Blitzkrieg allowed the Germans to win quick victories, after which they could plunder the food and raw materials of conquered countries in order to avoid diverting resources away from the civilian economy. After the German defeats on the Russian front and the American entry into the war, the economic situation changed. Early in 1942, Hitler finally ordered a massive increase in armaments production and the size of the army. Hitler's personal architect, Albert Speer (SHPAYR), was made minister for armaments and munitions in 1942. By eliminating waste and rationalizing procedures, Speer was able to triple the production of armaments between 1942 and 1943 despite the intense Allied air raids. Speer's urgent plea for a total mobilization of resources for the war effort went unheeded, however. Hitler, fearful of civilian morale problems that would undermine the home front, refused any dramatic cuts in the production of consumer goods. A total mobilization of the economy was not implemented until July 1944, when schools, theaters, and cafés were closed and Speer was finally permitted to use all remaining resources for the production of a few basic military items. But by that time, it was too late to save Germany from defeat.

The war produced a reversal in Nazi attitudes toward women. Nazi resistance to female employment declined as the war progressed and more and more men were called up for military service. Nazi magazines now proclaimed, "We see the woman as the eternal mother of our people, but also as the working and fighting comrade of the man."[10] But the number of women working in industry, agriculture, commerce, and domestic service increased only slightly. The total number of employed women in September 1944 was 14.9 million, compared to 14.6 million in May 1939. Many women, especially those of the middle class, resisted regular employment, particularly in factories.

JAPAN Wartime Japan was a highly mobilized society. To guarantee its control over all national resources, the government set up a planning board to control prices, wages, the utilization of labor, and the allocation of resources. Traditional habits of obedience and hierarchy, buttressed by the concept of imperial divinity, were emphasized to encourage citizens to sacrifice their resources, and sometimes their lives, for the national cause. Especially important was the code of *bushido* (BOO-shee-doh), or the way of the warrior, the old code of morality of the samurai, who had played a prominent military role in medieval and early modern Japanese history. The code of bushido was revived during the nationalistic fervor of the 1930s. Based on an ideal of loyalty and service, the code emphasized the obligation to honor and defend emperor, country, and family and to sacrifice one's life if one failed in this sacred mission. The system culminated in the final years of the war, when young Japanese were encouraged to volunteer en masse to serve as pilots in suicide missions—known as *kamikaze* (kah-mi-KAH-zee) ("divine wind")—against U.S. battleships.

Women's rights, too, were to be sacrificed to the greater national cause. Already by 1937, Japanese women were being exhorted to fulfill their patriotic duty by bearing more children and by espousing the slogans of the Greater Japanese Women's Association. Nevertheless, Japan was extremely reluctant to mobilize women on behalf of the war effort. Female employment increased during the war, but only in areas where women traditionally worked, such as the textile industry and farming. Instead of using women to meet labor shortages, the Japanese government brought in Korean and Chinese laborers.

Front-Line Civilians: The Bombing of Cities

Bombing was used in World War II in a variety of ways: against nonhuman military targets, against enemy troops, and against civilian populations. The use of bombs made World War II as devastating for civilians as for front-line soldiers (see the box on p. 682). A small number of bombing raids in the last year of World War I had given rise to the argument that the public outcry generated by the bombing of civilian populations would be an effective way to coerce governments into making peace. Consequently, European air forces began to develop long-range bombers in the 1930s.

LUFTWAFFE ATTACKS The first sustained use of civilian bombing contradicted this theory. Beginning in early September 1940, the German Luftwaffe subjected London and many other British cities and towns to nightly air raids, making the Blitz (as the British called the German air raids) a national experience. Londoners took the first heavy blows and set the standard for the

rest of the British population by refusing to panic. But London morale was helped by the fact that German raids were widely scattered over a very large city. Smaller communities were more directly affected by the devastation. On November 14, 1940, for example, the Luftwaffe destroyed hundreds of shops and 100 acres of the city center of Coventry. Although morale sank as wild rumors of heavy casualties spread in these communities, it soon rebounded.

THE BOMBING OF GERMANY The British failed to learn from their own experience, however, and soon proceeded to bomb German cities. Churchill and his advisers believed that destroying German communities would break civilian morale and bring victory. Major bombing raids began in 1942 under the direction of Arthur Harris, the wartime leader of the British air force's Bomber Command, which was rearmed with four-engine heavy bombers capable of taking the war into the center of occupied Europe. On May 31, 1942, Cologne became the first German city to be subjected to an attack by one thousand bombers.

With the entry of the Americans into the war, the bombing strategy changed. American planes flew daytime missions aimed at the precision bombing of transportation facilities and wartime industries, while the British Bomber Command continued nighttime saturation bombing of all German cities with populations over 100,000. Bombing raids added an element of terror to circumstances already made difficult by growing shortages of food, clothing, and fuel. Germans especially feared the incendiary bombs, which created firestorms that swept destructive paths through the cities. Four raids on Hamburg in August 1943 produced temperatures of 1,800 degrees Fahrenheit, obliterated half the city's buildings, and killed thousands of civilians. The ferocious bombing of Dresden from February 13 to 15, 1945, created a firestorm that may have killed as many as 35,000 inhabitants and refugees.

Germany suffered enormously from the Allied bombing raids. Millions of buildings were destroyed, and possibly half a million civilians died in the raids. Nevertheless, it is highly unlikely that Allied bombing sapped the morale of the German people. Instead, Germans, whether pro- or anti-Nazi, fought on stubbornly, often driven simply by a desire to live. Nor did the bombing destroy Germany's industrial capacity. The Allied Strategic Bombing survey revealed that the production of war matériel actually increased between 1942 and 1944. Even in 1944 and 1945, Allied raids cut German production of armaments by only 7 percent. Because of strong

The Bombing of Civilians

The home front became a battle front when civilian populations became the targets of mass bombing raids. Many people believed that mass bombing could effectively weaken the morale of the people and shorten the war. Rarely did it achieve its goal. In these selections, British, German, and Japanese civilians relate their experiences during bombing raids.

London, 1940

Early last evening, the noise was terrible. My husband and Mr. P. were trying to play chess in the kitchen. I was playing draughts with Kenneth in the cupboard.... Presently I heard a stifled voice: "Mummy! I don't know what's become of my glasses." "I should think they are tied up in my wool." My knitting had disappeared and wool seemed to be everywhere! We heard a whistle, a bang which shook the house, and an explosion.... Well, we straightened out, decided draughts and chess were no use under the circumstances, and waited for a lull so we could have a pot of tea.

Hamburg, 1943

As the many fires broke through the roofs of the burning buildings, a column of heated air rose more than two and a half miles high and one and a half miles in diameter.... This column was turbulent, and it was fed from its base by in-rushing cooler ground-surface air. One and one half miles from the fires this draught increased the wind velocity from eleven to thirty-three miles per hour. At the edge of the area the velocities must have been appreciably greater, as trees three feet in diameter were uprooted. In a short time the temperature reached ignition point for all combustibles, and the entire area was ablaze. In such fires complete burn-out occurred; that is, no trace of combustible material remained, and only after two days were the areas cool enough to approach.

Hiroshima, August 6, 1945

I heard the airplane; I looked up at the sky, it was a sunny day, the sky was blue.... Then I saw something drop—and pow!—a big explosion knocked me down. Then I was unconscious—I don't know for how long. Then I was conscious but I couldn't see anything.... Then I see people moving away and I just follow them. It is not light like it was before, it is more like evening. I look around; houses are all flat! ... I follow the people to the river. I couldn't hear anything, my ears are blocked up. I am thinking a bomb has dropped! ... I didn't know my hands were burned, nor my face.... My eyes were swollen and felt closed up.

Q What common elements do you find in these three different descriptions of bombing raids? What effect did aerial bombing have on the nature of modern warfare?

Source: From John Campbell, ed. *The Experience of World War II* (New York: Oxford University Press, 1989), p. 180.

German air defenses, air raids were also costly for the Allies. Nearly 40,000 Allied planes were destroyed, and 160,000 airmen lost their lives.

THE BOMBING OF JAPAN: THE ATOMIC BOMB The bombing of civilians eventually reached a new level with the dropping of the first atomic bomb on Japan. Japan was especially vulnerable to air raids because its air force had been virtually destroyed in the course of the war and its crowded cities were built of flimsy materials. Attacks on Japanese cities by the new American B-29 Superfortresses, the biggest bombers of the war, had begun on November 24, 1944. By the summer of 1945, many of Japan's factories had been destroyed along with one-fourth of its dwellings. After the Japanese government decreed the mobilization of all people between the ages of thirteen and sixty into the People's Volunteer Corps, President Harry Truman (1884–1972) and his advisers feared that Japanese fanaticism might mean a million American casualties. This concern led them to drop the newly perfected atomic bomb on Hiroshima (August 6) and Nagasaki (August 9). The destruction was incredible. Of 76,000 buildings near the center of the explosion in Hiroshima, only 6,000 remained standing, and 140,000 of the city's 400,000 inhabitants had died by the end of 1945. By the end of 1950, another 50,000 had perished from the effects of radiation.

The Destruction of Dresden. The bombing of an enemy's cities brought the war home to civilian populations. This picture shows the devastation in Dresden, Germany, as a result of British and American bombing raids on February 13 and 14, 1945. An area of 2.5 square miles in the city was destroyed, and as many as 35,000 people died.

© Bettman/Corbis

Aftermath of the War

Q FOCUS QUESTIONS: What were the costs of World War II? How did the Allies' visions of postwar Europe differ, and how did these differences contribute to the emergence of the Cold War?

World War II was the most destructive war in history. Much had been at stake. Nazi Germany followed a worldview based on racial extermination and the enslavement of millions in order to create an Aryan racial empire. The Japanese, fueled by extreme nationalist ideals, also pursued dreams of empire in Asia that led to mass murder and untold devastation. Fighting the Axis powers in World War II required the mobilization of millions of ordinary men and women in the Allied countries who rose to the occasion and struggled to preserve a different way of life. As Winston Churchill once put it, "War is horrible, but slavery is worse."

The Costs of World War II

The costs of World War II were enormous. At least 21 million soldiers died. Civilian deaths were even greater and are now estimated at around 40 million, of whom more than 28 million were Russian and Chinese. The Soviet Union experienced the greatest losses: 10 million soldiers and 19 million civilians. In 1945, millions of people around the world faced starvation; in Europe, 100 million people depended on food relief of some kind.

Millions of people had also been uprooted by the war and became "displaced persons." Europe alone may have had 30 million displaced persons, many of whom found it hard to return home. After the war, millions of Germans were expelled from the Sudetenland in Czechoslovakia, and millions more were ejected from former eastern German territories that were turned over to Poland, all of which seemed reasonable to people who had suffered so much at the hands of the Germans. In Asia, millions of Japanese were returned from the former Japanese empire to Japan, while thousands of Korean forced laborers returned to Korea.

Everywhere cities lay in ruins. Physical devastation was especially severe in eastern and southeastern Europe and in the cities of western and central Europe. In Asia, China also experienced extensive devastation from eight years of conflict. At the same time, millions of tons of shipping were now underneath the seas; factories, transportation systems, bridges, dams, and farms were in ruins. The total monetary cost of the war has been estimated at $4 trillion. The economies of most belligerents, with the exception of the United States, were left drained and on the brink of disaster.

Allied War Conferences

The total victory of the Allies in World War II was succeeded not by true peace but by a new conflict known as the **Cold War** that dominated world politics until the end of the 1980s. The Cold War grew out of military, political, and ideological differences, especially between the Soviet Union and the United States, that became apparent during the last years of the war. Although Allied leaders were preoccupied primarily with ending the war, they were also strongly motivated by differing and often conflicting visions of postwar Europe.

THE TEHRAN CONFERENCE Stalin, Roosevelt, and Churchill, the leaders of the Big Three powers of the Grand Alliance, met at Tehran, the capital of Iran, in November 1943 to decide the future course of the war. Their major tactical decision concerned the final assault on Germany. Stalin and Roosevelt argued successfully for an American-British invasion of the continent through France, which they scheduled for the spring of 1944. The acceptance of this plan had important consequences. It meant that Soviet and British-American forces would meet in defeated Germany along a north-south dividing line and that eastern Europe would most likely be liberated by Soviet forces. The Allies also agreed to a partition of postwar Germany.

THE YALTA CONFERENCE By the time of the conference at Yalta in Ukraine in February 1945, the defeat of Germany was a foregone conclusion. The Western powers, which had earlier believed that the Soviets were in a weak position, now faced the reality of 11 million Red Army soldiers taking possession of eastern and much of central Europe. Stalin was still operating under the notion of spheres of influence. He was deeply suspicious of the Western powers and desired a buffer to protect the Soviet Union from possible future Western aggression. At the same time, however, Stalin was eager to obtain economically important resources and strategic military positions. Roosevelt by this time was moving away from the notion of spheres of influence to the ideal of self-determination. He called for "the end of the system of unilateral action, exclusive alliances, and spheres of influence." The Grand Alliance approved the Declaration on Liberated Europe. This was a pledge to assist liberated European nations in the creation of "democratic institutions of their own choice." Liberated countries were to hold free elections to determine their political systems.

At Yalta, Roosevelt sought Soviet military help against Japan. The atomic bomb was not yet assured, and American military planners feared the possible loss of many men in amphibious assaults on the Japanese home islands. Roosevelt therefore agreed to Stalin's price for military assistance against Japan: possession of Sakhalin and the Kurile Islands, as well as two warm-water ports and railroad rights in Manchuria.

The creation of the United Nations was a major American concern at Yalta. Roosevelt hoped to ensure the participation of the Big Three powers in a postwar international organization before difficult issues divided them into hostile camps. After a number of compromises, both Churchill and Stalin accepted Roosevelt's plans for a United Nations organization and set the first meeting for San Francisco in April 1945.

The Victorious Allied Leaders at Yalta. Even before World War II ended, the leaders of the Big Three of the Grand Alliance, Churchill, Roosevelt, and Stalin (seated, left to right), met in wartime conferences to plan the final assault on Germany and negotiate the outlines of the postwar settlement. At the Yalta meeting (February 5–11, 1945), the three leaders concentrated on postwar issues. The American president, who died two months later, was already a worn-out man at Yalta.

The issues of Germany and eastern Europe were treated less decisively. The Big Three reaffirmed that Germany must surrender unconditionally and created four occupation zones (see Map 27.5). German reparations were set at $20 billion. A compromise was also worked out in regard to Poland. Stalin agreed to free elections in the future to determine a new government. But the issue of free elections in eastern Europe caused a serious rift between the Soviets and the Americans. The principle was that eastern European governments would be freely elected, but they were also supposed to be pro-Soviet. This attempt to reconcile two irreconcilable goals was doomed to failure, as soon became evident at the next conference of the Big Three powers.

Even as the war was ending, Western relations with the Soviets were deteriorating rapidly. The Grand Alliance had been one of necessity in which disagreements had been subordinated to the pragmatic concerns of the war. The Allied powers' only common aim was the defeat of Nazism. Once this aim had all but been accomplished, the many differences that troubled East-West

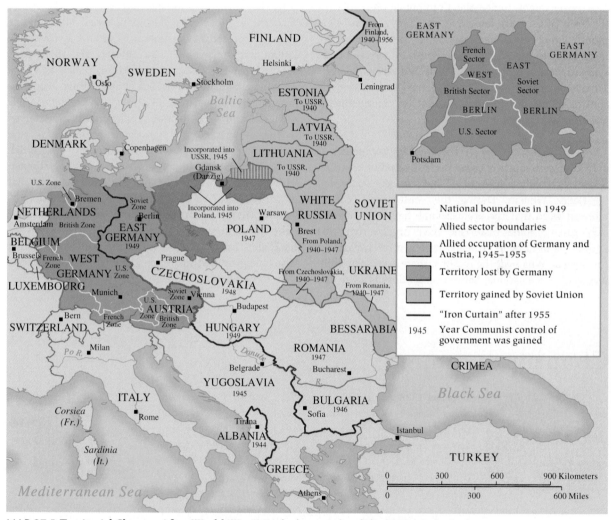

MAP 27.5 Territorial Changes After World War II. In the last months of World War II, the Red Army occupied much of eastern Europe. Stalin sought pro-Soviet satellite states in the region as a buffer against future invasions from western Europe, whereas Britain and the United States wanted democratically elected governments. Soviet military control of the territory settled the question.

Q Which country gained the greatest territory at the expense of Germany?

relations came to the surface. Each side committed acts that the other viewed as unbecoming of allies.

From the perspective of the Soviets, the United States' termination of Lend-Lease aid before the war was over and its failure to respond to a Soviet request for a $6 billion loan for reconstruction exposed the Western desire to keep the Soviet state weak. On the American side, the Soviet Union's failure to fulfill its Yalta pledge on the Declaration on Liberated Europe as applied to eastern Europe set a dangerous precedent. This was evident in Romania as early as February 1945, when the Soviets engineered a coup and installed a new government under the Communist Petra Groza (PET-ruh GRO-zhuh), known as the "Little Stalin." One month later, the Soviets sabotaged the Polish settlement by arresting West-leaning Polish leaders and their sympathizers and placing Soviet-backed Poles in power. To the Americans, the Soviets seemed to be asserting control of eastern European countries under puppet Communist regimes.

THE POTSDAM CONFERENCE The Potsdam Conference of July 1945 consequently began under a cloud of mistrust. Roosevelt had died on April 12 and had been succeeded by Harry Truman. During the conference, Truman received word that the atomic bomb had been successfully tested. Some historians have argued that this knowledge resulted in Truman's stiffened resolve against the Soviets. Whatever the reasons, there was a new chilliness in the relations between the Soviets and the Americans. At Potsdam, Truman demanded free elections throughout eastern Europe. Stalin responded, "A freely elected government in any of these East European countries would be anti-Soviet, and that we cannot allow."[11] After a bitterly fought and devastating war, Stalin sought absolute military security. To him, it could be gained only by the presence of Communist states in eastern Europe. Free elections might result in governments hostile to the Soviets. By the middle of 1945, only an invasion by Western forces could undo developments in eastern Europe, and after the world's most destructive conflict had ended, few people favored such a policy.

As the war slowly receded into the past, the reality of conflicting ideologies had reappeared. Many in the West interpreted Soviet policy as part of a worldwide Communist conspiracy. The Soviets, for their part, viewed Western, especially American, policy as global capitalist expansionism or, in Leninist terms, economic imperialism. Vyacheslav Molotov (vyich-chiss-SLAHF MAHL-uh-tawf), the Russian foreign minister, referred to the Americans as "insatiable imperialists" and "warmongering groups of adventurers."[12] In March 1946, in a speech to an American audience, former British prime minister Winston Churchill declared that "an iron curtain" had "descended across the continent," dividing Germany and Europe into two hostile camps. Stalin branded Churchill's speech a "call to war with the Soviet Union." Only months after the world's most devastating conflict had ended, the world seemed once again to be bitterly divided.

Chapter Summary

Between 1933 and 1939, Europeans watched as Adolf Hitler rebuilt Germany into a great military power. For Hitler, military power was an absolute prerequisite for the creation of a German racial empire that would dominate Europe and the world for generations to come. During that same period, the nation of Japan fell under the influence of military leaders who conspired with right-wing forces to push a program of expansion at the expense of China and the Soviet Union as well as territories in Southeast Asia. The ambitions of Germany in Europe and those of Japan in Asia led to a global conflict that became the most devastating war in human history.

The Axis nations, Germany, Italy, and Japan, proved victorious during the first two years of the war, which began after the German invasion of Poland on September 1, 1939. By 1942, the war had begun to turn in favor of the Allies, an alliance of Great Britain, the Soviet Union, and the United States. The Japanese advance was ended at the naval battles of the Coral Sea and Midway in 1942. In February 1943, the Soviets won the Battle of Stalingrad and began a push westward. By mid-1943, Germany and Italy were driven out of North Africa; in June 1944, Rome fell to the Allies, and an Allied invasion force landed in Normandy in France. After the Soviets linked up with British and American forces in April 1945, Hitler committed suicide, and the war in Europe came to an end. After atomic bombs were dropped on Hiroshima and Nagasaki in August 1945, the war in Asia also ended.

During its domination of Europe, the Nazi empire brought death and destruction to many, especially Jews, minorities, and others that the Nazis considered racially inferior peoples. The Japanese New Order in Asia, while claiming to promote a policy of "Asia for the Asians," also brought economic exploitation, severe hardships, and often death for the subject peoples under Japanese control. All sides bombed civilian populations, thus making World War II as devastating for civilians as for front-line soldiers.

If Hitler had been successful, the Nazi New Order, built on authoritarianism, racial extermination, and the brutal oppression of peoples, would have meant a triumph of barbarism and the end of freedom and equality, which, however imperfectly realized, had become important ideals in Western civilization.

The Nazis lost, but only after tremendous sacrifices and costs. Much of European civilization lay in ruins, and the old Europe had disappeared forever. Europeans, who had been accustomed to dominating the world at the beginning of the twentieth century, now watched helplessly at midcentury as the two new superpowers created by the two world wars took control of their destinies. Even before the last battles had been fought, the United States and the Soviet Union had arrived at different visions of the postwar European world. No sooner had the war ended than their differences gave rise to a new and potentially even more devastating conflict known as the Cold War.

CHAPTER TIMELINE

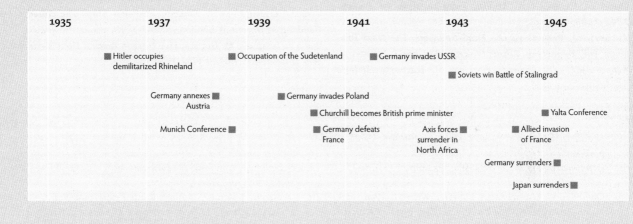

1935	1937	1939	1941	1943	1945
Hitler occupies demilitarized Rhineland		Occupation of the Sudetenland	Germany invades USSR		
				Soviets win Battle of Stalingrad	
	Germany annexes Austria	Germany invades Poland			
			Churchill becomes British prime minister		Yalta Conference
	Munich Conference	Germany defeats France	Axis forces surrender in North Africa	Allied invasion of France	
				Germany surrenders	
				Japan surrenders	

CHAPTER REVIEW

Upon Reflection

Q How do you account for the early successes of the Germans from 1939 to 1941?

Q How did the Nazis attempt to establish a New Order in Europe after their military victories, and what were the results of their efforts?

Q How did the attempt to arrive at a peace settlement after World War II lead to the beginnings of a new conflict known as the Cold War?

Key Terms

appeasement (p. 665)
Blitzkrieg (p. 667)
panzer division (p. 667)
unconditional surrender (p. 671)
Nazi New Order (p. 675)

Final Solution (p. 676)
Einsatzgruppen (p. 676)
Holocaust (p. 678)
Cold War (p. 683)

Suggestions for Further Reading

PRELUDE TO WAR   On the causes of World War II, see **A. J. Crozier, *Causes of the Second World War*** (Oxford, 1997). On the origins of the war in the Pacific, see **A. Iriye, *The Origins of the Second World War in Asia and the Pacific*** (London, 1987).

GENERAL WORKS   For general works on World War II, see **G. Weinberg, *A World at Arms: A Global History of World War II*,** 2d ed. (Cambridge, 2005), and **A. Roberts, *The Storm of War: A New History of the Second World War*** (New York, 2011). For a good military history of World War II, see **W. Murray** and **A. Millett, *A War to Be Won: Fighting the Second World War*** (Cambridge, Mass., 2000). On the impact of the war on civilians, see **J. Bourke, *The Second World War: A People's History*** (Oxford, 2003).

THE NEW ORDER   A standard work on the German New Order in Russia is **A. Dallin, *German Rule in Russia, 1941–1945*,** rev. ed. (London, 1985). On Poland, see **P. T. Rutherford, *Prelude to the Final Solution: The Nazi Program for Deporting Ethnic Poles, 1939–1941*** (Lawrence, Kans., 2007). On foreign labor, see **U. Herbert, *Hitler's Foreign Workers: Enforced Foreign Labor in Germany Under the Third Reich*,** trans. **W. Templer** (Cambridge, 1997).

THE HOLOCAUST   The best studies of the Holocaust include **R. Hilberg, *The Destruction of the European Jews*,** rev. ed., 3 vols. (New York, 1985), and **S. Friedlander, *The Years of Extermination: Nazi Germany and the Jews, 1939–1945*** (New York, 2007). For a brief study, see **D. Dwork** and **R. J. van Pelt, *Holocaust: A History*** (New York, 2002). Other Nazi atrocities are examined in **R. C. Lukas, *Forgotten Holocaust: The Poles Under German Occupation, 1939–44*,** 2d ed. (Lexington, Ky., 2001).

THE HOME FRONT   On the home front in Germany, see **M. Kitchen, *Nazi Germany at War*** (New York, 1995). The Soviet Union during the war is examined in **M. Harrison** and **J. Barber, *The Soviet Home Front, 1941–1945*** (London, 1991).

THE BOMBING CAMPAIGNS   On the Allied bombing campaign against Germany, see **R. Hansen, *Fire and Fury: The Allied Bombing of Germany*** (London, 2008). On the use of the atomic bomb in Japan, see **M. Gordin, *Five Days in August: How World War II Became a Nuclear War*** (Princeton, N.J., 2006).

Notes

1. A. Hitler, *Mein Kampf*, trans. R. Manheim (Boston, 1971), p. 654.
2. *Documents on German Foreign Policy* (London, 1956), ser. D, vol. 7, p. 204.
3. Quoted in W. Murray and A. Millett, *A War to Be Won: Fighting the Second World War* (Cambridge, Mass., 2000), p. 137.
4. Quoted in A. Speer, *Spandau*, trans. R. Winston and C. Winston (New York, 1976), p. 50.
5. Quoted in *Nazi Conspiracy and Aggression* (Washington, D.C., 1946), vol. 6, p. 262.
6. *International Military Tribunal, Trial of the Major War Criminals* (Nuremberg, 1947–1949), vol. 22, p. 480.
7. *Nazi Conspiracy and Aggression*, vol. 6, pp. 341–342.
8. Ibid., 6, p. 789.
9. Quoted in J. Campbell, *The Experience of World War II* (New York, 1989), p. 170.
10. Quoted in C. Koonz, "Mothers in the Fatherland: Women in Nazi Germany," in *Becoming Visible: Women in European History*, ed. R. Bridenthal and C. Koonz (Boston, 1977), p. 466.
11. Quoted in N. Graebner, *Cold War Diplomacy, 1945–1960* (Princeton, N.J., 1962), p. 117.
12. Quoted in W. Loth, *The Division of the World, 1941–1955* (New York, 1988), p. 81.

MindTap   **MindTap** is a fully online, highly personalized learning experience built upon Cengage Learning content. MindTap combines student learning tools—readings, multimedia, activities, and assessments—into a singular Learning Path that guides students through the course.

Cold War and a New Western World, 1945–1965

Survivors in the ruins of Berlin, Germany, at the end of World War II

© SZ Photo/SV-Bilderdienst/The Bridgeman Art Library

CHAPTER OUTLINE AND FOCUS QUESTIONS

Development of the Cold War

Q Why were the United States and the Soviet Union suspicious of each other after World War II, and what events between 1945 and 1949 heightened the tensions between the two nations? How and why did the Cold War become a global affair after 1949?

Europe and the World: Decolonization

Q Why and how did the European colonies in Africa, the Middle East, and Asia gain independence between 1945 and 1965?

Recovery and Renewal in Europe

Q What were the main developments in the Soviet Union, eastern Europe, and western Europe between 1945 and 1965?

The United States and Canada: A New Era

Q What were the main political developments in North America between 1945 and 1965?

Postwar Society and Culture in the Western World

Q What major changes occurred in Western society and culture between 1945 and 1965?

CRITICAL THINKING

Q What were the similarities and differences in the political, social, and economic history of eastern Europe and western Europe between 1945 and 1965?

CONNECTIONS TO TODAY

Q In what ways are the developments in the Cold War between 1945 and 1965 still evident in international affairs today?

THE END OF World War II in Europe was met with great joy. One visitor to Moscow reported, "I looked out of the window [at 2 A.M.], almost everywhere there were lights in the window—people were staying awake.

Everyone embraced everyone else, someone sobbed aloud." But after the victory parades and celebrations, Europeans awoke to a devastating realization: their civilization was in ruins. Some wondered if Europe would ever regain its former prosperity and importance. Winston Churchill wrote, "What is Europe now? A rubble heap, a charnel house, a breeding ground of pestilence and hate." There was ample reason for his pessimism. Forty million people (both soldiers and civilians) had been killed during the last six years. Massive air raids and artillery bombardments had reduced many of the great cities of Europe to heaps of rubble. An American general described Berlin: "Wherever we looked we saw desolation. It was like a city of the dead. Suffering and shock were visible in every face. Dead bodies still remained in canals and lakes and were being dug out from under bomb debris." Millions of Europeans faced starvation because grain harvests were only half of what they had been in 1939. Millions were also homeless. In the parts of the Soviet Union that had been occupied by the Germans, almost 25 million people were without homes. The destruction of bridges, roads, and railroads had left transportation systems paralyzed. Untold millions of people had been uprooted by the war—11 million prisoners of war had to be returned to their native countries, and 15 million Germans and eastern Europeans were driven out of countries where they were no longer wanted. Yet despite the chaos, Europe was soon on the road to a remarkable recovery. Already by 1950, Europe's industrial and agricultural output was 30 percent above prewar levels.

World War II had also destroyed European supremacy in world affairs. After 1945, the colonial empires of the European nations rapidly disintegrated, and Europe's place in the world changed radically. As the Cold War conflict between the world's two superpowers—the United States and the Soviet Union—intensified, the European nations were divided into two armed camps dependent on one or the other of these two major powers. The United States and the Soviet Union, whose rivalry raised the specter of nuclear war, seemed to hold the survival of Europe and the world in their hands.

Development of the Cold War

Q **Focus Questions:** Why were the United States and the Soviet Union suspicious of each other after World War II, and what events between 1945 and 1949 heightened the tensions between the two nations? How and why did the Cold War become a global affair after 1949?

Even before World War II had ended, the two major Allied powers—the United States and the Soviet Union—had begun to disagree on their vision for postwar Europe. Unity had been maintained during the war because of the urgent need to defeat the Axis powers, but once their defeat was assured, differences between the Americans and Soviets again surged to the front.

Confrontation of the Superpowers: Who Started the Cold War?

There has been considerable historical debate about who was responsible for starting the Cold War. In the 1950s, most scholars in the West assumed that the bulk of the blame must fall on the shoulders of Joseph Stalin, whose determination to impose Soviet rule on eastern Europe snuffed out hopes for freedom and self-determination there and aroused justifiable fears of communist expansion in the West. During the next decade, however, revisionist historians—influenced in part by their dislike of aggressive U.S. policies in Southeast Asia—began to argue that the fault lay primarily in the United States, where President Harry Truman and his anticommunist advisers sought to encircle the Soviet Union with a group of pliant U.S. client states. More recently, many historians have adopted a more nuanced view, noting that both the United States and the Soviet Union took steps at the end of World War II that were unwise or might have been avoided.

Both nations, however, were working within a framework conditioned by the past. Ultimately, the rivalry between the two superpowers stemmed from their different historical perspectives and their irreconcilable political ambitions. Intense competition for political and military supremacy had long been a regular feature of Western civilization. The United States and the Soviet Union were the heirs of that European tradition of power politics, and it should not surprise us that two such different systems would seek to extend their way of life to the rest of the world. Because of its need to feel secure on its western border, the Soviet Union was not prepared to give up the advantages it had gained in eastern Europe from Germany's defeat. But neither were American leaders willing to give up the power and prestige the United States had gained throughout the world. Suspicious of each other's motives, the United States and the Soviet Union soon raised their mutual fears to a level of intense competition (see the box on p. 692). In recent years, some historians have emphasized Soviet responsibility, especially in view of new evidence from previously closed Soviet archives that Joseph Stalin had even been willing to go to war to spread communism to all of Europe. Regardless of who was responsible, however, a number of events between 1945 and 1949 entangled the two in irreconcilable conflict.

Eastern Europe was the first area of disagreement. The United States and Great Britain had championed self-determination and democratic freedom for the liberated nations of eastern Europe. Stalin, however, fearful that the eastern European nations would return to traditional anti-Soviet attitudes if they were permitted free elections, opposed the West's plans. Having liberated eastern Europe from the Nazis, the Red Army proceeded to install pro-Soviet governing regimes in Poland, Romania, Bulgaria, and Hungary. These pro-Soviet governments satisfied Stalin's desire for a buffer zone against the West, but the local populations and their sympathizers in the West regarded the regimes as an expansion of Stalin's empire.

THE TRUMAN DOCTRINE A civil war in Greece provided another arena for confrontation between the superpowers. In 1946, the Communist People's Liberation Army and anticommunist forces supported by the British were fighting each other for control of Greece. Great Britain had initially assumed primary responsibility for promoting postwar reconstruction in the eastern Mediterranean, but in 1947, ongoing economic problems caused the British to withdraw from the active role they had been playing in both Greece and Turkey. The U.S. president Harry Truman, alarmed by British weakness and the possibility of Soviet expansion into the eastern Mediterranean, responded with the **Truman Doctrine**, which said, in essence, that the United States would provide money to countries that claimed they were threatened by communist expansion. If the Soviets were not stopped in Greece, so the argument went, the United States would have to face the spread of communism throughout the free world. As Dean Acheson, the American secretary of state, explained, "Like apples in a barrel infected by disease,

the corruption of Greece would infect Iran and all the East … likewise Africa … Italy … France.… Not since Rome and Carthage has there been such a polarization of power on this earth."[1] Truman asked the U.S. Congress to provide $400 million in economic and military aid for Greece and Turkey.

The proclamation of the Truman Doctrine was soon followed in June 1947 by the European Recovery Program, better known as the **Marshall Plan**. Intended to rebuild prosperity and stability, this program included $13 billion for the economic recovery of war-torn Europe. Underlying it was the belief that communist aggression fed off economic turmoil. General George C. Marshall had noted in a speech at Harvard, "Our policy is not directed against any country or doctrine but against hunger, poverty, desperation, and chaos."[2] From the Soviet perspective, the Marshall Plan guaranteed "American loans in return for the relinquishing by the European states of their economic and later also their political independence." To some scholars, the Marshall Plan encouraged Stalin to push for even greater control of eastern Europe to safeguard Soviet interests.

CONTAINMENT By 1947, the split in Europe between East and West had become a fact of life. At the end of World War II, the United States had favored a quick end to its commitments in Europe. But American fears of Soviet aims caused the United States to play an increasingly large role in Europe. In an important article in *Foreign Affairs* in July 1947, George Kennan, a well-known American diplomat with much knowledge of Soviet affairs, advocated a policy of **containment** against further aggression by the Soviets. Kennan favored the "adroit and vigilant application of counterforce at a series of constantly shifting geographical and political points, corresponding to the shifts and maneuvers of Soviet policy." By 1948, containment of the Soviet Union had become the formal American policy.

CONTENTION OVER GERMANY The fate of Germany also became a source of heated contention between East and West. Besides the partitioning of Germany (and Berlin) into four occupied zones, the Allied powers had agreed on little else with regard to the conquered nation. The Soviets, hardest hit by the war, took reparations from Germany in the form of booty. The technology-starved Soviets dismantled and removed to Russia 380 factories from the western zones of Berlin before transferring their control to the Western powers. At the same time, the German Communist Party was reestablished under

OPPOSING VIEWPOINTS

Who Started the Cold War? American and Soviet Perspectives

Although the United States and the Soviet Union had cooperated during World War II to defeat the Germans and the Japanese, differences began to appear as soon as victory became certain. The year 1946 was an especially important turning point in the relationship between the two superpowers. George Kennan, an American diplomat regarded as an expert on Soviet affairs, was asked to write an analysis of one of Stalin's speeches. His U.S. Foreign Service dispatch, which came to be known as the Long Telegram, was sent to U.S. embassies, U.S. State Department officials, and military leaders. The Long Telegram gave a strong view of Soviet intentions. A response to Kennan's position was written by Nikolai Novikov, a former Soviet ambassador to the United States. His response was read by Vyacheslav Molotov, the Soviet foreign minister, but historians are not sure if Stalin or other officials also read it and were influenced by it.

George Kennan, The Long Telegram, February 1946

At the bottom of [the Soviet] neurotic view of world affairs is a traditional and instinctive Russian sense of insecurity. Originally, this was the insecurity of a peaceful agricultural people trying to live on a vast exposed plain in the neighborhood of fierce nomadic peoples. To this was added, as Russia came into contact with the economically advanced West, the fear of more competent, more powerful, more highly organized societies.... For this reason they have always feared foreign penetration, feared direct contact between the Western world and their own.... And they have learned to seek security only in patient but deadly struggle for total destruction of rival power, never in compacts and compromises with it....

    In summary, we have here a political force committed fanatically to the belief that with the United State there can be no permanent modus vivendi, that it is desirable and necessary the internal harmony of our society be disrupted, our traditional way of life be destroyed, the international authority of our state be broken, if Soviet power is to be secure.... In addition it has an elaborate and far-flung apparatus for exertion of its influence in other countries, an apparatus of amazing flexibility and versatility, managed by people whose experience and skill in underground methods are presumably without parallel in history. Finally, it is seemingly inaccessible to considerations of reality in its basic reactions.... This is admittedly not a pleasant picture.... But I would like to record my conviction that the problem is within our power to solve—and that without recourse to any general conflict.... I think we may approach calmly and with good heart the problem of how to deal with Russia ... [but] we must have the courage and self-confidence to cling to our own methods and conceptions of human society. After all, the greatest danger that can befall us in coping with this problem of Soviet communism is that we shall allow ourselves to become like those with whom we are coping.

Nikolai Novikov, Telegram, September 27, 1946

One of the stages in the achievement of dominance over the world by the United States is its understanding with England concerning the partial division of the world on the basis of mutual concessions. The basic lines of the secret agreement between the United States and England regarding the division of the world consist, as shown by facts, in their agreement on the inclusion of Japan and China in the sphere of influence of the United States in the Far East.... The American policy in China is striving for the complete economic and political submission of China to the control of American monopolistic capital....

    Obvious indications of the U.S. effort to establish world dominance are also to be found in the increase in military potential in peacetime and in the establishment of a large number of naval and air bases both in the United States and beyond its borders....

Careful note should be taken of the fact that the preparation by the United States for a future war is being conducted with the prospect of war against the Soviet Union, which in the eyes of American imperialists is the main obstacle in the path of the United States to world domination. This is indicated by facts such as the tactical training of the American army for war with the Soviet Union as the future opponent, the placing of American strategic bases in regions from which it is possible to launch strikes on Soviet territory, intensified training and strengthening of Arctic regions as close approaches to the USSR, and attempts to prepare Germany and Japan to use those countries in a war against the USSR.

Q In Kennan's view, what was the Soviet policy after World War II? What did he believe determined that policy, and how did he think the United States should respond? In Novikov's view, what was the goal of U.S. foreign policy, and how did he believe the Americans planned to achieve it? Why was it so difficult to find a common ground between the two positions?

Source: *Origins of the Cold War: The Novikov, Kennan, and Roberts 'Long' Telegrams of 1946* (Kenneth M. Jensen, editor). Washington, DC: Endowment of the United States Institute of Peace, 1993. pp. 20–21, 28–31, 8, 16. Reprinted with permission.

the control of Walter Ulbricht (VAHL-tuh OOL-brikkt) (1893–1973) and was soon in charge of the political reconstruction of the Soviet zone in eastern Germany.

At the same time, the British, French, and Americans gradually began to merge their zones economically and by February 1948 were making plans for the unification of these three western sections of Germany and the formal creation of a West German federal government. The Soviets responded with a blockade of West Berlin that allowed neither trucks nor trains to enter the three western zones of Berlin.

The Western powers faced a dilemma. Direct military confrontation seemed dangerous, and no one wished to risk World War III. Therefore, an attempt to break through the blockade with tanks and trucks was ruled out. The solution was the Berlin Air Lift. It was an enormous undertaking. Western Allied air forces worked around the clock for almost a year to supply the city of Berlin with foodstuffs as well as the coal, oil, and gasoline needed to run the city's power stations, sewer plants, and factories and heat its dwellings. At the peak, 13,000 tons of supplies were flown to Berlin daily. Altogether the Western allies shipped 2.3 million tons of food on 277,500 flights. Seventy-three Allied airmen lost their lives due to accidents. The Soviets, also not wanting war, did not interfere and finally lifted the blockade in May 1949. The blockade of Berlin had severely increased tensions between the United States and the Soviet Union and resulted in the separation of Germany into two states. The Federal Republic of Germany, known as West Germany, was formally created in September 1949, and a month later, the separate German Democratic Republic was established in East Germany. Berlin remained a divided city and the source of much contention between East and West.

NEW MILITARY ALLIANCES The Soviet Union also detonated its first atomic bomb in 1949, and all too soon, both powers were involved in an escalating arms race that resulted in the construction of ever more destructive nuclear weapons. Soon the search for security took the form of **mutual deterrence**, the belief that an arsenal of nuclear weapons prevented war by ensuring that if one nation launched nuclear weapons in a preemptive first strike, the other nation would be able to respond and devastate the attacker. It was assumed that neither side would risk using the massive arsenals that had been assembled.

The search for security in the uncertain atmosphere of the Cold War also led to the formation of military alliances. The North Atlantic Treaty Organization (**NATO**) was formed in April 1949 when Belgium, Britain, Denmark, France, Iceland, Italy, Luxembourg, the Netherlands, Norway, and Portugal signed a treaty with the United States and Canada. All the powers agreed to provide mutual assistance if any one of them was attacked. A few years later, West Germany, Greece, and Turkey joined NATO.

The eastern European states soon followed suit. In 1955, Albania, Bulgaria, Czechoslovakia, East Germany, Hungary, Poland, Romania, and the Soviet Union organized a formal military alliance known as the **Warsaw Pact**. As had happened so many times before, Europe was divided into hostile alliance systems.

The Berlin Air Lift. During the Berlin Air Lift, the United States and its Western allies flew 13,000 tons of supplies daily to Berlin and thus were able to break the Soviet land blockade of the city. In this photograph, residents of West Berlin watch an American plane land at Berlin's Templehof Airport with supplies for the city.

Globalization of the Cold War

The Cold War soon spread from Europe to the rest of the world. The victory of the Chinese Communists in 1949 in the Chinese civil war brought a new communist regime and intensified American fears about the spread of communism. Shortly thereafter, the Korean War turned the Cold War into a worldwide struggle, eventually leading to a system of military alliances around the globe.

THE KOREAN WAR Korea had been liberated from the Japanese in 1945 but soon split into two parts. The land north of the 38th parallel became the Democratic People's Republic of Korea (North Korea) and was supported by the Soviet Union. The Republic of Korea (South Korea) received aid from the United States. In 1950, probably with Stalin's approval, North Korean forces invaded South Korea. The Americans, seeing this as yet another example of communist aggression and expansion, gained the support of the United

The Korean War

Nations and intervened by sending American troops to turn back the invasion. When the American and South Korean forces pushed the North Koreans back toward the Chinese border, Chinese forces entered the fray and forced the American and South Korean troops to retreat back to South Korea. Believing that the Chinese were simply the puppets of Moscow, American policymakers created an image of communism as a monolithic force directed by the Soviet Union. After two more years of inconclusive fighting, an uneasy truce was reached in 1953, leaving Korea divided. To many Americans, the policy of containing communism had succeeded in Asia, just as it had earlier in Europe.

ESCALATION OF THE COLD WAR The Korean experience seemed to confirm American fears of communist expansion and reinforced American determination to contain Soviet power. In the mid-1950s, the administration of President Dwight D. Eisenhower (1890–1969) adopted a policy of massive retaliation, which advocated the full use of American nuclear bombs to counteract even a Soviet ground attack in Europe. Moreover, American military alliances were extended around the world. The Central Treaty Organization (CENTO) of Britain, Iran, Iraq, Pakistan, Turkey, and the United States was intended to prevent the Soviet Union from expanding at the expense of its southern neighbors. In addition, Australia, Britain, France, New Zealand, Pakistan, the Philippines, Thailand, and the United States formed the Southeast Asia Treaty Organization (SEATO). By the mid-1950s, the United States found itself allied militarily with forty-two states around the world.

Despite the continued escalation of the Cold War, hopes for a new era of peaceful coexistence also appeared. The death of Stalin in 1953 caused some people in the West to think that the new Soviet leadership might be more flexible in its policies. But this optimism proved premature. All talk of **rapprochement** (ra-prohsh-MAHN) between East and West temporarily ceased in 1956 when the Soviet Union used its armed forces to crush Hungary's attempt to assert its independence from Soviet control.

A crisis over Berlin also added to the tension in the late 1950s. In August 1957, the Soviet Union had launched its first intercontinental ballistic missile (ICBM) and, shortly thereafter, *Sputnik I*, the first space satellite. Fueled by partisan political debate, fears of a "missile gap" between the United States and the Soviet Union seized the American public. Nikita Khrushchev (nuh-KEE-tuh KHROOSH-chawf) (1894–1971), the new leader of the Soviet Union, attempted to take advantage of the American frenzy over missiles to solve the problem of West Berlin. Khrushchev had said that Berlin was like "the testicles of the West: every time I want to make the West scream, I squeeze on Berlin."[3] West Berlin had remained a "Western island" of prosperity in the midst of the relatively poverty-stricken East Germany. Many East Germans also managed to escape by fleeing to West Berlin.

In November 1958, Khrushchev announced that unless the West removed its forces from West Berlin within six months, he would turn over control of the access routes to Berlin to the East Germans. Unwilling to accept an ultimatum that would have abandoned West Berlin to the Communists, Eisenhower and the West stood firm, and Khrushchev eventually backed down. In 1961, the East German government built a wall separating West Berlin from East Berlin, and the Berlin issue faded.

It was revived when John F. Kennedy (1917–1963) became the U.S. president. During a summit meeting in Vienna in June 1961, Khrushchev threatened Kennedy with another six-month ultimatum over West Berlin. Kennedy left Vienna convinced of the need to deal firmly with the Soviet Union, and Khrushchev was forced once again to lift his six-month ultimatum. Determined to achieve some foreign policy success, however, the Soviet leader soon embarked on an even more dangerous adventure in Cuba.

THE CUBAN MISSILE CRISIS The Cold War confrontation between the United States and the Soviet Union reached frightening levels during the Cuban Missile Crisis. In 1959, a left-wing revolutionary named Fidel Castro (fee-DELL KASS-troh) (b. 1927) had overthrown the Cuban dictator Fulgencio Batista (FULL-jen-see-oh bah-TEES-tuh) (1901-1973) and established a Soviet-supported totalitarian regime. In 1961, an American-supported attempt to invade Cuba via the Bay of Pigs and overthrow Castro's regime ended in utter failure. The next year, the Soviet Union decided to station nuclear missiles in Cuba. The United States was not prepared to allow nuclear weapons within such close striking distance of the American mainland, even though it had placed nuclear weapons in Turkey within easy range of the Soviet Union. Khrushchev was quick to point out that "your rockets are in Turkey. You are worried by Cuba . . . because it is 90 miles from the American coast. But Turkey is next to us."[4] When U.S. intelligence discovered that a Soviet fleet carrying missiles was heading to Cuba, President Kennedy decided to blockade Cuba and prevent the fleet from reaching its destination. This approach to the problem had the

CHRONOLOGY The Cold War	
Truman Doctrine	1947
European Recovery Program (Marshall Plan)	1947
Berlin blockade	1948–1949
Communist victory in Chinese civil war	1949
Soviet Union's first atomic bomb	1949
Formation of North Atlantic Treaty Organization	1949
Korean War	1950–1953
Formation of Warsaw Pact	1955
Berlin Crisis	1958
Cuban Missile Crisis	1962

The Cuban Missile Crisis: Khrushchev's Perspective

The Cuban Missile Crisis was one of the most sobering experiences of the Cold War. It led the two superpowers to seek new ways to lessen the tensions between them. This version of the events is taken from the memoirs of Nikita Khrushchev.

Nikita Khrushchev, *Khrushchev Remembers*

I will explain what the Caribbean crisis of October 1962 was all about.... At the time that Fidel Castro led his revolution to victory and entered Havana with his troops, we had no idea what political course his regime would follow.... All the while the Americans had been watching Castro closely. At first they thought that the capitalist underpinnings of the Cuban economy would remain intact. So by the time Castro announced that he was going to put Cuba on the road toward Socialism, the Americans had already missed their chance to do anything about it by simply exerting their influence: there were no longer any forces left which could be organized to fight on America's behalf in Cuba. That left only one alternative—invasion! ...

After Castro's crushing victory over the counterrevolutionaries we intensified our military aid to Cuba.... We were sure that the Americans would never reconcile themselves to the existence of Castro's Cuba. They feared, as much as we hoped, that a Socialist Cuba might become a magnet that would attract other Latin American countries to Socialism.... It was clear to me that we might very well lose Cuba if we didn't take some decisive steps in her defense.... We had to think up some way of confronting America with more than words. We had to establish a tangible and effective deterrent to American interference in the Caribbean. But what exactly? The logical answer was missiles. We knew that American missiles were aimed against us in Turkey and Italy, to say nothing of West Germany.... My thinking went like this: if we installed the missiles secretly and then if the United States discovered the missiles were there after they were already poised and ready to strike, the Americans would think twice before trying to liquidate our installations by military means.... I want to make one thing absolutely clear: when we put our ballistic missiles in Cuba we had no desire to start a war. On the contrary, our principal aim was only to deter America from starting a war....

President Kennedy issued an ultimatum, demanding that we remove our missiles and bombers from Cuba.... We sent the Americans a note saying that we agreed to remove our missiles and bombers on the condition that the President give us his assurance that there would be no invasion of Cuba by the forces of the United States or anybody else. Finally Kennedy gave in and agreed to make a statement giving us such an assurance.... It had been, to say the least, an interesting and challenging situation. The two most powerful nations of the world had been squared off against each other, each with its finger on the button. You'd have thought that war was inevitable. But both sides showed that if the desire to avoid war is strong enough, even the most pressing dispute can be solved by compromise. And a compromise over Cuba was indeed found. The episode ended in a triumph of common sense.... It was a great victory for us, though, that we had been able to extract from Kennedy a promise that neither America nor any of her allies would invade Cuba.... The Caribbean crisis was a triumph of Soviet foreign policy and a personal triumph in my own career as a statesman and as a member of the collective leadership. We achieved, I would say, a spectacular success without having to fire a single shot!

Q According to his memoirs, why did Nikita Khrushchev decide to place missiles in Cuba? Why did he later agree to remove them? What did each side "lose" and what did each side "win" in the Cuban Missile Crisis?

Source: From Strobe Talbot, ed., *Krushchev Remembers*, copyright © Andrew Nurnberg Associates.

benefit of delaying confrontation and giving each side time to find a peaceful solution (see the box above). Khrushchev agreed to turn back the fleet if Kennedy pledged not to invade Cuba. The intense feeling that the world might have been annihilated in a few days had a profound influence on both sides. A telephone "hotline" between Moscow and Washington was installed in 1963 to expedite rapid communication between the two superpowers in time of crisis. The same year, both powers agreed to ban nuclear tests in the atmosphere, a step that served to lessen the tensions between the two nations.

Europe and the World: Decolonization

Q **FOCUS QUESTION**: Why and how did the European colonies in Africa, the Middle East, and Asia gain independence between 1945 and 1965?

As noted in Chapter 26, movements for independence had begun in earnest in Africa and Asia in the years between the wars. After World War II, these movements gained momentum. The continued subjugation of peoples by colonial powers seemed at odds with the goals the Allies had pursued in overthrowing the repressive regimes of Germany, Italy, and Japan. Then, too, indigenous peoples everywhere took up the call for national self-determination and expressed their determination to fight for independence.

The ending of the colonial European empires did not come easy, however. In 1941, Churchill had said, "I have not become His Majesty's Chief Minister in order to preside over the liquidation of the British Empire." Britain and France in particular seemed reluctant to let go of their colonies, but for a variety of reasons, both eventually gave in to the obvious: the days of empire were over.

The power of the European states had been destroyed by the exhaustive struggles of World War II. The greatest colonial empire builder, Great Britain, no longer had the energy or the wealth to maintain its colonial empire after the war. A rush of **decolonization** swept the world. Between 1947 and 1962, virtually every colony achieved independence and attained statehood. Although some colonial powers willingly relinquished their control, others had to be driven out by national wars of liberation. Decolonization was a difficult and even bitter process, but it created a new geopolitics as the long era of Western domination of non-Western states ended.

Africa: The Struggle for Independence

After World War II, Europeans reluctantly realized that colonial rule in Africa would have to come to an end, but little had been done to prepare Africans for self-rule. Political organizations that had been formed by Africans before the war to gain their rights became formal political parties with independence as their goal. In the Gold Coast, Kwame Nkrumah (KWAH-may en-KROO-muh) (1909–1972) formed the Convention People's Party, the first African political party in sub-Saharan Africa. In the late 1940s, Jomo Kenyatta (JOH-moh ken-YAHT-uh)

(1894–1978) founded the Kenya African National Union, which focused on economic issues but also sought self-rule for Kenya.

In North Africa, the French granted full independence to Morocco and Tunisia in 1956 (see Map 28.1). Since Algeria was home to 2 million French settlers, however, France chose to retain its dominion there. But a group of Algerian nationalists organized the National Liberation Front (FLN) and in 1954 initiated a guerrilla war to free their homeland. The French people became so divided over this war that the French leader, Charles de Gaulle (SHAHRL duh GOHL), accepted the inevitable and granted Algeria independence in 1962. The liberation of Algeria led to a massive movement of

Algerian Independence. Although the French wanted to retain control of their Algerian colony, a bloody war of liberation finally led to Algeria's freedom. This photograph shows a group of Algerians celebrating the announcement of independence on July 3, 1962.

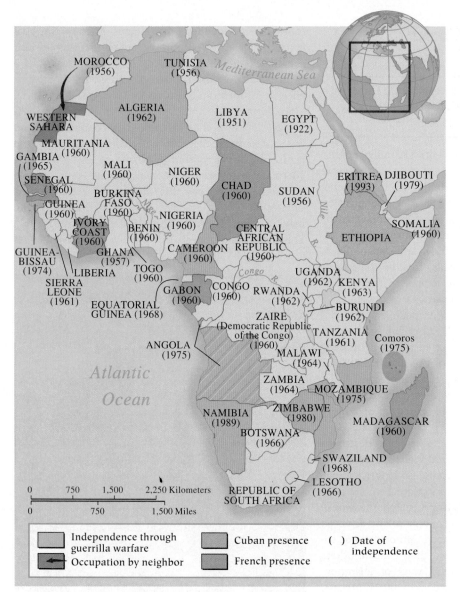

MAP 28.1 **Decolonization in Africa.** By the late 1950s, Britain and France had decided to grant independence to most of their African colonies, although France fought hard before relinquishing Algeria. Most of the new states had difficulty promoting economic growth and dealing with internal ethnic animosities.

Q What is a significant characteristic shared by a majority of the countries that gained independence from 1975 onward?

Map labels:
MOROCCO (1956)
TUNISIA (1956)
Mediterranean Sea
ALGERIA (1962)
LIBYA (1951)
EGYPT (1922)
WESTERN SAHARA
MAURITANIA (1960)
GAMBIA (1965)
MALI (1960)
NIGER (1960)
SENEGAL (1960)
BURKINA FASO (1960)
GUINEA (1960)
CHAD (1960)
SUDAN (1956)
ERITREA (1993)
DJIBOUTI (1979)
IVORY COAST (1960)
NIGERIA (1960)
BENIN (1960)
CENTRAL AFRICAN REPUBLIC (1960)
SOMALIA (1960)
ETHIOPIA
GUINEA-BISSAU (1974)
GHANA (1957)
CAMEROON (1960)
Congo R.
LIBERIA
TOGO (1960)
SIERRA LEONE (1961)
GABON (1960)
CONGO (1960)
RWANDA (1962)
UGANDA (1962)
KENYA (1963)
EQUATORIAL GUINEA (1968)
ZAIRE (Democratic Republic of the Congo) (1960)
BURUNDI (1962)
TANZANIA (1961)
Comoros (1975)
ANGOLA (1975)
MALAWI (1964)
ZAMBIA (1964)
MOZAMBIQUE (1975)
NAMIBIA (1989)
ZIMBABWE (1980)
MADAGASCAR (1960)
BOTSWANA (1966)
SWAZILAND (1968)
LESOTHO (1966)
REPUBLIC OF SOUTH AFRICA
Atlantic Ocean
Nile

0   750   1,500   2,250 Kilometers
0   750   1,500 Miles

Legend:
Independence through guerrilla warfare
Occupation by neighbor
Cuban presence
French presence
( ) Date of independence

peoples as 2 million French settlers repatriated to France and thousands of *harkis* (har-KEES), Muslim Algerians who had fought alongside the French, also fled in fear of retaliation. Their fears were not unwarranted; the new Algerian authorities executed almost sixty thousand harkis who remained behind.

In areas such as South Africa, where European settlers dominated the political system, the transition to independence was more complicated. In South Africa, political activity by local blacks began with the formation in 1912 of the African National Congress (ANC), whose goal was to gain economic and political reforms within the framework of the existing system. The ANC's efforts, however, met with little success. At the same time, by the 1950s, South African whites were strengthening the laws separating whites and blacks, creating a system of racial segregation in South Africa known as **apartheid** (uh-PAHRT-hyt). When blacks demonstrated against the apartheid laws, the white government brutally repressed the demonstrators. After the arrest of Nelson Mandela (1918–2013), the ANC leader, in 1962, members of the ANC called for armed resistance to the white government.

When both the British and the French decided to let go of their colonial empires, most black African nations achieved their independence in the late 1950s and 1960s. The Gold Coast, now renamed Ghana and under the guidance of Kwame Nkrumah, was first in 1957.

Nigeria, the Belgian Congo (renamed Zaire), Kenya, Tanganyika (later joined with Zanzibar and renamed Tanzania), and others soon followed. Seventeen new African nations emerged in 1960. Another eleven followed between 1961 and 1965. By the late 1960s, only parts of southern Africa and the Portuguese possessions of Mozambique and Angola remained under European rule. After a series of brutal guerrilla wars, the Portuguese finally gave up their colonies in the 1970s.

Conflict in the Middle East

Although Turkey, Iran, Saudi Arabia, and Iraq had become independent states between the two world wars, the end of World War II led to the emergence of other independent states in the Middle East. Jordan, Syria, and Lebanon, all European mandates before the war, became independent (see Map 28.2). Sympathy for the idea of Arab unity led to the formation of the Arab League in 1945, but different points of view among its members prevented it from achieving anything of substance.

The one issue on which all Muslim states in the area could agree was the question of Palestine. As tensions between Jews and Arabs intensified in that mandate during the 1930s, the British reduced Jewish immigration into the area and firmly rejected Jewish proposals for an independent state in Palestine. The Zionists, who wanted Palestine as a home for Jews, were not to be denied, however. Many people had been horrified at the end of World War II when they learned of the Holocaust, and sympathy for the Jewish cause grew dramatically. As a result, the Zionists turned for support to the United States, and in March 1948, the Truman administration approved the concept of an independent Jewish state in Palestine, even though Jews comprised only about one-third of the local population. When a United Nations resolution divided Palestine into a Jewish state and an Arab state, the Jews in Palestine acted. On May 14, 1948, they proclaimed the state of Israel.

Its Arab neighbors saw the new state as a betrayal of the Palestinian people, 90 percent of whom were Muslim. Outraged at the lack of Western support for Muslim interests in the area, several Arab countries invaded the new Jewish state. The invasion failed, but both sides remained bitter. Many of the Arab inhabitants of the new state fled to surrounding areas, and the Arab states refused to recognize the existence of Israel.

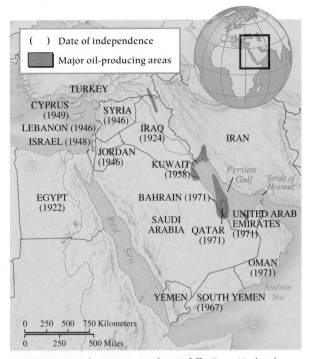

MAP 28.2 Decolonization in the Middle East. Under the control of the Ottoman Empire prior to World War I, much of the Middle East was ruled directly or indirectly by the British and French after the war. Britain, the main colonial power, granted independence to most of its holdings in the first years after World War II, although it did maintain control of small states in the Persian Gulf and Arabian Sea region until 1971.

Q Which countries are major oil producers?

The growing Arab hostility was a constant threat to the security of Israel. At a meeting of Arab leaders held in Jerusalem in 1964, the Egyptians took the lead in forming the Palestine Liberation Organization (PLO) to represent the interests of the Palestinians. The PLO believed that only the Palestinian peoples (and not Jewish immigrants from abroad) had the right to form a state in Palestine. During the 1960s, the dispute between Israel and other states in the Middle East intensified. Fearing an imminent attack by Arab forces, especially those of Egypt, Israel launched pre-emptive air strikes against Egypt and several of its Arab neighbors on June 5, 1967. During the Six-Day War, as it came to be called, Israeli forces defeated the Egyptians, seized Jordanian territory on the West Bank of the Jordan River, and occupied all of Jerusalem (formerly divided between Israel and Jordan). Israel tripled the size of its territory. The new Israel aroused even more bitter hatred among the Arabs. Furthermore, another million Palestinians now lived inside Israel's new borders, most of them in the Gaza Strip and on the West Bank.

Asia: Nationalism and Communism

In Asia, the United States initiated the process of decolonization in 1946 when it granted independence to the Philippines (see Map 28.3). Britain soon followed suit with India. Over the years, Mohandas "Mahatma" Gandhi (1869–1948) and his civil disobedience movement had greatly furthered the drive for India's independence. But unable to resolve the conflict between the Hindu and Muslim populations within India, in 1947 the British created two states—a mostly Hindu India and a predominantly Muslim Pakistan.

Other areas of Asia also gained independence. In 1948, Britain granted independence to Ceylon (modern Sri Lanka) and Burma (modern Myanmar). When the Dutch failed to reestablish control over the Dutch East

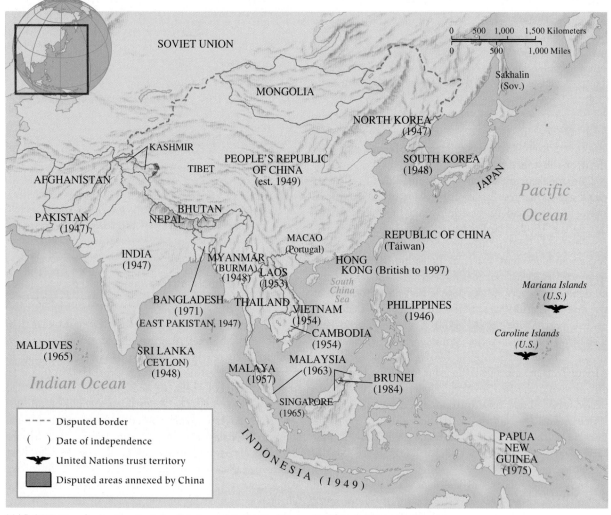

MAP 28.3 Decolonization in Asia. Britain and the United States facilitated relatively peaceful transitions to independence for their possessions in Asia. France fought hard to hold Indochina but left after major military defeats. Cold War tensions in Asia led to both the Korean War and the Vietnam War.

Q What two neighboring countries' presence helps explain why Korea has had difficulty maintaining complete independence throughout much of its history?

Indies, Indonesia emerged as an independent nation in 1949. The French effort to remain in Indochina led to a bloody struggle with the Vietminh (vee-et-MIN), Vietnamese nationalist guerrillas, led by Ho Chi Minh (HOH CHEE MIN) (1890–1969), the Communist and nationalist leader of the Vietnamese. After their defeat in 1954, the French granted independence to Laos and Cambodia, and Vietnam was temporarily divided in anticipation of elections in 1956 that would decide its fate. But the elections were never held, and the division of Vietnam into Communist and pro-Western regimes eventually led to the Vietnam War (see Chapter 29).

CHINA UNDER COMMUNISM At the end of World War II, two Chinese governments existed side by side. The Nationalist government of Chiang Kai-shek (1887–1975), based in southern and central China, was supported by the Americans. The Communists, under the leadership of Mao Zedong (1893–1976), had built a strong base in north China. Their People's Liberation Army included nearly a million troops.

When efforts to form a coalition government in 1946 failed, full-scale war between the Nationalists and the Communists broke out. In the countryside, millions of peasants were attracted to the Communists by promises of land, and many joined Mao's army. By 1948, the People's Liberation Army had routed Chiang's government, and Chiang and 2 million of his followers fled to the island of Taiwan, off the coast of mainland China. On October 1, 1949, Mao mounted the rostrum of the Gate of Heavenly Peace in Beijing and made a victory statement to the thousands gathered in the square before him. The Chinese people have stood up, he said, and no one will be able to humiliate us again.

The newly victorious Communist Party, under the leadership of its chairman, Mao, had a long-term goal of building a socialist society. In 1955, the Chinese government collectivized all private farmland and nationalized most industry and commerce. When the collective farms failed to increase food production, Mao began a more radical program, known as the Great Leap Forward, in 1958. Existing collective farms, normally the size of the traditional village, were combined into vast "people's communes," each containing more than thirty thousand people. Mao hoped this program would mobilize the population for a massive effort to speed up economic growth and reach the final stage of communism—the classless society—before the end of the twentieth century. But the Great Leap Forward was a disaster. Bad weather and peasant hatred of the new system combined to drive food production downward. Nevertheless, despite his failures, Mao was not yet ready to abandon his dream of a totally classless society, and in 1966 he launched China on a new forced march toward communism (see Chapter 29).

Recovery and Renewal in Europe

Q FOCUS QUESTION: What were the main developments in the Soviet Union, eastern Europe, and western Europe between 1945 and 1965?

Just a few years after the defeat of Germany and Italy in World War II, economic revival brought renewed growth to European society, although major differences remained between western and eastern Europe.

The Soviet Union: From Stalin to Khrushchev

World War II devastated the Soviet Union. To create a new industrial base, Stalin returned to the method that he had used in the 1930s—the acquisition of development capital from Soviet labor. Working hard for little pay, poor housing, and precious few consumer goods, Soviet laborers were expected to produce articles for export that they themselves could not even afford. The incoming capital from abroad could then be used to purchase machinery and Western technology. The loss of millions of men in the war meant that much of this tremendous workload fell on Soviet women, who performed almost 40 percent of heavy manual labor.

Economic recovery in the Soviet Union was nothing less than spectacular. By 1947, Russian industrial production had attained prewar levels; three years later, it had surpassed them by 40 percent. New power plants, canals, and giant factories were built, and new industrial plants and oil fields were established in Siberia and Soviet Central Asia.

STALIN'S POLICIES Although Stalin's economic policy was successful in promoting growth in heavy industry, primarily for the benefit of the military, consumer goods were scarce. The development of thermonuclear weapons in 1953, MIG fighter planes from 1950 to 1953, and the first space satellite (*Sputnik*) in 1957 may have elevated the Soviet state's reputation as a world power abroad, but domestically the Russian people were short-changed. Heavy industry grew at a rate three times that of personal consumption. Moreover, the housing shortage was acute. A British military attaché in Moscow reported that "all houses, practically without exception, show lights from every window after dark. This seems to indicate that every room is both a living room by day and a bedroom by night. There is no place in overcrowded Moscow for the luxury of eating and sleeping in separate rooms."[5]

When World War II ended in 1945, Stalin had been in power for more than fifteen years. During that time, he had removed all opposition to his rule and remained the undisputed master of the Soviet Union. Stalin's morbid suspicions fueled the constantly increasing repression that was a characteristic of his regime. In 1946, the government decreed that all literary and scientific works must conform to the political needs of the state. Along with this anti-intellectual campaign came political terror. A new series of purges seemed imminent in 1953, but Stalin's death on March 5, 1953, prevented more bloodletting.

KHRUSHCHEV'S RULE A new collective leadership succeeded Stalin until Nikita Khrushchev emerged as the chief Soviet policymaker. Khrushchev ended the system of forced-labor camps, a regular feature of Stalinist Russia. At the Twentieth Congress of the Communist Party in 1956, Khrushchev also condemned Stalin for his "administrative violence, mass repression, and terror."

Once in power, Khrushchev took steps to undo some of the worst features of Stalin's repressive regime. A certain degree of intellectual freedom was now permitted; Khrushchev said that "readers should be given the chance to make their own judgments" regarding the acceptability of controversial literature and that "police measures shouldn't be used."[6] In 1962, he allowed author Alexander Solzhenitsyn (sohl-zhuh-NEET-sin) (1918–2008) to publish his novel *A Day in the Life of Ivan Denisovich*, a grim portrayal of the horrors of Russia's forced-labor camps. Most important, Khrushchev extended the process of **de-Stalinization** by reducing the powers of the secret police and closing some of the Siberian prison camps. Nevertheless, Khrushchev's revelations about Stalin at the Twentieth Congress caused turmoil in Communist ranks everywhere and encouraged a spirit of rebellion in Soviet satellite countries in eastern Europe. Soviet troops reacted by crushing an uprising in Hungary in 1956, and Khrushchev and the Soviet leaders, fearful of further undermining the basic foundations of the regime, downplayed their campaign of de-Stalinization.

Economically, Khrushchev tried to place more emphasis on light industry and consumer goods. His attempts to increase agricultural output by cultivating vast lands east of the Ural Mountains proved less successful and damaged his reputation within the party. These failures, combined with increased military spending, hurt the Soviet economy. The annual rate of industrial growth, which had soared in the early 1950s, now declined dramatically from 13 percent in 1953 to 7.5 percent in 1964.

Khrushchev's personality also did not endear him to the higher Soviet officials, who frowned at his tendency to crack jokes and play the clown. Foreign policy failures caused additional damage to Khrushchev's reputation among his colleagues. His rash plan to place missiles in Cuba was the final straw. While he was on vacation in 1964, a special meeting of the Soviet Politburo voted him out

Ralph Crane/Time Life Pictures/Getty Images

Khrushchev's Visit to Yugoslavia. The leadership of Nikita Khrushchev appeared for a while to open the door to more flexible Soviet policies. In 1955, he visited Yugoslavia in an attempt to improve relations with a Communist state that had deviated from Soviet policies. Khrushchev is shown here making a conciliatory speech with Marshal Tito, the leader of Yugoslavia, looking on.

of office (because of "deteriorating health") and forced him into retirement. Although a group of leaders succeeded him, real power came into the hands of Leonid Brezhnev (lee-oh-NYEET BREZH-neff) (1906–1982), the "trusted" supporter of Khrushchev who had engineered his downfall.

Eastern Europe: Behind the Iron Curtain

At the end of World War II, Soviet military forces remained in all the lands they had liberated from the Nazis in eastern Europe and the Balkans except Greece, Albania, and Yugoslavia. All of the occupied states came to be part of the Soviet sphere of influence and, after 1945, experienced similar political developments. Between 1945 and 1947, one-party Communist governments became firmly entrenched in East Germany, Bulgaria, Romania, Poland, and Hungary. In Czechoslovakia, where there was a strong tradition of democratic institutions, the Communists did not achieve their goals until 1948 when all other parties were dissolved and Klement Gottwald (KLEM-ent GUT-vald) (1896–1953), the leader of the Communists, became the country's new president.

Albania and Yugoslavia were exceptions to this progression of Soviet dominance in eastern Europe. Both had had strong Communist resistance movements during the war, and in both countries, the Communist Party simply assumed power when the war ended. In Albania, local Communists established a rigidly Stalinist regime that grew increasingly independent of the Soviet Union.

In Yugoslavia, Josip Broz (yaw-SEEP BRAWZ), known as Tito (TEE-toh) (1892–1980), the leader of the Communist resistance movement, seemed to be a loyal Stalinist. After the war, however, he moved toward the establishment of an independent Communist state in Yugoslavia. In 1958, the Yugoslav party congress asserted that Yugoslav Communists would pursue a more decentralized economic and political system in which workers could manage themselves and local communes could exercise some political power.

Between 1948 and Stalin's death in 1953, the eastern European satellite states followed a policy of **Stalinization**. They instituted Soviet-type five-year plans with an emphasis on heavy industry rather than consumer goods. They began to collectivize agriculture. They established the institutions of repression—secret police and military forces. But communism—a foreign import—had not developed deep roots among the peoples of eastern Europe. Moreover, Soviet economic exploitation of eastern Europe resulted in harsh living conditions for most people.

1956: UPHEAVAL IN EASTERN EUROPE   After Stalin's death, many eastern European states began to pursue a more nationalistically oriented course while the new Soviet leaders, including Khrushchev, interfered less in the internal affairs of the satellites. But in the late 1950s, the Soviet Union also made it clear, particularly in Poland and Hungary, that it would not allow its eastern European satellites to become independent of Soviet control.

In 1956, worker protests erupted in Poland. In response, the Polish Communist Party adopted a series of reforms in October and elected Wladyslaw Gomulka (vlah-DIS-lahf goh-MOOL-kuh) (1905–1982) as first secretary. Gomulka declared that Poland had the right to follow its own socialist path. Fearful of Soviet armed response, however, the Poles compromised. Poland pledged to remain loyal to the Warsaw Pact, and the Soviets agreed to allow Poland to follow its own path to socialism.

The developments in Poland in 1956 inspired national Communists in Hungary to seek the same kinds of reforms and independence. Intense debates eventually resulted in the ouster of the ruling Stalinist and the selection of Imre Nagy (IM-ray NAHJ) (1896–1958) as the new Hungarian leader. Internal dissent, however, was not directed simply against the Soviets but against communism in general, which was viewed as a creation of the Soviets, not the Hungarians. The Stalinist secret police had also bred much terror and hatred. This dissatisfaction, combined with economic difficulties, created a situation ripe for revolt. To quell the rising rebellion, Nagy declared Hungary a free nation on November 1, 1956. He promised free elections, and the mood of the country made it clear that this could mean the end of Communist rule in Hungary. But Khrushchev was in no position at home to allow a member of the Communist flock to leave. Just three days after Nagy's declaration, the Red Army attacked Budapest. The Soviets re-established control over the country while János Kádár (YAH-nush KAH-dahr) (1912–1989), a reform-minded cabinet minister, replaced Nagy. By collaborating with the Soviet invaders, Kádár saved many of Nagy's economic reforms. The developments in Poland and Hungary in 1956 discouraged any similar upheavals elsewhere in eastern Europe.

Western Europe: The Revival of Democracy and the Economy

Western European countries recovered relatively rapidly from the devastation of World War II. The Marshall Plan played a significant role in this process. Between 1947 and 1950, European countries received $9.4 billion to be used for new equipment and raw materials. By 1950, industrial output in Europe was 30 percent above prewar levels. And this economic recovery continued well into the 1950s and 1960s, which saw dramatic economic growth and prosperity in western Europe. Indeed, western Europe experienced virtually full employment during these decades.

FRANCE: THE DOMINATION OF DE GAULLE The history of France for nearly a quarter century after the war was dominated by one man—Charles de Gaulle (1890–1970)—who possessed an unshakable faith that he had a historic mission to re-establish the greatness of the French nation. De Gaulle had played an important role in ensuring the establishment of a French provisional government after the war. The declaration of the Fourth Republic, with a return to a parliamentary system based on parties that de Gaulle considered weak, led him to withdraw from politics. Eventually, he formed the French Popular Movement, a decidedly rightist organization, which called for an even stronger presidency, a goal that de Gaulle finally achieved in 1958.

The fragile political stability of the Fourth Republic had been badly shaken by the Algerian crisis. The French army had suffered defeat in Indochina in 1954 and was determined to resist Algerian demands for independence. But a strong antiwar movement among French intellectuals and church leaders led to bitter divisions within France that opened the door to the possibility of civil war. The panic-stricken leaders of the Fourth Republic offered to let de Gaulle take over the government and revise the constitution.

In 1958, de Gaulle immediately drafted a new constitution for the Fifth Republic that greatly enhanced the power of the office of president, who now had the right to choose the prime minister, dissolve parliament, and supervise both defense and foreign policy. As the new president, de Gaulle sought to return France to the position of a Great Power. He believed that playing a pivotal role in the Cold War might enhance France's stature. For that reason, he pulled France out of the NATO high command. With an eye toward achieving the status of a world power, de Gaulle invested heavily in the nuclear arms race. France exploded its first nuclear bomb in 1960. Despite his successes, de Gaulle did not really achieve his ambitious goals of world power. Although his successors maintained that France was the "third nuclear power" after the United States and the Soviet Union, in truth France was too small for such global ambitions.

Although the cost of the nuclear program increased the defense budget, de Gaulle did not neglect the French economy. Economic decision making was centralized. Between 1958 and 1968, the French gross domestic product experienced an annual increase of 5.5 percent, greater than that of the United States. By the end of de Gaulle's era, France was a major industrial producer and exporter, particularly in such areas as automobiles and armaments. Nevertheless, problems remained. The nationalization (government ownership) of traditional industries, such as coal, steel, and railroads, led to large government deficits. The cost of living increased faster in France than in the rest of Europe. Consumer prices were 45 percent higher in 1968 than they had been ten years earlier.

Increased dissatisfaction with the inability of de Gaulle's government to deal with these problems soon led to more violent action. In May 1968, a series of student protests, followed by a general strike by the labor unions, shook the government. Although de Gaulle managed to restore order, the events of May 1968 had seriously undermined the French people's respect for their aloof and imperious president. Tired and discouraged, de Gaulle resigned from office in April 1969 and died within a year.

WEST GERMANY: A NATION REBORN As a result of the pressures of the Cold War, the unification of the three western zones into the Federal Republic of Germany became a reality in 1949. Konrad Adenauer (AD-uh-now-ur) (1876–1967), the leader of the Christian Democratic Union (CDU) who served as chancellor from 1949 to 1963, became the "founding hero" of the

Federal Republic. Adenauer sought respect for West Germany by cooperating with the United States and the other western European nations. He was especially desirous of reconciliation with France—Germany's long-time enemy. The beginning of the Korean War in June 1950 had unexpected repercussions for West Germany. The fear that South Korea might fall to the Communist forces of the North caused many Germans and Westerners to worry about the security of West Germany and led to calls for the rearmament of West Germany. Although many people, concerned about a revival of German militarism, condemned this proposal, Cold War tensions were decisive. West Germany rearmed in 1955 and became a member of NATO.

Adenauer's chancellorship saw the resurrection of the West German economy, often referred to as the "economic miracle." It was largely guided by the minister of finance, Ludwig Erhard (LOOD-vik AYR-hart) (1897–1977). Although West Germany had only 75 percent of the population and 52 percent of the territory of prewar Germany, by 1955 the West German gross domestic product exceeded that of prewar Germany. Real wages doubled between 1950 and 1965 even though work hours were cut by 20 percent. Unemployment fell from 8 percent in 1950 to 0.4 percent in 1965. To maintain its economic expansion, West Germany even imported hundreds of thousands of **guest workers**, primarily from Italy, Spain, Greece, Turkey, and Yugoslavia.

Throughout its postwar existence, West Germany was troubled by its Nazi past. The surviving major Nazi leaders had been tried and condemned as war criminals at war crimes trials held in Nuremberg in 1945 and 1946. As part of the denazification of Germany, the victorious Allies continued war crimes trials of lesser officials, but these diminished as the Cold War brought about a shift in attitudes. It was not until the 1960s, however, that Germans began to address the Nazi past more publicly by including the history of Nazism as part of the school curriculum (see the box on p. 706).

Adenauer resigned in 1963, after fourteen years of firmly guiding West Germany through its postwar recovery. Adenauer had wanted no grand experimentation at home or abroad; he was content to give Germany time to regain its equilibrium. Ludwig Erhard succeeded Adenauer and largely continued his policies. But an economic downturn in the mid-1960s opened the door to the rise of the Social Democrats, and in 1969 they became the leading party.

GREAT BRITAIN: THE WELFARE STATE The end of World War II left Britain with massive economic problems. In elections held immediately after the war, the Labour Party overwhelmingly defeated Churchill's Conservative Party. Labour had promised far-reaching reforms, particularly in the area of social welfare, and in a country with a tremendous shortage of consumer goods and housing, its platform was quite appealing. The new Labour government, with Clement Atlee (1883–1967) as prime minister, proceeded to enact reforms that created a modern **welfare state**.

The establishment of the British welfare state began with the nationalization of the Bank of England, the coal and steel industries, public transportation, and public utilities, such as electricity and gas. In the area of social welfare, the new government enacted the National Insurance Act and the National Health Service Act in 1946. The insurance act established a comprehensive social security program and nationalized medical insurance, thereby enabling the state to subsidize the unemployed, the sick, and the aged. The health act created a system of **socialized medicine** that forced doctors and dentists to work with state hospitals, although private practices could be maintained. This measure was especially costly for the state, but within a few years, 90 percent of medical professionals were

The British Welfare State: Free Milk at School. The creation of the welfare state was a prominent social development in postwar Europe. The desire to improve the health of children led to welfare programs that provided free food for young people. Pictured here are boys at a grammar school in England during a free milk break.

© Sally & Richard Greenhill/Alamy

The Burden of Guilt

In the years after World War II, West Germany focused primarily on rebuilding the country. Beginning in the 1960s, German educators started teaching Germany's Nazi past in schools. This selection is from *The Burden of Guilt: A Short History of Germany, 1914–1945*, published in 1961. The book was written by Hannah Vogt, a civil servant, and was widely used in secondary schools.

Hannah Vogt, *The Burden of Guilt*

A nation is made up of individuals whose ideas—right or wrong—determine their actions, their decisions, and their common life, and for this reason a nation, too, can look back at its history and learn from it. As Germans, we should not find it too difficult to understand the meaning of the fourteen years of the Weimar Republic and the twelve years of the Hitler regime....

We have paid dearly once before for the folly of believing that democracy, being an ideal political arrangement, must function automatically while the citizens sit in their parlors berating it, or worrying about their money. Everybody must share in the responsibility and must be prepared to make sacrifices....

Only if the citizens are thoroughly imbued with democratic attitudes can we put into practice those principles of political life which were achieved through centuries of experience.... The first such principle is the need for a continuous and vigilant control of power. For this, we need not only a free and courageous press but also some mechanism for shaping a vital political opinion in associations, parties, and other organizations. Equally necessary are clearly drawn lines of political responsibility, and a strong and respected political opposition....

More than anything else we must base our concept of law on the idea of justice. We have had the sad experience that the principle "the law is the law" does not suffice, if the laws are being abused to cover up for crimes and to wrap injustices in a tissue of legality. Our actions must once again be guided by that idea which is the basic of a just life: no man must be used as a means to an end....

Thus we are now faced with the difficult task of regaining, by peaceful means, the German unity that Hitler has gambled away. We must strive for it tirelessly, even though it may take decades. At the same time, we must establish a new relationship, based on trust, with the peoples of Europe and the nations of the world....

We owe it to ourselves to examine our consciences sincerely and to face the naked truth, instead of minimizing it or glossing over it. This is also the only way we can regain respect in the world. Covering up or minimizing crimes will suggest that we secretly approve of them. Who will believe that we want to respect all that is human if we treat the death of nearly six million Jews as a "small error" to be forgotten after a few years?

Q What does Vogt think is necessary for citizens to remain free? What lessons does she think Germans should learn from the Nazi era?

Source: From Hannah Vogt, *The Burden of Guilt*, translated by Herbert Strauss (Oxford University Press, 1964), pp. 283–286.

participating. The British welfare state became the model for most European states after the war.

The cost of building a welfare state at home forced the British to reduce expenses abroad. This meant the dismantling of the British Empire and the reduction of military aid to such countries as Greece and Turkey. It was not a belief in the morality of self-determination but economic necessity that brought an end to the British Empire.

Continuing economic problems brought the Conservatives back into power from 1951 to 1964. Although they favored private enterprise, the Conservatives accepted the welfare state and even extended it when they undertook an ambitious construction program to improve British housing. Although the British economy had recovered from the war, it had done so at a slower rate than other European countries. Moreover, the slow rate of recovery masked a long-term economic decline caused by a variety of factors. The demands of British trade unions for wages that rose faster than productivity were a problem in the 1950s and 1960s. The unwillingness of the British to invest in modern industrial machinery and to adopt new methods also did not help. Underlying the immediate problems, however, was a deeper issue. As a result of World War II, Britain had lost much of its prewar revenue from abroad but was left with a burden of debt from its many international commitments. At the same time, with the rise of the United States and the Soviet Union, Britain's ability to play the role of a world power had declined substantially.

Western Europe: The Move Toward Unity

As we have seen, the divisions created by the Cold War led the nations of western Europe to form the North Atlantic Treaty Organization in 1949. But the destructiveness of two world wars caused many thoughtful Europeans to consider the need for some form of European unity beyond the military. National feeling was still too powerful for European nations to give up their political sovereignty, so the desire for a sense of solidarity came to focus primarily on the economic arena.

In 1951, France, West Germany, the Benelux countries (Belgium, the Netherlands, and Luxembourg), and Italy formed the European Coal and Steel Community (ECSC). Its purpose was to create a common market for coal and steel products among the six nations by eliminating tariffs and other trade barriers. Freer trade curtailed the power of monopolies and cartels and encouraged participating counties to concentrate on the production of goods in which they had a comparative advantage. The success of the ECSC encouraged its members to proceed further, and in 1957 they signed the Treaty of Rome, which created the European Economic Community (EEC), also known as the Common Market. The EEC eliminated customs barriers for the six member nations and created a large free-trade area protected from the rest of the world by a common external tariff. By promoting free trade, the EEC also encouraged cooperation and standardization in many aspects of the six nations' economies. All the member nations benefited economically. With a total population of 165 million, the EEC became the world's largest exporter and purchaser of raw materials. Only the United States surpassed the EEC in steel production.

The United States and Canada: A New Era

Q Focus Question: What were the main political developments in North America between 1945 and 1965?

At the end of World War II, the United States emerged as one of the world's two superpowers. As the Cold War with the Soviet Union intensified, the United States worked hard to prevent the spread of communism throughout the world. American domestic political life after 1945 was played out against a background of U.S. military power abroad.

European Economic Community, 1957

American Politics and Society in the 1950s

Between 1945 and 1970, the ideals of Franklin Roosevelt's New Deal largely determined the patterns of American domestic politics. The New Deal had brought basic changes to American society, including a dramatic increase in the role and power of the federal government, the rise of organized labor as a significant force in the economy and politics, the beginning of a welfare state, and a grudging realization of the need to deal fairly with the concerns of minorities.

The New Deal tradition in American politics was bolstered by the election of Democratic presidents—Harry Truman in 1948, John Kennedy in

1960, and Lyndon Johnson in 1964. Even the election of a Republican president, Dwight Eisenhower, in 1952 and 1956 did not change the basic direction of the New Deal. As Eisenhower stated, "Should any political party attempt to abolish Social Security and eliminate labor laws and farm programs, you would not hear of that party again in our political history."

The economic boom after World War II fueled confidence in the American way of life. A shortage of consumer goods during the war left Americans with both extra income and the desire to buy those goods after the war. Then, too, the growth of labor unions brought higher wages and gave more and more workers the ability to buy consumer goods. After 1945, real wages grew an average of 3 percent a year, the most prolonged advance in American history.

Prosperity was not the only characteristic of the early 1950s. Cold War confrontations abroad had repercussions at home. The takeover of China by Mao Zedong's Communist forces in 1949 and Communist North Korea's invasion of South Korea in 1950 aroused fear that Communists had infiltrated America. President Truman's attorney general warned that Communists "are everywhere—in factories, offices, butcher stores, on street corners, in private businesses. And each carried in himself the germ of death for society." A demagogic senator from Wisconsin, Joseph R. McCarthy, helped intensify a massive "Red Scare" with his exposés of supposed Communists in high government positions. McCarthy went too far when he attacked alleged "Communist conspirators" in the U.S. Army and was censured by Congress in 1954. Very quickly, his anti-Communist crusade came to an end.

An Age of Upheaval: America in the 1960s

During the 1960s, the United States experienced a period of upheaval that brought to the fore problems that had been glossed over in the 1950s. The 1960s began on a youthful and optimistic note. At age forty-three, John F. Kennedy became the youngest elected president in the history of the United States. His own administration, cut short by an assassin's bullet on November 22, 1963, focused primarily on foreign affairs. Kennedy's successor, Lyndon B. Johnson, who won a new term as president in a landslide in 1964, used his stunning mandate to pursue what he called the Great Society, the heir to the welfare state first begun in the New Deal. Johnson's programs included health care for the elderly, a "war on poverty" to be fought with food stamps and a "job corps," a new Department of Housing and Urban Development to deal with the problems of the cities, and federal assistance for education.

THE CIVIL RIGHTS MOVEMENT Johnson's other domestic passion was equal rights for African Americans. The civil rights movement had its beginnings in 1954 when the United States Supreme Court took the dramatic step of striking down the practice of racially segregating public schools. The eloquent Martin Luther King, Jr. (1929–1968) became the leader of a growing movement for racial equality, and by the early 1960s, a number of groups, including King's Southern Christian Leadership Conference (SCLC), were organizing sit-ins and demonstrations across the South to end racial segregation. In August 1963, King led the March on Washington for Jobs and Freedom to dramatize black Americans' desire for equal treatment under the law. This march and King's impassioned plea for racial equality had an electrifying effect on the American people.

President Johnson took up the cause of civil rights. As a result of his initiative, Congress passed the Civil Rights Act of 1964, which created the machinery to end segregation and discrimination in the workplace and all public places. A voting rights act the following year made it easier for nonwhites to vote in southern states. But laws alone could not guarantee the Great Society, and Johnson soon faced bitter social unrest, both from African Americans and from the burgeoning movement opposing the Vietnam War.

African Americans had officially had voting rights for many years, but local patterns of segregation led to higher unemployment rates for blacks than for whites and left African Americans segregated in urban ghettos. In these ghettos, the calls for action by radical black leaders, such as Malcolm X (1925–1965) of the Black Muslims, attracted more attention than the nonviolent appeals of Martin Luther King. In the summer of 1965, race riots broke out in the Watts district of Los Angeles. Thirty-four people died and more than a thousand buildings were destroyed. Cleveland, San Francisco, Chicago, Newark, and Detroit exploded in the summers of 1966 and 1967. The riots led to a "white backlash" and a severe division of the American population.

The Development of Canada

Canada experienced many of the same developments that the United States did in the postwar years. For twenty-five years after World War II, a prosperous

Canada set out on a new path of industrial development. Canada had always had a strong export economy based on its abundant natural resources. Now it developed electronic, aircraft, nuclear, and chemical engineering industries as well on a large scale. Much of the Canadian growth, however, was financed by capital from the United States, which led to American ownership of Canadian businesses. Although many Canadians welcomed the economic growth, others feared American economic domination of Canada.

Canadians also worried about playing a secondary role politically and militarily to the neighboring superpower. Canada agreed to join NATO in 1949 and even sent military forces to fight in Korea the following year. At the same time, to avoid subordination to the United States, Canada actively supported the United Nations. Nevertheless, concerns about the United States did not keep Canada from maintaining a special relationship with its southern neighbor. The North American Air Defense Command (NORAD), formed in 1957, was based on close cooperation between the air forces of the two countries for the defense of North America against missile attack.

After 1945, the Liberal Party continued to dominate Canadian politics until 1957, when John Diefenbaker (1895–1979) achieved a Conservative Party victory. But major economic problems returned the Liberals to power, and under Lester Pearson (1897–1972), they created Canada's welfare state by enacting a national social security system (the Canada Pension Plan) and a national health insurance program.

Postwar Society and Culture in the Western World

Q FOCUS QUESTION: What major changes occurred in Western society and culture between 1945 and 1965?

During the postwar era, Western society and culture witnessed remarkably rapid change. Computers, television, jet planes, contraceptive devices, and new surgical techniques all dramatically and quickly altered the pace and nature of human life. The rapid changes in postwar society, fueled by scientific advances and rapid economic growth, led many to view it as a new society.

The Structure of European Society

The structure of European society was altered after 1945. Especially noticeable were the changes in the middle class. Such traditional middle-class groups as businesspeople and professionals in law, medicine, and the universities were joined by a new group of managers and technicians as large companies and government agencies employed increasing numbers of white-collar supervisory and administrative personnel. Whether in eastern or western Europe, the new managers and experts were very much alike. Everywhere their positions depended on specialized knowledge acquired from some form of higher education. Because their positions usually depended on their skills, they took steps to ensure that their own children would be well educated.

Changes also occurred among the traditional lower classes. Especially noticeable was the dramatic shift of people from rural to urban areas. The number of people engaged in agriculture declined drastically; by the 1950s, the number of farmers throughout most of Europe had dropped by 50 percent. Nor did the size of the industrial working class expand. In West Germany, industrial workers made up 48 percent of the labor force throughout the 1950s and 1960s. Thereafter, the number of industrial workers began to dwindle as the number of white-collar service employees increased. At the same time, a substantial increase in their real wages enabled the working classes to aspire to the consumption patterns of the middle class, leading to what some observers have called the **consumer society**. Buying on the installment plan, introduced in the 1930s, became widespread in the 1950s and gave workers a chance to imitate the middle class by buying televisions, washing machines, refrigerators, vacuum cleaners, stereos, and other appliances. Shopping for everyday commodities, such as food products, also became easier and cheaper with the introduction of supermarkets. Between 1956 and 1961, the number of supermarkets increased dramatically, rising from 1,380 to 30,680 in West Germany. But the most visible symbol of mass consumerism was the automobile. Before World War II, cars were reserved mostly for the European upper classes. In 1948, there were 5 million cars in all of Europe, but by 1957, the number had tripled. By the 1960s, there were almost 45 million cars.

Rising incomes, combined with shorter working hours, created an even greater market for mass leisure activities. Between 1900 and 1960, the workweek was reduced from sixty hours to about forty, and the number of paid holidays increased. All aspects of popular culture—music, sports, media—became commercialized and offered opportunities for leisure activities, including concerts, sporting events, and television viewing.

Another very visible symbol of mass leisure was the growth of tourism. Before World War II, travel for pleasure was largely confined to the upper and middle classes. After the war, the combination of more vacation time, increased prosperity, and the flexibility provided by package tours, with their lower rates and budget-priced rooms, enabled millions to expand their travel possibilities. By the mid-1960s, some 100 million tourists were crossing European boundaries each year.

Women in the Postwar Western World

Despite their enormous contributions to the war effort, women were removed from the workforce at the end of World War II to provide jobs for the soldiers returning home. After the horrors and separations of the war, people seemed willing for a while to return to traditional family life. Female participation in the workforce declined, and birthrates began to rise, creating a "baby boom." This increase in the birthrate did not last, however, and the size of families began to decline by the end of the 1950s. Largely responsible for this decline was the widespread practice of birth control. Invented in the nineteenth century, the condom was already in wide use, but in the 1960s the development of oral contraceptives, known as birth control pills (or simply "the pill"), provided an effective means of birth control that quickly spread to all Western countries.

WOMEN IN THE WORKFORCE The trend toward smaller families contributed to the change in the nature of women's employment in both Europe and the United States as women spent considerably more years not involved in rearing children. The most important development was the increased number of married women in the workforce. At the beginning of the twentieth century, even working-class wives tended to stay at home if they could afford to do so. In the postwar period, this was no longer the case. In the United States, for example, in 1900, married women made up about 15 percent of the female labor force; by 1970, their number had increased to 62 percent. The percentage of married women in the female labor force in Europe showed similar increases.

But the greater number of women in the workforce did not change some old patterns. Working-class women in particular still earned salaries lower than those of men for equal work. In the 1960s, women earned only 60 percent of men's wages in Britain, 50 percent in France, and 63 percent in West Germany.

In addition, women still tended to enter traditionally female jobs. Many European women also still faced the double burden of earning income on the one hand and raising a family and maintaining the household on the other.

SUFFRAGE AND THE SEARCH FOR LIBERATION The participation of women in World Wars I and II helped them achieve one of the major aims of the nineteenth-century feminist movement—the right to vote. After World War I, many governments acknowledged the contributions of women to the war effort by granting them suffrage, although women in France and Italy did not obtain the vote until 1945. After World War II, European women tended to fall back into the traditional roles expected of them, and little was heard of feminist concerns.

A women's liberation movement would arise in the late 1960s (see Chapter 29), but much of the theoretical foundation for the emergence of the postwar women's liberation movement was evident in the earlier work of Simone de Beauvoir (see-MUHN duh boh-VWAR) (1908–1986). Born into a Catholic middle-class family and educated at the Sorbonne in Paris, she supported herself as a teacher and later as a writer. She maintained a lifelong relationship (but not marriage) with the existentialist writer Jean-Paul Sartre (ZHAHNH-POHL SAR-truh) and became actively involved in political causes. De Beauvoir believed that she lived a "liberated" life for a twentieth-century European woman, but for all her freedom, she still came to perceive that as a woman she faced limits that men did not. In 1949, she published her highly influential work, *The Second Sex*, in which she argued that as a result of male-dominated societies, women had been defined by their differences from men and consequently received second-class status. De Beauvoir played an active role in the French women's movement of the 1970s, and her book was a major influence on the feminist movement on both sides of the Atlantic (see the box on p. 711).

Postwar Art

Following the war, so many artists and writers fled to the United States to avoid persecution that the United States became the dominant art world. New York City replaced Paris as the artistic center of the West. The Guggenheim Museum, the Museum of Modern Art, and the Whitney Museum of American Art, together with New York's numerous art galleries, promoted modern art and helped determine artistic tastes

The Voice of the Women's Liberation Movement

Simone de Beauvoir was an important figure in the emergence of the postwar women's liberation movement. This excerpt is taken from her influential book *The Second Sex*, in which she argued that women have been forced into a position subordinate to men.

Simone de Beauvoir, *The Second Sex*

Now, woman has always been man's dependent, if not his slave; the two sexes have never shared the world in equality. And even today woman is heavily handicapped, though her situation is beginning to change. Almost nowhere is her legal status the same as man's and frequently it is much to her disadvantage. Even when her rights are legally recognized in the abstract, long-standing custom prevents their full expression in the mores. In the economic sphere men and women can almost be said to make up two castes; other things being equal, the former hold the better jobs, get higher wages, and have more opportunity for success than their new competitors. In industry and politics men have a great many more positions and they monopolize the most important posts. In addition to all this they enjoy a traditional prestige that the education of children tends in every way to support, for the present enshrines the past—and in the past all history has been made by men. At the present time, when women are beginning to take part in the affairs of the world, it is still a world that belongs to men—they have no doubt of it at all and women have scarcely any. To decline to be the Other, to refuse to be a party to a deal—this would be for women to renounce all the advantages conferred upon them by their alliance with the superior caste. Man-the-sovereign will provide woman-the-liege with material protection and will undertake the moral justification of her existence; thus she can evade at once both economic risk and the metaphysical risk of a liberty in which ends and aims must be contrived without assistance. Indeed, along with the ethical urge of each individual to affirm his subjective existence, there is also the temptation to forgo liberty and become a thing. This is an inauspicious road, for he who takes it—passive, lost, ruined—becomes henceforth the creature of another's will, frustrated in his transcendence and deprived of every value. But it is an easy road; on it one avoids the strain involved in undertaking an authentic existence. When man makes of woman the *Other* he may, then, expect her to manifest deep-seated tendencies toward complicity. Thus woman may fail to lay claim to the status of subject because she lacks definite resources, because she feels the necessary bond that ties her to man regardless of reciprocity, and because she is often very well pleased with her role as the *Other*.

Now, what peculiarly signalizes the situation of woman is that she—a free and autonomous being like all human creatures—nevertheless finds herself living in a world where men compel her to assume the status of the *Other*.

Q What factors or values do you think informed de Beauvoir's implicit call for a new history of women? Why was she outraged by the neglect of women in the Western historical consciousness?

Source: From *The Second Sex* by Simone de Beauvoir, translated by Constance Borde and Sheila Malovany-Chevallier, translation copyright © 2009 by Constance Borde and Sheila Malovany-Chevallier. Introduction copyright © 2010 by Judith Thurman.

throughout much of the world. One of the styles that became synonymous with the emergence of the New York art scene was **Abstract Expressionism**.

Dubbed "action painting" by one critic, Abstract Expressionism was energetic and spontaneous, qualities evident in the enormous canvases of Jackson Pollock (1912–1956). In such works as *Lavender Mist* (1950), paint seems to explode, enveloping the viewer with emotion and movement. Pollock's swirling forms and seemingly chaotic patterns broke all conventions of form and structure. His drip paintings, with their total abstraction, were extremely influential with other artists, and he eventually became a celebrity. Inspired by Native American sand painters, Pollock painted with the canvas on the floor. He explained, "On the floor I am more at ease. I feel nearer, more a part of the painting, since this way I can walk around in, work from four sides and be literally in the painting. When I am in the painting, I am not aware of what I am doing. There is pure harmony."

Jackson Pollock Painting. After World War II, Abstract Expressionism moved to the center of the artistic mainstream. One of its best-known practitioners was the American Jackson Pollock, who achieved his ideal of total abstraction in his drip paintings. He is shown here at work in his Long Island studio. Pollock found it easier to cover his large canvases with exploding patterns of color when he laid them on the floor.

The early 1960s saw the emergence of Pop Art, which took images of popular culture and transformed them into works of fine art. Andy Warhol (1930–1987), who began as an advertising illustrator, was the most famous of the Pop artists. Warhol adapted images from commercial art, such as Campbell's soup cans, and photographs of such celebrities as Marilyn Monroe.

Postwar Literature

In postwar literature, the most significant new trend was called the Theater of the Absurd. Its most famous proponent was the Irishman Samuel Beckett (1906–1990), who lived in France. In Beckett's *Waiting for Godot* (1952), two men wait for the appearance of someone with whom they may or may not have an appointment. No background information on the two men is provided. During the course of the play, the men talk, but nothing seems to happen. The audience is never told if what they see in front of them is real or imagined. Unlike traditional theater, suspense is maintained by having the audience wonder not "What is going to happen next?" but simply "What is happening now?"

The sense of meaninglessness that inspired the Theater of the Absurd also underscored the philosophy of **existentialism** of Albert Camus (ahl-BAYR ka-MOO) (1913–1960) and Jean-Paul Sartre (1905–1980). The central point of the existentialism of Sartre and Camus was the absence of God in the universe. The death of God, though tragic, meant that humans had no preordained destiny and were utterly alone in the universe, with no future and no hope. As Camus expressed it:

> A world that can be explained even with bad reasons is a familiar world. But, on the other hand, in a universe suddenly divested of illusions and lights, man feels an alien, a stranger. His exile is without remedy since he is deprived of the memory of a lost home or the hope of a promised land. This divorce between man and his life, the actor and his setting, is properly the feeling of absurdity.[7]

According to Camus, then, the world was absurd and without meaning; humans, too, are without meaning and purpose. Reduced to despair and depression, humans have but one source of hope—themselves.

The Attempt to Revive Religion

Existentialism was one response to the despair generated by the apparent collapse of civilized values in the twentieth century. The revival of religion was another. Ever since the Enlightenment of the eighteenth century, Christianity and religion had been on the defensive. But a number of religious thinkers and leaders attempted to bring new life to Christianity in the twentieth century.

One expression of this religious revival was the attempt by the Protestant theologian Karl Barth (1886–1968) to infuse traditional Christian teachings with new life. In his numerous writings, Barth attempted to reinterpret the religious insights of the Reformation era for the modern world. To Barth, the sinful and hence imperfect nature of human beings meant that humans could know religious truth not through reason but only through the grace of God.

In the Catholic Church, an attempt at religious renewal came from a charismatic pope. Pope John XXIII (1881–1963) reigned as pope for only a short time (1958–1963) but sparked a dramatic revival of

Catholicism when he summoned the twenty-first ecumenical council of the Catholic Church. Known as Vatican II, the council liberalized a number of Catholic practices. For example, the liturgy of the Mass, the central feature of Catholic worship, was now to be spoken in the vernacular, not in Latin.

But these attempts to redefine Christianity were not necessarily successful in rekindling people's faith. Although many churches experienced an upswing in involvement in the late 1940s and 1950s, no doubt as a response to the war, by the late 1950s and 1960s, attendance was declining in European churches. Even in Italy, regular attendance by members of the Catholic Church fell from 69 percent in 1956 to 48 percent in 1968.

The Explosion of Popular Culture

Since World War II, popular culture has played an increasingly important role in helping Western people define themselves. The history of popular culture is also the history of the economic system that supports it, for this system manufactures, distributes, and sells the images that people consume as part of their culture. As popular culture and its economic support system became increasingly intertwined, industries of leisure emerged. As one historian of popular culture has argued, "Industrial societies turn the provision of leisure into a commercial activity, in which their citizens are sold entertainment, recreation, pleasure, and appearance as commodities that differ from the goods at the drugstore only in the way they are used."[8] Modern popular culture is therefore inextricably tied to the mass consumer society in which it emerged.

POPULAR CULTURE AND THE AMERICANIZATION OF THE WORLD The United States has been the most influential force in shaping popular culture in the West and, to a lesser degree, the rest of the world. Through movies, music, advertising, and television, the United States has spread its particular form of consumerism and the American dream to millions around the world. Already in 1923, the *New York Morning Post* noted that "the film is to America what the flag was once to Britain. By its means Uncle Sam may hope some day . . . to Americanize the world."[9] In movies, television, and music, the impact of American popular culture on the Western world was pervasive.

Motion pictures were the primary vehicle for the diffusion of American popular culture in the years immediately following the war, and they continued to dominate both European and American markets in the next decades. Although developed in the 1930s, television did not become readily available until the late 1940s. By 1954, there were 32 million sets in the United States as television became the centerpiece of middle-class life. In the 1960s, as television spread around the world, American networks sold their products in Europe and the Third World at extraordinarily low prices. The United States also dominated popular music. Jazz, blues, rhythm and blues, and rock-and-roll became the most popular music forms in the Western world—and much of the non-Western world—in the decades after World War II. All of them originated in the United States, and all are rooted in African American musical innovations. As these forms spread to the rest of the world, they inspired local artists, who then transformed the music in their own ways.

Chapter Summary

At the end of a devastating world war, a new kind of conflict erupted in the Western world as two of the victors, the United States and the Soviet Union, emerged as superpowers and began to argue over the political organization of a Europe liberated from Nazi Germany. Europeans, whether they wanted to or not, were forced to become supporters of one side or the other. The Western world was soon divided between supporters of a capitalistic West and adherents of a communist East. In 1949, the North Atlantic Treaty Organization (NATO) was created by the United States, Canada, and ten nations of western Europe as a defensive alliance against Soviet aggression. In 1955, the Soviet Union formed a military alliance with seven eastern European states, and Europe was once again divided into hostile alliance systems.

Western Europe emerged as a new community in the 1950s and the 1960s and staged a remarkable economic recovery. While the western European economy boomed, eastern Europe seemed to stagnate under the control of the Soviet Union. The economic integration of the western European nations began in 1951 with the European Coal and Steel Community and continued in 1957 with the formation of the European Economic Community, also known as the Common Market. Regardless of their economic differences, however, both western and eastern

Europeans were well aware that their future still depended on the conflict between the two superpowers.

A new European society also emerged after World War II. White-collar workers increased in number, and installment plan buying helped create a consumer

society. Rising incomes, combined with shorter working hours, created an ever-greater market for mass leisure activities. The welfare state provided both pensions and health care. Birth control led to smaller families, and more women joined the workforce.

In addition to the Cold War conflict, the postwar era was also characterized by decolonization. After World War II, the colonial empires of the European states were largely dissolved, and the liberated territories of Africa, Asia, and the Middle East emerged as sovereign states. All too soon, these newly independent nations often found themselves caught in the Cold War rivalry between the United States and the Soviet Union. After the United States fought in Korea to prevent the spread of communism, the ideological division that had begun in Europe quickly spread to the rest of the world.

CHAPTER TIMELINE

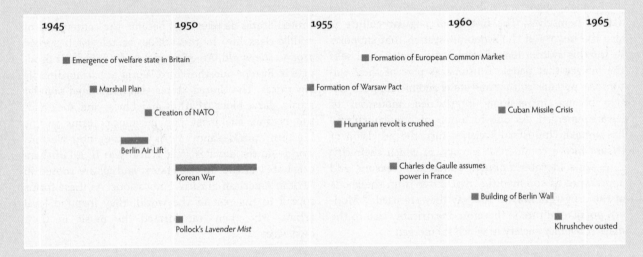

CHAPTER REVIEW

Upon Reflection

Q What were the major turning points in the development of the Cold War through 1965?

Q How did Soviet policies affect the history of eastern Europe between 1945 and 1965?

Q What role did popular culture play in the Western world between 1945 and 1965?

Key Terms

Truman Doctrine (p. 691)
Marshall Plan (p. 691)

containment (p. 691)
mutual deterrence (p. 693)

NATO (p. 693)
Warsaw Pact (p. 693)
rapprochement (p. 695)
decolonization (p. 697)
apartheid (p. 698)
de-Stalinization (p. 702)
Stalinization (p. 703)

guest workers (p. 705)
welfare state (p. 705)
socialized medicine (p. 705)
consumer society (p. 709)
Abstract Expressionism (p. 711)
existentialism (p. 712)

Suggestions for Further Reading

GENERAL WORKS   For a well-written survey on Europe since 1945, see **T. Judt, Postwar: A History of Europe Since 1945** (New York, 2005). See also **W. I. Hitchcock, The Struggle for Europe: The Turbulent History of a Divided Continent, 1945–2002** (New York, 2003).

COLD WAR   There is a detailed literature on the Cold War. A good account is **J. L. Gaddis, The Cold War: A New History** (New York, 2005). On the Berlin Wall and the Cold War in Germany, see **F. Taylor, The Berlin Wall: A World Divided, 1961–1989** (New York, 2006). For a good introduction to the arms race, see **E. M. Bottome, The Balance of Terror: A Guide to the Arms Race**, rev. ed. (Boston, 1986). On the Cuban Missile Crisis, see **D. Munton** and **D. A. Welch, The Real Thirteen Days: A Concise History of the Cuban Missile Crisis** (Oxford, 2006).

DECOLONIZATION   On decolonization after World War II, see **R. F. Betts, Decolonization,** 2d ed. (London, 2004). To put the subject into a broader context, see **D. Newsom, Imperial Mantle: The United States, Decolonization, and the Third World** (Bloomington, Ind., 2001).

SOVIET UNION AND EASTERN EUROPE   On the Khrushchev years, see **W. Taubman, Khrushchev: The Man and His Era** (New York, 2004). For a general study of the Soviet satellites in eastern Europe, see **M. Pittaway, Brief Histories: Eastern Europe, 1945–2000** (London, 2003).

POSTWAR WESTERN EUROPE   The rebuilding of postwar Europe is examined in **D. W. Ellwood, Rebuilding Europe: Western Europe, America, and Postwar Reconstruction** (London, 1992), and **M. A. Schain,** ed., **The Marshall Plan: Fifty Years After** (New York, 2001).

POSTWAR SOCIETY AND CULTURE   On Simone de Beauvoir, see **T. Keefe, Simone de Beauvoir** (New York, 1998). On women and the welfare state, see **R. Cleave et al., Gender and the Welfare State** (New York, 2003). A classic work on existentialism is **W. Barrett, Irrational Man** (Garden City, N.Y., 1962), but see also **T. Flynn, Existentialism: A Very Short History,** 5th ed. (Oxford, 2006). On the arts, see **A. Marwick, Arts in the West Since 1945** (Oxford, 2002).

Notes

1. Quoted in J. M. Jones, *The Fifteen Weeks* (February 21–June 5, 1947), 2d ed. (New York, 1964), pp. 140–141.
2. Quoted in W. Laqueur, *Europe in Our Time* (New York, 1992), p. 111.
3. Quoted in W. I. Hitchcock, *The Struggle for Europe: The Turbulent History of a Divided Continent, 1945–2002* (New York, 2003), p. 215.
4. Quoted in P. Lane, *Europe Since 1945: An Introduction* (Totowa, N.J., 1985), p. 248.
5. R. Hilton, *Military Attaché in Moscow* (London, 1949), p. 41.
6. N. S. Khrushchev, *Khrushchev Remembers*, trans. S. Talbott (Boston, 1970), p. 77.
7. Quoted in H. Grosshans, *The Search for Modern Europe* (Boston, 1970), p. 421.
8. R. Maltby, ed., *Passing Parade: A History of Popular Culture in the Twentieth Century* (New York, 1989), p. 8.
9. Quoted in ibid., p. 11.

MindTap   **MindTap** is a fully online, highly personalized learning experience built upon Cengage Learning content. MindTap combines student learning tools—readings, multimedia, activities, and assessments—into a singular Learning Path that guides students through the course.

Protest and Stagnation: The Western World, 1965–1985

The barricades go up in Paris in May 1968.

© Alain Nogues/Sygma/Corbis

CHAPTER OUTLINE AND FOCUS QUESTIONS

A Culture of Protest

Q What were the goals of the revolt in sexual mores, the youth protests and student revolts, the feminist movement, and the antiwar protests? To what extent were their goals achieved?

A Divided Western World

Q What were the major political developments in the Soviet Union, eastern Europe, western Europe, and the United States between 1965 and 1985?

The Cold War: The Move to Détente

Q What were the main events in the Cold War between 1965 and 1985, and how important was the role of détente in those events?

Society and Culture in the Western World

Q What were the major social and cultural developments in the Western world between 1965 and 1985?

CRITICAL THINKING

Q What are the similarities and differences between the feminist movement of the nineteenth century and the post–World War II feminist movement?

CONNECTIONS TO TODAY

Q During the 1960s, young people in the Western world protested against established political and social structures. What are the grievances of the young people protesting throughout Europe today?

BETWEEN 1945 AND 1965, Europe not only overcame the devastating effects of World War II but actually experienced an economic recovery that seemed nothing less than miraculous to many people. Economic growth and virtually full employment continued so long that the first post–World War II recession in 1973 came as a shock to western Europe.

In 1968, Europe had experienced a different kind of shock. May 1968 is now remembered as a historic month because of a student revolt in Paris. It erupted at the University of Nanterre outside Paris but soon spread to the Sorbonne (sawr-BON *or* sawr-BUHN), the main campus of the University of Paris, where about five hundred students gathered for demonstrations and demanded a greater voice in the administration of the university. The authorities decided to react with force and arrested a number of the demonstrators, although as one police officer said, "To tell the truth, we were not enthusiastic about it if we could avoid it, knowing too well, from experience, that our interventions created more problems than they solved." Indeed, students fought back, prying up paving stones from the streets to use as weapons. On May 3, eighty policemen and about three hundred students were hurt; almost six hundred were arrested. Demonstrations then spread to other universities, which served to embolden the students in Paris. On the night of May 10, barricades, formed by overturning cars, went up in the streets of Paris. When police moved in to tear down the barricades, violence ensued. One eyewitness recounted, "A young girl came rushing out into the street practically naked and was manhandled from one cop to another; then beaten like the other wounded students." Students expanded the scale of their protests by inviting workers to support them. Half of France's workforce went on strike in May 1968. After Charles de Gaulle's government instituted a hefty wage hike, the workers returned to work, and the police repressed the remaining student protesters.

The year 1968 saw widespread student protests around the world, and for a brief moment, students and radicals everywhere believed the time had come for a complete renovation of society and government. But the moment passed, and the Western world was left with the new order created in the twenty years after World War II. In eastern Europe, the crushing of Czechoslovakia in 1968 by Soviet troops left eastern Europeans with little choice but to continue as Soviet satellites. In western Europe, democracies continued to evolve. But everywhere, resignation and stagnation seemed to prevail as the new order established in the Western world during the two decades after World War II appeared to have become permanent: a prosperous, capitalistic West and an impoverished communist East.

A Culture of Protest

Q FOCUS QUESTIONS: What were the goals of the revolt in sexual mores, the youth protests and student revolts, the feminist movement, and the antiwar protests? To what extent were their goals achieved?

In the late 1960s, the Western world was rocked by a variety of protest movements relating to sexual mores, education, and women's rights as well as a strong movement against the Vietnam War (see "The Vietnam War" later in this chapter). Although many of the dreams of the protesters were not immediately realized, the forces they set in motion helped transform Western society.

A Revolt in Sexual Mores

Critics dubbed the society of postwar Europe the **permissive society**. World War I had opened the first significant crack in the rigid code of manners and morals of the nineteenth century. The 1920s had witnessed experimentation with drugs, the appearance of pornography, and a new sexual freedom (police in Berlin, for example, issued cards that permitted female and male homosexual prostitutes to practice their trade). But these indications of a new attitude appeared mostly in major cities and touched only small numbers of people. After World War II, changes in manners and morals were far more extensive and far more noticeable.

Sweden took the lead in the propagation of the so-called sexual revolution of the 1960s. Sex education in the schools and the decriminalization of homosexuality were but two aspects of Sweden's liberal legislation. The rest of Europe and the United States soon followed Sweden's example. A gay rights movement emerged in California in 1969 and had spread to France, Italy, and Britain by 1970.

The introduction of the birth control pill, which became widely available by the mid-1960s, gave people more freedom in sexual behavior. Meanwhile, sexually explicit movies, plays, and books broke new ground in the treatment of once taboo subjects.

The new standards were evident in the breakdown of the traditional family. Divorce rates increased dramatically, especially in the 1960s, and premarital and extramarital sexual experiences also rose substantially. A survey in the Netherlands in 1968 revealed that 78 percent of men and 86 percent of women had engaged in extramarital sex. The appearance of *Playboy* magazine in the 1950s had also already added a new dimension to the sexual revolution for adult males. Along with photographs of nude women, *Playboy* offered well-written articles on various aspects of masculinity. *Playboy*'s message was clear: men were encouraged to seek sexual gratification outside marriage.

Youth Protest and Student Revolt

The decade of the 1960s also saw the emergence of a drug culture. For most college and university students, marijuana was the recreational drug of choice. For young people more interested in mind expansion into higher levels of consciousness, Timothy Leary, who had done psychedelic research at Harvard on the effects of LSD (lysergic acid diethylamide), became the high priest of hallucinogenic experiences.

New attitudes toward sex and the use of drugs were only two manifestations of a growing youth movement in the 1960s that questioned authority and fostered rebellion against the older generation (see Images of Everyday Life on p. 719). Spurred on by opposition to the Vietnam War and a growing political consciousness, the youth rebellion became a full-fledged protest movement by the second half of the 1960s (see the box on p. 720).

Before World War II, higher education had largely remained the preserve of Europe's wealthier classes. After the war, European states began to foster greater equality of opportunity in higher education by reducing or eliminating fees, and universities experienced an influx of students from the middle and lower classes. Enrollments grew dramatically; in France, 4.5 percent of young people attended a university in 1950. By 1965, the figure had increased to 14.5 percent.

But there were problems. Classrooms with too many students, professors who paid little attention to their students, administrators who acted in an authoritarian fashion, and an education that to many seemed irrelevant to the modern age led to an outburst of student revolts in the late 1960s. In part, these protests were an extension of the spontaneous disruptions in American universities in the mid-1960s, which were often sparked by student opposition to the Vietnam War. Perhaps the most famous student revolt occurred in France in 1968, as described in the introduction to this chapter.

The student protest movement reached its high point in 1968, although scattered incidents lasted into the early 1970s. There were several reasons for the student radicalism. Some students were genuinely motivated by the desire to reform the universities. Others were protesting the Vietnam War, which they viewed as a product of Western imperialism. They also attacked other aspects of Western society, such as its materialism, and expressed concern about becoming cogs in the large and impersonal bureaucratic jungles of the modern world. For many students, the calls for democratic decision making within the universities were a reflection of their deeper concerns about the direction of Western society. Although the student revolts fizzled out in the 1970s, the larger issues they raised were revived in the 1990s and early 2000s.

The Feminist Movement

By the late 1960s, women began to assert their rights and speak as feminists. Along with the student upheavals of the late 1960s came renewed interest in **feminism**, or the women's liberation movement, as it was now called. Increasingly, women protested that the acquisition of political and legal equality had not brought true equality with men. In the words of a British "women's liberation workshop" in 1969:

> We are economically oppressed: in jobs we do full work for half pay, in the home we do unpaid work full time. We are commercially exploited by advertisement, television, and the press; legally, we often have only the status of children. We are brought up to feel inadequate, educated to narrower horizons than men. This is our specific oppression as women. It is as women that we are, therefore, organizing.[1]

An important contributor to the growth of the women's movement in the 1960s was Betty Friedan (free-DAN) (1921–2006). A journalist and the mother of three children, Friedan grew increasingly uneasy with her attempt to fulfill the traditional role of the "ideal housewife and mother." In 1963, she published *The Feminine Mystique*, in which she analyzed the problems of middle-class American women in the 1950s and argued that women were being denied equality with men (see the box on p. 721). She wrote, "The problem that has no name—which is simply the fact that American women are kept from growing to their full human capacities—is taking a far greater toll on the physical and mental health of our country than any known disease."[2]

The Feminine Mystique became a bestseller and propelled Friedan into a newfound celebrity. In 1966,

IMAGES OF EVERYDAY LIFE
Youth Culture in the 1960s

PROTEST WAS AN integral part of the youth movement in the 1960s. Young people questioned authority and fostered rebellion in an attempt to change the social thinking of the older generation. The illustration at the bottom left shows a group of young protesters facing the bayonets of National Guardsmen who had been called in by Governor Ronald Reagan to restore order on the Berkeley campus of the University of California during an antiwar rally. The "love-in" at the top left shows another facet of the youth movement. In the 1960s, a number of outdoor public festivals for young people combined music, drugs, and sex. Flamboyant dress, face painting, free-form dancing, and drugs were vital ingredients in creating an atmosphere dedicated to "love and peace." A popular slogan was "Make Love, Not War." Shown here are dozens of hippies dancing around a decorated bus at a "love-in" during the Summer of Love, 1967. Many young people were excited about creating a new culture based on love and community. In the photograph at the bottom right, a member of the Diggers, a communal group in San Francisco, is shown feeding a flower child.

© Henry Diltz/Corbis

© Ted Streshinsky/Corbis

© Ted Streshinsky/Corbis

"The Times They Are A-Changin'": The Music of Youthful Protest

In the 1960s, the lyrics of rock and folk music reflected the rebellious mood of many young people. Bob Dylan (b. 1941) expressed the feelings of the younger generation. His song "The Times They Are A-Changin'," released in 1964, has been called an "anthem for the protest movement."

Bob Dylan, "The Times They Are A-Changin'"

Come gather round people
Wherever you roam
And admit that the waters
Around you have grown
And accept it that soon
You'll be drenched to the bone
If your time to you
Is worth savin
Then you better start swimmin'
Or you'll sink like a stone
For the times they are a-changin'

Come writers and critics
Who prophesize with your pen
And keep your eyes wide
The chance won't come again
And don't speak too soon
For the wheel's still in spin
And there's no tellin' who
That it's namin'
For the loser now
Will be later to win
For the times they are a-changin'

Come senators, congressmen
please heed the call
Don't stand in the doorway
Don't block up the hall

For he that gets hurt
Will be he who has stalled
There's a battle outside
And it is ragin'
It'll soon shake your windows
And rattle your walls
For the times they are a-changin'

Come mothers and fathers
Throughout the land
And don't criticize
What you can't understand
Your sons and your daughters
Are beyond your command
Your old road
Is rapidly agin'
Please get out of the new one
If you can't lend your hand
For the times they are a-changin'

The line it is drawn
The curse it is cast
The slow one now
Will later be fast
As the present now
Will later be past
The order is
Rapidly fadin'
And the first one now
Will later be last
For the times they are a-changin'

Q What caused the student campus revolts of the 1960s? What and whom does Dylan identify in this song as the problem?

she founded the National Organization for Women (NOW), whose stated goal was to take "action to bring women into full participation in the mainstream of American society now, exercising all the privileges and responsibilities thereof in truly equal partnership with men." Friedan's voice was also prominent in calling for an amendment guaranteeing equal rights for women to be added to the U.S. Constitution.

Betty Friedan: The Problem That Has No Name

Betty Friedan, an American journalist, published *The Feminine Mystique* in 1963. The book became a bestseller and made her an influential voice in the women's liberation movement. In this selection, Friedan discusses in detail what she called the "the problem that has no name."

_____

Betty Friedan, *The Feminine Mystique*

The problem lay buried, unspoken, for many years in the minds of American women. It was a strange stirring, a sense of dissatisfaction, a yearning that women suffered in the middle of the twentieth century in the United States. Each suburban wife struggled with it alone. As she made the beds, shopped for groceries, matched slipcover material, ate peanut butter sandwiches with her children, chauffeured Cub Scouts and Brownies, lay beside her husband at night—she was afraid to ask even of herself the silent question—"It this all?"

For over fifteen years there was no word of this yearning in the millions of words written about women, for women, in all the columns, books, and articles by experts telling women their role was to seek fulfillment as wives and mothers. Over and over women heard in voices of tradition and of Freudian sophistication that they could desire no greater destiny than to glory in their own femininity.... They were taught to pity the neurotic, unfeminine, unhappy women who wanted to be poets or physicists, or presidents. They learned that truly feminine women do not want careers, higher education, political rights— the independence and the opportunities that the old-fashioned feminists fought for.... All they had to do was devote their lives from earliest girlhood to finding a husband and bearing children....

Gradually I came to realize that the problem that has no name was shared by countless women in America.... If I am right, the problem that has no name stirring in the minds of so many American women today is not a matter of loss of femininity or too much education, or the demands of domesticity. It is far more important than anyone recognizes. It is the key to these other new and old problems which have been torturing women and their husbands and children, and puzzling their doctors and educators for year. It may well be the key to our future as a nation and a culture. We can no longer ignore that voice within women that says: "I want something more than my husband and my children and my home."

_____

Q According to Friedan, what was the problem that had no name? Why is Friedan such a highly regarded figure in the women's movement?

_____

Antiwar Protests

One of the major issues that mobilized youthful European protesters was the U.S. war in Vietnam, which they viewed as an act of aggression and imperialism. In 1968, demonstrations broke out in universities in Italy, France, and Britain. In London, thirty thousand demonstrators took to the streets protesting America's war in Vietnam. But student protests in Europe also backfired in that they provoked a reaction from people who favored order over the lawlessness of privileged young people. As Pier Paolo Pasolini (PYER PAH-loh pah-SOH-lee-nee) (1922–1975), an Italian poet and intellectual, wrote, "Now all the journalists of the world are licking your arses ... but not me, my dears. You have the faces of spoiled brats, and I hate you, like I hate your fathers.... When yesterday at Valle Giulia [in Rome] you beat up the police, I sympathized with the police because they are the sons of the poor."[3]

Antiwar protests also divided the American people after President Lyndon Johnson sent American troops to war in Vietnam. As the war dragged on and a military draft ensued, protests escalated. Teach-ins, sit-ins, and the occupation of buildings at universities alternated with more radical demonstrations that led to violence. The killing of four student protesters at Kent State University in 1970 by the Ohio National Guard caused a reaction, and the antiwar movement began to decline. By that time, however, antiwar demonstrations had worn down the willingness of many Americans

The Women's Liberation Movement. In the late 1960s, as women began once again to assert their rights, a revived women's liberation movement emerged. Feminists in the movement maintained that women themselves must alter the conditions of their lives. During this women's liberation rally, some women climbed the statue of Admiral Farragut in Washington, D.C., to exhibit their signs.

to continue the war. The combination of antiwar demonstrations and ghetto riots in the cities also heightened the appeal of a call for "law and order," used by Richard Nixon, the Republican presidential candidate in 1968.

A Divided Western World

Q FOCUS QUESTION: What were the major political developments in the Soviet Union, eastern Europe, western Europe, and the United States between 1965 and 1985?

Between 1945 and 1965, economic recovery had brought renewed growth to Europe. Nevertheless, the political divisions between western and eastern Europe remained; so did disparities in prosperity.

Stagnation in the Soviet Union

Between 1964 and 1982, significant change in the Soviet Union seemed highly unlikely. After the overthrow of Khrushchev in 1964, Leonid Brezhnev (1906–1982) had become head of both the Communist Party and the state. He was optimistic but reluctant to reform. The **Brezhnev Doctrine**—the right of the Soviet Union to intervene if socialism was threatened in another socialist state—became an article of faith and led to the use of Soviet troops in Czechoslovakia in 1968.

THE BREZHNEV YEARS Brezhnev benefited from the more relaxed atmosphere associated with **détente** (day-TAHNT) (see "The Cold War: The Move to Détente" later in this chapter). The Soviets had reached a rough parity with the United States in nuclear arms and enjoyed a sense of external security that seemed to allow for a relaxation of authoritarian rule. The regime permitted more access to Western styles of music, dress, and art, although dissenters were still punished.

In his economic policies, Brezhnev continued to emphasize heavy industry. Overall industrial growth declined, although the Soviet production of iron, steel, coal, and cement surpassed that of the United States. Two problems bedeviled the Soviet economy. The government's insistence on vigorous central planning led to a huge, complex bureaucracy that discouraged efficiency and reduced productivity. Moreover, the Soviet system, based on guaranteed employment and a lack of incentives, bred apathy, complacency, absenteeism, and drunkenness. Agricultural problems added to Soviet economic woes. Bad harvests in the mid-1970s, caused by a series of droughts, heavy rains, and early frosts, forced the Soviet government to buy grain from the West, particularly the United States.

By the 1970s, party and state leaders—as well as leaders of the army and the secret police (KGB)—had come to expect numerous privileges. Brezhnev was unwilling to tamper with the party leadership and state bureaucracy despite the inefficiency and corruption the system encouraged. By 1980, the Soviet Union was ailing. A declining economy, a rise in infant mortality rates, a dramatic surge in alcoholism, and a deterioration in working conditions all gave impetus to a decline in morale and a growing perception that the system was foundering. Within the party, a small group of reformers emerged who understood the real condition of the Soviet Union; they included a young visionary, Mikhail Gorbachev (meek-HAYL GOR-buh-chof) (b. 1931), who was climbing the rungs of the party ladder. When party leaders chose Gorbachev as party secretary in March 1985, an astonishing new era began (see Chapter 30).

Conformity in Eastern Europe

As we saw in Chapter 28, the attempt of the Poles and Hungarians to gain their freedom from Soviet domination had been repressed in 1956. This year of discontent had consequences, however. Soviet leaders now recognized that Moscow could maintain control over its satellites in eastern Europe only by granting them leeway to adopt domestic policies appropriate to local conditions. As a result, eastern European Communist leaders now adopted reform programs to make socialism more acceptable to their subject populations.

In Poland, continued worker unrest led to the rise of an independent labor movement called Solidarity. Led by Lech Walesa (LEK vah-WENT-sah) (b. 1943), Solidarity gained the support of the workers, many intellectuals, and the Catholic Church and was able to win a series of concessions. The Polish government seemed powerless to stop the flow of concessions until December 1981, when it arrested Walesa and other Solidarity leaders, outlawed the union, and imposed military rule.

The government of János Kádár (1912–1989) in Hungary enacted the most far-reaching reforms in eastern Europe. In the early 1960s, Kádár legalized small private enterprises, such as retail stores, restaurants, and artisan shops. His economic reforms were termed "communism with a capitalist facelift." Under his leadership, Hungary moved slowly away from its strict adherence to Soviet dominance and even established fairly friendly relations with the West.

THE PRAGUE SPRING Czechoslovakia did not share in the thaw of the mid-1950s and remained under the rule of Antonín Novotný (AHN-toh-nyeen NOH-vahtnee) (1904–1975), who had been placed in power by Stalin himself. By the late 1960s, however, Novotný had alienated many members of his own party and was particularly resented by Czechoslovakia's writers, including the playwright Václav Havel (VAHT-slahf HAH-vul) (1936–2011). A writers' rebellion late in 1967, in fact, led to Novotný's resignation. In January 1968, Alexander Dubček (DOOB-chek) (1921–1992) was elected first secretary of the Communist Party and soon introduced a number of reforms, including freedom of speech and of the press, freedom to travel abroad, and a relaxation of secret police activities. Dubček hoped to create "communism with a human face." A period of euphoria erupted that came to be known as the "Prague Spring" (see the box on p. 724).

Soviet Invasion of Czechoslovakia, 1968. The attempt of Alexander Dubček, the new first secretary of the Communist Party, to liberalize Communist rule in Czechoslovakia failed when Soviet troops invaded and crushed the reform movement. This photograph, taken on August 21, shows Soviet tanks in Wenceslas Square while Prague residents look on.

© CTK/Alamy

OPPOSING VIEWPOINTS

Czechoslovakia, 1968: Two Faces of Communism

In the summer of 1968, a serious rupture began to appear in the Soviet-dominated communist world. Under the guidance of Alexander Dubček, Czechoslovakia appeared poised to take a path that deviated from Soviet communist ideals. The first selection is taken from a manifesto written by a group of Czech communist intellectuals in June 1968. The manifesto became the symbol of the "Prague Spring." The second selection is taken from a letter written in July to the Communist Party of Czechoslovakia by Soviet leader Leonid Brezhnev to justify intervention in Czechoslovakia. In August military forces of several Soviet bloc nations entered Czechoslovakia and imposed a new government. The move was justified by the principle that came to be known as the Brezhnev Doctrine.

Two Thousand Words Manifesto

The first threat to our national life was from the war. Then came other evil days and events that endangered the nation's spiritual well being and character. Most of the nation welcomed the socialist program with high hopes. But it fell into the hands of the wrong people....

After enjoying great popular confidence immediately after the war, the communist party by degrees bartered this confidence away for office, until it had all the offices and nothing else. We feel we must say this, it is familiar to those of us who are communists and who are as disappointed as the rest at the way things turned out. The leaders' mistaken policies transformed a political party and an alliance based on ideas into an organization for exerting power, one that proved highly attractive to power-hungry individuals eager to wield authority.... The influx of members such as these affected the character and behavior of the party, whose internal arrangements made it impossible, short of scandalous incidents, for honest members to gain influence and adapt it continuously to modern conditions. Many communists fought against this decline, but they did not manage to prevent what ensued.

We all bear responsibility for the present state of affairs. But those among us who are communists bear more than others, and those who acted as components or instruments of unchecked power bear the greatest responsibility of all. The power they wielded was that of a self-willed group spreading out through the party apparatus into every district and community. It was this apparatus that decided what might and might not be done....

Since the beginning of this year we have been experiencing a regenerative process of democratization. It started inside the communist party, that much we must admit, even those communists among us who no longer had hopes that anything good could emerge from that quarter know this. It must also be added, of course, that the process could have started nowhere else. For after twenty years the communists were the only ones able to conduct some sort of political activity. It was only the opposition inside the communist party that had the privilege to voice antagonistic views. The effort and initiative now displayed by democratically minded communists are only then a partial repayment of the debt owed by the entire party to the noncommunists whom it had kept down in an unequal position....

In this moment of hope, albeit hope still threatened, we appeal to you. It took several months before many of us believed it was safe to speak up; many of us still do not think it is safe. But speak up we did exposing ourselves to the extent that we have no choice but to complete our plan to humanize the regime. If we did not, the old forces would exact cruel revenge. We appeal above all to those who so far have waited on the sidelines. The time now approaching will decide events for years to come.

A Letter to Czechoslovakia

To the Central Committee of the Communist Party of Czechoslovakia

                                Warsaw, July 15, 1968

Dear comrades!

On behalf of the Central Committees of the Communist and Workers' Parties of Bulgaria, Hungary, the German Democratic Republic, Poland, and the Soviet Union, we address ourselves to you with this letter, prompted by a feeling of sincere friendship based on the principles of Marxism-Leninism and proletarian internationalism and by the concern of our common affairs for strengthening the positions of socialism and the security of the socialist community of nations.

The development of events in your country evokes in us deep anxiety. It is our firm conviction that the offensive of the reactionary forces, backed by imperialists, against your Party and the foundations of the social system in the Czechoslovak Socialist Republic, threatens to push your country off the road of socialism and that consequently it jeopardizes the interests of the entire socialist system....

We neither had nor have any intention of interfering in such affairs as are strictly the internal business of your Party and your state, nor of violating the principles of respect, independence, and equality in the relations among the Communist Parties and socialist countries....

At the same time we cannot agree to have hostile forces push your country from the road of socialism and create a threat of severing Czechoslovakia from the socialist community.... This is the common cause of our countries, which have joined in the Warsaw Treaty to ensure independence, peace, and security in Europe, and to set up an insurmountable barrier against aggression and revenge.... We shall never agree to have imperialism, using peaceful or nonpeaceful methods, making a gap from the inside or from the outside in the socialist system, and changing in imperialism's favor the correlation of forces in Europe....

That is why we believe that a decisive rebuff of the anticommunist forces, and decisive efforts for the preservation of the socialist system in Czechoslovakia are not only your task but ours as well....

We express the conviction that the Communist Party of Czechoslovakia, conscious of its responsibility, will take the necessary steps to block the path of reaction. In this struggle you can count on the solidarity and all-round assistance of the fraternal socialist countries.

Q What communist ideals are expressed in the manifesto? How do those ideals differ from those expressed by Leonid Brezhnev? How do you explain the differences?

Sources: Two Thousand Words Manifesto. From *The Prague Spring* 1968, Jaromir Navratil, 1998. Used with the permission of Central European Press. A Letter to Czechoslovakia. From "A Letter to Czechoslovakia," Moscow News, Supplement to No. 30917 (1968), pp. 3–6.

It proved short-lived. The euphoria had led many to call for more far-reaching reforms, including neutrality and withdrawal from the Soviet bloc. To forestall the spreading of this "spring" fever, the Red Army invaded Czechoslovakia in August 1968 and crushed the reform movement. Gustáv Husák (goo-STAHV HOO-sahk) (1913–1991), a committed nonreformist, replaced Dubček, abolished his reforms, and reestablished the old order.

REPRESSION IN EAST GERMANY AND ROMANIA Elsewhere in eastern Europe, Stalinist policies continued to hold sway. In the early 1950s, the ruling Communist government in East Germany, led by Walter Ulbricht, had consolidated its position and become a faithful Soviet satellite. Industry was nationalized and agriculture collectivized. After Soviet tanks crushed a workers' revolt in 1953, a steady flight of East Germans to West Germany ensued, primarily through the divided city of Berlin. This exodus of mostly skilled laborers led the East German government in 1961 to build the infamous Berlin Wall separating West from East Berlin, as well as equally fearsome barriers along the entire border with West Germany. After building the wall, East Germany succeeded in developing the strongest economy among the Soviet Union's eastern European satellites. In 1971, Ulbricht was succeeded by Erich Honecker (AY-reekh HOH-nek-uh) (1912–1994), a party hardliner who made use of the Stasi (SHTAH-see), the secret police, to rule with an iron fist for the next eighteen years.

Repression was also an important part of Romania's postwar history. By 1948, with Soviet assistance, the Communist People's Democratic Front had assumed complete power in Romania. In 1965, leadership of the Communist government passed into the hands of Nicolae Ceaușescu (nee-koh-LY chow-SHES-koo) (1918–1989), who with his wife, Elena, established a rigid and dictatorial regime. Ceaușescu ruled Romania with an iron grip, using a secret police force—the Securitate— as his personal weapon against dissent.

Western Europe: The Winds of Change

After two decades of incredible economic growth, Europe experienced severe economic recessions in 1973–1974 and 1979–1983. Both inflation and unemployment rose dramatically. A substantial increase in the price of oil in 1973 was a major cause for the first downturn. Moreover, a worldwide recession had led to a decline in demand for European goods. The economies of the western European states recovered in the course of the 1980s, although problems remained.

WEST GERMANY After the Adenauer era, West German voters moved politically from the center-right politics of the Christian Democrats to center-left politics, and in 1969, the Social Democrats became the leading party. The first Social Democratic chancellor was Willy Brandt (VIL-ee BRAHNT) (1913–1992). Brandt was especially successful with his "opening toward the east"—known as Ostpolitik (OHST-paw-li-teek)—for which he received the Nobel Peace Prize in 1972. In that year, Brandt made a treaty with East Germany that called for "good neighborly" relations, which led to greater cultural, personal, and economic contacts between West and East Germany.

Brandt's successor, Helmut Schmidt (HEL-moot SHMIT) (b. 1918), was more of a technocrat than a reform-minded socialist and concentrated primarily on the economic problems largely brought about by high oil prices between 1973 and 1975. Schmidt was successful in eliminating a deficit of 10 billion marks in three years. In 1982, when the coalition of Schmidt's Social Democrats with the Free Democrats fell apart over the reduction of social welfare expenditures, the Free Democrats joined with the Christian Democratic Union of Helmut Kohl (HEL-moot KOHL) (b. 1930) to form a new government.

GREAT BRITAIN: THATCHER AND THATCHERISM Between 1964 and 1979, the Conservative and Labour Parties alternated in power. Neither could solve the problem of fighting between Catholics and Protestants in Northern Ireland. Violence increased as the Irish Republican Army (IRA) staged a series of dramatic terrorist acts in response to the suspension of Northern Ireland's parliament in 1972 and the establishment of direct rule by London. Nor was either party able to deal with Britain's ailing economy. Failure to modernize made British industry less and less competitive. Moreover, Britain was hampered by frequent labor strikes, many of them caused by conflicts between rival labor unions.

In 1979, the Conservatives returned to power under Margaret Thatcher (1925–2013), who became the first woman to serve as prime minister in British history.

Margaret Thatcher. Great Britain's first female prime minister, Margaret Thatcher was a strong leader who dominated British politics in the 1980s. Thatcher is shown here shaking hands with Soviet leader Mikhail Gorbachev in 1984.

Peter Jordan/Time Life Pictures/Getty Images

Thatcher pledged to lower taxes, reduce government bureaucracy, limit social welfare, restrict union power, and end inflation. The "Iron Lady," as she was called (see the Film & History feature on p. 728), did break the power of the labor unions. Although she did not eliminate the basic components of the social welfare system, she did use austerity measures to control inflation. "Thatcherism," as her economic policy was termed, improved the British economic situation, but at a price. The south of England, for example, prospered, but the old industrial areas of the Midlands and north declined and were beset by high unemployment, poverty, and sporadic violence. Cutbacks in education seriously undermined the quality of British education, long regarded as among the world's finest.

In the area of foreign policy, Thatcher, like Ronald Reagan in the United States, took a hard-line approach toward communism. She oversaw a large military buildup aimed at replacing older technology and re-establishing Britain as a world police officer. In 1982, when Argentina attempted to take control of the Falkland Islands (one of Britain's few remaining colonial outposts; known to Argentines as the Malvinas) three hundred miles off its coast, the British successfully rebuffed the Argentines, although at considerable economic cost and the loss of 255 lives.

UNCERTAINTIES IN FRANCE The worsening of France's economic situation in the 1970s brought a shift to the left politically. By 1981, the Socialists had become the dominant party in the National Assembly, and the Socialist leader, François Mitterrand (frahnh-SWAH MEE-tayr-rahnh) (1916–1995), was elected president. His first concern was with France's economic difficulties. In 1982, Mitterrand froze prices and wages in the hope of reducing the huge budget deficit and high inflation. He also passed a number of liberal measures to aid workers: an increased minimum wage, expanded social benefits, a mandatory fifth week of paid vacation for salaried workers, a thirty-nine-hour workweek, and higher taxes on the rich. Mitterrand's administrative reforms included both centralization (nationalization of banks and industry) and decentralization (granting local governments greater powers). The party's victory had convinced the Socialists that they could enact some of their more radical reforms. Consequently, the government nationalized the steel industry, major banks, the space and electronics industries, and important insurance firms.

The Socialist policies largely failed, however, and within three years, a decline in support for the Socialists

caused the Mitterrand government to turn portions of the economy back over to private enterprise. Some economic improvement in the late 1980s enabled Mitterrand to win a second seven-year term in the 1988 presidential elections.

The European Community

After 1970, western European states continued to pursue the goal of integrating their economies. Beginning with six states in 1957, the European Economic Community expanded in 1973 when Great Britain, Ireland, and Denmark joined what its members now renamed the European Community (EC). Greece joined in 1981, followed by Spain and Portugal in 1986. The economic integration of the members of the EC led to cooperative efforts in international and political affairs as well. The foreign ministers of the twelve members consulted frequently and provided a common front in negotiations on important issues.

The United States: Turmoil and Tranquility

With the election of Richard Nixon (1913–1994) as president in 1968, American politics made a shift to the right. Nixon ended American involvement in Vietnam by 1973 by gradually withdrawing American troops. Politically, he pursued a "southern strategy," carefully calculating that "law and order" issues and a slowdown in racial desegregation would appeal to southern whites. The South, which had once been a Democratic stronghold, began to form a new allegiance to the Republican Party.

As president, Nixon was paranoid about conspiracies and began to use illegal methods to gather intelligence on his political opponents. One of the president's advisers explained that their intention was to "use the

CHRONOLOGY Western Europe, 1965–1985	
Willy Brandt becomes chancellor of West Germany	1969
Helmut Schmidt becomes chancellor of West Germany	1974
Margaret Thatcher becomes prime minister of Britain	1979
François Mitterrand becomes president of France	1981
Falklands War	1982
Helmut Kohl becomes chancellor of West Germany	1982

FILM & HISTORY

The Iron Lady (2011)

THE IRON LADY, directed by Phillida Lloyd, is a film based on the life of Margaret Thatcher, the first and only female British prime minister. In power from 1979 to 1990, she was also Britain's longest-serving prime minister. Much of the film focuses on Thatcher's later years, when she suffered from dementia. The film shows Thatcher (Meryl Streep) talking regularly to her recently deceased husband Denis (Jim Broadbent), as if he were still alive. Thatcher's early life and career as prime minister are depicted through flashbacks.

The Iron Lady is strong on presenting Thatcher's personality but weak on historical events. The film offers little to explain her development as a strongly principled conservative, other than that she was influenced by her father's conservative values as a small shopowner. She is also portrayed as a potential feminist, who sought to break away from the traditional female roles of wife and mother. As she so aptly informs her husband-to-be in the film when he proposes marriage, she will not be a "domestic woman, silent and pretty" because she wants to "live a life that matters."

Thatcher was a divisive figure in British politics; she was loved and hated in equal measure for her policies and actions. Unfortunately, the film touches only briefly on some of the most important events in her career as prime minister: her fight for the leadership of the Conservative Party, reform of the labor unions, privatization of state-owned industries, military intervention in the Falkland Islands, and reduction in social welfare benefits. All of these deserve more time in a film about Thatcher's life.

The strength of the film is the performance by Meryl Streep, who won her third Academy Award for Best Actress. Streep prepared diligently for her role, watching films of Thatcher, talking to people who knew her, and attending sessions in Parliament to obtain background. In many ways, Streep's performance captures much of the essence of Thatcher as a person. Clearly portrayed is her ideological rigidity; Thatcher believed firmly in her principles and that she was always right: "I do what I know to be right," she says in the film. She reveled in her toughness in dealing with any situation. On the use of British forces to recapture the Falklands from Argentina she says, "I will not negotiate with thugs. We must stand on principle. Right will triumph over wrong." Despite the reservations of her advisers, Thatcher is shown being adamant about imposing a poll tax: "You haven't got the courage to fight; you are cowards." As Streep portrays her, however, Thatcher's lack of flexibility and her conviction that she was always right turned to arrogance and led to her downfall. When members of her party turned against her over the poll tax, she had no choice but to resign as prime minister.

Prime Minister Margaret Thatcher (Meryl Streep) at a cabinet meeting.

available federal machinery to screw our political enemies." Nixon's zeal led to the Watergate scandal—the attempted bugging of Democratic National Headquarters, located in the Watergate apartment and hotel complex in Washington, D.C. Although Nixon repeatedly lied to the American public about his involvement in the affair, secret tapes of his own conversations in the White House revealed the truth. On August 9, 1974, Nixon resigned the presidency rather than face possible impeachment and then trial by the U.S. Congress.

ECONOMIC PROBLEMS After Watergate, American domestic politics focused on economic issues. Vice President Gerald Ford (1913–2006) became president when Nixon resigned, only to lose in the 1976 election to the former governor of Georgia, Jimmy Carter (b. 1924). Both Ford and Carter faced severe economic problems. The period from 1973 to the mid-1980s was one of economic stagnation, which came to be known as **stagflation**—a combination of high inflation and high unemployment. In part, the economic downturn stemmed from a dramatic change in oil prices. An oil embargo and price increases by the Organization of Petroleum Exporting Countries (OPEC) cartel in the aftermath of the Arab-Israeli War in 1973 quadrupled oil prices. Additional price hikes increased oil prices twentyfold by the end of the 1970s, encouraging inflationary tendencies throughout the economy.

By 1980, the Carter administration faced two devastating problems. High inflation and a noticeable decline in average weekly earnings were causing a drop in American living standards. At the same time, a crisis abroad had erupted when fifty-three Americans were taken hostage by the Iranian government of Ayatollah Khomeini (khoh-MAY-nee). Carter's inability to gain the release of the hostages led to perceptions at home that he was a weak president. His overwhelming loss to Ronald Reagan (1911–2004) in the election of 1980 enabled the chief exponent of right-wing Republican policies to assume the presidency and initiate a new political order.

THE REAGAN REVOLUTION The Reagan Revolution, as it has been called, consisted of a number of new policies. Reversing decades of increased spending on social welfare, Reagan cut back on the welfare state by reducing spending on food stamps, school lunch programs, and job programs. At the same time, his administration fostered the largest peacetime military buildup in American history. Total federal spending rose from $631 billion in 1981 to more than $1 trillion by 1986. But instead of raising taxes to pay for the new expenditures, which far outweighed the budget cuts in social areas, Reagan convinced Congress to rely on "supply-side economics." Massive tax cuts would supposedly stimulate rapid economic growth and produce new revenues. Much of the tax cut went to the wealthy. Reagan's policies seemed to work in the short run as the United States experienced an economic upturn that lasted until the end of the 1980s. The spending policies of the Reagan administration, however, also produced record government deficits, which loomed as an obstacle to long-term growth. In 1980, the total government debt was around $930 billion. By 1988, the total debt had almost tripled, reaching $2.6 trillion.

Canada

In 1963, during a major economic recession, the Liberals had been returned to power in Canada. The most prominent Liberal government was that of Pierre Trudeau (PYAYR troo-DOH) (1919–2000), who came to power in 1968. Although French Canadian in background, Trudeau was dedicated to Canada's federal union, and in 1968, his government passed the Official Languages Act that allowed both English and French to be used in the federal civil service. Although Trudeau's government vigorously pushed an industrialization program, high inflation and Trudeau's efforts to impose the will of the federal government on the powerful provincial governments alienated voters and undermined his popularity. Economic recession in the early 1980s brought Brian Mulroney (b. 1939), leader of the Progressive Conservative Party, to power in 1984.

The Cold War: The Move to Détente

Q FOCUS QUESTION: What were the main events in the Cold War between 1965 and 1985, and how important was the role of détente in those events?

The Cuban Missile Crisis (described in Chapter 28) led to a lessening of tensions between the United States and the Soviet Union. But within another year, the United States had been drawn into a new confrontation that had an important impact on the Cold War: the war in Vietnam.

The Vietnam War

In 1964, under President Lyndon B. Johnson (1908–1973), increasing numbers of U.S. troops were sent to Vietnam to keep the Communist regime of the north from uniting the entire country under its control. Although nationalism played a powerful role in this conflict, American policymakers saw it in terms of a **domino theory** concerning the spread of communism. If the Communists succeeded in Vietnam, the argument went, all the other countries in Asia freeing themselves from colonial domination would fall, like dominoes, to communism.

Southeast Asia at the Time of the Vietnam War

Despite their massive superiority in equipment and firepower, U.S. forces failed to prevail over the persistence of the North Vietnamese and especially the Vietcong. These guerrilla forces were extremely effective against U.S. troops. Natives of Vietnam, they were able to live off the land, disappear among the people, and attack when least expected. Many South Vietnamese villagers were so opposed to their own government that they sheltered and supported the Vietcong.

The mounting destruction and increasing brutalization of the war, brought into American homes every evening on television, also turned American public opinion against the war. Finally, in 1973, President Richard Nixon reached an agreement with North Vietnam that allowed the United States to withdraw its forces. Within two years, Communist armies from the North had forcibly reunited Vietnam. Despite the success of the North Vietnamese Communists, the domino theory proved unfounded. A noisy rupture between Communist China and the Soviet Union put an end to the idea of a monolithic communism directed by Moscow. Under President Nixon, American relations with China were resumed. New nations in Southeast Asia also managed to avoid Communist governments. Above all, Vietnam helped show the limitations of American power. By the end of the Vietnam War, a new era in American-Soviet relations, known as détente, had begun to emerge.

China and the Cold War

The Johnson administration had sent U.S. combat troops to South Vietnam in 1965 in an effort to prevent the expansion of communism in Southeast Asia. The primary concern of the United States, however, was not the Soviet Union but Communist China. By the mid-1960s, U.S. officials viewed the Soviet Union as an essentially conservative power, more concerned with protecting its vast empire than with expanding its borders. Mao Zedong's attempt to create a totally classless society had received much attention, and despite his failures with the Great Leap Forward (see Chapter 28), he now launched China on an even more dramatic forced march toward communism.

THE GREAT PROLETARIAN CULTURAL REVOLUTION Mao was convinced that only an atmosphere of constant revolutionary fervor could enable the Chinese to overcome the past and achieve the final stage of communism. Accordingly, in 1966 he unleashed the Red Guards, revolutionary units composed of unhappy Communist Party members and discontented young people who were urged to take to the streets to cleanse Chinese society of impure elements guilty of taking the capitalist road. Schools, universities, factories, and even government ministries were all subject to the scrutiny of the Red Guards. This so-called Great Proletarian Cultural Revolution (literally, the Chinese name translates as "great revolution to create a proletarian culture") lasted for ten years, from 1966 to 1976. Red Guards set out across the nation to eliminate the "four olds"—old ideas, old culture, old customs, and old habits. They destroyed temples, books written by foreigners, and jazz records.

Mao found, however, that it was not easy to maintain a constant mood of revolutionary enthusiasm. Key groups, including party members, urban professionals, and many military officers, did not share Mao's desire for "permanent revolution." People began to turn against the movement, and in September 1976, when Mao died, a group of practical-minded reformers seized power from the radicals and adopted a more rational approach to China's problems.

U.S.-CHINA RELATIONS For years, U.S. policy toward Communist China was determined by American fears of Communist expansion in Asia. Already in 1950, the Truman administration had adopted a new national improve. In 1979, diplomatic ties were established between the two countries, and by the end of the 1970s, China and the United States had forged a "strategic relationship" in which they would cooperate against the threat of Soviet intervention in Asia.

The Practice of Détente

By the 1970s, American-Soviet relations had entered a new phase known as détente, marked by a reduction of tensions between the two superpowers. An appropriate symbol of détente was the Antiballistic Missile Treaty, signed in 1972, in which the two nations agreed to limit their systems for launching antiballistic missiles (ABMs). The U.S. objective in pursuing the treaty was to make it unlikely that either superpower could win a nuclear exchange by launching a pre-emptive strike against the other. U.S. officials believed that a policy of "equivalence," in which there was a roughly equal power balance on each side, was the best way to avoid a nuclear confrontation.

In 1975, the Helsinki Accords provided yet another example of reduced tensions between the superpowers. Signed by the United States, Canada, and all European nations, these accords recognized all borders that had been established in Europe since the end of World War II, thereby acknowledging the Soviet sphere of influence in eastern Europe. The Helsinki Accords also committed the signatory powers to recognize and protect the human rights of their citizens.

The Limits of Détente

This protection of human rights became one of the major foreign policy goals of the next American president, Jimmy Carter. Although hopes ran high for the continuation of détente, the Soviet invasion of Afghanistan in 1979, undertaken to restore a pro-Soviet regime, hardened relations between the United States and the Soviet Union. President Carter canceled American participation in the 1980 Olympic games in

Hulton Archive/Getty Images

The Great Proletarian Cultural Revolution. The Cultural Revolution, which began in 1966, was a massive effort by Mao Zedong and his radical supporters to eliminate rival elements within the Chinese Communist Party and achieve the final stage of communism—a classless society. Shown here in front of a picture of Chairman Mao Zedong is a group of Chinese children in uniform holding Mao's *Little Red Book* (a collection of Mao's thoughts that became a sort of bible for Chinese Communists) during the Cultural Revolution in 1968.

policy that implied that the United States would take whatever steps were necessary to stem expansion of communism in the region, a policy that Truman invoked when he sent troops to Korea in 1950 (see "The Korean War" in Chapter 28). The Vietnam War raised additional concerns about Communist China's intentions.

President Richard Nixon, however, opened a new door in American relations when he visited China and met with Mao in 1972. Despite Nixon's reputation as a devout anti-Communist, the visit was a success as the two leaders agreed to put aside their most bitter differences in an effort to reduce tensions in Asia. During the 1970s, Chinese-American relations continued to

Moscow and placed an embargo on the shipment of American grain to the Soviet Union.

The early administration of President Ronald Reagan witnessed a return to the harsh rhetoric, if not all of the harsh practices, of the Cold War. Calling the Soviet Union an "evil empire," Reagan began a military buildup that stimulated a renewed arms race. By providing military support to the anti-Soviet insurgents in Afghanistan, the Reagan administration helped maintain a Vietnam-like war in Afghanistan that would embed the Soviet Union in its own quagmire. Like the Vietnam War, the conflict in Afghanistan resulted in heavy casualties and demonstrated that the influence of a superpower was limited in the face of strong nationalist, guerrilla-type opposition.

Society and Culture in the Western World

Q FOCUS QUESTION: What were the major social and cultural developments in the Western world between 1965 and 1985?

Dramatic social and cultural developments accompanied political and economic changes after 1965. Even as scientific and technological achievements began to revolutionize people's lives, environmental problems were becoming increasingly apparent. Intellectually and culturally, the Western world after 1965 was notable for its diversity and innovation. New directions led some observers to speak of a "Postmodern" cultural world.

The World of Science and Technology

During World War II, university scientists were recruited to work for their governments and develop new weapons and practical instruments of war. British physicists played a crucial role in the development of an improved radar system that helped defeat the German air force in the Battle of Britain in 1940. German scientists designed self-propelled rockets and jet airplanes to keep Hitler's hopes alive for a miraculous turnaround in the war. The computer, too, was a wartime creation. The British mathematician Alan Turing (1912–1954) designed a primitive computer to assist British intelligence in breaking the secret codes of German ciphering machines. The most famous product of wartime scientific research was the atomic bomb, created by a team of American and European scientists under the guidance of the American physicist J. Robert Oppenheimer (1904–1967). Obviously, most wartime devices were created for destructive purposes, but merely to mention computers and jet airplanes demonstrates that they could easily be adapted for peacetime uses.

THE COMPUTER The alliance of science and technology has led to an accelerated rate of change that has become a fact of life in Western society. One product of this alliance—the computer—may be the most revolutionary of all the technological inventions of the twentieth century. Early computers, which required thousands of vacuum tubes to function, were large and took up considerable space. An important figure in the development of the early computer was Grace Hopper (1906–1992), a career navy officer. Hopper was instrumental in inventing COBOL, a computer language that enabled computers to respond to words as well as numbers.

The development of the transistor and then the silicon chip produced a revolutionary new approach to computers. In 1971, the invention of the microprocessor, a machine that combined the equivalent of thousands of transistors on a single, tiny silicon chip, opened the road for the development of the personal computer.

DANGERS OF SCIENCE AND TECHNOLOGY Despite the marvels that were produced by the alliance of science and technology, some people came to question the underlying assumption of this alliance—that scientific knowledge gave human beings the ability to manipulate the environment for their benefit. They maintained that some technological advances had far-reaching side effects damaging to the environment. For example, the chemical fertilizers that were touted for producing larger crops wreaked havoc with the ecological balance of streams, rivers, and woodlands. *Small Is Beautiful*, written by the British economist E. F. Schumacher (1911–1977), was a fundamental critique of the dangers of the new science and technology (see the box on p. 733). The proliferation of fouled beaches and dying forests and lakes made environmentalism one of the important issues of the late twentieth century.

The Environment and the Green Movements

By the 1970s, serious ecological problems had become all too apparent. Air pollution, produced by nitrogen oxide and sulfur dioxide emissions from road vehicles,

The Limits of Modern Technology

Although science and technology have produced an amazing array of achievements in the postwar world, some voices have been raised in criticism of their sometimes destructive aspects. In 1975, in his book *Small Is Beautiful*, the British economist E. F. Schumacher examined the effects that modern industrial technology has had on the earth's resources.

E. F. Schumacher, *Small Is Beautiful*

Is it not evident that our current methods of production are already eating into the very substance of industrial man? To many people this is not at all evident. Now that we have solved the problem of production, they say, have we ever had it so good? Are we not better fed, better clothed, and better housed than ever before—and better educated? Of course we are: most, but by no means all, of us: in the rich countries. But this is not what I mean by "substance." The substance of man cannot be measured by Gross National Product. Perhaps it cannot be measured at all, except for certain symptoms of loss. However, this is not the place to go into the statistics of these symptoms, such as crime, drug addiction, vandalism, mental breakdown, rebellion, and so forth. Statistics never prove anything.

I started by saying that one of the most fateful errors of our age is the belief that the problem of production has been solved. This illusion, I suggested, is mainly due to our inability to recognize that the modern industrial system, with all its intellectual sophistication, consumes the very basis on which it has been erected. To use the language of the economist, it lives on irreplaceable capital which it cheerfully treats as income. I specified three categories of such capital: fossil fuels, the tolerance margins of nature, and the human substance. Even if some readers should refuse to accept all three parts of my argument, I suggest that any one of them suffices to make my case. And what is my case? Simply that our most important task is to get off our present collision course. And who is there to tackle such a task? I think every one of us, whether old or young, powerful or powerless, rich or poor, influential or uninfluential. To talk about the future is useful only if it leads to action now. And what can we do now, while we are still in the position of "never having had it so good"? To say the least—which is already very much—we must thoroughly understand the problem and begin to see the possibility of evolving a new lifestyle, with new methods of production and new patterns of consumption: a lifestyle designed for permanence. To give only three preliminary examples: in agriculture and horticulture, we can interest ourselves in the perfection of production methods which are biologically sound, build up soil fertility, and produce health, beauty and permanence. Productivity will then look after itself. In industry, we can interest ourselves in the evolution of small-scale technology, relatively nonviolent technology, "technology with a human face," so that people have a chance to enjoy themselves while they are working, instead of working solely for their pay packet and hoping, usually forlornly, for enjoyment solely during their leisure time.

Q What was Schumacher's critique of modern technology? To what extent has this critique been substantiated by developments since 1975?

Source: From E. F. Schumacher, *Small Is Beautiful–From Small Is Beautiful: Economics as if People Mattered* by E.F. Schumacher

---

power plants, and industrial factories, was causing respiratory illnesses and having corrosive effects on buildings and monuments. Many rivers, lakes, and seas had become so polluted that they posed serious health risks. Dying forests and disappearing wildlife alarmed more and more people. A disaster at the nuclear power plant at Chernobyl (chur-NOH-buhl) in Ukraine in the Soviet Union in 1986 made Europeans even more aware of potential environmental hazards. The opening of eastern Europe after the revolutions of 1989 (see Chapter 30) brought to the world's attention the incredible environmental destruction of that region caused by unfettered industrial pollution. Environmental concerns forced the major political parties in Europe to advocate new regulations for the protection of the environment.

Growing ecological awareness also gave rise to the Green movements and Green parties that emerged throughout Europe in the 1970s. Most started at the local level and then gradually expanded to include activities at the national level, where they became formally organized as political parties. Green parties competed successfully in Sweden, Austria, and Switzerland. Most visible was the Green Party in Germany, which was officially organized in 1979. By 1987, the Green Party had elected forty-two delegates to the West German parliament. In 1998, when the Green Party became a coalition partner with the Socialists under Gerhard Schröder, one of the Green Party members, Joschka Fischer, became the nation's foreign minister.

Although the Green movements and parties have played an important role in making people aware of ecological problems, they have not replaced the traditional political parties, as some political analysts in the mid-1980s forecast. For one thing, the coalitions that made up the Greens found it difficult to agree on all issues and tended to splinter into cliques. Moreover, traditional political parties co-opted the environmental issues of the Greens. More and more European governments began to sponsor projects to safeguard the environment and clean up the worst sources of pollution.

Postmodern Thought

The term *Postmodern* covers a variety of artistic and intellectual styles and ways of thinking prominent since the 1970s. In the broadest sense, **Postmodernism** rejects the modern Western belief in an objective truth and instead focuses on the relative nature of reality and knowledge.

While existentialism wrestled with notions of meaning and existence, a group of French philosophers in the 1960s attempted to understand how meaning and knowledge operate through the study of language and signs. **Poststructuralism**, or **deconstruction**, which was formulated by Jacques Derrida (ZHAHK DEH-ree-duh) (1930–2004), holds that culture is created and can therefore be analyzed in a variety of ways, according to the manner in which people create their own meaning. Hence, there is no fixed truth or universal meaning.

Michel Foucault (mih-SHELL foo-KOH) (1926–1984) likewise used poststructural concepts to explore relationships of power. Believing that "power is exercised rather than possessed," Foucault argued that the diffusion of power and oppression marks all relationships. For example, any act of teaching entails components of assertion and submission, as the student adopts the ideas of the person in power. Therefore, all norms are culturally produced and entail some degree of power struggle.

Trends in Art, Literature, and Music

Beginning in the 1960s and continuing well into the 1980s, artistic and literary styles emerged that some have referred to as "Postmodern." Postmodernism tends to move away from the futurism or "cutting-edge" qualities of Modernism. Instead it favors "tradition," whether that means using earlier styles of painting or elevating traditional crafts to the level of fine art. Weavers, potters, glassmakers, metalsmiths, and furniture makers have gained respect as artists. Postmodern artists and architects frequently blur the distinction between the arts, creating works that include elements of film, performance, popular culture, sculpture, and architecture.

ART In the 1960s and 1970s, artists often rejected the notion of object-based artworks. Instead, performances and installations that were either too fleeting or too large to appear in the traditional context of a museum were produced. Allen Kaprow (1927–2006) suggested that "happenings," works of art rooted in performance, grew out of Jackson Pollock's process of action painting. Rather than producing abstract paintings, however, Kaprow created events that were unscripted chance occurrences. Kaprow's emphasis on the relationship of art to its surroundings was continued in the "land art" of the early 1980s. In one such example, *Spiral Jetty* (1970), Robert Smithson (1938–1973) used a bulldozer to move more than 6,000 tons of earth into a 1,500-foot-long corkscrew in Utah's Great Salt Lake. Responding to the founding of the Environmental Protection Agency as well as to the cycles of nature, Smithson's artwork resembled a science-fiction wasteland while challenging notions of traditional fine art.

Postmodernism's eclectic mixing of past tradition with Modernist innovation became increasingly evident in architecture. One example is provided by Charles Moore (1929–1993). His *Piazza d'Italia* (1976–1980) in New Orleans is an outdoor plaza that combines classical columns with stainless steel and neon lights. This blending of modern-day materials with historical references distinguished the Postmodern architecture of the late 1970s and 1980s from the Modernist glass box.

LITERATURE Postmodernism was also evident in literature. European Postmodernism is well represented by the work of the Czech writer Milan Kundera (MEE-lahn koon-DAYR-uh) (b. 1929). Kundera blends fantasy with realism, using fantasy to examine moral issues while remaining optimistic about the human condition. Indeed, in his novel *The Unbearable Lightness of Being*

Robert Smithson, *Spiral Jetty*. Built on an abandoned industrial site, *Spiral Jetty* disappears and reappears according to the rise and fall of the Great Salt Lake's water level. As seen in this 2002 photograph, the surface has become encrusted in salt as drought has lowered the lake level. Robert Smithson filmed the construction of *Spiral Jetty*, carefully noting the various geological formations included in his creation. Earthworks like *Spiral Jetty* increased in number as the welfare of the world's ecosystems became a growing concern in the 1960s and 1970s.

(1984), Kundera does not despair because of the political repression in his native Czechoslovakia that he so aptly describes but allows his characters to use love as a way to a better life. The human spirit can be diminished but not destroyed.

MUSIC Like modern art, modern music has focused on variety and radical experimentation. The major musical trend since the war has been serialism. Serialism is a compositional procedure in which an order of succession is set for specific values: pitch (for tones of the tempered scale), loudness (for dynamic levels), and units of time (for rhythm). By predetermining the order of succession, the composer restricts his or her intuitive freedom as the work to some extent creates itself.

An offshoot of serialism that has won popular support, but not the same critical favor, is minimalism. Like serialism, this style uses repeated patterns and series and steady pulsation with gradual changes occurring over time. But whereas serialism is often atonal,

minimalism is usually tonal and more harmonic. Perhaps the most successful minimalist composer is Philip Glass (b. 1937), who demonstrated in *Einstein on the Beach* that minimalist music could be adapted to full-scale opera. Like other modern American composers, Glass found no contradiction in moving between the worlds of classical music and popular music. His *Koyaanisqatsi* (koh-YAH-niss-kaht-see) was used as background music to a documentary film on the disintegrative forces in Western society.

Popular Culture: Image and Globalization

The period from 1967 to 1973 was probably the true golden age of rock. During this brief period, much experimentation in rock music took place, as it did in society in general. Straightforward rock-and-roll competed with a new hybrid blues rock, created in part by British performers such as the Rolling Stones, who were in turn inspired by African American blues artists.

Many musicians also experimented with non-Western musical sounds, such as Indian sitars. Some of the popular music of the 1960s also focused on social issues. It was against the Vietnam War and materialism and promoted "peace and love" as alternatives to the prevailing "establishment" culture.

The introduction of the video music channel MTV in the early 1980s radically changed the music scene by making image as important as sound in selling records. Artists like Michael Jackson (1958–2009) became superstars by treating the music video as an art form. Jackson's videos often were short films with elaborate staging and special effects set to music. Technological advances became prevalent in the music of the 1980s with the advent of the synthesizer, an electronic piano that produced computerized sounds. Some performers replaced ensembles of guitar, bass, and drums with synthesizers, creating a futuristic and manufactured sound.

Paralleling the rise of the music video was the emergence of rap or hip-hop. Developed in New York City in the late 1970s and early 1980s, rap combined rhymed lyrics with disco beats and turntable manipulations. One scholar noted that hip-hop "also encompassed break dancing, graffiti art, and new styles of language and fashion." Early rap groups like Public Enemy and Grandmaster Flash and the Furious Five instilled social commentaries into their songs, using the popularity of hip-hop to raise awareness about social conditions in American cities.

THE GROWTH OF MASS SPORTS Sports became a major product of both popular culture and the leisure industry. The development of satellite television and various electronic breakthroughs helped make sports a global phenomenon. The Olympic games could now be broadcast around the globe from anywhere in the world. Sports were a cheap form of entertainment because fans did not have to leave their homes to enjoy athletic competitions. In fact, some sports organizations initially resisted television, fearing that it would hurt ticket sales. Soon, however, the tremendous revenues possible from television contracts overcame this hesitation. As sports television revenue escalated, many sports came to receive the bulk of their yearly revenue from television contracts. The Olympics, for example, are now funded primarily by American television. These contracts are paid for by advertising sponsors, mostly for products to be consumed while watching the sport: beer, soda, and snack foods.

Chapter Summary

The late 1960s experienced a rash of protest movements. A revolt in sexual mores was the result of the so-called sexual revolution of the 1960s, which was encouraged by the birth control pill as well as sexually explicit movies, plays, and books. A growing youth movement in the 1960s questioned authority and fostered rebellion against the older generation. Numerous groups of students and radicals protested the war in Vietnam and unsatisfactory university conditions. Women actively sought equality of rights with men. The women's movement gained momentum in the 1970s and 1980s, but the student upheavals were not a "turning point in the history of postwar Europe," as some people

thought at the time, especially in 1968, when the student protest movement reached its height. In the 1970s and 1980s, student rebels became middle-class professionals, and revolutionary politics remained mostly a memory.

In the 1970s, the Cold War took a new direction known as détente as the Soviet Union and the United States moved, if ever

fitfully, toward a lessening of tensions. With the Antiballistic Missile Treaty in 1972, the United States and the Soviet Union believed that they had reached a balance, or "equivalence," that would ensure peace. The early 1980s, however, saw renewed tensions between the superpowers. The Soviet invasion of Afghanistan in 1979 and the military buildup and harsh rhetoric of the American president Ronald Reagan brought a decline in détente. As we shall see in the next chapter, however, a dramatic shift in Soviet leadership would soon bring an unexpected end to the Cold War.

Between 1965 and 1985, the Western world remained divided between a prosperous capitalistic and democratic West and a stagnant, politically repressed eastern Europe. After two decades of incredible economic growth, western

European states experienced severe economic recessions in 1973–1974 and 1979–1983, although their economies largely recovered in the course of the 1980s. In eastern Europe, Soviet

leaders continued to exercise control over their satellite states while recognizing the need to allow some leeway for them to adopt domestic policies appropriate to local conditions.

Dramatic social and cultural developments accompanied political and economic changes after 1965. Scientific and technological developments, especially the rapid advance of the computer, began to revolutionize people's lives, while ecological problems became increasingly apparent and led to the Green movements and Green parties that emerged throughout Europe in the 1970s. Intellectually and culturally, the Western world after 1965 was notable for its diversity and innovation. New directions led some observers to speak of a Postmodern world in both literature and the arts.

CHAPTER TIMELINE

	1965	1970	1975	1980	1985

Eastern Europe/Soviet Union — Era of Brezhnev

■ Emergence of Solidarity in Poland

■ Soviets crush "Prague Spring" in Czechoslovakia

The West — ■ Student revolts

Golden age of rock

■ Common Market expands (European Community)

■ Margaret Thatcher becomes prime minister of Britain

Second Vietnam War

■ Organization of Green Party in Germany

Watergate scandal

CHAPTER REVIEW

Upon Reflection

Q What were the major turning points in the Cold War between 1965 and 1985?

Q What were the major successes and failures of the western European democracies between 1965 and 1985, and how did Soviet policies affect the eastern European states during the same time period?

Q What role did popular culture play in the Western world between 1965 and 1985?

Key Terms

permissive society (p. 717)
feminism (p. 718)
Brezhnev Doctrine (p. 722)
détente (p. 722)

stagflation (p. 729)
domino theory (p. 730)
Postmodernism (p. 734)
poststructuralism (deconstruction) (p. 734)

Suggestions for Further Reading

GENERAL WORKS   For a well-written survey on Europe between 1965 and 1985, see **T. Judt, *Postwar: A History of Europe Since 1945*** (New York, 2005).

A CULTURE OF PROTEST   On the sexual revolution of the 1960s, see **D. Allyn, *Make Love, Not War: The Sexual Revolution—An Unfettered History*** (New York, 2000). On the turbulent 1960s, see **A. Marwick, *The Sixties: Social and Cultural Transformation in Britain, France, Italy, and the United States*** (Oxford, 1999). On the women's liberation movement, see **D. Meyer, *The Rise of Women in America, Russia, Sweden, and Italy***, 2d ed. (Middletown, Conn., 1989), and **K. C. Berkeley, *The Women's Liberation Movement in America*** (Westport, Conn., 1999).

SOVIET UNION AND EASTERN EUROPE   On the Brezhnev era in the Soviet Union, see **E. Bacon**, ed., ***Brezhnev Remembered*** (New York, 2003). On events in eastern Europe, see the surveys listed in Chapter 28. On the Czech upheaval in 1968, see **K. Williams, *The Prague Spring and Its Aftermath: Czechoslovak Politics, 1968–1970*** (Cambridge, 1997).

WESTERN EUROPE   For general works on western Europe, see the works cited in Chapter 28. More specific works dealing with the period 1965–1985, include **E. J. Evans, *Thatcher and Thatcherism*** (New York, 1977); **D. S. Bell, *François Mitterrand*** (Cambridge, 2005); and **R. J. Dalton, *Politics in West Germany*** (Glenview, Ill., 1989).

THE COLD WAR: THE MOVE TO DÉTENTE   For general studies on the Cold War, see the works listed in Chapter 28. On the Vietnam War, see **M. Hall, *The Vietnam War***, 2d ed. (London, 2007). On China's cultural revolution, see **R. MacFarquhar** and **M. Schoenhals, *Mao's Last Revolution*** (Cambridge, Mass., 2006), and **T. Cheek, *Mao Zedong and China's Revolutions: A Brief History*** (Boston, 2002).

SOCIETY AND CULTURE   On the development of the Green parties, see **M. O'Neill, *Green Parties and Political Change in Contemporary Europe*** (Aldershot, England, 1997). The space race is examined in **W. A. McDougall, *The Heavens and the Earth: A Political History of the Space Age*** (New York, 1987). For a general view of postwar thought and culture, see **J. A. Winders, *European Culture Since 1848: From Modem to Postmodern and Beyond***, rev. ed. (New York, 2001). On Postmodernism, see **C. Butler, *Postmodernism: A Very Short Introduction*** (Oxford, 2002). The cultural impact of sports is examined in **W. Vamplew, *Mud, Sweat and Beers: A Cultural History of Sport and Alcohol*** (London, 2002).

Notes

1. Quoted in M. Rowe et al., *Spare Rib Reader* (Harmondsworth, England, 1982), p. 574.
2. B. Friedan, *The Feminine Mystique* (New York, 1963), p. 10.
3. Quoted in T. Judt, *Postwar: A History of Europe Since 1945* (New York, 2005), p. 390.

MindTap   **MindTap** is a fully online, highly personalized learning experience built upon Cengage Learning content. MindTap combines student learning tools—readings, multimedia, activities, and assessments—into a singular Learning Path that guides students through the course.

C H A P T E R

30

After the Fall: The Western World in a Global Age (Since 1985)

With clenched fist, Boris Yeltsin speaks out against an attempted right-wing coup.

CHAPTER OUTLINE AND FOCUS QUESTIONS

Toward a New Western Order

Q What reforms did Gorbachev institute in the Soviet Union, and what role did he play in its demise? What are the major political developments in eastern Europe, western Europe, and North America since 1985?

After the Cold War: New World Order or Age of Terrorism?

Q How and why did the Cold War end? What are the main issues in the struggle against terrorism?

New Directions and New Problems in Western Society

Q What are the major developments in the women's movement since 1985? What problems have immigrants created for European society?

Western Culture Today

Q What major Western cultural trends have emerged since 1985? What is the Digital Age, and what are its products, results, and dangers?

Toward a Global Civilization

Q What is globalization, and what are its main characteristics in the twenty-first century?

CRITICAL THINKING

Q In what ways were the major social, economic, and political developments in the second half of the twentieth century similar to those in the first half of the century? In what ways were they different?

CONNECTIONS TO TODAY

Q Twenty-five years ago, the destruction of the Berlin Wall brought forth great promise for a new Europe. What will be the challenges of the next twenty-five years for Western civilization?

BY 1985, AFTER four decades of the Cold War, Westerners had become accustomed to a division of Europe between West and East that seemed to be permanent. A prosperous western Europe allied with the United States stood opposed to a still-struggling eastern Europe that remained largely subject to the Soviet Union. The division of Germany symbolized the new and seemingly well-established order. Yet in just a few years, a revolutionary upheaval in the Soviet Union and eastern Europe brought an end to the Cold War and to the division of postwar Europe. Even the Soviet Union ceased to exist as a nation. And much of this can be traced to the reform efforts of one man, Mikhail Gorbachev.

On August 19, 1991, a group of Soviet leaders opposed to reform arrested Gorbachev, the president of the Soviet Union, and tried to seize control of the government. Spontaneously, hundreds of thousands of Russians, led by Boris Yeltsin, poured into the streets of Moscow and Leningrad to protest the attempted coup. Some army units, sent out to enforce the wishes of the rebels, defected to Yeltsin's side, and within days, the rebels were forced to surrender. This failed attempt to seize power had unexpected results as Russia and many of the other Soviet republics turned their backs on the government and declared their independence. By the end of 1991, the Soviet Union—one of the largest empires in world history—had come to an astonishingly swift end, and a new era of cooperation between the successor states of the old Soviet Union and the nations of the West had begun.

As the world adjusted to the transformation from Cold War to post–Cold War sensibilities, other changes shaped the Western outlook. The demographic face of European countries changed as massive numbers of immigrants created more ethnically diverse populations. New artistic and intellectual currents, the continued advance of science and technology, the emergence of a Digital Age, the surge of the women's liberation movement—all spoke of a vibrant, ever-changing world. At the same time, a devastating terrorist attack on the World Trade Center in New York City and the Pentagon outside Washington, D.C., in 2001 made the Western world vividly aware of its vulnerability to international terrorism. Moreover, a financial collapse in 2008 threatened the economic security of the Western world as well as the entire global economy. But most important of all, Western nations, like all nations on the planet, had become acutely aware of the political and economic interdependence of the world's nations and the global nature of the challenges of the twenty-first century.

Toward a New Western Order

Q Focus Questions: What reforms did Gorbachev institute in the Soviet Union, and what role did he play in its demise? What are the major political developments in eastern Europe, western Europe, and North America since 1985?

Between 1945 and 1985, a new political order following the devastation of World War II had left the Western world divided between a prosperous, capitalistic West and an impoverished, communist East. But in the late 1980s and early 1990s, the Soviet Union and its eastern European satellite states underwent a revolutionary upheaval that dramatically altered the European landscape (see Map 30.1) and left many Europeans with both new hopes and new fears.

The Revolutionary Era in the Soviet Union

By 1980, it was becoming apparent to a small number of reformers in the Communist Party that the Soviet Union was seriously ailing. When one of these young reformers, Mikhail Gorbachev, was chosen as party secretary in March 1985, a new era began in the Soviet Union.

THE GORBACHEV ERA After receiving his law degree at the University of Moscow in 1955, Mikhail Gorbachev returned to his native southern Russia, where he eventually became first secretary of the Communist Party in the city of Stavropol (he had joined the party in 1952). In 1980, Gorbachev became a full member of the ruling Politburo and secretary of the Central Committee. In March 1985, party leaders elected him general secretary of the party, and he became the new leader of the Soviet Union.

Educated during the years of reform under Khrushchev, Gorbachev seemed intent on taking earlier reforms to their logical conclusions. He had said to his wife on achieving power, "We cannot go on living like this."[1] By the 1980s, Soviet economic problems were obvious. Rigid, centralized planning had led to mismanagement and stifled innovation. Although the Soviets still excelled in space exploration, they had fallen behind the West in high technology, especially in the development and production of computers for private and public use. Most noticeable to the Soviet people was the decline in the standard of living. From the start, Gorbachev preached the need for radical reforms.

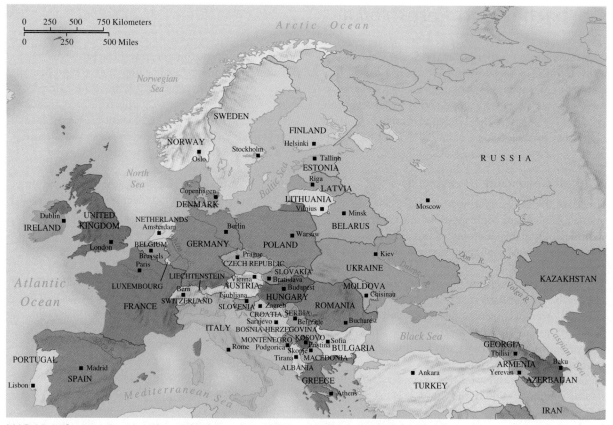

MAP 30.1 The New Europe. The combination of an inefficient economy and high military spending had led to stagnation in the Soviet Union by the early 1980s. Mikhail Gorbachev came to power in 1985, setting in motion political, economic, and nationalist forces that led to independence for the former Soviet republics and also for eastern Europe.

Q What new countries emerged out of the collapse of the Soviet Union?

The cornerstone of Gorbachev's radical reforms was **perestroika** (per-uh-STROI-kuh) or "restructuring" (see the box on p. 742). At first, this meant only a reordering of economic policy, as Gorbachev called for the beginning of a market economy with limited free enterprise and some private property. Gorbachev soon perceived, however, that in the Soviet system, the economic sphere was intimately tied to the social and political spheres. Attempting to reform the economy without political or social reform would be doomed to failure. One of the most important instruments of perestroika was **glasnost** (GLAHZ-nohst), or "openness." Soviet citizens and officials were encouraged to discuss openly the strengths and weaknesses of the Soviet Union. *Pravda* (PRAHV-duh), the official newspaper of the Communist Party, began for the first time to include reports of official corruption, sloppy factory work, and protests against government policy.

Political reforms were equally revolutionary. At the Communist Party conference in 1988, Gorbachev called for the creation of a new Soviet parliament, the Congress of People's Deputies, whose members were to be chosen in competitive elections. It convened in 1989, the first such meeting in Russia since 1918. Early in 1990, Gorbachev legalized the formation of other political parties and struck Article 6, which had guaranteed the "leading role" of the Communist Party, from the Soviet constitution. At the same time, Gorbachev attempted to consolidate his power by creating a new state presidency. Hitherto, the position of first secretary of the party had been the most important post in the Soviet Union, but as the Communist Party became

Gorbachev and *Perestroika*

After assuming the leadership of the Soviet Union in 1985, Mikhail Gorbachev worked to liberalize and restructure the country. His policies opened the door to rapid changes in eastern Europe and in Soviet-American relations at the end of the 1980s. In his book *Perestroika*, Gorbachev explained some of his "New Thinking."

Mikhail Gorbachev, *Perestroika*

Great are the dangers facing mankind. There are enough elements of confrontation, but the forces wishing and capable of stopping and overcoming that confrontation are growing in strength and scope before our very eyes.

Moving from suspicion and hostility to confidence, from a "balance of fear" to a balance of reason and goodwill, from narrow nationalist egoism to cooperation—this is what we are urging. This is the goal of our peace initiatives, and for this we shall continue, tirelessly to work.

There is a great thirst for mutual understanding and mutual communication in the world. It is felt among politicians, it is gaining momentum among the intelligentsia, representatives of culture, and the public at large. And if the Russian word "perestroika" has easily entered the international lexicon, this is due to more than just interest in what is going on in the Soviet Union. Now the whole world needs restructuring, i.e., progressive development, a fundamental change.

People feel this and understand this. They have to find their bearings, to understand the problems besetting mankind, to realize how they should live in the future. The restructuring is a must for a world overflowing with nuclear weapons; for a world ridden with serious economic and ecological problems; for a world laden with poverty, backwardness and disease; for a human race now facing the urgent need of ensuring its own survival.

We are all students, and our teacher is life and time. I believe that more and more people will come to realize that through RESTRUCTURING in the broad sense of the word, the integrity of the world will be enhanced. Having earned good marks from our main teacher—life—we shall enter the twenty-first century well prepared and sure that there will be further progress.

We want freedom to reign supreme in the coming century everywhere in the world. We want peaceful competition between different social systems to develop unimpeded, to encourage mutually advantageous cooperation rather than confrontation and an arms race. We want people of every country to enjoy prosperity, welfare and happiness. The road to this lies through proceeding to a nuclear-free, non-violent world. We have embarked on this road, and call on other countries and nations to follow suit.

Q What impact did Gorbachev's idea of restructuring have on communism and the Soviet Union's ability to reform itself?

Source: Pages 140–141, 253–254 from *Perestroika* by Mikhail Gorbachev. Copyright © 1987 by Mikhail Gorbachev. Reprinted by permission of HarperCollins Publishers.

---

less closely associated with the state, the powers of this office diminished correspondingly. In March 1990, Gorbachev became the Soviet Union's first president.

One of Gorbachev's most serious problems stemmed from the nature of the nation he led. The Union of Soviet Socialist Republics was a truly multiethnic country, containing 92 nationalities and 112 recognized languages. Previously, the iron hand of the Communist Party, centered in Moscow, had kept a lid on the centuries-old ethnic tensions that had periodically erupted. As Gorbachev released this iron grip, tensions resurfaced, a byproduct of glasnost that Gorbachev had not anticipated. Ethnic groups took advantage of the new openness to protest what they perceived as ethnically motivated slights. When violence erupted, the Soviet army, in disrepair since its ill-fated decade-long foray into Afghanistan, had difficulty controlling the situation.

The years 1988 to 1990 also witnessed the appearance of nationalist movements in the republics that made up the Soviet Union. Many were motivated by ethnic concerns, with calls for sovereignty and independence from Russian-based rule centered in Moscow. These movements sprang up first in Georgia in late 1988 and then in Latvia (LAT-vee-uh), Estonia (ess-TOH-nee-uh), Moldova (mohl-DOH-vuh), Uzbekistan (ooz-BEK-i-stan), Azerbaijan (az-ur-by-JAHN), and Lithuania (li-thuh-WAY-nee-uh). On March 11, 1990, the Lithuanian Supreme Council proclaimed Lithuania an independent state.

THE END OF THE SOVIET UNION During 1990 and 1991, Gorbachev struggled to deal with Lithuania and the other problems unleashed by his reforms. On the one hand, he tried to appease conservatives who complained about the growing disorder within the Soviet Union. On the other hand, he tried to accommodate the liberal forces, especially those in the Soviet republics, who increasingly favored a new kind of decentralized Soviet federation. In particular, Gorbachev labored to cooperate more closely with Boris Yeltsin (YELT-sun) (1931–2007), who had been elected president of the Russian Republic in June 1991.

By 1991, the conservative leaders of the traditional Soviet institutions—the army, government, KGB, and military industries—had grown increasingly worried about the impending dissolution of the Soviet Union and its impact on their own fortunes. On August 19, 1991, a group of these discontented rightists arrested Gorbachev and attempted to seize power. Gorbachev's unwillingness to work with the conspirators and the brave resistance in Moscow of Yeltsin and thousands of Russians who had grown accustomed to their new liberties caused the coup to disintegrate rapidly. The actions of these right-wing plotters, however, served to accelerate the very process they had hoped to stop—the disintegration of the Soviet Union. Despite desperate pleas by Gorbachev, the Soviet republics soon moved for complete independence. Ukraine voted for independence on December 1, 1991, and a week later, the leaders of Russia, Ukraine, and Belarus announced that the Soviet Union had "ceased to exist." Gorbachev resigned on December 25, 1991, and turned over his responsibilities as commander in chief to Boris Yeltsin, the president of Russia. By the end of 1991, one of the largest empires in world history had evaporated, and a new era had begun in its lands.

WHY DID THE SOVIET UNION COLLAPSE? What caused the sudden collapse of the Soviet system? Some analysts in the United States argue that the ambitious defense policies adopted by the Reagan administration forced the Soviet Union into an arms race that it could not afford and that ultimately led to the collapse of the Soviet economy. Most observers, however, believe that the fall of the Soviet Union was primarily a consequence of conditions inherent in the system, some of which have been pointed out in this and the previous chapter. For years, Soviet leaders had denied or ignored the massive inefficiencies in the Soviet economy. In the 1980s, time began to run out. The perceptive Mikhail Gorbachev tried to stem the decline with radical reforms, but by then it was too late.

One other factor should also be considered. One of the weakest aspects of the Soviet Union was its multiethnic character, with only a little more than half of the total population made up of ethnic Russians. As we have seen, many of the minority nationalities were demanding more autonomy or even independence for their regions. By the end of the 1980s, such demands brought about the final collapse of the Soviet system.

THE NEW RUSSIA A new power struggle soon ensued within Russia, by far the largest of the former Soviet republics. Yeltsin was committed to introducing a free-market economy as quickly as possible, but the transition was not easy. Economic hardships and social disarray, made worse by a dramatic rise in the activities of organized crime mobs, led increasing numbers of Russians to support both former Communists and hard-line nationalists, who criticized Russia's loss of prestige in world affairs.

During the mid-1990s, Yeltsin sought to implement reforms that would set Russia on a firm course toward a pluralistic political system and a market economy. But the new post-Communist Russia remained as fragile as ever. A nagging war in the Caucasus—where the Muslim people of Chechnya (CHECH-nee-uh) sought national independence from Russia—drained the government's budget and exposed the decrepit state of the once vaunted Red Army. Yeltsin won re-election as president in 1996, although his precarious health raised serious questions about his ability to govern.

THE PUTIN ERA At the end of 1999, Yeltsin suddenly resigned and was replaced by Vladimir Putin (POO-tin) (b. 1952), a former member of the KGB. Putin vowed to strengthen the role of the central government in managing the affairs of state. During the succeeding months, the parliament approved his proposal to centralize power in the hands of the federal government in Moscow.

Putin also vowed to return the breakaway state of Chechnya to Russian authority and to adopt a more assertive role in international affairs. Fighting in Chechnya continued throughout 2000, nearly reducing the republic's capital city of Grozny to ruins. In July 2001, Putin launched reforms, which included the unrestricted sale and purchase of land and tax cuts aimed at boosting economic growth and budget revenues. Although Russia soon experienced a budget surplus and a growing economy, serious problems remained.

Putin attempted to deal with the chronic problems in Russian society by centralizing his control over the system and by silencing critics—notably in the Russian media. Although Putin was criticized in the West for these moves, many Russians expressed sympathy with Putin's attempts to restore a sense of pride and discipline in Russian society.

In 2008, Dmitry Medvedev (di-MEE-tree mehd-VYEH-dehf) (b. 1965) became president of Russia when Putin could not run for a third consecutive term under Russia's constitution. Instead, Putin became prime minister, and the two men shared power. In 2012, despite public protests, Putin was again elected president to a six-year term. In 2014, an uprising in neighboring Ukraine led to the annexation of Crimea and the city of Sevastopol by Russian forces. In response, the United States and the European Union issued sanctions against Russia. By 2015, Russia's economy faced an uncertain future, as low oil prices and the unresolved Ukrainian crises destabilized the Russian economy.

Eastern Europe: The Revolutions of 1989 and the Collapse of the Communist Order

Stalin's postwar order had imposed Communist regimes throughout eastern Europe. The process of sovietization seemed so complete that few people believed that the new order could be undone. But discontent with their Soviet-style regimes always simmered beneath the surface of these satellite states, and after Mikhail Gorbachev made it clear that his government would not intervene militarily, the Communist regimes fell quickly in the revolutions of 1989.

THE FALL Martial law had not solved Poland's problems after it had been imposed in 1981, and in 1988, new demonstrations led the Polish regime to agree to hold parliamentary elections—the first free elections in eastern Europe in forty years. Bowing to the inevitable, the military regime allowed the newly elected Solidarity coalition to form a new government, thus ending forty-five years of Communist rule. In December 1990, Lech Walesa, the head of Solidarity, was elected president of Poland.

In Hungary, the economy had sagged by the late 1980s, and in 1989, the Communist regime, aware of growing dissatisfaction, began to undertake reforms. But they came too late as new political parties called for Hungary to become a democratic republic. After elections in March 1990, a new coalition government was formed that committed Hungary to democratic government.

Czechoslovakia, too, found a peaceful way to a new political system. Government attempts to suppress mass demonstrations in Prague and other cities in 1988 and 1989 only led to more and larger demonstrations. In December 1989, as protest continued, the Communist government, lacking any real support, collapsed. President Gustáv Husák resigned and at the end of December was replaced by Václav Havel, the dissident playwright who had played an important role in bringing the Communist government down. Havel set out on a goodwill tour to various Western countries, where he proved to be an eloquent spokesman for Czech democracy and a new order in Europe (see the box on p. 745).

Czechoslovakia's revolutionary path was considerably less violent than Romania's, where opposition grew as the dictator Nicolae Ceauşescu rejected the reforms in eastern Europe promoted by Gorbachev. Ceauşescu's extreme measures to reduce Romania's external debt led to economic difficulties and angered many Romanians. A small incident became the spark that ignited heretofore suppressed flames of discontent. The ruthless crushing of a demonstration in Timisoara in December 1989 led to other mass demonstrations. After the dictator was booed at a mass rally on December 21, the army refused to support any more repression. Ceauşescu and his wife were captured on December 22 and tried and executed on Christmas Day. Leadership now passed into the hands of the hastily formed National Salvation Front.

AFTER THE FALL The fall of Communist governments in eastern Europe during the revolutions of 1989 brought a wave of euphoria to Europe. The new structures meant an end to a postwar European order that had been imposed on unwilling peoples by the victorious forces of the Soviet Union. In 1989 and 1990, new governments throughout eastern Europe worked diligently to scrap the remnants of the old system and introduce the democratic procedures and market systems they believed would revitalize their scarred lands. But this process proved to be neither simple nor easy.

Most eastern European countries had little, if any, experience with democratic systems. Then, too, ethnic divisions, which had troubled these areas before World War II and had been forcibly submerged under Communist rule, re-emerged with a vengeance. Finally, the rapid conversion to market economies proved painful, and the adoption of austerity measures caused much suffering. Unemployment, for example, climbed to over 13 percent in Poland in 1992.

Václav Havel: The Call for a New Politics

In attempting to deal with the world's problems, some European leaders have pointed to the need for a new perspective, especially a moral one, if people are to live in a sane world. These two excerpts are taken from speeches by Václav Havel, who was elected president of Czechoslovakia at the end of 1989. The first is from his inaugural address as president on January 1, 1990; the second is from a speech given to the U.S. Congress.

Václav Havel, Address to the People of Czechoslovakia, January 1, 1990

But all of this is still not the main problem [the environmental devastation of the country by its Communist leaders]. The worst thing is that we live in a contaminated moral environment. We fell morally ill because we became used to saying something different from what we thought. We learned not to believe in anything, to ignore each other, to care only about ourselves. Concepts such as love, friendship, compassion, humility, or forgiveness lost their depth and dimensions, and for many of us they represented only psychological peculiarities, or they resembled gone-astray greetings from ancients, a little ridiculous in the era of computers and spaceships. Only a few of us were able to cry out loud that the powers that be should not be all-powerful, and that special farms, which produce ecologically pure and top-quality food just for them should send their produce to schools, children's homes and hospitals if our agriculture was unable to offer them to all. The previous regime—armed with its arrogant and intolerant ideology—reduced man to a force of production and nature to a tool of production. In this it attacked both their very substance and their mutual relationship. It reduced gifted and autonomous people, skillfully working in their own country, to nuts and bolts of some monstrously huge, noisy, and stinking machine, whose real meaning is not clear to anyone.

Source: From *The Washington Post*, February 22, 1990, p. 28d.

Václav Havel, Speech to Congress, February 21, 1990

For this reason, the salvation of this human world lies nowhere else than in the human heart, in the human power to reflect, in human meekness and in human responsibility.

Without a global revolution in the sphere of human consciousness, nothing will change for the better in the sphere of our being as humans, and the catastrophe toward which this world is headed—be it ecological, social, demographic or a general breakdown of civilization—will be unavoidable....

We are still a long way from that "family of man." In fact, we seem to be receding from the ideal rather than growing closer to it. Interests of all kinds—personal, selfish, state, nation, group, and if you like, company interests—still considerably outweigh genuinely common and global interests. We are still under the sway of the destructive and vain belief that man is the pinnacle of creation and not just a part of it and that therefore everything is permitted....

In other words, we still don't know how to put morality ahead of politics, science and economics. We are still incapable of understanding that the only genuine backbone of all our actions, if they are to be moral, is responsibility.

Responsibility to something higher than my family, my country, my company, my success—responsibility to the order of being where all our actions are indelibly recorded and where and only where they will be properly judged.

The interpreter or mediator between us and this higher authority is what is traditionally referred to as human conscience.

Q How different is Havel's view of politics from the views of mainstream politicians? What broader forces working in modern European society do you believe shaped Havel's thinking? How can Havel's view of our common humanity and responsibility to conscience help revitalize Western civilization?

Nevertheless, by the beginning of the twenty-first century, many of these states were making a successful transition to both free markets and democracy. In Poland, Aleksander Kwaśniewski (kwahsh-NYEF-skee) (b. 1954), although a former Communist, was elected president in November 1995 and pushed Poland toward an increasingly prosperous free-market economy. His successor, Lech Kaczyński (LEK kuh-ZIN-skee) (1949–2010), emphasized the need to combine modernization with tradition. In July 2010, Bronislaw Komorowski (brah-NEE-swahf koh-moh-RAHV-skee) (b. 1952) was elected president to succeed Kaczyński, who had died in a plane crash in April. In Czechoslovakia, the shift to non-Communist rule was complicated by old problems, especially ethnic issues. Czechs and Slovaks disagreed over the makeup of the new state but were able to agree to a peaceful division of the country. On January 1, 1993, Czechoslovakia split into the Czech Republic and Slovakia. Václav Havel was elected the first president of the new Czech Republic. In Romania, the current president, Traian Băsescu (trih-YAHN buh-SES-koo) (b. 1951), leads a country that is just beginning to show economic growth and the rise of a middle class. In 2012, however, austerity measures imposed to deal with the country's rising debt led to protests against the government.

The revival of the post–Cold War eastern European states is evident in their desire to join both NATO and the European Union (EU), the two major Cold War institutions of western European unity. In 1997, Poland, the Czech Republic, and Hungary became full members of NATO. In 2004, ten nations—including Hungary, Poland, the Czech Republic, Slovenia, Estonia, Latvia, and Lithuania—joined the EU, and Romania and Bulgaria joined in 2007. Yet eastern Europeans fear that their countries will be dominated by their more prosperous neighbors, while their counterparts in western Europe are concerned about a possible influx of low-wage workers. The global financial crises that began in 2008 added to the economic problems of eastern European countries.

The Reunification of Germany

Perhaps the most dramatic events took place in East Germany, where a persistent economic slump and the ongoing oppressiveness of the regime of Erich Honecker led to a flight of refugees and mass demonstrations against the regime in the summer and fall of 1989. After more than half a million people flooded the streets of East Berlin on November 4, shouting, "The wall must go!" the German Communist government soon

CHRONOLOGY The Fall of the Soviet Bloc	
1989	
Collapse of Communist government in Czechoslovakia	December
Collapse of East German government	December
Execution of Ceauşescu in Romania	December 25
1990	
Lithuania declares independence	March 11
East German elections—victory of Christian Democrats	March 18
Reunification of Germany	October 3
Lech Walesa becomes president of Poland	December
1991	
Boris Yeltsin becomes president of Russia	June
Slovenia and Croatia declare independence	June
Right-wing coup in the Soviet Union	August 19
Dissolution of the Soviet Union	December

capitulated to popular pressure and on November 9 opened the entire border with the West. The Berlin Wall, long a symbol of the Cold War, became the site of massive celebrations as thousands of people used sledgehammers to tear it down. By December, new political parties had emerged, and on March 18, 1990, in East Germany's first free elections ever, the Christian Democrats won almost 50 percent of the vote. After months of political negotiations between West and East German officials as well as the original four postwar occupying powers (the United States, Great Britain, France, and the Soviet Union), political reunification was achieved on October 3, 1990. What had seemed almost impossible at the beginning of 1989 had become a reality by the end of 1990.

The Disintegration of Yugoslavia

From its formation in 1918 as the Kingdom of the Serbs, Croats, and Slovenes, Yugoslavia had been an artificial creation. After World War II, the dictatorial Marshal Tito had managed to hold the nation's six republics and two autonomous provinces together. After his death in 1980, no strong leader emerged, and his responsibilities passed to a collective state presidency and the League of Communists of Yugoslavia. At the end of the 1980s, Yugoslavia was caught up in the reform movements sweeping through eastern Europe.

And the Wall Came Tumbling Down. The Berlin Wall, long a symbol of Europe's Cold War divisions, became the site of massive celebrations after the East German government opened its border with the West. On November 11, East German border guards demolished a section of the wall to create a new crossing point. As seen in this photograph, West Germans celebrated the opening of the new crossing point.

The League of Communists collapsed, and new parties quickly emerged.

In 1990, the republics of Slovenia, Croatia, Bosnia-Herzegovina, and Macedonia began to lobby for a new federal structure of Yugoslavia that would fulfill their separatist desires. Slobodan Milošević (sluh-BOH-dahn mi-LOH-suh-vich) (1941–2006), who had become the leader of the Serbian Communist Party in 1987 and had managed to stay in power by emphasizing his Serbian nationalism, rejected these efforts. He asserted that these republics could be independent only if new border arrangements were made to accommodate the Serb minorities in those republics who did not want to live outside the boundaries of a Greater Serbian state. Serbs constituted 11.6 percent of Croatia's population and 32 percent of Bosnia-Herzegovina's in 1981.

After negotiations among the six republics failed, Slovenia and Croatia declared their independence in June 1991. Milošević's government sent the Yugoslavian army, which it controlled, into Slovenia, without much success. In September 1991, it began a full assault against Croatia. Increasingly, the Yugoslavian army was becoming the Serbian army. Before a cease-fire was arranged, the Serbian forces had captured one-third of Croatia's territory in brutal and destructive fighting.

THE WAR IN BOSNIA The recognition of independent Slovenia, Croatia, and then Bosnia-Herzegovina by many European states and the United States early in 1992 did not stop the Serbs from turning their guns on Bosnia. By mid-1993, Serbian forces had occupied 70 percent of Bosnian territory. The Serbian policy of **"ethnic cleansing"**—killing or forcibly removing Bosnian Muslims from their lands—revived memories of Nazi atrocities during World War II. This account by one Muslim survivor from the town of Srebrenica

A Child's Account of the Shelling of Sarajevo

When Bosnia-Herzegovina declared its independence in March 1992, Serbian army units and groups of Bosnian Serbs went on the offensive and began to shell the capital city of Sarajevo. One of its residents was Zlata Filipovic, the ten-year-old daughter of a middle-class lawyer. Zlata was a fan of MTV and pizza, but when the Serbs began to shell Sarajevo from the hills above the city, her life changed dramatically, as is apparent in this excerpt from her diary.

Zlata Filipovic, *Zlata's Diary: A Child's Life in Sarajevo*

April 3, 1992: Daddy came back . . . all upset. He says there are terrible crowds at the train and bus stations. People are leaving Sarajevo.

April 4, 1992: There aren't many people in the streets. I guess it's fear of the stories about Sarajevo being bombed. But there's no bombing. . . .

April 5, 1992: I'm trying hard to concentrate so I can do my homework (reading), but I simply can't. Something is going on in town. You can hear gunfire from the hills.

April 6, 1992: Now they're shooting from the Holiday Inn, killing people in front of the parliament. . . . Maybe we'll go to the cellar. . . .

April 9, 1992: I'm not going to school. All the schools in Sarajevo are closed. . . .

April 14, 1992: People are leaving Sarajevo. The airport, train and bus stations are packed. . . .

April 18, 1992: There's shooting, shells are falling. This really is WAR. Mommy and Daddy are worried, they sit up late at night, talking. They're wondering what to do, but it's hard to know. . . . Mommy can't make up her mind—she's constantly in tears. She tries to hide it from me, but I see everything.

April 21, 1992: It's horrible in Sarajevo today. Shells falling, people and children getting killed, shooting. We will probably spend the night in the cellar.

April 26, 1992: We spent Thursday night with the Bobars again. The next day we had no electricity. We had no bread, so for the first time in her life Mommy baked some.

April 28, 1992: SNIFFLE! Everybody has gone. I'm left with no friends.

April 29, 1992: I'd write to you much more about the war if only I could. But I simply don't want to remember all these horrible things.

Q How do you think Zlata Filipovic was able to deal with the new conditions in her life?

Source: From *Zlata's Diary* by Zlata Filipovic, copyright © 1994 by Fixot et editions Robert Laffont. Used by permission of Viking Penguin, a division of Penguin Putnam, Inc.

(sreb-bruh-NEET-suh) is eerily reminiscent of the activities of the Nazi *Einsatzgruppen* (see Chapter 27):

> When the truck stopped, they told us to get off in groups of five. We immediately heard shooting next to the trucks. . . . About ten Serbs with automatic rifles told us to lie down on the ground face first. As we were getting down, they started to shoot, and I fell into a pile of corpses. I felt hot liquid running down my face. I realized that I was only grazed. As they continued to shoot more groups, I kept on squeezing myself in between dead bodies.[2]

Almost eight thousand men and boys were killed in the Serbian massacre at Srebrenica. Nevertheless, despite worldwide outrage, European governments failed to take a decisive and forceful stand against these Serbian activities. By 1995, some 250,000 Bosnians (mostly civilians) had been killed, and 2 million others were left homeless (see the box above).

Renewed offensives by mostly Muslim Bosnian government army forces and by the Croatian army regained considerable territory that had been lost to Serbian forces. Air strikes by NATO bombers, strongly advocated by U.S. president Bill Clinton, were launched in retaliation for Serb attacks on civilians and weakened the Serb military positions. A formal peace treaty was signed in Paris on December 14 that split Bosnia into a loose union of a Serb republic (with 49 percent of the land) and a Muslim-Croat federation (with 51 percent of the land). NATO agreed to send a force of 60,000 troops (20,000 American troops made up the largest single contingent) that would monitor the frontier between the new political entities (see Map 30.2).

MAP 30.2 The Lands of the Former Yugoslavia, 1995. By 1991, resurgent nationalism and the European independence wave overcame the forces that held Yugoslavia together. Declarations of independence by Slovenia, Croatia, and Bosnia-Herzegovina led to war with the Serbian-dominated rump Yugoslavia of Slobodan Milošević.

Q What aspects of Slovenia's location help explain why its war of liberation was briefer and less bloody than others in the former Yugoslavia?

THE WAR IN KOSOVO Peace in Bosnia, however, did not bring peace to the remnants of Yugoslavia. A new war erupted in 1999 over Kosovo, which had been granted the status of an autonomous province within Yugoslavia in 1974. Kosovo's inhabitants were mainly ethnic Albanians. But Kosovo also had a Serbian minority who considered Kosovo a sacred territory because it contained the site where the Ottoman Turks had defeated Serbian forces in the fourteenth century in a battle that became a defining moment in Serbian history.

In 1989, Yugoslav president Milošević stripped Kosovo of its autonomous status and outlawed any official use of the Albanian language. In 1993, some groups of ethnic Albanians founded the Kosovo Liberation Army (KLA) and began a campaign against Serbian rule in Kosovo. When Serb forces began to massacre ethnic Albanians in an effort to crush the KLA, the United States and its NATO allies sought to arrange a settlement. After months of negotiations, the Kosovo Albanians agreed to a peace plan that would have given the ethnic Albanians in Kosovo broad autonomy for a three-year interim period. When Milošević refused to sign the agreement, the United States and its NATO allies began a bombing campaign that forced the Yugoslavian government into compliance.

THE AFTERMATH By 2000, the Serbian people had finally tired of the violence and in the fall elections ousted Milošević from power. The new Serbian government under Vojislav Koštunica (VOH-yee-slav kuh-STOO-nit-suh) (b. 1944) moved quickly to cooperate with the international community and begin rebuilding the Serbian economy. On June 28, 2001, the Serbian government agreed to allow Milošević to be put on trial by an international tribunal for crimes against humanity for his ethnic cleansing policies throughout Yugoslavia's disintegration. He died in 2006 before his trial could be completed.

The fate of Bosnia has not yet been finally determined. Troops from the European Union remain in Bosnia to keep the peace between the Serb republic and the Muslim-Croat federation. More than thirty international organizations are at work rebuilding schools, roads, and sewers, but only the presence of the EU troops keeps old hatreds from erupting again.

In Kosovo, NATO military forces were brought in to maintain an uneasy peace, while United Nations officials worked to create democratic institutions and the EU provided funds for rebuilding the region's infrastructure. These efforts are ongoing but are made difficult by the festering hatred between Kosovo Albanians and the remaining Serbs.

The last political vestiges of Yugoslavia ceased to exist in 2004 when the Koštunica government officially renamed the truncated country "Serbia and Montenegro." Two years later, Montenegrins voted in favor of independence, and in 2008, Kosovo declared independence as well. Thus, ninety years after Yugoslavia was cobbled together, all six of its constituent republics (Slovenia, Croatia, Bosnia-Herzegovina, Serbia, Macedonia, and Montenegro) were once again independent nations, and a new one (Kosovo) had been born.

Western Europe and the Search for Unity

With the revolutions of 1989, western Europe faced new political possibilities and challenges. Germany was once again united, delighting the Germans but frightening their neighbors. At the same time, new opportunities for thinking of all of Europe as a political entity also emerged. Eastern Europe was no longer sealed off from western Europe by the Iron Curtain of the Cold War.

GERMANY RESTORED In the mid-1980s, West German chancellor Helmut Kohl had benefited greatly from an economic boom. Gradually, however, discontent with the Christian Democrats increased, and by 1988, their political prospects seemed diminished. But the 1989 revolution in East Germany led to the swift and unexpected reunification of the two Germanies, making the new German nation, with 79 million people, the leading power in Europe. Reunification, which was accomplished during Kohl's administration and owed much to his efforts, brought rich political dividends to the Christian Democrats.

But the excitement over reunification soon dissipated as new problems arose. All too soon, the realization set in that the revitalization of eastern Germany would take far more money than was originally thought, and Kohl's government was soon forced to face the politically undesirable task of raising taxes substantially. Moreover, the virtual collapse of the economy in eastern Germany led to extremely high levels of unemployment and severe discontent.

East Germans were also haunted by another memory from their recent past. The opening of the files of the secret police (the Stasi) showed that millions of East Germans had spied on their neighbors and colleagues, and even their spouses and parents, during the Communist era (see the Film & History feature on p. 751). A few senior Stasi officials were put on trial for their past actions, but many Germans preferred simply to close the door on an unhappy period in their lives.

As the century neared its close, then, Germans struggled to cope with the challenge of building a new, united nation. In 1998, voters took out their frustrations at the ballot box. Kohl's conservative coalition was defeated in elections, and a new prime minister, Social Democrat Gerhard Schröder (GAYR-hahrt SHRUR-duh) (b. 1944), came into office. But Schröder had little success at solving Germany's economic woes, and as a result of elections in 2005, Angela Merkel (AHNG-uh-luh MERK-uhl) (b. 1954), leader of the Christian Democrats, became the first female chancellor in German history. Merkel pursued health-care reform and new energy policies at home while taking a leading role in the affairs of the European Union. Merkel has since been re-elected and is currently the longest-serving elected head of state in the European Union. Merkel has led the European Union (EU) nations in attempting to solve the EU economic crises, while negotiating the Ukrainian crises and combating a surging anti-immigration movement in Germany.

POST-THATCHER BRITAIN While Margaret Thatcher dominated British politics in the 1980s, the Labour Party, beset by divisions between its moderate and radical wings, offered little effective opposition. Only in 1990 did Labour's fortunes seem to revive when Thatcher's government attempted to replace local property taxes with a flat-rate tax that would enable the rich to pay the same rate as the poor. In 1990, after antitax riots broke out, Thatcher's once remarkable popularity fell to an all-time low. At the end of November, she resigned and was replaced by John Major (b. 1943), whose Conservative Party won a narrow victory in the general elections held in April 1992. His government, however, failed to capture the imagination of most Britons.

In elections on May 1, 1997, the Labour Party won a landslide victory. The new prime minister, Tony Blair (b. 1953), was a moderate whose youthful energy immediately instilled new vigor into the political scene. Blair was one of the prominent leaders in forming an

FILM & HISTORY

The Lives of Others (2006)

DIRECTED BY FLORIAN HENCKEL VON DONNERSMARCK, *The Lives of Others*, which won the Academy Award for Best Foreign Film, is a German film (*Das Leben der Anderen*) that brilliantly recreates the depressing debilitation of East German society under its Communist regime and especially the Stasi, its secret police. Georg Dreyman (Sebastian Koch) is a successful playwright in the German Democratic Republic (East Germany). Although he is a dedicated socialist who has not offended the authorities, they try to determine whether he is completely loyal by wiretapping his apartment, where he lives with his girlfriend, Christa-Maria Sieland (Martina Gedeck), an actress in some of Dreyman's plays. Captain Gerd Wiesler (Ulrich Mühe) of the Stasi takes charge of the spying operation. He is the epitome of the perfect functionary—a cold, calculating, dedicated professional who is convinced he is building a better society and is only too eager to fight the "enemies of socialism." But in the course of listening to the everyday details of Dreyman's life, Wiesler begins to develop a conscience and becomes sympathetic to the writer. After a close friend of Dreyman's commits suicide, Dreyman turns against the Communist regime and anonymously writes an article on the alarming number of suicides in East German society for *Der Spiegel*, a West German magazine. Lieutenant Colonel Grubitz (Ulrich Tukur), Wiesler's boss, suspects that Dreyman is the author. His girlfriend is brought in for questioning and provides some damning information about Dreyman's involvement. Horrified by what she has done, she commits suicide, but Wiesler, who is now determined to save Dreyman, fudges his reports and protects him from being arrested. Wiesler's boss suspects what Wiesler has done and demotes him. The film ends after the fall of the Berlin Wall when the new German government opens the Stasi files.

When Dreyman reads his file, he realizes how Wiesler saved him and writes a book dedicated to him.

The film brilliantly captures the stifling atmosphere of East Germany under Communist rule. The Stasi had about ninety thousand employees but also recruited a network of hundreds of thousands of informers who submitted secret reports on their friends, family, bosses, and coworkers. Some volunteered the information, but as the film makes clear, others were bribed or blackmailed into cooperating with the authorities. As the movie demonstrates, the Stasi were experts at wiretapping dwellings and compiling detailed written reports about what they heard, including conversations, arguments, jokes, and even sexual activities. Ironically, Ulrich Mühe, who plays Captain Wiesler in the film, was an East German who himself had been spied on by the Stasi.

The Lives of Others has been praised by East Germans for accurately depicting the drab environment of their country and the role of the Stasi in fostering a society riddled by secrecy, fear, and the abuse of power. The dangers of governments that monitor their citizens are apparent and quite relevant in an age of laws such as the USA Patriot Act designed to fight terrorism. The police state is revealed for what it is, a soulless and hollow world with no redeeming features or values.

Creado Film/BR/Arte/The Kobal Collection at Art Resource, NY

Georg Dreyman (Sebastian Koch) examines his Stasi files.

international coalition against terrorism after the terrorist attack on the United States in 2001. Three years later, his support of the U.S. war in Iraq, when a majority of Britons opposed it, caused his popularity to plummet, although the failure of the Conservative Party to field a popular candidate kept him in power until the summer of 2007, when he stepped down and allowed the new Labour leader, Gordon Brown (b. 1951), to become prime minister. Elections held in early May 2010 were inconclusive: the Conservatives won the largest number of seats in Parliament but were twenty short of a majority. When Brown resigned a few days after the elections, Conservative David Cameron (b. 1966) became prime minister on the basis of a coalition with the Liberal Democrats. Cameron promised to decrease the government debt by reducing government waste and welfare benefits, cutting social services, and introducing legislation to overhaul Britain's health-care system. Cameron's austerity measures led to a sharp increase in unemployment in the public sector, while private sector jobs maintained steady growth. Despite government cuts, government deficits have almost doubled since 2007.

FRANCE: A MOVE TO THE RIGHT Although François Mitterrand was able to win a second term as president in 1988, France's economic decline continued. In 1993, French unemployment stood at 10.6 percent, and in the elections in March of that year, the Socialists won only 28 percent of the vote as a coalition of conservative parties gained 80 percent of the seats in the National Assembly. The move to the right in France was strengthened when the conservative mayor of Paris, Jacques Chirac (ZHAHK shee-RAK) (b. 1932), was elected president in 1995 and re-elected in 2002.

By 1995, resentment against foreign-born residents had become a growing political reality. Spurred by rising rates of unemployment and large numbers of immigrants from North Africa (often identified in the public mind with terrorist actions committed by militant groups based in the Middle East), many French voters advocated restrictions on all new immigration. Chirac himself pursued a plan of sending illegal immigrants back to their home countries.

In the fall of 2005, however, antiforeign sentiment provoked a backlash of its own as young Muslims in the crowded suburbs of Paris rioted against dismal living conditions and the lack of employment opportunities for foreign residents in France. After the riots subsided, government officials promised to adopt measures to respond to the complaints, but tensions between the Muslim community and the remainder of the French population have become a chronic source of social unrest—an unrest that Nicolas Sarkozy (nee-kohl-AH sar-koh-ZEE) (b. 1955), elected as president in 2007, promised to address but without much success. In 2009, unemployment among those under twenty-five was almost 22 percent, but in the suburbs that are home to many Muslims, youth joblessness exceeded 50 percent. Sarkozy lost his bid for a second term to Socialist Party candidate François Hollande (frahnh-SWAH oh-LAWND) (b. 1954) in a runoff election in May 2012.

Since 2012, Hollande has increased taxes for those making over 150,000 euros, increased the spending for renewable energy over nuclear power, and increased spending on education. Hollande also reformed France's entrenched labor laws, making it easier to fire employees. Although Hollande's approval ratings declined in response to his numerous policy changes, they rose after his handling of the Paris terrorist attacks on *Charlie Hebdo*, a French satirical magazine, in early 2015.

The Unification of Europe

With the addition of Austria, Finland, and Sweden in 1995, the European Community (EC) had grown to fifteen members. The EC was primarily an economic union, not a political one. The Treaty on European Union (also called the Maastricht Treaty after the city in the Netherlands where the agreement was reached) represented an attempt to create a true economic and monetary union of all EC members. On January 1, 1994, the EC renamed itself the European Union (EU). By 2000, the EU contained 370 million people and constituted the world's largest single trading entity, transacting one-fourth of the world's commerce. Another of its goals was to introduce a common currency, called the euro, which was adopted by twelve EU nations early in 1999. The European Central Bank was created on June 1, 1999, and by January 2012, the euro had officially replaced seventeen national currencies.

GOALS In addition to having a single internal market for its members and a common currency, the EU also established a common agricultural policy, under which subsidies are provided to farmers to enable them to sell their goods competitively on the world market. The policy also provides aid to the EU's poorest regions as well as subsidies for job training, education, and modernization. The end of national passports gave millions of Europeans greater flexibility in travel.

The EU has been less successful in setting common foreign policy goals, primarily because individual nations still see foreign policy as a national prerogative and are reluctant to give it up to an overriding institution. In 2009, however, the EU ratified the Lisbon Treaty, which created a full-time presidential post and a new voting system that reflects the size of each country's population. It also provided more power for the European Parliament in an effort to promote the EU's foreign policy goals.

TOWARD A UNITED EUROPE At the beginning of the twenty-first century, the EU has established a new goal: to incorporate into the union the states of eastern and southeastern Europe. Many of these states are considerably poorer than the older members, which raised the possibility that adding these nations might weaken the EU itself. To lessen the danger, EU members established a set of qualifications that focus on demonstrating a commitment both to market capitalism and to democracy, including not only the rule of law but also respect for minorities and human rights. In May 2004, the EU took the plunge and added ten new members: Cyprus, the Czech Republic, Estonia, Hungary, Latvia, Lithuania, Malta, Poland, Slovakia, and Slovenia. Their addition enlarged the population of the EU to 455 million people. In January 2007, the EU expanded again as Bulgaria and Romania joined the union, and in July 2013 Croatia joined (see Map 30.3).

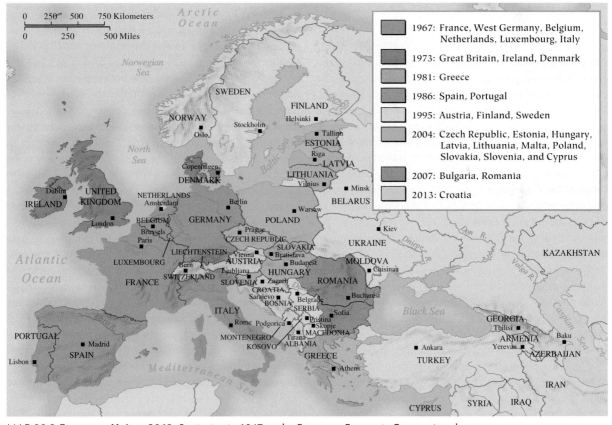

MAP 30.3 European Union, 2013. Beginning in 1967 as the European Economic Community, also known as the Common Market, the union of European states seeking to integrate their economies gradually grew from six members to twenty-eight in 2013. By 2002, the European Union had achieved two major goals—the creation of a single internal market and a common currency—although it has been less successful at working toward common political and foreign policy goals.

Q What additional nations do you think will eventually join the European Union?

The United States: Move to the Center

After twelve years of Republican administrations, the Democratic Party captured the U.S. presidency in the elections in November 1992. The inability of George H. W. Bush (b. 1924), Ronald Reagan's successor, to deal with the deficit problem, as well as an economic downturn, enabled Democrat Bill Clinton (b. 1946) to become president. The new president was a southerner who claimed to be a "new Democrat"—one who favored fiscal responsibility and a more conservative social agenda—a clear indication that the rightward drift in American politics had not been reversed by his victory. During his first term in office, Clinton reduced the budget deficit and signed a bill turning the welfare program back to the states while pushing measures to provide job opportunities for those Americans removed from the welfare rolls. By seizing the center of the American political agenda, Clinton was able to win re-election in 1996, although the Republican Party now held a majority in both houses of Congress.

Clinton's political fortunes were helped considerably by a lengthy economic revival. Much of Clinton's second term, however, was overshadowed by charges of presidential misconduct stemming from the president's affair with a White House intern. After a bitter partisan struggle, the U.S. Senate acquitted the president on two articles of impeachment brought by the House of Representatives. But Clinton's problems helped the Republican candidate, George W. Bush (b. 1946), win the presidential election in 2000. Although Bush lost the popular vote to Al Gore, he narrowly won the electoral vote after a highly controversial victory in the state of Florida was ultimately decided by the U.S. Supreme Court.

The first four years of Bush's administration were largely occupied with the war on terrorism and the U.S.-led war on Iraq. The Department of Homeland Security was established after the 2001 terrorist assaults to help protect the United States from future terrorist acts. At the same time, Bush pushed tax cuts through Congress that mainly favored the wealthy and helped produce record deficits reminiscent of the Reagan years. Environmentalists were especially disturbed by the Bush administration's efforts to weaken environmental laws and impose regulations to benefit American corporations. In November 2004, Bush was narrowly elected to a second term, after which his popularity plummeted drastically as discontent grew over the Iraq War and financial corruption in the Republican Party, as well as the administration's poor handling of relief efforts after Hurricane Katrina in 2005.

The many failures of the Bush administration led to the lowest approval ratings for a modern president and opened the door for a dramatic change in American politics. A fresh and often inspiring voice—that of Barack Obama (b. 1961)—who campaigned on a platform of change "we can believe in" and ending the war in Iraq, led to an overwhelming Democratic victory in the elections of 2008. The dramatic collapse of the American financial system in the fall of 2008 also favored the Democrats. Obama moved quickly at the beginning of 2009 to deal with the worst economic recession since the Great Depression.

At the same time, Obama persuaded Congress to pass a sweeping health-care bill to provide most Americans with medical insurance and to enact legislation aimed at regulating the financial institutions that had helped bring about the financial crisis. He also emphasized the need to combat global warming and the decline in the educational system. Obama was re-elected for a second term in 2012. In his second term, Obama has pursued policies for marriage equality for the LGBT (lesbian, gay, bisexual, and transgender) community and in the summer of 2014 began limited U.S. involvement in Iraq against the Islamic State of Iraq and the Levant (ISIL) (see "Islam and the West" later in this chapter). Obama also negotiated the normalizing of relations between Cuba and the United States.

Contemporary Canada

The government of Brian Mulroney, who came to power in 1984, sought greater privatization of Canada's state-run corporations and negotiated a free-trade agreement with the United States. Bitterly resented by many Canadians, the agreement cost Mulroney's government much of its popularity. In 1993, the ruling Conservatives were overwhelmingly defeated, and the Liberal leader, Jean Chrétien (ZHAHNH kray-TEN) (b. 1934), became prime minister. Chrétien's conservative fiscal policies, combined with strong economic growth, enabled his government to have a budgetary surplus by the late 1990s and led to another Liberal victory in the elections of 1997.

Charges of widespread financial corruption in the government, however, led to a Liberal defeat. In 2006, Stephen Harper (b. 1959), leader of the Conservative Party, was elected prime minister and has since been re-elected twice. Harper led Canada through the 2008 economic crises, stabilizing the Canadian economy by 2013. Despite his economic successes, Harper and the Conservative Party have been heavily criticized for cutting funding for environmental causes and censoring scientists in the press.

Mulroney's government had been unable to settle the ongoing crisis over the French-speaking province of Quebec. In the late 1960s, the Parti Québécois (par-TEE kay-bek-KWAH), headed by René Lévesque (ruh-NAY luh-VEK), ran on a platform of Quebec's secession from the Canadian union. To pursue their dream of separation, some underground separatist groups even resorted to terrorist bombings. In 1976, the Parti Québécois won Quebec's provincial elections and in 1980 called for a referendum that would enable the provincial government to negotiate Quebec's independence from the rest of Canada. Quebec voters narrowly rejected the plan in 1995, however, and debate over the province's status continues to divide Canada.

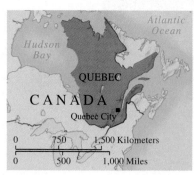

Quebec

After the Cold War: New World Order or Age of Terrorism?

Q FOCUS QUESTIONS: How and why did the Cold War end? What are the main issues in the struggle against terrorism?

Even before the collapse of the Soviet Union, there had been tantalizing signs of a thaw in the Cold War. China and the United States had decided in 1979 to establish mutual diplomatic relations, a consequence of Beijing's decision to focus on domestic reform and stop supporting wars of national liberation in Asia. Six years later, the ascent of Mikhail Gorbachev to leadership, culminating in the demise of the Soviet Union in 1991, brought a decisive end to almost half a century of bitter rivalry between the world's two superpowers.

The End of the Cold War

The accession of Mikhail Gorbachev to power in the Soviet Union in 1985 eventually brought a dramatic end to the Cold War. Gorbachev was willing to rethink many of the fundamental assumptions underlying Soviet foreign policy, and his "New Thinking," as it was called, opened the door to a series of stunning changes. For one, Gorbachev initiated a plan for arms limitation that led in 1987 to an agreement with the United States to eliminate intermediate-range nuclear weapons (the INF Treaty). Both sides had incentives to tamp down the expensive arms race. Gorbachev hoped to make extensive economic and internal reforms, and the United States had serious deficit problems. During the Reagan years, the United States had moved from being a creditor nation to being the world's biggest debtor nation. By 1990, both countries were becoming aware that their large military budgets made it difficult for them to solve their serious social problems.

The years 1989 and 1990 were a crucial period in the ending of the Cold War. As described earlier, the postwar settlements came unstuck as a mostly peaceful revolutionary upheaval swept through eastern Europe. Gorbachev's policy of allowing greater autonomy for the Communist regimes of eastern Europe meant that the Soviet Union would no longer militarily support Communist governments that faced internal revolt. The unwillingness of the Soviet regime to use force to maintain the status quo, as it had in Hungary in 1956 and in Czechoslovakia in 1968, opened the door to the overthrow of the Communist regimes. The reunification of Germany on October 3, 1990, marked the end of one of the most prominent legacies of the Cold War.

The Persian Gulf War provided the first major opportunity for testing the new relationship between the United States and the Soviet Union in the post–Cold War era. In early August 1990, Iraqi military forces

By the end of 1991, the Soviet Union had disintegrated, making any renewal of global rivalry between the superpowers impossible and leaving the United States as the world's leading military power. With the end of superpower rivalry and the collapse of the Soviet Union in 1991, attention focused on the new post–Cold War era. Many observers were optimistic. The U.S. president George H. W. Bush looked forward to a new era of peace and international cooperation that he called the "New World Order." But the voices of optimism began to fade as it became clear that forces were now being released that had long been held in check by the ideological rigidities of the Cold War. The age of conflict that had long characterized the twentieth century was not at an end but was simply beginning to take a different form.

An Age of Terrorism?

Acts of terror by individuals and groups opposed to governments have become a frightening aspect of modern Western society and indeed of all the world. In 1996, President Clinton called terrorism "the enemy of our generation," and since the end of the Cold War, it has often seemed as though terrorism has replaced communism as the West's number one enemy.

Already during the late 1970s and 1980s, concern about terrorism was often at the top of foreign policy agendas in the United States and many European countries. Small bands of terrorists used such tactics as assassination, indiscriminate killing of civilians (especially by bombing), the taking of hostages, and the hijacking of airplanes to draw attention to their demands or to destabilize governments in the hope of achieving their political goals. Terrorist acts garnered considerable media attention. When Palestinian terrorists kidnapped and killed eleven Israeli athletes at the Munich Olympic games in 1972, hundreds of millions of people watched the drama unfold on television.

Reagan and Gorbachev. The willingness of Mikhail Gorbachev and Ronald Reagan to slow the arms race was a significant factor in ending the Cold War confrontation between the United States and the Soviet Union. Reagan and Gorbachev are shown here standing before Saint Basil's Cathedral during Reagan's visit to Moscow in 1988.

invaded and occupied the small neighboring country of Kuwait, at the top of the Persian Gulf. The Iraqi invasion of Kuwait sparked a worldwide outcry, and an international force led by the United States liberated Kuwait and destroyed a substantial portion of Iraq's armed forces in the early months of 1991. Gorbachev and the Soviets played a minor role in the crisis and supported the American action.

Motivations for terrorist acts varied considerably. Left-wing groups, such as the Baader-Meinhof (BAH-durr-MYN-huff) gang (also known as the Red Army Faction) in Germany and the Red Brigades in Italy, consisted chiefly of affluent middle-class young people who denounced the injustices of capitalism and supported acts of revolutionary terrorism in an attempt to bring down the system. Right-wing terrorist groups, such as the New Order in Italy and the Charles Martel Club in France, used bombings to foment disorder and bring about authoritarian regimes. These groups received little or no public support, and authorities were able to crush them fairly quickly.

But terrorist acts were also committed by militant nationalists who wished to create separatist states. Because they received considerable support from local populations sympathetic to their cause, these terrorist groups could maintain their activities over a long period of time. Most prominent was the Irish Republican Army (IRA), which resorted to vicious attacks against the ruling government and innocent civilians in Northern Ireland. Over a period of twenty years, IRA terrorists were responsible for the deaths of two thousand people in Northern Ireland; three-fourths of the victims were civilians.

Terrorist Attack on the United States

One of the most destructive acts of terrorism occurred on September 11, 2001, in the United States. Four groups of terrorists hijacked four commercial jet airplanes after takeoff from Boston, Newark, and Washington, D.C. The hijackers flew two of the airplanes directly into the towers of the World Trade Center in New York City, causing these buildings, as well as a number of surrounding buildings, to collapse. A third hijacked plane slammed into the Pentagon near Washington, D.C. The fourth plane, apparently headed for Washington, crashed instead in an isolated area of Pennsylvania, evidently as the result of an attempt by a group of heroic passengers to overcome the hijackers. In total, nearly three thousand people were killed, including everyone aboard the four airliners.

These coordinated acts of terror were carried out by hijackers connected to an international terrorist organization known as al-Qaeda ("the Base"), run by Osama bin Laden (1957–2011). A native of Saudi Arabia, bin Laden used an inherited fortune to set up terrorist training camps in Afghanistan, under the protection of the nation's militant fundamentalist Islamic rulers known as the Taliban. On May 2, 2011, Osama bin

Terrorist Attack on the World Trade Center in New York City. On September 11, 2001, hijackers flew two commercial jetliners into the twin towers of the World Trade Center. The photograph shows the second of the two jetliners about to hit one of the towers while smoke billows from the site of the first attack.

Laden was killed by American military and Central Intelligence Agency operatives in a compound in Pakistan, under a directive of President Obama.

WAR IN AFGHANISTAN After the September 11 attacks, President George W. Bush vowed to wage a lengthy war on terrorism and worked to create a coalition of nations to assist in ridding the world of al-Qaeda and other terrorist groups. In October 2001, U.S. and NATO air forces began bombing Taliban-controlled command centers, airfields, and al-Qaeda hiding places in Afghanistan. On the ground, Afghan forces opposed to the Taliban, assisted by U.S. special forces, pushed the Taliban out of the capital city of Kabul and seized control of nearly all of the country by the end of November. A multiethnic government was installed but faced problems from renewed Taliban activity. In 2009, President Obama decided to deal with the deteriorating situation by sending an additional thirty thousand troops to Afghanistan. In 2014, American troops largely withdrew from Afghanistan.

WAR IN IRAQ In 2002, President Bush, charging that Iraqi dictator Saddam Hussein (1937–2006) had not only provided support to bin Laden's terrorist organization but also sought to develop "weapons of mass destruction" to be used against the nation's enemies, threatened to invade Iraq and remove the dictator from power. Both claims were denied by the Iraqis and widely doubted by other members of the United Nations; nevertheless, the United States decided to move against Iraq despite the lack of international support. The U.S. plan upset many Arab leaders and fanned anti-American sentiment throughout the Muslim world.

In March 2003, a predominantly American army invaded Iraq. The Iraqi troops were quickly defeated, and in the months that followed, occupation forces sought to restore stability to the country while setting forth plans to lay the foundations of a future democratic society. But although Saddam Hussein was later captured by U.S. troops, Saddam's supporters, foreign terrorists, and Islamic militants continued to battle the American-led forces.

U.S. efforts focused on training an Iraqi military capable of defeating the insurgents and establishing an Iraqi government that could hold free elections and create a democracy. Establishing a new government was difficult, however, because of differences among the three major groups in Iraqi society: Shi'ite Muslims, Sunni Muslims, and ethnic Kurds. Although a new Iraqi government came into being, it proved unable to establish a unified state. By 2006, violence had increased dramatically, and Iraq seemed to be descending into civil war between the Shi'ites, who control southern Iraq, and the Sunnis, who control central Iraq. An increase in American troops in 2007 helped stabilize conditions within a year. The U.S. and Iraqi governments then agreed to a complete withdrawal of American troops by 2011, a goal that President Obama affirmed after taking office and then achieved three years later.

The West and Islam

One of the major sources of terrorist activity against the West, especially in the United States, has come from some parts of the Muslim world. No doubt, the ongoing Israeli-Palestinian conflict, in which the United States has steadfastly supported Israel, helped give rise to anti-Western and especially anti-U.S. feeling among many Muslims. In 1979, a revolution in Iran that led to the overthrow of the shah and the creation of a new Islamic government led by Ayatollah Khomeini, also fed anti-Western sentiment. In the eyes of the ayatollah and his followers, the United States was the "great Satan," the powerful protector of Israel, and the enemy of Muslim peoples everywhere.

The involvement of the United States in the liberation of Kuwait in the Persian Gulf War in 1991 also had unexpected consequences in the relationship of Islam and the West. During that war, U.S. forces were stationed in Saudi Arabia, the location of many sacred Islamic sites. The presence of Americans was considered an affront to Islam by anti-Western Islamic groups, especially that of Osama bin Laden and his followers. These anti-Western attitudes came to be shared by a number of radical Islamic groups, as was evident in the 2003 bombing in Madrid, the 2005 bombing on subway trains in London, and the 2015 attack in Paris at the headquarters of *Charlie Hebdo*, a French satirical magazine.

In early 2014, a Muslim jihadist rebel group, the Islamic State of Iraq and Levant (ISIL), captured significant territory in western Iraq and northern and central Syria. ISIL's use of extreme violence, ethnic cleansing, and Internet videos of beheadings of their captives has led to worldwide repudiation of the group and commitment from over sixty countries to directly confront ISIL.

New Directions and New Problems in Western Society

Q **FOCUS QUESTIONS:** What are the major developments in the women's movement since 1985? What problems have immigrants created for European society?

Dramatic social developments have accompanied political and economic changes since 1985. New opportunities for women have emerged, and a reinvigorated women's movement has sought to bring new meaning to the principle of equality with men. New problems for Western society have also arisen with a growing reaction against foreign workers and immigrants.

Transformation in Women's Lives

Parents need to produce an average of 2.1 children to maintain the level of a country's population. In many European countries, birthrates first fell short of that number in the 1960s, and the decline has continued since then. By the 1990s, among the nations of the European Union, the average number of children per mother was 1.4. Spain's rate of 1.15 was among the lowest in the world in 2002.

At the same time, the number of women in the workforce continued to rise. In Britain, for example, women made up 44 percent of the labor force in 1990, up from 32 percent in 1970. Moreover, women were entering new employment areas. Greater access to universities and professional schools enabled women to take jobs in law, medicine, government, business, and education. In the Soviet Union, for example, about 70 percent of doctors and teachers were women. Nevertheless, economic inequality still often prevailed; women received lower wages than men for comparable work and found fewer opportunities for advancement to management positions.

THE WOMEN'S MOVEMENT Feminists in the women's liberation movement came to believe that women themselves must transform the fundamental conditions of their lives. They did so in a variety of ways. First, they formed numerous "consciousness-raising" groups to heighten awareness of women's issues. Women got together to share their personal experiences and become aware of the many ways that male dominance affected their lives. This consciousness-raising helped many women become activists.

Women also sought and gained a measure of control over their own bodies by insisting that they had a right to both contraception and abortion. In the 1960s and 1970s, hundreds of thousands of European women worked to repeal the laws that outlawed contraception and abortion. In 1968, a French law permitted the sale of contraceptive devices, and in the 1970s, French feminists began calling for the legalization of abortion. In 1979, abortion became legal in France. Even in Catholic countries where the church remained adamantly opposed to abortion, legislation allowing contraception and abortion was passed in the 1970s and 1980s.

As more women became activists, they also became involved in new issues. In the 1980s and 1990s, women faculty in universities concentrated on influencing cultural attitudes through the new academic field of women's studies, which stressed the role and contributions of women in history. As a result, courses in women's studies proliferated in both American and European colleges and universities.

Other women began to try to affect the political environment by allying with the antinuclear movement. In 1982, a group of women protested American nuclear missiles in Britain by chaining themselves to the fence of an American military base. Thousands more joined in creating a peace camp around the military compound. Enthusiasm ran high; one participant said, "I'll never forget that feeling; it'll live with me forever.... We walked round, and we clasped hands.... It was for women; it was for peace; it was for the world."[3]

Some women joined the ecological movement. As one German writer who was concerned with environmental issues said, it is women "who must give birth to children, willingly or unwillingly, in this polluted world of ours." Especially prominent were the female members of the Green Party in Germany (see "The Environment and the Green Movements" in Chapter 29), which supported environmental issues and elected forty-two delegates to the West German parliament in 1987. Among the delegates was Petra Kelly (1947–1992), one of the founders of the German Green Party and a tireless campaigner for the preservation of the environment as well as human rights and equality.

Women in the West have also reached out to work with women from the rest of the world in international conferences to change the conditions of their lives. Between 1975 and 1995, the United Nations held women's conferences in Mexico City, Copenhagen, Nairobi, and Beijing. These meetings made clear that women from Western and non-Western countries had different priorities. Whereas women from Western countries spoke about political, economic, cultural, and sexual rights, women from developing countries in Latin America, Africa, and Asia focused on bringing an end to the violence, hunger, and disease that haunted their lives. Despite these differences, the meetings were an indication of how women in both developed and developing nations were organizing to make all people aware of women's issues.

Guest Workers and Immigrants

As the economies of the western European countries revived in the 1950s and 1960s, a severe labor shortage encouraged them to rely on foreign workers. Government and businesses actively recruited so-called **guest workers** to staff essential jobs. Scores of Turks and eastern and southern Europeans came to Germany, North Africans to France, and people from the Caribbean, India, and Pakistan to Great Britain. Overall, there were probably 15 million guest workers in Europe in the 1980s. They constituted 17 percent of the labor force in Switzerland and 10 percent in Germany.

In the 1980s, there was an influx of other refugees, especially to West Germany, which had liberal immigration laws that permitted people seeking asylum for political persecution to enter the country. During the 1970s and 1980s, West Germany absorbed over a million refugees from eastern Europe and East Germany. In 1986 alone, 200,000 political refugees from Pakistan, Bangladesh, and Sri Lanka entered the country. Other parts of Europe saw a similar influx of foreigners. Between 1992 and 2002, London and the southeast region of England witnessed an increase of 700,000 foreigners, primarily from Yugoslavia, Southeast Asia, the Middle East, and Africa. A survey in 1998 found that English was not the first language of one-third of inner-city children in London.

The arrival of so many foreigners strained not only the social services of European countries but also the patience of many native residents who opposed the sudden ethnic diversification of their countries. Antiforeign sentiment increased, especially as domestic unemployment grew, and it was stoked by right-wing political parties that catered to people's complaints. Although these parties had only limited success in elections, their modest accomplishments encouraged traditional parties to adopt more nationalistic policies. Occasionally, an antiforeign party enjoyed particular success. In Austria, Jorg Haider (YORG HY-dur) (1950–2008), whose Freedom Party received 27 percent of the vote in 1999, cushioned his rejection of foreigners by appealing to Austrian nationalism and attacking the European Union: "We Austrians should answer not to the European Union, not to Maastricht, not to some international idea or other, but to this our Homeland."[4] Even more frightening than the growth of these right-wing political parties were the organized campaigns of violence in the early 1990s, especially against African and Asian immigrants, by radical, right-wing groups.

Even nations that have been especially tolerant in opening their borders to immigrants and seekers of asylum are changing their policies. In the Netherlands, 19 percent of the people have a foreign background, representing almost 180 nationalities. In 2004, however, the Dutch government passed tough new immigration laws, including a requirement that newcomers pass a Dutch language and culture test before being admitted to the Netherlands. Sometimes these policies have been aimed at religious practices. In 2004, France enacted a law prohibiting female students from wearing a headscarf (*hijab*) to school. Critics of the law argue that it will exacerbate ethnic and religious tensions in France, while supporters maintain that it upholds the traditions of secularism and equality for women in France (see the box on p. 761).

Western Culture Today

Q **Focus Questions:** What major Western cultural trends have emerged since 1985? What is the Digital Age, and what are its products, results, and dangers?

Western culture has expanded to most parts of the world, although some societies see it as a challenge to their own culture and national identity. At the same time, other societies are also strongly influencing Western cultural expressions, making recent Western culture a reflection of the evolving global response to the rapid changes in human society today.

Varieties of Religious Life

Despite the revival of religion after World War II, church attendance in Europe and the United States declined dramatically in the 1960s and 1970s as a result of growing secular attitudes. Yet even though the numbers of regular churchgoers in established Protestant and Catholic churches continued to decline, the number of fundamentalist churches and churchgoers has been growing, especially in the United States.

Fundamentalism was originally a movement within Protestantism that arose early in the twentieth century. Its goal was to maintain a strict traditional interpretation of the Bible and the Christian faith, especially in opposition to the theory of Darwinian evolution and secularism. In the 1980s and 1990s, fundamentalists became involved in a struggle against "secular humanism," "godless communism," legalized abortion, and homosexuality. Especially in the United States, fundamentalists organized politically to elect candidates who supported their views.

THE GROWTH OF ISLAM Fundamentalism, however, was not unique to Protestantism. In Islam, the term *fundamentalism* is used to refer to a return to traditional Islamic values, especially in opposition to a perceived weakening of morality due to the corrupting influence of Western ideas and practices. After the Iranian Revolution of 1979, the term was also applied to radical Islamic movements, such as the Taliban in Afghanistan, who favored militant action against Western influence.

OPPOSING **VIEWPOINTS**

Islam and the West: Secularism in France

The banning of headscarves in schools in 2004 was preceded by a debate on the secular state in France. Secularism in France extends beyond the separation of church and state: while recognizing the right to religious expression, French law dictates that religious expression must remain in the private sphere and cannot enter the public realm. Before the law banning headscarves was enacted, President Jacques Chirac set up a committee to interview school, religious, and political leaders on whether students should be allowed to wear headscarves in schools. The commission decided in favor of prohibiting all conspicuous religious symbols in schools.

The first selection below is taken from a speech by President Chirac, who favored the ban. The second selection is taken from interviews with French Muslim women, many of them from the Maghreb (the Arabic term for Northwest Africa, chiefly Morocco, Algeria, and Tunisia). Many of these women questioned how the law protects their individual rights and freedom of religious expression.

French President Jacques Chirac on Secularism in French Society

The debate on the principle of secularism goes to the very heart of our values. It concerns our national cohesion, our ability to live together, our ability to unite on what is essential.... Many young people of immigrant origin, whose first language is French, and who are in most cases of French nationality, succeed and feel at ease in a society which is theirs. This kind of success must also be made possible by breaking the wall of silence and indifference which surrounds the reality of discrimination today. I know about the feeling of being misunderstood, of helplessness, sometimes even of revolt, among young French people of immigrant origin whose job applications are rejected because of the way their names sound, and who are too often confronted with discrimination in the fields of access to housing or even simply of access to leisure facilities.... All of France's children, whatever their history, whatever their origin, whatever their beliefs, are the daughters and sons of the republic. They have to be recognized as such, in law but above all in reality. By ensuring respect for this requirement, by reforming our integration policy, by our ability to bring equal opportunities to life, we shall bring national cohesion to life again. We shall also do so by bringing to life the principle of secularism, which is a pillar of our constitution. It expresses our wish to live together in respect, dialogue and tolerance. Secularism guarantees freedom of conscience. It protects the freedom to believe or not to believe.... We also need to reaffirm secularism in schools, because schools must be preserved absolutely....

There is of course no question of turning schools into a place of uniformity, of anonymity, where religious life or belonging would be banned. It is a question of enabling teachers and head teachers, who are today in the frontline and confronted with real difficulties, to carry out their mission serenely with the affirmation of a clear rule. Until recently, as a result of a reasonable custom which was respected spontaneously, nobody ever doubted that pupils, who are naturally free to live their faith, should nevertheless not arrive in schools, secondary schools or A-level colleges, in religious clothes. It is not a question of inventing new rules or of shifting the boundaries of secularism. It is a question of expressing, with respect but clearly and firmly, a rule which has been part of our customs and practices for a very long time.... In all conscience, it is my view that the wearing of clothes or of symbols which conspicuously demonstrate religious affiliations must be banned in state schools.

North African Women in France Respond to the Headscarf Ban

Labiba (Thirty-Five-Year-Old Algerian)

I don't feel that they should interfere in the private life of people in the respect that we're in a secular country; France shouldn't take a position toward one religion to the detriment of another.... I think that in a secular school, we should all be secular, otherwise we need to have religious school and then everyone is free to wear what he wants.

(continued)

(Opposing Viewpoints continued)

Nour (Thirty-Four-Year-Old Algerian)

Honestly, you know the secular school, it doesn't miss celebrating Easter, and when they celebrate Easter, it doesn't bother me. My daughter comes home with painted Easter eggs and everything; it's pretty; it's cute. There are classes that are over 80 percent Maghrebin in the suburbs, and they celebrate Easter, they celebrate Christmas, you see? And that's not a problem for the secular school. And I don't find that fair.

I find that when it's Ramadan, they should talk about Ramadan. Honestly, me, it wouldn't be a problem. On the contrary, someone who comes into class ... with a veil, that would pose a question actually, that we could discuss in class, to know why this person wears the veil. So why punish them, amputate them from that part of their culture without discussing it? Why is it so upsetting to have someone in class who wears a veil, when we could make it a subject of discussion on all religions? ...

For a country that is home to so many cultures, there's no excuse.

Isma (Thirty-Six-Year-Old Algerian)

The girls who veil in France, especially in the high school and junior high students, it's first of all a question of identity, because these girls are born in France to foreign parents.... At a given time an adolescent wants to affirm himself, so he thinks, I'd say, he thinks that it's by his clothes that he shows that he comes from somewhere, that he's from someone. So then, I think you should let them do it, and afterwards, by themselves, people come back to who they really are.

Q What were the perspectives of the French president and the French Muslim women who were interviewed? How do they differ? Do you think there might be a way to reconcile the opposing positions? Why or why not?

Sources: French President Jacques Chirac on Secularism in French Society. From "France's President Lays Out His Views on the Principle of Secularism in the French State—in Schools and the Public Sector" from http://news.bbc.co.uk/go/em/fr/-/2/hi/europe/3330679.stm. North African Women in France Respond to the Headscarf Ban. Caitlin Killian, *Gender and Society*, Vol. 17, No. 4, pp. 567–590, copyright © 2003 by SAGE Publications. Reprinted by Permission of SAGE Publications.

Despite the wariness of Islamic radicalism in the aftermath of the September 11, 2001, terrorist attacks on the United States, Islam is growing in both Europe and the United States, thanks primarily to the migration of people from Muslim countries. As Muslim communities became established in France, Germany, Britain, Italy, and Spain during the 1980s and 1990s, they built mosques for religious worship and religious education.

POPE JOHN PAUL II AND THE CATHOLIC CHURCH Although changes have also occurred in the Roman Catholic Church, much of its history in the 1980s and 1990s was dominated by the charismatic Pope John Paul II (1920–2005). Karol Wojtyla (KAH-rul voy-TEE-wah), who had been the archbishop of Krakow in Poland before his elevation to the papacy in 1978, was the first non-Italian to be elected pope since the sixteenth century. Although he alienated a number of people by reasserting traditional Catholic teaching on such issues as birth control, women in the priesthood, and clerical celibacy, John Paul's numerous travels around the world helped strengthen the Catholic Church throughout the non-Western world. John Paul was a powerful figure in reminding Europeans of their spiritual heritage and the need to temper the pursuit of materialism with spiritual concerns.

The global nature of the Catholic Church became apparent on March 13, 2013, with the election of a new pope. Cardinal Jorge Mario Bergoglio (b. 1936), the archbishop of Buenos Aires, became the first Latin American as well as the first non-European since the eighth century to be elected pope. He chose to be called Pope Francis in honor of the humble Saint Francis of Assisi (see Chapter 10).

Art in the Age of Commerce: The 1980s and 1990s

Throughout the 1980s and 1990s, the art industry increasingly adopted the techniques of marketing and advertising. With large sums of money invested in artists, pressure mounted to achieve critical and commercial success. Negotiating the distinction between art and popular culture was essential because many people equated merit with sales or economic value.

In the art world, Neo-Expressionism reached its zenith in the mid-1980s. The economic boom and free spending of the Reagan years contributed to a thriving art scene in the United States. Neo-Expressionist artists like Anselm Kiefer (AN-selm KEEF-uhr) (b. 1945) became increasingly popular as the art market soared. The German-born Kiefer combines aspects of Abstract Expressionism, collage, and German Expressionism to create works that are stark and haunting. His *Departure from Egypt* (1984) is a meditation on Jewish history and its descent into the horrors of Nazism. Kiefer hoped that a portrayal of Germany's atrocities could free Germans from their past and bring some good out of evil.

The Digital Age

Since the invention of the microprocessor in 1971, the capabilities of computers have continued to grow, resulting in the Information Age or Digital Age we know today. Beginning in the 1980s, companies such as Apple and Microsoft created the technology that made possible ever more powerful computers. By the 1990s, the booming technology industry had made Microsoft founder Bill Gates the richest man in the world. Much of this success was due to several innovations that made computers virtually indispensable in the fields of communication, information, and entertainment.

THE TECHNOLOGICAL WORLD The advent of electronic mail, or e-mail, in the mid-1990s transformed the way that people communicate. As the capacity of computers to transmit data increased, e-mail messages could carry document and image attachments, making them a workable and speedier alternative to conventional postal mail. Perhaps even more transformative was the Internet, a network of smaller, interlinking webpages with sites devoted to news, commerce, entertainment, and academic scholarship. At first, websites were limited to text-based documents, but as computer processors became more powerful, video and music were added.

Advances in telecommunications led to wireless cellular or mobile telephones. Although cellular phones existed in the 1970s and 1980s, it was not until the digital components of these devices were reduced in size in the 1990s that the phones became truly portable. The ubiquity of cell phones today and their ability to transfer data electronically have made text messaging and electronic mail the primary form of global communication. Open-forum social media sites, such as Twitter and Facebook, have increased the availability and speed of information.

MUSIC AND ART IN THE DIGITAL AGE In 2001, Apple introduced the iPod, a portable digital music player. The pocket-sized device revolutionized the music industry by allowing users to download music from the Internet. Whereas the iPod altered the way we listen to, store, and access music, innovations in digital technology have changed the sound and production of music. In the late 1990s, musicians such as Moby and Fatboy Slim became internationally famous for creating music layered with synthesizers, distorted guitars, and simulated drum beats. These artists "sampled" snippets of earlier soul music to create albums and film scores.

Many visual artists have also adopted digital effects in producing artworks that fuse photography, sculpture, and cinema. Bill Viola (b. 1951) was one of the

Bill Viola, The Crossing, 1996. Two-channel video and sound installation, continuous loop 16 feet × 27 feet 6 inches × 57 feet (4.9 × 8.4 × 17.4 m) Solomon R. Guggenheim Museum (2000.61), New York. Gift, The Bohen Foundation, 2000. Photograph by Sally Ritts © The Solomon R. Guggenheim Foundation, New York.

Bill Viola, *The Crossing* (1996). In this video piece, Viola projected two films, one on each side of a sixteen-foot-high screen. On one side, a man is inundated with water, while on the other side, he is consumed by flames. The events occur in slow motion and, when experienced in conjunction with the sound of the deluge and/or flames, evoke feelings of spiritual regeneration.

first artists to exclusively employ video in his exhibits. By projecting films in a gallery space, Viola created powerful sensory experiences. He evoked mystical sensations with his allusions to rebirth and mysticism, contrasting light, sound, and focus with techniques of slow motion and editing.

FILM: FANTASY AND EPICS The films, video games, and literature of the late 1990s and early 2000s made fantasy and historical epics internationally popular. The successful adaptation of the *Lord of the Rings* trilogy, the Harry Potter series, and *The Hobbit* indicated the manner in which mythology, magic, and medieval fantasies appeal to contemporary sensibilities. At the heart of these epic motion pictures, *Troy* and *Gladiator* included, is a mythical struggle between good and evil that is governed by a moral sense of right and wrong, love, and companionship. These romanticized tales also featured non-Western cultures, as Japanese animé and martial arts films increased in worldwide popularity. The computer animation and digitized special effects of these movies reflect the impact of computers on the film industry as it too enters the Digital Age.

Toward a Global Civilization

Q FOCUS QUESTION: What is globalization, and what are its main characteristics in the twenty-first century?

Multiculturalism in the arts reminds us that more and more people are becoming aware of the political, economic, and social interdependence of the world's nations and the global nature of our contemporary problems. We are coming to understand that destructive forces generated in one part of the world soon affect the entire world. Smokestack pollution in one nation can produce acid rain in another. Oil spills and dumping of wastes in the ocean have an impact on the shores of many nations. As crises of food, water, energy, and natural resources proliferate, one nation's solutions often become other nations' problems. The new globalism includes the recognition that the challenges that seem to threaten human existence today are global.

As noted in the discussion of the Digital Age, an important part of global awareness is the technological dimension. The growth of new technology has made possible levels of world communication that simply did not exist before. At the same time that Osama bin Laden and al-Qaeda were denouncing the forces of modernization, they were doing so using advanced telecommunication systems that had only recently been developed. The technology revolution has tied peoples and nations closely together and contributed to **globalization**, the term that is frequently used to describe the process by which peoples and nations have become more interdependent. Economically, globalization has taken the form of a global economy.

The Global Economy

Especially since the 1970s, the world has developed a **global economy** in which the production, distribution, and sale of goods are accomplished on a worldwide scale. Several international institutions have contributed to the rise of the global economy. Soon after the end of World War II in 1945, the United States and other nations established the World Bank and the International Monetary Fund (IMF). The World Bank is a group of five international organizations, largely controlled by developed countries, which provides grants, loans, and advice for economic development to developing countries. The goal of the IMF is to oversee the global financial system by supervising exchange rates and offering financial and technical assistance to developing nations. Today, 187 countries are members of the IMF. However, critics have argued that both the World Bank and the IMF push inappropriate Western economic practices on non-Western nations that only aggravate the poverty and debt of developing nations.

Another reflection of the new global economic order is the **multinational corporation** or **transnational corporation** (a company that has divisions in more than two countries). Prominent examples of multinational corporations include Siemens, Wal-Mart, Exxon-Mobil, Mitsubishi, and the Sony Corporation. These companies are among the two hundred largest multinational corporations, which are responsible for more than half of the world's industrial production (see Images of Everyday Life on p. 765). A recent comparison of corporate sales and national gross domestic product disclosed that only half of the world's largest economies are nations; the other half are corporations.

THE END OF EXCESS? One consequence of the global economic order has been the growing interconnectedness of financial markets, which has contributed to the world's economic problems in recent years. In late 2007, the global economy faced a severe economic crisis following the collapse of the U.S. housing market. Spurred by low interest rates in the early 2000s, easily

IMAGES OF EVERYDAY LIFE

The New Global Economy: Fast Fashion

AN EXAMPLE OF the new global company is Inditex, best known for Zara, its oldest brand. The owner of the company, Amancio Ortega Gaona, is one of the wealthiest people in the world. His company pioneered a new business model, known as "fast fashion." It sells fashionable clothes for a fraction of the price of designer clothes in high-end retail stores, often located on some of the most fashionable shopping streets. Zara has capitalized on the new global economy of the late twentieth and early twenty-first centuries by using new technological, transportation, and communication systems to design and produce a garment in less than three weeks. Zara makes 840 million garments a year and has around 5,900 stores in eighty-five countries. Seen below (top left) is the design area in the Zara factory in La Coruña, Spain, where a number of designers are working together. The photo at bottom left shows a line of shoppers waiting for a Zara store to open in Australia in 2011. The image at the right of Kate, the duchess of Cambridge, photographed in Zara clothing, is emblematic of Zara's appeal.

Xurxo Lobato/Cover/Getty Images

Cameron Spencer/Getty Images

Niki Nikolova/FilmMagic/Getty Images

available mortgages drove up housing values in the United States. Investment banks capitalized on the housing boom by selling financial investments based on bundled mortgages. Banks in New York sold mortgage-based investments to Europe and elsewhere, spreading the wealth and risk of investment. Many European countries, such as Spain, also experienced a housing bubble, with housing prices rising 44 percent between 2004 and 2008. In Greece, low interest rates and the strength of the euro encouraged investments in government bonds, leading to higher government debt. Following the collapse of the housing market, investments rapidly lost their value, leaving banks and other financial institutions without enough capital to cover their debts and countries with insufficient funds. A worldwide recession quickly ensued and unemployment rose dramatically.

The U.S. government responded to the crisis with a series of measures including bank recapitalization and an economic stimulus package. In Europe, the efforts of the European Central Bank and International Monetary Fund (IMF), as well as the creation of a European Financial Stability Facility, supplied rescue packages for many eastern European countries, while Europe's stronger economies, primarily Germany and France, provided emergency funds to recapitalize their banks. In Greece, the severity of the crises led to a harsh bail-out agreement. The austerity measures put into place have reduced pensions, wages, and health-care services, leading to a wave of homelessness and hardship. Many of the severely affected European countries resent the policies imposed by the wealthier EU states, especially Germany.

Globalization and the Environmental Crisis

Taking a global perspective at the beginning of the twenty-first century has led many people to realize that everywhere on the planet, human beings are interdependent in regard to the air they breathe, the water they drink, the food they consume, and the climate that affects their lives. At the same time, however, human activities are creating environmental challenges that threaten the very foundation of human existence on earth.

One problem is population growth. As of March 2012, the world population was estimated at more than 7 billion people, only twenty-four years after passing the 5 billion mark. At its current rate of growth, the world population could reach 12.8 billion by 2050,

according to the United Nations' long-range population projections. The result has been an increased demand for food and other resources that has put great pressure on the earth's ecosystems. At the same time, the failure to grow enough food for more and more people has created a severe problem, as an estimated 1 billion people worldwide today suffer from hunger. Every year, more than 8 million people die of hunger, many of them young children.

Yet another threat to the environment is **global warming**, which has the potential to cause great chaos. Virtually all of the world's scientists agree that the **greenhouse effect**, the warming of the earth because of the buildup of carbon dioxide in the atmosphere, is contributing to devastating droughts and storms, the melting of the polar ice caps, and rising sea levels that could inundate coastal regions in the second half of the twenty-first century. Scientists reported that 2014 was the hottest year on record in the United States. Also alarming is the potential loss of biodiversity. Seven out of ten biologists believe that the planet is now experiencing an alarming extinction of both plant and animal species.

The Social Challenges of Globalization

Since 1945, tens of millions of people have migrated from one part of the world to another. These migrations have occurred for many reasons. Persecution for political reasons caused many people from Pakistan, Bangladesh, Sri Lanka, and eastern Europe to seek refuge in western European countries, while brutal civil wars in Asia, Africa, the Middle East, and Europe led millions of refugees to seek safety in neighboring countries. Most people who have migrated, however, have done so to find jobs. Latin Americans seeking a better life have migrated to the United States, while guest workers from Turkey, southern and eastern Europe, North Africa, India, and Pakistan have migrated to more prosperous western European lands. In 2005, nearly 200 million people, about 3 percent of the world's population, lived outside the country where they were born. As discussed earlier, the migration of millions of people has created a social backlash in many countries.

Another challenge of globalization is the wide gap between rich and poor nations. The rich nations, or **developed nations**, include countries such as the United States, Canada, Germany, and Japan, which have well-organized industrial and agricultural systems, advanced technologies, and effective educational systems. The poor nations, or **developing nations**, include many countries in Africa, Asia, and Latin America, which often have primarily agricultural economies with little technology. A serious problem in many developing nations is explosive population growth, which has led to severe food shortages often caused by poor soil but also by economic factors. Growing crops for export to developed countries, for example, may lead to enormous profits for large landowners but leaves many small farmers with little land on which to grow food.

New Global Movements and New Hopes

As the heirs of Western civilization have become aware that the problems humans face are not just national but global, they have responded to this challenge in different ways. One approach has been to develop grassroots social movements, including environmental, women's and men's liberation, human potential, appropriate-technology, and nonviolence movements. "Think globally, act locally" is frequently the slogan of these grassroots groups. Related to the emergence of these social movements is the growth of nongovernmental organizations (NGOs). According to one analyst, NGOs are an important instrument in the cultivation of global perspectives: "Since NGOs by definition are identified with interests that transcend national boundaries, we expect all NGOs to define problems in global terms, to take account of human interests and needs as they are found in all parts of the planet."[5] NGOs are often represented at the United Nations and include professional, business, and cooperative organizations; foundations; religious, peace, and disarmament groups; youth and women's organizations; environmental and human rights groups; and research institutes. The number of international NGOs increased from 176 in 1910 to 40,000 in 2007.

And yet hopes for global approaches to global problems have also been hindered by political, ethnic, and religious disputes. Pollution of the Rhine River by factories along its banks provokes angry disputes among European nations, and the United States and Canada have argued about the effects of acid rain on Canadian forests. The bloody conflict in the former Yugoslavia indicates the dangers inherent in the rise of nationalist sentiment among various ethnic and religious groups in eastern Europe. The widening gap between wealthy nations and poor, developing nations threatens global economic stability. Many conflicts begin with regional issues and then develop into international concerns. International terrorist groups seek to wreak havoc around the world.

Thus, even as the world becomes more global in culture and interdependent in its mutual relations, centrifugal forces are still at work attempting to redefine the political, cultural, and ethnic ways in which the world is divided. Such efforts are often disruptive and can sometimes work against measures to enhance our human destiny.

Many lessons can be learned from the history of Western civilization, but one of them is especially clear. Lack of involvement in the affairs of one's society can lead to a sense of powerlessness. In an age that is often crisis-laden and chaotic, an understanding of our Western heritage and its lessons can be instrumental in helping us create new models for the future. For we are all creators of history, and the future of Western and indeed world civilization depends on us.

Chapter Summary

When Mikhail Gorbachev came to power in the Soviet Union in 1985, he proposed radical reforms in both the Soviet economy and government. With these reforms, the pressure for more drastic change began to mount. In 1989, a wave of revolution swept through eastern Europe as communist regimes were overthrown and a new, mostly democratic order emerged, although serious divisions remained, especially in Yugoslavia. In 1991, the attempt of reactionary forces to undo the reforms of Gorbachev led instead to the complete disintegration of the Soviet Union and the emergence of a new Russia. The Cold War, which had begun at the end of World War II and had led to a Europe divided along ideological lines, was finally over.

Although many people were optimistic about a new world order after the collapse of communism, uncertainties still prevailed. Germany was successfully reunited, and the European Union became even stronger with the adoption of a common currency in the euro. Yugoslavia, however, disintegrated into warring states that eventually all became independent, and ethnic groups that had once been forced to live under distinct national banners began rebelling to form autonomous states. Although some were successful, others, such as the Chechnyans, were brutally repressed.

While the so-called new world order was fitfully developing, other challenges emerged. The arrival of many foreigners, especially in western Europe, not only strained the social services of European countries but also led to antiforeign sentiment and right-wing political parties that encouraged it. Environmental abuses led to growing threats not only to Europeans but also to all humans. Terrorism, especially that carried out by some parts of the Muslim world, emerged as a threat to many Western states. Since the end of World War II, terrorism seemed to have replaced communism as the number one enemy of the West.

At the beginning of the twenty-first century, a major realization has been the recognition that the problems afflicting the Western world have also become global problems. The nation-state, whose history dominated the nineteenth and twentieth centuries and which still plays an important role in contemporary affairs, nevertheless appears to be an outmoded structure if humankind is to resolve its many challenges. Nations and peoples have become more interdependent, and many Westerners recognize that a global perspective must also now become a part of the Western tradition.

CHAPTER TIMELINE

	1985	1990	1995	2000	2005	2010
Eastern Europe/Soviet Union	■ Gorbachev comes to power in the Soviet Union	■ Revolutions in Eastern Europe ■ Dissolution of the Soviet Union		■ War in Kosovo ■ Putin era begins in Russia		■ Independence of Kosovo ■ Putin reelected as president of Russia
Western and Central Europe	Reign of Pope John Paul II		■ European Union	Expansion of European Union ■ Merkel becomes first female chancellor of Germany ■ Expansion of European Union ■		■ Merkel reelected in Germany ■ Greek financial crisis ■ Hollande elected in France ■ Pope Francis elected
United States		■ Reunification of Germany		■ Terrorist attack on United States ■ War against terrorists in Afghanistan ■ U.S. invasion of Iraq	■ Election of Barack Obama	■ U.S. troops leave Iraq ■ Obama reelected

CHAPTER REVIEW

Upon Reflection

Q What roles did Mikhail Gorbachev and Ronald Reagan play in bringing an end to the Cold War? Which played a more important role? Why?

Q What directions did eastern European nations take after they became free from Soviet control? Why did they react as they did?

Q What is globalization, and how does it relate to the technological and social concerns of our age?

Key Terms

perestroika (p. 741)
glasnost (p. 741)
ethnic cleansing (p. 747)
guest workers (p. 759)
globalization (p. 764)
global economy (p. 764)

multinational corporation (transnational corporation) (p. 764)
global warming (p. 766)
greenhouse effect (p. 766)
developed nations (p. 766)
developing nations (p. 766)

Suggestions for Further Reading

GENERAL WORKS For a well-written survey on Europe from 1985 to 2004, see **T. Judt, *Postwar: A History of Europe Since 1945*** (New York, 2005).

TOWARD A NEW WESTERN ORDER Aspects of the revolutionary upheaval in the Soviet Union and its aftermath are covered in **M. Kramer, *Collapse of the Soviet Union*** (Boulder, Colo., 2007), and **M. Garcelon, *Revolutionary Passage: From Soviet to Post-Soviet Russia, 1985–2000*** (Philadelphia, 2005). On eastern Europe, see **P. Kenney, *The Burden of Freedom: Eastern Europe Since 1989*** (London, 2006).

AFTER THE COLD WAR On the end of the Cold War, see **S. Dockrill, *The End of the Cold War Era*** (London, 2005), and **J. L. Gaddis, *The Cold War: A New History*** (New York, 2005). On terrorism, see **W. Laqueur, *History of Terrorism*** (New York, 2001).

NEW DIRECTIONS AND NEW PROBLEMS IN WESTERN SOCIETY The changing role of women is examined in **R. Rosen, *The World Split Open: How the Modern Women's Movement Changed America*** (New York, 2001), and **J. W. Scott,**

The Politics of the Veil (Princeton, N.J., 2009). The problems of guest workers and immigrants are examined in **W. Laqueur, *The Last Days of Europe: Epitaph for an Old Continent*** (New York, 2007), and **R. Chin, *Guest Worker Question in Germany*** (Cambridge, 2007).

WESTERN CULTURE TODAY For a comprehensive examination of the Digital Age, see **M. Castells, *The Information Age*,** 3 vols. (Oxford, 1996–1998). On the role of the media in the Digital Age, see **J. R. Dominick, *Dynamics of Mass Communication: Media in the Digital Age*** (New York, 2006). On art, see **B. Wands, *Art of the Digital Age*** (London, 2007).

TOWARD A GLOBAL CIVILIZATION Useful books on different facets of the new global civilization include **M. B. Steger, *Globalization: A Very Short Introduction*** (New York, 2003); **J. H. Mittelman, *The Globalization Syndrome*** (Princeton, N.J., 2000); **P. O'Meara et al., eds., *Globalization and the Challenges of the New Century*** (Bloomington, Ind., 2000); and **H. French, *Vanishing Borders*** (New York, 2000), on globalization and the environment.

Notes

1. Quoted in T. Judt, *Postwar: A History of Europe Since 1945* (New York, 2005), p. 585.
2. Quoted in W. I. Hitchcock, *The Struggle for Europe: The Turbulent History of a Divided Continent, 1945–2002* (New York, 2003), pp. 399–400.
3. Quoted in R. Bridenthal, "Women in the New Europe," in *Becoming Visible: Women in European History*, ed. R. Bridenthal, S. M. Stuard, and M. E. Weisner, 3d ed. (Boston, 1998), pp. 564–565.
4. Quoted in Judt, *Postwar*, p. 743.
5. E. Boulding, *Women in the Twentieth-Century World* (New York, 1977), pp. 186–187.

MindTap **MindTap** is a fully online, highly personalized learning experience built upon Cengage Learning content. MindTap combines student learning tools—readings, multimedia, activities, and assessments—into a singular Learning Path that guides students through the course.

Glossary

abbess   the head of a convent or monastery for women.

abbot   the head of a monastery.

absolutism   a form of government in which the sovereign power or ultimate authority rested in the hands of a monarch who claimed to rule by divine right and was therefore responsible only to God.

Abstract Expressionism   a post–World War II artistic movement that broke with all conventions of form and structure in favor of total abstraction.

abstract painting   an artistic movement that developed early in the twentieth century in which artists focused on color to avoid any references to visual reality.

aediles   Roman officials who supervised the public games and the grain supply of the city of Rome.

agricultural revolution   the application of new agricultural techniques that allowed for a large increase in productivity in the eighteenth century.

Agricultural (Neolithic) Revolution   *see* Neolithic Revolution.

anti-Semitism   hostility toward or discrimination against Jews.

apartheid   the system of racial segregation practiced in the Republic of South Africa until the 1990s that involved political, legal, and economic discrimination against nonwhites.

appeasement   the policy, followed by the European nations in the 1930s, of accepting Hitler's annexation of Austria and Czechoslovakia in the belief that meeting his demands would assure peace and stability.

Arianism   a Christian heresy that taught that Jesus was inferior to God. Though condemned by the Council of Nicaea in 325, Arianism was adopted by many of the Germanic peoples who entered the Roman Empire over the next centuries.

aristocracy   a class of hereditary nobility in medieval Europe; a warrior class who shared a distinctive lifestyle based on the institution of knighthood, although there were social divisions within the group based on extremes of wealth.

Ausgleich   the "Compromise" of 1867 that created the dual monarchy of Austria-Hungary. Austria and Hungary each had its own capital, constitution, and legislative assembly but were united under one monarch.

authoritarian state   a state that has a dictatorial government and some other trappings of a totalitarian state but does not demand that the masses be actively involved in the regime's goals as totalitarian states do.

balance of power   a distribution of power among several states such that no single nation can dominate or interfere with the interests of another.

Baroque   an artistic movement of the seventeenth century in Europe that used dramatic effects to arouse the emotions and reflected the search for power that was a large part of the seventeenth-century ethos.

bicameral legislature   a legislature with two houses.

Black Death   the outbreak of plague (mostly bubonic) in the mid-fourteenth century that killed 25 to 50 percent of Europe's population.

Blitzkrieg   "lightning war." A war conducted with great speed and force, as in Germany's advance at the beginning of World War II.

Bolsheviks   a small faction of the Russian Social Democratic Party who were led by Lenin and dedicated to violent revolution. They seized power in Russia in 1917 and were subsequently renamed the Communists.

bourgeoisie (burghers)   inhabitants (merchants and artisans) of boroughs and burghs (towns).

boyars   the Russian nobility.

Brezhnev Doctrine   the doctrine, enunciated by Leonid Brezhnev, that the Soviet Union had a right to intervene if socialism was threatened in another socialist state; used to justify moving Soviet troops into Czechoslovakia in 1968.

Bronze Age   the period from around 3000 to 1200 B.C.E. It was characterized by the widespread use of bronze for making tools and weapons.

caliph   the secular leader of the Islamic community.

capital   material wealth used or available for use in the production of more wealth.

cartel   a combination of independent commercial enterprises that work together to control prices and limit competition.

Cartesian dualism   Descartes's principle of the separation of mind and matter (and mind and body) that enabled scientists to view matter as something separate from themselves that could be investigated by reason.

Catholic Reformation   the movement for the reform of the Catholic Church in the sixteenth century. It included a revived papacy; the regeneration of old religious orders and the founding of new ones, most notably the Jesuits; and the reaffirmation of traditional Catholic doctrine at the Council of Trent.

centuriate assembly   the chief popular assembly of the Roman Republic. It passed laws and elected the chief magistrates.

chansons de geste   a form of vernacular literature in the High Middle Ages that consisted of heroic epics focusing on the deeds of warriors.

chivalry   the ideal of civilized behavior that emerged among the nobility in the eleventh and twelfth centuries under the influence of the church; a code of ethics knights were expected to uphold.

Christian (northern) humanism   an intellectual movement in northern Europe in the late fifteenth and early sixteenth centuries that combined the interest in the classics of the Italian Renaissance with an interest in the sources of early Christianity, including the New Testament and the writings of the church fathers.

civic humanism   an intellectual movement of the Italian Renaissance that saw Cicero, who was both an intellectual and a statesman, as the ideal and held that humanists should be involved in government and use their rhetorical training in the service of the state.

civil disobedience   a policy of peaceful protest against laws or government policies in order to achieve political change.

civilization   a complex culture in which large numbers of humans share a variety of common elements, including cities; religious, political, military, and social structures; writing; and significant artistic and intellectual activity.

Cold War the ideological conflict between the Soviet Union and the United States after World War II.

collective farms large farms created in the Soviet Union by Stalin by combining many small holdings into large farms worked by the peasants under government supervision.

Columbian Exchange the reciprocal importation and exportation of plants and animals between Europe and the Americas.

commercial capitalism beginning in the Middle Ages, an economic system in which people invested in trade and goods in order to make profits.

common law law common to the entire kingdom of England; imposed by the king's courts beginning in the twelfth century to replace the customary law used in county and feudal courts that varied from place to place.

conciliarism a movement in fourteenth- and fifteenth-century Europe that held that final authority in spiritual matters resided with a general church council, not the pope. It emerged in response to the Avignon papacy and the Great Schism and was used to justify the summoning of the Council of Constance (1414–1418).

condottieri leaders of bands of mercenary soldiers in Renaissance Italy who sold their services to the highest bidder.

conquistadors "conquerors." Leaders in the Spanish conquests in the Americas, especially Mexico and Peru, in the sixteenth century.

conscription a military draft.

conservatism an ideology based on tradition and social stability that favored the maintenance of established institutions, organized religion, and obedience to authority and resisted change, especially abrupt change.

consuls the chief executive officers of the Roman Republic. Two were chosen annually to administer the government and lead the army in battle.

consumer society Western society that emerged after World War II as the working classes adopted the consumption patterns of the middle class and payment plans, credit cards, and easy credit made consumer goods such as appliances and automobiles affordable.

containment a policy adopted by the United States in the Cold War. Its goal was to use whatever means, short of all-out war, to limit Soviet expansion.

Continental System Napoleon's effort to bar British goods from the Continent in the hope of weakening Britain's economy and destroying its capacity to wage war.

cosmopolitan the quality of being sophisticated and having wide international experience.

cottage industry a system of textile manufacturing in which spinners and weavers worked at home in their cottages using raw materials supplied to them by capitalist entrepreneurs.

council of the plebs a council only for plebeians. After 287 B.C.E., however, its resolutions were binding on all Romans.

crusade in the Middle Ages, a military campaign in defense of Christendom.

Cubism an artistic style developed at the beginning of the twentieth century, especially by Pablo Picasso, that used geometric designs to re-create reality in the viewer's mind.

cultural relativism the belief that no culture is superior to another because culture is a matter of custom, not reason, and derives its meaning from the group holding it.

cuneiform "wedge-shaped." A system of writing developed by the Sumerians that consisted of wedge-shaped impressions made by a reed stylus on clay tablets.

Dadaism an artistic movement in the 1920s and 1930s founded by artists who were revolted by the senseless slaughter of World War I and used their "anti-art" to express contempt for the Western tradition.

decolonization the process of becoming free of colonial status and achieving statehood. It occurred in most of the world's colonies between 1947 and 1962.

deconstruction (poststructuralism) a system of thought, formulated by Jacques Derrida, that holds that culture is created in a variety of ways, according to the manner in which people create their own meaning. Hence, there is no fixed truth or universal meaning.

deism belief in God as the creator of the universe who, after setting it in motion, ceased to have any direct involvement in it and allowed it to run according to its own natural laws.

demesne the part of a manor retained under the direct control of the lord and worked by the serfs as part of their labor services.

de-Stalinization the policy of denouncing and undoing the most repressive aspects of Stalin's regime; begun by Nikita Khrushchev in 1956.

détente the relaxation of tension between the Soviet Union and the United States that occurred in the 1970s.

developed nations a term used to refer to rich nations, primarily in the Northern Hemisphere, that have well-organized industrial and agricultural systems, advanced technologies, and effective educational systems.

developing nations a term used to refer to poor nations, mainly in the Southern Hemisphere, that are primarily farming nations with little technology and serious population problems.

divination the practice of seeking to foretell future events by interpreting divine signs, which could appear in various forms, such as in entrails of animals, in patterns in smoke, or in dreams.

domino theory the belief that if the Communists succeeded in Vietnam, other countries in Southeast and East Asia would also fall (like dominoes) to communism; cited as a justification for the U.S. intervention in Vietnam.

economic imperialism the process in which banks and corporations from developed nations invest in underdeveloped regions and establish a major presence there in the hope of making high profits; not necessarily the same as colonial expansion in that businesses invest where they can make a profit, which may not be in their own nation's colonies.

economic liberalism the idea that government should not interfere in the workings of the economy.

Einsatzgruppen in Nazi Germany, special strike forces in the SS that played an important role in rounding up and killing Jews.

empiricism the practice of relying on observation and experiment.

encomienda in Spanish America, a form of economic and social organization in which a Spaniard was given a royal grant that enabled the holder of the grant to collect tribute from the Indians and use them as laborers.

enlightened absolutism an absolute monarchy in which the ruler follows the principles of the Enlightenment by introducing reforms for the improvement of society, allowing freedom of speech and the press, permitting religious toleration, expanding education, and ruling in accordance with the laws.

Enlightenment an eighteenth-century intellectual movement, led by the philosophes, that stressed the application of reason and the scientific method to all aspects of life.

Epicureanism a philosophy founded by Epicurus in the fourth century B.C.E. that taught that happiness (freedom from emotional turmoil) could be achieved through the pursuit of pleasure (intellectual rather than sensual pleasure).

equestrian order a group of extremely wealthy men in the late Roman Republic who were effectively barred from high office but sought political power commensurate with their wealth; called equestrians because many had gotten their start as cavalry officers (*equites*).

estates (orders) the traditional tripartite division of European society based on heredity and quality rather than wealth or economic standing, first established in the Middle Ages and continuing into the eighteenth century; traditionally consisted of those who pray (the clergy), those who fight (the nobility), and those who work (all the rest).

ethnic cleansing the policy of killing or forcibly removing people of another ethnic group; used by the Serbs against Bosnian Muslims in the 1990s.

Eucharist a Christian sacrament in which consecrated bread and wine are consumed in celebration of Jesus's Last Supper; also called the Lord's Supper or communion.

evolutionary socialism a socialist doctrine espoused by Eduard Bernstein who argued that socialists should stress cooperation and evolution to attain power by democratic means rather than by conflict and revolution.

existentialism a philosophical movement that arose after World War II that emphasized the meaninglessness of life, born of the desperation caused by two world wars.

fascism an ideology or movement that exalts the nation above the individual and calls for a centralized government with a dictatorial leader, economic and social regimentation, and forcible suppression of opposition; in particular, the ideology of Mussolini's Fascist regime in Italy.

feminism the belief in the social, political, and economic equality of the sexes; also, organized activity to advance women's rights.

fief a landed estate granted to a vassal in exchange for military services.

Final Solution the attempted physical extermination of the Jewish people by the Nazis during World War II.

Five Pillars of Islam the core requirements of the faith, observation of which would lead to paradise: belief in Allah and his Prophet Muhammad; prescribed prayers; observation of Ramadan; pilgrimage to Mecca; and giving alms (charitable contributions) to the poor.

functionalism the idea that the function of an object should determine its design and materials.

genocide the deliberate extermination of a people.

gentry well-to-do English landowners below the level of the nobility. They played an important role in the English Civil War of the seventeenth century.

geocentric conception the belief that the earth was at the center of the universe and that the sun and other celestial objects revolved around the earth.

glasnost "openness." Mikhail Gorbachev's policy of encouraging Soviet citizens to openly discuss the strengths and weaknesses of the Soviet Union.

global economy an interdependent economy in which the production, distribution, and sale of goods are accomplished on a worldwide scale.

globalization the trend in which peoples and nations have become more interdependent. The term is often used to refer to the development of a global economy and culture.

global warming the increase in the temperature of the earth's atmosphere caused by the greenhouse effect.

good emperors the five emperors who ruled from 96 to 180 (Nerva, Trajan, Hadrian, Antoninus Pius, and Marcus Aurelius), a period of peace and prosperity for the Roman Empire.

Gothic a term used to describe the art and especially architecture of Europe in the twelfth, thirteenth, and fourteenth centuries.

Gothic literature a form of literature used by Romantics to emphasize the bizarre and unusual, especially evident in horror stories.

Great Schism the crisis in the late medieval church when there were first two and then three popes; ended by the Council of Constance (1414–1418).

greenhouse effect the warming of the earth caused by the buildup of carbon dioxide in the atmosphere as a result of human activity.

guest workers foreign workers working temporarily in European countries.

guild an association of people with common interests and concerns, especially people working in the same craft. In medieval Europe, guilds came to control much of the production process and to restrict entry into various trades.

heliocentric conception the belief that the sun, not the earth, is at the center of the universe.

Hellenistic literally, "imitating the Greeks"; the era after the death of Alexander the Great when Greek culture spread into the Near East and blended with the culture of that region.

helots serfs in ancient Sparta who were permanently bound to the land that they worked for their Spartan masters.

heresy the holding of religious doctrines different from the official teachings of the church.

Hermeticism an intellectual movement beginning in the fifteenth century that taught that divinity is embodied in all aspects of nature. It included works on alchemy and magic as well as theology and philosophy. The tradition continued into the seventeenth century and influenced many of the leading figures of the Scientific Revolution.

hieroglyphics a pictorial system of writing used in ancient Egypt.

high culture the literary and artistic culture of the educated and wealthy ruling classes.

Holocaust the mass slaughter of European Jews by the Nazis during World War II.

hoplites heavily armed infantry soldiers in ancient Greece who entered battle in a phalanx formation.

Huguenots French Calvinists.

humanism an intellectual movement in Renaissance Italy based on the study of the Greek and Roman classics.

ideology a political philosophy such as conservatism or liberalism.

imperium in the Roman Republic, the right to command troops that belonged to the chief executive officers (consuls and praetors). A military commander was known as an *imperator.* In the Roman Empire, the title *imperator* (emperor) came to be used for the ruler.

Impressionism an artistic movement that originated in France in the 1870s. Impressionists sought to capture their impressions of the changing effects of light on objects in nature.

individualism emphasis on and interest in the unique traits of each person.

indulgence in Christian theology, the remission of part or all of the temporal punishment in purgatory due to sin; granted for charitable contributions and other good deeds. Indulgences became a regular practice of the Catholic Church in the High Middle Ages, and their abuse was instrumental in sparking Luther's reform movement in the sixteenth century.

inflation a sustained rise in the price level.

interdict in the Catholic Church, a censure by which a region or country is deprived of receiving the sacraments.

intervention, principle of the idea, after the Congress of Vienna, that the great powers of Europe had the right to send armies into countries experiencing revolution to restore legitimate monarchs to their thrones.

jihad "striving in the way of the Lord." In Islam, the attempt to achieve personal betterment, although it can also mean fair, defensive fighting to preserve one's life and one's faith.

joint stock company a company or association that raises capital by selling shares to individuals who receive dividends on their investment while a board of directors runs the company.

justification the primary doctrine of the Protestant Reformation, teaching that humans are saved not through good works but by the grace of God, bestowed freely through the sacrifice of Jesus.

Kulturkampf "culture conflict." The name given to Bismarck's attack on the Catholic Church in Germany, which has come to refer to conflict between church and state anywhere.

laissez-faire "let (them) do (as they please)." An economic doctrine that holds that an economy is best served when the government does not interfere but allows the economy to self-regulate according to the forces of supply and demand.

latifundia large landed estates in the Roman Empire (singular: *latifundium*).

lay investiture the practice in which someone other than a member of the clergy chose a bishop and invested him with the symbols of both his temporal office and his spiritual office; led to the Investiture Controversy, which was ended by compromise in the Concordat of Worms in 1122.

Lebensraum "living space." The doctrine, adopted by Hitler, that a nation's power depends on the amount of land it occupies. Thus, a nation must expand to be strong.

legitimacy, principle of the idea that after the Napoleonic wars, peace could best be reestablished in Europe by restoring legitimate monarchs who would preserve traditional institutions; guided Metternich at the Congress of Vienna.

liberal arts the seven areas of study that formed the basis of education in medieval and early modern Europe. Following Boethius and other late Roman authors, they consisted of grammar, rhetoric, and dialectic or logic (the *trivium*) and arithmetic, geometry, astronomy, and music (the *quadrivium*).

liberalism an ideology based on the belief that people should be as free from restraint as possible. Economic liberalism is the idea that the government should not interfere in the workings of the economy. Political liberalism is the idea that there should be restraints on the exercise of power so that people can enjoy basic civil rights in a constitutional state with a representative assembly.

mandates a system established after World War I whereby a nation officially administered a territory (mandate) on behalf of the League of Nations. Thus, France administered Lebanon and Syria as mandates, and Britain administered Iraq and Palestine.

Mannerism a sixteenth-century artistic movement in Europe that deliberately broke down the High Renaissance principles of balance, harmony, and moderation.

manor an agricultural estate operated by a lord and worked by peasants who performed labor services and paid various rents and fees to the lord in exchange for protection and sustenance.

Marshall Plan the European Recovery Program, under which the United States provided financial aid to European countries to help them rebuild after World War II.

Marxism the political, economic, and social theories of Karl Marx that included the idea that history is the story of class struggle and that ultimately the proletariat will overthrow the bourgeoisie and establish a dictatorship en route to a classless society.

mass education a state-run educational system, usually free and compulsory, that aims to ensure that all children in society have at least a basic education.

mass leisure forms of leisure that appeal to large numbers of people in a society, including the working classes; emerged at the end of the nineteenth century to provide workers with amusements after work and on weekends; used during the twentieth century by totalitarian states to control their populations.

mass politics a political order characterized by mass political parties and universal male and (eventually) female suffrage.

mass society a society in which the concerns of the majority—the lower classes—play a prominent role; characterized by the extension of voting rights, an improved standard of living for the lower classes, and mass education.

materialism the belief that everything mental, spiritual, or ideal is an outgrowth of physical forces and that truth is found in concrete material existence, not through feeling or intuition.

mercantilism an economic theory that held that a nation's prosperity depended on its supply of gold and silver and that the total volume of trade is unchangeable. Its adherents therefore advocated that the government play an active role in the economy by encouraging exports and discouraging imports, especially through the use of tariffs.

Middle Passage the journey of slaves from Africa to the Americas as the middle leg of the triangular trade.

militarism a policy of aggressive military preparedness; in particular, the large armies based on mass conscription and complex, inflexible plans for mobilization that most European nations had before World War I.

ministerial responsibility a tenet of nineteenth-century liberalism that held that ministers of the monarch should be responsible to the legislative assembly rather than to the monarch.

mir   a peasant village commune in Russia.

mobilization   the organization of troops and supplies for service in time of war.

Modernism   the artistic and literary styles that emerged in the decades before 1914 as artists rebelled against traditional efforts to portray reality as accurately as possible (leading to Impressionism and Cubism) and writers explored new forms.

monasticism   a movement that began in early Christianity whose purpose was to create communities of men and women who practiced a communal life dedicated to God as a moral example to the world around them.

monk   a man who chooses to live a communal life divorced from the world in order to dedicate himself totally to the will of God.

monogamy   the practice of being married to one person at a time.

monotheism   the doctrine or belief that there is only one God.

multinational corporation   a company with divisions in more than two countries.

mutual deterrence   the belief that nuclear war could best be prevented if both the United States and the Soviet Union had sufficient nuclear weapons so that even if one nation launched a preemptive first strike, the other could respond and devastate the attacker.

mystery religions   religions that involve initiation into secret rites that promise intense emotional involvement with spiritual forces and a greater chance of individual immortality.

nationalization   the process of converting a business or industry from private ownership to government control and ownership.

nation in arms   the people's army raised by universal mobilization to repel the foreign enemies of the French Revolution.

NATO   the North Atlantic Treaty Organization, a military alliance formed in 1949 in which the signatories (Belgium, Canada, Denmark, France, Great Britain, Iceland, Italy, Luxembourg, the Netherlands, Norway, Portugal, and the United States) agreed to provide mutual assistance if any one of them was attacked; later expanded to include other nations.

natural laws   a body of laws or specific principles held to be derived from nature and binding on all human societies even in the absence of written laws governing such matters.

natural rights   certain inalienable rights to which all people are entitled, including the right to life, liberty, and property; freedom of speech and religion; and equality before the law.

natural selection   Darwin's idea that organisms that are most adaptable to their environment survive and pass on the variations that enabled them to survive, while less adaptable organisms become extinct; "survival of the fittest."

Nazi New Order   the Nazis' plan for their conquered territories. It included the extermination of Jews and others considered inferior, ruthless exploitation of resources, German colonization in the east, and the use of Poles, Russians, and Ukrainians as slave labor.

Neolithic Revolution   the shift from hunting animals and gathering plants for sustenance to producing food by systematic agriculture that occurred gradually between 10,000 and 4000 B.C.E. (the Neolithic or "New Stone" Age).

Neoplatonism   a revival of Platonic philosophy in the third century C.E., associated with Plotinus; a similar revival in the Italian Renaissance, associated with Marsilio Ficino, who attempted to synthesize Christianity and Platonism.

nepotism   the appointment of family members to important political positions; derived from the regular appointment of nephews (Latin, *nepos*) by Renaissance popes.

New Economic Policy   a modified version of the old capitalist system introduced in the Soviet Union by Lenin in 1921 to revive the economy after the ravages of the civil war and war communism.

new imperialism   the revival of imperialism after 1880 in which European nations established colonies throughout much of Asia and Africa.

new monarchies   the governments of France, England, and Spain at the end of the fifteenth century, whose rulers succeeded in reestablishing or extending centralized royal authority, suppressing the nobility, controlling the church, and insisting on the loyalty of all people living in their territories.

nobiles   "nobles." The small group of families from both patrician and plebeian origins who produced most of the men who were elected to office in the late Roman Republic.

nuclear family   a family group consisting only of a father, a mother, and one or more children.

nuns   women who withdrew from the world and joined a religious community; the female equivalent of monks.

old order (old regime)   the political and social system of France in the eighteenth century before the Revolution.

oligarchy   rule by a few.

optimates   "best men." Aristocratic leaders in the late Roman Republic who generally came from senatorial families and wished to retain their oligarchical privileges.

orders   *see* estates.

organic evolution   Darwin's principle that all plants and animals have evolved over a long period of time from earlier and simpler forms of life.

Paleolithic Age   the period of human history when humans used simple stone tools (ca. 2,500,000–10,000 B.C.E.).

pantheism   a doctrine that equates God with the universe and all that is in it.

panzer division   in the German army under Hitler, a strike force of about three hundred tanks and accompanying forces and supplies.

papal curia   the administrative staff of the Catholic Church, composed of cardinals who assist the pope in running the church.

paterfamilias   the dominant male in a Roman family whose powers over his wife and children were theoretically unlimited, though they were sometimes circumvented in practice.

patriarchy   a society in which the father is supreme in the clan or family; more generally, a society dominated by men.

patricians   great landowners who became the ruling class in the Roman Republic.

patronage   the practice of awarding titles and making appointments to government and other positions to gain political support.

pax Romana   "Roman peace." A term used to refer to the stability and prosperity that Roman rule brought to the Mediterranean world and much of western Europe during the first and second centuries C.E.

perestroika   "restructuring." A term applied to Mikhail Gorbachev's economic, political, and social reforms in the Soviet Union.

perioikoi   in ancient Sparta, free inhabitants but not citizens who were required to pay taxes and perform military service.

permissive society   a term applied to Western society after World War II to reflect the new sexual freedom and the emergence of a drug culture.

phalanx   a rectangular formation of tightly massed infantry soldiers.

philosophes   intellectuals of the eighteenth-century Enlightenment who believed in applying a spirit of rational criticism to all things, including religion and politics, and who focused on improving and enjoying this world, rather than on the afterlife.

pig iron   a type of iron produced by smelting iron ore with coke; of lower quality than wrought iron.

plebeians   the class of Roman citizens that included nonpatrician landowners, craftspeople, merchants, and small farmers in the Roman Republic. Their struggle for equal rights with the patricians dominated much of the Republic's history.

plebiscita   laws passed by the council of the plebs during the Roman Republic.

pluralism   the practice of holding several church offices simultaneously; a problem of the late medieval church.

plutocrats   members of the wealthy elite.

pogroms   organized massacres of Jews.

polis   an ancient Greek city-state encompassing both an urban area and its surrounding countryside; a small but autonomous political unit where all major political and social activities were carried out centrally.

political democracy   a form of government characterized by universal suffrage and mass political parties.

politiques   a group who emerged during the French Wars of Religion in the sixteenth century, placed politics above religion, and believed that no religious truth was worth the ravages of civil war.

polytheistic   believing in or worshiping more than one god.

popular culture   as opposed to high culture, the unofficial written and unwritten culture of the masses, much of which was traditionally passed down orally and centered on public and group activities such as festivals. In the modern age, the term refers to the entertainment, recreation, and pleasures that people purchase as part of the mass consumer society.

populares   "favoring the people." Aristocratic leaders in the late Roman Republic who tended to use the people's assemblies in an effort to break the stranglehold of the *nobiles* on political offices.

Post-Impressionism   an artistic movement that began in France in the 1880s. Post-Impressionists sought to use color and line to express inner feelings and produce a personal statement of reality.

Postmodernism   a term used to cover a variety of artistic and intellectual styles and ways of thinking prominent since the 1970s.

poststructuralism   *see* deconstruction.

praetor   a Roman executive official responsible for the administration of the law.

praetorian guard   the military unit that served as the personal bodyguard of the Roman emperors.

predestination   the belief, associated with Calvinism, that God, as a consequence of his foreknowledge of all events, has predetermined those who will be saved (the elect) and those who will be damned.

price revolution   the dramatic rise in prices (inflation) that occurred throughout Europe in the sixteenth and early seventeenth centuries.

principate   the form of government established by Augustus for the Roman Empire. It continued the constitutional forms of the Republic and consisted of the *princeps* ("first citizen") and the senate, although the *princeps* was clearly the dominant partner.

principle of intervention   *see* intervention, principle of.

principle of legitimacy   *see* legitimacy, principle of.

procurator   the head of the Holy Synod, the chief decision-making body for the Russian Orthodox Church.

proletariat   the industrial working class. In Marxism, the class that will ultimately overthrow the bourgeoisie.

propaganda   a program of distorted information put out by an organization or government to spread its policy, cause, or doctrine.

psychoanalysis   a method developed by Sigmund Freud to resolve a patient's psychic conflict.

quadrivium   arithmetic, geometry, astronomy, and music; four of the seven liberal arts (the others made up the *trivium*) that formed the basis of medieval and early modern education.

quaestors   Roman officials responsible for the administration of financial affairs.

rapprochement   the rebuilding of harmonious relations between nations.

rationalism   a system of thought based on the belief that human reason and experience are the chief sources of knowledge.

Realism   a nineteenth-century school of painting that emphasized the everyday life of ordinary people, depicted with photographic accuracy.

Realpolitik   "politics of reality." Politics based on practical concerns rather than theory or ethics.

reconquista   in Spain, the reconquest of Muslim lands by Christian rulers and their armies.

relativity theory   Einstein's theory that, among other things, (1) space and time are not absolute but are relative to the observer and interwoven into a four-dimensional space-time continuum and (2) matter is a form of energy ($E = mc^2$).

relics   the bones of Christian saints or objects intimately associated with saints that were considered worthy of veneration.

Renaissance   the "rebirth" of Classical culture that occurred in Italy between ca. 1350 and ca. 1550; also, the earlier revivals of Classical culture that occurred under Charlemagne and in the twelfth century.

rentier   a person who lives on income from property and is not personally involved in its operation.

reparations   payments made by a defeated nation after a war to compensate another nation for damage sustained as a result of the war; required from Germany after World War I.

revisionism   a socialist doctrine that rejected Marx's emphasis on class struggle and revolution and argued instead that workers should work through political parties to bring about gradual change (*see also* evolutionary socialism).

rhetoric   the art of persuasive speaking; in the Middle Ages, one of the seven liberal arts.

Rococo an eighteenth-century artistic movement that emphasized grace, gentility, lightness, and charm.

Romanesque a term used to describe the art and especially architecture of Europe in the eleventh and twelfth centuries.

Romanticism a nineteenth-century intellectual and artistic movement that rejected the emphasis on reason of the Enlightenment. Instead, Romantics stressed the importance of intuition, feeling, emotion, and imagination as sources of knowing.

sacraments rites considered imperative for a Christian's salvation. By the thirteenth century, these consisted of the Eucharist or Lord's Supper, baptism, marriage, penance, extreme unction, holy orders, and confirmation of children; Protestant reformers of the sixteenth century generally recognized only two—baptism and communion (the Lord's Supper).

salons gatherings of philosophes and other notables to discuss the ideas of the Enlightenment; so called from the elegant drawing rooms (salons) where they met.

sans-culottes "without breeches." The common people, who did not wear the fine clothes of the upper classes and played an important role in the radical phase of the French Revolution.

satrap a governor with both civil and military duties in the ancient Persian Empire, which was divided into satrapies, or provinces, each administered by a satrap.

satrapy the name of a province in the Persian Empire.

scholasticism the philosophical and theological system of the medieval schools that emphasized rigorous analysis of contradictory authorities; often used to try to reconcile faith and reason.

scientific method a method of seeking knowledge through inductive principles, using experiments and observations to develop generalizations.

Scientific Revolution the transition from the medieval world-view to a largely secular, rational, and materialistic perspective that began in the seventeenth century and was popularized in the eighteenth.

scriptoria writing rooms for the copying of manuscripts in medieval monasteries.

scutage in the fourteenth century, a money payment for military service that replaced the obligation of military service in the lord-vassal relationship.

secularism the process of becoming more concerned with material, worldly, temporal things and less with spiritual and religious things.

self-determination the doctrine that the people of a given territory or a particular nationality should have the right to determine their own government and political future.

senate the leading council of the Roman Republic; composed of about three hundred men (senators) who served for life and dominated much of the political life of the Republic.

separation of powers a doctrine enunciated by Montesquieu in the eighteenth century that separate executive, legislative, and judicial powers serve to limit and control each other.

serf a peasant who is bound to the land and obliged to provide labor services and pay various rents and fees to the lord; considered unfree but not a slave because serfs could not be bought and sold.

skepticism a doubtful or questioning attitude, especially about religion.

Social Darwinism the application of Darwin's principle of organic evolution to the social order; led to the belief that progress comes from the struggle for survival as the fittest advance and the weak decline.

socialism an ideology that calls for collective or government ownership of the means of production and the distribution of goods.

socialized medicine health services for all citizens provided by government assistance.

social security government programs that provide social welfare measures such as old-age pensions and sickness, accident, and disability insurance.

Socratic method a form of teaching that uses a question-and-answer format to enable students to reach conclusions by using their own reasoning.

Sophists wandering scholars and professional teachers in ancient Greece who stressed the importance of rhetoric and tended toward skepticism and relativism.

soviets councils of workers' and soldiers' deputies that were formed throughout Russia in 1917 and played an important role in the Bolshevik Revolution.

squadristi in Italy in the 1920s, bands of armed Fascists used to create disorder by attacking Socialist offices and newspapers.

stagflation a combination of high inflation and high unemployment that was prevalent in the United States and elsewhere from 1973 to the mid-1980s.

Stalinization the adoption by Eastern European Communist countries of features of the economic, political, and military policies implemented by Stalin in the Soviet Union.

Stoicism a philosophy founded by Zeno in the fourth century B.C.E. that taught that happiness could be obtained by accepting one's lot and living in harmony with the will of God, thereby achieving inner peace.

subinfeudation the practice whereby a lord's greatest vassals subdivided their fiefs and had vassals of their own, who in turn subdivided their fiefs, and so on down to simple knights, whose fiefs were too small to subdivide.

suffragists advocates of extending the right to vote to women.

sultan "holder of power." A title taken by Turkish leaders who took command of the Abbasid Empire in 1055.

Surrealism an artistic movement that arose between World War I and World War II. Surrealists portrayed recognizable objects in unrecognizable relationships in order to reveal the world of the unconscious.

syncretism the combining of different forms of belief or practice, as, for example, when two gods are regarded as different forms of the same underlying divine force and are fused together.

tariffs duties (taxes) imposed on imported goods, usually to raise revenue and to discourage imports and protect domestic industries.

theocracy a government ruled by a divine authority.

tithe a portion of one's harvest or income, paid by medieval peasants to the village church.

totalitarian state a state characterized by government control over all aspects of economic, social, political, cultural, and intellectual life, the subordination of the individual to the state, and insistence that the masses be actively involved in the regime's goals.

total war warfare in which all of a nation's resources, including civilians at home as well as soldiers in the field, are mobilized for the war effort.

trade union an association of workers in the same trade, formed to help members secure better wages, benefits, and working conditions.

transnational corporation another term for "a multinational corporation," or a company with divisions in more than two countries.

transubstantiation a doctrine of the Roman Catholic Church that during the Eucharist, the substance of the bread and wine is miraculously transformed into the body and blood of Jesus.

trench warfare warfare in which the opposing forces attack and counterattack from a relatively permanent system of trenches protected by barbed wire; characteristic of World War I.

triangular trade a pattern of trade in early modern Europe that connected Europe, Africa, and the Americas in an Atlantic economy.

tribunes of the plebs beginning in 494 B.C.E., Roman officials who were given the power to protect plebeians against arrest by patrician magistrates.

trivium grammar, rhetoric, and dialectic or logic; three of the seven liberal arts (the others made up the *quadrivium*) that were the basis of medieval and early modern education.

Truman Doctrine the doctrine, enunciated by Harry Truman in 1947, that the United States would provide economic aid to countries that said they were threatened by Communist expansion.

tyrant in an ancient Greek *polis* (or an Italian city-state during the Renaissance), a ruler who came to power in an unconstitutional way and ruled without being subject to the law.

uncertainty principle a principle in quantum mechanics, posited by Heisenberg, that holds that one cannot determine the path of an electron because the very act of observing the electron would affect its location.

unconditional surrender complete, unqualified surrender of a belligerent nation.

utopian socialists intellectuals and theorists in the early nineteenth century who favored equality in social and economic conditions and wished to replace private property and competition with collective ownership and cooperation.

vassalage the granting of a fief, or landed estate, in exchange for providing military services to the lord and fulfilling certain other obligations such as appearing at the lord's court when summoned and making a payment on the knighting of the lord's eldest son.

viceroy the administrative head of the provinces of New Spain and Peru in the Americas.

war communism Lenin's policy of nationalizing industrial and other facilities and requisitioning the peasants' produce during the civil war in Russia.

War Guilt Clause the clause in the Treaty of Versailles that declared that Germany (with Austria) was responsible for starting World War I and ordered Germany to pay reparations for the damage the Allies had suffered as a result of the war.

Warsaw Pact a military alliance, formed in 1955, in which Albania, Bulgaria, Czechoslovakia, East Germany, Hungary, Poland, Romania, and the Soviet Union agreed to provide mutual assistance.

welfare state a sociopolitical system in which the government assumes primary responsibility for the social welfare of its citizens by providing such things as social security, unemployment benefits, and health care.

wergeld "money for a man." In early Germanic law, a person's value in monetary terms, paid by a wrongdoer to the family of the person who had been injured or killed.

world-machine Newton's conception of the universe as one huge, regulated, and uniform machine that operated according to natural laws in absolute time, space, and motion.

wrought iron a high-quality iron first produced during the eighteenth century in Britain; manufactured by puddling, a process developed by Henry Cort that involved using coke to burn away the impurities in pig iron.

zemstvos local assemblies established in Russia in 1864 by Tsar Alexander II.

ziggurat a massive stepped tower on which a temple dedicated to the chief god or goddess of a Sumerian city was built.

Zionism an international movement that called for the establishment of a Jewish state or a refuge for Jews in Palestine.

Zoroastrianism a religion founded by the Persian Zoroaster in the seventh century B.C.E., characterized by worship of a supreme god, Ahuramazda, who represents the good against the evil spirit, identified as Ahriman.

Index

Italicized page numbers show the locations of illustrations. Maps (map) and tables (tab.) are indicated separately.

Abolition of slavery, 339
Abortion, 640, 650, 759, 760
Absolutism: in central Europe, 366–68, 431–33; in eastern Europe, 368–70, 433, 435; enlightened, 427–28, 434–36; limits of, 370–71; in Ottoman Empire, 370; in Russia, 368–70, 535, 574; in western Europe, 358, 362–66. *See also* Enlightened absolutism
Abstract Expressionism, 711, *712*, 763
Abstract painting, 583–84, 654
Acheson, Dean, 691
Acid rain, 767
Act of Supremacy (England), 313, 322
Address to the Nobility of the German Nation (Luther), 305
Address to the Reichstag (Bismarck), 573
Adenauer, Konrad, 704, 705, 726
Administration. *See* Government
Adrianople: Treaty of, 506
Advertising, 570, 713
Affonso of Congo (Bakongo), 339
Afghanistan, 760; imperialism and, 600; Russia and, 597; Soviet Union and, 731, 732, 742; war on terrorism in, 757
Africa: in 1914, 596 (map); decolonization in, 697–99, 698 (map); imperialism in, 594–96, 596 (map), 599; Paris Peace Conference and, 627–28; Portugal and, 329; slaves and, 338–39, 340; World War I and, *616*, 616–17, 639; after World War I, 638, 639, 697
African Americans, 538, 708; music and, 713, 735; in World War II, 680
African National Congress (ANC), 698
Afrika Korps, 671
Afrikaners (Boers), 594
Agricultural revolution, 440, 478
Agriculture: in 16th century, 352; in 18th century, 440; Columbian Exchange and, 351; Great Depression and, 635; industrial economy and, 553; population growth and, 558, 767; in Soviet Union, 648, 649, 702, 722; World War I and, 635; World War II and, 690. *See also* Collective farms; Land
Airplanes, 552, 652, 732
Air pollution, 490, 491, 732–33
Akbar (Mughal Empire), 342
Albania and Albanians: Balkan wars and, 601; Kosovo and, 749–50; after World War II, 703
Albany, New York, 347
Albert (England), 539

Albuquerque, Afonso d', 330
Alchemy, 387
Alcohol: in 18th century, 420; factory workers and, 481; in Soviet Union, 722
Alexander I (Russia), 470, 508
Alexander II (Russia), 535, 536, *536*, 537, 573, 574
Alexander III (Russia), 536, 573
Alexandra (Russia), *591*, 621
Alexis (Russia), 621
Algeria, 515, 594, *697*, 697–98, 704, 761
Alliances: of Bismarck, 601; during Cold War, 693; after Napoleonic wars, 503; in Seven Years' War, 437; in War of the Austrian Succession, 436; World War I and, 606, 626, 630; World War II and, 671, *684*, 684–86. *See also* specific alliances
Allied Strategic Bombing, 681
Allies: World War I, 609, 616, 617, 624, 625, 626, 628, 638; World War II, 671, 672, 681–82, 683–86
All Quiet on the Western Front (Remarque), 614
Al-Qaeda, 757, 764
Alsace, 533, 628
Alva, duke of, 321
Amalgamated Society of Engineers, 497
Amazon region, 336
Amendments to Constitution (U.S.), 453
America(s): crops from, 440; European empires in, 345–47; horses in, 348; naming of, 333; voyages to, *327*, 328; and War of the Austrian Succession, 436. *See also* New World; specific locations
American Federation of Labor, 591
American Indians. *See* Indians (Native Americans)
Americanization, of culture, 713
American Revolution, 451–53, 504
American system, 487
Amish, 312
Amsterdam, 353
Amusement parks, *550*, 551, 569
Anabaptists, 312
Anatomy, 394, 397
Ancestors: Chinese, 349
Andersen, Hans Christian, 518
Andes Mountains, 336
Angkor kingdom (Cambodia), 342
Anglican Church. *See* Church of England
Anglo-Dutch trade wars, 351
Angola, 594, 699
Animals: in Columbian Exchange, 351
Animé films: in Japan, 764
Annam, 597
Anne (England), 376, 430
Antiballistic missiles (ABMs), 731
Anti-Comintern Pact, 663
Antinuclear movement, women in, 759
Anti-Semitism: in Austria, 586; Dreyfus affair and, 589; in Germany, 586, 645–46; of Hitler, 643, 645, 674. *See also* Jews and Judaism
Antiwar protests, 721–22; in France, 704; in United States, 721. *See also* Student protests
Antwerp, 353

Apartheid, 698
Appeasement: of Nazi Germany, 665
Apprentices: in 18th century, 447
Appropriate-technology movement, 767
Arab-Israeli disputes: in 1973, 729. *See also* Israeli-Palestinian conflict
Arab League, 699
Arabs and Arab world: Jews and, 699; Portugal and, 330; World War I and, 616, 628. *See also* Islam; Middle East
Archimedes and Archimedian screw, 386
Architecture: of country houses, 445; functionalism in, *655*, 655–56; neo-Gothic, 518; Postmodernism in, 734; Rococo, 417–18, *418*
Argentina, 504, 727
Aristocracy. *See* Nobility
Aristotle: medieval learning and, 386; on motion, 387
Armada (Spain), 324
Armed forces. *See* Military; Navy; Wars and warfare
Armenian people: genocide of, 625
Armistice, after World War I, 625
Arms and armaments. *See* Weapons
Arms race: of 1890s, 586; Cold War and, 722, 732, 756
Arouet, François-Marie. *See* Voltaire
Art(s): in 1980s and 1990s, 762–63; artists, society, and, 654–56; Baroque, 378–79, *379*; Classicism in, 380; in Digital Age, 763–64; in Enlightenment, 406, 417–19; "land," 734; Mannerism in, 378; Modernism in, 582–84, 656; multiculturalism and, 764; in Nazi Germany, 656; Neo-Expressionism in, 763; Postmodernism in, 734–35; Realism in, 544, *546*, 547; Rococo style in, *417*, 417–18; Romanticism in, 520; World War I and, 652, 654–56; after World War II, 710–12. *See also* specific arts and artists
Articles of Confederation (U.S.), 452
Artisans: in Industrial Revolution, 492
Aryan racial empire, Hitler and, 675, 683
"Aryans," racist concept of, 581, 644, 645, 646, 662
Ashkenazic Jews, 422
Asia: in 1914, 598 (map); decolonization in, 700–701, 700 (map); European involvement in, 339–42, *341*, 353; immigrants from, 766; imperialism in, 596–98, 598 (map), 599–600; Portugal and, 339–40, 342, 348; trade with, 442; water route to, 329; World War I in, 617; after World War I, 638, 697; in World War II, 666, 669–70, 670 (map), 674, 679. *See also* Southeast Asia; specific locations
Asia Minor, 639
Assemblies: in Russia, 536. *See also* Diet (legislative body); Parliament
Assembly line, 553
Assimilation: of Jews, 422, 586
Associated Shipwrights Society, *497*
Astell, Mary, 414
Astrolabe, 329
Astrology, 387

Journalism: mass, 578. *See also* Newspapers
Journeymen, 447
Joyce, James, 656
Judaism. *See* Jews and Judaism
Judith Beheading Holofernes (Gentileschi), 379, *379*
July Ordinances (France), 512
July Revolution (France, 1830), 512–13, *513*
Jung, Carl, 656–57
Junkers, 367, 432
Justification by faith alone, 304–5, 307

Kaczyński, Lech, 746
Kádár, János, 703, 723
Kamikaze, 681
Kandinsky, Wassily, 583–84
Kangxi (China), 344
Kant, Immanuel, 406
Kaprow, Allen, 734
Karelia, 369
Kelly, Petra, 759
Kemal, Mustafa (Atatürk), 638, 639
Kennan, George, 691, 692
Kennedy, John F., 695, 707, 708
Kent State University, protesters at, 721
Kenya African National Union, 697
Kenyatta, Jomo, 697
Kepler, Johannes, 387, 388–89, 391
Keynes, John Maynard, 638
KGB, 722
Khomeini, Ayatollah, 729, 758
Khrushchev, Nikita, 695–96, *702,* 702–3, 740
Khrushchev Remembers (Khrushchev), 696
Khubilai Khan, 328
Kiefer, Anselm, 763
Kiel mutiny, 625
King, Martin Luther, Jr., 708
Kingdom of the Serbs, Croats, and Slovenes, 746
Kingdom of the Two Sicilies, 507, 531
Kings and kingdoms. *See* Monarchs and monarchies; specific rulers
Kipling, Rudyard, 593
Kirch, Gottfried, 395
Kitchener (Lord), 600
Kivshenko, Alexei, *536*
Knox, John, 314
Koch, Robert, 543
Kohl, Helmut, 726, 750
Kolkhozes, 649
Komorowski, Bronislaw, 746
Königgrätz (Sadowa), battle at, 532–33
Korea, 597, 679, 683, 708; split of, 694
Korean War, 694, 694 (map), 705, 709, 730–31
Kosovo, 749–50
Kosovo Liberation Army (KLA), 749
Kossuth, Louis, 516, 535
Koštunica, Vojislav, 750
Koyaanisqatsi (Glass), 735
Kraft durch Freude (Strength Through Joy), 652
Kristallnacht, 647
Kuchuk-Kainarji, Treaty of, 435
Kulturkampf, 572

Kundera, Milan, 734–35
Kurds: in Iraq, 758
Kurile Islands, 684
Kursk, Battle of, 673
Kuwait, 756, 758
Kwaśniewski, Aleksander, 746
Kyushu, 349

Labor: in 18th century, 442; in British 1851 census, 492; in factories, 481–82, *482,* 483, 487; in Japan, 553; May Day and, 557; migration of, 558; in Russia, 590; in United States, 487; walkouts by, 557; women as, 618–19, *619,* 620; World War I and, 617, 618–19, 620; World War II and, 675, 678, 679, 680, 681, 683. *See also* Forced labor; Labor unions; Slavery; Trade unions; Workers; Working class
Labor unions: in England, 727; in United States, 708. *See also* Strikes; Trade unions
Labour Party (England), 589, 726, 750; in Great Depression, 636; after World War II, 705
La Bruyère, Jean de, 397
Laissez-faire doctrine, 412, 466, 508, 589; Great Depression and, 636
Lake Texcoco, 334
Lampi, Johann, *426*
Land: in 18th century, 440; European conquerors and, 351; industry and, 492. *See also* Agriculture
"Land art," 734
Landed estates, 560
Language(s): in 19th century Europe, 511 (map); in Canada, 591–92. *See also* specific languages
Laos, 597, 701
Lateran Accords (1929), 642
Latin America: in early 19th century, 505 (map); European colonies in, 348; immigrants from, 766; independence and, 466, 504–5; revolts in, 504–6. *See also* Colonies and colonization; specific locations
La Tour, Maurice-Quentin de, *410*
Latvia, 628, 666, 742, 746, 753
Launay, marquis de, 450–51
Laurier, Wilfred, 591–92
Lavasseur, E., 554
Lavender Mist (Pollock painting), 711
Lavoisier, Antoine and Marie-Anne, 394
Law(s). *See* Law codes; Scientific laws; specific laws
Law codes: Napoleonic, 468–70; in Prussia, 443; in Russia, 434, 435
Law of the General Maximum, 465
Lawrence, T. E. (Lawrence of Arabia), 616
Lay Down Your Arms (Suttner), 586
League of Communists of Yugoslavia, 746–47
League of German Girls, 645
League of Nations: Africa and, 639; beginning of, 634; mandates and, 626
League of Nations Covenant, 635
Learning. *See* Education; Intellectual thought
Leary, Timothy, 718

Lebanon, 628, 638, 699
Lebensraum, 643, 664 (map)
Lee, Robert E., 540
Legal issues. *See* Law codes
Legislative Assembly (France), 460, 466
Legislative Corps (France), 526
Legitimacy principle, Metternich and, 502
Leisure, 551, 569
Lend-Lease, 686
Lenin, V. I., 621–22, *622,* 647
Leningrad, 668, 673, 679
Leo X (Pope), 305
Leonardo da Vinci, 387
Leopold I (Holy Roman Empire), 367
Leopold II (Belgium), 594
Leopold II (Holy Roman Empire), *433,* 460
Lepanto, Battle of, 320, 370
Lerma, duke of (Spain), 366
Lesbian, gay, bisexual, and transgender (LGBT) community, 754. *See also* Homosexuals and homosexuality
Lesueur brothers, *462*
"Letter from a Peasant to the Bolshevik Leaders," 623
"Letter from a Soldier in Leningrad to Lenin," 623
Letters: between Louis XIV and King of Tonkin, 343–44
"Letter to Paolo Foscarini" (Bellarmine), 392–93
"Letter to the Grand Duchess Christina" (Galileo), 392
Lettow-Vorbeck, Paul von, 616
Lévesque, René, 755
Leviathan (Hobbes), 378
LGBT community. *See* Lesbian, gay, bisexual, and transgender (LGBT) community
Liberalization, in France, 526
Liberal Party: in Canada, 709, 729, 755; in England, 538, 589
Liberals and liberalism: in central Europe, 507; defeat of, 524–25; economic, 412, 508; nationalism and, 502, 509; political, 508–9
Liberia, 595
Liberty: Locke on, 378; Mill on, 509
Libya: Tripoli as, 594
Liebknecht, Wilhelm, 557
Lifestyle: in 18th century, 442–47; of 19th-century workers, 495–96; aristocratic, 445, *445*; Columbian Exchange and, 351; in country houses, 445, *445*; of Dutch, 373, *373*; improvements in, 559–60; in Industrial Revolution, 489–90; of Louis XIV (France), 363, 364; of middle class, 562, 567; of nobility, 443; in Russia, 368; of urban poor, 491, *491*; of workers, 578; in World War I trenches, 612–13, *613*
Lima, Pizarro in, 336
Limited monarchies, 358
Lincoln, Abraham, 537, 538, 539
Linen Cupboard, The (de Hooch), 373, *373*
Lisbon Treaty, 753
Literacy, 568
Literature: in late 1900s and early 2000s, 764; Elizabethan, 381; in England, 381; feminist, 718, 721; in France, 381–82;

Empire of, 470–72, 471 (map); psychological warfare and, 468; rise of, 467–68; slavery and, 466; Spain and, 504

Napoleon II (France), 526

Napoleon III (France), 515, *525*, 525–29, 531, 533, 570

Napoleonic wars, 502, 594

Narva, Battle of, 369

Naseby, battle at, 375

National Assembly (France), 455–57, 458, 460, 526, 570, 571, 727, 752

National Convention (France), 461, 462, 463, 465

National debt, 442

National Government (England), 636

National Guard (France), 460, 466

National Guard (U.S.), 719, *719*, 721

National Health Service Act, 705

National Insurance Act (1911), 589, 705

Nationalism, 509; in Africa, 599; in Asia, 700–701; in Austria, 507, 516; in central Europe, 507; in China, 701; defeat of, 524–25; in former Yugoslavia, 767; in France, 462, 473; in Franco's Spain, 651; German, 473, 507, 531, 580, 590; in Greece, 506; of Hitler, 643; in India, 600; in Italy, 507, 531; languages and, 511 (map); liberalism and, 502, 509; Napoleon and, 472–73; in Prussia, 473; revolutions of 1830 and, 512; socialism and, 557; in Soviet Union, 742; Spanish, 473; in Turkey, 639; in United States, 517, 597; in World War I, 701; World War I and, 606–7

Nationalist Chinese, 670

Nationalists (Spain), 651

Nationalities: revolutions of 1848 and, 517. *See also* Ethnic cleansing; Minorities; specific groups

Nationalities problem (Austria-Hungary), 572–73, 590

Nationalization: in Britain, 705; in France, 727; in Russia, 624; in World War I, 618

National Liberation Front (Algeria), 697

National Organization for Women (NOW), 720

National Salvation Front, 744

National Socialist German Workers' Party, 643. *See also* Nazi Germany

National workshops (France), 513, 515

Nation building, 525, 533–36, 538–40

Native Americans. *See* Indians

Native peoples: Christianization of, 348. *See also* Decolonization; Indians (Native Americans)

NATO, 693, 707, 746; Canada and, 709; France and, 704; Kosovo and, 749, 750; Serbia and, 748

Naturalism, in literature, 582

Natural law: of economics, 412; natural rights and, 427–28; reason and, 406, 408

Natural philosophers, 386, 405

Natural rights, 427–28, 452, 457, 458–59

Natural selection, 543–44

Nature: Romanticism and, 518–20

Navarre, 320

Navigational aids, 387; astrolabe, 329; compass, 329

Navy: British, 438, 472; French, 472; Russian, 369. *See also* Armada (Spain); Merchant marine; Military; Ships and shipping; specific battles and wars

Nazi Empire, 675

Nazi Germany, 640, 642–47, 662, 683; anti-Semitism in, 645–46; Great Depression and, 637; Japan and, 666; mass meetings in, *645*, 646; resistance to, 671, 673; Rhineland and, 663, 664 (map); Soviet nonaggression pact and, 666; war crimes and, 705; West German school curriculum and, 705, 706; women in, 645, 680. *See also* Germany; Holocaust; World War II

Nazi New Order, 675

Nazi Party, 643

Neo-Expressionism, 763

Neo-Gothic architecture, 518

Netherlands: in 1968, 717; Anabaptists in, 312; Calvinism in, 314, 321; France and, 470; immigration laws of, 760; Maastricht Treaty and, 752; sciences and, 391; Spain and, 320–21, 321 (map), 366; in World War II, 667, 675. *See also* Austrian Netherlands; Dutch; Dutch Republic; Low Countries; Spanish Netherlands

Neumann, Balthasar, 418, *418*

Neumann, Solomon, 559

New Brunswick, 591

New Caledonia, 571

New Deal, 638, 707–8

New Economic Policy (NEP), 647

New England: exploration of, 333; factories of, 487

New Europe (1980s), 741 (map)

New France, 540. *See also* Canada

New Guinea, 617, 671

New imperialism: in Africa, 594–96, 596 (map), 599; in Asia, 596–98, 598 (map), 599–600; factors in emergence of, 592, 594; responses to, 599–600; by United States, 597–98. *See also* Imperialism

New Lanark, Scotland, 509, 511, *512*

New Model Army (England), 374

New Netherland, 346–47

New Order: in Asia, 679; in Italy, 757; Nazi, 675–78

New Spain, 337

Newspapers, 419, 568

New Testament, 305. *See also* Bible

"New Thinking," 755

Newton, Isaac, 387, 391, 393, 399, 406, 407–8, 578–79

"New woman," 586

New World: European diseases in, 335, 336, *337*; exploration of, 331, 333–37; Portugal and, 328; Spain and, 320, 331, 333–37; voyages to, *327*, 328, 331, 333–37; women in, 351. *See also* America(s)

"New World Order," 756

New York, 347, 766; as artistic center, 710; September 11, 2001, terrorist attack on, 740, 752, 757, *757*, 762

New Zealand, 407, 597, 616

NGOs. *See* Nongovernmental organizations

Nice, 531

Nicholas I (Russia), 508, *508*, 513, 516

Nicholas II (Russia), 574, 590, *591*; capture and murder of, 624; Russian Revolutions and, 620, 621; World War I and, 608

Nietzsche, Friedrich, 579–80

Nigeria, 699

Nightingale, Florence, 529, *529*, 585

Night Watch, The (Rembrandt), *380*

"Night witches," 679

Niña (ship), 333

Nineteenth Amendment (U.S.), 619

Ninety-Five Theses (Luther), 305, 306

Nixon, Richard, 722, 727, 729, 730–31

Nkrumah, Kwame, 697, 698

Nobility: in 18th century, 443; in England, 428, 506–7; as entrepreneurs, 492; in France, 363–64, 453, 454, 455, 457, 463, 470, 472; in Prussia, 367, 432; in Russia, 368, 435; in Spain, 366

"Noble savage" idea, 407

Nocturnal Spectator (Restif de la Bretonne), 421

Nongovernmental organizations (NGOs), 767

Nonindustrial world, 487

Nonviolence movements, 767

Normandy, 672

North Africa: France and, 594, 697; guest workers from, 766; immigrants from, 752; World War II and, 668, 669 (map), 671

North America: in 1763, 451 (map); in 1783, 452 (map); British in, 347, 351, 436; Dutch in, 346–47; European migration to, 558; French in, 347, 351, 436; in Seven Years' War, 437, 437 (map), 438; Spain and, 351

North American Air Defense Command (NORAD), 709

North Atlantic Treaty Organization. *See* NATO

Northern Europe: sciences in, 391

Northern Ireland, 726, 757. *See also* Ireland

Northern Renaissance humanism, 302–3

North German Confederation, 533

North Korea. *See* Korea; Korean War

North Vietnam. *See* Vietnam; Vietnam War

Norway: voting rights in, 586; in World War II, 667, 675. *See also* Scandinavia

Notre-Dame Cathedral (Paris): as Temple of Reason, 465

Novalis, Friedrich, 520

Nova Scotia, 591

Novels, 419, 518. *See also* Literature

Novikov, Nikolai, 692–93

Novotný, Antonín, 723

Nuclear power disaster, at Chernobyl, 733

Nuclear weapons, 693, 731, 755; arms race and, 722, 732, 756; intermediate-range, 755; missiles in Cuba, 695–96

Nuns, 348

Nuremberg, 644, 646, 653; war crime trials at, 705

Nuremberg laws, 646

Nursing, 529, *529*, 556, 585

Nutrition, 351, 558

Nystadt, Peace of, 369

Royal Council (Britain), 347
Royal council (France), 363
Royal Observatory, at Greenwich, England, 400
Royal Society (England), 395, 396, 399
Rudolf II (Holy Roman Empire), 389
Rugby Football Union (England), 569
Ruhr region, 558
Rural areas, 488; aristocratic lifestyle in, 446
Russell, W. H., *529*
Russia: in 18th century, 433–35; in late 1800s, 573–74; in 1990s, 743; absolutism in, 368–70; alliances of, 601; Asian expansion by, 597; Balkans and, 601, 608; China and, 345; civil war in, 624–25; Communist Party in, 622, 624; in Concert of Europe, 503; Crimean War and, 528–29; Enlightenment in, 427; government of, 369; industrialization in, 487, 553; military in, 369, 370, 437; Napoleon and, 470, 473; after Napoleonic wars, 507–8; Ottoman Empire and, 506, 528; Peter the Great and, 369–70, *370*; Poland and, 435, 513; Quintuple Alliance and, 503; reforms in, 535–36; revolts in, 362, 368–69, 435, *435* (map); in Seven Years' War, 437; Soviet Union and, 743; Triple Entente and, 601; West and, 369; women in, 369, 621; World War I and, 609–10, 628. *See also* Soviet Union; World War I; World War II
Russian Empire, 528
Russian Orthodox Church, 368–69. *See also* Eastern Orthodoxy
Russian Republic, 743
Russian Revolutions: of 1905, 590; Bolshevik Revolution (1917), 617, 621–22; of March, 1917, 621
Russian-Turkish war, 506
Russo-Japanese War, 590, 597, 601
Rutherford, Ernest, 657

SA. *See* Storm Troops (SA)
Sacraments: Calvin on, 313; Luther on, 305, 307, 311
Saddam Hussein, 758
Sailors and sailing: navigational aids for, 329; Portuguese, 330–31. *See also* Ships and shipping
Saint-Domingue, 346, 465–66, *466* (map). *See also* Haiti
Saint Helena, Napoleon on, 474
Saint Lawrence River region, 436, 438
Saint Matthew's Passion (Bach), 418
St. Peter's Basilica (Rome), 379
St. Petersburg, Russia, 369, 371 (map), 621; in 18th century, 446
"Saints," Anabaptists as, 312
Saint-Simon, duc de (Louis de Rouvroy), 358, 364
Sakhalin Island, 684
Salons, 414, 416, *416*
Salt, Titus, *490*
Saltaire, England, *490*
Salvation: Calvin on, 313; Luther and, 304–5, 307; before Reformation, 304

Samurai (Japan), 599
Samurai revolt (1867), 599
Sanford, Elizabeth Poole, 564
Sanger, Margaret, 654
Sanitation: in cities, 447, 490, 491, *491*, 492, 559
San Martín, José de, 505, *506*
Sans-culottes, 460–61
Santa María (ship), 333
Sarajevo, 606
Sardinia: Congress of Vienna and, 507; in kingdom of Piedmont, 530
Sarkozy, Nicolas, 752
Sartre, Jean-Paul, 710
Sati, 600
Saudi Arabia, 699, 757, 758
Savoy: house of, 507, 530, 531
Scandinavia: Lutheranism in, 308
Schleswig, 532
Schlieffen, Alfred von, 608
Schlieffen Plan, 608, *608,* 609
Schmidt, Helmut, 726
Scholarship. *See* Intellectual thought
Schönberg, Arnold, 656
Schönborn prince-bishop (Würzburg): palace of, 418
Schools: Jesuit, 317; monastic, 348. *See also* Education; Universities and colleges
Schröder, Gerhard, 734, 750
Schumacher, E. F., 732, 733
Schurz, Carl, 514–15
Schuschnigg, Kurt von, 663
Schutzstaffel (SS), 644–45, 675, 676
Science(s): agriculture and, 440; in Enlightenment, 406–7, *407*; in nineteenth century, 543–44; religion and, 400–402; society and, 400; in Soviet Union, 702; technology and, 553, 732, 733; women in, 395–97; before World War I, 578–79; World War II and, 732. *See also* Medicine; Scientific Revolution
Science of man, 412
Scientific laws: of Kepler, 389; of Newton, 393
Scientific method, 398–99, 543
Scientific research, 543
Scientific Revolution: astronomy in, 387–93; background of, 386–87; chemistry in, 394–95; Eurocentrism and, 352; impact of, 385–86, 543; medicine in, 393–94
Scientific societies, 396, 398, *399,* 399–400
Scotland: Calvinism in, 314; England and, 372; Knox in, 314; Presbyterian Church in, 372; in United Kingdom, 428
Scott, Walter, 518
Scout, The, 567, *567*
Scripture, 303, 310, 319. *See also* Catholic Church; Protestantism; Theology
Sculpture: Baroque, 379, *379*
Seasons, The (Haydn), 419
SEATO, 695
Secondary education, 566
Second Balkan War, 601, 602 (map)
Second Battle of the Marne, 625
Second Continental Congress, 452
Second Empire (France), 526, 528–29, 570
Second Estate: in France, 453, 455

Second German Empire, 533
Second Industrial Revolution, 550, 551–57, *552,* 568
Second International, 557
Second Republic (France), 515
Second Sex, The (de Beauvoir), 710, 711
Second World War. *See* World War II
Secret police: in Czechoslovakia, 723; in eastern Europe, 703; in East Germany (*stasi*), 725, 750, 751; in Romania, 725; in Russia, 508, 573, 624, 722; in Soviet Union, 702, 703
Secret societies: in Enlightenment, 416; in Russia, 508
Sectionalism, in Italy, 571
Secular humanism, 760
Secularism, 357–58, 386; France and, 761–62; fundamentalism and, 760; materialism and, 543
Sedan, battle at, 533
Segregation: in colonies, 599, 698; in United States, 708
Self-determination: for eastern Europe, 691; World War I and, 626, 628, 629; after World War II, 691, 697
Self-Help (Smiles), 493
Self-interest: as economic principle, 412
Senate: in France, 571
Separation of church and state, 312, 508
Separation of powers, Montesquieu on, 409–10
Sephardic Jews, 422
Sepoys, 597
September 11, 2001, terrorist attacks, 740, 752, 757, *757,* 762
Serbia, 750; Austria and, 601, 606; Balkan wars and, 601; independence of, 528; World War I and, 608, 609, 610, 628
Serbs, 517; Bosnia and, 747–50
Serfs and serfdom: in 16th century, 353; in eastern Europe, 443; in Prussia, 432; in Russia, 435, 536, *536,* 537. *See also* Peasants
Serialism, in music, 735
Serious Proposal to the Ladies, A (Astell), 414
Servants: as urban workers, 495, 563; women as, 495
Sevastopol, 529, 743
Seven Years' War: alliances in, 437; battlefields of, 437 (map); England and, 430; Europe in, 437, 437 (map); India and, 344, 437, 437 (map), 438, 439; North America in, 437, 437 (map), 438; Prussia in, 432
Sewage and sewer systems, 447, 558, 559–60
Sex and sexuality: in 1950s, 718; in 1960s, 717; Freud on, 580; in marriage, 314; after World War I, 652, 654, 717; after World War II, 717. *See also* Gender and gender issues
Sexual revolution, 717, 718
Seymour, Jane, 313
Seyss-Inquart, Arthur, *663*
Shakespeare, William, 381
Shelley, Mary, 518
Shelley, Percy Bysshe, 518

Trading companies: British East India Company, 344, 345, *438*, 487, 597; Dutch East India Company, 341, *341, 353*
Trading empire: of Portugal, 330
Trading posts: European, 342
Trafalgar, Battle of, 472
Trains. *See* Railroads
Transistor, 732
Transportation: in Britain, 705; in cities, 558; internal combustion engine and, 552; mass leisure and, 569; in United States, 487; after World War II, 690, 705
Transportation revolution, 480–81, 487, 555–56
Transubstantiation, Luther on, 307
Transvaal, 594
Transylvania, 367
Travel, 407, 446, 652, 710
Travels (Polo), 328–29
Travels of John Mandeville, The, 328
Treaties. *See* specific treaties
Treatise on Toleration (Voltaire), 410
Treaty on European Union. *See* Maastricht Treaty
Trench warfare, in World War I, 606, 609, 610, *611,* 612–14, *613*
Trent, Council of, 319
Trevithick, Richard, 480
"Trial of Suzanne Gaudry, The," 360
Trials: for witchcraft, 358, 359, 360
Triangular trade, 338–39, 338 (map)
Triple Alliance, 578, 601
Triple Entente, 578, 601
Tripoli: as Libya, 594
Triumph of the Will, The (movie), 652, *653,* 653–54
Trotsky, Leon, 622, *622,* 624, 647
Troy (movie), 764
Trudeau, Pierre, 729
Truman, Harry, 690, 707, 730–31; atomic bomb and, 674, 682; at Potsdam Conference, 686; Zionism and, 699
Truman Doctrine, 691
Tsar (Russia), 507–8, 573–74
Tudor dynasty (England), 372
Tunisia, 594, 671, 697
Turing, Alan, 732
Turkestan, 597
Turkey: guest workers from, 766; missiles in, 695; NATO and, 693; after World War I, 638–39, 691, 699
Turks, 320, 435, 506. *See also* Ottoman Empire; Ottoman Turks
Two Treatises of Government (Locke), 378
Two Women Teach a Child to Walk (de Hooch), 373, *373*
Tyrol, 367
Tzara, Tristan, 654

Ukraine, 733, 744; independence of, 743; Stalin and, 648; World War I and, 624; World War II in, 668, 673, 678
Ulbricht, Walter, 693, 725
Ulianov, Vladimir. *See* Lenin, V. I.
Ulm, Battle of, 470
Ultra-Catholics, 320

Ultraroyalists (France), 512
Ulysses (Joyce), 656
Unbearable Lightness of Being, The (Kundera), 734–35
Uncertainty principle, 657
Unconditional surrender, 671
Unconscious, 580, 581, 656–57
Unemployment: benefits for workers, 497; in East Germany, 750; after end of communism, 744; in England, 752; in France, 752; in Great Depression, 635–38; Keynes on, 638; in Nazi Germany, 644; in United States, 708, 729; in western Europe, 726–27; worldwide, 766. *See also* Economy
Unification: of Germany, 511 (map), 516, *524,* 525, 531–33, 532 (map); of Italy, 511 (map), 516, 530–31, 530 (map)
Union of French Indochina, 597
Union of South Africa, 594
Union of Soviet Socialist Republics (USSR). *See* Soviet Union
Unions. *See* Labor unions; Trade unions
United Kingdom, 428. *See also* England (Britain)
United Nations, 684, 758; Canada and, 709; Korean War and, 694; in Kosovo, 749–50; NGOs at, 767; Russia and, 743; women's conferences by, 759
United Netherlands. *See* Dutch Republic
United Provinces. *See* Dutch Republic
United States: in 1960s, 708, 717–22; in 1990s and 2000s, 754; Allied war conferences and, 683–86; antiwar protests in, 721; Canada and, 709; China and, 730–31, 755; civil rights movement in, 708; Civil War in, 538–40, 585, 609; containment policy of, 691, 694; creation of, 452–53; cultural influence of, 713; decolonization by, 700; economy in, 538, 638, 708, 729, 766; European migration to, 558; fundamentalism in, 760; Great Depression in, 638; housing market in, 764, 766; imperialism of, 597–98; industrialization of, 486–87, 591; Iraq invaded by, 758; Islam and, 758; Israel and, 758; Japan and, 597, 666; Japanese Americans during World War II, 680; Kuwait and, 758; Latin America and, 506, 766; military alliances of, 671, 683–86, *684;* national unity in, 517; NATO and, 693; Neo-Expressionism in, 763; under Nixon, 727, 729; Persian Gulf War and, 755–56; postwar art in, 710–12; Progressive Era in, 591; religion in, 760; Russia and, 744; slavery and, 339, 537, 538–40; Soviet Union and, 690–93, 722, 731–32, 755–56; stagflation in, 729; terrorism against, 757; Versailles Treaty and, 630; western Europe and, 739; World War I and, 617; in World War II, 668, 670, 671–74, 679–80; after World War II, 685 (map), 707–8, 710–12; Zionism and, 699. *See also* Cold War
Universal law of gravitation, 393
Universe: atomic theory of, 657; geocentric view of, 387; heliocentric view of, 388,

389, 390; Kepler on, 388–89; medieval conception of, *388;* Scientific Revolution and, 387–88. *See also* Astronomy
Universities and colleges: antiwar protests at, 719, *719;* student revolts at, 717; women and, 568, 759. *See also* Education; Student protests
Upper Austria, 367
Upper classes: in 18th century, 420; in late 1800s, 560; birth control in, 441; families in, 440–41; lifestyle of, 445. *See also* Classes
Urban areas: in 18th century, 443, 446–47; in 19th century, 488–92, *490;* transformation of, 558–60. *See also* Cities and towns; Ghettos
Urbanization, 488, 558, 591
USA Patriot Act, 751
USSR. *See* Soviet Union
Utopian socialists, 509, 511–12
Uzbekistan, 742

Vacations, mass leisure and, 569
Vaccinations, 558
Valley of Mexico, 334. *See also* Mexico
Valois dynasty (France), 308, 320
Vanderbilt, Consuelo, 560
Van de Velde, Theodore, 654
Van Gogh, Vincent, 583, *584*
Vanity Fair… (Thackeray), 544
Vatican II, 713
Vatican City, 642
Venetia, 507, 516, 531
Venice: republic of, 516
Venezuela, 504–5
Veracruz, Cortés in, 334
Verdun: battle at, 610
Vernet, Horace, *513*
Versailles: architecture and, 417–18; Hall of Mirrors at, *365, 524,* 525, 533; lifestyle at, 363; Treaty of, 628, 633, 634, 662, 663, 666; women's march to, 457
Vesalius, Andreas, 394, 397
Vespucci, Amerigo, 333
Viceroy, 337
Victor Emmanuel II (Italy), 530, 531
Victor Emmanuel III (Italy), 641
Victoria (England), *484,* 513, 538, 539, *552,* 597
Victorian England, 536, 538, 562, 566
Video: in art, 763–64
Video games, 764
Video music channel, 736
Vienna: Congress of, *501,* 501–2, 503 (map), 504, 507, 512; Hitler in, *663;* Jews in, 586; Ottomans and, 309, 367, 370; revolution of 1848 in, 516
Vierzehnheiligen, church of, 418, *418*
Vietcong, 730
Vietminh, 701
Vietnam, 342, 344, 701; Japanese expansionism and, 679
Vietnam War, 701, 708, 721, 729–30, *730;* China and, 731; music focused on, 736; protests against, 718, 721–22
Villages, 443

Vindication of the Rights of Woman
(Wollstonecraft), 414, 415–16
Viola, Bill, *763*, 763–64
Violence: in domestic politics, 466
Virchow, Rudolf, 559
Virginia: Jamestown in, 347
Vodka, 420
Vogt, Hannah, 706
Volga River region, 671
Voltaire (François-Marie Arouet): on gender
equality, 414; portrait of, *410*; on religion
and religious intolerance, 410, 411; salons
and, 416
Von Bora, Katherina, 308
Voting and voting rights: in Austria-
Hungary, 590; in England, 430, 507, 513,
514, 538, 538 (tab.), 570; in France, 512,
513, 515, 526, 570; in Italy, 571; political
liberalism and, 508; in United States, 517,
708; women and, 586, 587–88, *588*, 619,
710
Voyages of exploration, *327*, 328, 329–31,
333–37

Wages: industrialization and, 497, 553; price
revolution and, 352; for workers, 563
Waiting for Godot (Beckett), 712
Walesa, Lech, 723, 744
Wallachia, 506, 528, 529
Walpole, Robert, 430
Walsingham, Francis, 323
Wanderer Above the Sea of Fog, The
(Friedrich), 520, *520*
War, The (Dix), 654
War communism, in Russia, 624
War for Independence. *See* American
Revolution
"War Girls" (poem), 619
War Guilt Clause, 628
Warhol, Andy, 712
War of 1812, 517
War of the Austrian Succession, 432, 436,
438
"War on poverty," 708
War on terrorism, 754
Wars and warfare: in 18th century, 436–38;
over colonies, 351; Dutch and, 372;
guerrilla, 594; of Louis XIV, 365–66; slave
trade and, 339; trench warfare, 606, 609,
610, *611*, 612–14, *613*. *See also* specific
battles and wars
Warsaw, 674
Warsaw Pact, 693, 701
Wars of Religion, 319–20
Wartburg Castle: Luther at, 305
Washington, George, 452
Wastewater treatment, 560
Water: clean, 559–60; for drinking, 447, 492
Watergate scandal, 729
Waterloo, battle at, 473–74
Water pollution, 491
Watt, James, 479
Watteau, Antoine, 417, *417*
Wealth: in late 1800s, 560; in England, 589;
industrial, 497; Physiocrats on, 412
Wealth gap: industrialization and, 497, 591

Wealth of Nations, The (Smith), 412
Weapons: in African trade, 348; Portuguese,
331; in World War I, 610, *611*, 612, 613,
613, 617; in World War II, 732. *See also*
Atomic bomb; Nuclear weapons
Weapons of mass destruction, 758
Weather: uncertainty principle and, 657. *See
also* Climate
Weaving: in Industrial Revolution, 479
Weimar Republic, 642–43
Welfare state: in Canada, 709; in Great
Britain, 589, *705*, 705–7; in United
States, 638, 707, 708, 729. *See also* Social
welfare
Wellington, duke of, 474
Wesley, John, 423
West, the. *See* Western civilization; Western
world
West Africa, 338, 339, 347–48, 594, 616,
616
West Bank (Jordan River), 699, 700
West Berlin, 693, 695. *See also* Berlin
Western civilization: colonial populations
and, 597–98; globalization and, 767;
Southeast Asia and, 339–42; World War I
and, 606. *See also* Western world
Western Europe: absolutism in, 358, 362–66;
Cold War and, 704–7; democracy in,
570–71, 634, 636, 638, 704–7; economic
recovery in, 704; end of Cold War in,
739–40; inflation in, 726–27; prosperity
in, 704, 722; recessions in, 726–27;
Russia and, 369; unemployment in,
726–27; unity in, 707, 750–52; after
World War II, 704–7, 716. *See also* World
War I; World War II; specific locations
Western Front, in World War I, 609, 611
(map), 612, 614, 616, 617
Westernization: of Russia, 369
Western world: in 1965–1985, 716–36;
culture of, 760, 762–64; divided, 722–29;
in global age, 739–67; Islam and, 758;
Postmodern culture in, 732–36; postwar
society and culture in, 709–13; postwar
society in, 709–13; society after 1965 in,
732–36
West Germany, 693, 704–5, 706, 725;
economy in, 705; ECSC and, 707; Green
Party in, 734; guest workers and
immigrants in, 705, 760; industrial
workers in, 709; NATO and, 693, 705;
Nazi Germany studied in, 705, 706;
women in, 759. *See also* East Germany;
Germany
West Indies, 346 (map), 465
Westphalia: Peace of, 361–62, 366, 372
Whigs (Britain), 507, 513, 514
White-collar workers, 556–57, 562, 709
White forces, in Russia, 624, 678
"White man's burden," 592, 593, 595
White Man's Burden, The (Kipling), 593
Whitney Museum of Modern Art, 710
William I (Germany), 531, 533
William II (Germany): authoritarianism of,
590; Balkan region and, 601; Bismarck
and, 572, *572*; submarine warfare and,
617; World War I and, 608, 625

William III (Orange), 372, 376, 377
William and Mary (England), 376, 377
William of Nassau (prince of Orange), 321
William of Orange, 372
Wilson, Richard, 445, *445*
Wilson, Woodrow, 591; mandate system
and, 628–29; at Paris Peace Conference,
625–26, 627; World War I and, 618, 634,
639
Windischgrätz, Alfred, 516
Winkelmann, Maria, 395–96
Witchcraft, 358–59
"With Germany's Unemployed" (Hauser),
637
Wittenberg, Luther in, 304, 305, *307*
Wojtyla, Karol, 762
Wolfe, James, 438
Wollstonecraft, Mary, 414, 415–16
Woman in Her Social and Domestic Character
(Sanford), 564
Women: in late 1800s, 563–66; in
antinuclear movement, 759; as British
prime minister, 726; as Chartists, 498;
debates on nature of, 396–97; education
and, 414, 568; in Enlightenment, 413–14,
415–16; environmental movements and,
759; in factories, 478, 487, 494–95,
618–19, *619*, 620, 650, 679, 680; in
France, 457, 458–59, 465, *465*, 469–70,
717, 760, 761–62; headscarves (hijabs)
and, 760–61; in India, 600; Italian
Fascists and, 642; missionary nunneries
and, 348; natural rights of, 457, 458–59;
in Nazi Germany, 645, 680; "new woman"
and, 586; in New World, 351; Paris
Commune and, 570–71; in postwar world,
710; Protestant, 315; in Roaring
Twenties, 651; Rousseau on, 413; in
Russia, 369; salons and, 414, 416, *416*; in
sciences, 395–97; as servants, 495; as
socialists, 511; in Soviet Union, 648, 650,
679, 700, 701, 759; as teachers, 568; in
Turkey, 639; voting by, 619; witchcraft
and, 359; as workers, 442, 478, 494–95,
495, *556*, 556–57, 650, 679, 680, 681,
710, 759; World War I and, 618–20, *619*,
652, 654; after World War I, 640, 651,
710; in World War II, 679, 681. *See also*
Birth control; Gender and gender issues;
Sex and sexuality; Women's rights
Women's liberation movement, 710, 711,
722, 740, 759, 767
Women's march, to Versailles, 457
Women's rights: in Japan, 681; Mill on, 509;
movements for, 585–86, 587–88, 619,
710, 711; Wright, Frances, and, 511–12.
See also Feminism
Women's Social and Political Union
(England), 586
Women's suffrage movement, 586, 587–88,
588
Woolen industry, 442
Wordsworth, William, 518–20
Workday, 498, 563
Workers: in 18th century, 446–47; children
as, 442; in factories, 478, 481–82, *482*,
483; in French Revolution, 463; guest,

ARCTIC OCEAN

ALASKA RANGE

80°N

60°N

ROCKY MOUNTAINS

CANADIAN SHIELD

NORTH
AMERICA

40°N

NORTH PACIFIC OCEAN

Mississippi R.

APPALACHIAN MTS.

NORTH
ATLANTIC
OCEAN

Arctic

Rio Grande

Tropic of Cancer

20°N

0°   Equator

Amazon R.

SOUTH
AMERICA

ANDES MOUNTAINS

20°S

Tropic of Capricorn

SOUTH PACIFIC OCEAN

SOUTH
ATLANTIC
OCEAN

40°S

Cape Horn

60°S

Antarctic Circle

80°S

180°

Sea ice
Ice cap
Tundra
Forest
Grassland
Desert
Mountains